DICTIONARY OF EAST EUROPEAN HISTORY SINCE 1945

EASTERN EUROPE

1945

0   50   100
Miles

DICTIONARY OF EAST EUROPEAN HISTORY SINCE 1945

Joseph Held

GREENWOOD PRESS
Westport, Connecticut

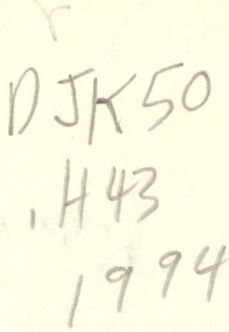

Library of Congress Cataloging-in-Publication Data

Held, Joseph.
    Dictionary of East European history since 1945 / Joseph Held.
        p. cm.
    Includes index.
    ISBN 0–313–26519–4 (alk. paper)
      1. Europe, Eastern—History—1945- —Dictionaries. I. Title.
  DJK50.H43   1994
  947.08′03—dc20   93–35840

British Library Cataloguing in Publication Data is available.

Library of Congress Catalog Card Number: 93–35840
ISBN: 0–313–26519–4

First published in 1994

Greenwood Press, 88 Post Road West, Westport, CT 06881
An imprint of Greenwood Publishing Group, Inc.

Printed in the United States of America

The paper used in this book complies with the
Permanent Paper Standard issued by the National
Information Standards Organization (Z39.48–1984).

10 9 8 7 6 5 4 3 2 1

Copyright Acknowledgments

The author and publisher thank Margaret Held for the maps appearing in this book. The illustration of The Congress of Gyorffy Collegium is from Laszlo Kardos, *Sej, a mi lobogonkat fenyes szelek fujjak Nepi Kollegiumok, 1939–1949*. The illustrations of Laszlo Rajk and Jozef Cardinal Mindszenty are from Domokos Kosary, ed., *Magyarorszag Tortenete Kepekben*.

Every reasonable effort has been made to trace the owners of copyright materials in this book, but in some instances this has proven impossible. The author and publisher will be glad to receive information leading to more complete acknowledgments in subsequent printings of the book and in the meantime extend their apologies for any omissions.

CONTENTS

Photo essays follow pp. 174 and 300.

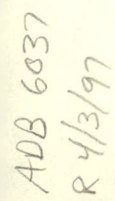

MAPS

PREFACE

This work is intended as a guide for serious students of East European history since World War II. It deals with major events, personalities, and policies in the region on a country-by-country basis. Consequently, its scope is all encompassing. However, since the East European countries have retained their individual characteristics based on centuries of historical traditions, they are treated separately in this work. East Germany, the only country under Soviet rule in the time period under discussion that had no such historical traditions, and that had disappeared from the map in 1990, is included because it was part of the Soviet Union's East European empire. Other countries situated in Eastern Europe—such as Austria and Greece—have been excluded, because they were outside the Soviet empire.

Thus, the reader can survey each country separately. Within the country sections the entries are listed in alphabetical order to make locating them easier. In addition, a map of each country is included. Unfortunately, it is not yet possible to draw an accurate, up-to-date map of the former Yugoslavia. Therefore, the map of that country lists the various republics, most of which have either become independent since 1991 or are being fought over at the present time (January, 1994). The book also includes chronologies of the countries in question at the beginning of each section. This should help the reader place events of interest in their proper settings. In addition, a general chronology of the world events that influenced the course of East European history since 1945 is included after the introduction. In order to make readers' orientation easier, cross-references are listed when warranted. Finally, a detailed index at the end of the volume provides the locations of specific entries.

The discussion of events and personalities who shaped them had, by necessity, to end by June 1993. This is, however, an ongoing story; and the unfolding events and the appearance of new personalities shaping the course of history in Eastern Europe will require further research by interested students. The tortuous road of the countries of the region toward democracy, and their efforts to establish market-based economies since the conclusion of this work, are being reported by various news organizations. These reports are, however, not yet history. They are current events that, at best, will receive treatment by historians at a later time.

This book is the only one of its kind at the present time. Various encyclopedias certainly do treat East European events, policies, and personalities, but they do not concentrate on the subjects included in this volume. Finally, I must warn the reader that, in spite of the vast amount of information included in this work, the history of Eastern Europe in the communist era is still unfinished. The works written on the various countries vary in quantity and quality, but their number is overwhelming. Moreover, the researcher must understand several languages of the region in order to study individual countries and properly evaluate their characteristics. The present work includes some sources, mostly in the English language, to help those lacking the knowledge of local languages to study the countries in question. It is hoped, however, that this book will arouse the interest of students about a history of Eastern Europe, and will spur them on to further study.

NOTE: Because of technical difficulties, diacritical marks had to be omitted from the text.

DICTIONARY OF
EAST EUROPEAN
HISTORY SINCE 1945

EASTERN EUROPE

1990

Miles

INTRODUCTION: EASTERN EUROPE

The concept, the title of this introduction, is not entirely a geographic one. Historians, geographers, and political scientists cannot fully agree whether Eastern Europe should include the landmass usually referred to as European Russia—and today, also Ukraine—the arbitrarily defined territory between the ever-changing western borders of the state of the former tsars, and then the commissars, on the one hand, and the Ural mountains on the other. The political boundaries of Eastern Europe have also been controversial. Should they include, for instance, the Baltic states of Estonia, Latvia, and Lithuania? How about the Balkan states? Should Greece be included in the concept? Not surprisingly, a number of terms have been used to describe the region, such as Central Europe, East Central Europe, and, of course, Eastern Europe. East Central Europe has usually referred only to Poland, Czechoslovakia, and Hungary. Central Europe usually included Germany, Poland, Hungary, and Czechoslovakia. Eastern Europe has included Poland, Hungary, Czechoslovakia, and European Russia. What is certain, however, is that Austria, that leftover state of the defunct Habsburg empire, which, by rights of geography, and history should be part of Eastern Europe, is not. The safest way to handle the problem of definition is to include in the region all the countries that were part of the colonial empire of the Soviet Union in the second half of the twentieth century. Complicating the situation will be the fact that the list will include East Germany—the so-called German Democratic Republic (GDR)—and the southeast European countries of the Balkans, including Romania, the former Yugoslavia, Bulgaria, and Albania. The current volume will, therefore, take this "easy way" out of the dilemma of definition.

Once the definition of the dimensions of Eastern Europe is accepted, further problems will intrude into our deliberations. The concept of Eastern Europe is a relatively new one from the historical perspective. The peoples of this amorphously defined region have considered themselves Europeans without any qualifying adjectives. The term "East Europeans" was never used to refer to them until World War I. Furthermore, the designation denotes a homogeneity that has never existed—not when the region was controlled by the three great empires of the Ottoman Turks, the Russian

Romanovs, and the Austrian Habsburgs and, from 1945 to 1989, the Soviet Union. In fact, most people familiar with the region stress the variety of historical, social, and economic experiences, and traditions; the often conflicting nationalisms; and the different cultures that the peoples have created in this vast area of Europe during their millennia of existence. To discuss Eastern Europe, therefore, as a homogeneous entity would hardly be valid; if it happens, it is the result of the misreading of the region's history. This being said, one must mention some of the important forces that shaped the characters of the various peoples of Eastern Europe, and in this process some generalizations will be unavoidable.

First of all, one must point out the role of religion in the history of East Europeans. For centuries, various ethnic groups and nations identified themselves with certain religions. If, for instance, one would have been able to ask a Serb to describe himself in the fifteenth century, he would have said that he was an Orthodox Christian of Eastern Rites. If he were pressed, he would say that he was the subject of such and such a landlord. The next level of identification would have been his village, and then his family. After repeated questioning, he would have finally said that he was also a member of the Natio Serbica, a Latin term used for such a purpose at the time. The meaning of this exercise is that the churches of Eastern Europe were instrumental in keeping the national and ethnic cultures and languages alive even in hard times, when the occupying great powers pressed hard on the populations. What is even more interesting to note is that, in the process, the universal churches, such as Roman Catholicism, Orthodox Christianity, and Islam had become "nationalized" and contributed to the gradual separation of peoples and ethnic groups from each other. Thus, to be an Albanian was to be a Muslim. A Romanian was an Orthodox Christian first, separated from other Orthodox Christians only by his language. Bulgarians were also Orthodox Christians. Croatians were, by definition, Roman Catholics and so were Slovenians. Orthodox Christians-except Romanians-adopted the Cyrillic alphabet designed by the great Greek missionaries Cyril and Methodius in the course of the eighth century. Culturally, therefore, they were affiliated with the Byzantine, or Eastern Roman, empire whose capital city, Constantinople, fell to the Ottoman Turks in 1453. Istanbul, the new name for this once great city, is still only sporadically accepted by peoples of the Orthodox faith.

National or ethnic identification was much less important during the long centuries of East European history than was religious affinity. This was true especially after the Ottoman conquest of the southern tier of Eastern Europe when the preservation of ethnic identity went hand in hand with religious affiliation. This was also the case for East Europeans who lived outside the control of the Ottoman empire. For instance, Czech history and culture were certainly shaped by the memories of the great reformer, Jan Hus, forerunner to Martin Luther, burned at the stake by the Council of Constance in 1415. The Czech Hussites and their non-Czech sympathizers translated the Bible into their own languages and conducted a series of wars against the Popists, that is, the adherents of the Pope. They provided a cultural shield for the Czech people at a time when they were subjected to the Habsburg empire. Poles were ardent Roman Catholics and they conducted crusades against the non-Christian Lithuanians until, at the end of the fourteenth century, Queen Jadwiga (Hedwig of the Hungarian branch of the Anjou family) married the Lithuanian Jagiello and brought about the conversion of Lithuanians into Catholicism. When Poland was partitioned at the end of the eighteenth century between Orthodox Russia, Lutheran Prussia and the Catholic Habsburg empire, it was the Roman Catholic church that maintained a sense of Polishness in the separate realms. Hungarians have also been the beneficiaries of religious affiliation in preserving their culture. To be a Hungarian in the sixteenth and seventeenth centuries meant to be a Christian first, opposed to Islam, whose armies occupied central Hungary. Then, it meant to be Protestant, preferably a Calvinist, in opposing the Habsburg Counter-Reformation. The influence of religion and the cultures fostered by the various religious institutions in Eastern Europe were, therefore, very much part of national historical traditions. When the openly atheistic Soviet empire imposed its own version of culture on the peoples of Eastern Europe, its leaders were underestimating the historical role of religious traditions. Perhaps one of the many—and not the least important—reasons for the surprisingly speedy collapse of the communist system in Eastern Europe could be found in its rejection of the role of traditional religions in the respective countries.

Another factor that must be considered in this context is nationalism. The peoples of Eastern Europe began to assert their national identities rather late in history, not earlier than the late eighteenth century. While nationalism was a unifying force in the historical development of the English, French, German, and Italian peoples, in Eastern Europe it was a disruptive force. It was directed against the unifying great empires of the region and eventually it led to their dissolution. However, East European nationalism did not go through the calming passage of generations. It became and remained a radical force. Eventually it splintered into as many versions as there are nations and ethnic groups in the region. When the time was ripe, competing East European nationalisms contributed to the creation not of national states, but of miniature replicas of the multinational empires; Poland, Czechoslovakia; the kingdom of Serbs, Croats, and Slovenians, later to become Yugoslavia; the new Romanian state; even Bulgaria gathered as much territory as was possible, which included large numbers of ethnic minorities, within their borders in 1918. Their nationalism was aggressive, chauvinistic, and imperialistic. The argument that was eagerly accepted by France and Great Britain at the peace conference following World War I, according to which the strategic interests of the new states required borders that included large ethnic minorities was, of course, false. In fact, the situation destabilized Eastern Europe, making it impossible for the new states to fulfill their intended role as a replacement for the Habsburg empire, to be a cordon sanitaire between Soviet Russia and defeated Germany. Competing nationalisms were sufficient to create the new states, but by their very nature, they were unable to form viable alliances. The millions of Germans, Hungarians, Albanians, Russians, Ukrainians, and others included in the new states dominated by nations with different cultures, languages, and historical experiences, could only spell trouble, and they did. The disregard of the principles of national self-determination, espoused by the president of the United States, Woodrow Wilson, contributed to the eventual destruction of the interwar order in Eastern Europe and subjected the region's peoples first to Nazi, then to communist rule.

When the Soviet colonial empire came to control Eastern Europe, it attempted to impose a version of "internationalism" on the peoples of the region. It was argued by its Marxist-Leninist ideologues that proletarian internationalism was an antidote to chauvinistic, radical nationalism. The latter was allegedly only a product of bourgeois society and when that society was abolished, there would be no longer a basis for nationalism. However, proletarian internationalism, in the Soviet context, meant the subordination of the interests of the East European nations to those of the "international proletariat," allegedly represented by the Soviet state. In other words, the concept simply denoted a Soviet version of great power nationalism.

The first sign that this would not work appeared when Josip Broz Tito of Yugoslavia rejected the primacy of Soviet interests over those of his own country and opted for a Yugoslav road to socialism. In 1956, the Hungarians had shown in a glorious revolution that proletarian internationalism was dead. Soon the Romanians followed suit, and the Albanians broke their dependence on the Soviet Union in the early 1960s. Four and a half decades of oppression did nothing to eliminate East European nationalism. When the Soviet restraints were removed, nationalism, the elementary force that it is, came out into the open once again. The revived nationalism proved to be just as destructive as it had been in the pre-World War I empires. In Yugoslavia, it led to the terrible civil war witnessed since 1992. In the case of Czechoslovakia, it led to the dissolution of the state into its Czech and Slovak components. It revived Hungarian-Romanian hostility over Transylvania and its large Hungarian minority. The new Yugoslav federation of Serbia and Montenegro will have to face the problem of the large Albanian ethnic group in Kosovo. Bulgaria, Greece, and Yugoslavia will undoubtedly have another go at the problem of Macedonia.

Poland and Hungary present the only hopeful picture in Eastern Europe in regard to the nationalistic revival. Poland was deprived of its Russian and Ukrainian minorities thanks to Joseph Stalin's annexation of their homelands into the Soviet Union in 1945. The Polish state also divested itself of its huge German minority population when ethnic Germans were expelled from the western territories following World War II. Hungary lost its huge minority populations (really a majority) after World War I and after World War II. In both countries, there is not much support for chauvinistic nationalism. But the absence of minorities does not mean that the danger of the revival of chauvinism is over. For instance, hardly any Jews are left in Poland, and only about 80,000 Hungarian Jews still live in Hungary. Yet, anti-Semitism of the East European variety, an expression of chauvinistic nationalism, continues to flourish in both societies.

Another factor that causes all sorts of problems in Eastern Europe in the 1990s is the absence of true democratic traditions in most states of the region. With the exception of interwar Czechoslovakia, none of the states in the area had any truly democratic institutions during their long history. It is true that there were diets (only for noblemen) before the modern era; there were also parliamentary elections ever since the establishment of the new states. However, the diets included, at the most, about 5 percent of the population and elections were rigged more often than not. In consequence, the parliaments were hardly more than rubber stamping institutions for the decisions of kings, regents, and dictators. Even the much praised democracy of Czechoslovakia was flawed during the interwar years. The minorities had no representation in parliament until 1926, and after that, discrimination did not end against them, although it was more subtle than elsewhere. The three major elements of East European statehood—religion, nationalism, and authoritarianism—went hand in hand throughout much of the history of the peoples of the region.

Two more observations about the few general characteristics of East European history are due here. One of these concerns civil society. The institutions characteristic of such a society usually develop spontaneously and consist of numerous associations, clubs, and private groups whose membership joins them voluntarily. Civil society is characterized by the fact that it is largely—though not entirely—independent of any government, or at least its connections are tenuous with the ruling institutions. It may include soccer clubs, bridge partnerships, and many other loose organizations, providing a sense of autonomy and companionship to their members. Such associations cannot exist in a totalitarian environment and their survival even in a "normal" dictatorship could be questionable. The reverse of this assertion is also true. There is no true democracy without the existence of civil society. The history of the East European countries points to the fact that this important component of democracy has been missing. Since the collapse of the communist system, civil society has emerged in every country in the region, an important sign of the nature of the new societies that are being built.

The other factor that should be mentioned in this context is a special kind of extremism that seems typical of all East European societies. This extremism is so deeply ingrained in the public mind that is has become second nature for the population. It is based on the belief that there exists only "one truth" and the one who is in possession of it will consider everyone doubting his "truth" either as feebleminded or a scoundrel. As a consequence, there are no disputing partners in, for instance, politics, but either supporters or enemies. The term, "opponent," meaning someone who might be in possession of a slightly different "truth," is simply rejected. East European societies from Prague to Tirana are permeated through and through by such intolerance of differing opinions. It is present in the schools and universities, in private homes, and in scholarly conferences. In politics, it permeates to the core of organizations and parties, leading to brawls in party headquarters and parliaments.

In summing up our findings, one must say that religion, often taking on an intolerant hue; chauvinistic nationalism and hatred of different ethnic and racial minorities;

lack of true democratic historical traditions; the lateness of the development of civil society; and deeply ingrained intolerance of differing opinions are in the baggage that East European societies are carrying into the twenty-first century. They will need an extraordinary amount of luck to succeed in building democratic societies.

Let us now turn our attention to the outlines of the history of East European societies before the establishment of communist regimes in the region.

ALBANIA

The smallest country in Eastern Europe—but by no means on the European continent—Albania was the last of the Balkan nations to become independent. After 450 years of Ottoman Turkish rule, Albania was established by the Great Powers in 1912. Independence, however, did not mean instant development. Albania's economy was backward and her cultural institutions were underdeveloped. Only in 1908 was an Albanian alphabet created, although this did not mean that Albanians lacked national consciousness. The new state, harboring 740,000 inhabitants (the rest of the 1,300,000 of its total population were scattered in Serbia and Macedonia), had some mineral resources, but it was mainly agricultural. Its population was mostly illiterate. Divided into two subgroups, the northern Gegs and the southern Tosks, tribal and clan relations were still important. Ancient customs, among them the blood feud, were still observed. Ethnically, however, Albania was about 95 percent Albanian populated. The Sunni and Bektashi Islamic sects dominated national religion. There were only three cities in the country with populations over 10,000 each, and 88 percent of the people lived in rural areas. The new Albanian state was constantly threatened by its neighbors. Greece wanted southern Albania, claiming that its Orthodox Christian minority-about 10 percent of the population-was Greek. Serbians, Bulgarians, and Montenegrines all wanted pieces of the country, and they were prevented from partitioning it only by the Great Powers.

The major task of any Albanian government was, therefore, to guard independence and prevent encroachment on the nation's territory. The Great Powers designated William, Prince of Wied, as king of Albania in 1912, but his brief rule which extended until September 1914, brought little progress. Between 1914 and 1920, Albania was invaded and occupied by armies of the neighboring states and Italy, the Habsburg empire, and eventually France. At the peace conference, however, Albanian independence was recognized and the occupational armies were withdrawn. In December 1920, the country was admitted to the League of Nations.

However, political stability was not yet established. The two competing groups were the populists and the progressives. For a brief time, the populists succeeded in establishing a government. Headed by Father Fan Noli, a Harvard-educated clergyman of the Eastern Orthodox church, they argued that a new Albania could not be established until the power of the old bureaucracy was broken. However, the prime minister, Ahmed Zogu, the leader of the progressives, argued that law and order had primacy over social reorganization. In 1924, the Noli-led group seized power for a brief time, lasting only six months. Ahmed Zogu overthrew the Noli regime with British and Yugoslav backing in December 1924. In 1928, the state was transformed into a monarchy headed by King Zog, the former Ahmed Zogu. Although Zog had ruled in a dictatorial manner, he succeeded in laying the foundations of an Albanian state. He established a state bureaucracy and a national police force. He disarmed the tribesmen of the north and ended the practice of the blood feud. He promulgated criminal and commercial law codes based on Western models. Although elections were held in Albania during King Zog's rule, no political parties were permitted to be formed, and the elections were rigged. The number of cities grew to six, and the population increased to over one million. A national educational system was also established, although illiteracy remained high. But Albania's need for foreign economic assistance soon drew the country into the sphere of influence of Benito Mussolini's Italy. The first economic agreement between the two countries had already been signed in 1926. A year later, a twenty-year alliance was concluded. In 1939, Italian troops entered Albania and king Zog fled abroad with his wife and infant son. The Allies, however, were unwilling to recognize him as king-in-exile, and the period during World War II was a prelude to the communist conquest of power in the country.

BULGARIA

In the spring of 1879, an assembly of Bulgarian noblemen met, as stipulated by the Treaty of Berlin following the Russo-Turkish war of the year before, and established a constitution for the newly autonomous Bulgarian state. This state was still nominally under the suzerainty of the Ottoman Turkish empire, but in reality, it was, for all practical purposes, independent of the authorities in Istanbul. The Turnovo constitution guaranteed freedom of religion, the franchise for all male citizens over the age of twenty-one, eligibility for office for all citizens over thirty years of age and literate, a unicameral parliament, freedom of speech and assembly, and free elementary education for all. The head of state, however, not only had the power to command the armed forces, but also the power to promulgate and approve the laws and control the executive branch of government. Predictably, the two decades before 1900 saw many conflicts between ruler and parliament.

The first king, Prince Alexander von Battenberg, a young officer of the Prussian Guards in Berlin, was installed in Bulgaria by the Great Powers. He was a favorite nephew of Tsar Alexander II of Russia. He ran a personal regime with the backing of the tsar. When Tsar Alexander III came to the Russian throne, however, he lost the new tsar's favor and abdicated in 1885. His replacement was Prince Ferdinand of Saxe-Coburg-Gotha, who was related to practically every monarch in Europe. When Tsar Alexander III died and was replaced by Nicholas II in 1894, Ferdinand made up his differences with the new tsar. He also built a personal regime and disregarded the opposition. Bulgaria nevertheless made unprecedented progress during the years of

Ferdinand's rule. However, much of the progress was made possible by heavy borrowing from abroad. By 1912, the national foreign debt was so high that it required special taxes and the establishment of all sorts of state monopolies to pay the interests. Since the population was still mainly agricultural, the heavy taxes fell on the peasants who were gradually ruined by them.

All this was suddenly cut short by Bulgaria's participation in the two Balkan wars, in 1912 and 1913. The cause of the debacles was the Macedonian question. Bulgaria and Greece contested the territory and, after 1878, Serbia joined in the struggle. In 1894, Bulgarian Macedonians created the Internal Macedonian Revolutionary Organization (IMRO), demanding either autonomy within the Ottoman empire or annexation by Bulgaria. In 1912, an Italian-Turkish war threatened the possibility of either further Habsburg expansion into the Balkans or Italian intervention, or both. Thus, an alliance was concluded between Serbia and Bulgaria for the partitioning of Macedonia. Bulgaria also concluded an alliance with Greece. They both financed the war efforts of Montenegro, which became the fourth member of the Balkan alliance directed against Ottoman Turkey. The war began in October 1912, and Bulgaria bore the brunt of the fighting. In the meantime, Macedonia fell into Greek and Serbian hands. The peace conference that followed was deadlocked. Serbia and Greece argued that occupation determined possession. Bulgaria had three choices. It could demand Russian arbitration-as the treaty with Serbia demanded-or it could accept the loss of Macedonia. The third choice was war. Ferdinand decided on war and the Bulgarian army attacked Serb and Greek positions, beginning the Second Balkan War. Romania, taking advantage of the opportunity, attacked Bulgaria from the rear, and threatened Sofia. Turkey reopened the war on its front and took Adrianople. Bulgaria had no choice but to surrender. The peace treaty, signed in Bucharest, Romania, divided Macedonia between Greece and Serbia. Bulgaria received a small region called the Pirin. Romania took Bulgaria's southern Dobrudja, while Bulgaria was allowed to annex Western Thrace.

While the demands for revenge were strong, Bulgaria remained neutral at first in World War I. The British approached Ferdinand, but they could offer little inducement because of their commitments to Serbia and Greece. On the other hand, the Central Powers could offer all of Serb-held Macedonia and lands from Greece and Romania in case these two states sided with the Allies. In September 1915, therefore, Bulgaria entered the war on the side of the Central Powers. Its attack on Serbia ended Serb resistance. Bulgarian troops were soon in possession of all Macedonia up to the Greek borders, and they settled down to hold the line. But the entrance of the United States in the war soon had its over all effects. The Bulgarian army which faced a massive concentration of Allied armies, asked for peace. An armistice was signed in December 1918, and it required complete Bulgarian withdrawal from Serbian and Greek territories including Macedonia. By then, Ferdinand had already abdicated in favor of his son, Boris, and had left Bulgaria.

The new government was headed by Alexander Stamboliiski, the head of the

Agrarians, a Populist party, who signed the peace treaty with the Allies. He wanted a regime favoring the peasants. He and his allies considered the cities as alien bodies in the nation that would have to be reduced in size and in influence. Stamboliiski dreamed of setting up a Green International, in opposition to V. I. Lenin's Red International, advancing the peasants' cause in the world.

New elections were held in 1920 and the populist Agrarians won 110 seats out of 229 in parliament. Stamboliiski began to put through his reforms; he wanted to reduce the bureaucracy, eliminate government pensions, and alter the taxation system to stop rural folks from supporting the cities. He wanted to end the existing party system and introduce a sort of direct democracy in which the majority-the peasants-would rule the nation. Stamboliiski lasted for three years. He was violently overthrown and killed by an alliance of IMRO activists and military men in 1923, and many of his supporters shared his fate.

The Bulgarian communists, established following the Bolshevik Revolution in Russia, tried to fish in troubled waters. The COMINTERN dispatched an agent, Vassily Kolarov, to organize an uprising. It was, of course, a complete failure. The following year, the Communist party was declared outside the law. The party participated in brigandage and assassinations, but it played no role in Bulgarian politics until 1944.

Several political circles had more influence than the communists in Bulgarian politics. One of these, the ZVENO (Link), was cooperating with the Military League and favored the monarchy.

King Boris was more successful than his father in establishing his rule in subtle ways. He acted through loyal military officers and civilians. His government concluded a pact with Yugoslavia in 1937, and an agreement with Bulgaria's neighbors permitting Bulgarian rearmament. Boris came to know Adolf Hitler through several personal meetings with the German dictator. It was obvious that if war came, Bulgaria would once again be drawn into it on the German side.

In the summer of 1940, following the Soviet Union's reconquest of Bessarabia from Romania, Bulgaria received southern Dobrudja from its besieged neighbor. Before the German attack on the Soviet Union, Bulgaria was offered Greek and Turkish Thrace by Soviet diplomats if Bulgaria would be willing to assist Soviet security in the Dardanelles and Black Sea regions. King Boris declined, and within three months of this offer, his government concluded a treaty of alliance with Turkey. Germany, however, needed to cross Bulgaria on its way to Greece, when Hitler needed to secure the southern flank of the Central Powers, and the Bulgarian government agreed.

Prime Minister Filov signed the Tripartite Pact in Berlin. Soon thereafter, a law was passed that placed the same disabilities on Bulgaria's Jews as the German Jews suffered. This was a preliminary step to later anti-Jewish legislation and actions. Before the invasion of the Soviet Union by Germany, the Nazi armies attacked Yugoslavia and Greece, the latter through Bulgarian territory. As a reward, Bulgaria received Yugoslav Macedonia. Although Bulgaria's claims on Greece were not fulfilled, the

Bulgarian army was permitted to expand its control over some regions. But the Germans made sure to exploit all conquered areas for their own use, and the Italians quarreled with Bulgaria over territories which they claimed were Albanian populated. Although Bulgaria joined the Anti-Comintern Pact in November 1942, its relations with the Soviet Union were not broken.

In August 1943, King Boris suddenly died. Almost simultaneously, and encouraged by the final German defeat at Stalingrad, the Bulgarian communists started an organized guerilla movement directed by the likes of Georgy Dimitrov and Vassily Kolarov from Moscow. The communists created a front organization in the Fatherland Front which soon attracted some left-wing Agrarians, Social Democrats, members of ZVENO, and a few people from the Military League. In September 1944, the Soviet Red Army had reached Bulgaria's borders. By then, the resistance movement attracted some 10,000 people.

When King Boris died, his son, Simeon, was only six years old. Thus, a regency, consisting of conservative royalists, took over. In January and March 1944, severe allied bombing raids devastated whole sections of the major Bulgarian cities with no other purpose than to show that the war was real. On September 5, the Soviet Union declared war on Bulgaria. However, before the Red Army reached Sofia, a coup d'etat, organized by the Military League and the communists, succeeded in arresting the ministers and installing a government of the Fatherland Front. Bulgaria thus became Stalinized earlier than most other East European countries, and its people ended communist rule exactly forty-five years later.

CZECHOSLOVAKIA

The Czechoslovak republic was established in 1918 as the result of Czech and Slovak emigres signing an agreement in Pittsburgh. The leading Czech politicians, Tomas Garrigue Masaryk and Eduard Benes, engineered the establishment of the new state by convincing the Allied leaders, especially Woodrow Wilson, that the dismemberment of the Austro-Hungarian empire was a necessity for the creation of a new, democratic order in the eastern part of the European continent.

The Czech people have, of course, a long historical tradition of independence and even greatness in European history. Their medieval rulers had created a powerful state out of Moravia, Bohemia, and Silezia and had influenced European politics for centuries. Not so the Slovaks. While the Czechs were becoming an increasingly urbanized people in the course of the nineteenth century, the Slovaks remained basically rural. Their lands were part and parcel of the Kingdom of Hungarians, and their national consciousness was undeveloped. Czechs were a highly literate people; in 1918, only about 5 percent of the population over the age of ten lacked reading and writing skills. In contrast, over 60 percent of the Slovaks were still illiterate. The Slovaks were to argue later that their national and cultural development was retarded by the oppressive Hungarian state. This was only partly true.

In Slovakia—until 1918, the Highlands of northern Hungary—the Roman Catholic church had a much greater influence than in the largely secularized Czech lands, and this fact may have had something to do with Slovakia's cultural development. While in Prague, Charles University, established in the fourteenth century, was the center of intellectual life, no such institution existed in Slovakia.

The fusion of these two peoples immediately presented serious problems for the new state. Although Czechs and Slovaks basically spoke the same language, their historical and cultural experiences were so different that there could scarcely be agreement on any question except the independence of their new state. Slovaks expected a wide-ranging autonomy within Czechoslovakia, but the Czechs wanted a unitary state. In addition, Czechoslovakia was "enriched" by the victorious Allies; they gave the new state huge ethnic minorities who were unwilling participants in this new state. About three million Sudeten Germans, close to a million Hungarians, and large Ukrainian and Russian minorities were included in the new Czechoslovakia. All this could only spell trouble, and it did. Nevertheless, the interwar Czechoslovak republic was considered the only democratically organized state in Eastern Europe. Its economy was largely industrial; the Austro-Hungarian empire established some heavy and light industries in the Czech lands before 1918, and these now became the property of the new state. The Skoda factory, producing heavy machinery and war material, and the Bata shoe factory were already well known in Europe. Consequently, there was a relatively large stratum of industrial workers with advanced ideas about social and political organization, and a large intelligentsia that was Western in its orientation.

The political system that emerged was based on the willingness of the participants to compromise over issues that created conflict in other East European societies. There was general respect for democratic processes among the five major parties that participated in the government during the interwar years. Consequently, there was continuity in politics, a quality sorely lacking in the rest of the states of Eastern Europe.

The Czechoslovak Communist party was legal, and it attracted a sizable following. However, by its very need to participate in the give and take of everyday political life, the party was less radical than it was in other societies. Although the Communist party did not participate in government, it had many parliamentary deputies. In 1929, Klement Gottwald, the leader of the communists, tried to radicalize the party on Stalin's orders, but even this produced a less militant organization than similar efforts elsewhere.

Although Czech-German relations became overwhelmingly important as the 1930s progressed, it was the conflict between Czechs and Slovaks that caused most of the problems for the new state. The Czech lands were, as indicated above, far more advanced in every area of national and social life than were those of the Slovaks. There was a rich civil society in existence, allowing large numbers of the population to participate in public life. In Slovakia, Roman Catholicism heavily influenced national consciousness and many priests, as public figures, spoke up for Slovak national culture.

After the establishment of the Czechoslovak state in 1918, Slovak hopes for autonomy did not materialize. The disappointment that this engendered created a great deal of dissatisfaction among the people, fueled by nationalist intellectuals. Slovaks perceived that the industrialized Czech lands provided a better living for the Czechs than their own agricultural economy. Consequently, they demanded that either Czech industries be transplanted to Slovakia, or that new industries be established in their half of the Czechoslovak republic. This did not happen.

The Great Depression of the 1930s caused severe difficulties for the country as a whole, and the economy stagnated. Even after the recovery in the mid-1930s, Slovakia's development was a lot slower than that of the Czech lands. Considerable progress was made in education, literacy among the Slovaks increased, and the growth of the intelligentsia was noticeable. Yet, this was not considered sufficient progress by nationalistic Slovaks.

Radical nationalist leaders soon emerged. Among them was Vojtech Tuka, who received his inspirations from Germany. The People's party, led by Father Andrej Hlinka (until his death in 1938), and his successor, Josef Tiso, no longer demanded autonomy for Slovakia, but independence. Yet the breakup of the Czechoslovak state in 1939 was not the result of these disputes. It was caused by the grievances of the German minority, skillfully exploited by Hitler.

The Germans made up 22.3 percent of the population of the Czechoslovak state. They were the descendants of settlers invited to the Czech lands by earlier kings and noblemen, residing in the country for many, many generations. Some of them were imposed on the Czechs by the Habsburg rulers in the sixteenth-seventeenth centuries. Their grievances centered on the conflict between German and Czech cultures that was extended into politics and economics. Most important, the Germans found themselves a minority in the country in 1918, after having been the dominant ethnic group, at least since the early seventeenth century.

The land reform following the establishment of the new state had hit them hard, which was its real purpose. Most estates that were confiscated had German owners, but the land so gained by the state was given to Czechs. Industry and banking in the region was closely associated with foreign capital, mostly German, and pressure from those quarters heavily influenced the behavior of the German population. The Sudetenland was also hit hard by the Depression because of its close ties to depressed economies abroad. In addition, the Czechoslovak state consciously encouraged the migration of Czechs into lands with heavy German populations in order to counterbalance German dominance in those regions.

On the other hand, the state did not interfere with the educational and cultural activities of the German minority. German language schools were maintained, and cultural organizations functioned freely. In 1926, parliamentary representation was made available to the Germans—until then, no minorities were permitted to vote and have deputies in the Czechoslovak parliament—and several parties took advantage of the opportunity.

With the accession of Adolf Hitler to power in Germany in 1933, extremism grew in the Sudenten areas. Konrad Henlein formed the Sudeten German party with the express intention of separating the area from Czechoslovakia. Hitler used the party's propaganda as an excuse for the dismemberment of the Czechoslovak state. However, the participation in the appeasement of the German dictator by Great Britain and France was among the major causes of Hitler's success. When World War II broke out, the Czechoslovak state no longer existed. In its place there was a puppet Slovak state, beholden to Hitler for its very existence, and a German "protectorate" of Bohemia and Moravia.

GERMAN DEMOCRATIC REPUBLIC (EAST GERMANY)

Germany had many ties to Eastern Europe, some going back centuries, but when the East German state emerged in the late 1940s, it took on an unprecedented role in the region. Germany had been divided by religion ever since the activities of Martin Luther in the sixteenth century. The east, including Prussia, became Lutheran, while the west and the south of the country remained Roman Catholic. German influence entered Eastern Europe in the shape of German settlers, many of them skilled craftsmen, miners, and also peasants, who were invited by various kings and landlords who needed their skills. Many of the cities and towns of Eastern Europe were founded by German settlers. Many of these settlers preserved their German language even if their culture reflected those of the receiving nations.

In the course of the late nineteenth century, however, nationalism and national revival in Eastern Europe began to regard the Germans as alien bodies in the polities in question. The Habsburg rulers' culture was German. German political influence and the expansionism of the Second German empire certainly contributed to this phenomenon. During World War I, most East European nations were on the side of the Allies except Hungary and Bulgaria.

With the dismemberment of the Habsburg empire in 1918, the new states, formed in its former territories, regarded German influence as hostile. Romanians, Czechs and Slovaks, Yugoslavs, and Poles, were all anti-German, and their Germanophobia was often colored by racism. On the other hand, Hungary and Bulgaria once again looked upon Germany and its struggles against the peace treaties as an example to be followed. Even when Hitler came into power, Hungary and Bulgaria remained favorably disposed to German penetration of the region as a way to change the borders that were drawn by the victorious Allies often arbitrarily, usually at their expense. Most East Europeans also feared the Soviet Union and its radical Marxist-Leninist ideology.

When Germany proceeded to redraw the map of Europe, first at the expense of Czechoslovakia, and Italy annexed Albania, the East European countries remained inactive. When the German army attacked Poland and France and forced their surrender, there was apprehension among the East Europeans, but there was also a grudging acceptance of Germany as the dominant power of the continent.

Romania and Hungary joined Germany in the attack on the Soviet Union. The former did so in order to keep Transylvania Romanian, the latter to gain Hitler's support for revisionism. Yugoslavia was defeated and dismembered by then, and Bulgaria cautiously edged closer to Germany.

Between 1939 and 1943, Germany was the dominant power in Eastern Europe, and the East Europeans began to hedge their bets only after the decisive defeat of the German army at Stalingrad. By 1944, the liquidation of the Jews of Eastern Europe was in high gear. Resistance movements, usually led by communists and other leftists, but also by such nationalists as Dragoljub Mihajlovic in Yugoslavia, began to gather strength. However, with the notable exception of Tito's partisan army, most East European resistance was small and did not decisively affect the outcome of the war. This was the case even in Poland, where an underground army existed.

By the end of World War II, there emerged a general dislike of Germans throughout the region. There was sentiment in favor of getting rid of ethnic Germans in Yugoslavia, Poland, Hungary, and Romania. And when these populations were deported to defeated Germany, few voices were raised on their behalf.

When the German Democratic Republic emerged, it was only grudgingly accepted by other East Europeans as a member of the Soviet bloc. When its leaders, especially Walter Ulbricht, insisted on a special relationship with the Soviet Union, and buttressed this demand with a strong East German economy, many East Europeans, even communists, were resentful. When East German troops and secret police were active in Africa, most East Europeans considered this unnecessary. When the communist system and the Berlin Wall collapsed and German unification became a fact of life, most East Europeans were apprehensive of the future influence in their region by a strong, rich Germany.

HUNGARY

Hungarians, like Poles and Czechs, could look back on a long history, during which the Hungarian state had played an important role in shaping European affairs. The medieval Hungarian kingdom expanded at one time to include most of the northern Balkans, and it was a worthy competitor of the Polish and Czech powers. In 1526, however, Hungary lost its independence and great power status to the conquering armies of the Ottoman Sultan, Suleiman the Magnificent. Its central and southern regions, including Transylvania, were incorporated into the Ottoman empire, while the north and west became part of the increasingly powerful and expansive Habsburg realms.

Hungarian national consciousness was stimulated by the assimilationist policies of the absolutist Habsburg emperor, Joseph II, who wanted his subjects to become

German speaking people with German culture. Resistance to Germanization brought about the revision of the Hungarian language which soon became the language of literature and intelligent conversation. Soon demands for Hungarian independence began. These led to a revolution in 1848 which eventually resulted in the declaration of the dethroning of the House of Habsburg. The Hungarians fought with incredible bravery. But the revolution was suppressed by the armies of Tsar Nicholas I of Russia, whose help was solicited by Francis Joseph, the young Habsburg emperor. However, it proved impossible to rule Hungary by royal decrees.

By 1867, a compromise between the House of Habsburg and the Hungarian nation was reached that gave Hungary autonomy in all internal matters except the armed forces, finance, and foreign policies. A separate Hungarian government was established that ruled the country from Budapest and was in constant squabbles with the imperial administration stationed in Vienna. There was also a separate Hungarian army, the national guard, and a joint armed force composed of all peoples of the empire.

Hungary had seen considerable economic progress during the dualistic era. The economy developed with great speed, industrialization progressed. However, Hungary was a true multinational state, and assimilationist policies were causing a great deal of resentment among the ethnic minorities. The defeat of the Austro-Hungarian empire in World War I brought these resentments to the fore. In 1918, the Romanian, Serb, Croatian, Slovak and Slovene minorities decided to secede from Hungary and were supported by the victorious Allied powers. Hungary lost two-thirds of its territory and about 60 percent of its former population to the Successor States and Romania. This had created a nationalistic fervor that became dominant throughout the interwar years in Hungarian foreign and internal policies.

Rump Hungary was the first country to establish a communist dictatorship in Eastern Europe in 1919. Although it lasted for only three months, it left lasting imprints on the national psyche.

During the 1920s and 1930s, Hungarian politics were dominated by right-wing parties. The country also had a regent, Miklos Horthy de Nagybanya, a former rear admiral of the Habsburg navies, and adjutant to Emperor Francis Joseph. As the years went by, Hungary increasingly sought support for its revisionist demands at the governments of European dictators. First, Mussolini came to Hungary's support. When it turned out that his agenda was mainly expansion of Italian power into the Balkans, relations between the two countries cooled. When Hitler came into power in Germany and voiced his radical plans for the remaking of the map of Europe, the Hungarians approached his regime cautiously at first. However, it soon became evident that Hitler was sympathetic to Hungary's territorial claims.

Nazi Germany had, by then, established deep inroads into the Hungarian economy. Germans provided armaments for the Hungarian armed forces and supplied other industrial goods for the country. In exchange, they bought up Hungary's agricultural surpluses. The whole exchange was conducted on a barter basis, since neither country had sufficient amounts of hard currency. German ideological penetration followed this process. Native Nazism was never strong in Hungary, although the Hungarian Nazis, who called themselves the Nyilaskeresztes part (Arrow Cross party), gained considerable notoriety. However, they could never have gained power by their own effort.

The Communist party of Hungary was devastated by the failure of the first communist dictatorship. Its membership dwindled to insignificance. Its leaders were either in jail or in exile in the Soviet Union during the entire interwar period. However, Hungary entered the war against the Soviet Union in 1941, and lost an entire army on the Stalingrad front. When the Soviet army reached Hungary in 1944, the regent tried to arrange for a separate armistice. By then, Hungary was occupied by German forces which made the attempt fail.

The war caused great devastation in the country. By 1945, most of Hungarian factories were looted of their equipment either by the Germans or by the Soviet armies. Bridges, roads, and buildings were destroyed or damaged. The country faced a period of hard times rebuilding a shattered infrastructure.

POLAND

The medieval Polish state was among the great European powers. Its boundaries extended at one point in time from the Baltic to the Black sea. It was responsible for the conversion of the Lithuanians to Christianity in the late fourteenth century. Its king, John III Sobieski, saved Vienna from the Ottoman Turks in 1683. Yet, the Polish state had weaknesses that were exploited by its neighbors. By the end of the eighteenth century, the Russian and Habsburg empires and Prussia had partitioned the Polish state three times so that, by 1795, Poland disappeared from the map of Europe. The bulk of the Polish territories were taken by Russia. The Russian tsars made every effort to turn Poles into Russians. Polish language schools were closed, and the administration was conducted in the Russian language. Several attempts were made by Polish patriots to reassert Polish independence, but all of them were suppressed. After 128 years, in 1918, Poland was reconstituted as an independent state. The new state took several years to establish stable borders. The economy was also rebuilt, and the political system was reconstituted. However, the new Polish state included large ethnic minorities who had been included within its borders without their consent. The large German minority in the west, numbering close to 6 million people, was matched by millions of Ukrainians and Russians in the east. Poland's Jewish population came to 3.5 million. Although Poles were in the majority, their state could hardly be called a national state. Nation building was, therefore, a difficult task indeed and it had not yet been completed when World War II broke out. The situation was similar with state building. Polish people in the German-dominated regions were generally more prosperous and better educated than their brothers in Russian-dominated Poland. On the other hand, the latter had a better chance to participate in administrative work and were, therefore, more experienced in the ways of bureaucracy. The Poles in the

Poles in the Austro-Hungarian monarchy were neither prosperous, nor better educated, but they experienced the gemutlichkeit so typical of the last decades of the empire. To bring these three elements "into the state" was a difficult task indeed.

The three parts of Poland that were united in the new state continued to experience differences in terms of economic, social, and cultural development right up to the end of the interwar period. Despite all these problems, institutional and legal integration progressed and, given more time, it would have been completed within a reasonable period. But Poland was not given the time.

The political life of Poland was deeply influenced by the Western democracies. When the Polish state was established, it was expected to become a democracy. Its initial problems with this system were ascribed to the war that Poland fought against Bolshevik Russia in 1920, which the Polish army won. General Jozef Pilsudski, one of the founders of the Polish state, commanded the Polish forces, and he became the grand old man of the new state.

The most troubling economic issue was the problem of the peasantry. There were too many peasants who had no land or had such small holdings that they had to hire themselves out as laborers. The new state tried land reforms twice, once in 1920 and again in 1925, but the political influence of large landowners prevented a thoroughgoing reform, and the general situation of the peasantry was barely changed.

Polish industry was unevenly developed. Firms around the larger cities were modern factories, but with the developing customs barriers it became more and more difficult for them to find buyers for their products. Furthermore, the large Russian market suddenly closed before them. Not surprisingly, industrial production declined in the 1920s. When the Depression came, Polish industry was already in stagnation.

With the slump in agricultural prices, the Polish economy was in difficulties throughout the 1930s. The state designated an area with the highest industrial development as a Central Industrial Region, which was a successful experiment, but the outbreak of the war ended this process.

The Polish intelligentsia, whose members came from various social strata, very quickly acquired dominance over all phases of national life. Its members believed that it was their destiny to rule Poland and, therefore, they neglected the other social strata as politically immature and, therefore, insignificant.

The intelligentsia in Poland had never been able to develop its ideas for ruling the state. Democracy and dictatorship were equally abhorred. The only system they favored was one in which their special position was not threatened. Since the national minorities objected to the continuation of the status quo, the intelligentsia became very nationalistic and attempted to turn the minorities into Poles. Although anti-Semitism existed in Poland, it occurred mainly among the workers and peasants.

Poles, almost without exception, mistrusted authority of any kind. Yet, most Poles recognized the special relationship that existed between their nation and the Roman Catholic church. The church enjoyed privileges and was closely intertwined with the government bureaucracy. In turn, the church's hierarchy was strongly supportive of Polish nationhood.

The new Polish state did not have outstanding political leaders. Jozef Pilsudski came closest to that ideal, but he was also often hesitant and capricious. He was strongly nationalistic, did not care much for democracy, and was loyal to his supporters to an unlimited degree. He enjoyed popular support, in spite of his unconcern for economic and social issues. In 1926, Pilsudski assumed dictatorial powers through a coup d'etat, but he soon gave up his powers. His major challenger was Roman Dmowski, who represented Poland at the peace negotiations after World War I, and who successfully argued for Poland's new borders. Dmowski was pushed aside by Pilsudski and he left the country. He returned to Poland just before he died in 1939.

On the eve of World War II, Poland projected the image of a country that, after some turmoil, had finally reached the takeoff point for dynamic development. If the war could have been avoided, Poland would have reached a point in about a decade that would have made it a country similar to Hungary and Czechoslovakia in economic and social developments. In history, of course, such suppositions do not count.

ROMANIA

The Romanian people present an enigma for historians. There are several versions about the origin of Romanians. Romanians believe that their people descended from the ancient Dacians who mixed with the soldiers of the Roman legions. When the legions were withdrawn, the people moved into the southern slopes of the Carpathian mountains where they survived the Barbarian invasions.

Others, however, present a different story. According to them, the Vlachs (or Wlachs), as the Romanians were called in the late Middle Ages, were shepherds who originated in the western parts of the Balkans and gradually moved north until they reached their present homeland. Practicing trans-humance, they gradually penetrated Transylvania. Whatever the truth in these theories, the fact is that the forerunners of present-day Romanians did not appear in East European history until the twelfth century. If they spent the centuries of Barbarian invasions and the establishment of the early East European kingdoms in the mountains, then they do indeed represent remarkable powers of survival. The two principalities of Wallachia and Moldavia, the kernels of the later Romanian state, struggled for existence throughout the fourteenth and fifteenth centuries. Eventually they were subjected to Ottoman Turkish rule from which they were liberated only in the 1870s.

The new Romanian state had all the trappings of democracy, but without the traditions and values to make such a system work. Elections were indeed held, and representation, and the procedures for the rotation of leadership, were based on them. Political parties emerged, and the press was free. Beyond the facade, however, there were flaws that eventually proved fatal for the system.

During the 1920s, politics in Romania went on with stops and starts. The Populist party had a powerful message for the peasantry, combining nation and God. It preached that politicians in general were the bane of society, and that the nation and the people must be made one. In typical populist fashion, the cities were proclaimed the home of "alien" peoples, especially Jews and Hungarians, who were bent on exploiting the poor Romanian peasants. The populists were also authoritarians; their two most powerful movements, the Legion of St. Michael and the Iron Guard, were basically right-wing groups who resorted to terrorism when they could not reach their goals otherwise. Members of the Iron Guard murdered Nicolae Jorga, the most prominent critic of violence and authoritarian methods.

In the 1930s, these organizations intimidated most politicians and were on the verge of taking power into their own hands. The Iron Guards were openly fascist; the Legionnaires preached an agrarian radicalism. In 1938, the king had taken matters into his own hands. The royal coup d'etat ended the reign of terror by the extremists, although it did not usher in a society safe for democracy.

The corruption that was so typical of all Romanian regimes continued unabated. In such a situation one would expect extremism of both kinds—left wing and right wing—to flourish. But this was not the case with the traditionally leftist groups. The Romanian Communist party was established in the early 1920s, and it exerted itself in preparing the revolt of the workers. But the party was small and insignificant. It was outlawed in the early 1920s, and its known leaders were arrested and jailed. Such people as Gheorghe Gheorghiu-Dej, Ana Pauker, and others spent most of the 1930s in prison, although they were not badly treated. They would never have been able to establish a communist dictatorship without direct support from the Soviet Red Army in 1944.

YUGOSLAVIA

Yugoslavia came into being only in 1926. Following World War I, in whose instigation Serb terrorists played a leading role, a kingdom of Serbs, Croats, and Slovenes was established. This mini-multinational state included large numbers of ethnic minorities. Of the participating nations, Serbia and Montenegro achieved autonomy, then independence from the Ottoman empire early in the nineteenth century. Croatia and Slavonia were part of the Austro-Hungarian empire. Kosovo, with its large Albanian population, was included in Serbia in the late nineteenth century. Hungarians, Germans, and Romanians were also included in the new state.

Throughout the interwar years, there were disagreements among the constituent nationalities and politicians over the shape the state should take. In 1926, the name of the country was changed to that of Yugoslavia, that is, the state of the South Slavs. But the change did not mean any significant alteration in the nature of the government.

The Croats and Slovenes wanted a federal state organization, with wide-ranging autonomy for the constituent parts. But the Serbs who spent most of the effort—and blood—in the establishment of the new state, brought with them a tradition of unitary state organization. Since they were the most numerous in the new country, amounting to 39 percent of the population, as opposed to 24 percent Croatians and 8.5 percent Slovenes, and since they controlled the armed forces, their will prevailed. The Serbs also believed that they could assimilate the minorities, amounting to 16.6 percent of the population, making them into South Slavs. Deprived of their national rights and with their cultures suppressed, the minorities became a constant source of discontent and turmoil in the South Slavic state.

Between 1919 and 1929, the country experienced a weak democratic system. Parliament, freely elected, was beset by constant bickering among various ethnic and political parties. The disputes ranged from the form of government—whether monarchy or republic, whether unitarism or federalism—to territorial autonomy for the constituent nations. The Croatian Peasant party emerged as the strongest challenger of unitarism. Its leader, Stjepan Radic, was a controversial figure who inspired unbounded love by his co-nationals and hatred by his opponents.

In 1921, a constitution was accepted, based on the 1903 Serb document that provided for parliamentary democracy in a unitary state. The constitution was challenged from the very beginning, and the disputes resulted in twenty-three governments between 1921 and 1928. There was no trust among the antagonists, and King Alexander meddled in politics behind the scenes. All this culminated in 1928 in the assassination of the Croatian Radic in parliament. The turmoil that followed threatened the existence of the state.

In January 1929, the king suspended the constitution and declared his own personal dictatorship. He was supported by the army whose officers were mainly Serbian. In 1931, a new constitution reestablished parliamentarism, but the representative body was subordinated to the king. In 1934, the king himself was assassinated by Croatian and Macedonian terrorists while on a visit to Marseilles, France. He was succeeded by a minor under the name of Peter II, and a regency was set up. But this did not change the system, showing that royal dictatorship was supported by the powerful members of the political establishment.

During the interwar years, the South Slav state maintained its French foreign policy orientation. However, it also inherited rivalries from pre-World War I days with Bulgaria over Macedonia, and with Albania over Kosovo. It also faced a revisionist Hungary, whose government constantly agitated for the revision of the borders. Yugoslavia refused to recognize Lenin's Bolshevik regime in the Soviet Union, and it also had disputes with Romania over the province of the Banat.

In order to break out of its isolation, the South Slav state concluded a series of treaties with Romania and Czechoslovakia, establishing an alliance system, known as the Little Entente, in 1921. French inspired, the alliance was intended as a substitute for the defunct Habsburg empire, a cordon sanitaire against the Soviet Union and a buffer against defeated Germany. The weak alliance should have included Poland as well as Hungary. But Poland had a serious dispute with Czechoslovakia over the territory around the city of Teschen that almost led to war, and Hungary was an out-and-out enemy of the new order established by the peace treaties. The South Slav state also had to face a resurgent Italy under Mussolini, a real danger to its very existence.

Internally, Yugoslavia had its share of extremists. The most dangerous groups on the right included ultranationalist Croatians and Macedonians. They were outright fascists and enemies of the state, and they received support from Italy. The Croatian terrorists called themselves Ustashi, and their major means were violence and intimidation. Their goal was the establishment of a separate Croatia as an independent state. Their leader, Ante Pavelic, who was in Italian exile, directed his faction from abroad. The Internal Macedonian Revolutionary Organization (IMRO) was split; one segment demanded annexation to Bulgaria, and the other wanted communism and a Balkan federation. The communists had a surprisingly strong showing in the elections in 1920, but, because they conducted terror, their support declined. In 1924, the party was outlawed and it dwindled into insignificance. In 1937, after Josip Broz Tito returned to Yugoslavia from his exile in Moscow, he reorganized the party and, on the eve of World War II, it had nearly 10,000 members.

Economically, Yugoslavia had made little progress during the interwar years. In 1941, 75 percent of the population was still agricultural. Although the number of industrial firms doubled in two and a half decades, and the number of industrial workers grew correspondingly, Yugoslavia's main exports continued to be agricultural goods and raw materials, while the country imported industrial, finished goods.

The country collapsed in 1941 under German assault, and the resistance, led by the communist Josip Broz Tito, and the nationalist Dragolyub Mihailovich, fought not only against the Germans but also against each other. Population losses were enormous, and rebuilding the country took tremendous effort.

GENERAL CHRONOLOGY

1939   *March-April.* German-Polish relations became strained. The Czech lands were proclaimed a German protectorate. Britain and France guaranteed Polish territorial integrity. The Spanish civil war ended with the victory of General Francisco Franco's forces. Italy invaded Albania, forcing King Zog to flee, first to Greece, then to Turkey.

May. Jewish participation in Hungarian professional life was severely restricted by anti-Jewish legislation. Italy and Germany established a military alliance.

June-August. Great Britain and France began to negotiate with the Soviet Union for a possible military alliance against Adolf Hitler's Germany. Simultaneously, Josip V. Stalin began secret discussions with German representatives for a partition of East European territory between the two totalitarian dictatorships. On August 23, Germany and the Soviet Union concluded a pact for cooperation and mutual assistance and divided their spheres of influence in Eastern Europe at the expense of Poland, Romania, and other states. In secret protocols they agreed to partition Poland; the Soviet Union was to annex Bessarabia, taken by Romania in 1919, and the three Baltic states of Lithuania, Latvia and Estonia. The Soviet Union was to supply Germany's needs in raw materials and food.

September-October. World War II began with a German attack on Poland and the British-French declaration of war on Germany. The Polish armed forces were defeated in sixteen days. The Soviet Red Army invaded Poland and occupied territories taken from the Russian state in the Polish-Soviet war of 1919–1920.

December. The League of Nations expelled the Soviet Union from its membership when the Soviet army invaded Finland.

1940 *May-June.* In Britain, Winston Churchill was named prime minister. The Soviet army occupied the three Baltic states. France was defeated and forced to sign an armistice with Germany. The act was performed in the same railroad car in which the German armistice was signed in 1918.

September-October. German troops entered Romania to secure oil deliveries for Germany. Italy entered the war by attacking Greece, but its troops, needing German help, were defeated.

1941 *March-April.* German troops, assisted by Bulgarian and Hungarian forces, quickly defeated Yugoslavia. The resistance movements crystallized around the communist partisan army of Josip Broz Tito and the Yugoslav nationalist Dragoljub Mihailovic's Chetniks.

June-November. Germany attacked the Soviet Union, in spite of the Soviet Union's scrupulous fulfillment of its obligations to Germany according to the treaty of 1939. Rapid German advances necessitated the evacuation of the Soviet government from Moscow.

December. The German attack stalled before it reached Moscow. Japan attacked The United States naval base at Pearl Harbor. The United States entered the war.

1942 *June-August.* After reverses in the Philippines, the U.S. Navy defeated Japan's fleet at Midway island, beginning a battle of attrition. German forces, in a new offensive, reached Stalingrad where they bogged down.

December. Enrico Fermi, leading a team of brilliant scientists, most of whom had escaped from Eastern Europe, achieved the first sustained nuclear reaction in Chicago.

1943 *May-July.* The Soviet Union, in order to allay the fear of its Western allies about its expansionist ambitions, dissolved the COMINTERN. Benito Mussolini was overthrown by a coup d'etat led by the Italian king, and his fascist party was dissolved.

September-December. Italy surrendered unconditionally to the Allies. Three days later, German troops occupied Rome and began a campaign to delay the

Allied offensive to the north. The three major Allied leaders met at Teheran. They agreed on the attack on Germany through France by Britain and the United States, and through Poland and Eastern Europe by the Soviet army.

1944 *March-August.* The last Jewish enclave in Hungary was invaded by German SS troops, after occupying the country. The Soviet army was approaching Warsaw, and its leaders appealed to the Polish home army to rise against the Germans. However, when the Polish resistance attacked the Germans, the Red Army stopped its advance permitting the Germans to slaughter the Poles. Warsaw was almost completely destroyed. The Red Army occupied Bucharest.

September-December. The Soviet Union declared war on Bulgaria when its troops neared the Bulgarian border. After Bulgaria asked for an armistice, Bulgarian troops were used by the Red Army as shields and advanced forces in fighting Germany. The Allied forces occupied Athens. Hungary asked for an armistice, but its efforts were thwarted by the Germans. The Red Army reached Budapest.

1945 *January-February.* Soviet troops finally entered devastated Warsaw. At Yalta on the Black Sea (in the Soviet Union) Churchill, Stalin and Franklin D. Roosevelt met in order to discuss the conclusion of the war and their views on post-World War II Europe. They agreed on a concerted attack on Germany and, after the conclusion of hostilities in Europe, on a joint attack on Japan. They agreed to divide post war Germany into four occupational zones on a temporary basis. The Western leaders noted that the Soviet Union unilaterally established communist regimes in Romania and Bulgaria. They reached no agreement on the shape of the Polish government after the war. The government of the Yugoslav communists was recognized by all the Allied powers.

March-April. A Romanian government headed by crypto-communist Petru Groza was established. The Red Army entered Vienna. President Roosevelt died, and his vice president, Harry Truman, replaced him. The Soviet, British, and American forces met at Torgau on the Elbe river, ending the existence of Nazi Germany. Italian resistance fighters caught and executed Mussolini. Hitler committed suicide. The war in Europe had ended.

June-July. The Allied Control Commission was established in Germany and the former allies of the Nazis in Eastern Europe. The four zones of occupation of Germany were established. Berlin was taken under the control of the four occupying powers; the French were given a part from the zones of the Western Allies. In San Francisco, the Allied powers and China signed the United Nations charter. A communist-dominated government was established in Poland, but it included five members from the Polish government-in-exile in London. Churchill, Truman, and Stalin met for the last wartime conference in Potsdam, where Truman notified his allies of the United States' possession of the atomic bomb. A council of foreign ministers was established with the task of drafting a peace treaty with the defeated nations. German reparations were agreed upon and trials for war criminals were to be held. The western borders of the Polish state were to be extended to the Oder-Neisse rivers, and the German population from the new Polish lands was to be deported to the zones of occupation. Similarly, ethnic Germans were to be expelled from Czechoslovakia and Hungary and they, too, were to be deported to Germany. *August-December.* Atomic bombs were dropped on the Japanese cities of Hiroshima and Nagasaki. Japan surrendered. World War II. At the first conference of Allied foreign ministers, the Western powers unsuccessfully tried to remove Soviet-installed communist governments from Bulgaria, Hungary, and Romania. War crime trials began in the city of Nuremberg. Hungary expelled about 150,000 ethnic Germans followed by another 100,000 two years later. The process was reminiscent of the deportation of Jews during the war. The second meeting of Allied foreign ministers reached agreements on the peace treaties.

1946 *January-March.* The first meeting of the general assembly of the United Nations was held. Albania proclaimed itself the first People's Republic in Eastern Europe. Churchill delivered a speech at Westminster College at Fulton, Missouri, declaring that an "iron curtain" now separated Eastern and Western Europe.

July-October. The Paris Peace Conference reestablished the pre-World War II borders in Eastern Europe, except areas annexed by the Soviet Union and Poland. The Nuremberg tribunal sentenced twelve former Nazi leaders to death, and three to life imprisonment and it acquitted nine.

1947 *January-March.* The British and U.S. occupational zones in Germany were united as one economic unit. Peace treaties were signed with Italy, Hungary, Romania, Finland, and Germany. The Allies could not agree on peace terms for Germany and Japan. Truman declared his famous doctrine for the containment of communism.

May-June. The Marshall Plan was proclaimed, aimed at rebuilding war-torn Europe. The Soviet Union and the East European states declined an invitation to participate.

October. The Communist Information Bureau, an organization intended to supervise the Stalinization of East European countries and to coordinate the supremacy of the Soviet Union in the international socialist movement, was established. Its first headquarters was in Belgrade.

1948 *March.* Five countries, including Great Britain, France, Holland, Belgium, and Luxemburg, agreed to cultural and economic cooperation. This group was to become the kernel for the North Atlantic Treaty Organization, or NATO. The Allied Control Commissions stopped operating in the conquered European countries.

June. The Soviet Union, angered by the introduction of financial reform in the

Western zones of occupation in Germany, suddenly blockaded Berlin. An air lift, organized by the three Western powers, kept the city supplied with necessities until the blockade ended in 1949.

1949 *January-April.* The Soviet Union, Bulgaria, Czechoslovakia, Hungary, Poland, and Romania established the Council of Mutual Economic Assistance (COMECON). The basic agreement for the establishment of NATO was signed by Britain, the United States, France, Italy, Portugal, Denmark, Norway, Iceland, and Canada.
May. Ten Western European states established the Council of Europe. The Federal Republic of (West) Germany was established with its capital at Bonn. The (East) German Democratic Republic was created.
September. Konrad Adenauer was elected president of West Germany.
October. China proclaimed its People's Republic. The communist insurgency in Greece was defeated and the communist troops were driven out of the country. They kidnapped and carried with them thousands of Greek children who were then raised in the Soviet bloc.

1950 *February-June.* A thirty-year alliance between the Soviet Union and communist China was signed. The Korean war began with an attack by North Korea on the South Korean state.
August. The Council of Europe proclaimed the need for the establishment of a European army, including German troops. This was the signal for the rearmament of West Germany.

1951 *April-May.* France, the Benelux countries, Italy, and West Germany agreed to a European Coal and Steel Union. Radio Free Europe began broadcasting from Munich. Soviet jamming stations immediately tried to disrupt the broadcasts.
July-September. France, Britain, and the United States declared the end of hostilities with Germany. The peace treaty with Japan was signed by forty-nine countries. On the same day, the United States and Japan signed an agreement for U.S. help in case of an unprovoked attack on Japan.

1952 *March-May.* The Soviet Union protested the signing of a Western peace treaty with Germany. France, Great Britain, and the United States agreed to treat West Germany as an equal partner. Western troops in West Germany were to protect the country against Soviet aggression.
October-November. The first British atomic bomb was exploded off Australia. The Marshall islands were the scene of the explosion of the first American hydrogen bomb.

1953 *March-June.* Stalin died. Nine days later Nikita Sergeyevich Khrushchev was named first secretary of the Soviet Communist Party. The United States signed a treaty of friendship and cooperation with West Germany. Demonstrations in East Germany were suppressed by the use of Soviet tanks. Over 200 people were killed and wounded. About 1,200 people were jailed.

July-September. Lavrenty Pavlovich Beria, chief of the Soviet secret police, was arrested. Prime Minister Georgy Maksimilianovich Malenkov announced the explosion of the first Soviet hydrogen bomb. Beria and six associates were tried and executed.

1954 *January-May.* French expeditionary forces were defeated at Dien Bien Phu in northwestern Vietnam.

June-December. The first nuclear power plant was opened in the Soviet Union. Chou En-lai and Jawaharlal Nehru signed the Five Principles of International Relations, declared to be the basis of peaceful coexistence. The United Nations established its own Atomic Energy Agency. The Soviet government notified France and Great Britain that if the Paris agreements for the West European Union were ratified, its treaties with the two countries would be considered void.

1955 *January.* The Supreme Soviet declared that the state of belligerence with Germany had ended.

May-July. The three Western powers proclaimed the end of the occupation of Germany. West Germany, now a fully sovereign nation, joined NATO. The Western European Union was ratified and the Soviet Union declared the end of its treaties with France and Great Britain. The Soviet Union established the Warsaw Pact with its East European satellites. The commanding officer of the forces was always to be a Soviet general. The Austrian state treaty was signed by the four occupying powers, declaring the country's neutrality and the withdrawal of all occupying forces.

May-July. Khrushchev and Nikolay Aleksandrovich Bulganin visited Yugoslavia. The foreign ministers of the great powers met in Geneva in order to try to lessen tensions among them.

September. Adenauer, the West German chancellor, visited Moscow. Over 10,000 German soldiers, still being kept in Soviet concentration camps, were repatriated.

December. The United Nations accepted Albania, Bulgaria, Hungary, and Romania into membership in the organization.

1956 *February-April.* The Twentieth Congress of the Soviet Communist party was the scene of the denunciation by Khrushchev of Stalin's crimes. The Congress declared its acceptance of peaceful coexistence and the notion of "different roads to socialism." The COMINFORM was disbanded.

June-July. Riots occurred in the Polish city of Poznan. The Hungarian dictator, Matyas Rakosi, was dismissed by the Soviet leaders.

October. Revolution broke out in Hungary. Wladyslaw Gomulka became first secretary of the Polish Communist party despite Soviet objections. Israel attacked Egypt over the latter's refusal to permit the passage of Israeli ships over the nationalized Suez canal. Five days later, Britain and France jointly attacked Egyptian targets. The United States condemned the attack and joined other nations in the United Nations to call for an immediate cease fire.

November. Soviet troops suppressed the Hungarian revolution with great brutality. As many as 200,000 thousand Hungarians fled to the West. Britain and France accepted the cease-fire demanded by the United Nations.

1957 *March.* The Treaty of Rome, the founding document of the European Economic Community (the Common Market), was signed. The signatories included France, West Germany, Italy, and the Benelux states. They also established the European Atomic Energy Union.

May. In a television interview, Khrushchev declared, "we will bury you," meaning that Soviet-style socialism would soon triumph throughout the world.

October. The first satellite, the Soviet Sputnik, circled the earth.

1958 *March-May.* Khrushchev declared the unilateral ending of all Soviet nuclear testing. Warsaw Pact troops were withdrawn from Romania.

October. Pope Pius XII died. He was succeeded by Pope John XIII.

December. Boris Pasternak received the Nobel Prize for his novel, *Doctor Zhivago.* He declined the prize, fearing that he would not be permitted to return home if he left the Soviet Union. He was thrown out of the Soviet Writers Union.

1959 *January.* A revolution in Cuba, led by Fidel Castro, overthrew Fulgencio Batista.

August. A Soviet pipeline for oil deliveries, linking Soviet oil fields with East European satellites, was announced.

September. Lunik II, a Soviet satellite, landed on the moon.

1960 *February.* The first French atomic bomb was exploded in the Sahara desert.

May. Gary Power, an American piloting a U2 spy plane, was shot down over the Soviet Union. The summit meeting between Khrushchev and Dwight Eisenhower ended in mutual recriminations. Cuba became a communist dictatorship, a source fomenting unrest in South and Central America.

September. Khrushchev appeared at the general assembly meeting of the United Nations and exhibited scandalous behavior during a debate of the General Assembly by banging his shoes on his table.

November. John F. Kennedy was elected president of the United States.

1961 *April-June.* Yuri Gagarin was the first man in space. Cuban exiles, encouraged and supplied by the U.S. government, invaded Cuba at the Bay of Pigs. The invasion was defeated, and the exiles were captured. The first summit meeting was held between President Kennedy and Khrushchev.

August. The Berlin Wall, cutting off the major avenue of escape for refugees from East Germany, was built. The Soviet Union resumed testing of nuclear bombs.

October-December. Stalin's body was removed from the tomb of Lenin in

Moscow. Moscow severed relations with Albania, and Beijing signed a treaty of friendship with the Balkan nation.

1962 *March-May.* A disarmament conference opened in Geneva, but it ended in disputes between the Eastern and Western powers. Adolph Eichman was executed in Israel.

October. The Cuban missile crisis began, and the Soviet Union was forced to remove its missiles from the country. In exchange, the United States pledged not to invade Castro's fortress, now depending entirely on Soviet resources for the survival of its regime.

November. The Cuban crisis ended.

1963 *June-August.* The Chinese openly accused the Soviet Union of deviating from Marxism-Leninism. John Profumo, British secretary of state for defense, was censored for sharing a mistress with the Soviet military attache in London. Negotiations between the Chinese and the Soviet leaders to end their disagreements failed. The foreign ministers of the United States, Soviet Union, and Great Britain signed the first partial nuclear test-ban treaty. France refused to join the treaty, and the Chinese berated the Soviet Union for signing.

November. President Kennedy was assassinated in Dallas, Texas.

1964 *August.* The Tonkin Gulf incident, in which North Vietnamese boats fired at U.S. warships, resulted in congressional authorization of the use of American forces in Vietnam.

October. In a coup d'etat, Khrushchev was ousted from leadership. He was the first Soviet leader not to be exterminated after such a change since Lenin. Leonid Ilyich Brezhnev and Alexey Nikolayevich Kosigin became joint Soviet dictators.

November. Lyndon B. Johnson was elected president of the United States.

1965 *March.* The first contingent of 3,500 U.S. marines landed in Vietnam.

1966 *March-August.* The Congress of the Soviet Communist party was boycotted by the Chinese. France withdrew its troops from NATO. The Chinese cultural revolution began, intended to tighten the party's grip on every phase of human activity. French president Charles DeGaulle visited the Soviet Union as a symbol of France's independence from NATO. The Soviet Union signed an agreement with the Italian Fiat automobile firm to set up a factory in the Soviet Union to produce 600,000 automobiles.

October. China announced the successful testing of its atomic bomb.

1967 *January-February.* A congress of European socialist and communist parties met in Rome. The Chinese leaders ended the cultural revolution. A treaty banning nuclear weapons in outer space was signed by Britain, the United States and the Soviet Union.

March-June. Svetlana Alliluieva, Stalin's daughter, asked asylum in the West. A military coup d'etat in Greece established a dictatorship. In Karlovy Vary, Czechoslovakia, European Socialist and Communist parties met but refused to acknowledge the supremacy of the Soviet Communist party in the international socialist movement. China exploded its first hydrogen bomb.

September-October. Che Guevara, a Cuban communist, was killed in guerilla fighting in Bolivia. Demonstrations against the Vietnam war began on a large scale in Western capitals.

1968   *April-May.* The Reverend Martin Luther King was assassinated in Memphis, Tennessee. Paris witnessed violent student demonstrations. De Gaulle resigned.

June-July. Senator Robert Kennedy was shot and killed in Los Angeles. The Warsaw Pact threatened Czechoslovakia with intervention if the new course of the Czechoslovak Communist party was not altered.

August-September. Troops of five nations, members of the Warsaw Pact, invaded Czechoslovakia, ending the period called the Prague Spring. Albania, in protest against the invasion, withdrew from the Warsaw Pact.

November. Richard Nixon was elected president of the United States. The Brezhnev doctrine was announced, stating that the Soviet Union would intervene in socialist countries where the survival of socialism was threatened.

1969   *March.* Large scale clashes between Chinese and Soviet troops occurred on the borders between the two socialist states.

June-September. Seventy-five Communist parties met in Moscow, but they refused to condemn the Chinese party leadership for its split with Moscow. The U.S. military began large-scale troop withdrawals from Vietnam. Neil Armstrong, a U.S. astronaut, was the first man to walk on the moon.

November. The United States and the Soviet Union ratified the Nuclear Non-Proliferation Treaty.

1970   *August.* West German chancellor Willy Brandt and Soviet prime minister Kosygin signed a nonaggression treaty in Moscow.

October. French president Georges Pompidou visited the Soviet Union.

November. After a two-year hiatus, the United States resumed its bombing of North Vietnam.

December. West German Chancellor Willy Brandt signed a treaty with Poland, recognizing the Oder-Neisse line as the boundary between Germany and the Polish state.

1971   *June.* The United States lifted a twenty-year embargo on trade with China.

October. The United Nations general assembly recognized communist China as the rightful holder of a Security Council seat. Taiwan was expelled. West German chancellor Brandt received the Nobel Peace Prize.

1972   *February-May.* President Nixon went to China on an official visit. During his visit to the Soviet Union, president Nixon signed the Strategic Arms Limitation Treaty.

June. Five burglars were caught in the Watergate Hotel in Washington, DC, breaking into the national headquarters of the Democratic party.

July–December. President Anwar Sadat of Egypt expelled all Soviet advisors and technical personnel and reoriented his country's foreign policies toward the West. The two Germanies concluded a basic agreement establishing diplomatic relations as a preliminary to their admittance to the United Nations.

1973 *January–May.* Britain, Ireland, and Denmark joined the European Common Market. A cease-fire agreement was signed between the United States and North Vietnam. Great Britain and France exchanged ambassadors with East Germany. Brezhnev visited West Germany and signed agreements on economic and cultural cooperation between the two states.

June–October. Brezhnev visited the United States, but no agreement was signed on Salt II. Brezhnev's visit to France served as an occasion to create dissension between the United States and Western Europe. Egypt and Syria launched a surprise attack on Israel during Yom Kippur. The attack was repelled, but it started an Arab attempt to coerce the West through the use of an embargo on oil exports.

December. Gerald Ford was appointed vice president of the United States, replacing Spiro Agnew who had resigned in disgrace.

1974 *January–June.* Twenty-four European Communist parties meeting in Brussels announced some general principles for their cooperation. Gunther Guillaume, West German chancellor Brandt's close advisor, was arrested for spying for East Germany. Brandt was forced to resign and was replaced by Helmut Schmidt. India exploded its first atomic bomb. President Nixon's visit to the Soviet Union resulted in an agreement to limit the underground testing of nuclear warheads.

July–November. Following ethnic strife on Cyprus, Turkish troops invaded the island and partitioned it into Turkish and Greek regions. The military dictatorship in Greece was overthrown. Nixon resigned the presidency of the United States before Congress would have impeached him. Elections were held in Greece.

1975 *February–April.* British Prime Minister Harold Wilson visited Moscow and signed several economic and cultural agreements with the Soviet leadership. The North Vietnamese took over Saigon, and the United States had lost the war.

July–November. The first summit of the Conference on Security and Cooperation in Europe, meeting in Helsinki, Finland, attended by thirty-three European nations, the United States, and Canada, signed the "Helsinki accords," finalizing the borders of the European states and strengthening human rights. Follow-up conferences were scheduled.

October–November. Andrei Sakharov received the Nobel Peace Prize. Two days after the death of Generalissimo Franco, Juan Carlos was crowned king of Spain.

1976 *January.* Chou En-lai died. Mao Tse-tung died.

October. The wife of Mao Tse-tung, Chiang Ching, was arrested with three others and charged with planning a coup d'etat.

November. Jimmy Carter was elected president of the United States.

1977 *April-July.* The Falangist party of Spain was dissolved. Ali Bhutto was overthrown in Pakistan.

October-November. A new Soviet constitution replaced the Stalinist document of 1936. On the sixtieth anniversary of the Russian Revolution, Brezhnev offered to end testing and production of nuclear weapons.

1978 *April.* President Carter stopped the production of neutron bombs.

October. A new pope, John Paul II, was elected; a Pole, Karol Cardinal Woytila. His new name is John Paul II.

1979 *January-March.* Full diplomatic relations established between China and the United States. Mohammad Reza Pahlavi fled Iran, and the Ayatolla Ruholla Khomeini established a fundamentalist regime. Egyptian president Anwar Sadat and Israeli leader Menachem Begin signed a peace accord between their two countries in Washington, D.C.

April. The Chinese government notified Moscow that its treaty with the Soviet Union would not be renewed when it expired in 1980.

May-June. Greece was admitted to the European Common Market. Pope John Paul II visited his homeland. Hundreds of thousands celebrated his visit. Brezhnev and Carter signed SALT II, limiting the number of nuclear strategic missiles.

November-December. The U.S. embassy in Teheran was attacked, and its personnel were taken prisoners with the approval of the fundamentalist regime. In reaction to the installment of new missiles in Eastern Europe, NATO decided to accept Pershing II and cruise missiles. The U.S. Congress refused to ratify the SALT II treaty, but the treaty was observed by both contracting parties. The Soviet Union attacked Afghanistan. The U.S. president stopped food deliveries to the Soviet Union as well as equipment for oil exploration.

1980 *January.* The United States signed a mutual help treaty with Turkey. The Soviet leaders ordered that Andrey Dmitriyevich Sakharov be stripped of all his awards and decorations. He and his wife were banished to the remote city of Gorky. Israel and Egypt exchanged ambassadors.

May. Tito died.

July-August. The Olympic Games were held in Moscow. The United States and other Western countries refused to participate. Shah Reza Pahlavi died. Strikes occurred in Poland. The Solidarity trade union emerged, led by Lech Walesa.

September. The Iraq-Iran war began.

November. Ronald Reagan was elected president of the United States.

1981 *February.* King Juan Carlos intervened and stopped an attempt at a military coup in Spain.

May. An unsuccessful attempt was made on the life of Pope John Paul II by a Turk, Ali Agca. The Bulgarian secret service, acting for the Soviet KGB, was suspected.

June-August. Israeli planes destroyed an Iraqi nuclear plant under construction. The United States decided to renew the building of neutron bombs.

October. Egyptian President Anwar Sadat was murdered by mutinous soldiers.

November. Disarmament talks between the two superpowers began in Geneva and continued for two years.

December. Martial law was introduced in Poland.

1982   *January-April.* Members of NATO and the Common Market decided to introduce measures against the Soviet Union for its share in imposing martial law in Poland.

October. Helmut Schmidt's government received a no-confidence vote in the West German parliament. In the new elections, the Christian Democrats won a majority, and Helmut Kohl became West Germany's new chancellor.

November. Brezhnev died, and was succeeded by Yuri Vladimirovich Andropov, former head of the KGB.

December. The Soviet government offered to reduce the number of its intermediate nuclear missiles by two-thirds if NATO cancelled the installation of Pershing II and cruise missiles in Western Europe. The proposal was rejected.

1983   *January-March.* The Warsaw Pact offered a non-aggression treaty to NATO. The United States began experiments for a Strategic Defense Initiative, to defend the country against strategic missiles.

June. Pope John Paul II visited Poland for the second time. He discussed the situation with Lech Walesa and General Woyciech Jaruzelski.

October. Walesa won the Noble Peace Prize. New Soviet missile bases were established in Czechoslovakia.

November. West Germany accepted the Pershing missiles on its territory. In retaliation, the Soviet Union cancelled the START II treaty with the United States.

1984   *January-March.* The European Free Trade Association and the Common Market abolished all customs duties on industrial products. Andropov died. His successor was Constantin Chernenko, who was seventy-three years old.

October. Economic reforms were introduced in China, allowing private businesses on a small scale. Factory managers were allowed to compete for customers.

December. After Chernenko's death, Mikhail Gorbachev was named new Soviet leader. His first visit abroad was to London.

1985   *April.* The Warsaw Pact nations signed an agreement for a ten-year extension of the alliance.

June. Spain and Portugal were admitted to the Common Market.

July. Eduard Shevardnadze replaced Andrey Andreyevich Gromyko as foreign minister of the Soviet Union.

November. The first meeting between President Reagan and First Secretary Gorbachev was held in Geneva.

1986 *February-March.* At a meeting of the Supreme Soviet, Gorbachev announced the introduction of fundamental economic reforms in the Soviet Union. Boris Yeltsin castigated power abusers, creating a furor at the meeting.

April. One of four power plants at the Chernobyl nuclear facility had a most serious accident. Radioactive clouds spread over much of Eastern and Western Europe. Large areas in the Ukraine were evacuated.

June. The Soviet leaders abolished censorship.

1987 *July.* The Soviet Union reestablished diplomatic relations with Israel.

November. After criticizing Gorbachev for the slowness of economic reforms, Yeltsin was dismissed as head of the Moscow branch of the Communist party.

1988 *February.* Unrest began in Nagorno-Karabakh in Azerbaijan between Armenians and Azeris, the first ethnic conflict to occur in the Soviet Union since World War II.

April. The Soviet Union agreed to withdraw all its troops from Afghanistan.

May. The withdrawal of Soviet troops began. More than 13,000 dead and 35,000 wounded soldiers were the casualties on the Soviet side. Soviet troops suppressed a huge demonstration with large casualties in Yerevan, the capital of the Soviet Socialist republic of Armenia. Reagan and Gorbachev met in Moscow and signed the Intermediate-range Nuclear Forces treaty.

June. Gorbachev announced sweeping political reforms, including the election of Soviet presidents by the Congress of People's Deputies. He also proposed the establishment of elected legislatures in the Soviet republics with powers to introduce reforms.

November. George Bush was elected president of the United States.

December. Gorbachev announced unilateral reduction of Soviet forces in Europe and Asia.

1989 *February.* Sayed Ali Khameini, the Iranian president, visited Romania and established trade relations with that country.

April. The West German government recalled its ambassador to Romania in protest against the human rights violations of the regime. The European Community suspended talks with Romania over the same issue.

May. Walesa was given the Human Rights Prize of the Council of Europe. Romania declared that the Warsaw Pact forces should be used to reestablish the unity of the alliance.

July. President Bush visited Warsaw. He addressed a huge crowd at the monument commemorating the victims of the strikes of 1970.

August. Turkey closed its borders with Bulgaria after 250,000 ethnic Turks fled from the Bulgarian state.

November. The Berlin Wall was dismantled.

1990 *January.* After difficult negotiations, the COMECON summit meeting agreed to adopt a free market approach to economic development. Trade among the participating nations was to be conducted by hard currencies. Multilateral barter was to be changed into bilateral trade.

February. The phased withdrawal of the Soviet army from Czechoslovakia began.

May. The parliament of the new Russian Republic elected Boris Yeltsin its president.

June. The Conference on Security and Cooperation in Europe concluded its conference in Copenhagen with a resolution for multiparty elections in all member states. The resolution also included provisions for the separation of political parties from the state, independent judiciaries, and respect for minority rights. Included also were the rights to freedom of expression, organization, and assembly. The Soviet Union signed the document.

July. Boris Yeltsin resigned from the Soviet Communist party. Gorbachev at a meeting with German Chancellor Kohl, agreed to the unification of Germany. Kohl agreed to pay the cost of removing Soviet troops and to build housing for them in the Soviet Union. The new Germany was to assume financial obligations of the former East German state to the Soviet Union.

August. East and West Germany ratified the reunification treaty.

October. Germany was unified. President Gorbachev received the Nobel Peace Prize. The Cold War was declared to have ended.

December. Shevardnadze resigned and warned the Soviet peoples of the danger of reestablishing a dictatorship.

1991 *January-March.* KGB forces attacked the radio station in Vilnius, Lithuania. Yeltsin declared on Soviet television that he favored the abolition of the Soviet presidency. U.S. forces, in alliance with European and Arab states, attacked the Iraqi army in Kuwait and decisively defeated it. The forces of Saddam Hussein were withdrawn from Kuwait after setting most oil wells on fire. Only nine Soviet republics participated in a referendum over the preservation of the Soviet Union, and six did not act on the proposal. The referendum was supported by a majority in each republic.

April-June. At a meeting in the republic of Novo-Ogarevo, Gorbachev tried to convince the leaders of Soviet republics to preserve the union, but he failed. The Ukrainian leaders refused even to discuss Gorbachev's proposal. Yeltsin elected president of the Russian Republic, and he visited George Bush in Washington.

August-September. Communist leaders launched a coup d'etat against Soviet President Gorbachev; however, the coup collapsed because regular and special troops refused to arrest Yeltsin, who led the opposition against the coup. Yeltsin became a symbol of democratization.

October-November. Economic agreements were signed for the reorganization of the Soviet economic system by the heads of constituent republics. However, the Russian Republic immediately broke the agreement by instituting economic reforms without consultation.

December. The epidemic of death by starvation in Somalia finally moved the United States to send 28,000 troops to the country in order to ensure the delivery of food to the starving people. An agreement was signed in Moscow by the leaders of Russia, Ukraine, and Belarus for the establishment of a Commonwealth of Independent States. Eight other republics joined the new state later. This signalled the end of the former Soviet Union. Gorbachev resigned as president.

1992 *January-February.* Boris Yeltsin, president of Russia, visited London and conferred with Prime Minister John Major. Afterward, he appeared at the United Nations, where he pledged Russia's observation of human rights. A friendship treaty was signed between Turkey and the new Russia. The U.S. secretary of state, James Baker, visited Moscow and offered help to destroy Russian nuclear warheads. Russia recognized the independent Croatian state.

March-April. Military clashes in Nagorno-Karabakh continued. A European Community office was opened in Bulgaria. Fighting between ethnic Serbs and Bosnian Muslim Slavs flared. Germany recognized Croatia and Slavonia. Walesa, the Polish president, visited Germany. The United States established diplomatic relations with Bosnia, Croatia, and Slavonia.

May-June. Local authorities in Odessa, the Ukraine, told a visiting German delegation that thirteen districts were prepared to welcome German settlers, and in two-to-three years, 6,000 German families could move in. Member states of the European Community withdrew their ambassadors from Belgrade. Serious fighting erupted in the Moldovan Republic between ethnic Russians and Romanians. The Russian Fourteenth Army supported the breakaway "Dniester republic." Its commander, General Lebed, became virtual dictator in the region. UN sanctions were imposed on rump-Yugoslavia for supporting "ethnic cleansing" by Bosnian Serbs. All trade and air traffic was reduced, and Yugoslav assets abroad were frozen. Yeltsin and Bush agreed in Washington to reduce the number of nuclear warheads on multiple-warhead missiles possessed by the two states by one-third. The first Earth Summit opened in Rio de Janeiro, Brazil, and the United States refused to sign its declaration.

July-August. The fighting in Moldova escalated. The Council of Europe expelled rump-Yugoslavia. Serb heavy artillery and mortars pounded Sarajevo in Bosnia. The independence of Slovakia was intensively debated.

September-October. An international conference on Bosnia opened in London under UN sponsorship. No agreement was reached. The United Nations banned Serbian airplanes from flying over Bosnia, but the ban was widely disregarded. The murder of 21,000 Polish prisoners of war by Soviet secret police in 1941 was documented by Yeltsin's special envoy to Poland. He delivered copies of deliberations of the Soviet Politburo, headed by Stalin, approving the murders.

November-December. William Jefferson Clinton was elected president of the United States. The presidents of Slovakia and the Czech Republic agreed to end the existence of the Czechoslovak state after seventy-five years. Slovakia was to become independent on January 1, 1993. The common assets of the two states were to be split through negotiations. Germany began the expulsion of tens of thousands of illegal Romanian gypsies to repatriate them to Romania. Special envoy Cyrus Vance and Lord Owen of Great Britain presented a plan to divide Bosnia into ten provinces along ethnic lines. Yeltsin visited Hungary and turned documents over to the Hungarian government concerning the Red Army's invasion of Hungary in suppressing the Hungarian Revolution in 1956. The United Nations voted to tighten sanctions against rump-Serbia. Listening devices were discovered in the consulate building of the United States in Bratislava, Slovakia. The Islamic Council meeting held in Jidda, called on the United Nations to intervene militarily in Bosnia. Turkey had offered its forces to assist the United Nations.

1993 *January-March.* The Council of Europe took under advisement the Romanian request to be received into membership. Opposition to Yeltsin's reformist course mounted in the Russian parliament whose membership consisted mostly of former communists. Slovakia became an independent state. Efforts in Moscow to impeach Yeltsin began in the Russian parliament. The Belarusian parliament ratified the START II treaty. The impeachment of Boris failed. The START II treaty was signed in Moscow. Seven new republics signed a treaty and joined the Commonwealth of Independent States. Croat and Serb forces renewed their battle. Croatians also fought against their former Bosnian allies.

April-May. The referendum in Russia on Yeltsin's reforms was approved by a majority of the people, handing a defeat to the parliament. A May day demonstration by communists and their sympathizers erupted into violence when the demonstrations attacked police in Moscow. Inflation in Russia in the first quarter of the year was 93 percent. Two constitutions were being prepared for Russia: one by a committee convened by President Yeltsin, and another drafted by the parliament. New fighting began in Bosnia.

June. President Clinton proposed joint United States-United Nations intervention in Bosnia in parallel with lifting the arms embargo on Muslim Slavs. The European powers rejected the proposal.

July. The G-7 nations held a summit in Tokyo, Japan and agreed to provide $3 billion in aid to Russia.

ALBANIA

General Information. *Area:* 11,099 square miles. *Population:* approximately 3 million. *Communist party membership:* 101,500 (in 1986). *Major cities:* Tirana, Durres, Vlore, Elbasan, Korce. *Urban population:* approximately 40 percent, rural population about 60 percent. *Total school enrollment:* 430,000 students (1987). Twenty-five newspapers are published of which two are dailies (1987). *Road network:* 6,900 kilometers paved. *Railroad network:* 603 kilometers. *Natural resources:* oil, chrome, copper, iron, nickel, timber, water power. *Major trading partners:* Soviet Union (until 1961), China (until 1974), Soviet Bloc countries (until 1985), Italy, Germany, France, Czechoslovakia, Romania, Poland (after 1985). *Currency:* Albanian lek, not convertible. *Geography:* borders on Serbia on the north and east, on Greece in the south and southeast, and on the Adriatic sea on the west. The southwestern tip of Albania controls the strait of Otranto, a major port of embarkation for trade with the Near East. The country is predominantly mountainous. Seventy percent of the land is over 1,000 feet high. Thirty percent covers the coastal plains, some river valleys, and low hills. The soil is generally of low quality. Because communications between the north and south of the country have been difficult in the past, there are several dialects of the Albanian language. Social customs are also varied. Two distinct tribal societies have developed in the past. In the northern hilly regions live the Gegs who also populate the Kosovo-Metohija area now under Serbian control. The southern people, who call themselves Tosks, spill over in small communities to northern Greece. The Shkumbi river separates the Gegs from the Tosks. The more numerous Gegs account for about 67 percent of the total population. Tosks constitute about 30 percent; scattered groups of Greeks, Serbs, and Bulgarians make up the rest. Large Albanian minority populations live in the provinces of Macedonia, and they constitute the overwhelming majority of the population of Kosovo (in Albanian; Kosova). Anthropologically, the Gegs belong to the Dinarian types, while the Tosks are Alpine. The Gegs have been divided into ten tribes that resemble the Scottish clans in many ways. Until the twentieth century, the Gegs had few contacts with the outside world, including the Tosks. Gegs are generally self-reliant, proud, and independent. They are fierce warriors who have always resented any control by a central government. The Tosks have lived, until recently, in small villages. Since their settlements are located in less rugged country, they have had more outside contacts than

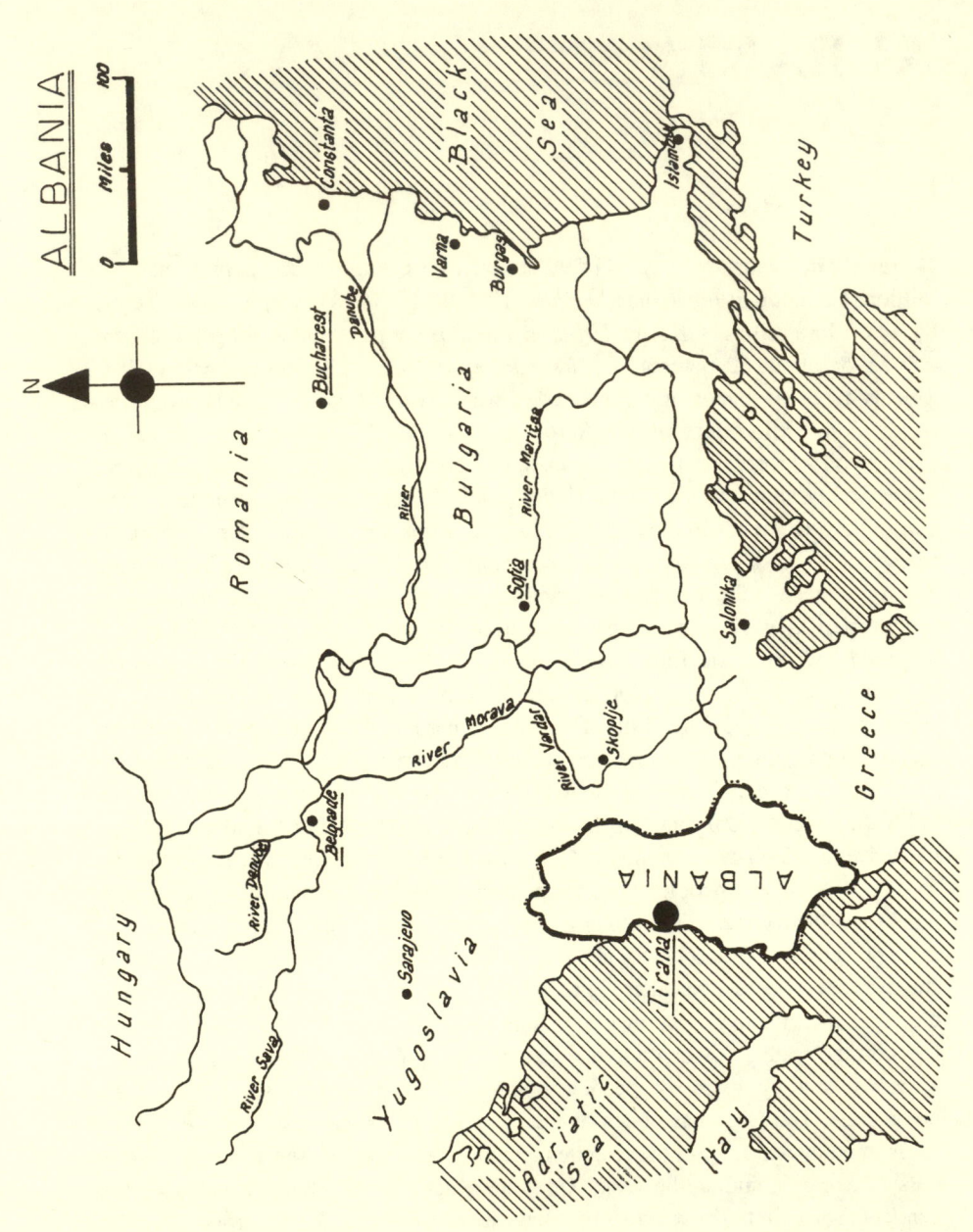

the Gegs. Some travelled overseas and brought with them news of different ways of life than their own. The Tosks provided most of the leadership of the Albanian Communist party as well as the backbone of the membership. They are, of course, all Albanians. About 98 percent of the population belongs to the Albanian ethnicity.

Bibliography
Gewehr, W.M., and Scheill, F. *A History of the Balkans Peninsula*. New York, 1933; Pano, N.C. *The People's Republic of Albania*. Baltimore, 1968; ——, "Albania," in J. Held, ed. *The Columbia History of Eastern Europe in the Twentieth Century*. New York, 1992.

CHRONOLOGY

1944 *November.* Communist government was installed in Tirana.

1946 *January.* The newly "elected" communist parliament, whose single-list candidates received 95 percent of the votes cast, declared Albania a People's Republic.

1950 *May.* Rigged elections resulted in 98.18 percent of the votes cast for candidates of the Albanian Communist party. The Politburo banned all religious teachings and institutions, and imprisoned most clergymen.

1951 *January-December.* The Stalinization of Albania was completed. All industrial enterprises, banks, and other businesses were nationalized without compensation. The collectivization of land was being undertaken. The Albanian Workers party (AWP) was in control of all political, social, and economic processes in the nation. The first secretary of the AWP, Enver Hoxha, was the most powerful man in the country. Koci Xoxhe, his rival, and an agent of the Yugoslav Communist party, was purged.

1952 *January-December.* Soviet technicians and engineers began to build a naval base for Soviet submarines and supply ships in Albania's ports on the Adriatic sea.

1955 *December.* Albania was admitted to membership in the United Nations.

1961 *July.* After severe rifts, originating from Albania's refusal to play its assigned role in the Soviet Bloc, all Soviet technicians were withdrawn from the country. Hoxha openly denounced Khrushchev, and the Soviet Union withdrew its diplomatic representatives from Tirana. It also began to dismantle its naval facilities.

1962 *January.* A treaty of friendship and cooperation was signed between Albania and communist China. It was followed by the arrival of Chinese technicians and economic and military aid. China contributed heavily to the development of Albania's mining industry.

1966 *February.* The cultural revolution began.

1968 *September.* In response to the Warsaw Pact invasion of Czechoslovakia, Albania withdrew from the alliance, the first among East European socialist states to do so. When the Brezhnev doctrine was proclaimed in Warsaw in

November, Albania vehemently denounced it as an imperialist, hegemonic plot.

1971 *May.* Greece and Albania resumed diplomatic relations and established embassies. There had been no such relations between the two countries since 1940. China broke off relations with Albania and withdrew its technicians and economic aid.

1976 *June.* Albania refused to send delegates to a meeting of European Communist parties called to reaffirm the primacy of the Soviet Communist party in world communist affairs. The fact that the communique skipped the issue supported Albania's position. However, Albania was and remained an outcast in international affairs. During the rest of the 1970s and until 1989, Albania isolated itself from foreign affairs.

1989 *June.* The new Albanian leader, Ramiz Alia, announced that the reforms in the Soviet Union, Poland, and Hungary should be considered the restoration of capitalism.

August. Albanian radio announced that the Prime Ministership of Stanys-law Mazowiecki in Poland was an act of bourgeois counter-revolution.

1990 *March.* A treaty of cultural exchange and cooperation was signed between Bulgaria and Albania. The treaty included agreements on health care and aviation. It was the first occasion that an Albanian premier visited Bulgaria.

June. Thousands of Albanians invaded Western embassies in Tirana seeking refuge abroad. At first, the communist government stopped food deliveries to the embassies, but then it permitted the evacuation of the refugees.

July. The Council for Security and Cooperation in Europe gave Albania observer status in exchange for a promise to improve the country's human rights record. Diplomatic relations between the Soviet Union and Albania, broken off in 1961, were restored.

December. Army troops were deployed in several cities where anticommunist riots broke out. Shooting occurred in Shkoder and four civilians, including the head of the major oppositional group, were killed. Great hatred for Hoxha and his regime was expressed everywhere. Over 3,000 Albanians, claiming to be ethnic Greeks, sought asylum in Greece. Under great public pressure, Ramiz Alia gave in to the demand for the establishment of a multiparty political system.

1991 *January–March.* Over 10,000 Albanians, mostly young people, sought refuge in Greece. Albania was on the verge of civil war. Huge crowds demonstrated against the communist government. In Tirana and elsewhere statues of Hoxha and other communist monuments were toppled. Nearly 20,000 Albanians on makeshift boats fled to Italy. The first multi-party elections were held, and the Albanian Workers party (communists) won over 60 percent of the votes cast, mainly in the rural areas. The opposition was deprived of the media, which helped the communists.

April-August. Sali Berisha became the first democratically elected president of Albania. Violence was renewed, however, because communist holdovers in the government continued to obstruct democratization. A coalition government was installed, but Alia was reelected president of parliament. The last congress of the Albanian Workers party was held. After another crowd of 22,000 Albanians fled to Italy, a new prime minister, Ylli Bufi was appointed. The economy was in a state of paralysis.

September-December. Italian troops were sent to Albania to guard relief supplies looted by the population. A German-Albanian commission was created to oversee relief operations for which Germany provided 75 million deutsche marks. The Serbian province of Kosovo, whose population consists of over 90 percent Albanians, declared its independence from rump-Yugoslavia. Only Albania recognized the new state.

1992 *March.* In the national elections, the Albanian Democratic party, the major opposition party, won an overwhelming victory.

April-May. The Serb government began supplying the Serb minority in Kosovo with heavy weapons. Albania signed a cooperation agreement with the European Community, providing for regular contacts and liberalized trade. In an election declared illegal by the Serb government, over 95 percent of Albanians in Kosovo elected a parliament, headed by Ibrahim Rugova.

June-August. In Pristina, Kosovo, Serb police prevented the meeting of the newly elected Albanian parliament and arrested five deputies.

September-December. Albanians in Montenegro declared that they were seeking autonomy. Albanian observers from Kosovo, Montenegro, Macedonia, and Albania proper participated in the London conference on rump-Yugoslavia as observers. Albanian demonstrations broke out in cities in Kosovo. They demanded the reopening of the Albanian language schools that had been closed by Slobodan Milosevic's Serb government in 1990. The Serb police clashed with protesters. Serb president Nicola Panic visited Kosovo where discussions were held with Serb and Albanian representatives. He promised to reopen Albanian schools. Police in Macedonia killed four Albanian demonstrators. Ethnic Albanians make up from 20 to 40 percent of Macedonia's population. Albanian army commanders claimed that they were ready for war with Serbia if the Serbs tried "ethnic cleansing" in Kosovo. Sali Berisha visited Egypt and Saudi Arabia in an effort to broaden Albania's international relations. The socialists (former communists) criticized the effort as dangerous.

1993 *January-March.* After the late 1992 elections, five parties gained parliamentary representation. Albania signed a treaty of cooperation with Turkey. President Ozal of Turkey visited Albania for the occasion. He offered Turkish support for the renovation of Albanian port facilities. He also offered help in developing Albania's tourist industry and financial institutions. Ozal declared that, in case of a new Balkan war caused by unprovoked aggression against Albanians, Turkey would come to the aid of the country. A Turkish military delegation, headed by Lieutenant General Erol Tutali, visited Tirana and held discussions with Albanian government and military leaders.

Alia, Ramiz (1925–). Born on October 18, 1925, in the city of Shkoder, Alia's parents were Gegs from Kosovo who fled to Albania after the Balkan Wars of 1912–1913. Between 1939 and 1940, Alia was a member of Albanian Youth of the Lictor, a fascist youth organization. In 1942, he changed sides and joined the Albanian Communist Youth organization while still a student. A year later, he became a member of the Albanian Communist party. He was then sent to Berat to work in the regional committee as organizational secretary. In 1943, he was appointed political officer, with the rank of lieutenant colonel in the Albanian division that assisted the Yugoslav Partisan army in the liberation of Kosovo from German occupation. In 1945, Alia held leadership positions in the Albanian Communist Youth organization. He was also appointed as a member of the Communist party's Central Committee. In 1947, Alia was appointed secretary-general of the Youth League of Albania and remained in that post until 1948. In that year, he was transferred to head the Office of Propaganda and Agitation of the party's Central Committee, and the following year he was named president of the People's Youth Association. In 1950, he was a parliamentary deputy and in 1952 adopted by the Politburo as a candidate (nonvoting) member. In 1955, Alia was sent to the Lenin Academy of the Soviet Union in Moscow to study Marxism-Leninism. After his return, he was appointed minister of education. In February 1961, Alia was named director for propaganda and agitation of the Central Committee of the Albanian Communist party and a full (voting) member of the Politburo. He was also secretary of the Central Committee in charge of ideology and cultural policies. He remained a solid supporter of Enver Hoxha (*see* Hoxha, Enver) during the rupture of Soviet-Albanian relations. He was one of the subordinates of the Albanian dictator who organized the Cultural Revolution (*see* Cultural Revolution) of 1966–1967, and was made responsible for propaganda against Soviet, Yugoslav, and, after 1974, against Chinese "revisionists" (*see* Chinese-Albanian Relations).

Alia was the most competent member of the Communist party's Secretariat. He was widely recognized as the logical successor to Enver Hoxha. After the death of the communist dictator in 1985, Alia came into his own. But he inherited an economy that was on the verge of collapse, and a large number of young people who were completely alienated from society and politics. Albania was, thanks to the policies of Hoxha, isolated from the rest of the world, without allies and supporters. Alia proved incapable of cutting himself off from his and his nation's communist past. He did attempt to bring about institutional changes from above. He was, however, more interested in maintaining a reformed communist system than in replacing it with a pluralistic society. At first, his government tried to introduce incentives for workers and collective peasants and to establish a quasi-private market for the peasants' surplus products. He also tried to encourage the production of consumer goods. Yet none of these halfway measures succeeded in improving economic conditions in Albania. There was just too much bureaucracy, on the one hand, and too much apathy on the part of the population, on the other, to bring about desired change.

During the autumn of 1989, most East European communist regimes simply collapsed, their Communist parties assuming different names in which the term "socialist" dominated. Alia tried desperately to stave off the collapse of the communist regime in Albania. He courted young people, the largest group in Albanian society; he ordered the building of recreational facilities, the broadcast of youth programs by Albanian national radio and television, and the creation of job opportunities specifically for youth. He promised the introduction of educational reforms and led a campaign for improvements in cultural life. However, he was unwilling to eliminate Communist party control over social, intellectual, and economic affairs.

Alia also made great efforts to end Albania's isolation from the rest of the world. Relations with Greece, Germany, and Canada were normalized. For the first time, in 1988, Albania participated in the conference of Balkan foreign ministers, and repeatedly held meetings for these ministers in Tirana. He introduced a new term, new for Albania at least: the New Economic Mechanism (NEM), modeled after the Hungarian economic reforms of 1968 (*see* Economic Policies, Hungary). However, the NEM meant only modest reforms in the heavily centralized Hungarian economic system. Foreign investments were now encouraged, and consumer goods were imported. At the same time, Enver Hoxha's old collaborators were removed from the leadership. But an angry and disillusioned public could not be appeased. It wanted radical change and the complete disassociation of Albania from its communist past.

When Alia promoted Xhelil Gjoni, a despised hard-line crony of Hoxha, to the secretariat of the party's Central Committee, and to full membership in the Politburo, the honesty of his entire effort of reform was called into question. On December 8, 1990, a strike conducted by students at the University of Tirana was a signal for disturbances. A series of demonstrations began in the major cities. As a response, the presidium of the People's Assembly ended the one-party system on December 18. The first alternative, the Democratic party was legalized the following day. Opposition groups then flooded the country with newspapers openly critical of Alia and the Communist party.

Alia was still not ready to give up power. He removed several unpopular hardliners; he declared all the Stalinist laws null and void. Finally, he ordered the preparation of a new platform for the Communist party. All through 1990 and 1991, Alia desperately tried to hold the Communist party together. When over 5,000 young Albanians entered foreign embassies and consulates in Tirana, seeking asylum abroad, Alia's position became untenable. He still refused to speed up economic reforms. He made concessions, not real reforms. Elections were held in the atmosphere of crisis. Sali Berisha, a member of the Democratic Front, launched scathing attacks on Alia in the front's newspaper, *Union*. The economic situation continued to worsen, and Alia was unable to do anything about it. On February 20, 1991, more than 100,000 people demonstrated in Tirana and they pulled down Enver Hoxha's statue in the central square of the city. In response, Alia reintroduced censorship.

The Albanian Communist party (called Albanian Party of Labor) controlled the media. It polled 67 percent of the votes or 169 seats in parliament out of the available 250. The Democratic party won 30 percent or 75 seats. The countryside supported the communists, but the cities voted for change. Following the elections, Ramiz Alia was appointed president for a five-year term, and he resigned his positions in the party hierarchy. A new premier, Fatos Nano, took office. The Democratic party refused to join a coalition government and remained in opposition. In 1992, Alia was removed from the presidency.

Bibliography
Biberaj, Elez. "Albania, The Last Domino," in Ivo Banac, ed. *Eastern Europe in Revolution* (Ithaca-London, 1992).

Anti-Fascist Council for National Liberation. This organization, a cover group for the Albanian Communist party in its quest for power, was established on May 24, 1944. It was declared to be the Supreme Executive Council and Legislative Organ of the Albanian nation. The chairman of the council was Enver Hoxha, (*see* Hoxha, Enver) general secretary of the Communist party. He was also the supreme commander of the Albanian Army of National Liberation (*see* Army of National Liberation). In later 1944, the National Liberation Movement was renamed the National Liberation Front, but the name change did not alter the organization's composition or purposes. The first decree issued by its leadership forbade King Zog's return from exile. On October 24, 1944, the front was transformed into the Provisional Democratic Government of Albania. Hoxha was named prime minister. By November, the Germans were forced to withdraw from Albania, and the anticommunist resistance was crushed. The armed forces were controlled by the communists, and they were soon in control of Albania as a whole. This was the only country in Eastern Europe that did not have Soviet soldiers on its soil when communists came into power. Hoxha's support came mainly from the Yugoslavian communist agents directed by Josip Broz Tito.

Bibliography
Prifti, Peter R. *Socialist Albania Since 1944: Domestic and Foreign Developments* (Cambridge, MA, 1978).

Army of National Liberation. This army was formed by the communists in March 1943 in order to fight the Italian and German occupiers of Albania. It united guerrilla bands that had operated since 1941 in remote areas of the country. The leadership came almost entirely from the Albanian Communist party. Foreign advisors joined the army from the Partisans of Yugoslavia, headed by Josip Broz Tito. A general staff for the army was established on July 10, 1943. It was headed by Mehemet Shehu (*see* Shehu, Mehemet). The Army was also supervised by political commissars headed by Enver Hoxha (*see* Hoxha, Enver). Commander in chief was Spiro Moisiu, a member of the Central Committee of the Albanian Communist party. The army became and remained one of the mainstays of the communists in controlling Albanian society.

Bibliography
Skendi, Stavro. *Albania* (New York, 1956).

Balluku, Beqir (1917–1974). Balluku was born in Tirana into a Moslem family. He received a few years of grammar school education. Between 1935 and 1939, Balluku worked as a metal worker in a factory in Tirana. He had a reputation for being a lazy thief. In 1939, he was drafted into the regular Albanian army. When he was demobilized in 1941, he joined the antifascist guerrillas and became a member of the Albanian Communist party. In 1942, Balluku became political commissar of the Third Partisan Brigade. Two years later, he was named deputy commissar of the Third Army Corps. He was appointed political commissar of the First Army Corps in 1945 and was named a member of a special people's court for the prosecution of alleged war criminals and members of the former political elite. At the same time, Balluku was appointed Vice President for the General Council of the Democratic Front. In 1947, he was promoted to colonel and appointed commander of the Second Infantry Division. Promoted to major general in 1948, Balluku became chief of staff of the Albanian army. In the same year, he joined the Central Committee of the party and became a candidate (non-voting) member of the Politburo. Between 1952 and 1953, Balluku attended the Voroshilov Academy of the Soviet Union in Moscow and was a member of the Albanian communist delegation at Joseph V. Stalin's funeral. In that same year, Balluku was named minister of defense. The following year, he was named deputy prime minister while retaining his portfolio as minister of defense. In 1974, Balluku was placed on a show trial for allegedly being a Western spy and enemy of the people, and he was executed.

Bibliography
Skendi, Stavro. *Albania* (New York, 1956).

Belishova, Liri (1923–). Born in a village of the same name in southern Albania, she graduated from the Girls Pedagogical Institute of Tirana. Belishova became a convinced, fanatical communist while still in school. Between 1941 and 1944, she fought with the Albanian Partisans, was wounded, and lost one of her eyes. In 1945, Belishova married Nako Spiru, a member of the Central Committee and the Politburo of the Albanian Communist party, but she did not take her husband's name. Between 1944 and 1948, she was a member of the secretariat of the Albanian Antifascist Youth organization, a subsidiary of the Communist party. In 1946, Belishova led the Albanian delegation to the Third Congress of Yugoslav Youth, held in Zagreb, and to the Soviet Physical Culture Festival held in Moscow. Between 1946 and 1947, she was president of People's Youth, the Albanian version of the Soviet KOMSOMOL. After her husband committed suicide in 1947, Belishova was dismissed from her post and was sent to the city of Berat as a schoolteacher. She was rehabilitated after the purge of the Titoists. Belishova was elected to membership in the Central Committee and the Politburo of the Albanian Communist party, and in 1954, she was named secretary to the party's secretariat.

Bibliography
Skendi, Stavro. *Albania* (New York, 1956).

Chinese-Albanian Relations. In October 1954, China and Albania, the largest and the smallest countries ruled by Communist parties, signed an agreement for cultural, scientific, and technical cooperation. By then, Albanian leaders, especially Enver Hoxha (*see* Hoxha, Enver), began to look upon the Soviet Union as a threat to their own road to socialism. In December, China presented a gift of $2.5 million worth of commodities and a loan of $12.5 million for the years from 1955 to 1960.

In 1956, after the denunciation of Joseph Stalin by Nikita Khrushchev at the Twentieth Party Congress, Hoxha and his designated heir, Mehemet Shehu (*see* Shehu, Mehemet), attended the Eighth Congress of the Chinese Communist party and exchanged views with the Chinese leaders. On December 29, 1956, the Chinese published a long list, analyzing communist bloc relations and they sided with Albania against Yugoslavia. They also indirectly rebuffed Khrushchev by praising Stalin's achievements in building socialism in the Soviet Union.

Albanian-Chinese ties were strengthened in 1958 after the criticism of Josip Broz Tito was renewed. Albanian attacks on Tito and Titoism, the most vehement in all the socialist countries, were spurred on by Albania's renewed fears of Yugoslav expansionism and the increasing restiveness of the Albanian population of Kosovo.

China and Albania agreed upon the coordination of their agrarian policies and the global strategy to be followed by communist countries outside the Soviet Bloc. By 1960, China and Albania were in complete agreement on most policy issues. When the Sino-Soviet arguments became public, Albania joined the Chinese side. When Khrushchev called a communist summit meeting in the Romanian capital, Bucharest, with the ostensible purpose of reading China out of the socialist camp, Albania refused to attend.

On February 2, 1961, an Albanian delegation concluded an agreement with the Chinese for economic cooperation. China was to underwrite the construction of twenty-five Albanian industrial enterprises. China announced on April 25, 1961, that it was giving $125 million in aid for Albania for the 1961 to 1965 five-year-plan period. Altogether, China provided about $5 billion in aid to its Albanian ally between 1961 and 1971. The aid included the construction of industrial firms, food shipments, military hardware, and the salary of technical advisers. Blueprints for construction, material for building port facilities, and all-around economic support were also provided. In turn, Albania gave ideological and diplomatic support to China in its struggle with the Soviet Union and drummed up support for the Chinese in the international Marxist communities.

In 1971, however, relations between the two countries began to cool down. After border clashes between Soviet and Chinese troops took place in 1969, the Albanians began to have doubts about their giant ally's real strength. When the Chinese leadership decided to renew its relations with the United States, the Albanians openly objected. The verbal support given by the Chinese to NATO and the Common Market further discomfited the Albanians. After the death of Mao Tse-tung and Chu-en-lai, Enver Hoxha criticized the foreign policies of the new Chinese leaders calling them a departure from the teachings of Marx and Lenin. In 1978, Albania endorsed Vietnam's stand against China and praised the Vietnamese invasion of Kampuchea.

By 1977, China had withdrawn all technicians and military advisers from Albania and had discontinued economic aid. Although diplomatic relations were not severed, they remained cool throughout the 1980s.

Bibliography

Biberaj, Elez, *Albania and China: A Study of an Unequal Alliance* (Boulder, CO, 1968); Griffith, William, *Albania and the Sino-Soviet Rift* (Cambridge, MA, 1963); Hamm, Harry, *Albania: China's Beachhead in Europe* (New York, 1963); Marmullaku, Ramadan *Albania and the Albanians* (London, 1975).

Civil War in Albania (1943–1944). A fierce struggle, conducted by guerrilla bands, who called themselves Partisans during 1943 and 1944, eventually led to the formation of the communist state in Albania. The communists organized the struggle against the foreign troops of occupation as well as the internal enemies of communism whom they called the bourgeoisie.

The first attacks were hit-and-run affairs directed against the Italians in 1942. In November of that year, Midhat Frasheri formed the Balli Kom-betar, a noncommunist, nationalist resistance group, which joined in the struggle against the occupiers. There was, at first, some cooperation between the communists and the nationalists, but each group harbored deep suspicions against the other. There were also mutual recriminations if an operation did not succeed. The Balli Kombetar accused the communists of being Soviet agents and of deliberately exposing civilians to retaliation by the enemy. The communists insisted that the Balli Kombetar cooperated with the fascists. Before things got out of hand, the communists proposed to hold a joint meeting. The Balli Kombetar accepted the proposal, and the two sides met at the village of Mukaj in August 1943. The representatives agreed to establish a common front against the Germans and Italians. They also agreed to work for an ethnic Albanian state which would include the province of Kosovo within its borders. There would be free elections after the conclusion of the struggle to determine the shape of the state for all Albanians.

Enver Hoxha (*see* Hoxha, Enver) rejected the agreement. He charged that the Balli Kombetar intended to seize power after the war. But he acted under Yugoslav pressure, since Tito's men would not want to give up the province of Kosovo to a socialist Albania. All contacts between the leaders of the two groups were cut off, and civil war began in Albania.

In the summer of 1943, Allied forces landed in Sicily, and Italy surrendered to the Allies. The Italian soldiers in Albania surrendered to the Partisans and handed over their military equipment. The Germans continued the struggle, however. The communists then decided to eliminate the Balli Kombetar because the leaders of this group were no longer fighting the occupiers. The Balli Kombetar could not resist effectively. Its leaders were forced to turn to the Germans for help. Their joint offensive inflicted great harm on the Partisans, but they lost public support. After one last offensive in the summer of 1944 which proved ineffective, the Germans withdrew from Albania. The communists could then concentrate on fighting the nationalists.

By November 1944, the Balli Kombetar lost and its leaders fled the country. However, new challengers appeared on the scene. Abas Kupi, a member of the General Council of the National Liberation Front, established a so-called Legality Organization in September 1944. Kupi was a respected Geg leader who supported the return of King Zog to Albania. Kupi was then declared an enemy of the Albanian people by the communists. He was also accused of being a British agent. The Partisans conducted a successful offensive against the ill-equipped forces of the Legality Organization and annihilated them. In September 1944, the communists were the victors of the civil war in Albania.

Bibliography
Prifti, Peter R., *Socialist Albania Since 1944: Domestic and Foreign Developments* (Cambridge, MA, 1978).

Collective Leadership in Albania. After Stalin's death in 1953, Enver Hoxha (*see* Hoxha, Enver) endeavored to copy the new Soviet leaders' method of rule, called "collective leadership." Fearful of Tito's Yugoslavia, and of possible internal disturbances after the passing of the Soviet dictator, Hoxha dropped several of his titles and offices. These included the posts of foreign and defense ministers. However, he still retained his title of prime minister and general secretary of the Albanian Communist party. At the same time, he combined several ministries reducing their numbers from nineteen to ten. Mehemet Shehu (*see* Shehu, Mehemet) was removed from his post as secretary of the secretariat of the Communist party, but he retained his membership in the Central Committee.

In July 1954, Hoxha even gave up the prime ministership and gave that post to Shehu. Albania broke its relations with the Soviet Union in 1961, and Hoxha once again resumed his various posts, including that of prime minister. It appears that collective leadership—in other words, an oligarchy, based on the monopoly of power by a single party—was not really suitable as a form of government in the communist system. Such a system needed a single dictator to function.

Bibliography
Pano, Nicholas C., "Albania," in Joseph Held, ed. *The Columbia History of Eastern Europe in the Twentieth Century* (New York, 1992).

Committee for the Salvation of Albania. This committee, established on August 2, 1943, united the communist National Front and the coalition included in the National Liberation Movement. Its purpose was to direct and coordinate the war efforts against the Axis armies and to provide local administration for the liberated areas.

The agreement between the communists and the noncommunist forces united in the committee stipulated that the fate of Kosovo-Metohija, an Albanian-populated territory, formerly belonging to Yugoslavia but given to Albania by the Germans in 1941, was to be decided by a plebiscite after the war. The Yugoslav communist agents attached to the Albanian Partisan army forced the communists to repudiate this agreement. As a consequence, the Committee broke up. This led to the civil war (*see* Civil War in Albania 1943–1944).

Bibliography
Prifti, Peter R., "The Labor Party of Albania," in Stephen Fischer-Galati, ed. *The Communist Parties of Eastern Europe* (New York, 1979), pp. 5-48.

Communist Party of Albania (*see* Albanian Party of Labor). Established in 1941, this party was a nationalistic and, at the same time, a radical Marxist-Leninist organization. It emphasized the struggle for national identity for Albanians in the past, and it glorified the fighters for the cause. It was especially fond of George Kastriota or Skanderbeu (Skanderbeg), a fifteenth-century general who successfully fought against Ottoman imperialism in the Balkans. The party also extolled, among others, Kristofor Idhi and Naim Frasheri, two nationalistic writers, and Abdul Frasheri, another advocate of Albanian independence. It observed the important national holidays, paid tribute to national monuments and historical places and buildings, and emphasized the national heritage of the Albanian people.

The party's leaders, especially Enver Hoxha (*see* Hoxha, Enver), considered Marxism-Leninism as a universally valid source of social change for all times and all societies, and denied that the ideology was changeable. The party, therefore, rejected any form of coexistence with the non-communist world.

The party was anxious to overcome the general backwardness of Albania which its leaders recognized. They tried to combine modernization with egalitarianism, not realizing that modernity was characterized by the stratification of society. The party was also centralist, strictly enforcing the party's monopoly in politics, the economy, culture, and social policies. It has remained the last bastion of Stalinism in Europe (the other is Castro's Cuba) long after communists system disappeared in Eastern Europe and the Soviet Union. Characteristically, the Albanian Communist party was also utopian and nepotistic.

The party's organization was based on the pattern set by the Soviet Communist party in the 1930s. It consisted of small cells; regional units; and the national leadership. In 1986, the party had 101,500 members out of a population of approximately 3 million. The Central Committee consisted of 115 members. The Politburo, with fifteen members, was the real seat of power. The Politburo operated on the basis of the so-called principle of democratic centralism. This meant that, after a decision had been made by the central party organs, no further discussions were permitted. Periodic purges of leaders and party members occurred in the Communist party of Albania (*see* Purges). Even Mehemet Shehu (*see* Shehu, Mehemet) could not avoid being purged in 1981, after which he committed suicide. In 1945, only 15 percent of party members were industrial workers. By 1976, their ratio increased to 37 percent. However, this number included the members of the huge party bureaucracy who were all classified as workers.

The party consciously fostered the country's isolation from the outside world. It was "building socialism" under conditions of "fierce encirclement" by imperialist and revisionist enemies. But the idea of encirclement was ideological only. It was disseminated to the population by radio, newspapers, and television. It led to campaigns against Western fashions in clothing, even against Western tourists who were considered to be nothing less than spies.

The communist system lasted in Albania until 1990. Then the Communist party (already renamed the Albanian Party of Labor) changed names once again, calling itself the Albanian Socialist party. Ramiz Alia (*see* Alia, Ramiz), the successor to Enver Hoxha, continued as premier, and the socialists won the elections that year. Only in 1991 was Alia finally ousted from power ending the communist period in Albanian history.

Bibliography
Marmalluku, Ramadan, *Albania and the Albanians* (London, 1975); Pano, Nicholas C. *The Socialist Republic of Albania* (Baltimore, 1968); Prifti, Peter R., "The Labor Party of Albania," in Stephen Fischer-Galati, ed. *The Communist Parties of Eastern Europe* (New York, 1979).

Constituent Assembly. The assembly was established in December 1945, after the elections, as a front organization for the Albanian Communist party. It was intended to placate Western public opinion. The task of creating a new constitution was assigned to the assembly. However, a law that was passed in October 1945 made it practically impossible to field opposition candidates in the coming elections. The elections, held on December 2, witnessed 89 percent of the electorate eligible to vote casting their ballots. Ninety-three percent allegedly cast their votes in favor of the candidates of the Democratic Front, another front organization of the Communist party. There was only one list of candidates for the elections. The Constituent Assembly met on January 10, 1946. It abolished the monarchy and proclaimed Albania to be a People's Republic on the Yugoslav pattern.

Bibliography
Biberaj, Elez, *Albania* (Boulder CO, 1990).

Constitutions of Albania. Three constitutions were adopted in Albania during the communist regime. The first, enacted in 1946, established Albania as a People's Republic on the Yugoslav model. The constitution declared the Communist party to be the leading force of the country, allegedly ruling in the name of the "proletariat." All political power was vested in the leaders of the Communist party.

The next constitution was enacted in 1950 after the Soviet-Yugoslav rift. Albania was now firmly in the Soviet Bloc, and the new constitution was patterned after the Stalinist Soviet constitution of 1936. Its basic law was the "dictatorship of the proletariat," embodied in the Communist party. The constitution regulated the economy by declaring that the already accomplished nationalization of industry, banking, finance, and land was in line with building socialism.

The constitution of 1976 replaced both previous documents. It proclaimed Albania to be a socialist republic. It prohibited the stationing of foreign troops on Albanian soil and the establishment of foreign military bases. This paragraph was certainly aimed at the Soviet Union which withdrew its military advisers and submarine fleet from Albania in the early 1960s. It also declared that Albania's ruling ideology was Marxism-Leninism and it created a defense council headed by Enver Hoxha (*see* Hoxha, Enver). The constitution stressed that Albania was building a new society under the severe conditions of enhanced class struggle that would ensure the final victory of socialism. It asserted that Albania had entered the final phase of socialist construction. "Albania," the constitution declared, "is the state of the dictatorship of the proletariat and the Albanian party of Labor is its only leading force in politics." All trade was placed under the control of the state as were all aspects of economic and social life. Religion was completely banned by the constitution. This document aimed at the continuation of the general line of the Albanian Communist party after the expected departure of Enver Hoxha and his presumed successor, Mehemet Shehu (*see* Shehu, Mehemet).

Bibliography
Prifti, Peter R., "The Labor Party of Albania," in Stephen Fischer-Galati, ed. *The Communist Parties of Eastern Europe* (New York, 1979); Starr, Richard, *The Communist Parties of Eastern Europe* (Stanford, CA, 1989).

Cultural Policies in Communist Albania. There were several motives for state-sponsored development of cultural life in Albania. First of all, it was a means to indoctrinate the people in the ideology of Marxism-Leninism. Second, culture was to serve as a tool in creating a socialist society. At the same time, culture was to promote "communist patriotism," really Albanian nationalism under another name. Culture was also to play a decisive role in promoting the class struggle against perceived internal and external enemies of the communist regime, including the "revisionists," a euphemism for the Soviet Union. Promoting Albanian culture was also considered by the party to be a means for getting Albanians to drop habits leftover from the feudal, Ottoman-dominated past.

In 1960, an Institute for Folklore was established. In little more than a decade, the members of the institute collected over 10,000 folk songs and published them in forty volumes. A network of local and national museums was established which exhibited the results of the excavations conducted by archeologists. Historical buildings were restored, and Albanian artists of earlier ages were publicized. Despite the ban on religious activities, old churches, such as that of Saints Triadha and Nikolla in the city of Berat and the Muslim monastery in the same city, were restored. The late medieval master painters of Onufri and Nikolla were "resurrected," and David Selenica, an eighteenth-century artist, was reintroduced to the public. A new Institute for the Preservation of Monuments of Culture was also created. Albanian scholars or artists who acquired a reputation outside the country were publicized. Such favorably presented personages included Andrea Aleksi, a fifteenth-century sculptor; Elena Gijka (known as Dora d'Istria), a nineteenth-century poet; and Albanian nationalist Aleksander Moisiu, a well-known character actor in Western Europe in the 1930s. Viktor Efthimiu, a Romanian of Albanian origins, a writer who was named member of the Romanian Academy of Sciences (together with Elena Ceausescu), received the Order of Naim Frasheri, named after Albania's national poet.

The regime promoted a series of folk festivals. A Theater Olympiad, the Radio and TV's Song Festival, became annual events. The National Festival of Folklore assembled nearly 20,000 participants. Party anniversaries dedicated to women, to the armed forces, or to the working class, were celebrated by festivals. The 500th anniversary of the death of Skanderbeu was celebrated by a huge festival in 1968. The purpose of these festivals was to identify the Albanian Communist party with the nation's "progressive" past and to impress the people with the power of the regime.

Specific cultural policies were directed toward the creation of "socialist man." This was to be a citizen whose life was focused on the building of socialism. Every one of his endeavors was to be dedicated to this purpose. Theaters, film, television, and radio were all producing shows glorifying the guerrilla struggle of the party against the Italians and Germans.

Most of state-sponsored culture was, therefore, propaganda that saturated the lives of the people. There were plays about "erring intellectuals" who were brought to their senses by the wise party secretary (Ibrahim Uruci's *Doktor Aleksi* and his *Shembja*). The nationalization of industry was the subject of Fadil Pacrami's *Mbi germadha*. A national puppet theater was created in order to expose the "exploiters of the people" for young children. Even the national opera company served propaganda purposes. A work, composed by Prenk Jakova, for instance, entitled *Mrika*, told in song about a dedicated party worker, a young woman, who worked for socialism. Tish Daija's opera portrayed the struggle against the Germans.

In 1954, a Gallery of Fine Arts was established in Tirana. It provided space for exhibitions by "socialist realist" works. Albanian filmmakers worked in the new National Film Studio. Their productions usually discussed the building of socialism and the struggle of heroic party members against the hidden enemy. Television was introduced in Albania in 1971. Most television sets produced in Albania were restricted to the use of one channel. In each village, town, and city, the state established and subsidized a "house of culture," the local propaganda arm of the Communist party. The buildings had small reading rooms whose shelves were stacked with cheap reprints of Stalin's, Lenin's, and Hoxha's works. They also contained socialist realist novels. Some houses had a movie projector, and a stage for amateur theater and propaganda meetings.

The Committee for Cultural Relations with the Outside World controlled all contacts with foreigners and foreign countries. All meetings with foreign scholars, sportsmen, and the small tourist exchange were under its auspices. The purpose of the committee was to present an image of "progressive socialist Albania" and to denigrate the "decadent" cultures of noncommunist countries.

In 1972, the party began a campaign against "harmful foreign ideas." Ramiz Alia (*see* Alia, Ramiz), later the successor to Enver Hoxha (*see* Hoxha, Enver), complained at a meeting of the League of Albanian Writers and Artists that people were reading books by Jean-Paul Sartre and Albert Camus, and that Freudian psychology was being discussed by some intellectuals. He also stated that Albanians were being corrupted by television and the cinema.

The campaign against Western influences gathered force the following year when meetings were held in factories, collective farms, and other institutions condemning "foreign capitalist and bourgeois influences." This was emphasized at the fifth conference of the party in April 1973, when it was charged that the Albanian media as well as theaters and ballets made concessions to bourgeois ideologies. They were all instructed to serve only the party's aim in building socialism. Italian television, which could be received in Albania, was accused of spreading "Vatican propaganda" and a decadent American way of life. Party ideologues asserted that the "people" (they meant, of course, the party leaders) had the right to demand Marxist-Leninist commitment from its writers. They also stated that the party's control of cultural life was fully justified and that nothing would budge them from this position. Although previous efforts to impose strict uniformity on culture failed (*see* the Cultural Revolution of 1966–1967), the Albanian communists did not cease their efforts until the collapse of their system.

Bibliography
Marmullaku, Ramadan, *Albania and the Albanians* (London, 1975); Prifti, Peter R., *Socialist Albania Since 1944: Domestic and Foreign Developments* (Cambridge, MA, 1978).

Cultural Revolution of 1966–1967. Deeply concerned about the alienation of the people from the communist regime, and attributing this fact to the tremendous growth of the party—and state—bureaucracy that apparently isolated the leaders from the people, Enver Hoxha (*see* Hoxha, Enver) proclaimed a Cultural Revolution to begin in 1966. This was not the consequence of an intraparty struggle as was the case in China, but the idea had its origin in Beijing. Hoxha wanted to reassert the Communist party's authority over the local and regional party bureaucracies and strengthen the influence of the Communist party over all segments of Albanian society.

The Cultural Revolution began in February 1966 with an announcement that high party and state functionaries had been assigned to work with local and regional party and state institutions. Excess personnel were "encouraged" to volunteer for work in factories and collective farms. The party leaders promised to correct their mistakes in an open letter to the people issued by the party's secretariat. Ranks in the armed forces were abolished next, and the institution of political commissars was reintroduced. The salaries of middle and high-ranking officials were reduced. The cabinet shrank from nineteen ministers to thirteen. The number of civil servants was cut. Next, so-called dissident intellectuals were attacked.

In February 1967, the second phase of the Albanian Cultural Revolution began. Hoxha urged Albanians to eliminate the "last vestiges of bourgeois culture" from their thinking and to intensify their struggle against what he called "bureaucratism." He appealed to the young people of Albania to strive for the preservation of the purity of the ideology of Marxism-Leninism. During the late spring and early summer of 1967, the Cultural Revolution reached its climax.

The Albanian Red Guards, patterned after their Chinese counterparts, criticized intellectuals on wall posters and conducted a vicious anti-religion campaign in the cities. But they did not get out of hand as did their Chinese brothers. They continued to be controlled by the party's bureaucrats throughout the Cultural Revolution. The party leaders now proclaimed the emancipation of women and suggested that they enter the industrial and agricultural labor force. This was a response to the growing labor shortage in every area of the economy. By the end of 1967, the Cultural Revolution had petered out.

Bibliography

Prifti, Peter R. *Socialist Albania Since 1944: Domestic and Foreign Developments* (Cambridge, MA, 1978).

Economic Policies of the Communist Regime. In 1944, Albania was an underdeveloped country. Its meager industries were destroyed by World War II. For this very reason, rebuilding the economy after the war was over did not take a long time. The aim of the Communist party was, however, not only reconstruction, but the building of a modern industrial state with a highly developed, mechanized agriculture. It embraced the Stalinist methods of centralized planning and management systems. The regime's economic policies show remarkable consistency, more so than those of any other socialist country in Europe. Rapid industrialization, the forced collectivization of agriculture, and the upgrading of centralized social services were to be the means to achieve these goals.

The wartime experiences of Albanian communist leaders deeply influenced their thinking. They were quite conscious of the fact that, without foreign assistance, they would not be able to achieve their aims, yet they were wary of the possible consequences. As a result, they were determined to make Albania as self-sufficient economically as possible. This effort necessarily created tensions with their various patrons, first with Yugoslavia, then with the Soviet Union, and, finally, with communist China. In the end, all outsiders had given up efforts at building up Albania's economy, and they considered the country to be the victim of an inconsiderate, unreasonable leadership.

In 1950, long-range planning began in Tirana. Its basis was the accelerated exploitation of the country's natural resources in building up industry. During the first five-year plan, industry grew by an incredibly high rate of 20 annually. This was, however, partly the result of starting from an almost zero-base.

By the mid-1950s, the post-Stalinist Soviet leaders, especially Khrushchev, began to emphasize economic integration among the members of the Soviet Bloc with a new "socialist division of labor." The major contribution of Albania and Romania was to be the supplying of abundant agricultural products and raw materials for the more advanced countries of the Soviet Bloc. Both Albania and Romania refused to go along with this requirement. Such a role would have required them to remain industrially underdeveloped, and their leaders had already committed too much of their prestige to industrialization. Enver Hoxha (*see* Hoxha, Enver) was especially vehement in his objections. He considered the Soviet Politburo too soft on capitalism, and, in time, he began to see himself as the only original Marxist-Leninist thinker in Eastern Europe.

In 1961, the formal break between Albania and the Soviet Union occurred. Hoxha then allied his country with China, a country that was contesting Soviet leadership in the world communist movement. The Chinese initially were eager to replace Soviet economic help with their own for Albania. They provided scarce funds, raw materials, and technical and military advisers to help Albania to continue its drive for industrialization. They helped the Albanians to develop an extensive hydroelectric system, to build oil refineries, and to create machine and tool-making industries. They were particularly helpful in supporting the development of Albania's food-processing industry.

When China began to open its closed doors to Western contacts in 1973, the Albanians objected. The Chinese response was the reduction of economic aid. By 1978, all aid had stopped. In spite of this, the Albanian communist leadership continued to cling to its outdated policies. As a consequence, industrial growth slowed down and, by 1985, when Hoxha died, it reached zero level.

When the communist regime finally collapsed, the Albanian economy was in complete shambles. As the Albanian communists came into power in 1944, they were determined to collectivize agriculture. The first collectivization drive began in 1946, but it was largely unsuccessful. Two years later, the drive was resumed but at a much slower pace. By 1960, 86 percent of all arable land of the country belonged to collective farms. The results were achieved by the well-known Stalinist methods of terror and intimidation. The immediate result was the decline of production in agriculture. But the leaders did not let up the pressure. By 1967, they reported that 100 percent of the land of Albania was in the hands of collective farmers. So were all farm implements and draft, dairy, and meat animals. The families of collectivized farmers were each allocated one-quarter of an acre of land as a household plot. However, the produce from these plots could not be sold, since there was no open market for food products in the country. Not surprisingly, Albanian food production reached only 50 percent of the planned output.

Believing that larger collective farms would be more efficient, the government began combining smaller collective farms into larger units in the 1970s. At the same time, the remaining animals of the collective farmers were confiscated and placed into commonly held herds. These policies contributed to growing discontent among the peasants. Nevertheless, in 1976, the propaganda apparatus of the party proclaimed that Albania had achieved self-sufficiency in the production of bread grains and said that collective farmers would be able to fulfill all food needs of the Albanian people by the early 1980s. This proved to be empty propaganda.

In the meanwhile, the government made tremendous efforts at mechanizing agricultural production, providing artificial fertilizers, and raising a new generation of agricultural technicians. Yet, all these efforts proved futile; they did not result in the increase of agricultural production. During much of the 1980s, Albania was forced to import food, and this drained the country's hard currency reserves. Other ill-considered interventions in agriculture continued to plague Albanian food producers.

Although new lands were brought into cultivation during the 1960s and 1970s, further land resources were not available. In the 1980s, the population increased yearly by nearly 2 percent, and the leaders were forced to modify their policies somewhat. Even so, food production increases remained below that of the increase of the population.

Bibliography

Kaser, Michael, "Albania Under and After Hoxha," *East European Economies: Slow Growth in the 1980s* (Washington, DC., 1986), vol. 3, pp. 1-21; Kaser, Michael and Schnitzer, Adi, "Albania's Uniquely Socialist Economy," *East European Economies: Post-Helsinki* (Washington, DC., 1977), pp. 567-646; Schnitzer, Adi, *Stalinist Economic Strategy in Practice: The Case of Albania* (New York, 1982).

Educational Policies. The communist states everywhere placed great emphasis upon expending educational opportunities for the population under their control. This was true also for Albania. Education was a means of indoctrinating young people in the ideology of Marxism-Leninism. But it was also necessary if Albania was to fulfill its ambitious program of industrialization.

In 1944, the majority of the population, especially those living in the rural areas, was illiterate. By 1973, 700,000 students were studying at various levels. These included 569,600 young people in eight-grade schools, 102,600 in middle-level schools, and 28,600 in higher schools. This meant that the number of young people receiving some form of schooling had grown by twelve times since 1938. This, however, has to be compared to the absolute increase of the Albanian population which had the highest rate of growth in all of Europe.

The country was, however, the most in need of higher educational institutions. One important step was taken in 1947 when an Institute for Science was established, and it became the foundation for the first Albanian university. The university was formally established in 1957. Its seven faculties provided instruction in traditional subjects . In its first year the university enrolled 3,600 students, taught by 200 faculty members. By 1985, enrollment was up to 18,000 students who were instructed by 800 faculty members. In 1972, the Albanian Academy of Sciences was established to study the sciences and Marxist-Leninist ideology. Twenty-five top scholars of the country were admitted to the institution. They represented a mixture of true scholars and party ideological pundits.

The academy included six institutions and the Institute of Figurative Arts (painting), the State Conservatory of Music, and the Academy of Theater Arts.

Bibliography

Prifti, Peter R., *Socialist Albania Since 1944: Domestic and Foreign Developments* (Cambridge, MA, 1978); Thomas, John E., *Education for Communism: Schools and State in the People's Republic of Albania* (Stanford, CA, 1969).

Greek Minority in Albania. The situation of ethnic Greeks living in Albania has been a perennial issue of contention between Greece and the Albanian state ever since the existence of independent Albania. In 1914, the Florence Protocol established the borders between the two countries. At that time, about 20 percent of the Albanian population was Orthodox Christian while the rest was Muslim. Consecutive Greek governments thereafter claimed that the Orthodox Christians were really ethnic Greeks who lived in the area the Greek governments called northern Epirus, and the Albanians named southern Albania. Although Greek premier Georgikos Mitsotakis declared, in his 1990 visit to Tirana, that Greece had no territorial claims against Albania, talks nevertheless continued in Athens, especially among leaders of the conservative New Democratic party, about the issue concerning northern Epirus. The Albanians on their part claim that ethnic Greeks moved to their current residence in the Dropuli region "only" in the eighteenth century as servants of Albanian feudal lords. While Greece claims to have from about 300,000 to 400,000 of their conationals living in Albania, the Albanians put the number at 60,000.

In December 1990, the ethnic Greeks created OMNIA, a political organization aimed at defending their ethnic rights. The organization fielded candidates in the first free elections and won five seats in the Albanian parliament. Its opponents claimed, however, that Ramiz Alia (*see* Alia, Ramiz), the last communist president of the country, supported the ethnic Greeks in exchange for their votes. Thus, the Albanian parliament changed OMNIA's status to that of a cultural organization and banned political activities by the group, in 1992. This act was considered by many as retaliation for Greek practices vis a vis Albanian refugees who were creating serious problems in Greek urban centers (*see* Politics in Post-Communist Albania). In turn, the parliamentary act could not fail to create adverse feelings toward Albania in Greece.

As pressure mounted on the Albanian government to honor its pledges of respecting human rights—pressure that was brought on not only by the Greek government but also by the Council of Europe—the Albanian parliament finally consented to permit the ethnic Greeks to form their own political party. The party was promptly established under the name of Union for Human Rights. This party was to participate in the coming elections. What this affair shows is that the sins of the past, created by the cynical disregard by the Western powers of ethnic problems in Eastern Europe after both world wars, are coming back to haunt the region. The disregard of ethnic boundaries in the name of the so-called principle of national self-determination could still result in a series of confrontations similar to those that are tearing apart Yugoslavia (*see* Kosovo).

Bibliography
Zanga, Louis, "Albania Between Democracy and Chaos," *Radio Free Europe Research Reports*, 1.1 (January 3, 1992), pp. 74-77.

Hoxha, Enver (1908–1985). Born in Gjirocaster in southern Albania, Hoxha graduated from the French lycaeum in the town of Korce in 1930. He enrolled at the University of Montpelier in France the following year on a government scholarship. While at Montpelier, Hoxha wrote articles for the French communist daily newspaper, *L'Humanite*, directed against Albanian King Zog. When his authorship was discovered, his Albanian state scholarship was terminated. Hoxha then moved to Brussels, Belgium, to work as a private secretary at the local Albanian consulate.

At Brussels, he studied law, but he also continued his antigovernment propaganda activities, which resulted in his dismissal. In 1936, he returned to Albania and found a job as a teacher at the gymnasium in Tirana and later at his alma mater at Korce.

After the Italian invasion of Albania in 1939, Hoxha was dismissed from his teaching position. Thereupon he moved back to Tirana and opened a tobacco shop, which became the center of clandestine anti-fascist activities. In November 1941, he was invited to head the recently established Albanian Communist party as secretary of the Provisional Central Committee.

He was a nationalist and, at the same time, a doctrinaire communist with a penchant for conspiracy. He believed in Marxist-Leninist doctrines with a messianic zeal. He was intent on modernizing Albanian society in a radical way. He spoke French, Russian, English, Italian, and Serbo-Croatian.

During the fateful years of 1943 and 1944, Hoxha was the guiding spirit behind the Albanian Communist party's single-minded drive for power. His party, together with the party of Josip Broz Tito, gained power without direct Soviet intervention. In 1946, he was named prime minister and commander in chief of the Albanian armed forces. He was also first secretary of the Albanian Communist party (later called the Albanian Party of Labor). In July 1946, Hoxha traveled to Belgrade and signed a treaty of friendship, cooperation, and mutual aid with the Yugoslav government of Tito. In 1949, however, Hoxha broke with the Yugoslavs and sided with Joseph Stalin. He used vile, vituperative language in denouncing his former mentor and the Yugoslav Communist party.

After Stalin's death, Hoxha became increasingly critical of Stalin's successors considering them, especially Nikita Khrushchev, as willfully deviating from Marxism-Leninism. In 1961, he openly broke relations with the Soviet Union and sided with communist China in the latter's struggle for liberation from Soviet tutelage. By 1971, however, Albanian-Chinese relations soured, and three years later Hoxha broke with the Chinese over the issue of the Chinese leaders' gradual accommodation with the United States.

By then, Hoxha exhibited signs of megalomania. He considered himself the only remaining true Marxist-Leninist leader in Europe, and his theoretical writings increased in intensity and vehemence. He remained Albania's Stalinist ruler until his death on April 11, 1985. He was in power for 41 years, longer than any other communist dictator except Kim Il Sung of North Korea.

Hoxha was indisputably the leader who brought Albania into the twentieth century. His regime succeeded in transforming age-old habits and customs of the people. He also successfully defended Albania's territorial integrity, although his denunciation of Tito prevented the satisfactory settlement of the Kosovo question (*see* Kosovo). Hoxha was also responsible for the transformation of the Albanian economy based on the Stalinist model and for the thorough transformation of Albania's social structure. Nevertheless, the "house that Hoxha built" eventually proved to be fundamentally unsound.

Among the positive changes that the Hoxha regime brought about was a new educational system, improved health care for the entire population, and a new cultural life basically different from anything that existed before in Albania. In comparison with prevailing conditions in the country before World War II, life certainly improved for Albanians during the Hoxha era. The nation and state building, begun by King Zog in the 1920s and 1930s, had been successfully completed by Hoxha. The central government finally acquired unquestioned authority even in the most remote areas of the country and reduced tribal and religious conflicts to a minimum. Hoxha's dogmatism and his ruthless enforcement of Marxist-Leninist-Stalinist doctrines and methods of government were, however, liabilities that eventually negated the positive aspects of his rule. His rigidity in enforcing his own ideological convictions created the conditions for eventual failure.

By the time of Hoxha's death, most young people, the largest segment of Albania's population; the intelligentsia; and the peasantry were completely alienated from his system. Nor was Hoxha able to instill ideological discipline in the industrial workers whose apathy contributed to the failure of the consecutive five-year plans. The frequent and repeated violations of the so-called socialist legality, the enforced ideological conformity, and the brutality of Hoxha's secret police, failed to advance the goal of gaining internal legitimacy for the regime that it would have needed to survive.

Bibliography

Artisien, Patrick, F.R., "Albania After Hoxha," *Sais Review* 6.1 (Winter-Spring 1986), pp. 159-160; Halliday, Jon, *The Artful Albanian: The Memoires of Enver Hoxha* (London, 1986).

Knives (*The Knives*, by author Neshat Tozaj). In August 1989, during the uncertainty and turmoil that followed the collapse of the Soviet colonial empire in Eastern Europe, a novel was published in Tirana by the writer Neshat Tozaj entitled *Thikat* (Knives). Tozaj, an employee of the Ministry of the Interior, was a veteran journalist. His novel opened a window upon the life of secret policemen during the Hoxha regime. The book showed the incredible callousness and brutality of secret police operatives, and their total disregard of the laws and the civil rights of ordinary citizens. Tozaj showed that the secret police obeyed only direct orders issued by Enver Hoxha (*see* Hoxha, Enver). It became a state within the state, a runaway system that served the individual whims of those who were in the top echelons of the communist *apparat*.

The publication of the novel created a great stir in Albania. It was reviewed in the October 15, 1989, issue of the weekly newspaper of the Writers' Union in a very favorable way, which enhanced its popularity. It also provided a wider platform for obtaining knowledge of the secret world of the political police. The book contributed to demands for reigning in the secret police and for the establishment of the rule of law instead of the whims of the leaders of the Communist party.

Bibliography

Neshat Tozaj, *Thikat (The Knives)* (Tirana, 1989).

Kosovo. The land of the province of Kosovo is inhabited by about 2 million Albanians and 200,000 ethnic Serbs. The historical antagonism that exists between the two nations is the most evident in this land. Religious divisions add fuel to the fire; most Albanians are Muslims and most Serbs are Orthodox Christians. None of these factors provides a better understanding between the two groups.

Kosovo has great historical significance for both nations. It was here that the Serbian culture originated. It was also in the "Kosovo polje," or field of blackbirds, where the Ottoman army of Sultan Murad I inflicted the greatest defeat on the opposing Serbian army in 1389, ending the existence of a quasi-independent Serbian state. On the other hand, Albanians have probably lived longer in Kosovo than any other ethnic group. Prizren, a town in the province, was the meeting place for Albanian tribal chieftains in 1878 from which the Albanian national movement began, leading to independence in the First Balkan War of 1912.

Kosovo was given to the Kingdom of Serbs, Croats, and Slovenians, in 1918, by the great powers (later to become Yugoslavia), in total disregard for the Wilsonian principles of the right of self-determination of nations.

Yugoslavia consistently employed discriminatory policies toward the Ko-sovo Albanians, a policy that differed little from the apartheid practices of South Africa against blacks. The properties of Albanians were often confiscated for no other reason than that they belonged to Albanians; police terror was an everyday occurrence, and Albanians were often forced to vacate their houses and even leave the province if the Serbian authorities so demanded. Albanian language schools were closed, and their teachers were fired. Even the speaking of Albanian in public places was prohibited. All this in a land overwhelmingly populated by Albanians! In response, the Albanians set up a Kosovo Committee, operating clandestinely, which encouraged passive resistance to the Serbian oppressors.

On April 7, 1939, fascist Italy invaded Albania. When Yugoslavia was dismembered by Nazi Germany in 1941, Kosovo was transferred to Albania, and the Albanian-populated areas of Macedonia and Montenegro were also united with the Nazi's Albanian client state. Although the Albanian resistance fought against the fascist armies (*see* Legality Organization), these territories were restored to Yugoslavia after the conclusion of World War II by the victorious Allies. The policy of oppression was then renewed. KGB-trained Yugoslav secret policemen intimidated and terrorized the Albanian population. When Yugoslavia was expelled from the COMINFORM in 1949, Enver Hoxha (*see* Hoxha, Enver), the Albanian communist chief, called on the Kosovo Albanians to rise up against their oppressors, but his call went unanswered.

Until 1966, the Kosovo Albanians were engaged in passive resistance. In that year, the dreaded Yugoslav secret police chief, Alexandar Rankovic (*see* Rankovic, Alexandar, in the chapter on Yugoslavia), was removed, and a policy of more relaxed control was introduced in Kosovo province.

Albanian language instruction was once again permitted, and Kosovo received an autonomous status in the Yugoslav federation. The Yugoslav constitution of 1974 recognized the status of Kosovo Albanians as equal citizens of Yugoslavia. At the same time, an Albanian language university was established in Prizren.

After the death of Tito, however, the Yugoslav government resorted to the same old methods of rule through intimidation and terror. In 1981, major riots broke out in the province; the Yugoslav secret police shot scores of people in suppressing the disorders. In 1987, Slobodan Milosevic, a former communist chief, became the premier of Yugoslavia. An ardent Serb chauvinist, he was determined to reassert Serbian supremacy in the Yugoslav federation. In June 1990, Milosevic's police simply disbanded the provincial legislature and, upon his urging, the Serbian parliament abolished Kosovo's autonomous status. The democratically elected Albanian legislators went underground.

On September 7, 1990, they met secretly at Kacanik and approved a separate constitution for the Kosovo province. In September 1991, Albanians voted overwhelmingly in favor of the Kacanik constitution, despite an all-out effort made by the Serbian government to stop the "illegal" election. On October 19, the underground legislature declared Kosovo an independent republic. Albania promptly recognized the new state, but other European states did not follow suit.

Currently, several political parties exist in the Kosovo province, and the Serb secret police does not seem to be able to keep them underground. The Democratic Alliance, headed by Ibrahim Rugova, has the largest membership. Next in size is the Parliamentary party, led by Veton Surroi. The third largest party is that of the Social Democrats led by Shkelzin Maliqi. All these parties are dedicated to the restoration of civil rights to the Albanian population, but they have not had much success so far. It is, however, only a matter of time until outside pressures will force the Serbian government, whether it is headed by Milosevic or someone else, to grant basic human rights to the large Albanian majority in the province of Kosovo. If that dos not happen soon, Serbia might have to face war over Kosovo which, in turn, could lead to another general conflagration in the Balkans.

Bibliography

Artisien, Patrick, F.R., "A Note on Kosovo and the Future of Yugoslav-Albanian Relations: A Balkan Perspective," *Soviet Studies*, 36.2 (April, 1984), pp. 267-276; Biberaj, Elez, *Albania* (Boulder, CO, 1990); Kosta, Nicholas, "Kosovo: a Tragedy in the Making," *East European Quarterly*, 21.1 (March, 1987), pp. 87-97; Moore, Patrick, "The 'Albanian Question' in the Former Yugoslavia," *Radio Free Europe Research Reports*, 1.14 (April 3, 1992), p. 7-15; Pipa, Arshi, *Albanian Stalinism: Ideo-Political Aspects* (Boulder, CO, 1990); Skendi, Stavro, *Albania* (New York, 1956).

League of Albanian Writers and Artists. Established as the Albanian Party of Labor's (Communist) intellectual arm, the league was intended to provide guidance to intellectuals and artists and keep them within the confines of party ideology. In 1957, the Writers League was joined to the League of Artists in one organization. The president of the new institution was Dhimiter Shuteriqi, a devoted communist party apparatchik. This step was taken in response to Khrushchev's denunciation of Stalin's crimes which inspired fear in the extremist Albanian communist leaders of the possible aftereffects of a trend toward relaxation of controls over the intellectuals. Some efforts had already been made by moderate intellectuals to mitigate the harsh terror exercised over personal expressions. They resented the stifling effects of conformism imposed on writers and artists. But the party leaders would have none of it. The combined league started out by continuing to impose the required uniformity of "socialist realism" on writers and artists, and it remained a tool of oppression of individual thought during the entire communist period.

Bibliography
Prifti, Peter R. *Socialist Albania Since 1944: Domestic and Foreign Developments* (Cambridge, MA, 1978).

Legality Organization in Albania. Established in the fall of 1943 by the Geg leader, Abas Kupi, this movement which resisted the fascist armies, was also dedicated to the return of the monarchy to Albania. Its membership came mainly from among the northern Gegs. The organization was contending for power with the Balli Kombetar and the communists in 1944. Kupi himself was an influential Geg leader, and a member of the Executive Committee of the National Liberation Front, until the communists began their attacks on the Balli Kombetar, another nationalist organization, in 1943. Kupi then decided to quit the front and establish his own organization for the return of King Zog to Albania. But his ragtag army was quickly destroyed by the communists after the Germans withdrew from the Balkans. By then, Italy had already surrendered to the Allies, and 15,000 Italian soldiers gave up their arms and other equipment to the communists.

Bibliography
Prifti, Peter R. *Socialist Albania Since 1944: Domestic and Foreign Developments* (Cambridge, MA, 1978).

Maleshova, Sejfulla (1917–1947). Maleshova was a charter member of the Albanian Communist party and a member of the Politburo. In 1945, Maleshova was appointed minister of culture and propaganda. He was the party's ideological watchdog and, at the same time, a poet of the guerrilla war against the Italian and German armies of occupation. In October 1945, Maleshova was instrumental in establishing the League of Albanian Writers which consisted of seventy-four members at that time. These included some noncommunist intellectuals. Maleshova was elected first president of the organization.

He was a moderate among the rabidly extremist Albanian communist leaders. He invited publications in the official journal of the league by both communist and noncommunist writers. He decreed that high quality writings be published with only moderate regard for their ideological content. He attempted to establish a modus vivendi between the ideologically committed intellectuals and those who were not so inclined. Consequently, Maleshova received increasingly vehement criticisms from high party officials. Enver Hoxha (*see* Hoxha, Enver) was especially suspicious of his moderation, and he attacked Maleshova over a wide range of issues. When the League of Albanian Writers appealed to President Harry Truman and Prime Minister Clement Attlee for Western recognition of the Albanian state, Maleshova was roundly denounced in Communist party circles.

At a meeting of the party's Central Committee held in February 1946, Maleshova was accused by Hoxha of rightist deviation and expelled from the party. He was also removed from the Politburo. Following Maleshova's dismissal, a wave of terror was directed against the writers' community. Many of them were arrested and imprisoned on false charges. About ten writers were executed; many others died of mistreatment in prison or in camps. Maleshova was also imprisoned and died an outcast.

Bibliography

Pipa, Arshi, *Area Handbook for Albania: Foreign Area Studies* (Washington, DC., 1971).

National Liberation Front. In September 1942, the communist leaders of the anti-fascist resistance movement called a meeting for all resistance forces at the city of Berat. This meeting created a National Liberation Front. Its purpose was to coordinate all efforts at ousting the Italian and German forces from the country. The communists controlled this organization which proceeded to establish local governments in areas cleared of the occupiers. The political rivals of the communists were the Balli Kombetar, a moderate group led by Midhat Frasheri an ardent Albanian patriot, and the Legality Organization, led by Abas Kupi, who was dedicated to the reestablishment of the monarchy under King Zog.

The agreement between these competing forces did not last long. During 1943, the moderate and monarchist groups fought bitterly against the communists as well as against the Italians and Germans. The Balli Kombetar attracted a relatively large number of fighters, but the communists were better organized. In 1943, the Balli Kombetar reduced its activities in order to avoid unnecessary casualties. This strategy was used by the communists to brand them as German collaborators. At the Mukja meeting, held in 1943, a tentative agreement was reached among the resistance forces for terminating the infighting, but this was eventually rejected by the communist leadership.

In August 1945, the National Liberation Front was renamed the Democratic Front. By then it was a front organization for the Albanian Communist party. The Democratic Front, under communist guidance, proceeded to create a single list of candidates for the coming national elections, the candidates being communists or communist sympathizers. The elections for the Constituent Assembly (*see* Constituent Assembly) took place in December 1945. Conducted under great terror by the communists, the elections resulted in an overwhelming victory for the Communist party. After the elections, the Democratic Front was turned into a mass organization serving as a transmission belt for the dissemination of Marxist-Leninist ideology in Albania.

Bibliography

Pipa, Arshi, *Albanian Stalinism: Ideo-Political Aspects* (Boulder, CO, 1990).

Nationalizations. Early in 1945, the new communist government of Albania confiscated all German and Italian assets in the country. It also revoked all foreign concessions and nationalized all means of transportation and communication, including the newspapers and radio stations. It nationalized all lands and began to create state-controlled agricultural cooperatives. In January 1945, all land debts were cancelled, and rents on remaining private holdings were reduced by 75 percent. Water resources and power-generating facilities were nationalized next. All forest lands became the property of the state. At first, landowners were permitted to work a maximum of 40 acres, but this concession was soon terminated. By the summer of 1946, all industrial firms had been taken over by the state, and retail trade had been declared state monopoly. Foreign trade was completely taken over by state organs. However, it was only in 1955 that the state began an all-out collectivization drive in the rural communities.

Bibliography
Prifti, Peter R. *Socialist Albania Since 1944: Domestic and Foreign Developments* (Cambridge, MA, 1978).

Politics in Post-Communist Albania. The collapse of the communist regimes in Eastern Europe and the Soviet Union had a profound effect on the most brutal regime of them all in the region. Ramiz Alia (*see* Alia, Ramiz), the heir to Enver Hoxha (*see* Hoxha, Enver), held onto power for the time being, but his situation was becoming ever more precarious. In December 1990, student strikes at the University of Tirana forced Alia to accede to the holding of multi-party elections. Nevertheless, unrest continued in the country.

In February 1991, an enraged mass demonstration ended by toppling the giant statue of Hoxha, located on Skanderbeu square in Tirana. Six new parties emerged, and they all participated in the elections held in March. Alia was still able to slow down the march of events. In February, he set up a Presidential Council which strengthened his control over governmental affairs. At the same time, he tried to calm the situation by acceding to some demands of the opposition.

The general elections were held on March 31, 1991. A huge number of people, about 95 percent of all those who were eligible, cast their votes. A new legislature of 257 members was elected. The Albanian Workers' (formerly Communist) party won two-thirds of the seats in the new parliament, but the opposition also had a strong showing. In June, the Albanian Workers' party changed its name once again, this time to the Albanian Socialist party. But this change was recognized by the population for what it was, namely, an effort to dissociate the current communist leaders from the sins of the party's past.

The major oppositional organization, the Democratic party, continued to point out that only the name of the Communist party has been changed, not the aims of its leaders. Alia on his part countered that the Democratic party was aiming at the reestablishment of a one-party dictatorship in Albania, this time its own. Meanwhile, bloody confrontations took place between police and demonstrators in the major cities. In Shkoder, whose population had a long anti-communist tradition, four people were killed by the police in early April 1991, including the leader of the local branch of the Democratic party. In response, police vehicles were burned, and the local headquarters of the Socialist party were torched.

During 1991, the Albanian economy slowly ground to a halt. Tens of thousands of Albanian citizens, mostly young people, were seeking refuge in neighboring countries, especially in Greece. When Greece introduced major restrictions on new emigration from Albania, the exodus did slow down, but not without creating ill feelings toward Greece in general. In August 1991, about 20,000 Albanians sought asylum in Italy; they commandeered a ship and landed at Bari. As a consequence, the Italian government was forced to involve itself in Albanian affairs which, in the light of its past, it was quite reluctant to do.

On September 1, however, Italy committed 800 soldiers to accompany food shipments to Albania, guarding the goods against looters. Italian emergency food shipments came to $70 million. At the same time, a three-year agreement on economic cooperation was signed by the two governments, which included $800 million in food shipments to Albania. In addition, Western European countries agreed to deliver 50,000 tons of wheat to Albania before June 1992. Germany conducted separate negotiations with the Albanian government and provided $75 million worth of technical and financial assistance. All this support notwithstanding, Albania continues to be economically depressed mainly because of the social habits and attitudes acquired by the population over four decades of state control.

By the end of 1991, total agricultural and industrial production was down from about 12 to 15 percent of the pre-World War II levels. There existed severe shortages of spare parts and machinery. Raw material resources were exhausted. The indebtedness of Albania increased to $400 million in 1991. Large-scale unemployment appeared, coupled with horrendous inflation. Agricultural cooperatives were dissolved, and their lands, implements, and animal stocks were taken over by individual peasant families. Food had to be severely rationed.

On May 2, 1991, Ramiz Alia was elected president of the country by parliament. A week later, he appointed a new government headed by Fatos Nano. However, a general strike, held on June 4, forced the government to resign. On June 11, the first Albanian coalition government was formed. Ylli Bufi, a former communist official, was appointed prime minister.

The new government proved itself just as incapable of solving Albania's economic collapse as its predecessors. Although it indeed enacted a series of economic reforms, including one for the orderly redistribution of land to the former collective peasants, and it discontinued the practice of centrally controlling prices, the economy did not recover. Finally, the Democratic party issued four demands, including the arrest and prosecution of former communist leaders, the punishment of the police who fired on the demonstrators at Shkoder, the replacement of the communist managers of the national television and radio stations, and the holding of elections no later than February 1992. The last of these demands was immediately accepted; elections were to be held within three months. In the meantime, there was no letup in the economic crisis.

The reemergence of the issue of securing the civil rights of the Albanian population in the Serbian-controlled province of Kosovo (*see* Kosovo) added to the social unrest. It seems certain that Albania will not be able to recover without the infusion of foreign aid on a massive scale into its economy. However, material aid must be matched by the recovery of Albanian self-esteem and Albanian history as well as the will to rebuild the ruined country. Without such a change, Albania will remain a society of angry, alienated people, a perpetual powder keg ready to explode at the slightest provocation, a danger to the peace of the Balkans and to that of the entire European continent.

Bibliography

Zanga, Louis, "Albania Between Chaos and Democracy," *Radio Free Europe Research Reports*, 1.1 (January 3, 1992), pp. 74-77; "Albania: Fall of Government Plunges Country into Chaos," *Radio Free Europe Research Reports*, 1.2 (January 10, 1992), pp. 17-19; "Albania's Local Elections," *Radio Free Europe Research Reports*, 1.35 (September 18, 1982), pp. 75-78.

Post-Communist Albanian-Greek Relations. After the collapse of communism in Eastern Europe, there was a temporary improvement in Albanian-Greek relations. Already in 1987, the Papandreau government of Greece unilaterally declared that the status of war between Greece and Albania, in existence since the Albanian support of Greek communist insurgency in the 1940s, was ended. In 1989, the two countries signed an economic cooperation agreement. But matters soon changed for the worse. Papandreau's socialist government was ousted, and his party suffered defeat in the Greek elections. Simultaneously, the Albanian economic situation deteriorated. This opened the floodgates of Albanian refugees seeking a better life in Greece.

The Prime Minister of Greece, Georgikos Mitsotakis, and his government, were perplexed; consequently, the prime minister visited Tirana. It happened for the first time in modern history that such a visit took place by a Greek prime minister. He tried to settle the issue of refugees. Mitsotakis appealed to ethnic Greeks in Albania to stay put and he promised economic aid of $20 million to help Albania improve the economic conditions of the country.

However, Greece is not a rich country despite being a member of the European Common Market. Its economy was seriously impacted by the flood of Albanian refugees. It was simply unable to absorb even the initial wave of 60,000 people. The number of refugees soon swelled to 200,000, and Greece simply had no choice but to send most of them back to Albania. Albanian refugees caused problems by moving to Greek cities where work was not always available. Many of them resorted to crime in order to maintain themselves. This inflamed Greek public opinion and forced the government to take strong measures.

When the Greek government strengthened its control over its border with Albania, the Albanians protested. Greek economic aid promised by Mitsotakis, was slow in coming and when it did it usually went to ethnic Greek communities. Albanians in the southern cities of Delvine and Saranode went on a three-day pogrom against ethnic Greeks, looting their stores and burning the Greek party's headquarters. In Greece, talk over the issue of Northern Epirus was revived. The declaration of independence by the former Yugoslav republic of Macedonia, with its sizable Greek and Albanian ethnic groups, created new bases for tensions.

So far, open, violent conflict have been avoided simply because neither Greece nor Albania can afford war. Greece itself has not yet recovered from the disastrous policies of the Andreas Papandreau government, and the Albanian economy is in shambles. There is no guarantee, however, that one or the other government would not find it necessary to go to war over Macedonia if the economic situation became so threatening that it would create social disintegration and revolution.

Bibliography

Zanga, Louis, "Albanian-Greek Relations Reach a Low Point," *Radio Free Europe Research Reports,* 1.5 (April 10, 1992), pp. 18-20.

Purges of the Communist Party. There have been four major periods of purges in Albania during the rule of the Communist party. The purges were related to what the communist leaders, especially Enver Hoxha (*see* Hoxha, Enver), declared to be "deviations." They included the issue of Titoism, Soviet "social imperialism," Maoism and Euro-communism.

After the end of World War II, Enver Hoxha was a junior partner to Tito and the Bulgarian leader, and veteran COMINTERN agent, Georgy Dimitrov (*see* Dimitrov, Georgy, in the section on Bulgaria). Tito's agents sponsored the fledgling Albanian Communist party and directed its affairs until at least 1947. Before that year, there was a strong possibility that Albania would become the seventh republic in the Yugoslav federation. Tito's spokesman in the Albanian Politburo was Koci Xoxhe (*see* Xoxhe, Koci), who belonged to the Korce group of early Albanian communists. He was groomed for his task by Vukmanovic-Tempo, an important member of Tito's entourage. The issues centered on the problem of Albanian independence. Sejfulla Maleshova (*see* Maleshova, Sejfulla), an old communist who had connections in the Soviet Union, competed with Hoxha for leadership of the party. He was secretary-general of the National Liberation Front and was opposed to the Stalinization of Albania based on the Yugoslav pattern. He was also minister of culture and propaganda and chairman of the state planning committee. He was anti-Tito, and when he was purged, both Xoxhe's and Hoxha's positions were strengthened.

Next came the turn of Naku Spiro, who studied political economy at the University of Turin in Italy. Spiru opposed Hoxha and he was eliminated in 1945. There was also personal rivalry between Spiru and Xoxhe. When Spiru was accused of being an "agent of imperialism," he could defend himself by pointing out that he was the one who had sponsored the invitation issued to Soviet economic and technical advisers. But this invitation was exactly the major point that Xoxhe used against him. Spiru did not wait to be imprisoned; he committed suicide on November 20, 1947.

By the early spring of 1948, however, there emerged some tension between Tito and Stalin. The Hoxha-led Albanian communist party had a sigh of relief. Xoxhe was dismissed from his posts, faced a show trial and was shot as a Titoist in 1949. A witch-hunt immediately began against Xoxhe's associates and friends. Pandi Kristo,

Nesti Kerenxhi, Xhoxhi Blushi, all Politburo members, were dismissed from their positions. The regional party organizations were decimated next. In April 1950, Abedin Shehu, the minister for industry, and Niazi Islami, deputy minister for communications were dismissed.

Hoxha took advantage of the anti-Tito hysteria to get rid of various additional personal enemies who were not Tito supporters. Beqir Ndou, president of the National Council, and Dukagjin Plain, former member of the Kosovo Regional National Liberation Council, were removed. Two army generals were also purged.

Between 1948 and 1951, about 25 percent of the general membership of the Albanian Communist party were purged. One-half of the Central Committee and one-third of the parliamentary deputies were eliminated. When a bomb exploded at the Soviet embassy in Tirana in February 1951, a terror campaign began against all those who were suspected of opposing the regime. When the relations between Hoxha and the successors of Stalin worsened, several Albanian party leaders voiced their reservations concerning the Stalinist methods of control used in Albania.

In June 1955, Bedri Spahiu openly accused Hoxha of being responsible for the show trials and executions that followed them. He was expelled from the party and ended his life in prison. In April 1956, taking their clue from Khrushchev, opponents of Hoxha demanded the rehabilitation of Xoxhe and other purged party leaders. Hoxha refused and he prevailed. Thereupon 27 high-level party apparatchiki were arrested, tried, and imprisoned. Liri Gega, a former member of the Politburo, her husband, general Dali Ndreu, were captured while allegedly trying to flee to Yugoslavia and were shot (Gega was pregnant at the time). During the following purges, general Panajot Plaku, deputy minister of defense, escaped to Yugoslavia and received asylum in the Soviet Union .

In 1964, Albania's leader was disenchanted with the relaxations of international tensions pursued by Khrushchev. In June, an Albanian delegation visited China and expressed support for the Chinese Communist party in its dispute with the Soviet Union. The break with the Khrushchev-led Soviet Union was followed up with a new set of purges. Rear Admiral Teme Sejko and former Albanian delegate to the COMECO, Tahir Demi, were the first victims. Both were executed in May 1964. Liri Belishova (*see* Belishova, Liri) and Koco Tashko were accused of treason—they both expressed their loyalty to the Soviet Union—and were imprisoned. Following their elimination, Enver Hoxha and his second-in-command, Mehemet Shehu (*see* Shehu, Mehemet), faced no further challenges for more than a decade.

The break with China resulted in another wave of show trials and executions. In 1973, a number of writers and prominent artists, among them Fadil Pacrami and Todi Lubonja, were eliminated. The former was editor in chief of the party's daily newspaper; the latter was director of national television and radio stations. The turn of the military commanders came next. Beqir Balluku (*see* Balluku, Beqir), the minister of defense, Petri Dume, the chief of the general staff and Hito Cako, the head of the army's political directorate were arrested for allegedly plotting against the party's leaders. All were executed.

In 1975, the chairman of the state planning commission and the minister of industry, as well as the minister of trade, were purged. The following year, the agricultural ministry and the ministry of education were "cleansed" of allegedly antiparty elements. The unspeakable atrocities culminated in "the conspiracy of Mehemet Shehu" in 1982. Shehu, a brutal military and police man, was designated to succeed the ailing dictator. He was, nevertheless, accused of being an agent for Yugoslavia, and, for good measure, of the Soviet Union and the United States. Before he could be arrested, Shehu committed suicide. Subsequently, his wife and other members of his family were arrested and executed. The personnel of three additional ministries and several members of the secret police apparatus were also eliminated.

The fierceness and brutality of the purges were matched only by Stalin's activities in the 1930s and 1940s. It is to be seen if the newly elected government would open the secret files and provide the outside world a glimpse of the murderously dirty world of intrigue and conspiracy that ruled Albanian life under Enver Hoxha.

Bibliography

Amnesty International, *Albania: Political Imprisonment and the Law* (London, 1984); Pipa, Arshi, *Albanian Stalinism: Ideo-Political Aspects* (Boulder, CO, 1990).

Religious Policies. When Albania was freed of the Italian and German occupational forces, the northern Gegs were mostly Muslim by religion. Twenty percent of the Tosks were Orthodox Christians, and 10 percent of them were Roman Catholics. The Gegs were mostly Sunnites, while the majority of Muslim Tosks were divided between the moderate Sunnites and the Bektashi sect. The Bektashi were the most liberal in their outlook on life and religion in general. While the Gegs were strict observers of Islamic law, the Tosks were less religiously inclined. The Roman Catholic clergy were educated in the European ways. The attraction of religion in general was weaker in the south than in the north.

Between 1948 and 1953, the state exerted increasing control over religious institutions. The Muslims were brought under control first by the appointment of Hafiz Musa Haxhi Ali, a procommunist clergyman, as head of all non-Bektashi Muslims. Mustafa Faja Martoneshi, a wartime communist leader, was then appointed to lead the Bektashi.

In 1947, Faja was assassinated and another communist, Ahmed Myfta Dade, took his place. The communist state actively discouraged all religious activities. Consequently, attendance at religious services declined and mosques were closed; many of them were razed to the ground. In 1949, the Orthodox Christian archbishop, Kristofer Kisi, an opponent of communism, was removed from his see.

In the 1950s, his successor strengthened his church's connections with the patriarchate of Moscow and made his church a tool of the communist government. The Roman Catholic church was severely persecuted during the entire communist era. In

1951, its independence from the state was ended by the new constitution issued for the church by the state. This prohibited the maintenance of any connections whatsoever with the Vatican. All Christian seminaries were then taken under the control of the state.

By 1953, there was hardly any trace of Roman Catholicism in Albania. Many churches were closed and only 22 of its 187 clergymen were still at liberty. The 1976 constitution specifically prohibited any religious practices. This situation was maintained until the end of the communist regime.

Bibliography

Marmullaku, Ramadan, *Albania and the Albanians* (London, 1975), pp. 75-78; Tonnes, Bernhard, "Religious Persecution in Albania," *Religion in Communist Lands,* 10.3 (1982).

Social Changes in Albania During the Communist System. The most significant social change that occurred was the result of a true demographic explosion. Between 1944 and 1990, the population of the country more than doubled from 1,122,000 to nearly 3 million. By the end of the era, more than two-thirds of the Albanian people knew no other system than communism. About 35 percent of the population is under sixteen years of age which makes Albania the youngest nation in Europe. By 1991, only 51 per-cent of the population earned their living from agriculture; 31 percent were industrial wage earners and 19 worked in nonindustrial, white-collar jobs. The last number points to an enormous increase in the party and state bureaucracies. The country had eighteen cities with populations of 10,000 or more each compared to three such cities at the turn of the century. Thirty-four percent of the population now lives in urban centers. The average life expectancy has increased to 71 years.

An area where customs have changed fundamentally was in the status of women. In pre-World War II Albania, women's place was strictly in the house. Many blood feuds started because of real or imagined insults to housewives. According to ancient customs, "women were for carrying things." With industrialization, and collectivization, women were increasingly drawn into the work force. They were given jobs regardless of the difficulty involved, and many of them found a place in the communist *apparat*. The state tried to help women by establishing state-run nurseries and day-care centers. They were given time off for childbirth and child care. Nevertheless, wherever women became dominant in a profession or occupation, salaries declined. It is certainly true that the Albanian communist leadership did bring Albanians into the twentieth century. In the process, age-old customs were abandoned and even forbidden.

Bibliography

Kolsti, John, "From Courtyard to Cabinet: The Political Emergence of Albanian Women," in Sharon Wolchick and Alfred E. Meyer, eds. *Women, State, and Party in Eastern Europe* (Durham, NC, 1985).

Shehu, Mehemet (1913–1981). Shehu was born January 10, 1913, in Corrush,

Mallakaster region, in southern Albania; he was a Tosk. He graduated from the American Vocational School in Tirana in 1932. He then went to Italy and enrolled at the Military Academy in Naples. Four months later, however, he was expelled for alleged communist sympathies. He then enrolled and attended the officer's training school of the Albanian armed forces in Tirana.

During the Spanish civil war, he served in the Garibaldi International Brigade on the side of the loyalists. He eventually rose to the command of the fourth battalion of the brigade. After the victory of General Francisco Franco, Shehu was sent to a French concentration camp and spent the years from 1939 to 1942 as a prisoner.

Shehu returned to Albania in 1942 following the French defeat by the Germans and immediately joined the clandestine Albanian Communist party. He was a commander of the Partisan army fighting the occupiers. He was also a commander of the forces engaged in the civil war in Albania, struggling against the non-communist resistance (*see* National Front for the Liberation of Albania). After the war, he was a faithful follower of Enver Hoxha (*see* Hoxha, Enver), and supported him in the struggle against the Titoists and against the Soviet "revisionists."

During 1945 and 1946, Shehu attended the Voroshilov Military Academy in Moscow. After his return, he held many high positions in the party and state as well as in the Albanian armed forces. At various times, he was army chief of staff, minister of the interior, and minister of defense.

He was a ruthless, radical Marxist-Leninist who gladly cooperated in the extermination of the opponents of the communist regime. He was considered for a long time the designated heir apparent for Enver Hoxha. When Hoxha decided otherwise and chose Ramiz Alia (*see* Alia, Ramiz), he also excluded Shehu from the succession and denounced him in the Politburo. Following the denunciation, Shehu committed suicide. True to communist practices, his wife and other family members were subsequently murdered.

Bibliography

Skendi, Stavro, *Albania* (New York, 1956); Pipa, Arshi, *Albanian Stalinism: Ideo-Political Aspects* (Boulder, CO, 1990).

Soviet-Albanian Relations. Until 1947, Albania was, for all practical purposes, a satellite of Yugoslavia. With the break between Stalin and Tito, however, Enver Hoxha (*see* Hoxha, Enver) saw an opportunity to untangle his country from the Yugoslav embrace. In January 1949, Albania applied for and was accepted for membership in COMECON, the economic organization of East European communist countries and the Soviet Union. These countries concluded separate trade agreements with Albania. Soviet technical advisers were sent to Albania and took the place of the departed Yugoslavs. At the same time, Albania became a base for the Greek communist insurgency.

In 1950, a Soviet naval base was built on the island of Sazan, threatening the opening of the Adriatic sea to the Mediterranean. By 1952, the naval base was operational, and twelve Soviet submarines were stationed there. But the base was vulnerable to attack by the Western powers, and the Soviet military refused to develop it any further.

In March 1949, Hoxha visited Stalin. The Soviet dictator encouraged him to proceed with the purges of Titoist elements in the Albanian party. Soon Koci Xoxhe (*see* Xoxhe, Koci) was tried and shot. His trial became a part of a vast spectacle of show trials sweeping through Eastern Europe. In Albania, fourteen members of the Central Committee and thirty-two parliamentary deputies were eliminated, and huge numbers of ordinary party members were expelled. Altogether about eight percent of the party was purged.

By the time Stalin had died in 1953, Albania was a fully committed satellite of the Soviet Union. The country's capital needs, its raw material supplies, were all coming from the Soviet Union. In 1950, the Soviet leaders had already sent 480 military advisers to Albania who trained the armed forces and the secret police in techniques of internal command and modern warfare.

With Stalin's death, a new chapter began in Soviet-Albanian relations. The disengagement from the Stalinist system began in the Soviet Union, and this did not sit well with Hoxha and his supporters. The fact was that they were all tainted by the crimes of Stalinism; they had copied the Soviet dictator in the unspeakable atrocities committed against their own people. In addition, Khrushchev began mending fences with Tito's Yugoslavia, and this caused further apprehension in the Albanian party leaders. They denounced Tito vehemently at the time of the Yugoslav leader's disagreement with Stalin and could rightly expect repercussions in the new situation.

On February 28, 1953, Greece, Turkey, and Yugoslavia signed a treaty of friendship and cooperation, and Albania felt intimidated. Soon Yugoslavia resumed relations with Albania broken off during the rift with the Soviet Union. Khrushchev now sought Yugoslavia's friendship and consequently reduced support for orthodox communist Albania.

After the twentieth congress of the Soviet Communist party in February 1955, in which Khrushchev openly denounced Stalin, the new Soviet leadership demanded that Hoxha rehabilitate Koci Xoxhe. In order to reinforce this demand, two members of the Soviet Politburo, Mikhail Suslov and P.N. Pospelov, visited Tirana. They succeeded in eliciting a declaration from Hoxha according to which the Albanian leader was "deceived" by the "wrecker Beria," and henceforth the Albanians would work for reconciliation with Yugoslavia.

The Hungarian revolution of 1956 created strong disagreements between Hoxha and Khrushchev. The Albanian leader charged that the "revisionists," that is Tito and Khrushchev, were responsible for the explosion since they had cooperated with the Western "imperialists" against true socialism. But in April 1957, Hoxha and Mehemet Shehu (*see* Shehu, Mehemet) did go to Moscow where Khrushchev seemingly succeeded in convincing them to cooperate with Yugoslavia. To encourage the Albanian leaders to follow the new course, the Soviet Union cancelled a $105 million debt and agreed to send another $7.5 million worth of foodstuffs to Albania, where severe food shortages began to appear once again.

In May 1957, a Soviet delegation of economic experts visited Tirana in order to help the Albanians prepare a long-range fifteen-year plan for the years from 1961 to 1975. Albania also signed a treaty with Hungary and Czechoslovakia for the purchase of industrial equipment and manufactured goods to be paid for by Albanian minerals and agricultural products. At the same time, the Soviet Union granted another loan of $40 million to Albania.

When Soviet criticism of Yugoslavia was renewed in 1958, the Albanians gleefully joined in the chorus of denunciations. The Chinese communist leaders were equally vehement in denouncing Titoist "revisionism," and their ties to Albania were strengthened.

The following year, the COMECON distributed the new economic "division of labor" among the Soviet dependencies and announced that Albania would supply minerals and agricultural goods for the rest of the Soviet Bloc. Hoxha saw this as an effort to keep Albania in a second-class status in the Soviet Bloc. In May-June 1959, Khrushchev visited Tirana. He was greeted by a speech by Hoxha in which the Albanian openly criticized Khrushchev's leadership. On his part, the Soviet leader made some threats against the West by suggesting that the Soviet Union would build a rocket base in Albania. This was a highly satisfactory development in the Albanian leaders' opinion. The Soviet leader endorsed another loan to Albania in the amount of $75 million. However, Hoxha was leaning ever more closely to the opinion of the Chinese communist leaders concerning the Soviet Union.

In the summer of 1960, Khrushchev turned to the Albanian communists with a suggestion that they should get rid of Hoxha and his supporters. In order to encourage them to change their direction, grain shipments to Albania were severely reduced in volume. The Soviet ambassador to Tirana worked behind the scene encouraging Politburo members Liri Belishova and Koco Tashko to work against Hoxha's Chinese orientation. The possibility of expelling Albania from the Warsaw Pact, which it had joined at the time of the pact's inception, was also raised. If these were to happen, so the Soviet leaders argued, Albania would be vulnerable once again to Yugoslav pressure.

As a response to the Soviet moves, Albania appealed to Beijing for help. Mao Tse-tung gladly accepted the appeal as a means of weakening Soviet influence in Eastern Europe. Chinese grain shipments soon began arriving in Albania, replacing the Soviet contributions to Albania's economy. Other economic and technical-military help was also arriving (see Chinese-Albanian Relations).

On November 10, 1960, eighty-one Communist parties convened in Moscow with the express purpose of confirming the leading role of the Soviet Union in the world communist movement. This was a direct challenge to the Chinese. The Albanian delegation was led by Hoxha and Shehu. At the meeting, they were openly castigated by Khrushchev for their allegedly anti-Soviet policies. In turn, Hoxha addressed the conference and supported the Chinese position. The Albanians departed from Moscow a week before the conclusion of the meeting. They refused to sign the joint declaration of the participants.

In 1961, all negotiations between Moscow and Tirana were broken off. The Soviet economic and technical advisers were withdrawn from Albania. In March, Czechoslovakia informed the Albanian leadership that all Soviet Bloc economic aid had been terminated. In response, Hoxha staged another show trial of the supporters of the Soviet Union in May 1961. The Soviet naval base was being dismantled, but the Albanians intervened in force. Four Soviet submarines and two submarine tenders were left behind as a consequence. All radar and other military equipment was also abandoned by the Soviet Union. In retaliation, two Albanian merchant ships were seized by Soviet naval forces.

Most East European communist regimes followed the example set by the Soviet Union in their dealings with Albania. They reduced the number of their embassies' staff and sent the Albanian diplomatic representatives packing. Albanian students, who were being educated in East Europe, were now sent home.

The Albanian Communist party was not invited to the twenty-second congress of the Soviet Communist party. At this meeting, Khrushchev denounced Albania while the Chinese derided their Soviet colleagues for making their dispute public. In December 1963, the Chinese foreign minister, Chu-En-lai, paid a visit to Tirana. Following the visit, anti-Soviet polemics were raised by several decibels by Albania.

With the fall of Khrushchev in 1964, Hoxha hoped for a reconciliation with the Soviet Union, but this did not happen. In July 1966, Alexandar Rankovic, the dreaded secret police chief of Yugoslavia, was ousted. Then, Yugoslavia approached Tirana for possible reconciliation. When the Greek junta overthrew the legitimate Greek government, Tirana felt relieved. A fellow dictatorship was less threatening than a neighboring democracy, or so Hoxha reasoned. When Warsaw Pact troops invaded Czechoslovakia in August 1968, however, Albanian fears of a Soviet-sponsored invasion were renewed. As a result, Albania withdrew from the Warsaw Pact alliance on September 1, 1968. It was the first communist country to do so. Hoxha declared, and rightly so, that the pact had become an instrument of aggression against socialist countries, and it was no longer a defensive alliance against imperialist intervention.

During the last phase of the existence of the Soviet Union, Soviet-Albanian relations did not improve. Although open polemics were more muted in the 1970s and the first half of the 1980s, Albania's mistrust of its socialist neighbors continued.

When Mikhail Gorbachev assumed the helm of the Soviet government in 1985, the Albanian communist leaders were absorbed in their own transition. Hoxha had died in the same year, and Ramiz Alia (*see* Alia, Ramiz), his successor, was not established well enough to initiate foreign policy changes at the time.

Bibliography
Hoxha, Enver, *Albania Challenges Khrushchev Revisionism* (New York, 1976); Pipa, Arshi, *Albanian Stalinism: Ideo-Political Aspects* (Boulder, CO, 1990).

Union of Working Youth. This mass organization was set up by the Albanian communist leadership to serve as a reserve for the Albanian Party of Labor (Communist), preparing people for membership in the party. Until 1973, it was a docile organization; its leaders submitted to orders coming from the higher party organs without a murmur. However, in 1973, young leaders began to complain that party leaders had no understanding of the problems facing young people and that they were neglecting young people's interests in society. They no longer shared the revolutionary fervor of the aging Enver Hoxha (*see* Hoxha, Enver) and were becoming restive under the stultifying policies of the party leaders. Above all, they hoped for an opening toward Europe; they wanted to listen to Western music, wanted to wear Western clothes, and, most of all, wanted to be able to visit Western countries. Their protests went unheeded. Rudi Monari, the secretary of the Youth League, was expelled from the organization shortly after the protest, and he was imprisoned on false charges.

The Communist party's control of the Union of Working Youth of Albania was exercised under the statute issued by the Politburo on November 23, 1941. According to this, two members of the Politburo of the Albanian Communist party were delegated to the Central Committee of the youth organization. (During the 1940s and early 1950s, these two were Qemal Stafa and Naku Spiro.) The organization was patterned on the KOMSOMOL of the Soviet Union, which prepared thousands of young people for party membership.

Bibliography
Pipa, Arshi, *Albanian Stalinism: Ideo-Political Aspects* (Boulder, CO, 1990).

Western-Albanian Relations after World War II. In the early 1940s, Albanian communist leaders hoped for the recognition of their government by the Western powers. However, when the United States and Great Britain did not respond to Albanian overtures, and even encouraged the Greek government to cast its eyes on southern Albania, they became violently anti-Western. No doubt, they were encouraged in their attitude by Tito's agents in their ranks.

In the early months of 1946, the Albanian communists went so far as to restrict the movements of American and British representatives to their country. Thereupon, Britain refused to upgrade its mission and forbade the establishment of an Albanian legation in London. The United States Senate's resolution of July 26, 1946, went so far as to suggest that northern Epirus (southern Albania) be transferred to Greek sovereignty. The United States eventually withdrew the corollary resolution its representatives had placed on the agenda of the Paris Peace Conference in 1947, but the damage to United States-Albanian relations had already been done. The Albanians intensified their anti-United States propaganda, and the United States withdrew its diplomatic mission from Tirana on November 6, 1947.

Albanian relations with Western states remained nonexistent through the 1950s and most of the 1960s. After the 1968 invasion of Czechoslovakia by the Warsaw Pact, however, the Albanian leaders became so frightened that they began a cautious approach to the West. However, they could never get over their anti-Western bias. Enver Hoxha (*see* Hoxha, Enver) tried to re-establish relations with West European countries, but he did not approach the United States.

In 1971, Albania exchanged ambassadors with Yugoslavia and Greece. Between 1970 and 1975, Albanian trade with Western Europe quadrupled, and diplomatic contacts multiplied. After 1979, Albanian economic relations with Western Europe as well as with select East European states such as Romania, intensified. Eastern Europe gradually replaced China as the main market for Albanian products. However, foreign trade remained of low volume since Albania had no hard currency and its constitution forbade the solicitation or acceptance of loans from abroad. As a consequence, the slowly expanding trade relations did not result in the improvement of the Albanian economy.

Bibliography
Biberaj, Elez, *Albania: A Socialist Maverick* (Boulder, CO, 1990).

Xoxhe, Koci (–1949). A member of the Yugoslav Communist party, he was delegated by Josip Broz Tito to assist the fledgling Albanian Communist party in 1941. Eventually, he rose to the position of vice premier of Albania. He became a member of the Politburo of the Albanian Communist party and was appointed a secretary of the party's Central Committee. In 1946, Xoxhe was made minister of the interior on Yugoslav suggestion and organizational secretary of the Albanian Communist party. He was instrumental in 1946 in Albania's break with the Western powers; he was concerned that their diplomatic presence in Tirana would be an impediment to Albania's absorption into the Yugoslav federation.

As minister of the interior, Xoxhe was responsible for the brutal repression that dominated Albanian politics and society in the 1940s. He was a rival of Enver Hoxha (*see* Hoxha, Enver) and, for a long period of time, he seemed to have the upper hand in the Albanian Politburo. Xoxhe was also a supporter of the idea of a Balkan federation, a notion advanced by Georgy Dimitrov of Bulgaria. After the Stalin-Tito break, however, Xoxhe fell victim to Hoxha's tenacity. He was arrested in October 1948, tried in early 1949, and executed.

Bibliography
Pipa, Arshi, *Albanian Stalinism: Ideo-Political Aspects* (Boulder, CO, 1990).

Yugoslav-Albanian Relations. Albania's relations with the neighboring states of the Balkans were complicated after the conclusion of World War II. Most Albanian communist leaders were from the south and were, consequently, Tosks. The northern Gegs were fearful of interference in their affairs by neighboring Yugoslavia, while the southerners were wary of Greece and Bulgaria. When the Tosk leaders accepted the return of Kosovo province to Yugoslavia with its overwhelmingly ethnic Albanian Geg population, the nationalistic feelings of the northern Gegs were aroused. Nevertheless, the will of the Tosk leaders prevailed.

Yugoslavia recognized the new communist Albanian government on April 28, 1945. The Albanians signed a treaty of friendship, cooperation, and mutual aid with Yugoslavia in July 1946, and this was followed by a series of economic and technical agreements. An agreement for the establishment of a joint economic company was signed on November 28, 1946. These agreements made Albania a Yugoslav satellite. However, friction developed in 1947 over the pricing of goods produced by the joint Albanian-Yugoslav companies. The Albanians complained that Yugoslavia was monopolizing their foreign trade. Further discord appeared when it became obvious that Yugoslav agents were preparing the ouster of Enver Hoxha (*see* Hoxha, Enver).

In April 1947, an Albanian delegation went to Belgrade to obtain Yugoslav support for the establishment of some light industry in Albania and the building of an oil refinery. The Yugoslavs refused to negotiate until the Albanians agreed to the establishment of a joint economic commission for the coordination of economic planning in the two countries. The Albanians refused this demand. The Yugoslavs then instructed their agents in Albania, led by Koci Xoxhe (*see* Xoxhe, Koci), to begin a campaign against the anti Yugoslav faction in the Albanian Communist party. Xoxhe succeeded in having nine members of the Albanian parliament arrested on May 20, 1947. In June, Yugoslavia openly accused Hoxha of conducting an anti-Yugoslav foreign policy. This, however, played into Hoxha's hands.

Tito realized his mistake and ordered that two billion dinars worth of credit be granted to Albania (about $40 million). But it was already too late; Hoxha turned to Stalin for support.

During the autumn of 1947, the Albanians frequently criticized Yugoslavia, especially the leadership practices of Tito. In December, Albania concluded a treaty of friendship and cooperation with Bulgaria. This treaty was intended to provide a counterbalance toward the Yugoslavs. Even then, Xoxhe attempted to have a clause inserted in the agreement that would have given Yugoslavia veto power over joint Albanian-Bulgarian ventures, but he failed.

By 1948, the Yugoslav-Albanian break was out in the open. In February, Stalin learned that a squadron of Yugoslav military airplanes had been moved to Albania and that Tito intended to follow this up with the transfer of two Yugoslav army divisions, ostensibly to defend Albania against Greek aggression. The Soviet Union then stepped in and forced Tito to abandon his plans.

In early 1948, the Central Committee of the Yugoslav Communist party sent a delegation to Tirana with the express purpose of convincing the Albanians to join the Yugoslav federation. The Albanian Central Committee met on February 26, 1948. The majority of its members supported Xoxhe against Hoxha. Hoxha was forced to "admit his errors" and denounce the anti-Yugoslav movement in his party. Liri Belishova (*see* Belishova, Liri), the strongest opponent of the Yugoslavs was expelled from the Politburo. Mehemet Shehu (*see* Shehu, Mehemet), Hoxha's man, was relieved of his post as chief of staff of the army.

The plan to merge the Albanian economy and the Albanian armed forces with their

Yugoslav counterparts was approved. Following up the meeting, Xoxhe called the Albanian Politburo into session in April, and proposed that a petition be drawn up, requesting Albania's admission to the Yugoslav federation. He also recommended the expulsion of Soviet military advisers from Albania and the merging of the armies of the two Balkan states. He also recommended the appointment of Yugoslav directors to joint Albanian-Yugoslav companies. At this time, however, Xoxhe's proposals were rejected by the majority. He then resorted to terror against his opponents. At the same time, the Stalin-Tito disputes grew in intensity. Hoxha, taking advantage of the situation, ordered the closing down of the Yugoslav information center in Tirana. In June 1948, he banned the selling of Yugoslav newspapers in Albania. Albania unilaterally and abruptly terminated all economic agreements with Yugoslavia on July 1, 1948. All Yugoslav technical and military advisers were expelled from the country.

Albanian radio and newspapers began a vicious anti-Tito campaign. Soviet technicians and military advisers replaced the Yugoslav personnel. Hoxha then proceeded to restore Shehu and Belishova to their former positions. In turn, Xoxhe was now removed from his posts in the party and the ministry of the interior.

On October 31, Xoxhe and many of his supporters were arrested. The following year, he was put on trial and executed. Many of his followers' turns came soon thereafter.

During the 1960s, Yugoslav-Albanian relations fluctuated. Sometimes it appeared that there would be reconciliation; at other times relations turned cool again. During the 1970s, however, Albania slowly began to improve relations with its northern neighbor. Between 1975 and 1980, trade increased, and diplomatic relations were renewed on the level of legations. The Albanians did not raise the question of Kosovo. Hoxha made it clear that the destabilization of Yugoslavia was not in the best interest of Albania.

After Hoxha's death in 1985, Ramiz Alia (*see* Alia, Ramiz) seemed more interested in renewing Albania's Yugoslav ties; nevertheless, he was also more closely identified with the cause of the Kosovo Albanians. The world can expect further disputes between the remnants of Yugoslavia and the Albanian state over this issue in the future.

Bibliography
Lee, Michele, "Yugoslavia's Albanian Crisis: Wrong Turn in Kosova [sic!]," *Labor Focus on Eastern Europe*, 5.1: 51 (London, 1988).

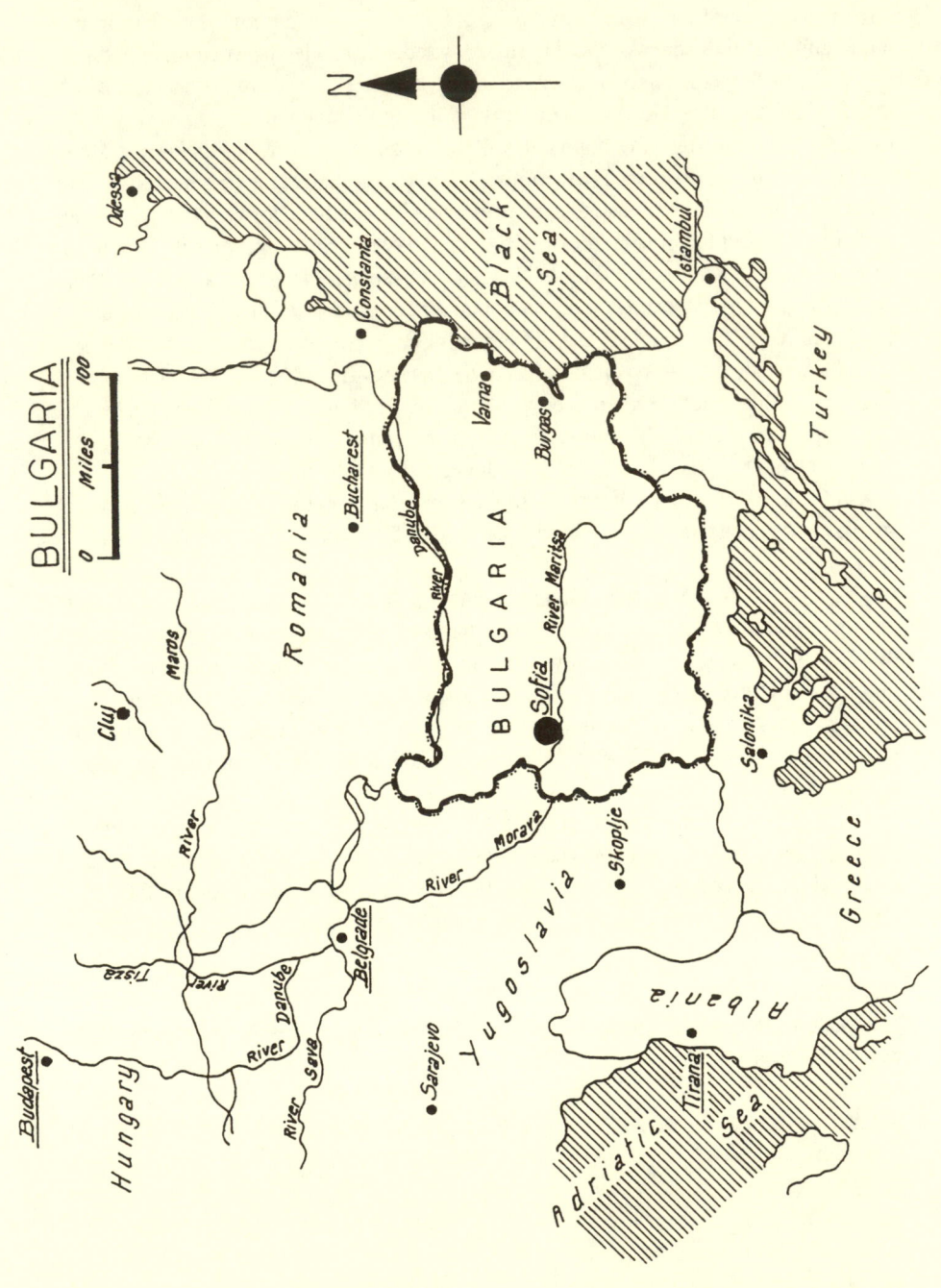

BULGARIA

BULGARIA

General Information. *Size of territory:* the Bulgarian state is smaller than New York state. Its total area comprises 42,818 square miles. *Population:* the population consists of 90 percent ethnic Bulgarians, about 8 percent ethnic Turks, and scattered groups of Gypsies and Armenians. There was also a Jewish population of about 5,000 people. Their total number in 1988 was 15.5 million people. The urban population includes about 66.2 percent of all the people; the rural population compose 35.4 percent. *Production:* the gross national product in 1985, the last year when data were available, came to 45.5 billion leva. Forty-three percent of the workers were laboring in industrial enterprises; 22 percent were agricultural workers; the rest worked in administration and the bureaucracy. *Roads and railways:* the length of the railway network was a modest 2,550 miles (4,094 kilometers), of which 1,569 miles (2,510 kilometers) were electrified. The length of the road network came to 16,410 miles (29,233 kilometers), of which 4,373 miles (6,998 kilometers) were paved. *Geography:* in the north, the Bulgarian territory encompasses the Danubian flatlands, the extensions of the great steppes of southern Russia; in the middle of the country, the Balkan Mountains rise on average to about 1,000 meters in height; in the northeast and north, Bulgaria borders on the former Yugoslavia and Romania; in the southeast, its next-door neighbor is Turkey. Greece encloses Bulgaria in the south. *Currency:* the currency is called the Bulgarian leva. It is, at the time of this writing (1993), exchangeable for hard currencies on a limited basis. *Communist party membership:* the membership of the Communist party developed as follows; in February 1945, there were 250,000 members; in December 1948, the numbers increased to 495,000; in November 1988, before the collapse of the communist system, there were 825,000 card-carrying members of the Communist party. *Cities:* the capital city of Bulgaria is Sofia. Its major cities include Varna on the Black sea, Plovdiv, Kardzhali, Pleven, Pernik, Vratsa, Borgas, and Ruse. *Literacy:* the educational system is highly developed. There were 1,231,560 elementary school students and 56,574 teachers in these schools. Professional-technical schools enrolled 94,694 students, with 6,422 teachers educating them. Technikums and arts schools had altogether 172,098 students enrolled and 8,902 teachers teaching them. Finally, university and college enrollments were 82,573 with 6,156 instructors. *Religious groups:* the religion of most of the population is Orthodox Christian. The ethnic Turks are

Muslims, and there were scattered groups of Roman Catholics and Protestants in the country. The Jewish population, of course, followed Judaism. At the present time, the form of government is parliamentary democracy.

Bibliography

Aspaturian, Vernon, "Eastern Europe in World Perspective," in Teresa Rakowska-Harmstone, ed. *Communism in Eastern Europe* 2nd Ed., (Bloomington, IN, 1984); Brzezinski, Zbigniew *The Soviet Bloc: Unity and Conflict* (Cambridge, MA, 1967); Pundeff, Marin, "Bulgaria," in Joseph Held ed. *The Columbia History of Eastern Europe in the Twentieth Century*. (New York, 1992), pp. 65-118.

CHRONOLOGY

1944   *September.* The Soviet government, its army nearing Bulgaria's borders, declared war on Bulgaria. Bulgaria then asked for an armistice. A few days afterward, it declared war on Germany. For the rest of the war, the Bulgarian army fought as the advance guard of the Soviet troops, sustaining horrendous casualties.

1945   *January–June.* In Bulgaria, the communists established firm control over the population. So-called class enemies were murdered or driven out of the country.
November. Rigged elections resulted in 90 percent of the vote being given to the Bulgarian National Front, an organization dominated by communists. The results were rejected by the United States as fraudulent.

1946   *October.* In the new national elections, terror and intimidation were used against the opponents of the Communist party. In consequence, the communists were given 277 seats in the national parliament, an absolute majority. Georgy Dimitrov, an old Stalinist and the hero of the European communist movement for his courage during the trial for the Reichstag fire in Germany in 1934, was appointed prime minister.

1947   *February.* Bulgaria signed a peace treaty with the victorious Allies returning all territories awarded to the country by Italy and Germany.
August. Nicola Petkov, the head of the Agrarian party, was arrested in the Bulgarian parliament. He was tried and sentenced to death. The trial was a farce.
December. The nationalization of all industrial firms, banks, and other economic institutions began the transformation of Bulgaria into a Stalinist state.

1948   *June.* Georgy Dimitrov died of cancer in Moscow.
August. The Bulgarian communists forced the Social Democratic party into an unwanted merger. The name of the united party: Bulgarian Communist party.

1949   *December.* A former assistant prime minister of Bulgaria, Traitcho Kostov, was tried for "nationalist deviation" and for allegedly spying for the West.

After a typical show trial he was sentenced to death and executed. Kostov's trial was part of the anti-Titoist witch-hunt that reached into every Communist party in Eastern Europe.

1950   *January.* Stalinist-style collectivization began in Bulgaria with great brutality. Thousands of peasants were killed, jailed, or sent to concentration camps.

1953   After Stalin's death, Bulgaria began experimenting with "collective leadership" on the basis of the example provided by the successors to Stalin.

1955   *May.* All the East European socialist states, except Yugoslavia, signed the Warsaw Pact Treaty.

December. Bulgaria was admitted to membership in the United Nations.

1956   *October.* The Polish and Hungarian revolutions shook the entire Soviet Bloc, including Bulgaria. Bulgaria responded by tightening control over society by increasing the use of the secret police.

1960   Bulgaria accelerated its industrialization with Soviet help. Soviet military and other technicians provided support, and the Soviet Union delivered blueprints and plans for industrial plants. The Bulgarian armed forces were thoroughly integrated into the forces of the Warsaw Pact.

1967   *April.* The Bulgarian delegation, attending a conference of twenty-four European Communist parties in Karlovy Vary, Czechoslovakia, sharply criticized China's communist leaders.

1968   *June.* Bulgarian troops participated in Warsaw Pact maneuvers held in Czechoslovakia.

August. The Bulgarian army sent a contingent to Czechoslovakia as part of the Warsaw Pact forces suppressing the Prague Spring.

1969   *June.* Bulgaria participated in a meeting of seventy-five Communist parties that failed to condemn the "Chinese deviation." The Bulgarian delegation strongly supported the Soviet position.

1971   *March-April.* Bulgaria sent representatives to the twenty-fourth Congress of the Soviet Communist party in Moscow.

1974   *January.* Bulgarian communist representatives, participating in a meeting of European Communist parties held in Brussels, Belgium, signed a statement of general principles of cooperation.

1975   *July-August.* Bulgaria was a signer of the Helsinki Declaration at the first summit meeting of the Conference on Security and Cooperation in Europe.

1976   *June.* Bulgaria strongly supported the Soviet Communist party's bid at a meeting of European Socialist and Communist parties for the condemnation of the Chinese party's "deviationism." The conference rejected the Soviet effort.

1981   *May.* An attempt made on the life of Pope John Paul II in Rome was connected with the Bulgarian secret service. The Bulgarian government strongly denied the allegations, but the involvement of Bulgarian travel officials was suspected. Since Bulgarian agents had been proven to have attempted assassinations in the West before—and succeeded in doing so—the attack on the Pope certainly had a Bulgarian connection. The Bulgarian secret service was also implicated in drug smuggling to the West.

1984 *May.* Bulgaria boycotted the Olympic games held in Los Angeles, siding with the Soviet Union.

September. Todor Zhivkov, the Bulgarian communist leader, canceled his visit to West Germany, after the Soviet government condemned Erich Honecker's alleged efforts to improve relations between the two Germanys.

1985 *April.* Bulgaria signed a ten-year extension of the Warsaw Pact. Zhivkov offered, to Mikhail Gorbachev, to have Bulgaria join the Soviet Union as the seventeenth Soviet republic. His offer was rejected.

1989 *March.* Dimitar and Diana Boyadzhiev, two prominent Bulgarian opposition leaders, were expelled from the country. They were guilty of organizing the first free trade union movement in Bulgaria, patterned after Poland's Solidarity.

June. Thousands of ethnic Turks living in Bulgaria were forced to leave the country. The communist government, at its last gasp, tried to direct the attention of the public away from pressing economic problems by this action.

August. Over 250,000 ethnic Turkish refugees entered Turkey from Bulgaria. The Bulgarian communists' campaign against ethnic Turks reached a crescendo. Turks were forced to change their names to Bulgarian-sounding names, and their schools and cultural centers were closed. Those who left Bulgaria had to leave everything behind. When the number of refugees reached 310,000, Turkey closed its borders with Bulgaria.

1990 Bulgaria abolished the secret police section of the ministry of internal affairs. Several Bulgarian secret police generals fled to the Soviet Union, seeking KGB protection. They took files of the ministry with them; among those were sensitive materials dealing with Ali Agca, the would-be assassin of Pope John Paul II.

January. The summit meeting of COMECON, meeting in the Bulgarian capital, Sofia, agreed to adopt a free market approach to economic development. The Bulgarian Communist party was forced by popular pressure to give up its monopoly of political power. Todor Zhivkov, the former dictator, was arrested. He was charged with inciting ethnic animosity, misuse of government property, and malfeasance in office.

February. Petar Mladenov, the secretary of the Bulgarian Communist party, was replaced by Alexander Lilov, but Mladenov remained head of state for the time being. Andrey Lukanov was named prime minister.

March. The Albanian minister of cultural affairs visited Sofia, the first time such a visit had taken place. The two countries had signed an agreement for cooperation in aviation, cultural affairs, and health care.

April. A new name was chosen for Bulgaria's Communist party: the Socialist

Party of Bulgaria. The Bulgarian government ordered the dismantling of the lethal fortifications and mine fields on the Yugoslav-Bulgarian border.

May. In the elections, the Socialist party of Bulgaria received the largest number of votes.

June. In the run off elections, the Socialists won amidst charges of intimidation and election fraud.

August. Zhelyu Zhelev, the new president of Bulgaria, announced that all anticonstitutional laws would be abolished, and he created a consultative group to confer with political parties for creating a new constitution. The headquarters of the ruling Socialist Party of Bulgaria was set afire by protesters in Sofia.

November. A general strike of industrial workers forced president Andrei Lukanov's resignation.

December. Independent politician Dimiter Popov was elected prime minister of Bulgaria by the Grand National Assembly. A coalition government, including ministers from the Socialist party, the Union of Democratic Forces (UDF) and the Agrarian Union, was formed in Sofia.

1991   *July.* A new constitution was promulgated, based on multiparty democracy and a parliamentary government. The document also spoke to the establishment of a market economy. It guaranteed freedom of speech, of assembly, and of religion.

October. In the first free elections held since 1945, Bulgarians gave a majority to the Union of Democratic Forces, a coalition of former opposition groups. The new government promised sweeping changes in the economy and politics. In the elections the Movement for Rights, and Freedoms, the ethnic Turkish party, gained twenty-four seats in the 400-member parliament. In the new parliament, besides the UDF and the Turkish MRF, the Socialist Party of Bulgaria (BSP), and the Bulgarian Agrarian National Union (Banu-United), received the most votes. The new prime minister was Filip Dimitrov. More than half of the 350,000 ethnic Turkish refugees returned to Bulgaria.

1992   *January-March.* The victims of the Bulgarian People's Courts, an instrument of communist warfare against the nation's intellectuals, were remembered at a church service in Sofia. Major political figures participated. Former Soviet KGB general Oleg Kalugin, who had revealed the connections between the KGB and the Bulgarian secret service in the murder of Bulgarian dissident Georgy Markov in London in 1978, arrived in Sofia on a private visit. He indicated his willingness to discuss matters with the Bulgarian authorities. The Directorate on Religious Faiths declared that the election of Patriarch Maxim in 1971 was invalid. It accused the Holy Synod of having buckled under those who "wanted to annihilate the faith and the church." Radio Free Europe began a two-hour daily program, broadcasting from its studio in Sofia.

April-June. The ministry of education stopped all teachings of Bulgarian history based on communist textbooks. New textbooks will be prepared by a commission set up by the ministry. A group of five parliamentary deputies proposed to open secret police files. A fistfight occurred between a UDF and a BSP representative in the Bulgarian parliament. There was a joint protest against economic policies organized by traditional and new trade unions. Three former wardens of the notorious communist concentration camp at Lovech were arrested and accused of extreme cruelty to political prisoners. Former prime minister Georgy Atanasov and minister of the economy Stoyan Ovcharov were remanded into custody for their crimes against the Bulgarian people. Former dictator Todor Zhivkov is also to be tried for illegally transferring Bulgarian funds to the Soviet Communist party in support of communist parties in capitalist countries. Georgy Dimitrov's mausoleum, in which his body lay in imitation of Vasily Ilyich Lenin's in Moscow, was symbolically dismantled during a rock concert in Sofia. A "Renewed" Holy synod was formed by church officials intent on eradicating the communist past in the Bulgarian Orthodox church. Information coming from the Bulgarian ministry of internal affairs revealed that the Bulgarian Communist party had aided international terrorists. In 1974, Greek communist exiles were smuggled across the border to Greece, and a clandestine radio station was given to them. They also received direct financial support from Bulgaria. In 1984, several Turkish terrorists were secretly received. Security agents from Angola, Nicaragua, Yemen, Cuba, Tanzania, and Ghana were trained by the Bulgarian secret police. They also received money.

July-October. Todor Zhivkov, the brutal communist dictator, now eighty years old, was indicted for embezzlement of state funds in connection with the transfer of millions of dollars to the Soviet Communist party. The indictments also charged him with deaths that occurred in Bulgarian concentration camps set up by the secret police during his rule. About twenty other high-ranking former communist officials are also to be charged with a variety of crimes. Andrey Lukanov, former prime minister, was arrested and charged with misappropriating state funds. Grisha Filipov, another former secretary of the Communist party, was also arrested. The Communist party's archives are to be opened to public scrutiny, reported the head of Bulgarian archives, Veselin Metodiev. Todor Zhivkov was found guilty of embezzlement of government funds, and he was sentenced to seven years' imprisonment.

November-December. Following a no-confidence vote in the government by parliament, prime minister Filip Dimitrov and his cabinet resigned. The vote was the result of secret negotiations the government conducted with Macedonian leaders for an arms deal. The nationalization decrees of the communist government were annulled, and property was returned to Bulgarian nationals and foreigners. The government crisis deepened when neither the Union of

Democratic Forces nor the Socialists were able to form a government.

1993   *January-March.* Serious problems emerged in Bulgarian cultural institutions. During the communist era, most of them were heavily subsidized in exchange for following party policies. When communist rule ended and freedom of artistic expression and freedom of the press were restored, state subsidies also ended. This produced stagnation and unemployment among creative people. A new government was formed, headed by prime minister Lyuben Berov, an economist. The ministers were mostly technocrats. The Bulgarian arms industry, long the supplier of arms to all sorts of dictators and terrorists in the world, began demanding special considerations from the government. It argued that the Bulgarian economy, receiving little support from the West, needed to renew its international ties. At the national conference of the Union of Democratic Forces, the majority supported president Zhelev and elected a hard-liner, Stefan Savov, as party chairman. This generated a split in the party's parliamentary forces.

April-June. A new budget was introduced that would satisfy the Internal Monetary Fund and the World Bank currently negotiating financial support for Bulgaria. Skirmishes occurred between police and old-style communists when the Red Army monument in the center of Sofia was beginning to be dismantled. Serbian freight trains were halted at the Bulgarian border in compliance with UN sanctions against rump-Yugoslavia. A new Confederation of Roma in Bulgaria was established in order to promote the rights of Gypsies. A new draft law on police and security matters was accepted by parliament. It regulates police behavior in fighting crime and maintaining public order. The law also regulates the activities of security agents and directs them to fight international terrorism, drug smuggling, and threats against the security of Bulgaria. The transportation ministers of Albania, Bulgaria, and Macedonia signed an agreement for creating a railroad link between the Adriatic and Black seas. Italy and Turkey have expressed interest in the project. Bulgaria has asked the United Nations to create a free transit corridor through rump-Yugoslavia. Bulgaria has been enforcing UN sanctions against Serbia and Montenegro and, as a consequence, it has lost hundreds of millions of dollars' worth of trade. Under current conditions Bulgaria cannot long sustain the situation. The Bulgarian defense minister proclaimed that Turkey has become a friend for Bulgaria. This comes at a time of increased tensions in the Balkans and signifies a minor diplomatic revolution in the region. Bulgaria, Hungary, and Romania signed an agreement to tighten the blockade of transit of Serbian and Montenegrine goods on the Danube river, in line with UN sanctions.

Agrarian Union. During the interwar years, a strong agrarian movement emerged in Bulgaria. In the early 1920s, it was led by a charismatic politician of peasant background, Alexander Stamboliiski. He was assassinated in 1923. The Agrarian Union eventually became a nation wide party whose aim was the improvement of the lot of the peasantry.

During the late 1930s, many of the leaders were murdered or forced to seek exile abroad. One of these leaders, George M. Dimitrov (not to be confused with Georgy Dimitrov, the communist leader) returned from Africa, where he had spent the years of World War II, and reorganized the leadership of the Agrarian Union. However, the party soon split into two major factions. One of them remained loyal to the ideals of the interwar Agrarian Union, while a smaller faction sided with the Bulgarian communists in reorganizing the country.

The minority faction was led by Nikola Petkov, while Dimitrov remained the leader of the majority. Petkov's group became a part of the Fatherland Front (*see* Fatherland Front), a political organization dominated by the communists. Eventually, George M. Dimitrov was forced to flee the country in 1945. Petkov now replaced Dimitrov as the leader of the Agrarian Union upon the orders of Soviet General S. S. Biriuzov, who headed the Allied Control Commission in Bulgaria after World War II. But Petkov was not a communist plant; he resented the growing terror that accompanied the communist conquest of power, and he spoke out openly against it. He was very successful and received strong public support.

The Soviet Union then intervened. Joseph Stalin sent deputy foreign minister Andrey Wyshinsky to Bulgaria to convince Petkov to keep the Agrarian Union in the Fatherland Front. Petkov was willing to oblige, but he set several conditions; the upcoming national elections, scheduled for November 1945, were to be postponed to give the opposition more time to organize its electorate, and the ministries of the interior and justice were to be turned over to ministers chosen from the membership of the Agrarian Union. The Communist party's leaders agreed to a compromise to appoint an Agrarian to the ministry of justice only.

However, Stalin vetoed the compromise and instructed the communists to use intimidation and terror to change the minds of Petkov and his supporters.

The postponed elections were finally held on October 27, 1946, under great communist terror. Nevertheless, Petkov's Agrarian Union was still able to garner eighty-nine mandates in the Grand National Assembly whose major task was the creation of a new constitution. Petkov then openly declared that, if the elections were truly free, his Union would have received at least 60 percent of the total votes.

On June 4, 1947, the Bulgarian peace treaty was ratified by the United States Senate. With all restrains now removed, the communists moved against Petkov. He was arrested in the building of the Grand National Assembly by Bulgarian secret policemen. The daily paper of the Agrarian Union was shut down by a communist-inspired pressmen's strike. In August 1947, Petkov was tried on false charges—the prosecutor charging him with subversion—and, on September 23, he was sentenced to death and was shortly thereafter executed.

The Agrarian Union was reorganized, and it simply became a subordinate organization of the Bulgarian Communist party. This sham of a party remained a member of the Fatherland Front organization throughout the communist era. Its membership was restricted to 120,000. Its leaders acknowledged the leading role of the Communist party in Bulgarian society and willingly supported the party's policies. Most leaders of the Agrarian Union henceforth received political training in the Communist party's ideological schools. They were permitted to retain some local units of their party and were even given 100 deputies in parliament out of 400. A member of the Agrarian Union was appointed deputy to premier Todor Zhivkov (*see* Zhivkov, Todor) in the 1960s.

In 1974, the Agrarian Union's leaders declared that they had transformed their organization into an educational institution.

Bibliography
Oren, Nissan, *Revolution Administered: Agrarianism and Communism in Bulgaria* (Baltimore, MY, 1973); *The Trial of Nikola Petkov, August 5-15, 1947: Record of Judicial Proceedings* (Sofia, 1947); Bell, John D., *Peasants in Power: Alexander Stamboliiski and the Bulgarian Agrarian National Union, 1899-1923* (Princeton, NJ, 1987); Petkov, Michael, *Dimitrov Wastes No Bullets. Nikola Petkov: A Test Case* (London, 1948).

Assassinations and Drug Trafficking. It has been suspected for a long time—as the recently opened East German and Hungarian secret archives proved—that the secret services of the Soviet satellites often acted as surrogates for the Soviet KGB in sponsoring international terrorism, espionage, and drug trafficking against the Western states. For instance, Hungary provided a safe haven for the notorious terrorist gang of Carlos in the mid-1980s.

Bulgaria's role in these clandestine activities was also suspected although never proved beyond a reasonable doubt. What threw some light on these activities was the attempted assassination of Pope John Paul II in 1981 by Mehmet Ali Agca, who claimed that he was prompted by Bulgarian nationals stationed in Rome. The investigation, however, never succeeded in proving the Bulgarian connection, although some sources have recently claimed that this was indeed the case.

With the collapse of communism in Eastern Europe and the Soviet Union, a trickle of documents have appeared. However, the Bulgarian files on Agca had disappeared, together with the chief of Bulgarian secret police, who ended up in Moscow. There is little doubt, however, that the Bulgarian secret service was directly involved in other clandestine activities. In October 1978, the Soviet KGB provided the Bulgarians, at the personal request of Todor Zhivkov (*see* Zhivkov, Todor), poison for the murder of Georgy Markov. Markov, a Bulgarian exile working for the BBC radio in London, had excellent sources within Bulgaria and often broadcast revelations of corruption. Evidently, he was so much detested by the party leaders that he was marked for assassination. Markov was killed in London by a poison pellet that was injected into his leg by a specially modified umbrella.

Another assassination attempt was made against Vladimir Kostov, an opponent of the communist Bulgarian regime, who lived at that time in Paris. This attempt, however, failed when French doctors were able to remove the poisoned pellet before it dissolved in Kostov's body. After the collapse of communism, high-ranking officers of the Bulgarian secret service removed the incriminating files and delivered them to the KGB in Moscow. Undoubtedly, however, more of the evidence will come to light in future years.

The Bulgarians were also involved in drug smuggling from the East or, at the least, provided a way station for the smugglers in their country. Once again, however, evidence has been destroyed.

Bibliography

Andrew, Christopher and Gordievsky, Oleg, *KGB: The Inside Story of its Foreign Operations from Lenin to Gorbachev* (New York, 1990); Broadhead, Frank, et al., "Darkness in Rome: The Bulgarian Connection Revisited," Covert Action Information Bulletin 23 (1988) pp. 3-38; Engelbrekt, Kjell, "Bulgaria's Communist Legacy: Settling Old Scores," *Radio Free Europe Research Reports*, 1.28 (July 10, 1992), pp. 6-10; Pundeff, Marin, "Bulgaria," in Joseph Held, ed., *The Columbia History of Eastern Europe in the Twentieth Century* (New York, 1992).

Blagoev, Dimitar (1856–1924). Blagoev, the first radical socialist-turned-communist leader in Bulgaria, was born in a small village into a peasant family. He became involved at an early age in the nationalist movement directed against the Ottoman occupiers of his country. In 1878, he went to study in Odessa, then a city in the Russian empire, then transferred to the University of St. Petersburg. The university was a hotbed of radical thinking and Blagoev was soon converted to Marxism. In 1883, he was a member of the first Marxist study circle at the university, and two years later he was expelled from Russia for antistate agitation. Returning to Bulgaria, Blagoev was among those who organized the Social Democratic party in 1890, and he became its ideological guru. When the Bulgarian Social Democrats split into a moderate ("broad") faction and a radical ("narrow") faction, Blagoev led the latter. In 1917, he and his followers joined Lenin's Third International, the COMINTERN, and Blagoev renamed his "narrow" Social Democratic faction "communist."

His party supported an uprising against the monarchy in 1918. The uprising failed, and those who participated in the action were killed, except Blagoev. He instinctively stayed out of physical trouble, directing his followers from the background. However, he also learned from his previous mistakes. He began to oppose the reckless adventurism of the COMINTERN and its agents, Georgy Dimitrov (*see* Dimitrov, Georgy) and Vassily Kolarov (*see* Kolarov, Vassily), who organized the communist rising of 1923 in Bulgaria. Blagoev was, by then, ill which prevented his active participation in the affair (*see* Communist Party of Bulgaria). In 1924, Blagoev died. The failure of the 1923 uprising contributed to the destruction of the organization of the Communist party for which Blagoev had labored all his life.

Bibliography

Dellin, L.A.D., "The Communist Party of Bulgaria," in Stephen Fischer-Galati, ed. *The Com-*

munist Parties of Eastern Europe (New York, 1979); Evans, Stanely, G., *A Short History of Bulgaria* (London, 1960).

Chervenkov, Vulko (1900–1963). Georgy Dimitrov (*see* Dimitrov, Georgy), the undisputed leader of the Bulgarian Communist party after 1945, was suffering from a long illness, possibly cancer. He went to the Soviet Union in 1949 for medical treatment and died there in the same year. He was first replaced by his longtime collaborator, Vassili Kolarov (*see* Kolarov, Vassily), but he, too, died within six months after Dimitrov. The Bulgarian communists then elected, upon Moscow's advice, Vulko Chervenkov as their first secretary. Chervenkov was the brother-in-law of Dimitrov. He was also a fervent Marxist-Leninist-Stalinist.

Born to a noncommissioned officer of the Bulgarian army, he received a good education. He joined the Bulgarian Communist party in 1919. In 1925, he was sent by his party to the Soviet Union where he entered the Marx-Engels Institute, run by the Soviet Communist party, and eventually he became an instructor at this institute. He also worked for the COMINTERN and maintained close relations with the Soviet secret police. He was a robust man, easily given to sarcasm and he was disliked by most of his fellow exiles.

During World War II, Chervenkov worked for the Bulgarian station of the Soviet Broadcasting Service, called Hristo Botev, sending communist propaganda programs to his native country. He acquired Soviet citizenship and was devoted to Stalin and his methods of government. The Soviet dictator appreciated Chervenkov's adulation, and, when the time came, he supported his elevation to the highest position in Bulgaria.

Chervenkov returned to Sofia only in 1946 and at first took up unimportant positions. He was appointed chairman of the State Committee on Science and the Arts. But this was only a temporary situation. When Chervenkov succeeded Kolarov in 1949, his first act was to purge the party of "opportunistic elements," who happened to be the local party leaders who had remained in Bulgaria in the 1930s. He combined the posts of party leader with that of premier of the cabinet, thus ensuring his domination of both organizations. He was the mastermind behind the show trial of Traicho Kostov (*see* Kostov, Traicho), although the Soviet secret police provided direct help in this trial. During the purges, 92,500 party members were expelled from the organization. Chervenkov eliminated Anton Yugov next (*see* Yugov, Anton). He also ordered the immediate, forcible collectivization of Bulgarian agriculture. The process was executed with great brutality. By 1958, Chervenkov was able to report to the meeting of the party's Central Committee that 92 percent of all arable lands were in the possession of collectives (that is, under the control of the state). Then he ordered the deportation of large numbers of ethnic Turks who resisted the collectivization drive. By November 1951, 155,000 ethnic Turks had been expelled from Bulgaria. At that point, the Turkish government refused to accept any more refugees.

In the field of religious affairs, Chervenkov arranged the reconciliation of the Bulgarian Exarchate with the Patriarchate of Istanbul (Constantinople). But he ordered the incarceration of Exarch Stephen because he was not willing to be a tool of the government; the Bulgarian Orthodox Christian church was completely subordinated to the Communist party.

Chervenkov dominated Bulgarian politics in a way not comparable to other communist leaders in Eastern Europe. He was particularly strict in enforcing Marxist-Leninist-Stalinist dogmas in cultural life. He completely Sovietized Bulgarian literature and the arts.

With the death of Stalin in 1953, Chervenkov was threatened by the new concept of "collective leadership" that ensued in the Soviet Union. But his position remained stable for the time being because the Soviet party leaders were not willing to risk instability in their empire. Chervenkov then brought into the highest party leadership a former guerilla leader, Todor Zhivkov, who, in 1954, became the general secretary of the Bulgarian Communist party. By then, Nikita S. Khrushchev emerged as the successor to Joseph Stalin, and the East European communist leaders, among them Chervenkov, who were implicated in the anti-Tito witch-hunt of the 1940s and 1950s, became a liability for the new Soviet leadership. Khrushchev was determined to settle the conflict with Tito and reestablish good relations with Yugoslavia. Consequently, Chervenkov was shorn of all his party and state positions, and he died a forgotten man in 1963.

Bibliography

Brown, J.F., *Bulgaria under Communist Rule* (New York, 1970); Mcintyre, Robert J., *Bulgaria: Politics, Economics and Society* (London-New York, 1988); Denoff, Dragomir, *The Bulgarian Communist Party* (New York, 1961); Skilling, Harold, *The Governments of Communist Eastern Europe* (New York, 1966).

Collapse of Communism. The first open manifestation of public discontent with the communist system in the 1980s was a demonstration held in a port on the Danube river in 1988. Romanian industrial plants, opposite the city of Ruse, caused so much ecological damage in the region that ecologists voiced their open opposition against such destruction. The demonstration was brutally suppressed by the Bulgarian secret police, as was a similar protest meeting held in Sofia led by the wife of Stanko Todorov, the current president of the National Assembly. Party members who had participated in these expressions of public outrage were expelled from the organization.

By early 1989, however, informal organizations began to appear in ever-increasing numbers. Civil society was organizing itself against all opposition from the Communist party. An independent labor union, patterned on the Polish Solidarity organization, appeared. Todor Zhivkov (*see* Zhivkov, Todor) ordered the arrest of the members and leaders of the organization, but such coercive acts no longer worked. They only focused the attention of the public on the protests. In October 1989, a conference was held in Sofia concerning environmental issues. The communist government, anxious to demonstrate its concern over the environment, had invited the conference to Bulgaria. By then, Zhivkov was getting desperate about the isolation of Bulgaria from the international community, especially since his fellow communist dictators were losing their positions in most East European countries. The meeting, sponsored by the Conference on Security and Cooperation in Europe, was a continuation of the Helsinki Process. But the Bulgarian secret police who kept ordinary Bulgarians away from the meeting, hauled away those who were imprudent enough to want to talk to the participating foreigners. These efforts misfired; they produced more bad publicity for the Bulgarian communist regime.

The simultaneous disappearance of communist systems in other East European countries finally convinced reform-minded Bulgarian communists that Zhivkov and his minions must go. Petar Mladenov, Zhivkov's foreign minister since 1971, led the anti-Zhivkov movement within the Politburo. His personal relations with Zhivkov deteriorated. On November 5, 1989, Mladenov visited Beijing, and on his way home he stopped in Moscow. He conferred with Gorbachev, but no communique of this meeting was published. Back in Sofia, he obtained the support of Dobri Dzhurov, a wartime guerrilla leader, and Stanko Todorov, and other Zhivkov associates. They confronted Zhivkov at a specially convened Central Committee meeting on November 10, and demanded his resignation. Surprising everyone, Zhivkov gave up without a fight.

The change in leadership was immediately announced to the population. Hundreds of thousands of ordinary citizens poured out into the streets in Sofia and in other major urban centers, demanding the end of communist rule. Mladenov refused to give a green light to the secret police and declared his belated respect for political pluralism. He also promised that the dreaded secret police would be dissolved. There was no bloodshed, although at one point Mladenov seemed to change his mind and threatened to call out the tanks, but even this threat fizzled. It was evident that the masses of citizens would no longer tolerate rule by intimidation.

In October, elections were held, and the Union of Democratic Forces gained the majority. The new government promised swift, fundamental changes. A new constitution, promulgated by the Grand National Assembly, provided the framework for a pluralistic society. It includes freedom of speech, religion, conscience and the press. The authority of the president of the republic is limited to security and ceremonial functions. He has no veto power over legislation. The new electoral law permitted the formation of a wide range of parties.

Forty-two of these parties took part in the elections, and a minimum of 4 percent of the votes was necessary for parliamentary representation. Of the 240 seats, the Union of Democratic Forces won 110, and the Bulgarian Socialist party (successor to the communists) won 106. The Turkish ethnic party, Movement for Rights and Freedom (MRF), and the Agrarian National Union-United shared the rest. This, in fact, gave the Turkish ethnic party a greater weight than its numbers would indicate, since it could decide in major matters if its members sided with either party. The new premier, Filip Dimitrov, the chairman of the Union, is a lawyer and was originally a founding member of the Bulgarian Greens.

The new government immediately introduced legislation for land reform. Its intention was to return the land, confiscated by the communist government, to its previous owners. However, a limit of forty hectares was set in order to prevent the establishment of large estates. A progressive income tax was also enacted, and a new commercial code was established. The government also began to eliminate state subsidies for food and transportation. This resulted in inflationary price increases. At the same time, consumer goods, especially food, became more widely available, and the shelves of stores were once again full. In the first quarter of 1991, inflation reached 300 percent; however, thereafter it was only 5 percent monthly.

The new government was successful in obtaining a moratorium on its debt to the Deutsche Bank, and this enabled it to introduce limited convertibility of the leva. On March 15, 1991, the International Monetary Fund announced the granting of a $300 million loan to Bulgaria. The Paris Club of European states rescheduled $2 billion worth of Bulgarian debt over the next ten years. In April, a trade agreement with the United States provided most favored nation status, and the World Bank provided a loan of $250 million. Bulgaria is the only country in the Balkans that has managed the transformation from the monolithic communist system to a pluralistic, democratic regime without bloodshed. This augurs well for Bulgaria's future.

Bibliography

Perry, Duncan M., "Bulgaria: A New Constitution and Free Elections," *Radio Free Europe Research Reports,* 1.178-82 (January 3, 1992), pp. 178-182; Pundeff, Marin, "Bulgaria," in Joseph Held, ed., *The Columbia History of Eastern Europe in the Twentieth Century* (New York, 1992); Todorova, Maria N., "Improbable Maverick or Typical Conformist? Seven Thoughts on the New Bulgaria," in Ivo Banac, ed., *Eastern Europe in Revolution* (Ithaca, NY, 1992).

Communist Party of Bulgaria. The Bulgarian Communist party emerged from a split within the Social Democratic party in 1903. During the interwar years, it developed a strong organizational structure in spite of the fact that most of the time it had to operate underground (*see* Blagoev, Dimitar). The Bulgarian Communist party (BCP) left the Second International and joined Lenin's COMINTERN in 1919. By that time, it could count on the prestige of Georgy Dimitrov (*see* Dimitrov, Georgy) and Vassily Kolarov (*see* Kolarov, Vassily), two members of the highest levels of the COMINTERN, who took refuge in the Soviet Union and acquired Soviet citizenship. In Bulgaria proper, the BCP attracted mostly students, intellectuals and a few industrial workers. It was not yet a mass party, but it was vigorous and quite dogmatic. Its membership may have been around 30,000 before 1944.

In 1923, a COMINTERN-inspired, badly organized attempt at revolution had disastrous effects on the BCP. In his pursuit of world revolution, V.I. Lenin misjudged the Bulgarian situation and dispatched Dimitrov and Kolarov to lead the uprising.

The two emissaries tried to gain the cooperation of the Agrarian Union (*see* Agrarian Union), only recently removed from power by a royal coup d'etat, but without success. The revolution began in September 1923 and ended a week later. It failed primarily because the Bulgarian masses refused to join it. The government used draconian measures and ended the affair swiftly. Dimitrov and Kolarov fled with a handful of their followers to Yugoslavia, and then to the West. Those who stayed behind—the majority of ordinary sympathizers and party members—were caught and severely punished. This ill-conceived adventure destroyed the organizational structure of the BCP. In January 1924 it was outlawed by the Bulgarian government. Full recovery did not come until the early 1940s.

After the disaster, the BCP resorted to terrorism in its efforts to overthrow the government. In 1925, the party, with the approval of its Moscow-based leaders, concocted a scheme to assassinate King Boris. A powerful bomb was hidden in the Sveta Nedelia cathedral in Sofia and it was detonated during a funeral service held for a prominent general, who had been previously assassinated by the communists for just this purpose. Over 300 people were killed or injured by the explosion, but Boris, who was late in attending, was not harmed. Nor were the members of his cabinet killed. The following police measures (the communists later referred to these as the White Terror) wiped out the remaining membership of the BCP and reduced it to a minuscule organization.

The party's fortunes were somewhat revived in 1931-1932, when the Bulgarians experimented with a Popular Front government promoted by Moscow, but the party sank back to obscurity when persecutions were reinstated. In 1939, the BCP merged with the Workers' party, an extremist left-wing organization. The new party claimed to have 10,600 members and 19,000 young people in its youth auxiliaries. There was a Politburo with five members inside Bulgaria, including Traicho Kostov (*see* Kostov, Traicho), the secretary of the party, Tsola Dragoicheva, and Anton Yugov (*see* Yugov, Anton). There was also a Politburo in exile consisting of Dimitrov, Kolarov, Georgy Damjanov, Stanko Dimitrov, and Vulko Chervenkov (*see* Chervenkov, Vulko).

The underground Communist party organized a resistance movement against the Germans during the Soviet-German war, but it was largely ineffective. Only in 1943, following the German defeat at Stalingrad did it become more active. But it was never comparable to Tito's Partisan movement or even to the Albanian communist resistance. It gained momentum only when the Red Army entered Romania in the summer of 1944. However, Bulgaria never declared war on the Soviet Union; therefore, the communists were content with conducting minor sabotage and infiltrating the army. About 10,000 members took part in the resistance. The most effective resistance leader was Slavcho Trunski, who operated near the Yugoslav border; while another such leader was Dobri Terpeshev.

The major political effort of the BCP during the war was the creation of a anti-fascist coalition. But the largest political parties, the Agrarians, the Social Democrats, and the Democratic party who were all opposed to king Boris' authoritarian rule, did not want any part of the communists' plan. The party's reputation for terrorism was too well established for such cooperation. However, there were some splinter groups in these parties that were not as squeamish as their leaders. Two members of the Social Democratic party's leadership, Grigor Cheshmedzhiev and Dimitar Niekov, agreed to enter the proposed antifascist alliance. Kimon Georgiev and Colonel Danayan Velchev from ZVENO (Link) also agreed (see ZVENO).

The agreement was concluded early in 1944, and resistance to the Germans intensified thereafter. King Boris died in August 1943. A three-men regency took over, since the successor to Boris, Simeon II, was only six years old. In the spring of 1944, premier Bagryanov briefly cooperated with the communists, but that cooperation did not last. On August 23, Romania capitulated and the Soviet army approached Bulgaria's borders. On September 4, the Soviet Union declared war on Bulgaria. Five days later, the communists succeeded by a coup d'etat in overthrowing the government in Sofia and, with the help of the Red Army, became the rulers of Bulgaria. The Bulgarian armed forces were now co-opted into the Soviet army and were sent to fight the Germans.

The army safely out of the way—it suffered horrendous losses, since neither its equipment nor its personnel were up to modern standards—the communists took control of the ministries of justice and interior. They proceeded to eliminate the noncommunist leaders of the antifascist alliance called the Fatherland Front (see Fatherland Front). According to some reports, the number of victims, including all those who opposed the dictatorship of the Communist party, came to nearly 20,000, although these numbers have never been confirmed. The terror, however, generated revulsion among the population. The Fatherland Front was now used to consolidate communist power. The brutal process was openly supported by the Soviet army and, after the war came to an end, by the Soviet KGB.

Stalin sent back to Bulgaria Georgy Dimitrov and Vassily Kolarov, both COMINTERN and KGB agents. Dimitrov immediately took over the reigns of the party and government. In 1946, the Agrarian Union was dissolved; its parliamentary deputies were summarily dismissed and later imprisoned on false charges. In 1948, the left wing of the Agrarians that had joined the Fatherland Front was also eliminated. The Social Democrats were forcibly merged with the Communist party, and a year later, the remnants of ZVENO and the Democratic party were also absorbed by the communist organization.

In 1944, the Communist party had only a small membership. By 1946, the number of party membership grew to 250,000 and by 1966, they counted over 600,000 card-carrying members. These numbers continued to grow until, by the collapse of the communist system, over 800,000 Bulgarians had joined the communist organization. This meant that the party was the largest Bulgarian mass organization.

In the 1950s and 1960s, the party instituted several purges (see Purges). The most infamous of these purges included that of Traicho Kostov, who was accused of being a Titoist and a Western spy and was executed in 1949. His alleged fellow conspirators were expelled from the party and jailed. Georgy Dimitrov died of cancer in 1949 while undergoing treatment for the illness in the Soviet Union. He was succeeded by Kolarov but he, too, died shortly thereafter. Kolarov was succeeded by Vulko Chervenkov, the brother-in-law of Dimitrov, as general secretary of the party. A Stalinist, his term in power was characterized by a relentless pursuit of the alleged "enemies of the people." The terror that lasted many years numbed Bulgarian society. About one-fourth of the membership of the Communist party fell victim to the purges, and countless individuals who were not party members came under suspicion and were persecuted. In 1953 and 1956, following the Berlin riots and the Hungarian Revolution, the secret police acted especially brutally against suspected opponents of the regime.

After the emergence of the "collective leadership" in the Soviet Union following Stalin's death, Chervenkov dutifully followed the Soviet example. Some political prisoners were released and detention camps were dissolved. More openness on the part of *apparatchiki* was urged, and greater accessibility of officials to the people was ordered. Joint Soviet-Bulgarian companies, which were a means of Soviet exploitation of the Bulgarian economy, were now purchased by Bulgaria. When Khrushchev began the attempt to reestablish Soviet-Yugoslav relations in 1955, however, Chervenkov and his followers became a liability. They were too closely identified with the vicious anti-Tito campaign of the late 1940s and early 1950s. On April 17, 1956, two months after Khrushchev's denunciation of Stalin's crimes, Chervenkov was replaced by Anton Yugov (*see* Yugov, Anton), himself a former victim of the purges.

In October 1961, Todor Zhivkov (*see* Zhivkov, Todor) replaced Yugov as general secretary of the party. In turn, Yugov was purged the following year. In the meantime, Kostov was posthumously rehabilitated. Zhivkov now combined the posts of general secretary of the party and prime minister of the government. In 1971, however, he gave up the prime minister's office and became president of the Bulgarian People's Republic. He ruled Bulgaria until the collapse of the communist system in 1989. In 1991, he was arrested and tried for crimes committed during his regime.

The Bulgarian Communist party was organized on the pattern set by the Communist party of the Soviet Union. The organizational principle was the so-called democratic centralism, a device of authoritarian rule. The highest elected organ of the party was the Central Committee. This group originally consisted of only a few members. By 1947, however, membership had grown to 147; in 1976, it had 154 members, and two years later, 173. Candidate members came to 110 in 1971 and 106 in 1978. Altogether, the Central Committee had 279 members in 1978. Thereafter the numbers remained stable. The average age of the membership of the Central Committee increased as time went on. In 1980, forty-five of the members were over seventy years of age. Women accounted for only twenty-seven of the members.

Government officials were increasingly dominant among the Central Committee's membership. Party *apparatchiki*, scientists, cultural figures, and leaders of mass organizations made up the rest. Only thirteen blue-collar workers were included in this elite group. There were no peasants represented. Over 80 percent of the committee's membership had some form of higher education in 1980. The Turkish minority, composing about 10 percent of the country's population, was represented by one member. The Central Committee "elected" the members of the Politburo, which was its executive branch.

The party was organized along hierarchical lines. The party congress, meeting at five-year intervals, "elected" the Central Committee from a single list. The ordinary membership consisted of 41 percent blue-collar workers, 31 percent of white-collar employees, and 23 percent peasants. Five percent of the membership was not accounted for. However, these percentages included party "workers" as blue-collar, making the numbers somewhat suspect. Twenty-seven percent of the members were women. Young people under twenty-four years of age made up only 15 percent of the membership. In 1989, most party members simply quit. Nevertheless, the party survived albeit under a different name. Its reformist leaders contributed to a bloodless transformation of the Bulgarian political system for which they have not yet received sufficient credit.

Bibliography

Bell, John D., *The Bulgarian Communist Party from Blagoev to Zhivkov* (Stanford, CA, 1986); Fischer-Galati, Stephen, *The Communist Parties of Eastern Europe* (New York, 1979); Nenoff, Dragomir, *The Bulgarian Communist Party* (New York, 1951); Oren, Nissan, *Bulgarian Communism: The Road to Power, 1934–1944* (New York, 1971); Rothschild, Joseph, *The Communist Party of Bulgaria: Origins and Development, 1883–1936* (New York, 1959); Staar, Richard, *The Communist Regimes of Eastern Europe* (Stanford, CA., 1987).

Constitution of 1971. On March 30, 1971, a draft of a new constitution was published. It was submitted to the Tenth Communist Party Congress in April and then to the National Assembly for final action. On May 16, a referendum was held which produced the usual 99.6 percent approval rate of the new constitution. Two days later, parliament accepted it to be the law of the land.

The constitution declared Bulgaria to be a People's Republic and also a socialist state. It was a "member of the world socialist community" and the "world socialist economic system." It declared Bulgaria's Communist party the leading force in the building of a new society. The document recognized that, besides state, cooperative, and public organizations' property, there existed individually owned private properties in Bulgaria. However, the state owned all means of production. The rights spelled out in the document for citizens were extensive just as they were under the previous constitution (*see* Dimitrov Constitution), but they were also hedged around with many restrictions. The document mandated education for young people "in the spirit of communism."

The constitution expounded upon the role of the National Assembly. It described the method of establishing permanent parliamentary commissions and committees, extending their control over the ministerial council and agencies of state. A new State Council was also created which, together with other parliamentary committees, the supreme court, the prosecutor general, and public mass organizations, had the right to initiate new legislation. The presidium of the National Assembly was replaced by the State Council, which was to act for parliament when it was not in session. Since the National Assembly met only twice a year for a short time in each case, real authority lay in the hands of the members of the State Council, who were members of the Politburo of the Bulgarian Communist party.

The composition of the government under the new constitution remained unchanged. The local administrative organs were granted a greater measure of autonomy than before. The concept of elected judges was introduced, and the post of the prosecutor general was made independent of the government—at least on paper.

Bibliography

Oren, Nissan, *Revolution Administered: Agrarianism and Communism in Bulgaria* (Baltimore, 1973).

Cultural Policies. The conquest of power by the Bulgarian Communist party in 1944 provided its leaders with the opportunity to reshape Bulgarian culture and orient it toward the Soviet Union. The basis of cultural policies was to be state subsidies provided for conforming writers, painters, musicians, and other "cultural workers." In turn, they were expected to be loyal to the Communist ideology of Marxism-Leninism and serve the party's aim of creating a socialist society. The instrument of these policies was the Ministry of Culture. It organized unions for writers, artists, filmmakers, and others. Each of the unions, in cooperation with the ministry, assigned subjects to be treated and arranged the production of art works. Membership in these unions was the sine qua non of cultural existence.

The unions also provided remuneration for the works produced. Creative people, who deviated from the party line, were disciplined by the unions. In the worst cases, they were expelled and their works were not popularized or were even removed from circulation. There was no artistic freedom to speak of, but this was compensated for by lavish rewards for those who conformed.

These policies created a new, privileged stratum of Bulgarian society who, together with talented sportsmen, were dedicated to the glorification of the socialist system, intending to prove that it was superior to the capitalist way of life. At a time when life was hard for ordinary Bulgarians, the creative people lived a life of leisure indeed.

Nevertheless, there was discontent among them because of the straightjacket imposed upon them by the official notion of "socialist realism." Many writers and artists who had real talent, could have been successful under competitive conditions. They eventually became impatient and grew disillusioned by the ever-widening gap between communist promises—and Marxist-Leninist ideology—on the one hand and real life on the other. Many of them were willing to give up their privileges for a more honest life.

Much of what had been produced by Bulgarian writers in the first flush of Stalinism was worthless as literature. The themes they pursued—the heroic workers overcoming difficulties in meeting production quotas, the heroic terrorism of the interwar years—were not worth the paper they were written on. The older, more talented writers such as Elizaveta Bagriana, Mladen Isev, and Georgy Karaslavov (a dedicated communist) to mention only a few, struggled hard to provide readable stories. Dimitar Angelov and Bogumil Rainov, members of the younger generation, were not so squeamish.

In theater, the situation was similar; only a few plays could be called by that name. But since genuine criticism did not exist, it hardly mattered. In 1951, an outstanding novel was published by Dimitar Dimov, entitled *Tobacco*. It described the revolutionary movement among tobacco factory workers before and during World War II. The book was condemned by the party censors, because its "positive heroes" were not revolutionary enough. Two years later, however, official opinion was revised, and the book was hailed as a masterpiece. This was the result of the changing atmosphere following Stalin's death, imitating the pattern of cultural policies pursued by the successors of Stalin in the Soviet Union. By then, over 2,700 Soviet books had been translated into Bulgarian and published, mostly of the "socialist realism" variety. Soviet styles were still slavishly imitated.

The party still stressed the importance of "socialist realism." Vulko Chervenkov (*see* Chervenkov, Vulko), in an address delivered to the meeting of the Writers' Union in 1955, condemned writers who were "unduly critical" of the union's leaders.

In 1956, some writers began complaining about the lifelessness of Bulgarian literature, about the deadening effect of the suppression of freedom of expression. A small group of writers now began to be referred to as dissidents. These were joined by other intellectuals and, in January 1957, a new literary magazine, *Plamuk* appeared, which published works that were denied dissemination by the censors. The writers now began openly to criticize the leadership, following the example of their colleagues in Poland and Hungary in 1956. Chervenkov, the personification of cultural oppression, was removed from his top party post, but he was appointed minister of education and culture, signaling that the new leadership did not really want to change cultural policies.

A new wave of oppression followed. Todor Pavlov, the president of the Bulgarian Academy of Sciences, was eager to land a helping hand to Chervenkov. In July 1957, a new attack was launched against dissidents. Revisionism, and the "exaggeration of errors" were condemned. The attacks did not let up. The writers responded by withholding publications. In early 1958, the president of the Journalists' Union was dismissed. Members of the Academy of Sciences were reminded that their privileges depended upon their loyalty to the Communist party. In April 1958, the Writers' Union was purged of most of its leaders. As a result of continued pressure, some of the writers capitulated and apologized to the party. Only then did the Politburo remove Chervenkov from the ministry of education and culture. But the criticism of the regime quieted down, and conformity once again became the order of the day.

In 1958, the Seventh Congress of the Bulgarian Communist party put three demands on intellectuals; they were to be more intimately involved in the political, economic, and cultural endeavors of the party; they had to raise the ideological level of their activities; and they had to commit themselves to the struggle against "bourgeois penetration" of Bulgarian cultural life. A year later, the writers were simply told that, if they wanted their works published, they had to become propagandists for the communist cause. Some of the writers continued to struggle against the stifling policies of the party. In 1959, two works caused official furor. These were Orlin Vassilev's play, *The Buried Sun*, and Dragomir Assenov's novel, *The Roads Bypass One Another*. The two authors were accused of presenting a distorted image of Bulgarian communists, of accusing communist leaders of having become "bourgeois" themselves after achieving power. According to the critics, the two works asserted that communists were no longer motivated to fight for a better life for the people.

The two authors were not imprisoned; nevertheless, the outcome was predictable. Bulgarian writers thereafter increasingly avoided themes that could land them in trouble. A gray uniformity settled over literature and the arts. The regime's monopoly of control over cultural affairs continued, but minor violations were overlooked.

In September 1966, the party finally reorganized its Committee for Culture and held a Congress of Culture the following year. The committee was the supervisor of the various unions of creative people. The new push was now against what the leaders considered to be the dangerous inroads made in Bulgaria by Western culture. By then, thanks to the general relaxation that had begun to characterize East-West relations, nearly a million tourists visited Bulgaria every year, half of them from the West. The continuation of the old policy of isolation of citizens from this movement was becoming impossible. In the end, all efforts at suppressing the longings of creative individuals for freedom of expression were bound to fail.

During the 1970s and most of the 1980s, the party leaders who were growing old (Zhivkov himself was reaching his late seventies by 1988) were fighting a holding action. Eventually all their efforts failed. There was an uneasy compromise until the very end of communist rule in Bulgaria, but writers and artists gradually freed themselves from the party censors. By 1989, all restraints had been removed, and society began to recover its balance with the disappearance of the communist system.

Bibliography

Brown, J.F., *Bulgaria under Communist Rule* (New York, 1970); Held, Joseph, "Cultural Developments," in Stephen Fischer-Galati, *Eastern Europe in the 1980s* (Boulder, CO, 1981).

Dimitrov, Georgy (1882–1949). Born in Radomir to a father who was an independent craftsmen, Dimitrov was involved in the Bulgarian trade union movement from an early age. His oldest brother, Konstantin, was secretary of the union of printers' apprentices and died in the Second Balkan War in 1913. Another brother, Nikola, joined the Russian revolutionaries in 1905 and died in Russia in 1917. A third brother, Todor, died in 1925 following the communist bombing of Sofia's cathedral. Georgy himself received a sixth-grade education and became an apprentice typesetter. When he turned eighteen, he was elected secretary of his union.

The apprentices' union was a sort of school for minors who were expected to join the adult printers' union when they reached a certain age. In 1902 Dimitrov joined the Bulgarian Social Democratic party where he came under the influence of Dimitar Blagoev (*see* Blagoev, Dimitar). A year later, when the party split, Dimitrov joined the "narrow" (radical) wing, the future communist party under Blagoev's leadership. In 1909, Dimitrov was elected a member of the fledgling party's Central Committee. In 1913, he was elected to the Bulgarian parliament on the Social Democratic ticket, and he also became an official of the municipal government of the capital city, Sofia. In 1919, Dimitrov was jailed for some unknown reason for eighteen months.

When he was released, he traveled to Moscow where he was appointed a member of the COMINTERN, together with another Bulgarian, Vassily Kolarov (*see* Kolarov, Vassily). In 1923, Dimitrov was sent back to Bulgaria by the COMINTERN together with other exiled communists to organize a communist uprising intended to topple the government of King Boris. The uprising which lasted for four days, ended in abject failure. Dimitrov and his fellow Muscovites fled to Yugoslavia and then to Vienna and other Western capitals where they were, ironically, safe. The ordinary communists who participated in the uprising were caught and punished. By then, Dimitrov was a full-fledged COMINTERN agent, working closely with Lenin's, and later with Stalin's, secret police in organizing the communist parties in Germany and Austria. In 1933, he was accused of participating in the fire set at the German parliament's building, the Reichstag, but was acquitted.

Returning to the Soviet Union, now a communist celebrity, Dimitrov was appointed by Stalin as secretary of the COMINTERN. He remained in the Soviet Union during the rest of the 1930s and during World War II, directing propaganda to his homeland. By the time Dimitrov returned to Bulgaria in late 1945, the communists were already in power, thanks to the Red Army of the Soviet Union and the Soviet secret police.

Dimitrov's task was to provide a "legal" framework for justifying the conquest of power. Working through the Grand National Assembly, Dimitrov "inspired" his fellow communists to create a constitution in 1947 (*see* Dimitrov Constitution). He also advanced the idea of creating a Balkan federation uniting all the states of the region. The concept was favored by Tito of Yugoslavia as a way of preventing future nationalist conflicts in the Balkans. However, Stalin would not agree to the plan, and it was eventually dropped. It would certainly have interfered with Soviet plans for the colonization of Eastern Europe.

In 1946, Dimitrov was ill, most probably with cancer. He went for treatment to the Soviet Union and died there in 1949. His body was returned to Bulgaria and was buried in a specially built mausoleum in the center of Sofia. In 1990, after the collapse of the system he helped to build, Dimitrov's body was removed and buried in a regular cemetery.

Bibliography

Brown, J.F., *Bulgaria Under Communist Rule* (New York-Washington, D.C.-London, 1970); Evans, Stanley G., *A Short History of Bulgaria* (London, 1960); Oren, Nissan, *Revolution Administered: Agrarianism and Communism in Bulgaria* (Maryland, 1973).

Dimitrov Constitution. Georgy Dimitrov (*see* Dimitrov, Georgy) returned to Bulgaria from exile in the Soviet Union in 1945. His first task was to create a quasi-legal framework for communist dictatorship. In 1946, his government held a plebiscite which, predictably, led to the abolition of the monarchy. It also approved the proclamation of Bulgaria as a People's Republic. Elections were then held for a Grand National Assembly whose major task was to write a new constitution.

In December 1947, the assembly approved the so-called "Dimitrov Constitution" which, in fact, replaced the Turnovo constitution of 1879. The new constitution was Dimitrov's in name only. It was, in fact, copied from the Soviet constitution of 1936, a document that had little effect on the politics of communist Bulgaria and which never stopped the judicial murders and other atrocities committed by the security organs.

The constitution proclaimed that Bulgaria was a People's Democracy. It vested all powers in the "people" who exercised it through universal suffrage of all citizens over the age of eighteen. All means of production were declared to be public property, that is, owned by the state. It also permitted the holding of some private property on a limited basis. The constitution, therefore, gave a green light for the state to nationalize all properties that it declared not in conformity with the "public interest." The state was empowered to regulate social activities.

The National Assembly was given authority to enact all laws. It was to elect a presidium and appoint a government. It had the right to declare war and approve peace and also approve the state budget. The assembly was also to appoint judges and the chief prosecutor of the state. It had the right to amend the constitution. Elections for the National Assembly were to be held every four years, and each group of 30,000 citizens was entitled to one deputy. The assembly was to meet twice a year; in between sessions, the presidium was to act as the executive institution.

The presidium was the authority entitled to promulgate laws. It was permanently in session. Its nineteen members were directed by the president of the assembly, who had two vice presidents and a secretary to assist in exercising his functions. The prime minister, his cabinet, and the chairmen of various parliamentary committees usually were members of the presidium. The government was responsible to the National Assembly, and when it was not in session, to the presidium. Any action taken by local governments was subject to governmental approval. The constitution also created a supreme court, appointed by the assembly for five-year terms.

The document guaranteed many civil rights, including equality before the law and the equality of women. Racial, national, and religious equality was also included in the document. Freedom of speech, and freedom of assembly were also proclaimed. The Dimitrov Constitution provided for a highly centralized state in which the leaders of the communist party had unlimited control in spite of all the high-sounding principles proclaimed in it.

Bibliography

Brown, J.F., *Bulgaria Under Communist Rule* (New York, 1970).

Dobrudja. The territory of Dobrudja, situated between Bulgaria and Romania, has been the subject of nationalist disputes between the two nations for at least a century. Each claims that the majority of the population of the province belongs to its ethnic group. In the first Balkan War of 1912, Serbia and Greece gained control of Dobrudja together with Macedonia. This created conditions for the Second Balkan War of 1913, in which Bulgaria suffered a disastrous defeat. Dobrudja was then incorporated into Romania, which belatedly joined the war against its southern neighbor. After World War I, Bulgaria was again among the losers. But this time Dobrudja was not taken away. Parts of its remained under Bulgarian sovereignty.

Bibliography

Evans, Stanley, G., *A Short History of Bulgaria* (London, 1960).

Education. There was only one university in Bulgaria, but other higher educational institutions were available for students seeking knowledge in practical fields. There were also a number of private schools, among them the American College at Simeonovo, organized by American missionaries, providing education in Western languages. The system was well organized, and it fulfilled its task outstandingly. By the outbreak of World War II, illiteracy had been reduced from the 90 percent level of 1878 to less than 25 percent among the adult population. The number was still relatively high because numerous Gypsy groups living in Bulgaria did not send their children to the schools.

The Bulgarian communists changed the educational system of the country by making it conform to the Soviet model. By 1948, all school textbooks were replaced, a large number of teachers and university instructors were dismissed, and loyal communists were installed in their places regardless of their qualifications. There was only one requirement, namely, loyalty to the Communist party.

The resolution of the party's Central Committee issued in August 1949 stipulated that education at all levels was to be conducted in the spirit of socialism and the unbreakable brotherhood between Bulgaria and the Soviet Union. In line with these policies, education in general and the acquisition of knowledge of Marxism-Leninism in particular were considered not so much a privilege but a duty of all citizens.

After the accession of Nikita Khrushchev to power in the Soviet Union, education in Bulgaria tended to move more and more in the direction of polytechnic instruction that required each student to spend time working in factories and collective farms a few hours each day.

By 1960, facilities for education had been greatly expanded. By 1980, 86 percent of all those eligible were enrolled in some form of education. The number of dropouts was significantly reduced. The number of two- and four-year colleges grew by leaps and bounds. In 1980, 21.7 percent of the people between the ages of twenty and twenty-four received some form of secondary education. In addition, about 8,500 Bulgarian students attended universities in the Soviet Union. Vocational schools performed well in Bulgaria.

In 1975, secondary education, including vocational schooling, became compulsory. Plans called for the addition of two years of study in the vocational schools' curriculum, making them four-year institutions. This provided ten years of schooling for all Bulgarian youngsters. At the same time, the curriculum of five-year colleges was reduced to four years. In addition to vocational schools, Bulgaria introduced apprentice training for young people not interested in education on other levels. These schools required the students to work in factories under the supervision of skilled workers and take a certain number of classes in a regular school. The students spent a minimum time studying "extraneous" subjects.

Higher educational institutions were very selective, but the criteria for selection had only partially been related to the student's abilities or preparations. Great stress was placed on a candidate's social origins and ideological preparation. When admitted, a student might be directed into a field for which he had no desire, depending on the space availability of all subjects.

The entire system was handicapped by its isolation from Western scientific and intellectual life, and by the insistence on conformity with communist perceptions. The official adulation of the achievements of Soviet science—real or imagined—and the assertion that it was superior to "capitalist" knowledge provided further problems for students and educators alike. University, or college, professorships were more often than not given to people who were good party men first and intellectuals second. The performance of graduates of these institutions were often not on the same level as their counterparts in Western countries. The system of counter selection was harmful for the entire educational system.

The special institutions attached to the Bulgarian Academy of Sciences probably functioned the best among all educational institutions. These institutions specialized in specific fields, and their members were, on the whole, freer to pursue their interests than were members of the professoriates. They were permitted to attend scholarly conferences in the West and study abroad when required by their scholarship. Western publications that were not available to ordinary college, or university, professors were usually available to members of the institutions of the Academy of Sciences. However, these scholars were usually not permitted to teach at the university or colleges for fear that they might "contaminate" the young people of Bulgaria.

In addition to regular schools, the mass organizations also conducted some form of education for their members. The Communist Youth Union, counterpart to the Soviet KOMSOMOL, and the Young Pioneers, also organized on the Soviet pattern, were instruments for educating young people in Marxism-Leninism and for preparing them for eventual membership in the Bulgarian Communist party.

With the collapse of the communist system in Bulgaria in 1989, the failure of indoctrination became apparent. Nevertheless, the educational achievements of the Communist system cannot be denied. It is likely, however, that the entire system will once again be reorganized to reflect the democratic values toward which Bulgaria is now striving.

Bibliography

Roucek, Joseph S. and V. Lottich, Kenneth V., *Behind the Iron Curtain: The Soviet Satellite States: East European Nationalism and Education* (Caldwell, Idaho, 1964); Thomas, John T., *Education for Communism* (Stanford, CA, 1969); Velichkov, Alexander, "Bulgarian Educational System in a Quagmire," *Radio Free Europe Research Reports*, 1.24 (June 12, 1992), pp. 52-56.

Fatherland Front. The idea of a united anti-fascist movement in Bulgaria was first proposed by the Moscow-based Politburo of the Communist party. This was simply a projection of the Popular Front idea of the 1930s to the Bulgarian scene. The proposal was broadcast by the Hristo Botev radio based in the Soviet Union in 1941. The broadcast described the Fatherland Front as an undertaking of all democratic forces, with a limited role for the Communist party. Although the major opposition parties rejected the idea, their splinter groups found it attractive. Grigor Chezhmedzhiev and Dimitur Niekov, the left-wing Social Democrats; Kimon Georgiev of ZVENO (*see* ZVENO), and left-wing Agrarians, led by Nikola Petkov, joined with the communists in the Fatherland Front. Of them, Petkov (*see* Petkov, Nikola) was the most courageous and most important political leader.

The first National Committee of the Fatherland Front was formed in September 1943. It was clearly dominated by the communists who became more and more aggressive and demanding as time went by and as the Red Army neared the Bulgarian borders. But the Fatherland Front served its purpose; it split the democratic forces in the country making it easier for the communists to gain power in postwar Bulgaria.

After the September 9, 1944, coup d'etat, the first Fatherland Front government was formed. This government, headed by Kimon Georgiev, included only two communist ministers, although their role proved crucial. They headed the ministries of the interior and of justice. These two ministries and the secret police under their control, were used to dismantle the opposition. Anton Yugov (*see* Yugov, Anton) was the first minister of the interior. He organized the so-called People's Militia that went on to conduct mass arrests. This was a preliminary to the mass terror that was to be used to gain power by the communists. Those who were arrested were tried at the so-called

People's Courts (*see* People's Courts), under the jurisdiction of the ministry of justice. The courts gave out death sentences freely.

All politicians of the wartime Bulgarian scene who did not leave the country met their deaths by the courts. The leaders of the democratic opposition were given long prison terms. It was officially stated later that the People's Courts had given out 2,138 death sentences and 1,940 long-term prison sentences; however, the actual numbers must have been much higher. This was the bloodiest conquest of power in all of Eastern Europe.

The Fatherland Front was also used to create communist-dominated local governments. Tsola Dragoicheva, a member of the Communist party's Central Committee, was instrumental in this process. The Fatherland Front's local committees effectively eliminated the opposition in the countryside, using the People's Militia for the purpose. The collaborators, Petkov and Chezhmedzhiev, and their followers became the next targets. Their "crime" was that each had an independent power base. Petkov was not only the leader of the left-wing Agrarians (*see* Agrarian Union), but after the leader of the majority Agrarians was hounded out of the country, Petkov became his successor.

Petkov was, at first, removed from his post in the Fatherland Front. Chezhmedzhiev shared Petkov's fate later. The front was, therefore, "cleansed" of its former leaders except the communists. For the rest of the communist rule of Bulgaria, the Fatherland Front remained an empty shell, used for the purposes of mass mobilization. As a mass organization, the Fatherland Front had 4 million members in 1980, including members of the Agrarian Union, the trade unions, and the Dimitrov Communist Youth Association. It was used to nominate people for the rigged elections that were held every four years and other efforts of social mobilization.

Bibliography

Brown, J.F., *Bulgaria Under Communist Rule* (New York, 1970); Dellin, L.A.D., *Bulgaria* (New York, 1956); Mcintyre, Robert J., *Bulgaria: Politics, Economics and Society* (London-New York, 1988); Skilling, Harold, *The Governments of Communist Eastern Europe* (New York, 1966).

Foreign Relations. Bulgaria was the most loyal ally of the Soviet Union for during four-and-a-half decades of Communist rule. In foreign policy, its regime kept strictly to the Soviet line even at the expense of sacrificing Bulgarian national interests. When discussing the refusal of the Bulgarian communist leaders to avail themselves of opportunities of gaining some measure of independence, several reasons must be considered. First of all, these leaders were devoted communists who honestly believed that the interests of the Soviet Union were the same as those of Bulgaria. In addition, there was a historical tradition of friendship between the two peoples. Common religion, and common cultural characteristics added to the historical traditions. Furthermore, by being the most loyal ally, Bulgaria received plenty of rewards.

Unlike Albania or Romania, Bulgaria was the recipient of Soviet economic help right up to the collapse of communism in Eastern Europe and the Soviet Union. Finally, the more frequent power struggles within the Bulgarian leadership made the position of each general secretary more insecure than in any other Soviet bloc country, and the Bulgarian leaders needed the Soviet Union to keep themselves in power.

In 1948, Bulgaria signed a treaty of friendship and mutual cooperation with Romania, a treaty that survived until 1990. However, the relations between the two countries became strained when Romania began to exercise some independent foreign policy in the 1980s. During the last years of the rule of the Ceausescu clan, relations became outright hostile.

Bulgarian-Greek relations also fluctuated. According to the Paris Peace Treaty of 1947, Bulgaria's reparations obligation came to $45 million, but the amount was never paid. In fact, during the Greek civil war, Bulgaria provided safe haven for Greek insurgents and permitted the transit of Soviet supplies. Bad relations survived into the early 1960s. In that year, there appeared an opportunity to settle some of Bulgaria's problems with Greece. A year before, in a speech to the National Assembly, Todor Zhivkov (*see* Zhivkov, Todor) proposed that Greece and Bulgaria reduce their armed forces to the minimum level necessary; only the border guards should remain as they were. The speech was considered an effort to weaken the southern flank of NATO, and it received no response from the Greek government. Zhivkov repeated his offer in an address delivered at the General Assembly of the United Nations in September 1960. He proposed the signing of a nonaggression treaty among the Balkan states, severe cuts in their armed forces, and the establishment of the region as an area of general disarmament. Neither Greece nor Turkey responded to this speech which was considered support for Soviet propaganda efforts to induce dissensions in NATO ranks.

In 1964, full diplomatic relations between Greece and Bulgaria were reestablished, although not yet on the ambassadorial level. Telephone and railway communications that had ben restricted until then were restored, and even a new railway line was built between Koulata in Bulgaria and Salonika in 1965. This opened an alternate route for Bulgarian goods since the Yugoslav port of Rijeka (Fiume) was practically closed because of the Tito-Stalin conflict.

When the anti-Western socialist government of Andreas Papandreau came into power in Athens, Bulgarian-Greek relations naturally improved. The Greek dispute with Turkey over Cyprus added fuel to Papandreau's hostility to NATO, and an accord with Bulgaria became a distinct possibility. Soon a series of agreements were signed in Athens. Bulgaria paid $7 million in reparations to Greece, and trade and communications were expanded. Cultural cooperation and the mutual fostering of tourism were also agreed upon.

Relations with Turkey, however, continued on the time worn pattern of centuries of hostility. In 1950 and 1951, the Bulgarians "encouraged" 150,000 ethnic Turks to seek refuge in Turkey permitting them to carry away only a very small amount of their possessions. In 1963, the still sizable Turkish minority grew restive because of rumors that a new wave of expulsions was in the works. The relatives of those who had left in the 1950s were not permitted to maintain contacts with their loved ones, let alone join them in Turkey. Turkish tobacco growers on the slopes of the Rhodope mountains were paid much lower wages than their Bulgarian counterparts, which added to their dissatisfaction.

In the 1970s, the Bulgarian communist authorities began a policy of "ethnic cleansing" of their own. They forced ethnic Turks to change their names into Bulgarian names and closed Turkish language schools. Open, blatant discrimination against ethnic Turks continued into the 1980s. This was the case even though Zhivkov visited Turkey in 1968, and he and the Turkish prime minister signed a non-aggression treaty. With the Soviet administration becoming more and more rigid in foreign policy, the Bulgarians themselves followed suit. In 1988, just before the collapse of his regime, Zhivkov's government expelled an additional 450,000 ethnic Turks from Bulgaria.

Yugoslav-Bulgarian relations were also an appendage of Soviet foreign policies. Immediately after the communist coup d'etat, relations were good. The two countries cooperated in supplying arms and provisions to the Greek insurgents and in providing safe haven for the treatment of their wounded. Georgy Dimitrov and Josip Broz Tito were on good personal terms, and the latter liked Dimitrov's idea of a Balkan confederation. However, Stalin rejected the idea of the federation, and it was dropped by the Bulgarians.

When the conflict between Tito and Stalin came into the open, Bulgaria joined the chorus of East European communist states denouncing Tito as an imperialist spy. Traicho Kostov's show trial (see Kostov, Traicho) and execution was a signal, followed by a witch hunt of his supporters, that the Bulgarian leadership adhered strictly to the Stalinist line. Foreign policy towards Yugoslavia thereafter continued along the gyrations of Soviet policies. There was a period of relaxation following Nikita Khrushchev's efforts to patch up Soviet-Yugoslav relations between 1955 and 1957, and outright hostility flared up after the invasion of Czechoslovakia in 1968. Normal relations were resumed only in the mid-1980s. The break up of Yugoslavia and the outbreak of the civil war kept Bulgaria's relations with its northern neighbor on a hold.

Relations with Western nations also followed the Soviet line. The Communist party's declarations usually began with the "assured collapse" of the capitalist world, allegedly accelerated by the continuously growing strength of the socialist bloc. In time, Bulgaria embraced the notion of "peaceful coexistence" and of detente. The Bulgarians signed the Helsinki Accord in 1975, but they have not been willing to observe its principles on individual freedoms and rights. All these actions on the part of the Bulgarian communist regime had one aim, namely, to obtain Western loans and technology. Relations with the United States were broken off in 1951. Only after the collapse of the communist regime were relations placed on a normal footing.

During the Sino-Soviet conflict, Bulgaria remained loyal to the Soviet Union. This loyalty was not dented when Albania sided with Beijing, and Romania tried to maneuver between the two giant antagonists.

Bibliography

Amnesty International, *Bulgaria: Imprisonment of Ethnic Turks* (New York, 1986); ———, *Bulgaria: Continued Human Rights Abuses Against Ethnic Turks* (New York, 1987); Aspaturian, Vernon, "Eastern Europe in World Perspective," in Teresa Rakowska-Harmstone, ed. *Communism in Eastern Europe* 2nd ed. (Bloomington, IN, 1984); Bell, John, D., *Cold War in the Balkans: American Foreign Policy and the Emergence of Communist Bulgaria, 1943–1947* (Lexington, KY, 1984); Brown, J.F., Bulgaria Under Communist Rule (New York, 1970); Burks, R.V., *The Dynamics of Communism in Eastern Europe* (Princeton, NJ, 1961); Kostalnick, H.L., *Turkish Resettlement of Bulgarian Turks, 1950–1953* (Berkeley, CA., 1957).

Grand National Assembly. Elections for Bulgaria's constitutional parliament, called the Grand National Assembly (Grand Sobranie), were held in October 1946, under communist terror and intimidation. The results were the "election" of 277 communist deputies out of 364 mandates won by the Fatherland Front (the wartime united antifascist alliance) and 101 deputies for the opposition parties. The Grand National Assembly was then declared to be the supreme legislative organ of the Bulgarian People's Democratic state; each deputy represented 30,000 voters.

The assembly met twice each year for a short session each time, rubber stamping decisions made by the Politburo of the Communist party. The assembly elected its own leaders, the judges of the state supreme court, and the prosecutor general. It appointed the ministers (proposed by leaders of the Communist party). It was empowered to amend the constitution. The presidium of the assembly consisted of nineteen members, all Communist party members or fellow travelers. Between sessions, the presidium acted as the executive of the assembly.

In June 1990, a new Grand National Assembly was elected, this time in free elections. Its first task was the enactment of a new constitution. Several parties participated in the elections, including the communists, who renamed their party to that of Socialist party of Bulgaria. The government emerging from the new parliament was led by Andrei Lukanov, a former communist apparatchik. The strongest opposition force that emerged was the Union of Democratic Forces, a grouping of sixteen parties, organizations, and movements. Its chairman was Zhelu Zhelev. This group which emerged in 1988, won 144 seats in the Assembly. The revived Agrarian Union won only sixteen seats. The Movement for Rights and Freedom, a Muslim-Turkish party, won twenty-three seats.

In new elections held in 1991, the Union of Democratic Forces became the strongest party, followed by the Socialist party and the Movement for Rights and Freedom party. The Agrarian Union came in fourth place. The new government was formed by the Union, and its chairman, Filip Dimitrov, became prime minister of Bulgaria.

Bibliography
Dainov, Evgenii. "Bulgaria: Politics after the October 1991 Elections," *Radio Free Europe Research Reports*, 1.2 (January 10, 1992), pp. 12-16; Perry, Duncan M. "A New Constitution and Free Elections," *Radio Free Europe Research Reports*, 1.1 (January, 3, 1992), pp. 78-82; Todorova, Maria N., "Improbable Maverick or Typical Conformist?" in Ivo Banac, ed., *Eastern Europe in Revolution* (Ithaca, NY, 1992).

Kolarov, Vassili (1887–1950). Born in the village of Shoumen (renamed Kolarovgrad by the communist authorities), he ran away from home at the early age of eight because he wanted to join the army, but was returned home by the officers. In the early 1900s, he went to Varna as a laborer where he came under the influence of the father of Bulgarian communism, Alexander Blagoev. Between 1904 and 1905, he was an editor of the *Student Voice*, a radical leftist newspaper that appeared irregularly. In 1906, he graduated from a teacher's college and soon thereafter was instrumental in the establishment of the first Bulgarian teachers' union. In 1907, Kolarov went to study in France at Aix-en-Provance, but he did not complete his studies for a law degree. Returning to the place of his birth, he worked as a lawyer and attended officers' school. In 1904, Kolarov began his career as a full-time politician and became one of the members of the "narrow" socialists, later communists, in the city of Plovdiv. He was elected parliamentary deputy on the Social Democratic ticket.

In World War I, Kolarov served as an officer in the Bulgarian army. After the war, Kolarov was elected secretary of the Bulgarian Communist party. In 1921, he became a COMINTERN agent and, two years later, was one of the organizers of the ill-fated communist uprising in Bulgaria. When the uprising ended, Kolarov fled to Vienna with Georgy Dimitrov (*see* Dimitrov, Georgy), and then returned to Moscow. As a member of the Bulgarian Communist party's Politburo-in-exile, Kolarov served the COMINTERN as a liaison with the Bulgarian underground Communist party, or what was left of it after the abortive uprising. He also continued working on assignments given him by Stalin.

During the Spanish civil war, Kolarov was a Soviet commissar, working with the KGB-NKVD, the Soviet secret police against Trotskyists and Anarchists. After the victory of General Francisco Franco's forces, Kolarov was evacuated by his Soviet friends and returned to Moscow where he worked in his posts during World War II.

In September 1944, after the communist coup d'etat in Bulgaria, he returned to Sofia and immediately became a member of the leadership of the Fatherland Front (*see* Fatherland Front). As such, Kolarov was engaged in the Stalinization of his country. Kolarov then worked in various posts and, after the death of Dimitrov, he took over as first secretary of the Bulgarian Communist party. He lasted in that post for only six months; in early 1950, he died of an unknown ailment.

Bibliography
Evans, Stanley G., *A Short History of Bulgaria* (London, 1960); Mcintyre, Robert J., *Bulgaria: Politics, Economics and Society* (London-New York, 1988); Rothschild, Joseph, *The Communist Party of Bulgaria: Origins and Development, 1883–1936* (New York, 1959).

Kostov, Traicho (?–1949). In Bulgaria, as in other East European countries under communist rule, a struggle developed in the late 1940s between the Muscovites (communists who spent years in exile in the Soviet Union and returned to their home countries with the Soviet and with citizenship) and the local communist leaders, who risked their lives during the interwar years in underground communist movements. The Muscovites not only were willing tools of Stalin, but were also mostly out of touch with the situation "back home." One would think that under such conditions, the local communists would have had an edge over the Muscovites, but this was not the case. Because the Muscovites established relations with Soviet leaders, the support of the Soviet secret police was extended to them.

In one sense, there was little difference between the two factions. They were all ruthless, unscrupulous individuals who craved power and were utterly devoted to the Soviet Union and to Stalin's leadership. These men included Wladislaw Gomulka in Poland, Klement Gottwald in Czechoslovakia, Matyas Rakosi in Hungary, Georghe Gheorghiu-Dej in Romania and, of course, Georgy Dimitrov (*see* Dimitrov, Georgy), and Vassily Kolarov in Bulgaria.

Traicho Kostov was the most powerful local communist leader. Dimitrov and Kolarov certainly had a great deal more prestige than any other leader among communist cadres, but Kostov was in charge of economic development after 1944, and he engineered the economic recovery of the country. He was entrusted with the nationalization of industry, banking, and, most important, agriculture.

Kostov, an educated man, from a family of railway workers, studied at the University of Sofia where he became a convinced Marxist radical. He faced constant scrutiny by the Bulgarian police during the 1930s, and he was even injured once when escaping from police interrogation. Yet, in March 1949, Kostov was arrested. In cooperation with the Soviet KGB, the Bulgarian secret police concocted a case against him charging him with being a nationalist and an enemy of the Soviet Union. He was also charged with allegedly wrecking the Bulgarian economy and being a British spy. The charges included the accusation that Kostov had been an informer for the Bulgarian police during the interwar years, and that he had sold out the leadership of the underground Communist party causing their arrest and imprisonment. Above all, he was accused of being a Titoist. But in fact, he and Tito genuinely disliked each other, and Kostov was by no means awed by the Yugoslav dictator whose pompousness he often compared to Benito Mussolini's. What singled out Kostov, however, for the role of scapegoat for the economic hardships descending on Bulgaria was that he often argued for Bulgarian national interests in negotiations with Bulgaria's Soviet partners. This, in the eyes of Stalin and his henchmen, was sufficient "proof" of Kostov's "dangerous nationalistic tendencies."

In December 1949 Kostov, who had not been broken by the hideous tortures inflicted on him by the secret police, was tried. During the course of the show trial that lasted ten days, he denied some of the accusations against him, a highly unusual phenomenon at these proceedings. All this mattered little, however, since his sentence was predetermined. He was condemned to death and executed together with several of his other—equally innocent—followers. In 1956, following Nikita Khrushchev's denunciation of Stalin's crimes, Kostov was rehabilitated.

Bibliography

Brown, J.F., *Bulgaria under Communist Rule* (New York, 1970); *The Trial of Traicho Kostov and His Group* (Sofia, 1949); Ulam, Adam, *Titoism and the COMINFORM* (Cambridge, MA, 1952).

Mobilization of Bulgarian Women. One important aspect of the economic policies of communist leaders everywhere in the Soviet bloc was their attempt to draw women into the labor force, since rapid industrialization created labor shortages that could be only partially alleviated by peasants displaced from the villages by the collectivization of agriculture. In addition, Marxist ideology proclaimed the equality of the sexes; this became an important consideration everywhere in Eastern Europe since most of these societies had traditionally considered women's role in raising a family more important than working outside the home.

In Bulgaria, the principle of the equality of sexes was included in the Dimitrov constitution of 1947 (*see* Dimitrov, Georgy). In subsequent years, the Bulgarian communist government introduced a whole series of measures to enable women to work outside the home. Abortion was legalized; a network of state-run kindergartens and nursery schools was created; privileges—although at lower pay—were extended to pregnant women and nursing mothers. The law gave leaves for child care as long as a whole year if so desired.

On the other hand, women were not expected to enter the hierarchy of the communist leadership. There were always one, or at the most two, token women in the Politburo and there were some in the Central Committee. But no one comparable to a Margaret Thatcher would emerge in a communist system in Eastern Europe. Ana Pauker of Romania came closest, but she was purged during the anti-Tito hysteria. The two women in Bulgaria who rose to membership in the Politburo were Tsola Dragoicheva, a long-time, radical communist, and Ludmilla Zhivkova, the daughter of the general secretary of the Bulgarian Communist party after 1965. The Central Committee of the party which consisted of 195 full (voting) members, included only twelve women in 1986.

The social changes induced by rapid industrialization did make women enter the labor force in large numbers. It should also be noted that wherever a profession or craft became dominated by women, salaries or wages dropped. Communist policies concerning women's roles were also extended to education. In 1953, over half of the students at the University of Sofia, as well as at the four-year and two-year colleges, were women. In the professions, especially in health care and teaching, women came to be employed in overwhelming numbers.

Bibliography

McIntyre, Robert J., *Bulgaria: Politics, Economics and Society* (London, 1988).

Monarchy in Bulgaria. The monarchy, established at the same time as the long-forgotten Turnovo constitution in 1878, was an institution that created a great deal of controversy. The first tsar (King), Alexander of Battenberg, a young lieutenant of the Prussian Guards in Berlin, lasted for about six months. A Protestant, not an Orthodox Christian, he did not really know how to handle a government that was totally alien to German traditions.

His successor, Ferdinand of Saxe Coburg-Gotha, started off his reign similarly. He was not recognized by the Russian tsar as legitimate Bulgarian king, but he did succeed in retaining his kingship. When a new Russian tsar, Alexander III, was crowned in 1881, after the assassination of his father by the terrorists of the secret organization, called The People's Will, Ferdinand succeeded in placating him by promising to baptize his heir, Boris, as an Orthodox Christian.

Ferdinand ruled Bulgaria through the disastrous Balkan wars and through the equally disastrous World War I. In each of these wars, Bulgaria lost territory and manpower. Ferdinand abdicated on October 3, 1918, in favor of his son, Boris, and left for Germany where he lived for the rest of his life.

Tsar Boris proved himself more skillful and cunning in manipulating the competing parties and movements than was his father. He survived the rule of the Agrarian Union (*see* Agrarian Union), headed by the anti-monarchy Alexander Stamboliiski, and he certainly benefited from the murder of the Agrarian leader in 1923. He also survived an assassination attempt made by communist terrorists who exploded a bomb in Sofia's cathedral in 1925 (*see* Communist Party of Bulgaria).

Boris was a Germanophile who engaged Bulgaria, for the fourth time in the twentieth century, on the losers' side in World War II. He died in 1943, after a visit to Adolf Hitler, and it was rumored that he had been poisoned by the Germans. It is, however, difficult to see the reason for such an action, since Bulgaria was a loyal German ally, and Hitler had no reason to distrust Boris.

Boris' successor was his six-year-old son, Simeon II, named after the most renowned tsar of the early middle ages. A regency of three men took over the rule and managed the country until September 1944. After the communist coup d'etat that took place on September 9, Simeon II left Bulgaria never to return. A communist-orchestrated plebiscite abolished the institution of the monarchy in 1946. After the collapse of the communist system in Bulgaria in 1989, the possibility of inviting Simeon II to take his father's throne was discussed in the Grand National Assembly, but unofficial inquiries elicited a strongly negative response from Simeon II.

Bibliography
Pundeff, Marin, "Bulgaria," in Joseph Held ed. *The Columbia History of Eastern Europe in the Twentieth Century* (New York, 1992), pp. 65-118.

People's Councils. Established by the Fatherland Front (*see* Fatherland Front) under communist domination in 1944 and 1945, the councils were the organs of local government in Bulgaria. Their membership was not elected but was appointed by the local representatives of the Fatherland Front. Originally, the members were to serve three-year terms, but all subsequent elections were rigged, and the councils were simply surrogates of the Communist party. The dissemination of the decisions of the party's Politburo, as well as the decrees issued by the government, was the main task of these councils. They existed on village, district, and county levels; the larger cities had their own councils. They paralleled the hierarchy of party organizations taking their orders through the appropriate members of the nomenklatura. This was a dual system of government in which local initiatives were discouraged. It was also a system which, by its very nature, generated corruption and nepotism. In 1959, an effort was made to decentralize local governments. Some authority was transferred to the local councils, and district councils were restricted in their supervision. Development planning, the evaluation of projects initiated by the local People's Councils, and the production of designs were now the responsibility of local governments. Nevertheless, the central authorities had the final say in all important matters.

Bibliography
Brown, J.F., *Bulgaria under Communist Rule* (New York, 1970).

People's Courts. The Bulgarian court system was established in the late nineteenth-early twentieth centuries. The system was based on the enlightened principle of impartiality of judges and the equality of citizens before the law. Although, during the 1930s, the courts came increasingly under the domination of the government, judicial traditions survived even the fascist episode in Bulgaria. The communists began destroying this system in late 1944 and early 1945 by organizing the so-called People's Courts which were courts in name only. These courts were directed by the ministries of the interior and justice, were run by members of the Communist party's hierarchy, and they meted out sentences predetermined by the communist leaders. The People's Courts were ostensibly created to punish war criminals, but, in time, they became the instruments for the destruction of the previous political system and the judicial murder of prewar and World War II politicians. Most penalties given out by the courts were, in any case, disproportionate to the alleged crimes committed. The People's Courts murdered more than 2,000 former politicians and leading intellectuals, decapitating the system that could stand up against their usurpation of power. The officers of the Bulgarian army were similarly treated, and long prison terms were handed out to "lesser" offenders. The new secret police, created on the pattern and with the help of the Soviet KGB, had been the mainstay of the People's Courts and had often executed those who were sentenced to death.

By late 1946, the work of the People's Courts had been successfully completed, although later trials and executions were still processed through them. The communists' subordination of the entire judicial system to the vagaries of the changing party line seriously affected the prestige of the courts. It also created widespread cynicism among the population. The courts usually handled communists, who broke the law, leniently, but handed out serious sentences against offenders who were not affiliated with the party. Even after the collapse of the communist system, the Bulgarian judges did not acquit themselves creditably. They failed to examine impartially the activities of former communist officials. It will take a long time before the rule of law will again be as respected in Bulgaria as it was at the establishment of the modern judicial system.

A word about the supreme court is due here. This court was created by the Dimitrov constitution of 1946 (*see* Dimitrov Constitution) as the supreme judicial body in the land. This court also operated within the confines of Marxist-Leninist doctrines, and it was actually supervised by the Politburo of the Communist party. Together with twelve regional and ninety-three district courts, the task of the Supreme Court was the safeguarding of "socialist legality," a true oxymoron. The courts, including the supreme court, were composed of professional jurists and lay "judges" as well as lay assessors "elected" by the local Peoples Councils (*see* People's councils). The judges of the supreme court were ostensibly "elected" by the National Assembly, but they were approved by the party's Politburo. The prosecutor general was responsible for the enforcement of laws enacted by parliament and governmental decrees. He was especially responsible for pursuing "crimes against the state," a category that was never clearly defined.

Bibliography
Engelbrekt, Kjell, "Toward the Rule of Law: Bulgaria," *Radio Free Europe Research Reports*. 1.27 (July, 13, 1992), pp.4-9.

Perestroika in Bulgaria. Initially, the Bulgarian communists welcomed Gorbachev and his new policies, breaking with the Stalinist past. The Bulgarian version of reconstruction led to a series of minor changes, especially a much heralded decree that permitted the formation of workers' self-management units in state-owned factories and collective farms. The party went so far as to encourage workers' initiatives in transferring the supervision of the operations of state firms to workers' collectives. The small private sector that had operated mostly underground, forming the ever-present "second economy"—a phenomenon that emerged in every centrally managed East European country in the 1980s—was finally legalized in Bulgaria. It suddenly came to life with such vigor that it surprised everyone. However, all this did not mean a fundamental change in the system still dominated by old-style communist bosses. The state retained for itself the final decisions in the management of the economy through the national bank and the central planning apparatus, the latter of which continued to issue directives and production quotas to industrial enterprises.

By 1985, however, thanks to the development of the educational system, a new generation of technical experts emerged, and its members resented the continuing stream of often unreasonable directives issued by the planning organs. Symptoms of universal skepticism toward utopian ideologies, especially and including Marxism-Leninism, openly appeared. Demands for human rights and individual freedoms, especially the freedom to travel, were increasingly being voiced in society, demanding further fundamental changes. Independent groups appeared with increasing frequency, and a trade union, patterned on the Polish Solidarity movement, was organized. All the ferment had one result. It undermined the moral as well as the physical authority of the "leading force" of Bulgarian society, the Communist party. The aging leaders of the party were unable to understand what was going on and they desperately hung onto their power.

In 1984 and 1985, a serious economic crisis emerged. During the summer and fall of 1985, the party's Central Committee openly criticized corrupt party officials and incompetence among the members of the nomenklatura. In 1986, the younger members of the Politburo, Chudomir Alexandrov, Ognyan Doynov, Georgy Atanasov and Stoyan Markov, divided major responsibilities for running the country among themselves. This palace revolution pushed the old dogmatists aside. They followed the example set by Gorbachev in the Soviet Union. Eventually, they changed the name of their party to the Socialist party. In free elections held in 1990 and 1991, the party polled enough votes to survive, but its ideals of a socialist Bulgaria were rejected.

Bibliography

Engelbrekt, Kjell, "Bulgaria: The Weakening of the Postcommunist Illusions," *Radio Free Europe Research Report* 2.1 (January 1, 1993), pp. 78-83; McIntyre, Robert J., *Bulgaria: Politics, Economics and Society* (London-New York, 1988).

Purges. The Bulgarian Communist party conducted periodic purges of its leaders and membership, paralleling those held in the Soviet Communist party. In late 1944 and early 1945, the prewar political system was destroyed, and its politicians were executed or jailed. An entire generation of political leaders was, thus, eliminated. Military officers came next, and they were followed by Orthodox Christian priests.

In 1949, Bulgarian communists who had spent the war years in the country or in West European states—not in the Soviet Union—were expelled from the party. When the Yugoslav communists established their independence from Moscow and the conflict was fought on both the ideological and diplomatic levels, Bulgarian communists who favored cooperation with Josip Broz Tito were eliminated. In Bulgaria, this list was headed by Traicho Kostov (*see* Kostov, Traicho), who was suspected by Joseph Stalin of favoring Bulgarian national interests over those of the Soviet Union, just as Tito has done, and he had to be eliminated. He was arrested by the secret police and was charged with conspiring with Tito to restore capitalism in Bulgaria. He was also charged with being a British spy and other offenses against the "people." Georgy Dimitrov (*see* Dimitrov, Georgy), himself a KGB agent, former secretary of the COMINTERN, charged Kostov in a violent speech of being a "devious, refined scoundrel." Kostov's show trial was held between December 5-15, 1949. His sentence was, of course, predetermined, and he was executed on December 18. His codefendants received long prison sentences, some of them were executed. The American ambassador, Donald R. Heath, was accused of complicity and participation in Kostov's conspiracy with Tito, and he was declared persona non grata by the Bulgarian government. This was part of the campaign, originating in Stalin's chambers, to discredit the United States in world opinion. In February 1950, the United States broke diplomatic relations with the Bulgarian state.

The Bulgarian Communist party continued to have periodic purges in order to suggest to its members that there was a constant danger of "capitalist" penetration of society and, therefore, there was need for ideological vigilance. The atmosphere was saturated with suspicion and allegations, making it easy for the secret police to recruit informers against those who were suspected of opposition to the regime. In 1962, Vulko Chervenkov (*see* Chervenkov, Vulko) and his successor, Anton Yugov (*see* Yugov, Anton), former prime ministers and secretaries general of the Bulgarian Communist party, were dismissed from all their party—and government posts. With them went Georgy Tsankov, the minister of the interior. Their followers were also purged. Even ordinary party members were not spared. Between 1949 and 1980, more than a quarter of the membership were expelled. Nevertheless, the number of party members continued to increase. By 1986, there were over 800,000 card-carrying communists out of a population of about 9 million.

In 1965, the Bulgarian secret police, in cooperation with the Soviet KGB, "uncovered" an alleged conspiracy for the overthrow of the government. Five high-level officers of the Bulgarian armed forces who had fought against the Germans as guerrillas in World War II, were tried and executed under false charges. In reality, their views conflicted with those of Todor Zhivkov (*see* Zhivkov, Todod), who saw them as his opponents. In the same year, Ivan-Asen Khristov-Georgiev, an infamous radical and KGB agent, responsible for the organization of an attack on the former embassy building of the United States in Sofia in 1963 and again in 1965, was himself arrested and accused of spying for the United States. He was subsequently tried and hanged. Later purges included officers of the secret police, especially those who were involved in torturing prisoners.

Bibliography
The Trial of Fifteen Pastor-Spies (Sofia, 1949); *The Trial of Nikola Petkov, August 5-15, 1947: Record of Judicial Proceedings* (Sofia, 1947); *The Trial of Traicho Kostov and His Group* (Sofia, 1949).

Referendum of 1946. The referendum held in 1946 was an effort by the Bulgarian communist leadership to gain a legal basis for the abolition of the Bulgarian monarchy. Although the outcome of the referendum was a foregone conclusion, and the 99.6 percent vote for abolition was clearly unrealistic, there are good reasons to believe that the people's majority would have approved the measure even if the vote had not been rigged. All the more interesting to note that the communists were not taking any chances.

The king, Simeon II, escaped from the country after the coup d'etat of September 9, 1944, and, at the time of the referendum, was only nine years old. It is highly unlikely that he and his family would have contemplated returning to Bulgaria. The evidence was provided after the collapse of communism, when Simeon II declared his unwillingness to return.

Bibliography

Brown, J.F., *Bulgaria Under Communist Rule* (New York, 1970); Mcintyre, Robert J., *Bulgaria: Politics, Economics and Society* (London-New York, 1988)

Religious Policies. A census conducted in Bulgaria in 1934 showed that 85 percent of the population belonged to the Eastern Orthodox Christian church. Thirteen percent were Muslims and the rest of the people confessed Roman Catholic, various Protestant and Armenian-Gregorian beliefs. Before the Ottoman conquest, there was an Orthodox Bulgarian patriarchate, headed by a primate. After the loss of independence, the Bulgarian Orthodox church became part of an Ottoman religious district, administered from Constantinople (Istanbul) by the Greek patriarch. Greek priests were then installed in Bulgarian churches, and the language of the liturgy became Greek. This situation lasted until 1870, when the Turkish authorities consented to the establishment of an autocephalous Bulgarian exarchate. This was not the equivalent of a patriarchate, but it was at least independent of the patriarch of Istanbul. The area that was put under the jurisdiction of the exarchate included not only Bulgaria proper, but also Macedonia and most of Thrace. However, the patriarch of Istanbul refused to consent to the new arrangements, and the matter was not settled until later in the twentieth century. The cooperation between the exarchate and the Bulgarian state was always close. The clergy were paid by the state and were, for all practical purposes, civil servants.

After the communists took over the government, and forced the church to continue its cooperation with the existing authority, they followed the Bulgarian traditions. The major difference was, of course, that the communists openly professed atheism, and severe persecution of the religious ensued. Clergymen were constantly harassed, many of them were imprisoned or even killed. Others were banished from their parishes. Exarch Stefan was locked up in a monastery because he was considered an opponent of the regime. However, once the first wave of persecutions passed, the communists realized the possible advantages to be derived from church-state cooperation. Thus, they encouraged the reconciliation of the exarchate with the patriarchate of Istanbul and, in 1951, the exarchate was raised to the higher rank of a patriarchate. In 1953, Metropolitan Kiril of Plovdiv was appointed Bulgarian patriarch. The patriarch closely cooperated with the communist government and instructed the clergy not to resist the state authorities. By succeeding in the promotion of the exarchate to a patriarchate, the communists also had their eye on Moscow, since this strengthened the Russian Orthodox church in its struggle for supremacy among the Orthodox Christians with the Patriarchate of Istanbul. Through these efforts the hierarchs of the Bulgarian Orthodox Church became subordinates of the Soviet Union.

Bibliography

Brown, J.F., *Bulgaria under Communist Rule* (New York, 1970); Kjell, Engelbrekt, "Bulgaria's Religious Institutions under Fire," in *Radio Free Europe Research Reports* 1.38 (September 29,1992), pp. 60-66.

Savov, Stefan (1924–). Savov, the son of a businessman-politician, studied at the University of Sofia when, during early in World War II, he was drafted into the Bulgarian army. When the communists took power, Savov's father was arrested and imprisoned. The family was then exiled to Dob-rudja. From his student days on, Savov was an ardent anticommunist. Although he was permitted to complete his studies for a degree in law, he was arrested and sent to a concentration camp for his views. After his release, he worked in construction as a laborer for more than ten years. After that, he worked as a translator of Spanish language works.

In 1990, Savov became involved in politics. His impeccable anticommunist credentials led him to become the president of the Democratic party. In the first free elections held, he was sent to parliament by the voters as a deputy where he became deputy chairman of the assembly's Foreign Relations Committee. In 1991, he was elected president of the Bulgarian parliament. Savov, a founding member of the Democratic party, was elected president of the Union of Democratic Forces in 1992, and the leader of its parliamentary caucus.

Bibliography

Kjell, Engelbrekt, "Bulgaria: Union of Democratic Forces Closes Ranks," in *Radio Free Europe Research Report* 2.16 (April 16, 1993), pp. 10-13.

Trade Policies. In 1949, Bulgaria became a charter member of the CMEA or COMECON, an organization created by the Soviet Union. Its purpose was to become a counterpart of the European Common Market. However, the CMEA differed from the latter in that its members had bilateral treaties with the Soviet Union but not with each other. Various economic tasks were distributed not through agreements but through Soviet commands. By 1962, 82 percent of Bulgaria's foreign trade was flowing into the economies of CMEA members, the bulk of this volume going to the Soviet Union. Yet, Bulgaria's major produce, agriculture, was in serious decline; its industrial goods were of low quality. Thus, they could be sold only in the Soviet bloc.

The state organs in Bulgaria traditionally had a monopoly over foreign trade long before the communist conquest of power. In fact, the state institute conducting foreign trade before and during World War II was simply taken over when the communists assumed authority. There was some private trade, especially in agricultural products during the war, but this was now completely eliminated. The Bulgarian Agricultural Bank, also established during the old regime, and a network of credit-cooperatives financed by it, were now state agencies buying up all agricultural products at fixed prices, determined by the State Planning Office. Before World War II, Bulgaria borrowed heavily from French financial institutions. In 1944, Yugoslavia and Greece, as well as the Soviet Union, would not demand heavy reparations from a fellow People's Democracy. It was also very unlikely that Bulgaria would receive help from the Western powers, and help from the Soviet Union obviously depended upon the behavior of the Bulgarians in the post-World War II world.

Dependence on Nazi Germany which was heavy during the war, was now exchanged by dependence on the Soviet Union. In 1944 and 1945, the Soviet Union demanded higher levels of exports than Germany had ever done, and in 1945, almost the entire foreign trade of Bulgaria went to the Soviet Union. Soviet-Bulgarian trade thereafter never sank below 65 percent of the total trade. The great economic crisis that hit Bulgaria at the end of the 1980s was the result of the sudden cessation of Soviet-Bulgarian trade, itself the result of the collapse of the Soviet economy. This was especially serious in energy; since the trade in Soviet oil slowed down to a very low level, electric energy production faced a shut-down. Only Western help in propping up Bulgaria's foreign trade could turn the situation around quickly, but such help has been slow in reaching Bulgaria. At the present time, the new government is trying to rebuild its foreign trade with the West, but it does not have the hard currency necessary for such a change.

Bibliography

McIntyre, Robert J., *Bulgaria: Politics, Economics and Society* (London, 1988).

Union of Democratic Forces. Formed on December 7, 1989, the purpose of this political movement was the coordination of the activities of all groups that were opposed to the communist monopoly of power. The number of organizations that joined the Union of Democratic Forces (UDF) increased rapidly. By the end of 1989, a resurrected Social Democratic party, the Federation of Independent Student Associations, and many other such groups joined the UDF. In January 1990, the UDF consisted of sixteen organizations under the direction of a coordinating council, whose chairman, Zhelu Zhelev, was a Marxist philosopher at the University of Sofia. Zhelev had been in trouble with the communist authorities many times before, since his unorthodox views did not correspond to those of the dogmatic old guard of the party. Since the early 1960s, Zhelev had been constantly under suspicion for political deviation. Under his leadership, the Union of Democratic Forces began the peaceful dismantling of the communist system.

The UDF also began preparations to change the Bulgarian economy into a market-oriented system. The first step the UDF took was to arrange for a meeting with the communist reformists at a roundtable discussion. By then, the reformists had changed the name of the Communist party to the Socialist party, and they did everything possible to distance themselves from the discredited policies of their predecessors. But the "new" Socialist party was unwilling to cut its umbilical cord to its predecessor's economic institutions. These were typified by the huge party headquarters that continued to fly the red flag with the sickle and the hammer of the old party.

The bureaucracy established during the communist supremacy also remained in place. In addition, the national radio network and the television broadcasting station remained in communist hands. The negotiations between the reform communists (now socialists) dragged on for months. Agreement was finally reached on issues such as the availability of newsprint for all newspapers, access to national radio and television by the opposition, the basic principles of a future pluralistic, democratic system of government, and the procedures for holding elections for a Grand National Assembly.

The first task of the assembly was to enact a new constitution for Bulgaria. The elections were held on June 10, 1990; June 17, 1990, was reserved for the runoff elections. The elections were free for the first time since 1946. The Socialist party, thanks to its successful use of the media, received 47.15 percent of the total votes cast, a surprisingly large percentage. This vote came largely from the rural areas where the socialists were strong. The vote gave the socialists 211 seats in the 400-seat parliament. Thirty-nine other parties shared the rest of the votes, but only three of them received a meaningful number of deputies. The Union of Democratic Forces gained 144 seats; the Turkish Movement for Rights and Freedom received twenty-three. The Agrarian Union (*see* Agrarian Union) totally discredited during the communist era, received only sixteen mandates.

The most vocal critics of the results were the students of Sofia University who went on strike. They charged that the communists maintained a monopoly over the media and other means of communications and that they were intent on covering up their crimes. The students demanded that Petar Mladenov, the new prime minister, resign. Mladenov bowed to the demand and gave up the premiership. On August 1, the socialists agreed to the election of Zhelev as president of Bulgaria.

On August 12, the Socialist party's headquarters—formerly the headquarters of the Communist party—in Sofia were set on fire by demonstrators. The protesters also forced the removal of the embalmed corps of Georgy Dimitrov from its mausoleum erected in Skanderbeu square in the center of Sofia. President Zhelev worked hard to lessen tensions and he succeeded to some extent. In October 1991, new elections were held. The Union of Democratic Forces came out the strongest party with 110 parliamentary deputies; the Socialist party received 106 mandates; and the Agrarian Union and the Movement for Rights and Freedom shared the rest.

Bibliography
Perry, Duncan M., "Bulgaria: A New Constitution and Free Elections," *Radio Free Europe Research Reports* 1.1 (January 3, 1992), pp. 78-82.

Yugov, Anton (1904–). Yugov joined the Bulgarian Communist party when he was thirty-four years old. In 1944, he was named minister of the interior in the Fatherland Front government (*see* Fatherland Front), and he proved himself as ruthless a pursuer of the party's instructions as any communist leader in Eastern Europe. As a local communist leader, however, Yugov fell out of grace following the Traicho Kostov trial (*see* Kostov, Traicho). Shortly afterward he made it back and was appointed deputy prime minister. In 1950-1951, he was made minister of industry, and the following year he was appointed to head the ministry responsible for the rapid development of heavy industry. Yugov remained a member of the Politburo of the Communist party throughout this period.

In May 1953, riots among tobacco workers in the city of Plovdiv broke out. Yugov was dispatched to deal with the crisis. Although he had been born in Macedonia, he had lived most of his adult life in Plovdiv, and he had his power base in that city. In fact, he represented the city in the Bulgarian National Assembly. Even more opportune was the fact that, during World War II, Yugov himself was a tobacco worker and had close connections with the trade union movement in that city. The situation presented him with the opportunity to return to the pinnacle of power which he had lost when Vulko Chervenkov (*see* Chervenkov, Vulko) assumed the general secretary's post in 1950. He was successful in calming the workers and ending the disturbances. Nevertheless, he had eight of the leaders of the rioters executed.

Yugov then returned triumphantly to Sofia and, taking advantage of Nikita Khrushchev's genuine dislike of Vulko Chervenkov, he gained the Soviet leader's support. He was soon back in power. Upon Khrushchev's "advice," Chervenkov, Yugov, and Todor Zhivkov (*see* Zhivkov, Todor) formed a "collective leadership" based on the Soviet example. After Khrushchev's denunciation of Joseph Stalin's crimes at the Twentieth Congress of the Soviet Communist party, Yugov himself denounced Bulgaria's "little Stalin, Chervenkov." Nevertheless, Chervenkov was successful in rallying his supporters following the Hungarian Revolution of 1956, an event that shook the communist world to its foundations. Chervenkov was able to reimpose strict censorship and discipline over the restive Bulgarian intellectuals.

In March 1957, the post of general secretary of the Communist party, held by Chervenkov, was abolished. In its place, the Central Committee "elected" a secretariat of three persons and excluded Yugov from it. Yet he continued as a full (voting) member of the party's Politburo. In April 1957, Chervenkov finally resigned the premiership, but he retained his post in the party. Yugov was then named president of the Bulgarian state.

Khrushchev soon grew tired of the squabbles among the Bulgarian party leaders. By 1962, Bulgaria had come through the experiment with the "great leap forward," an effort at accelerated industrialization based on the workers' "initiatives," which proved to be a complete failure.

In November 1962, Todor Zhivkov assumed the leadership of the Bulgarian state and the Communist party. He dismissed both Chervenkov and Yugov as well as their supporters from the various party organs. They were dropped from the Central Committee, and Chervenkov was expelled from the Communist party altogether. In an open meeting of the leadership, Zhivkov denounced Yugov's many crimes and ridiculed him for his alleged cowardice during World War II. He painted an all-too vivid picture of the cruelty with which Yugov had treated innocent party members during the purges. Finally, Zhivkov had Yugov expelled from the Bulgarian Communist party without, however, giving him the ultimate punishment, that which Yugov had meted out so freely in the past to the party's real or imagined opponents.

Bibliography
Brown, J.F., *Bulgaria Under Communist Rule* (New York, 1970).

Zhivkov, Todor (1911–). Zhivkov was born in the village of Pravets, north of Sofia. He became an apprentice printer in his late teens and joined the Bulgarian Communist party in 1932. During World War II, he provided the link between the underground leadership of the local party workers and the communist guerrillas led by Dobri Dzhurov, who were active in the Pravets region. Legend had it that Zhivkov was the leader of the communist coup d'etat in September 1944; however, in 1989, it became clear that the legend was nothing but fiction. After the coup, Zhivkov entered Sofia with the guerrillas and immediately organized them as the new police force of the nation. They carried out murder on a large scale, eliminating all possible enemies of their party.

Zhivkov was soon rewarded for his "service to the people." He was made a candidate (nonvoting) member of the party's Central Committee in 1945. In 1948, he was promoted to regular (voting) membership in that organ. Two years later, he was appointed as a junior member of the Politburo and secretary to the Central Committee. He also worked as first secretary to the party's organization in the capital city of Sofia. In 1954, Zhivkov became secretary general to the Communist party. In April 1956, he formulated the so-called April line, which was a copy of the internal policies introduced in the Soviet Union by Nikita Khrushchev. In 1962, Zhivkov combined his post of general secretary with that of prime minister, taking control of both government and party organizations. In 1971, Zhivkov was instrumental in introducing a new constitution for Bulgaria, which created a State Council as the highest policy-making body. Zhivkov, as head of state, was also head of the State Council. He withdrew from the everyday running of the government and the party and concerned himself with policy formulation.

The Council of Ministers was charged with carrying out Zhivkov's policies, introduced through the State Council. Zhivkov was intent on making Bulgaria an inseparable ally of the Soviet Union. He often declared that the two countries were sharing a common circulation system. He did succeed in turning his country into a miniature replica of the Soviet Union. However, Zhivkov did not count on events taking a different turn than he had envisaged. When the Soviet economy began to deteriorate, Bulgaria also began to have economic difficulties. Zhivkov's regime borrowed heavily from Western banks and governments, using the funds to subsidize the production of substandard goods that could be sold only to the Soviet Bloc. His government also began trafficking in the illegal drug trade or, at least, provided transit for drug dealers for a fee. It also sponsored international terrorism. There were unconfirmed and unprovable reports that Zhivkov offered to incorporate Bulgaria into the Soviet Union as the sixteenth Soviet republic. If he made such an offer, it was not accepted. Zhivkov also maintained close relations with the murderous communist dictator Nicolae Ceausescu and his clan in Romania. Copying the dynastic policies of his Romanian friend, Zhivkov made his daughter, Ludmilla, a member of the party's Central Committee and appointed her minister of education. She was also made to serve as the president of the Committee on Culture which was responsible for education and propaganda.

Zhivkov remained in power for nearly thirty-five years. He was finally removed on November 10, 1989, by reform-communists who were also following the Soviet line, this time the one laid down by Mikhail Gorbachev. His legacy includes an economically and morally bankrupt society, a country whose rebuilding will take many years—if not decades.

Bibliography

Brown, J.F. *The New Eastern Europe: The Khrushchev Era and After* (New York, 1966); McIntyre, Robert J., *Bulgaria: Politics, Economics and Society* (London, 1988); Staar, Richard F., *The Communist Regimes of Eastern Europe* (Stanford, CA., 1989).

ZVENO (LINK). This small, politically active group in the 1930s gathered around a well-known Bulgarian intellectual, Dimo Kazasov. They called their organization Zveno, or Link, because their aim was to create conditions for greater national unity. They wanted to remain outside or, rather, above politics because the unity they envisaged was to be above political parties. They attracted several intellectual, political, and military leaders into their ranks. Zveno declared itself to have been alienated from the sterile struggles that characterized Bulgarian politics during the interwar years and wanted to solve what its members considered the perpetual moral and economic crisis of their fatherland. There were some strong supporters for Zveno's ideals among the higher echelons of Bulgaria's Military League. The league took advantage of the many cabinet crises and carried out a military coup d'etat on May 9, 1934, and installed a new government under the premiership of Kimon Georgiev. The real organizer of the coup, Damian Velchev, a member of the Zveno leadership, remained in the background. Zveno survived into the 1940s, but it never again played a prominent role in Bulgarian society. In 1948, it was merged into the Communist party.

Bibliography

Pundeff, Marin, "Bulgaria," in Joseph Held, ed. *The Columbia History of Eastern Europe in the Twentieth Century* (New York, 1992); Oren, Nissan, *Bulgarian Communism: The Road to Power, 1934–1944* (New York 1971).

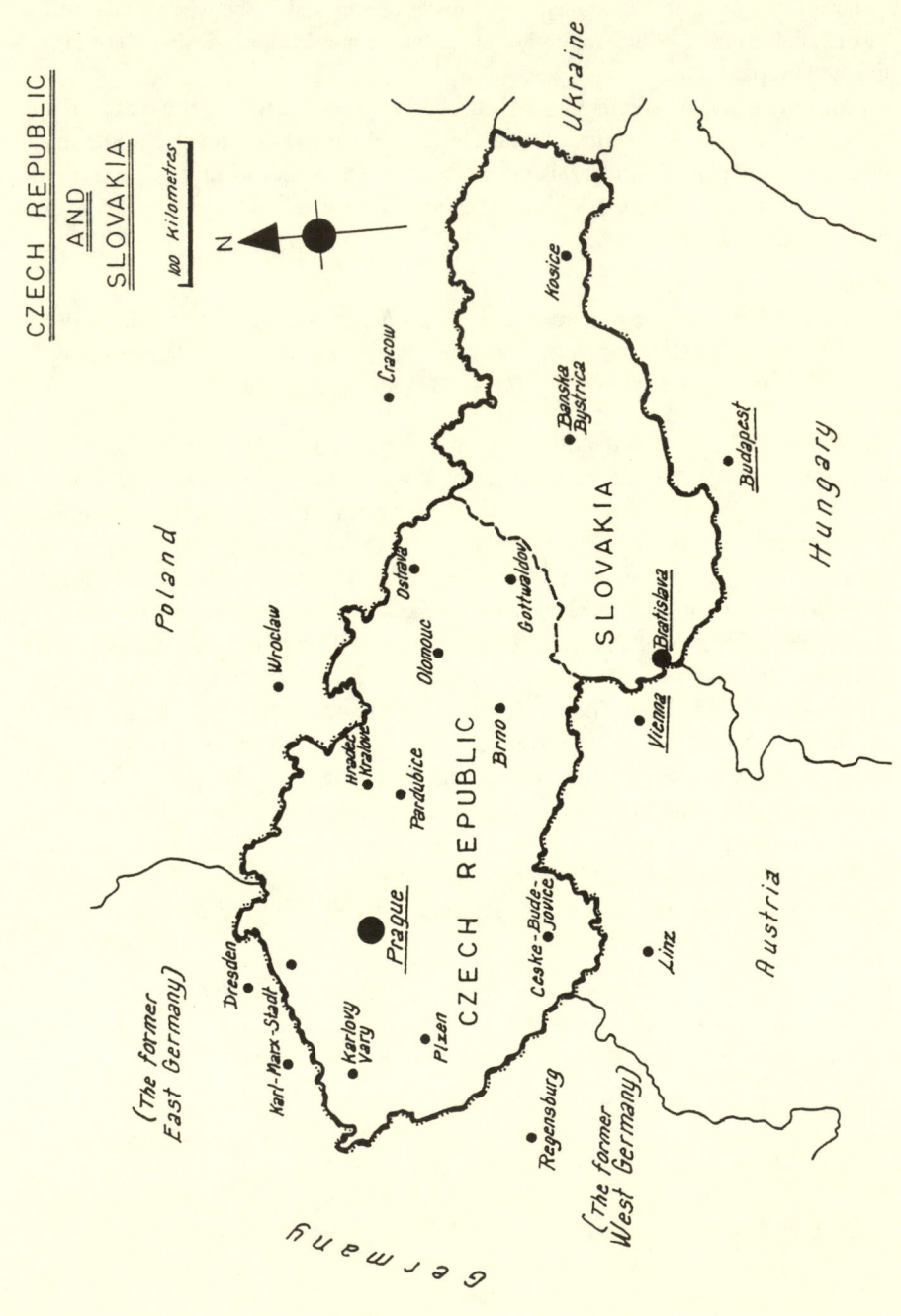

CZECHOSLOVAKIA

General Information. *Area:* 48.379 square miles (127,686 square kilometers). *Population:* 15.5 million. *Percentage of urban dwellers:* 66 percent. *Rural population:* 34 percent. *GNP:* 112,036 billion Czechoslovak crowns. *Distribution of the work force:* 64 percent in industry and trade, 14 percent in agriculture. *Length of railway network:* 13,130 kilometers of which 3,307 kilometers are electrified. *Length of road network:* 74,891 kilometers. *Currency:* Czechoslovak crowns. (Koruna) *Ethnicity:* 65 percent Czech, 30 percent Slovak, five percent Hungarian, scattered groups of Germans, Ruthenians and Gypsies. *Communist party membership:* 1,700,000 in 1988. *Capital cities:* Prague (Praha) for the Czech lands, and Bratislava for Slovakia.

Bibliography

Korbel, Joseph, *Twentieth Century Czechoslovakia: The Meanings of its History* (New York, 1977); Wolchick, Sharon, *Czechoslovakia: Politics, Economics and Society in the Transition to Post-Communist Rule* (London, 1991).

CHRONOLOGY

1944   The American army reached the borders and marched into Czechoslovakia. However, according to Allied agreements, it withdrew and permitted the Soviet army to occupy the country.

1945   *April.* Klement Gottwald, head of the Czechoslovak Communist party and deputy prime minister, declared that the restored state would be based on the equality of Czechs and Slovaks.

June. Eduard Benes, the president of Czechoslovakia, declared that the German and Hungarian minorities were to be expelled from the country. He thus initiated the first "ethnic cleansing" in Eastern Europe outside the Soviet Union and Nazi Germany.

1946   *February.* The Hungarian government under duress agreed to the exchange of Hungarians in Czechoslovakia and Slovaks in Hungary on a "voluntary" basis.

May. In general elections, the Czechoslovak Communist party received 38 percent of the votes cast and became the largest party in the state.

1948   *February.* Klement Gottwald was named prime minister. His government was dominated by communist ministers. The Stalinization of Czechoslovakia began.

March. All industrial firms, banks and trade were nationalized. No compensation was paid to their owners. All estates of more than fifty hectares were confiscated.

June. The forced merger of the Czechoslovak Social Democratic party with the Communist party eliminated possible competition for the communists.

1949   *January.* Czechoslovakia joined with five other East European countries and the Soviet Union in establishing the Council of Mutual Economic Assistance (COMECON).

1952   *November.* The show trial of Rudolf Slansky and Vladimir Clementis took place. They were charged with a variety of "crimes," including right-wing nationalism and Titoism. Both Slansky and Clementis were found guilty, sentenced to death, and executed. A whole series of other trials followed, and death sentences and long prison terms were given to lesser officials of the Communist party and government.

1955   *May.* Czechoslovakia signed the Warsaw Pact Treaty, subordinating its armed forces to the command of Soviet generals.

1968   *January.* Antonyn Novotny, the head of the Czechoslovak Communist party, was ousted from the leadership. He was succeeded by Alexander Dubcek, a reform-minded communist from Slovakia.

March. Novotny was removed from the presidency of the state, a position he had held since his ouster as party leader in January.

April. The new Czechoslovak cabinet included Otto Cernik as prime minister, assisted by the reform economist Ota Sik. The foreign minister was Jiry Hajek. The cabinet was decidedly reformist.

June. Seventy intellectuals issued an open letter to the Czechoslovak Communist party entitled "Two Thousand Words," which severely criticized the Stalinist policies of the past and demanded fundamental reforms.

August. The armies of five Warsaw Pact nations invaded Czechoslovakia in order to put an end to the "Prague Spring," the reforms pursued by the Czechoslovak Communist party. Gustav Husak, an old-line Slovak communist was placed at the head of the government. Dubcek and his followers, although not officially ousted, were relegated into oblivion. Later, many of them were tried on trumped-up charges and were imprisoned.

September. Warsaw Pact troops left Prague.

October. A two-state federation of the Czech lands and Slovakia was signed into law by Czechoslovak president Ludvik Svoboda. A Slovak Socialist republic was proclaimed in Bratislava.

1969 *April.* Alexander Dubcek was officially replaced by Gustav Husak as the head of the Czechoslovak Communist party.

September. Dubcek was deprived of his membership in the Czechoslovak Politburo.

October. Dubcek was ousted from the presidency of parliament.

1970 *June.* Dubcek was expelled from the Czechoslovak Communist party. He was named head of a forestry office in Slovakia.

1975 *August.* The Czechoslovak government of Gustav Husak signed the Helsinki Accord guaranteeing civil rights, and also the borders of the signatory states.

1976 *June.* Delegates of the Czechoslovak Communist party strongly supported Moscow's demand for a condemnation of the Chinese Communist party. The bid was resisted and eventually rejected by Western Communist parties.

1977 *January.* Two-hundred and fifty-seven Czechoslovak intellectuals issued what was to become known as Charter 77. They demanded the reestablishment of human rights in the country. The government and the Communist party condemned the document as anti-socialist.

1983 *January.* At the Prague meeting of the Warsaw Pact, an offer was made to NATO for a nonaggression treaty.

October. New missile bases were established in Czechoslovakia by the Soviet Union.

1984 *May.* Czechoslovakia joined the Soviet Union in boycotting the Olympic Games in Los Angeles in retaliation for the US boycott of the Moscow Olympics.

1985 *April.* Czechoslovakia joined with other Warsaw Pact members in signing a ten-year extension of the Pact.

1986 *September.* The Stalinist Czechoslovak party leaders ordered the arrest of the jazz section of the Czechoslovak Musicians Union. They were accused of performing antistate music.

1987 The discredited first party secretary, Gustav Husak, was replaced by a younger communist, Milos Jakes, as the new head of the Czechoslovak Communist party.

1988 *October.* The entire Czechoslovak government, headed by premier Lubomir Strougal, resigned. His replacement, Ladislav Adamec, was expected to slow down the changes pursued by Strougal.

1989 *February.* Most Czechoslovak artists demanded in a manifesto that the state release all political prisoners. Jakes, head of the still Stalinist Czechoslovak Communist party, refused to negotiate with so-called antistate groups. The official communist newspaper condemned playwright Vaclav Havel as a subversive.

May. Vaclav Havel was released from prison four months ahead of the end of his sentence for alleged subversion.

June. The daily paper of the Czechoslovak Communist party applauded the shooting of advocates of democracy in Tiannanmen Square in Beijing.

August. The official Czechoslovak radio declared that Lech Walesa, the head of Poland's Solidarity trade union, represented a danger to socialism everywhere.

November. The one-party dictatorship of the communists had ended in Czechoslovakia. In the presidential elections held in December, Vaclav Havel was elected president.

1990 *January.* President Havel declared amnesty for a large number of prisoners. In consequence, the Skoda armament factory had to stop production since most of its workers were prisoners. Of the total of 120 new parliamentary deputies, only 9 communists were elected to the Czechoslovak parliament.

February. Discussions with Radio Free Europe resulted in the establishment of the first broadcasting studio in a former communist country. The withdrawal of the troops of the Soviet army from Czechoslovakia began.

March. The name of the Czechoslovak state was changed to the hyphenated Czecho-Slovakia.

June. In the first free elections held in more than four decades, the Czech Civic Forum and its Slovak counterpart, Public Against Violence, won 170 seats in a parliament of 300 deputies. The communists won 47 seats.

August. The Skoda and Volkswagen factories established a joint automobile production plant in the Czech lands.

October. The Slovak parliament declared the Slovak language the official language of the state. Minorities will be allowed the use of their own language where they constitute 20 percent of the population.

December. The Czecho-Slovak federal parliament approved power sharing between the federal government and the Slovak and Czech republics.

1991 *February.* Talks about the remaking of the Czecho-Slovak state (the name was hyphenated by then)in the shape of a confederation were rejected by all Czech leaders.

April: The Christian Democratic Movement for Slovakia proposed that a new federal constitution be preceded by a state treaty between the Czech and Slovak republics.

June. At a meeting of republican representatives, an agreement was reached. Accordingly, the agreement between the two republics was to be an intrastate document. The actual treaty was to be drafted by the joint meeting of the Czech and Slovak National Councils. But the agreement was questioned immediately by both parties.

July. President Havel recommended that a referendum be held on the form of the Czecho-Slovak state.

September. The two National Councils met in Bratislava but were unable to agree on a new state treaty. Slovak nationalists, led by Vladimir Meciar, a former communist official began arguing for an independent Slovakia.

November. President Havel's recommendation of constitutional changes strengthening the hand of the federal government was rejected by parliament.

1992 *January.* A new law was introduced in the federal parliament, making the promotion of fascism or communism a crime. President Havel criticized the proposed law as injurious to human rights. A new electoral law was also introduced. It set a minimum threshold of 5 percent of the votes gained by any party for parliamentary representation. The law limited the time for campaigning to twenty-three days and gave any party with 10,000 members or current parliamentary representation the right to set up candidates. The Prime minister of Slovakia, Jan Carnogursky, declared that Slovakia's aim was to achieve independence like other European nations.

February. Parliament ordered the opening of police files on individual citizens.

March. The Slovak parliament rejected a proposal for a proclamation of sovereignty, but more and more signs pointed to just such a development. For instance, a new Czech foreign ministry was created, and Slovak parties spoke more and more openly of independence.

April. A list containing the names of suspected secret police agents was published for the use of parliamentary deputies only. The list included 262 Czech journalists and 114 Slovak newspapermen. The list was published by a Prague newspaper.

May. The Slovak parliament once again failed to approve a proposal for sovereignty.

June. The Civic Democratic party, led by Vaclav Klaus, won a majority of the votes in the Czech lands, while in Slovakia, the Movement for a Democratic Slovakia, led by Vladimir Meciar, triumphed. The president asked Klaus to form a new federal government. Meciar immediately contested the decision. In talks between Meciar and Havel, it became clear that the two sides were far apart concerning the form of the state.

July. Discussions between Klaus and Meciar led nowhere. It became clear that Slovak political leaders wanted a confederation or independence for their state. Twelve of the fourteen new members of the Slovak cabinet were chosen from Meciar's party. The nationalists in the party ignored the demands of minorities, especially those of the large Magyar group, for autonomy. The Czech parliament began discussions on a new constitution.

August. Prime ministers of the Czech and Slovak republics agreed to submit a proposal to the federal parliament for the break up of the federation.

September. At a meeting held in Brno, the prime ministers of the Czech and Slovak republics agreed that the affiliation of the two states would come to an end on January 1 1993, and on that day Slovakia would become an independent country. Alexander Dubcek had been involved in an automobile accident, and his condition was critical. A new Slovak constitution was signed into law. It did not contain provisions for the protection of minority rights.

October. Slovakia and the Czech Republic agreed to maintain a customs union after the separation.

November. The two republics agreed to maintain a common currency. However, since the Slovak budget had a huge deficit, this decision was soon rescinded. Alexander Dubcek succumbed to his injuries and died. Vaclav Havel, after declaring that he would not preside over the dissolution of Czechoslovakia, announced that he would be a candidate for the presidency of the Czech Republic after the separation. The federal parliament approved a law on the division of the assets of Slovakia and the Czech lands. A series of treaties were signed by the two governments to regulate postseparation relations. The Czech parliament approved the law on separation.

December. The Czech parliament was deeply divided over the new constitution.

1993   *January.* The new independent states of Slovakia and the Czech Republic began their separate existence. Slovakia immediately ran into difficulties over its budget and its relations with Hungary. The Hungarians demanded the abandonment of the building of the Gabcikovo-Bos, Nagymaros dam on the Danube river, a project forced on Hungary by the Soviet Union in 1977.

March. A new agreement to become effective on March 31, signed by Hungary, Poland, and predissolution Czecho-Slovakia, at the Hungarian town of Visegrad (hence the name, Visegrad Triangle) establishes a free-trade zone composed of the three countries by 2001. Discussions over the person of the new president and the membership in the senate to be formed in the Czech lands led to divisions. However, the parties eventually agreed to the election of Havel as president. In Slovakia, the former communist Meciar declared that the state would interfere with freedom of expression if journalists "besmirch his reputation."

April. The opposition parties in the Czech parliament were unable to agree on a common basis to confront the government. Slovakia experienced a serious crisis. The foreign minister, Milan Knazko, was dismissed after he criticized Meciar's handling of government affairs. Minister of economics Ludovit Cernak resigned. Some members of the cabinet disagreed with the prime minister in public. Meciar himself was increasingly on the defensive. Slovak relations with the Czech lands also deteriorated. The division of former federal assets created bitter disputes.

May. Church-state relations in the Czech lands were embittered by the controversy over a law on the restitution of the church properties confiscated by the communist authorities. The Czech ministry of labor reported that unemployment in the country fell below 3 percent, the lowest rate in Eastern Europe. After a ban imposed on livestock deliveries by the European Community on most East European countries, because of alleged danger of infectious animal diseases, the Czech lands, Slovakia, Hungary, and Poland, followed by Bulgaria, closed their borders to imports of animal origin from Western Europe.

June. Discussions between Slovak and Czech negotiators over the division of former federal properties continued. Although Slovakia sent a contingent of 418 soldiers to Croatia as part of the UN peacekeeping force, the Slovak government refused to participate in a similar mission in Bosnia-Herzegovina. Meciar, in comments to the German magazine Der Spiegel, suggested that the fact that Czech energy supplies pass through Slovakia might induce the Czech government to share some of its assets, such as gold and other property, with the Slovak state. He added that the Czech economy would collapse in ten days if energy supplies were disrupted. The Czech government demanded an explanation from Meciar. The Slovak prime minister announced, during a visit to Washington, D.C., that his country intends to increase arms production to help the conversion of the arms industry to regular products.

Agreement of Christmas, 1943. At the end of December 1943, before the beginning of the Slovak uprising against German domination, the underground organization in Slovakia, including the Slovak Communist party (largely independent from the Czech party during World War II), concluded an agreement for the organization of future political alignments after the war. The agreement stipulated that the Slovak democratic parties would have a considerable measure of autonomy in the republic. The agreement was later nullified by the Moscow-directed Communist party.

Bibliography

Toma, Peter, A., "The Communist Party of Czechoslovakia," in Stephen Fischer-Galati, ed. *The Communist Parties of Eastern Europe* (New York, 1979).

Bilak, Vasil (1917–). Bilak has been a member of the leadership of the Czechoslovak Communist party in one position or another after 1950. In 1954, he became a candidate (nonvoting) member of the party's Central Committee. An old-guard, dogmatic communist, he was the first secretary of the Slovak Communist party between January and September 1968, and he was a leading party member who stressed "normalization" after the invasion of the country by the Warsaw Pact forces. In January 1969, he was appointed as a member of the presidium (Politburo) of the Czechoslovak Communist party. He was eventually ousted from power in 1988.

Bibliography

Kusin, Vladimir, *From Dubcek to Charter 77: A Study of "Normalization" in Czechoslovakia, 1968–1978* (New York, 1978).

Bridge Episode. Between 1945 and 1948, the democratic parties of Czechoslovakia still believed that it was possible to establish a democratic and independent Czechoslovakia, and that such a state could exist side-by-side with the Soviet Union of Joseph Stalin. They presumed that the country would be a loyal ally of the Soviet Union, its big Slavic brother, but this would not mean a break with Western contacts and the general historical traditions of the Czech and Slovak peoples. According to President Eduard Benes, who was one of the major inventors of this idea, a rebuilt Czechoslovakia would be a bridge between East and West. This would have required the continuous cooperation between the Western Allies and the Soviet Union. In addition, the Czechoslovak Communist party would have had to play the role of a democratic party, participating in the parliamentary life of the country. In the elections of 1946, the Communist party gained 37.9 percent of all the votes cast, becoming the strongest party in the reconstituted Czechoslovak state. The following year, the Council of Ministers decided unanimously (with the participation of the communist members) to join the European Recovery Program, the Marshall Plan. However, swift Soviet intervention forced Czechoslovakia to withdraw from the preparatory conference held in Paris. This was the signal that the "bridge plan" was an illusion.

Bibliography

Ulc, Otto, "The Communist Party of Czechoslovakia," *East European Quarterly*, (June, 1972); Zinner, Paul E., *Communist Strategy and Tactics in Czechoslovakia, 1918–1948* (New York, 1963).

Charter 77. A combination of a statement, a petition, and a declaration, the Charter 77 document was intended to be delivered to the Czechoslovak government and party leadership in 1977. It was signed by 243 persons, mostly intellectuals. One of them withdrew his signature before the intended submission. The document began by citing the covenant of the United Nations and the Helsinki Accord on human rights. Its main assertion was that the human rights guaranteed by the UN charter and the Helsinki Accord constituted the framework of civilized life in the twentieth century. Although Czechoslovakia signed both documents, its government observed their provisions only on paper.

The Charter 77 document, in large part, detailed the violations of human rights by the communist government of Czechoslovakia. It referred to violations of the freedom of expression, and the right to an education, of freedom of information, and of religious convictions. It stated that the Marxist-Leninist doctrine of the leading role of the Communist party was at the root of most violations of human rights. There were specific charges against the police. The authors also stressed the fact that the government placed obstacles in the way of travel by the citizens and forbade them to leave the country.

The Charter 77 document defined its signatories as a group of people of different faiths, opinions, and convictions, who felt it to be their obligation to bring attention to the violations against the human rights of the Czech and Slovak peoples. The signers also declared that they were not engaging in any oppositional activity against the regime. Similarly, they were not interested in participating in politics or of proposing any economic or social reforms. They were interested only in expressing their opinions in areas of civic duty: They were pointing out infringements on individual human rights; they were proposing ways to correct abuses; they were working for the strengthening of the observation of human rights; and they offered their mediation between violators and victims.

The three major spokesmen for Charter 77 were Professor Jan Patocka, Vaclav Havel (*see* Havel, Vaclav), and Jiry Hajek (*see* Hajek, Jiry), a former communist minister of foreign affairs. As his case illustrated, the members of Charter 77 were a mixed group indeed. They were mostly intellectuals who supported Alexander Dubcek's efforts at reform in 1968 (*see* Dubcek, Alexander). They stressed the differences between Czechoslovak culture and that of the Soviet Union. They were also an alternate source of information contradicting official propaganda coming from the Communist party's agitprop department.

Charter 77 was instrumental in the establishment of a Committee for the Defense of the Unjustly Accused, another group that tried to establish the rule of law in the country. The members of both the Public against Violence in Slovakia and Charter 77 were undoubtedly brave people, and the persecution that they suffered did not discourage them. Yet the authorities succeeded in keeping both groups small, and only a relatively few people had the courage to join them aside from the original members.

One drawback for the Charter 77 group was the fact that, as intellectuals, they had few contacts with ordinary people. Nevertheless, they evoked wide responses throughout Eastern Europe. Prominent intellectuals signed the charter's call for respect for basic human rights. In Poland and Hungary, in particular, the document created a sense of a common struggle against the communist tyranny. By 1987, over 2,500 people had signed the Charter 77 document. Their influence on public opinion in their own countries was much greater than their numbers would indicate. Chartists played a leading role in the establishment of the Czech Civic Forum, which developed into a national liberation movement, ending communist rule in Czechoslovakia.

Bibliography
Skilling, Gordon, *Charter 77 and Human Rights in Czechoslovakia* (Boston, 1981).

Civic Forum and Public Against Violence. When the communist system was about to collapse in Czechoslovakia, following a brutal police attack on peaceful demonstrators in November 1989, there emerged an umbrella organization, really a national liberation movement, that was to negotiate with the government about a peaceful transformation from communist to democratic rule. This organization called itself the Civic Forum. Its counterpart in Slovakia called itself the Public against Violence. As with similar organizations in Hungary and Poland, the two groups in Czechoslovakia were not political parties, but movements. As such, they were uniquely suited to negotiate not only the ending of the communist regime, but also the new institutions that were to replace the authoritarian ones. They were not representing specific social strata as genuine political parties do in the West, and therefore they had great difficulty in governing their countries when they eventually came into power.

Most leaders of the Civic Forum and the Public against Violence were greatly surprised at the speed with which the communist system collapsed. Suddenly it was proven beyond a doubt that only brute Soviet force had kept the communist regimes in power, and once this force was made inactive by Mikhail Gorbachev, the leaders had nowhere to turn for support. Milos Jakes (*see* Jakes, Milos) resigned together with his cabinet. The privileged position of the Communist party and its nomenklatura ended. The first noncommunist government in more than four decades came into existence. Vaclav Havel (*see* Havel, Vaclav), a spokesman for Charter 77, and a prominent playwright, was elected president of the republic in December 1989. The Velvet Revolution, inducing no violence on the part of the opposition to the communist regime, was accomplished.

The name of the government was that of the Government of National Understanding. It found its task so enormous that it was almost impossible to accomplish. It had to restore a pluralistic, multiparty democracy, create a new market economy, and restore the country's traditional Western cultural orientation. It also had to begin to assess the enormous environmental damage left behind by an insane policy of industrialization at any price. Its tasks were complicated by the revival of traditional Slovak nationalism whose advocates were now demanding not only autonomy for Slovakia, but also the establishment of an independent Slovak national state. Almost immediately, the Communist party lost most of its members, and other political parties proliferated. The official trade unions, nothing more than the instruments of the Communist party, were also disbanded, and most of the membership disappeared. By February 1990, twenty-nine political parties were competing for public attention. They were all gearing up for the coming elections to be held in June.

In the elections, the Public Against Violence-Civic Forum formed a coalition, and they received 50 percent of the votes cast for the House of Nations (the upper house of parliament) and 53.2 percent of the votes cast for the House of the Peoples (the lower chamber). The Communist party won 13 percent of the total votes cast, which corresponded to about the actual numbers of the apparatchiki and the state bureaucracy.

Bibliography

Peche, Jiri, "Czech-Slovak Conflict Threatens State Unity," *Radio Free Europe Research Report*. 1.1 (January 3, 1992), pp. 83-86; Rothschild, Joseph, *The Return to Diversity*. (Oxford, 1992).

Collapse of Communism. The Husak-regime could probably have trudged along for a while longer after the cataclysmic changes that occurred in Eastern Europe and the Soviet Union in the late 1980s. While in Poland and Hungary the reform communists negotiated the transition from a one-party dictatorship to a multi-party democracy, and the hard-line regime of Erich Honecker came to an end in East Germany, in Czechoslovakia the communist system seemed to be durable enough to withstand change. But the widespread dissatisfaction of the population could not be suppressed forever.

In 1987, Gustav Husak (*see* Husak, Gustav) was removed from the leadership and replaced with a younger apparatchik, Milos Jakes (*see* Jakes, Milos). By then, however, the Czechoslovak communists could no longer face the legacy of the Prague Spring (*see* Prague Spring, 1968) and the "normalization" that followed its suppression. Yet, there was no reform-faction in the party leadership who would have had the courage to negotiate a peaceful transition to political pluralism as it happened in Poland and Hungary. In addition, the deterioration of the country's economy accelerated. The slump never reached the depth of that in Poland, yet it exposed the illegitimacy of the regime despite outward appearances of stability. When Jakes took over as first secretary of the Communist party, many hard-liners resigned with Husak, hoping that this would trigger another Soviet intervention in Czechoslovakia. But their replacements were not reformists, but younger hard-liners; the difference was that the newcomers did not have sufficient political experience comparable to those that they replaced. Nevertheless, the new leaders were less committed to the "normalization process," as the Husak-era was euphemistically called. This contributed to considerable disputes within the party leadership. The Politburo was too busy with its internal divisions to be able to respond to demands of change in a unified manner.

At the same time, the ordinary citizen began to realize that the communist system could be challenged, after all. Soon, many independent groups emerged from the masses, forming the basis of a civil society that had always been prevented by the communists. Unauthorized demonstrations began to attract ever larger crowds. Religious pilgrimages were held in spite of official objections.

In January 1989, an important breakthrough was achieved when a huge demonstration commemorated the self-immolation of the Prague student, Jan Palach, who was protesting the Soviet-led invasion of Czechoslovakia in August 1968. This demonstration was broken up with great brutality by the secret police. Vaclav Havel (*see* Havel, Vaclav), one of the leaders of the crowd, was arrested together with other dissidents. This action was seen by millions of Czechs and Slovaks thanks to the modern communication medium, television. The vivid pictures of bleeding demonstrators and brutal communist police thugs beating them without provocation created general revulsion against the hard-line communist leadership. Most people knew by then that these leaders were no longer capable of leading the country out of the morass.

A new sense of activism emerged in Czechoslovakia. Twenty years of passive resistance was changed overnight into active opposition to the regime. The new spirit brought together intellectuals, workers, and university and even high school students, creating an alliance that the dissident intellectuals had never been able to achieve before. This was a new phenomenon in the sorry history of communist Czechoslovakia. The party leaders were completely surprised by the way events turned out.

Ladislav Adamec, the premier who had replaced Ludomir Strougal in 1988, attempted to mediate between the government and the dissidents, but he was not recognized by the opposition as a reformist. When it became clear that Soviet tanks would not rescue the party leaders this time around, Jakes finally saw the light. He accepted the major demands of the opposition to end one-party rule in Czechoslovakia.

Bibliography

Peche, Jiri, "Czech-Slovak Conflict Threatens State Unity," *Radio Free Europe Research Report* 1.1 (January 3, 1992), pp. 83-86; Slay, Ben, "Economic Reformers Face High Hurdles," *Radio Free Europe Research Reports* 1.1 (January 3, 1992), pp. 100-104.

Communist Party of Czechoslovakia. The Communist party, established in 1921, soon acquired 350,000 members. In the elections held in 1925, the party received 13.3 percent of the total votes cast, and it gained 41 parliamentary deputies. By then, however, the card-carrying membership had declined to 280,000. The trend continued. In the elections of 1929, the party's share of the votes declined to 10.2 percent and its parliamentary representation shrank to 30 deputies. In 1935, membership and vote-gathering strength stabilized at around 10 percent and 30 deputies. Alone in the countries of Eastern Europe, the Czechoslovak Communist party was and remained legal throughout the interwar years. It participated in political life and in the parliamentary system without, however, giving up its revolutionary goals. Nevertheless, the fact that it had to participate in normal politics, making the necessary concessions and adjustment to its partners, made the party less prone to violence than other East European Communist parties.

The Czechoslovak Communist party was financed through illegal channels by the COMINTERN from Moscow. In 1938, the post-Munich government, headed by president Eduard Benes, dissolved the party and it went underground. The following year, the party split and its organization in Bohemia and Moravia became separate from the Slovak party. In 1945, the core of the leadership of the party, which spent most of the war years in the Soviet Union, returned home. By then, the hard-core membership was down to about 40,000. Yet, the number of members was higher than that of any other political party in the restored Czechoslovak republic. The Red Army of the Soviet Union and the Soviet secret police provided direct help for the reorganization of the Communist party while, at the same time, impeding the efforts of the other parties.

According to the Kosice Program, signed by president Benes and the Moscow-based Czech communist leaders in 1944 (*see* Kosice Program), no political parties that continued their activities during the Nazi occupation of Czechoslovakia were permitted to reorganize after liberation. In this way, the strongest party, the Agrarians, was eliminated. The Communist party won over a large number of its followers because the Ministry of Agriculture was in Communist hands, and it immediately redistributed the lands confiscated from the expelled Germans. In consequence, the Communist party had, by the end of 1945, over 1 million card-carrying members.

After the coup d'etat of 1948, the Communist party extended its control over every phase of Czechoslovak life and society. It forced Marxist-Leninist ideology on the people by making its knowledge a prerequisite for economic advancement.

In 1951, all non-communist organizations were banned, and their properties were confiscated. Newspapers, national radio, and television stations were all tightly controlled. Cultural institutions, such as the film industry, were also brought under communist control. The communist leaders paid special attention to the coercive forces; the military, the secret police, and the regular police force. Most officers of these organizations were under double control, namely, under the Czech communist leadership and under the corresponding Soviet institutions. The officers of the military were periodically purged, and the dismissed officers were replaced by loyal party members. Military ranks and uniforms were copied from those of the Soviet army. Political indoctrination and training in Marxism-Leninism were conducted by political commissars. Soviet military "advisers" were attached to both on the operational and strategic levels, and they instructed their Czechoslovak charges in Soviet military doctrine and strategic thinking. The officers and the ranks were directly observed by the Soviet NKVD-KGB, and many of them received training in the Soviet Union.

After 1948, the police and the judiciary were completely reorganized. They were given more or less a free hand in dealing with designated political opponents or suspected dissidents. The secret police could arrest anyone, except members of the party's Central Committee and the Politburo, without a warrant. Those arrested could be held "as long as necessary." The prosecutors presented the results of their "investigations" to the court, and no other proof was necessary for conviction. "Justice" in communist Czechoslovakia was a tool of the Communist leadership.

The party's organizational structure changed little over the decades. It consisted of local cells, supervised by regional units that reported to the central party organs in Prague. The Slovak section was ostensibly autonomous, but in reality it was simply a subordinate branch of the central party apparatus. The Central Committee "elected" members of the Politburo (the name was later changed to the Presidium), but such "elections" were predetermined. The Central Committee ostensibly appointed the first secretary of the party whose post was later renamed to that of the secretary general. The membership of the Politburo remained fairly constant, between thirteen and fifteen people.

The general practice of Communist parties in Eastern Europe was to keep some of the democratic parties in existence but under strict communist control. The exception everywhere was the Social Democratic parties whose long traditions of defense of workers' interests were considered a direct challenge to communist supremacy. These parties were merged with the Communist parties in their respective countries. Czechoslovakia followed this pattern in June 1948. The twenty-three parliamentary seats were simply declared to belong to the unified party. Many Social Democratic party members sympathized with the communists, and they swelled the membership in 1949 to 2.5 million. Outside the Soviet Union, this made the Czechoslovak Communist party the largest such organization in the world. The party operated on the principle of "democratic centralism," which actually meant tight control over the membership. Since such a large membership belied the party's avowed elite status, several purges were conducted to weed out the "opportunists." This process resulted in a serious decline in membership. By 1951, only 1.5 million card-carrying party members were registered. Intraparty disputes were usually settled by the use of the secret police since factionalism was severely prohibited.

The Stalinist phase of communist rule in Czechoslovakia did not end with the death of the Soviet dictator. Antonyn Novotny (*see* Novotny, Antonyn), the secretary general, was a rigid, dogmatic communist, and he and practically the entire surviving party leadership were implicated in the purges and show trials that were conducted with great barbarity in the late 1940s and early 1950s. In addition, despite the senseless Stalinization of the Czechoslovak economy, the economic system still functioned better than the economic systems in the other East European states. Consequently, the population was relatively quiet and satisfied with its lot.

Soviet pressure in the early 1960s, however, moved the Novotny leadership to a somewhat less rigid position. In 1961, a committee was established to review the trials of Communist party leaders and members. It took the leaders a full year to agree on the parameters of the Committee's charge. By that time, economic problems had undermined the prestige of Novotny in the Soviet Bloc. The Slovak communists were the first to openly challenge Novotny. They had gained support from communist intellectuals who had scrutinized the true history of the party and had published some damaging findings. Novotny's most outspoken critic was Alexander Dubcek (*see* Dubcek, Alexander), the secretary general of the Slovak Communist party.

By 1966, pressures were building against the hard-line leaders. Lawyers began to demand the restoration of the rule of law. The leaders made some concessions in introducing mild economic reforms but they were not willing to do more for fear of losing control of politics. In January 1968, however, Novotny was finally ousted, and Dubcek was named his replacement.

Dubcek's reform efforts led to the period referred to by the name of the "Prague Spring" (*see* Prague Spring, 1968) or "Socialism with a Human Face." During "normalization" (*see* "Normalization in Czechoslovakia"), the Communist leadership became a gerontocracy whose members were replaced by like-minded individuals only upon death. The institution appeared unchanging and unchangeable even after the emergence of Mikhail Gorbachev in the Soviet Union in 1985. The organization was characterized as "a party of no surprises." At the same time, the leaders were suspicious, unsure of themselves, and they were aware of the fact that they lacked mass public support. Gustav Husak (*see* Husak, Gustav), just as Novotny had done before him, resisted even Soviet pressure for change. He may have been right in the sense that Soviet-type socialism was unreformable. At the end of 1987, Husak was finally replaced by Milos Jakes (*see* Jakes, Milos) as secretary general; he remained president of the republic until 1989, when his regime finally was swept away by the

Velvet Revolution. Since then, the membership of the Czechoslovak Communist party has disappeared. In the elections held in 1990, it received about 13 percent of the votes, about the same ratio it had attracted during the interwar years.

Bibliography
Suda, Zdanek, *Zealots and Rebels: A History of the Ruling Communist Party of Czechoslovakia* (Stanford, CA., 1980); Toma, Peter A., "The Communist Party of Czechoslovakia," in Stephen Fischer-Galati, ed., *The Communist Parties of Eastern Europe* (New York, 1979).

Constitutions of 1948 and 1960. After the rigged elections of 1948 the newly elected National Assembly created a new constitution for Czechoslovakia. It was actually introduced a day after the elections, showing that it had been prepared well ahead of the elections. The document did not include any reference to the privileged position of the Communist party nor of the administrative decrees of nationalization introduced after the coup d'etat. However, it did contain enough restrictions on individual liberties to make it less than a democratic document. President Benes refused to sign the document. When he resigned, he was replaced by the dominant communist, Klement Gottwald, who signed the constitution.

The constitution of 1960 came about as the result of the decision of the Politburo to record the changes that had occurred after 1948. The new document was first approved by the party's Central Committee and rubber-stamped by the National Assembly in July 1960. The document "legalized' the " dictatorship of the proletariat" retroactively. It proclaimed the successful construction of socialism. However, since the document had mainly propaganda purposes, it had no real significance in Czechoslovak politics. The 1960 constitution proudly proclaimed that Czechoslovakia was the second nation in the world (after the Soviet Union, of course), to have completed the task of building true socialism. It also outlined the road to a future utopian communism.

The preamble stated that the establishment of a "people's democracy" was the correct way toward socialism. The document copied the major features of the Stalinist constitution of 1936 although it was less detailed. Article 4 declared that the Czechoslovak Communist party was the vanguard of the working class and the guiding force of society and the state. Article 8 provided for the abolition of private property (retroactively, of course) and defined state ownership as "ownership by the people." Articles 9 and 10 further defined the limits of property-ownership. Despite the overwhelming "triumphs" proclaimed by the communist leaders, they were showing in this document a desperate need for internal legitimacy. The 1960 constitution had no other purpose.

Bibliography
Kral, Vaclav, ed., *The Origin and Development of People's Democracy in Czechoslovakia* (In Czech) (Prague, 1961).

Cultural Policies. The Stalinization of Czechoslovak culture began immediately after the coup d'etat of 1948. The schools were transformed to base their curricula on Marxism-Leninism regardless of the subjects taught. Teachers and professors were retrained in the spirit of this ideology. Russian language instruction in the schools became compulsory. Large numbers of "socialist realist" Soviet novels were translated into Czech and Slovak and were published by state publishing houses at public expense. Lenin's and Stalin's multivolume works were also published in huge printings and were distributed free to public libraries and schools. Theaters and movie houses presented mostly Soviet plays or movies. The state also sponsored "socialist realist" works in every area of culture. Paintings, even music, had to conform to vague notions of "socialist realism." Writers were commanded to produce "optimistic" works, glorifying "creative workers" in factories and collective farms, struggling to fulfill state-set production targets. The "alliance of workers, peasants and the intelligentsia" had to be portrayed by painters. Perhaps the most distasteful musical events of the day were "odes to Stalin" and other "leaders of the world revolutionary movement." Every anniversary of the history of the communist party was to be celebrated by overproduction of the work-norms. The death of Stalin did not end these endeavors. Although in other Soviet Bloc nations, certain intellectual ferment began in the mid-1950s, the Czechoslovak party leaders remained faithful to the rigid Stalinist creed. Their policies stultified artistic creativity and the production of any original works.

During the short period of the Prague Spring (*see* Prague Spring, 1968), all restrictions on intellectual activity were removed, including censorship. Suddenly, a flood of new works appeared that had been hidden in the drawers of writers and other creative people. They described real life in a socialist country in unflattering terms. Writers openly criticized the past and demanded reforms. In this euphoria of sudden release, however, certain subjects were still avoided. The discussion of Soviet-Czechoslovak relations remained tabu, and socialism as a system was never questioned.

The Warsaw Pact invasion ended this cultural ferment. After the dust had settled, Gustav Husak (*see* Husak, Gustav), the new party chief, declared that the Czechoslovak communists had successfully defended the leading role of the party against those who wanted to restore capitalism, and that it had remained totally devoted to the Soviet Union. Miloslav Bruzek, a hard-line orthodox communist, was appointed minister of culture and education. He purged the reformers from the Writers' Union and had their works removed from the shelves. Censorship was reintroduced and tightened. In August 1975, a list of 140 Czechoslovak historians was published, and all of them were dismissed from their jobs. Leading the list was Josef Macek, formerly the director of the Historical Institute of the Czechoslovak Academy of Sciences. New artists' unions, organized by Bruzek's ministry, excluded those who supported the reformers in 1968, and their works were no longer disseminated. Throughout the 1970s and 1980s, the Husak government remained one of the most rigid, doctrinaire groups among the governments of Eastern Europe, with the exception of the Romanian and Albanian governments. But the repression of the reformists constituted only one step in the consolidation of the communist regime. After the proclamation of the Final Helsinki Act on Human Rights in 1975, which the Husak government signed, the leader declared that its provisions did not refer to "poisonous works disguised as culture."

Repression in the 1980s, however, became ever more difficult to maintain. Some reformers were released from jail, and the less prominent leaders of the experiment with "Socialism with a Human Face" were given employment. In 1975, Pavel Kohut, a prominent reformist writer, was given a passport to visit Austria and Switzerland in order to see his plays performed. Milan Kundera could accept an invitation from France to teach. In 1972, Bruzek was dismissed from the head of the ministry of culture and education. His replacement was Milan Klusak, who attempted to enlist recalcitrant intellectuals to cooperate with the regime. His condition was, however, that they denounce the reformists. Three major writers, Miroslav Holub, Jiri Sotola, and Bohumir Hrabal, obliged with the demand and exercised "self-criticism." The prominent Marxist philosopher, Jiri Cvetl, joined them and condemned Dubcek and the reformists.

Despite the vigilance of the secret police, underground cultural activities continued. Vaclav Havel (see Havel, Vaclav), Ludvik Vaculik, Karel Kasik, and Ivan Malek (a former president of the Czechoslovak Academy of Sciences), continued to criticize Husak's government. They were all harassed, sometimes jailed, and generally persecuted. Not until the collapse of the communist system in 1989 was Czechoslovak culture freed of the oppressive policies of the communist government.

Bibliography
Golan, Galia, *The Czechoslovak Reform Movement: Communism in Crisis* (Cambridge, England, 1971); Skilling, Gordon H., *Czechoslovakia's Interrupted Revolution* (Princeton, NJ, 1976); Vodinsky, Stanislow. *Czechoslovakia: Education* (Prague, 1963).

Czechoslovakia After 1990. The major issue following the collapse of the communist regime was the open hostility that broke out between Czech and Slovak politicians. In February 1991, president Vaclav Havel (see Havel, Vaclav) convinced the Czech and Slovak leaders of the necessity of creating a new constitution. He immediately encountered obstacles: The participants of the meeting were unable to agree on a federal, or a confederate, solution to the Czech and Slovak antagonism. The Slovaks wanted a very loose association between the two republics; the Czech statesmen argued for a "functional federation" with some common ministries and policies.

The Christian Democrats of Slovakia proposed in April that a state treaty be signed between the Czech lands and Slovakia even before the creation of a new constitution. This was a preliminary step in asserting complete autonomy for the Slovak republic. At a further discussion, held at the Moravian city of Kromeriz on June 17, the two sides agreed that a state treaty should indeed be signed, but this would not mean that two separate states had been created. The treaty to be prepared by the two

National Councils, would provide the basis for the new federal constitution. However, the agreement was immediately questioned by leading Slovak politicians, especially by Vladimir Meciar (*see* Meciar, Vladimir), the former prime minister. They all considered the treaty to be inadequate for Slovakia's needs. In response to the doubts raised in Slovakia, Havel called for a referendum in July to decide whether the country should be divided into two separate states. The Slovaks opposed an early referendum for the simple reason that opinion polls did not indicate overwhelming popular support for independence.

Early in September, the two National Councils met in order to start work on a new state treaty. It immediately became obvious that negotiations were going nowhere. After the meeting, Meciar called on the Slovak National Council to adopt a declaration of Slovak sovereignty, written by some Slovak intellectuals in March, and to write a new Slovak constitution independently of the Czechs. Although the council voted down this proposal on two separate occasions, the Czech reaction was swift. The Czech National Council declared that, if Meciar's proposal were acted upon, the Czech lands would immediately follow it up by declaring their independence from Slovakia. In two further meetings of the rival leaders one in October and the other the following month, no solution came to light. Further negotiations had shown that irreconcilable differences existed between the two sides. Finally, in 1992, it was agreed that the Slovak republic would become an independent state on January 1, 1993.

Bibliography

Peche, Jiri, "Czech-Slovak Conflict Threatens State Unity," *Radio Free Europe Research Report* 1.1 (January 3, 1992), pp. 83-84; ——, "Czechoslovakia's Political Balance Sheet," *Radio Free Europe Research Report* 1.25 (June 19, 1992), pp. 24-25; ——, "Czechs and Slovaks Prepare to Part," *Radio Free Europe Research Report* 1.37 (September 18, 1992), pp. 12-15.

Czechoslovak-Soviet Treaty of Friendship and Mutual Aid. In December 1943, president Eduard Benes of Czechoslovakia traveled to Moscow in order to discuss the role his country was to play after the end of World War II. In his talks with Joseph Stalin, president Benes raised the issue of the expulsion of German and Hungarian minorities from Czechoslovakia. Stalin agreed to Benes's proposal. On his part, Benes agreed with Stalin that the Communist party of Czechoslovakia, most of whose leaders had spent the war years in Moscow, would be included in the reconstituted state's government. Benes also agreed to Stalin's suggestion that all key industries in Czechoslovakia be nationalized, the property of German collaborators be confiscated, and extensive land reforms be introduced, using lands taken from the Germans and Hungarians after they were expelled from the country. They also agreed that the post-Munich political parties that had continued to function during the German domination would not be permitted to reemerge after the war. The two heads of state also signed a treaty of friendship and mutual cooperation valid for twenty years after the conclusion of the war (*see* Kosice Program).

Bibliography

Rothschild, Joseph, *Return to Diversity* (London, 1972); Zinner, Paul, *Communist Strategy and Tactics in Czechoslovakia, 1918–1948* (New York, 1963).

Dubcek, Alexander (1921–1992). Although Dubcek was conceived in Chicago, Illinois, he was born in Slovakia, and he spent his early years in the Soviet Union. Dubcek's Slovak father, dissatisfied with conditions in his homeland, emigrated to the United States. He settled in Chicago where he became a convinced communist. After he returned to Slovakia with his pregnant wife and children, he joined a local cell of the Slovak faction of the Communist party. Heeding the call of the COMIN-TERN, he took his family to a commune in Soviet Kirghizia. Alexander, together with his older brother, attended the local school and learned to speak perfect Russian. When conditions did not improve in Kirghizistan in the 1920s, the family moved to the city of Gorky, when Alexander was six years old.

Just before the Nazi invasion of Czechoslovakia, the Dubcek family returned home. In March 1939, an independent Slovak state was proclaimed, and the Slovak faction of the Communist party went underground, but it also became independent of its Czech counterpart. The male members of the Dubcek family, including Alexander, joined the party. This party was loyal to Joseph Stalin, even when the Soviet dictator signed the Nazi-Soviet pact in August 1939. When Hitler's armies invaded the Soviet Union, the Slovak underground communists organized resistance to the Germans. The Slovak revolt in 1944 found Alexander Dubcek among the fighters. When the revolt failed, he joined the guerrillas in the mountains.

In 1945, Dubcek returned to his home city, Trencin, and became a minor party functionary in a local yeast factory. In 1949, Dubcek was bypassed for higher office and did not become a major functionary until later. He participated in the collectivization drive and the nationalization of industrial enterprises in Slovakia. In 1951, Dubcek was summoned to Bratislava, the Slovak capital city, and was named a member of the party's highest bureaucracy, the administration of the Central Committee. His career was, thus, launched. While in this position, Dubcek became convinced that the Communist party of Czechoslovakia would have to be changed or, it would lose all its authority and prestige. But he was not a radical innovator and was, therefore, acceptable to the Soviet leadership. By 1967, Alexander Dubcek had become a leading opponent of the hard-line Novotny group in the Politburo, and he eventually defeated his opponents. It is possible that, initially, he received Soviet support.

When he came into power in January 1968, Dubcek immediately began a program that was to be known as the Prague Spring (*see* Prague Spring, 1968). Together with General Ludvik Svoboda, who became president of Czechoslovakia in March 1968, Dubcek introduced a series of reforms that could have led to a pluralistic society. His program was named "Socialism with a Human Face." Dubcek's aim was the reinvigoration of the Communist party and the revitalization of the country's economy. This included the separation of party and state and the liberation of public institutions from party dictatorship. Dubcek was quite aware of the limits acceptable to the Soviet Union and did not want to antagonize the Brezhnev-led Soviet government, but, at this stage in his life, Dubcek was by no means a committed democrat, and he still believed that the democratization of the Communist party could be accomplished without giving up its leading role in society. He often declared his belief in Marxism-Leninism and in the leading role of the Soviet Union in the socialist camp.

The Prague Spring was suppressed in August 1968, and the subsequent "normalization" (*see* Normalization in Czechoslovakia) was engineered by Leonid Brezhnev. Dubcek was not jailed, however. At first, he remained general secretary of the party, but the real power was in the hands of Gustav Husak (*see* Husak, Gustav), a hard-line Slovak communist. In a half a year, however, Dubcek was removed and appointed ambassador to Turkey. A year later, he was ordered home and appointed director of a factory in Slovakia. When the communist system collapsed in Czechoslovakia, Dubcek became the president of the newly elected Czechoslovak parliament. However, this was a largely ceremonial post, and Dubcek did not play an active role in politics any more.

His most famous appearance was in December 1989, when, at a huge rally, Dubcek symbolically hugged the demonstrators from a balcony. This became a symbol of the changes taking place in Czechoslovakia. In the summer of 1992, Dubcek suffered injuries in a serious automobile accident, and he died in November, 1992.

Bibliography
Kusin, Vladimir, *From Dubcek to Charter 77: A Study of 'Normalization' in Czechoslovakia, 1968–1978* (New York, 1978); Shawcross, William, *Dubcek* (New York, 1990).

Economic Policies in Communist Czechoslovakia. The development of the Czechoslovak economy went through several phases between 1945 and 1990. The first two years following the end of World War II, were taken up by reconstruction. It was a transitional phase, nevertheless, the economic system was already being changed and moved toward Stalinization. The conquest of power by the Czechoslovak Communist party in 1948 inaugurated a major redirection of the economy. The country was in a better position than most other East European countries because it possessed a rather developed industrial system, inherited from the interwar republic, considerable managerial talent, and an educated industrial labor force. It also suffered less from the ravages of war than her neighbors, and was, therefore, an instructive case of economic performance under Stalinist control.

For the first time in the history of the socialist movement, the communists came into power in an industrialized state, one that fit the prescriptions of Karl Marx and Friedrich Engels better than the Soviet Union. It could be considered a test case. The Stalinist method of economic development, however, was uniformly imposed on all the East European countries after 1948, regardless of the level of their economies. The method involved the rapid development of heavy industries, channeling the bulk of investment into that sector. This necessarily meant the neglect of consumer goods production and housing. The process depended upon the exploitation of the agricultural sector, which was achieved through the ruthless collectivization of private landed properties regardless of their size. The method required a tremendous amount of raw material resources, including electric power, metallurgy, and machine production.

In Czechoslovakia, as elsewhere, emphasis was placed on the rapid expansion of military industry. Price control, central planning of developmental targets that not only set overall goals but also micro-managed the entire economic system, was part of the Stalinist method of economic management. Soviet advisers attempted to introduce new products in the collectivized agricultural sector, such as citrus fruits, tea, and bamboo, totally unfit for the northern latitudes. Accompanying the Stalinist method was the concept of the intensification of class struggle in the developing socialist economy. This worked against expertise because a good manager was considered to be someone imbued with Marxist-Leninist ideology, who was willing to use harsh methods to meet production targets.

After 1948, the nationalization of large and small-scale industrial enterprises and the collectivization of agriculture were swiftly accomplished. By 1953, the Czechoslovak economy had been completely Stalinized; foreign trade had been redirected to the east; and, especially after the outbreak of the Korean War, it had begun the accelerated development of military production. The performance of the Czechoslovak economy during the first decade of communist control was moderately successful owing to the advantage of the country's relatively high industrial development prior to World War II. The first five year plan of 1949 to 1953, the two one-year plans of 1954 and 1955, and the second five year plan of 1956–1960 produced yearly growth rates of 8 percent in industry. But the system had no flexibility. It created hidden inflation and was incapable of eliminating the emerging imbalances. Above all, rigid adherence to the Stalinist concept of intensified class struggle created an atmosphere of fear in which quality production was subordinated to quantity, in as much as not meeting planned targets was considered to be sabotage. The Stalinist method also encouraged self-sufficiency which was impossible to achieve in a modern economy.

By 1958, it was already evident that, although rapid growth had been achieved overall, the introduction of new techniques had been retarded, and bureaucratic obstacles had made further progress difficult indeed. Industrial and agricultural wages remained low, keeping the living standards of the population at a low level and providing no incentives for the producers. The only incentive was fear of the secret police apparatus.

After the death of Joseph Stalin, his Czechoslovak disciples, Klement Gottwald and later Antonyn Novotny (*see* Novotny, Antonyn), did not change the country's economic system. Even the accession of Nikita Khrushchev and his relaxed economic policies in the Soviet Union changed the situation in Czechoslovakia little. Only at the end of the decade of the 1950s did this leadership take some hesitant steps toward economic reforms. Not even the economic decline that had set in by 1960 succeeded in shaking its complacency.

By then, some East European states had begun moving away from the Stalinist model of economic development. The Yugoslavs were first; they had broken with the model in the later 1940s. But the Poles went farthest and the most quickly. Their influence, however, was not felt in Czechoslovakia, because the Czechoslovak communists did not even permit the publication of the works of Polish economists.

The one man who championed economic reforms in Czechoslovakia was Ota Sik. He was not only a leading economist in the country but also a member of the party's Central Committee. He noted that the labor reserves were exhausted and that productivity had not increased sufficiently to offset this problem. He also observed that increases in raw material imports from the Soviet Union and other members of the Soviet Bloc could no longer be expected. Sik criticized the system of management as too rigid and totally neglectful of workers' interests. He proposed that reforms should be introduced in order to improve the mechanism of production-management, not the economic system of the whole. He knew that the shibboleths of the system could not be challenged in toto and, therefore, if improvements were to come they would have to be introduced piecemeal. Consequently, the few reforms that were introduced tried to lower the level of centralization. But they did not go far enough; they certainly did not go down to the level of individual enterprises. Although the central planning office and the ministries did transfer some authority to production units, these became trusts with their own planning functions that had to adhere to the overall economic plans. Priorities were not changed, however, and the existing imbalances in the economy were not eliminated. The reasons were political; the hard-line leadership was fearful that economic decentralization would bring about political consequences. Giving up central control over the economy was, therefore, rejected.

In the 1960s, Czechoslovakia did not make any progress toward reversing the economic decline. One of the major imbalances was in agriculture. By 1953, only 50 percent of the lands were collectivized, but the process had been completed by the end of the decade. This was accompanied by a vicious campaign against better-to-do peasants, the so-called kulaks. The consequence of all this was a serious decline in agricultural production. The officially reported decline was 6 percent in the 1960–1964 plan period. Shortages of food became part of everyday life; the food supplies of cities were often interrupted.

In January 1967, the Politburo introduced a series of measures intended to increase agricultural production. More authority was granted to managers of collective farms to plan products, and they were encouraged to determine their own production targets. However, the production of essential foodstuffs, such as bread grains, dairy products, and meat, remained under the control of the central planning office. A new price system was also introduced, but this permitted the fluctuation of only 15 percent of the prices of food products. The rest remained under central control. Investment policies remained unchanged; the share of the centrally controlled salaries of agricultural workers, however, was increased. But no special incentives were given to workers to increase the production of foodstuffs. Not surprisingly, they did not do so. After the Warsaw Pact invasion of Czechoslovakia in 1968, agricultural production further deteriorated. Large quantities of bread grain had to be imported to feed the population. The imports came from the Soviet Union but also from West Germany. However, since the Czechoslovak state had to pay with hard currency for Western deliveries, this created large budget deficits. The situation began to change at the end of the 1980s. Massive reprivatization had begun, and it continues to the present day (1993).

The efforts of economists to convince the leaders that reforms were unavoidable did not go on without some results in other sectors of the economy. In 1964, the third five year plan was simply abandoned, and preparations for changes began. In 1967, the so-called new economic model was introduced. Now financial goals replaced quantitative ones. A new, three-tiered system of prices was established; in one tier prices were freed of all controls, another retained regulated prices, and the third included a mixture of the two. However, the prices of major consumer goods remained in the second tier. There occurred a period of two years during which signs of recovery appeared.

In late 1966, the general framework of reforms, proposed by Ota Sik, was accepted in principle. However, the implementation of reforms was, once again, postponed. The invasion of 1968 not only put a stop to the reform efforts but reversed those that had already been introduced. The years of "normalization" (*see* Normalization in Czechoslovakia) between 1968 and 1975 began with the dismantling of whatever changes had been made in the previous few years. Czechoslovakia once again followed the Soviet line. Administrative decentralization was introduced, but it was not accompanied by the decentralization of economic management. The central authorities did go so far as to delegate some authority to the trusts and, in exceptional cases, to individual enterprises. They established funds for bonuses for managers in case the work norms were surpassed.

In 1975, a "new" type of economic unit, the so-called concern was established in order to channel research and technological innovations to the firms. At the same time, agriculture received a higher priority in investment allocation. Once again, tinkering with the system did not bring about the desired results. On the one hand, animal husbandry began to produce enough meat and dairy products for the needs of the population, and there were enough other supplies of foodstuffs. However, the dogmatism of the leadership prevented further improvements. In 1975, new taxes were imposed on collectives in order to prevent the rural population to live better than industrial workers. In the late 1970s, the world economy began to change rapidly. The situation in Czechoslovakia was not favorable to make adjustments to the changes. By the middle of that decade, it became clear that the communist approach to economic development was a complete failure. It was unavoidable to realize that the system could not be reformed; it had to be abolished. This is the task that postcommunist Czech and Slovak leaders are currently trying to solve.

Bibliography

Stevens, John N., *Czechoslovakia at the Crossroads: The Economic Dilemmas in Postwar*

Czechoslovakia (Boulder, CO, 1985); Teichova, Alice, *The Czechoslovak Economy, 1918–1980* (London, 1988); Wadekin, Karl-Eugen, *Agrarian Policies in Communist Europe: A Critical Introduction* (The Hague, 1982).

Educational Policies. The educational system of Czechoslovakia was based on the traditional West European model and its products were universally recognized in the West. The Communist party changed this system in order to conform to the Soviet model. Since the need for education was accepted by all social strata in the country, every child was expected to finish at least elementary school. After World War II, greater emphasis was placed on completing secondary education; however, the major aim of the school system after 1948 was the indoctrination of students in Marxism-Leninism.

After the accession of Nikita Khrushchev to power in the Soviet Union, the Czechoslovak educational system was once again altered in the direction of polytechnical education. This, in short, directed students to spend some of their time in factories or on collective farms, ostensibly to practice the unity of theories and everyday labor. In fact, the purpose of the device was to help alleviate the labor shortage.

The admission standards at schools and universities were also changed. Children of good communist cadres were assured entrance to these institutions; the children of noncommunist parents had to meet higher admission standards. Expertise and knowledge in the field of interest of the student counted for less than "correct" ideological preparation, or participation in the activities of the youth association sponsored by the Communist party. This was affirmative action, Stalinist style.

In 1980, the administration of postsecondary education was centralized in the office of the minister of education. The minister was made responsible for the hiring and dismissal of university faculty members. The government encouraged scientific education more than studies in the humanities, especially in history. Compulsory elementary education was expanded from eight to nine years, beginning at age six. Many primary schools held day long sessions. The curricula on every level corresponded to those of Soviet schools, and the study of the Russian language was made compulsory. Consecutive five-year plans demanded ever larger numbers of skilled, educated workers. However, it soon turned against state interests to prolong the education of children beyond a certain level of expertise and have larger numbers of them enter higher educational institutions. Eventually, the nine-year elementary school system was judged to be adequate for the training of skilled industrial workers. Thereafter, admissions to higher educational institutions became ever more restricted. Children of party members, the offspring of the nomenklatura, had priority for higher education. Children of the intelligentsia had several strikes against them.

Bibliography
Toma, Peter A, "The Communist Party of Czechoslovakia," in Stephen Fischer-Galati, ed. *The Communist Parties of Eastern Europe* (New York, 1979).

Expulsion of Ethnic Germans. The ethnic German population in Eastern Europe was to be removed after the war and repatriated to defeated Germany. With this step, centuries of German *Drang Nach Osten* (the march to the east) was to be reversed. This was also collective punishment for ethnic Germans, some of whom had served as a Nazi fifth column in Eastern Europe. This was the second "ethnic cleansing" in Europe, a response to the German "cleansing" of Jews from the European continent. It did not matter that most of the ethnic German populations went to Eastern Europe centuries before World War II, at the invitation of native rulers and were civilizing agents, introducing urban crafts to the region. Many of them did not sympathize with Nazism, but they were caught up in the nationalism of the time between the two world wars. They considered the East European countries in which they resided as their homelands.

The Sudeten Germans, some of whom did support the Henlein-led Nazi party in Czechoslovakia before World War II, were removed from their homes. They were permitted to carry only as many of their belongings as they could carry in their hands. First, they were herded into concentration camps under barbaric conditions, then they were marched on foot to the nearest railroad station where they were loaded into cattle wagons. They were deported to various parts of Germany under Allied occupation. About 3 million ethnic Germans were removed.

Eduard Benes also began the expulsion of ethnic Hungarians from Czechoslovakia in 1945, but this process was halted after more than 100,000 Hungarians had been driven across the borders with Hungary. However, large number of ethnic Hungarians were deported to Silezia and Moravia where they were put to forced labor in retaliation for Hungary's role in the dismemberment of Czechoslovakia in 1939. Many of them died under the barbaric conditions in which they were held.

In 1991, president Vaclav Havel (*see* Havel, Vaclav) apologized to Germany for the expulsion of ethnic Germans from Czechoslovakia, but no steps were taken to compensate the victims for the loss of their properties, and Havel did not mention the fate of Hungarians after 1945.

Bibliography
Luza, Radomir, *The Transfer of the Sudeten Germans: A Study of Czech-German Relations, 1933–1962* (New York, 1982).

Gorbachev's Impact on Czechoslovakia. After the death of Leonid Brezhnev, the change of leadership in the Soviet Union had hardly any effect on Czechoslovak politics. "Normalization" (*see* "Normalization in Czechoslovakia") under Gustav Husak (*see* Husak, Gustav) was too effective in preventing quick changes in political life. Husak praised the changes in the Soviet Union as was the custom among the East European satraps, but he had no intention of altering the course of Czechoslovak communism. There occurred scattered incidents in the country, people demanding greater freedoms and the observation of human rights, but none of these incidents were on a scale large enough to introduce Glasnost or Perestroika in the Czechoslovak lands. Husak was convinced in any case that Gorbachev's policies were only window dressing, and that the system would not substantially change in the Soviet Union. There were many proofs to the effect that the Husak regime was not about to loosen its reign over the country. Dissenters were persecuted as before, and religious people were singled out for especially brutal treatment by the communist secret police. There were perfunctory calls for the elimination of corruption and for the rejuvenation of the party leadership, but hardly anyone from among the hard-line nomenklatura was removed.

What changed the situation was that, by 1985, the Czechoslovak economy was sputtering. It was in economics that perestroika was finally employed. In July 1987, the leaders endorsed minor reforms in the style of management. The size of the central planning apparatus and its influence were reduced. Enterprise managers were promised greater latitude in determining production targets, and workers were going to receive the right to influence the selection of enterprise directors. The concept of profit was still considered to be tabu, but the idea of financial incentives for producers began to appear in official announcements. Next, prices were to be modified in order to relate them more closely to the costs of production. The general direction of foreign trade was also to be altered.

Many of these proposals resembled those offered during the Prague Spring of 1968, but there was one great difference. In 1968, the changes went against the wishes of Soviet leaders; the historical irony of 1987 was that now Soviet leaders were advocating reforms while Husak and his supporters dragged their collective feet in implementing them. Consequently, the changes were enacted and effected at such a slow pace that the communist system collapsed before full implementation had taken place.

Bibliography
Dawisha, Karen, *Eastern Europe, Gorbachev and Reform: The Great Challenge* (Cambridge, England 1988).

Hajek, Jiri (1913–). Hajek was a member of the Czechoslovak Social Democratic party in the interwar years, and was placed in a Nazi concentration camp during the occupation of Czechoslovakia. In 1945, he was freed and appointed Professor of Philosophy at Charles University in Prague. He was appointed a member of the Central Committee of the Czechoslovak Communist party and a parliamentary deputy in 1948. Between 1952 and 1954, Hajek was chairman of the committee on Foreign Affairs of the Czechoslovak parliament. In 1954, he was appointed ambassador to Britain where he remained until 1958. In 1958, he returned to Czechoslovakia and was appointed deputy foreign minister, a post in which he remained until 1962. In that year, he was named permanent Czechoslovak representative to the United Nations. He stayed in New York until 1965. In 1965, he returned to Czechoslovakia and was appointed minister of education and culture, then only of education between 1967 and 1968. Between April and September, he served as foreign minister.

After the invasion of Czechoslovakia by the Warsaw Pact armies in August 1968, Hajek turned to the United Nations and voiced complaints about the Soviet occupation of his country. For his action, he was expelled from the Central Committee of the Communist party and all his other posts in 1969. Until 1989, Hajek remained a dissident, who joined the group of writers and artists who openly voiced their objections to the restoration of Stalinism in Czechoslovakia.

Bibliography

Skilling, Gordon H., *Czechoslovakia's Interrupted Revolution* (Princeton, NJ, 1976).

Havel, Vaclav (1928–). As a young playwright, Havel quickly established himself as the conscience of the intellectuals. His plays, which probed the debt of the crises of national life, soon made him a spokesman for the discontented creative people. He had great difficulty in having his works performed in Czechoslovakia, yet he was recognized in the West as an important voice in the Czechoslovak theater. In June 1967, at the fourth congress of the Union of Czechoslovak Writers, there was an open confrontation between the dogmatic communists and the increasingly vocal dissidents. After Ludvik Vaculik roundly condemned the communist system and its failure to solve the problems of the country, Havel criticized the bureaucratic leadership of the Union of Writers. As a consequence, they were both excluded from the leadership, together with other dissidents.

In March 1968, Havel made a statement that was widely circulated in typewritten form among the leading intellectuals. His "On the Theme of Opposition" was eventually published in *Literarny Listi*; it advocated the establishment of a two-party system in Czechoslovakia with a new democratic party based on Czech historical traditions, namely, democracy. He argued that the only safeguard of human rights was "real choice where people will elect those who will govern them." This required two independent political parties with equal opportunity to compete for the votes of the population.

During the first half of 1968, discussions on the role of the Writers' Union in Czechoslovak intellectual life continued. The noncommunist writers, who continued to encounter difficulties in having their works published by the state publishing houses, finally had enough. They established a Circle of Independent Writers with the participation of sixty members and elected Vaclav Havel as the chairman of the group. The group demanded the independence of culture from political interference. They also proposed that the Writers' Union be transformed into an independent interest group, a truly democratic organization.

In 1977, Havel was among the signers of the Charter 77 document (*see* Charter 77). After this, Havel became the focus of government persecution. He was arrested several times, tried, and sentenced to various terms in jail. This inevitably made him a hero of the opposition. He never gave up his protest.

In 1989, Havel was a founding member of the Civic Forum (*see* Civic Forum and Public against Violence), a national liberation movement that eventually wrested power from the communists. In the following year he was elected president of the Czechoslovak republic. In 1990, he visited the United States, and he was the first East European leader since 1945, who addressed the joint meeting of the Congress of the United States. He received a tumultuous welcome. In 1991, he lost some of his popularity because of the difficulty of revitalizing Czechoslovakia's economy. As a consequence, Havel was not reelected president. His successor was Vaclav Klaus. Havel was unwilling to assume the presidency because, as he stated, he did not want to preside over the dissolution of Czechoslovakia into two independent states. After the separation took place on January 1, 1993, Havel stood for, and was elected president of, the Czech Republic.

Bibliography
Peche, Jiri, "Czech-Slovak Conflict Threatens State Unity," *Radio Free Europe Research Report* 1.1 (January 3, 1992), pp. 83-86; Skilling, Gordon H., *Czechoslovakia's Interrupted Revolution* (Princeton, NJ, 1976).

Hendrych, Jiri (1913–). In 1934, the 21-year-old Hendrych joined the legal Communist party of Czechoslovakia. He was a member of the regional leadership at Kladno. He remained active in the underground Communist party during the Nazi occupation of Czechoslovakia and ended up in the Mauthausen concentration camp for the duration of the war. He survived and, in 1945, he was appointed as a member of the secretariat of the Central Committee of the party, and from 1946 he was a parliamentary deputy. In 1951, Hendrych was appointed secretary to the Central Committee. He was adopted by the Politburo as a candidate (nonvoting) member in 1958, and in 1962 he was made a full member of the Presidium (formerly the Politburo) of the party. Between 1965 and 1968, Hendrych was the chairman of the Commission on Ideology of the party's Central Committee. As such, he issued violent criticisms of the Writers' Union and was dismissed from his posts by Alexander Dubcek (*see* Dubcek, Alexander) during the spring of 1968. After the Warsaw Pact invasion of Czechoslovakia, Hendrych joined the hard-liners and issued scathing criticisms of the reformers. After the collapse of communism, Hendrych, now in his late seventies, disappeared from Czechoslovak politics.

Bibliography
James, Robert R., *The Czechoslovak Crisis, 1968* (London, 1969); Ulc, Otto, *Politics in Czechoslovakia,* (San Francisco, CA., 1974); Wolchick, Sharon, "Czechoslovakia," in Joseph Held, ed. *The Columbia History of Eastern Europe in the Twentieth Century* (New York, 1992).

Husak, Gustav (1913–). Husak joined the Czechoslovak Communist party in 1933. Between 1938 and 1943, he worked underground, but he also served the party as a lawyer. In September 1943 he became vice chairman of the Slovak faction of the Communist party. In 1945, he was appointed a member of the party's Central Committee, and between 1945 and 1951, he was a member of its Politburo. In February

1951, he was arrested, tried on false charges of "Slovak bourgeois nationalism," and sentenced to life imprisonment. Released from jail in 1960, Husak was rehabilitated four years later. Between 1964 and 1968, Husak worked as a researcher at the Slovak Academy of Sciences. After the Warsaw Pact invasion of Czechoslovakia, Husak was among the hard-liners who supported the invasion. He was named first secretary of the Czechoslovak Communist party in April 1969 and was appointed president of the republic in 1975.

Husak had no use for the communist reformers. He eased them out of office and from national politics altogether but, unlike his counterpart in Hungary, Janos Kadar, did not have them killed or jailed. Eventually, Husak was forced by circumstances to adopt some of the economic policies proposed during the Dubcek era, except those that would have infringed upon the monopoly of the Communist party over politics. His politics, however, created a lethargic population. An atmosphere of hopelessness pervaded national life, and it was not lifted until the end of the 1980s. This was called "normalization" (*see* "Normalization" Czechoslovakia).

For two decades Husak maintained a rigidly conservative communist regime in Czechoslovakia. After 1985, he even resisted the influence of Mikhail Gorbachev in his own country, just as his predecessors, Klement Gottwald and Antonyn Novotny (*see* Novotny, Antonyn) refused to follow a relaxed policy after the death of Stalin. Old, ailing, and cynical, he was finally replaced by another hard-liner, Milos Jakes (*see* Jakes, Milos), as secretary general of the party in 1988, but he remained president of the republic. He was finally dismissed after the Velvet Revolution of 1989, and his entire regime went out with him.

Bibliography
Pelikan, Jiri, *The Czechoslovak Political Trials of 1950–1954* (Stanford, CA., 1971); Ulc, Otto "The 'Normalization' of Post-Invasion Czechoslovakia," in *Survey*. 24.3 (1979), pp. 201-214; Wolchik, Sharon, "Regional Inequality in Czechoslovakia," in Daniel J. Nelson, ed. *The Politics of Inequality* (Lexington, MA., 1983).

International Relations of Communist Czechoslovakia. Czechoslovakia, just as other members of the Soviet Bloc, had two types of international relations. One was conducted with bloc member states and Communist parties of the world; the other type was conducted with the capitalist countries. A third type emerged in the 1960s; relations with the Third World nations. Within the Soviet Bloc, Czechoslovakia was required to subordinate its national interests to that of "proletarian internationalism," namely, the Soviet Union. There was no autonomy of action for the country in any case. Relations with the Third World countries, as well as with the capitalist nations, were completely subordinated to Soviet diplomatic interests. When the Soviet Union began a campaign for peaceful coexistence, it appeared for a moment that there might emerge a possibility for independent Czechoslovak actions. However, there was no response from the leadership. In the 1960s, particularly, the Czechoslovak state simply echoed Soviet diplomatic moves.

The Czechoslovak-Soviet alliance was revived in 1963. Since the Czechoslovak economy almost completely depended upon the Soviet Union, this made independent foreign policy almost impossible. Although no Soviet troops were stationed in Czechoslovakia until 1968, this did not encourage the Novotny-leadership to follow Albania's or Romania's example of carving out a special diplomatic niche for themselves even in the Sino-Soviet dispute. Czechoslovakia had not hesitated to associate itself with "peaceful coexistence."

Prague campaigned for Soviet proposals for the codification of the principles of peaceful coexistence with Europe and for a European security conference in which special attention would have been placed on a Central European security arrangement. In the Middle East, Prague slavishly followed Soviet policies. It broke relations with Israel in 1967, following a similar action by the Soviet Union. Relations with the Western Allies were uniformly hostile. Special hostility was reserved for West Germany and the United States. When Prague negotiated with West Germany for a possible economic agreement, Moscow stepped in, and the negotiations went nowhere.

Czechoslovakia, a charter member of the Warsaw Pact, participated in its plans against NATO. Special military alliances were concluded with Poland and East Germany to reinforce Czechoslovak adherence to the Soviet military system. Yet, realities increasingly interfered with communist rigidity. In 1967, a two-year pact was signed with West Germany and, although this was not followed up because of Prague's solidarity with the rest of the Soviet Bloc, it did open the door for better relations.

Foreign relations were in the hands of the party's Presidium. Its membership having been maintained often for decades, this body was not given to innovations and independence. During the Prague Spring (*see* Prague Spring, 1968), even the reformers refrained from starting new foreign policy initiatives for fear of Soviet disapproval. After the collapse of the communist system, Czechoslovakia began rebuilding its international relations with the rest of the world on a more even keel.

Bibliography
Remington, Robert, *The Warsaw Pact* (Cambridge, MA., 1971); Skilling, Gordon H., *Czechoslovakia's Interrupted Revolution* (Princeton, NJ., 1976); Toma, Peter A., "The Communist Party of Czechoslovakia," in Stephen Fischer-Galati, ed. *The Communist Parties of Eastern Europe* (New York, 1979).

Invasion of Czechoslovakia by the Warsaw Pact. After the introduction of the reform program by the government headed by Alexander Dubcek (*see* Dubcek, Alexander), five members of the Warsaw Pact (the Soviet Union, East Germany, Poland, Hungary and Bulgaria) issued a stern warning to Czechoslovakia. In essence they accused the Czechoslovak reformists of endangering Communist party rule in their country and opening the Czechoslovak state to the penetration of the "imperialists," meaning the Western nations. They were warning the Czechoslovak leaders that they were jeopardizing the common cause of socialism and that the alliance would not stand by to see anticommunism triumph there.

In response, the entire Presidium of the Communist party of Czechoslovakia met members of the Soviet Politburo in July 1968 at the town of Cerna/Tisou. Dubcek agreed to tone down the parts of the reform program with which the Soviet leaders disagreed the most. However, Dubcek stood firm on Czechoslovakia's right to follow its own road to socialism. The compromise that was reached was confirmed at the meeting of the six Warsaw Pact members in Bratislava. It seemed that the matter was settled without violence.

However, Leonid Brezhnev and his fellow Soviet leaders could not accept the Czechoslovak reform program without endangering their control over the entire Soviet Bloc. Not only that; the hard-line states, especially East Germany, feared the impact of the Czechoslovak reforms on their own monopoly of power. A divided Soviet Politburo voted seven to four on August 14 to invade Czechoslovakia and restore the hard-liners to power. The decision was conveyed to the other Warsaw Pact members—except Czechoslovakia—on August 18. On the evening of August 20, troops of the Soviet Union, Poland, Hungary, Bulgaria, and East Germany entered the Czechoslovak state. Soviet paratroopers landed at the major airports in Prague and other cities and, led by Czechoslovak secret policemen, they rounded up the leaders of the reform movement. The Soviet leader declared at first that the invaders had been invited by Czechoslovak patriots who were worried about the restoration of capitalism in their country. However, when only lower level officials showed any willingness to cooperate with the invaders, the so-called Brezhnev doctrine was introduced. According to the doctrine, the Soviet Union-led bloc was duty-bound to intervene in any socialist country where one-party rule was being endangered. This doctrine was, in effect, the rejection of the sovereignty of the Soviet Union's socialist allies.

After the invasion, the Soviet Union installed a completely subservient dictatorship under the control of the Slovak communist, Gustav Husak (*see* Husak, Gustav). This rigid, dogmatic system set back reforms by two decades and created a sullen, cynical population. The system of Husak which was called "normalization" (*see* "Normalization" in Czechoslovakia) was eventually destroyed in the revolution of 1989.

Bibliography

Czerwinski, Eduard J., and Piekalkiewicz, Jaroslaw, eds. *The Soviet Invasion of Czechoslovakia: Its Effects on Eastern Europe* (New York, 1972); Oxley, Andrew, Alex Pravda, and Andrew Ritchie, eds. *Czechoslovakia: The Party and the People* (London, 1973); Skilling, Gordon H., *Czechoslovakia's Interrupted Revolution* (Princeton, NJ., 1976); Svitak, Ivan, *The Czech Experiment, 1968–1969* (New York, 1971).

Jakes, Milos (1922–). Jakes was a minor communist functionary, an apparatchik in the communist youth organization, the Czechoslovak equivalent of the Soviet KOMSOMOL. Between 1955 and 1958, he was sent to Moscow to study at the Lenin

Academy of the Communist (bolshevik) party of the Soviet Union. After his return to Czechoslovakia, Jakes was appointed an official in the ministry of the interior. In 1966, he became deputy minister of the interior, serving in that position until 1968. Jakes supported the Warsaw Pact invasion of his country and was, therefore, rewarded by the appointment to chair the Central Auditing and Control Commission of the Communist party. He remained in that post until 1977. Then he was appointed a candidate (nonvoting) member of the Presidium of the Communist party. In 1985, he replaced the ailing Gustav Husak (*see* Husak, Gustav) as prime minister of the Czechoslovak republic. In 1989, he was ousted and disappeared from political life.

Bibliography

Kusin, Vladimir V., *From Dubcek to Charter 77: A Study of 'Normalization' in Czechoslovakia, 1968–1978* (New York, 1978); Rothschild, Joseph, *Return to Diversity: A Political History of East Central Europe Since World War II* (Oxford, 1992).

Kosice Program. Based on the discussions between president Eduard Benes and Joseph Stalin in 1943, the Kosice program was signed in April 1945 at the city of the same name in the presence of Soviet and Czechoslovak party and state officials. The program described the method of cooperation among political parties in post-World War II Czechoslovakia, their system of work in the yet-to-be elected parliament, and the distribution of cabinet posts among the future coalition parties. This agreement went against Czechoslovakia's democratic traditions by prearranging the distribution of political power without the consent of the voters. It foreshadowed the communist dictatorship in coming years.

The agreement seemingly simplified Czechoslovakia's political system. Parties that either collaborated with the Nazis or even continued working during the German occupation of the country, were forbidden to revive their organizations. All coalition parties were to become members of the National Front of Urban and Rural Workers. No provision was made for oppositional parties. Accordingly, seven parties were to operate in postwar Czechoslovakia. These were the Communist party of Czechoslovakia, a separate Communist party for Slovakia, the Democratic party (in Slovakia only), the Slovak Labor party (only in Slovakia), the People's Socialist party (only in Bohemia, Moravia and Silezia), the Populist (or Christian Democratic) party (only in the Czech lands), and the Social Democratic party of Czechoslovakia. After the elections of 1946, the Slovak Labor party merged with the Social Democrats; however, at the same time, a new Slovak Liberal party was formed, and the number of parties remained the same.

The Czechoslovak Communist party and its Slovakian counterpart benefited from the agreement greatly. They were given control of key ministries, including the ministries of the interior, justice, and agriculture. The party immediately undertook the sponsorship of popular measures, including the efforts to rebuild the shattered economy and land reform, including the redistribution of the lands recovered from the expelled ethnic Germans. The program also included an economic plan. It decreed the nationalization of all major industries and enterprises owned by Germans and Czech collaborators. None of these generated popular opposition; the Nazi occupation had succeeded in muddling property relations to such an extent that the old rules no longer applied.

Bibliography
Toma, Peter A., "The Communist Party of Czechoslovakia," in Stephen Fischer-Galati, ed. *The Communist Parties of Eastern Europe* (New York, 1979).

Meciar, Vladimir (1942–). Meciar graduated from the Komsomol College in Moscow, an institute established by the Soviet communist leaders for the training of foreign youth in Marxist-Leninist doctrine. After his return to Czechoslovakia, Meciar occupied various positions in the Communist party apparatus. He was chairman of the Czechoslovak Socialist Youth Union, District National Committee at Ziar and Hronom, and was deputy chairman of the People's Control Committee between 1967 and 1969. However, Meciar expressed some opinions that conflicted with the official positions of the party and was therefore dismissed from these posts. In 1970, he was expelled from the Czechoslovak Communist party.

For the next three years, he worked as a smelter. In 1973, however, he completed his studies for a law degree and was appointed attorney for the Skloobal bottle factory in Nemsova, Slovakia. In 1990, Meciar was elected a deputy to the Czechoslovak National Assembly as a representative of the group, Public against Violence (*see* Civic Forum and Public against Violence). In January 1990, he was appointed minister of internal affairs and the environment of Slovakia. Six months later, he became prime minister of the Slovak half of Czechoslovakia. In April 1991, however, Meciar was dismissed from the prime ministership because of his abrasive, authoritarian style and his outspoken Slovak nationalism.

In 1991, he was elected chairman of the Slovak nationalist party, called Movement for a Democratic Slovakia. In March 1992, Meciar was accused in parliament of having been an informer for the Czechoslovak secret police during the communist regime, but these charges have not been proven. In June 1992, Meciar was elected once again as prime minister of Slovakia, and he engineered the separation of Slovakia from the Czech Republic in January 1993. Since then, he continued a nationalist Slovak course. He became involved in a bitter dispute with the Czech Republic over the distribution of the former assets of Czechoslovakia. His arguments with Hungary have centered on the treatment of Slovakia's large Hungarian minority and on the building of a dam on the Danube river, which is choking off water supplies for some Hungarian regions. Meciar has also battled with his own cabinet.

Bibliography
Kalniczky, Adele, "The Slovak Government's First Six Months in Office," *Radio Free Europe Research Report.* 2.6 (February 5, 1993), pp. 18-25.

Mikova, Marie (1920–). Mikova joined the Czechoslovak Communist party in

1946. Between 1962 and 1968, she was a candidate (nonvoting) member of the Central Committee of the party and a parliamentary deputy in 1964. Between April and September 1968, she was vice chairman of the Czechoslovak parliament. She was appointed a member of the Commission on Rehabilitation of the party's Central Committee and co-opted to membership in the Central Committee itself in August 1968. In 1969, she delivered a speech at the session of the Central Committee condemning the invasion of Czechoslovakia the previous year. For this, she was expelled from the Central Committee and from all other jobs she had held in the party and government.

Bibliography
Rothschild, Joseph, *Return to Diversity: A Political History of East Central Europe Since World War II* (Oxford, 1992).

Mlynar, Zdenek (1930–). Mlynar, the son of a craftsmen, joined the Czechoslovak Communist party in 1950. He rose rapidly, and he was soon sent to Moscow to study at Lomonosov University. After his return to Czechoslovakia in 1955, he worked in the office of the prosecutor general until 1956. He was then appointed secretary to the Institute of State and Law. In 1962, he became chairman of the department of political leadership and society in the Institute. Between 1964 and 1968, he was secretary to the Legal Commission of the party's Central Committee. During 1968 and 1969, Mlynar was a member of the Czechoslovak Communist party's Presidium. In 1969, he resigned from all his offices.

He worked during the 1970s and 1980s in the National Museum in Prague. In the 1970s, Mlynar was a member of a loose group of dissident intellectuals demanding the democratization of society. He was arrested and jailed several times by the authorities. He wrote for the underground press.

In early 1975, Mlynar had written a memorandum about the motivations of the reformers in 1968. It included a thoughtful criticism of Alexander Dubcek (*see* Dubcek, Alexander) and his leadership. This memorandum was circulated in typescript within Czechoslovakia and then published abroad. The memorandum provided the first critical analysis by a scholar of the reform movement of the 1960s. His conclusion was that, given the international context, the reforms were doomed to failure because of the inexperience of the Dubcek-leadership and the consequent mistakes that they committed.

Bibliography
Skilling, Gordon H., *Czechoslovakia's Interrupted Revolution* (Princeton, NJ., 1976).

National Committees. These committees were established in 1948 after the conquest of power by the Communist party by a special decree of the government. They were later approved by parliament. The committees which were established in every village, town, and city, were responsible for ensuring the control of the population by the Communist party cadres. Their power was considerable; they could send any recalcitrant citizen to a labor camp if such a person was judged to be dangerous for communist control. No judicial action was necessary for a two-year stint in such a camp; the sentences were given out at the discretion of the local committee. Many of these committees became hotbeds of corruption and nepotism as well as means of settling personal disputes in localities. During the collectivization drive, the National Committees were widely used against uncooperative peasants.

Bibliography

Wolchik, Sharon, "Czechoslovakia," in Joseph Held, ed. *The Columbia History of Eastern Europe in the Twentieth Century* (New York, 1992).

'Normalization' in Czechoslovakia. In April 1969, Alexander Dubcek (*see* Dubcek, Alexander), powerless since the Warsaw Pact invasion the year before, was officially removed from his posts in the Communist party and was replaced by the Slovak Gustav Husak (*see* Husak, Gustav). The personnel change brought about great efforts to undo the reforms introduced during Dubcek's leadership. Husak cleverly exploited the latent antagonism between Czechs and Slovaks in order to direct popular attention away from the national humiliation of the invasion. This was a time of "normalization," a euphemism for the elimination of reformers and reforms from politics and economics.

Husak restored the Communist party's monopoly of power. Censorship was reestablished, and strict controls were placed on radio and television broadcasting. A large number of people were dismissed from the Communist party, which usually meant the loss of jobs and income. Nonparty groups and dissident intellectuals were warned that discipline would be enforced. "Unlawful" assemblies were dispersed by the secret police. Dubcek's supporters were removed from all levels of the party and were replaced by pliant collaborators. The leaders of mass-organizations were also purged. The universities and research institutes were cleansed of their reformist scholars. Scores left the country in search of freedom of expression and research. Many talented experts were eliminated from Czechoslovak cultural and scientific life. The role of the secret police as the party secretary's private army was reestablished.

As a consequence, over 500,000 people lost their livelihoods. No wonder that the economic life of the country was seriously affected. Normalization also meant no reliance on mass-citizen support for the policies pursued by the Communist party. Instead, material advantages were offered to those willing to go along with neo-Stalinist policies. For those who were not willing, there was coercion. The regime paid more attention to previously neglected issues, such as the plight of the collective farmers. In the countryside, its unpopularity was, therefore, less.

Slovakia was appeased by the fact that Husak was a Slovak, and, for the first time in the twentieth century, a Slovak had real power in the republic (Alexander Dubcek, himself a Slovak, was not considered to have had real power). Nevertheless, the communist Husak ruled over a sullen people withdrawn into passive resistance.

Bibliography

Czerwinski, Eduard J., and Piekalkowicz, Jaroslaw, eds. *The Soviet Invasion of Czechoslovakia: Its Effects on Eastern Europe* (New York, 1972); Kusin, Vladimir V., *From Dubcek to Charter 77: A Study of 'Normalization' in Czechoslovakia 1968–1978* (New York, 1978); Mastny, Vojtech, ed. *Czechoslovakia: Crisis in World Communism* (New York, 1972); Remington, Robert A., *Winter in Prague* (Cambridge, MA, 1969).

Novotny, Antonyn (1904–1978). Novotny joined the Czechoslovak Communist party in 1921 and was elected a member of the regional party leadership of Prague in 1935. In 1941, he was arrested by the Nazis and he was kept in Mauthausen concentration camp until the end of World War II. His close friendship with Klement Gottwald helped his career along after the war. In 1945, Novotny was appointed to head the Prague regional party organization, and the following year he became a member of the Central Committee. Upon the death of Gottwald in 1953, Novotny became first secretary of the Communist party, and he inherited control over the party's apparatus.

He followed the time-honored practice of placing his reliable supporters in commanding posts of the party. Novotny moved quickly to consolidate his power in other ways as well. He abolished the former office of party president, a post that had been held by Gottwald before his death. He changed the name of the Politburo, the highest organ of the party, to the Presidium in order to conform to current usages in the Soviet Communist party, and he changed the title of first secretary to that of secretary general for the same reason. He appointed four new secretaries, each with responsibility for a different area of party work; these secretaries automatically became members of the Central Committee. The entire national organization of the party was similarly revised.

Novotny was and remained through the rest of his life a convinced Stalinist. He maintained the rigid policies of Stalinism long after they were modified even in the Soviet Union. He ignored Soviet attempts at relaxation during the mid-1950s. He and most of his supporters were deeply implicated in the show-trials of that period and in the terror of the late 1940s. Therefore, Novotny was not about to open the files for scrutiny. In January 1957, after the brutal Soviet attack on the Hungarian revolution, Novotny denounced de-Stalinization as a "reactionary process." As late as 1961, he refused proposals for the review of the show-trials as "irresponsible." No public apology was offered to victims of Stalinism in Czechoslovakia; the survivors of concentration and prison camps were quietly sent home. There was no rehabilitation of these people.

In January 1968, Novotny's protege was defeated for the first secretaryship of the Slovak section of the Czechoslovak Communist party. The man he did not want in that post was Alexander Dubcek (*see* Dubcek, Alexander). This was an open revolt against Novotny's leadership. He never again attended a meeting of the Central Committee or the Presidium of his party. At the end of April, the Slovak Central Committee declared the rehabilitation of Slovak victims of Stalinism and the restoration of some traditional Slovak organizations. By then, lawyers were clamoring for the restoration of the rule of law and the independence of the courts. Although Novotny was forced to give up his post as first secretary of the party in January 1968, he remained president of the republic. On March 30, he was ousted even from this position. He retired from politics and died in 1975 in obscurity.

Bibliography
Rothschild, Joseph, *Return to Diversity: A Political History of East Central Europe Since World War II* (Oxford, 1992); Skilling, Gordon H., *Czechoslovakia's Interrupted Revolution* (Princeton, NJ, 1976). Ulc, Otto, *Politics in Czechoslovakia* (San Francisco, 1974); Wolchik, Sharon, "Czechoslovakia," in Joseph Held, ed. *The Columbia History of Eastern Europe in the Twentieth Century* (New York, 1992).

Pelikan, Jiri (1923–). A member of the underground Czechoslovak Communist party in the late 1930s, Pelikan was arrested by the Germans in 1940. However, he escaped and was hidden by friends until the end of the war. He became the president of the Czechoslovak Students' Union in 1948 and was elected to parliament in the rigged elections of that year. He was appointed chairman of the University Committee of the Communist party from 1948 to 1951. From 1953 to 1963, he was the president of the International Union of Students. Between 1963 and 1968, he was director of Czechoslovak television. He also filled various party posts during this time. From October 1969 to September 1969, he served as cultural attache in the Czechoslovak embassy in Rome. When he was recalled, he refused to return to Czechoslovakia and went instead to London, where he edited a work on the Czechoslovak show-trials.

Bibliography
London, Arthur, *On Trial* (London, 1968); Pelikan, Jiri, ed. *The Czechoslovak Political Trials, 1950–1954* (London, 1971); Skilling, Gordon H., *Czechoslovakia's Interrupted Revolution* (Princeton, NJ, 1976).

Persistence of Stalinism in Czechoslovakia. There were many reasons for the survival of Stalinism in Czechoslovakia into the late 1980s. One of the most important of these reasons was that, given the relatively developed state of the Czechoslovak economy during the interwar years, Stalinist economic policies did not do as much damage as they did in other East European countries. To some extent, the country even derived some benefits from these policies and, above all, it could rid itself of the troublesome German minorities. Economic discontent and national feelings towards Soviet domination was, therefore, not as strong as in other East European countries. In any case, Czechoslovakia had a long history of affinity with Big Slavic Brother. The Czech intelligentsia quickly adapted to the Stalinist system and soon became its beneficiary. The Communist party, also part of the prewar political system, enjoyed considerable support after the war on account of the role it played in the defeat of Nazi Germany.

The terrorist apparatus that had been built up in Czechoslovakia after World War

II, with the help and supervision of the Soviet KGB, retained most of its power even after Stalin's death. Although show-trials were not repeated, the ever vigilant security organs with their tens of thousands of agents, stool pigeons, and other undercover operators simply prevented the emergence of a significant political opposition. Presidents Klement Gottwald and Antonyn Novotny, as well as most of their henchmen, were personally involved in the Stalinist and post-Stalinist terror, and they were not inclined to permit inquiries into their activities.

The fact that Czechoslovakia remained a multi-ethnic state after the expulsion of the ethnic Germans also contributed to the survival of Stalinism. Hungarians, the largest ethnic minority in Slovakia, were often used as scapegoats for the failures of the system. The emergence of opposition was made doubly difficult by the persistence of different degrees of development in the Czech and Slovak lands. All these factors, as well as the Czech national character, long accustomed to passive resistance to oppressors, symbolized by the fictional character, Good Soldier Schweik, contributed to the longevity of Stalinism.

Bibliography
Gilberg, Trond, "The Political Order," in Stephen Fischer-Galati, ed. *Eastern Europe in the 1980s* (Boulder, CO, 1981); Jowitt, Ken, "The Leninist Legacy," in Ivo Banac, ed. *Eastern Europe in Revolution* (New York, 1992); Judt, Tony R., "Metamorphosis: The Democratic Revolution in Czechoslovakia," in Ivo Banac, ed. *Eastern Europe in Revolution* (Ithaca, NY, 1992).

Prague Spring, 1968. During the spring of 1968, a series of public discussions began in Czechoslovakia which soon developed into an avalanche of expressions of outrage over two decades of communist oppression. Alexander Dubcek (*see* Dubcek, Alexander), the secretary general of the Communist party, realized that the party would have to respond to the public mood. He dismissed many of the hard-liners from leading positions in state and party. Ministries were now headed by his supporters. In the ministry of the interior, huge numbers of documents were discovered, implicating the Czechoslovak and Soviet secret police forces in manufactured show-trials and other repressive measures. Dubcek arranged for a presidential pardon for all the unjustly accused in early May. On June 25, a law cleared all victims of the terror of their alleged crimes. Censorship, already discontinued in March, was formally abolished in June. All these were responses not only to public pressure in politics, but also to the economic crisis that had persisted in the country from the mid-1960s. It was obvious to most observers that the crisis had originated in the mindless application of Stalinist methods of development. Radislaw Selucky, a well-known economist, aptly labeled the system as "the cult of the plan."

The atmosphere in Prague and Bratislava resembled the euphoria Hungarians felt in October 1956 when their revolution seemed about to succeed. Smiling people greeted each other on the streets as if a great burden had been lifted from their shoulders. What was remarkable was that, at least at this time, public opinion did not turn against the socialist system per se. The Communist party was not condemned, nor was the Soviet Union abused. There was no demand for the restoration of capitalism or for the dissolution of collective farms. Dubcek and his associate tried in every possible way to avoid offending Leonid Brezhnev and the other aging Soviet leaders.

Poland and East Germany were, however, terrified of the spectacle of freedom in Czechoslovakia and did everything in their power to incite the Soviet comrades against Prague. In April, the first Soviet criticisms were voiced. The attacks on the reformist Czechoslovak leadership became more and more serious as time went on. On the other hand, Czech intellectuals pressured Dubcek to stand up for the nation and refute the criticism. On June 27, a group of these intellectuals issued a statement entitled "Two Thousand Words" (*see* "Two Thousand Words"), which was an open condemnation of two decades of mismanagement of affairs by the Communist party. On July 11, the Soviet official daily, *Pravda*, compared the Czech developments with those that took place in Hungary in 1956.

Four days later, the Warsaw Pact members (actually, the Soviet Union in the name of the pact) demanded in a memorandum sent to Dubcek that censorship be restored and the liberalization of politics be reversed. Prague could not possibly comply with these demands without provoking a popular uprising. Further negotiations resulted in more disagreements. On August 10, a draft of new Communist party statutes was published, and the vote on these statutes by a special congress of the party was to occur in September. The statutes proclaimed that party leaders on all levels of the organization were to be elected by the membership by secret ballot. They also relaxed rules on factions within the party. This was apostasy in the eyes of conservative communists, especially those who ruled the Soviet Union.

In response, the Warsaw Pact, led by Soviet tanks and infantry, entered Czechoslovakia on August 20 1968, ending the "experiment with socialism with a human face." The invasion was not resisted by the people or by the Czechoslovak armed forces. Dubcek formally remained secretary general of the party until April 1969, when he was replaced by the rigidly dogmatic communist, the Slovak Gustav Husak (*see* Husak, Gustav). The invasion and the subsequent declaration of the "Brezhnev doctrine" had worldwide repercussions. In the Soviet Bloc, it halted the process that was the last chance to reform the tottering system of Soviet-style socialism and prolonged the existence of the corrupt, inefficient socialist regimes in Eastern Europe and the Soviet Union. Yugoslavia, Albania, and Romania, free of Soviet troops, were frightened anew of possible intervention in their own countries and became more hostile to the Soviet Union. New questions were raised about Soviet colonialism in Eastern Europe, and the Brezhnev doctrine was roundly condemned by the Western nations.

The invasion failed to solve Czechoslovakia's festering economic and political problems. Although the country had to endure two more decades of communist rule, often referred to as "normalization" (*see* "Normalization" in Czechoslovakia), and the reformer communists were shunted aside, humiliated, and even imprisoned, there was no way the communist system could have been salvaged.

Bibliography
Golan, Golia, *The Czechoslovak Reform Movement: Communism in Crisis 1962–1968* (Cambridge, 1971); Kusin, Vladimir, *The Intellectual Origins of the Prague Spring: The Development of Reformist Ideas in Czechoslovakia, 1956–1967* (Cambridge, England, 1971); Tigrid, Pavel, *Why Dubcek Fell* (London, 1971); Valenta, Jiri, Soviet Intervention in Czechoslovakia, 1968: Anatomy of a Decision (Baltimore, MD, 1979).

Prochazka, Jaroslaw (1897–). In 1917, Prochazka was a soldier in the Czech Legion that fought its way through Bolshevik lines in Russia on its way to the Pacific Ocean and evacuation by the British. He returned to Czechoslovakia in 1919. Soon, however, he went back to Moscow where he entered the Marx-Engels Institute in 1920. After finishing his schooling in the institute, Prochazka was appointed director of a state publishing firm in the Soviet Union. During the World War II, Prochazka was one of the founders of the Czechoslovak brigade and fought against the Germans. He returned to Czechoslovakia in 1945 as a general of the Soviet army. In 1948, he was appointed chief of staff of the armed forces of his homeland. The following year, he was appointed a member of the Central Committee of the Communist party. In 1950, he became deputy minister for defense. Seven years later, in 1957, he was named chairman of the Department of History at Charles University, although he did not have a college degree. In 1958, he was named rector of the University.

Bibliography
Toma, Peter A., "The Communist Party of Czechoslovakia," in Stephen Fischer-Galati, *The Communist Parties of Eastern Europe* (New York, 1979).

Religious Policies in Communist Czechoslovakia. The aim of all communist regimes has been the elimination of all religious influences from their respective societies. If this were not entirely possible, the party was content to subordinate religious institutions to its policies. The communists were aware indeed that religion was a powerful force, therefore, they copied religious rituals as substitutes for the real thing. Burials, baptisms, and marriages were performed by state functionaries, and the theory of the infallibility of the pope was substituted for by the doctrine of the infallibility of the Communist party. Even the Holy Trinity found a replacement in the trio of Marx-Engels-Lenin in communist mythology.

The Communist party of Czechoslovakia was no exception. Immediately after the coup d'etat of 1948, special administrative measures were introduced in order to eliminate religious instruction in schools. Church leaders of all denominations were persecuted. Many were jailed on trumped-up charges and were sent to concentration camps. They received especially brutal treatment from the prison guards at these jails. National Committees (*see* National Committees in Czechoslovakia) in villages singled out priests and ministers for deportation.

The Catholic Church tried to fight back. In 1949, the Bishops' Conference sent a pastoral letter to all its parishes, pointing out the incompatibility between Christianity and materialist Marxism. The response was increased repression against all churches. All religious and social organizations that were supervised by priests or ministers were now dissolved. Church properties were confiscated, seminaries and church-run schools were closed, and their teachers were fired. Many bishops were harassed and jailed. The state declared its open support of atheism and sponsored rallies, published books, and held lectures against religion. When a bishopric fell vacant, the regime refused to accept newly appointed replacements. The relations of the Catholic church with the Vatican were forbidden. Church attendance was monitored, and party members were forbidden to participate in church rituals and ceremonies. Anyone who was discovered to have religious convictions could lose a job.

After the Warsaw Pact invasion of 1968, the party continued to emphasize the antireligious nature of socialism. Yet tactics were changed. Agreements were soon reached with the Vatican over the appointment of four new bishops to vacant sees. A new cardinal was also appointed by the pope in the person of Stephan Trochta, the bishop of Litomerice. In spite of the seeming relaxation of anti religious policies, the publication of antireligious texts was continued and so were conferences in the name of atheism. The state presented an exhibition on Czechoslovak atheistic traditions at the Slovak National Museum in Bratislava in 1972. Only the collapse of the communist regime in 1989 put a stop to official persecution of religions in Czechoslovakia.

Bibliography

Ramet, Pedro, "Christianity and National Heritage among the Czechs and Slovaks," in Pedro Ramet, ed. *Religion and Nationalism in Soviet and East European Politics 2nd Ed.* (Durham, NC, 1989).

Sik, Ota (1919–). Sik spent his early years studying economics at Charles University in Prague. When the Germans occupied the Czech lands, Sik was taken to Mauthausen concentration camp where he was kept until 1945. After his liberation, Sik joined the Communist party. He was appointed a member of the party's regional committee. He attended the higher party school for cadres in 1950 and became chairman of the Department of Economics at his alma mater in 1953. In that year, he was appointed full professor.

Between 1958 and 1962, Sik was a candidate (nonvoting) member of the Central Committee of the Communist party. In 1962, he was appointed director of the Economics Institute of the Czechoslovak Academy of Sciences, and he became a recognized expert on socialist economics. In that same year, he became a full voting member of the Central Committee, and in 1968 he was appointed deputy prime minister in Alexander Dubcek's government. His theories served as the basis for the economic reform plans introduced during the Prague Spring (*see* Prague Spring, 1968). Following the Warsaw Pact invasion of Czechoslovakia in August 1968, Sik was unwilling to go along with the old, stodgy policies of "normalization" (*see* "Normalization" in

Czechoslovakia). His outspoken criticism of the whole system earned him expulsion from the Communist party. In 1969, Sik emigrated to Germany where he continues his studies today.

Bibliography
Kusin, Vladimir V., *From Dubcek to Charter 77: A Study of 'Normalization' in Czechoslovakia, 1968–1978* (New York, 1978).

Siroky, William (1902–1089). Siroky became a member of the Czechoslovak Communist party in 1921, and he served as a member of various regional party committees. He was a member of the party's Central Committee between 1930 and 1938. In 1935, he was elected to the Czechoslovak parliament on the Communist party ticket. In 1938, he was regional party secretary in Bratislava in Slovakia. When Germany invaded the Czech lands, Siroky escaped at first to France and then he went to the Soviet Union. In 1941, he returned to his homeland only to be arrested by the Nazis almost immediately. He was very lucky and managed to escape, and he ended up once again in Moscow. After the end of World War II, Siroky returned home and served, until 1953, as deputy prime minister. He was already a member of parliament and of the party's Politburo. Between 1950 and 1953 he was minister of foreign affairs and was prime minister of Czechoslovakia between 1953 and 1963. In 1968, he was dismissed and expelled from the Presidium (formerly the Politburo) of the party, and in May of that year his party membership was suspended. The Warsaw Pact invasion ended the suspension, but Siroky never returned to active party life.

Bibliography
Skilling, Gordon H., *Czechoslovakia's Interrupted Revolution* (Princeton, NJ., 1976).

Slansky Trial. Rudolf Slansky was among the early members of the Czechoslovak Communist party. When Germany invaded the Czech lands, Slansky left for the Soviet Union and spent several years there in exile. While in Moscow, he befriended Klement Gottwald who later became the general secretary of the Czechoslovak Communist party. In 1944, Slansky was sent back to Czechoslovakia to participate in the Slovak uprising against the Germans. A cold man, a narrow-minded dogmatic communist, he was totally devoted to Marxism-Leninism and to Stalin. After the Rajk-trial in Hungary, Matyas Rakosi, the Hungarian general secretary, urged Gottwald to follow the Hungarian's lead and purge the Czechoslovak Communist party of "subversive" elements. But Gottwald dragged his feet, until Stalin personally intervened and sent some KGB "experts" to arrange the Czechoslovak show trials.

With the help of KGB general Likachev, preparations began for a trial of Vladimir Clementis and Gustav Husak, (*see* Husak, Gustav), Slovak communists, who were to be accused of nationalism. Slansky himself selected them for this role in order to "prove" that Titoism in Slovakia was alive and that Slovak Titoists were preparing the overthrow of the socialist state and the separation of Slovakia.

By the winter of 1950, however, Stalin obviously believed that the anti-Tito campaign in Eastern Europe needed further reinforcement. By then, Israel had turned to the West and the Soviet Union started to cultivate the Arabs as potential clients against the Western alliance. This made it necessary for Stalin to find some Jews to sacrifice to this turn of affairs. Slansky was a Jew. He was also second-in-command in the Czechoslovak Communist party. On July 31, 1951, the entire country celebrated Slansky's birthday. He received the Order of Socialism, and streets and factories were named after him. By then, however, the secret police had several "witnesses" against him, and Gottwald, who was scared out of his wits of the KGB, finally consented to the Slansky's trial.

On November 23, 1951, Slansky was suddenly arrested. The accusations against him did not focus on his alleged Titoism, but on "cosmopolitanism," a Soviet euphemism for Zionism. He was also accused of ignoring Leninist teachings and of transforming the Czechoslovak Communist party into a mass organization. He allegedly supported the "imperialist Israeli state" between 1946 and 1947. Furthermore, the Slansky-trial was to be slanted in such a way as to discourage "national communism," a warning to other East European communists to beware of slighting the Soviet Union and its interests, defined by Stalin.

There was some truth in the accusations. Slansky, until his arrest, was certainly Stalin's staunchest supporter among Czechoslovak communists. He certainly was not a Czech nationalist who would want to chart an independent road for Czechoslovakia. It was also true that many of the Czech and Slovak communist leaders were uncomfortable with the policies forced on them by Stalin, especially since most of these policies were alien to Czechoslovak historical traditions. Slansky was the leader of one faction within the party that included intellectuals of Jewish background, and they all had shown contempt for the "uncouth ones" in the party leadership. Many among Slansky's supporters had fought in the Spanish civil war, traveled abroad, and, although they were convinced communists, had a broader political perspective than did Gottwald's cronies.

The population of the country had also developed a genuine dislike for Slansky, the celebrations of his birthday notwithstanding, since they held him responsible for the terrorist excesses of Stalinization. Thus, they were easy targets for the coming purges. Many of Slansky's supporters were also arrested, but his preparation for the trial lasted a whole year.

During the proceedings a brutally tortured Slansky "confessed" to all the charges. He "admitted" that he had conspired for the restoration of capitalism and that he had been an agent of the CIA. One of the most ridiculous of the charges was that he was taking his orders secretly for sabotage from the British left-wing Labor party deputy, Konni Ziliacus. He also admitted that he had planned the assassination of Klement Gottwald. On November 26, 1952, Slansky and ten of his fellow codefendants were sentenced to death. On December 3, they were all hanged. Three other defendants received prison terms. The bodies of the executed communists were cremated and their ashes were strewn around the outskirts of Prague.

The trial was a link in the chain of Stalinist terror, one of the most barbaric episodes in the modern history of Europe, and certainly of Czechoslovakia. The consequences of the Slansky trial for Czechoslovakia and the Communist party were long-lasting. The leaders who survived were all involved in the purges and approved of the judicial murders. Thereafter they were always worried about their roles being exposed to the public's view. In the mid-1960s, the reform communists attempted to rehabilitate Slansky and the others who had shared his fate, partly as a means of discrediting the hard-line party leaders, partly to cleanse the party of its sins. A commission was set up in 1967, but its report was not made public, and Slansky was not rehabilitated.

Bibliography
London, Arthur, *On Trial* (London, 1968); Pelikan, Jiri. ed. *The Czechoslovak Political Trials, 1950–1954* (Stanford, CA, 1971).

Slovakia and the Slovak Problem. Relations between Slovaks and Czechs have been rocky ever since the establishment of the Czechoslovak state in 1918. The Slovaks have always felt that their culture and nationality have never been appreciated appropriately by their Czech compatriots and that they were denied the autonomy promised in 1918. This led to the split of Czechoslovakia after the appeasement at Munich in 1938 and to the establishment of a puppet Slovak state, which was independent in name but was subordinated to the Germans in practice.

In August 1944, the Slovak Communist party led a national uprising against the Germans and their Slovak supporters. The uprising was easily suppressed by the German army with great losses to the resistance fighters and the civilian population. Nevertheless, the very fact that the uprising even occurred, gave self-confidence and stature to the Slovak communists, since there was no analogue to their heroic act on the part of the Czechs.

After 1945, the Slovak communists did not want their party to be merged with the Czech party in a centralized common organization. A compromise was eventually reached with Soviet mediation. The Slovak Communist party was included in the Communist party of Czechoslovakia as an autonomous body. Yet this was not a real concession because the supreme organization was that of the federal party as it was also the primary organization in Bohemia and Moravia. Thus, the solution did not really provide the autonomy demanded by the Slovak communists. It created perpetual discontent in party ranks until, with the show trial of Gustav Husak (*see* Husak, Gustav) and Vladimir Clementis, all muttering was silenced.

It was the Slovak Alexander Dubcek (*see* Dubcek, Alexander) who brought the controversy into the open once again in 1968. The Soviet leaders took advantage of Slovak discontent after the invasion of Czechoslovakia in that year and installed the Slovak Husak—who survived the purges—as the new Czechoslovak leader. In 1968, it was the Slovak wing of the Czechoslovak Communist party that became the strongest critic of the Novotny leadership. Its former leaders, who had fallen victim to the purges, became symbols of national oppression. Slovaks in general considered Rudolf Slansky (see Slansky Trial) and his group, executed in 1952, Jewish dogmatists who had largely been responsible for the Stalinist terror of the late 1940s and the Czechs who had been purged at that time simply as irrelevant to their situation. But the Slovaks who died or were imprisoned, including the Jewish Eugene Loebl, Vladimir Clementis, Laco Novomesky, and even Gustav Husak, were regarded as genuine national heroes. Traditionally, Slovak communists were more independent-minded than their Czech comrades. Above all, they were not part of the cabal who were partly responsible for the show trials. In addition, the sharp dividing line that separated the intellectuals in the Czech party from ordinary members did not exist in the Slovakian case. The national resentment over Czech domination became part and parcel of the Slovak party's ideology.

In 1968, during the Prague Spring, (*see* Prague Spring, 1968) the Slovak communists resurrected their claim to equality with the Czechs. They went so far as to demand the establishment of a completely independent Slovak party organization. They proposed to revive the Slovak National Council that had been created during the uprising of 1944. However, after the Soviet intervention, Slovak demands became more muted. The shrewd Soviet move to make Husak the leader of the Czechoslovak Communist party and of the government of the republic placated Slovak communists.

However, with the collapse of the communist regime in the state, Slovak nationalism was reborn with a vengeance. It led to the emergence of an autonomous Slovak government that became the leader of a newly independent Slovak state on January 1, 1993. The Czechoslovak state that existed for 75 years thus disappeared from the map of the world.

Bibliography

Mates, Pavel, "The New Slovak Constitution," *Radio Free Europe Research Report* 1.43 (October 30, 1992), pp. 39-42; Peche, Jiri, "Czech-Slovak Conflict Threatens State Unity," *Radio Free Europe Research Report* 1.1 (January 3, 1992), pp. 83-86; ——, "Czechoslovakia's Political Balance Sheet," *Radio Free Europe Research Report* 1.25 (June 19, 1992), pp. 24-25; ——, "Czechs and Slovaks Prepare to Part," *Radio Free Europe Research Report* 1.37 (September 18, 1992), pp. 12-15.

Smrkovsky, Josef (1911–1974). Smrkovsky joined the Czechoslovak Communist party in the early 1930s and was sent to Moscow to study at the school maintained by the COMINTERN for the indoctrination of foreign communists. In 1934, he returned to Czechoslovakia and became a functionary of the Communist party. During the German occupation of Czechoslovakia Smrkovsky worked in the underground communist movement and, after the German attack on the Soviet Union, he was one of the leaders of the resistance.

In 1945, Smrkovsky entered the inner circle of the party's leadership by becoming a member of the Politburo. However, he was swallowed up in the purges that followed the Slansky trial (*see* Slansky Trial). He was arrested, tried, and sentenced to life imprisonment in 1952. In 1955, he was released from prison, but he had to wait until 1963 to be rehabilitated.

In 1966, Smrkovsky once again became active in party politics. He was appointed as a member of the Central Committee and was also named minister of forestry and water conservation. He entered the Politburo in 1968 during the premiership of Alexander Dubcek (*see* Dubcek, Alexander). By then, he was a supporter of reforms, and he became chairman of the National Assembly. Smrkovsky strongly opposed the Warsaw Pact invasion of Czechoslovakia. As a consequence, he was expelled from the Communist party in 1970 and died as an outcast four years later.

Bibliography

Kusin, Vladimir V., *From Dubcek to Charter 77: A Study of 'Normalization' in Czechoslovakia, 1968–1978* (New York, 1978).

Svitak, Ivan (1926–). Svitak, a party member since 1945, became a Marxist philosopher at Charles University in Prague. During the purges, he was expelled from the party, but he retained his academic position.

He became a spokesman for reforms in 1968. He deplored the fact that the Czechoslovak Communist party had essentially remained a totalitarian organization. In a speech, entitled "With Head against the Wall," a reference to the practice of the secret police in treating political prisoners, Svitak declared totalitarian dictatorship enemy number one of the Czechoslovak people, and he called for its abolition in favor of an open society. He also declared that the people did not want democratization, but democracy. The aim, Svitak said, was to have free elections with true competition for the votes of the people. He proposed the creation of at least two new parties, one based on Christian and the other on socialist ideas, to provide alternatives to the communists' program. He rejected the existing "shadow parties" that the communists used to camouflage their real monopoly of power. Svitak especially condemned the disappearance of the Social Democratic party as a healthy alternative to the communists. He declared that without opposition, there is no democracy. In a later article, he proclaimed that the communists could never win a free election unless they became a normal, democratic organization. After the Warsaw Pact invasion, Svitak was harassed and he eventually left Czechoslovakia.

Bibliography

Oxley, Andrew, Alex Pravda, and Andrew Ritchie, *Czechoslovakia: The Party and the People* (London, 1973); Remington, Robert, ed., *Winter in Prague* (Cambridge, MA, 1972); Skilling, Gordon H., *Czechoslovakia's Interrupted Revolution* (Princeton, NJ, 1976); Svitak, Ivan, *The Czechoslovak Experiment, 1968–1969* (New York, 1971).

Svoboda, Ludvik (1895–1989). Svoboda served in the Habsburg army, then, after the establishment of Czechoslovakia, in the Czechoslovak armed forces. He became a communist during the 1930s. During World War II and the German occupation of the Czech lands, Svoboda went to the Soviet Union. When Germany attacked the

Soviet state, Svoboda joined the Czechoslovak Legion and fought alongside the Red Army.

In 1945, he returned to Czechoslovakia and was immediately appointed minister of defense. He participated in various coalition governments until the communist coup d'etat, in which Svoboda played a major role. Until 1950, he remained in his post as minister of defense. In that year, Svoboda became a victim of the purges; he was dismissed from his post and was expelled from the Communist party. For three years, he was kept in prison as an alleged Titoist.

Following Stalin's death, Svoboda was released and worked for a year as an accountant in Prague. In the following year, Svoboda's party membership was restored, and he was appointed commander of the country's chief military academy. In 1959, he retired. However, during Alexander Dubcek's premiership (*see* Dubcek, Alexander), Svoboda was elected president of the Czechoslovak republic and served in that capacity until October 1975. Although he opposed the Warsaw Pact invasion of Czechoslovakia, he made his accommodation with the Husak regime. He was even appointed to membership in the party's Central Committee and the Presidium (formerly the Politburo). In 1976, he retired once again, because he was ill and was no longer able to perform the functions of president.

Bibliography

Kusin, Vladimir V., *From Dubcek to Charter 77: A Study of 'Normalization' in Czechoslovakia, 1968–1978* (New York, 1978).

Two Thousand Words (1968). Ludvik Vaculik, a nonparty intellectual in Czechoslovakia, published a famous article as the expression of popular opinion about the reform process during the spring of 1968 (*see* Prague Spring, 1968). He reviewed the history of Czechoslovakia since 1945 and voiced sharp criticism of the leadership and policies of the Communist party. He also stressed his conviction that the revival process that had begun in the spring was grinding to a halt and that stronger measures than those proposed by the reformist leaders were needed to reform the system. The article was really a declaration, signed by more than sixty intellectuals, to alert the people to the dangers facing the movement for democracy in Czechoslovakia. The article and its signers were bitterly denounced by the party and government leaders and it stirred up a great deal of controversy. Conservatives and progressive all commented on it, according to their own points of view, and it polarized opinions. The conservatives who called it "an open appeal to counterrevolution," wanted the author prosecuted. The party's Presidium, the National Front, and even premier Alexander Dubcek contributed to the open debate. They especially denounced the article's call for independent mass organizations as an attack on the party and on socialism itself.

The "Two Thousand Words" became a center of intense discussions all over the country. Party district organizations, city councils, and people on the street were all aroused by its statement. A flood of letters, both for and against, arrived at newspaper editorial offices. In Slovakia, the nomen-klatura was generally negative about the article, but individuals were sometimes supportive of its demands.

In the final count, although the timing of the article (June) was perhaps debatable, it did achieve its purpose. It alerted the people of the dangers of opposition to democratization. In fact, "Two Thousand Words" did not represent the concerted action of a mass of people to change the system; it was not a call for a counterrevolution as its conservative critics maintained. It nevertheless stirred up public opinion in support of reform. It also provided an opportunity for hard-line conservatives to attack the reformist leadership.

Bibliography

Oxley, Andrew, Alex Pravda, and Andrew Ritchie, eds. *Czechoslovakia: The Party and the People* (London, 1973); Skilling, Gordon H., *Czechoslovakia's Interrupted Revolution* (Princeton, NJ, 1976).

Zapotocky, Antonin (1894–1957). Zapotocky, a member of the Czechoslovak Social Democratic party, headed its regional organization in Brno between 1907 and 1911. He changed over to the communists and was elected general secretary of the Communist party between 1922 and 1925. In 1925, he was elected parliamentary deputy on the Communist party's ticket and was also appointed to membership in the party's Politburo. Between 1929 and 1939, Zapotocky was secretary to the Red Trade Union Movement. When Germany occupied the Czech lands, Zapotocky was arrested and thrown in the Orienburg concentration camp where he remained until 1945. In 1945, he became the chairman of the Revolutionary Trade Union Movement. In 1948, he was appointed deputy prime minister of the new People's Democracy. He became prime minister and served in that post until 1953. Finally, he was named president of the Czechoslovak republic and died in office in 1957.

Bibliography

Ulc, Otto, *Politics in Czechoslovakia* (New York, 1967).

Sali Berisha of Albania

Mehemet Shehu of Albania (Library of Congress)

Enver Hoxha speaking at a congress of the Albanian Communist party (Library of Congress)

H. Lleshi, president of the People's Assembly of Albania

The headquarters of the Bulgarian Communist party in Sofia (Library of Congress)

Vulko Chervenkov, successor to Georgi Dimitrov, head of the Bulgarian Communist party (Library of Congress)

Georgi Dimitrov, secretary general of Comintern and premier of Bulgaria since 1945 (Library of Congress)

Rudolf Slansky, ruthless Communist minister of the interior in Czechoslovakia (Library of Congress)

The National Assembly of Czechoslovakia before 1968 voting for a governmental measure (Library of Congress)

Antonyn Novotny, secretary general of the Czechoslovak Communist party with Leonid Brezhnev (Library of Congress)

Klement Gottwald, premier of Czechoslovakia (Library of Congress)

Vaclav Havel, playwright and
president of Czech Republic
(© Peter Turnley, Black Star)

Erich Honecker, East Germany's Communist boss with U.S. Secretary General Cuellar in East Berlin

Demonstration in East Berlin in 1953, with Soviet tanks which later fired on the crowd

Soviet tanks fire on demonstrators in East Berlin in 1953, during the uprising against Communist policies

A section of the Berlin Wall, built in 1961, separating East Germany from the West (Library of Congress)

Wilhelm Pieck and Otto Grotewohl of East Germany (Library of Congress)

Walter Ulbricht, general secretary of the East German Communist Party, arriving on a visit to Warsaw, Poland (Library of Congress)

Soviet occupying forces in Budapest, Hungary, stopping photographer in November 1956

The sentencing to death of Imre Nagy on June 15, 1958

Jozef Antall, prime minister of Hungary, 1990–1993

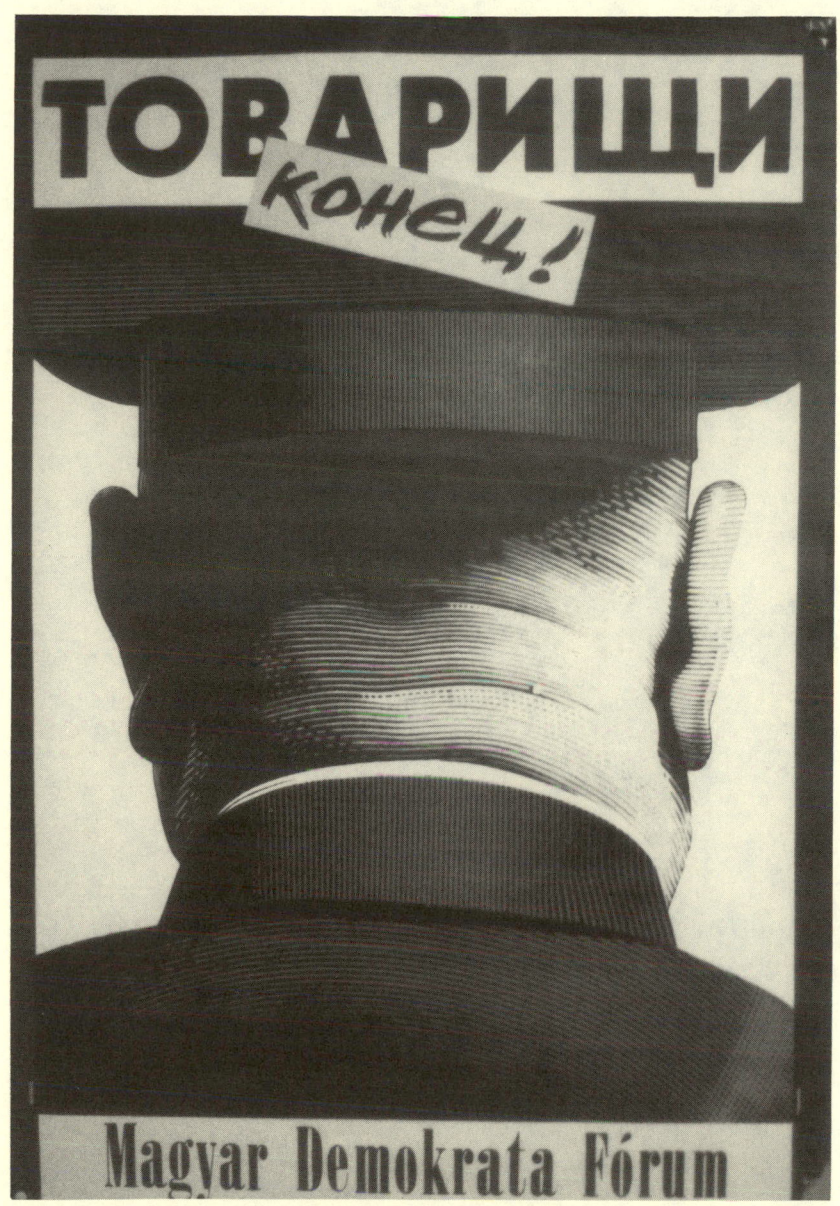

Election poster of the Hungarian Democratic Forum in the spring of 1990. Caption at the top: "Comrades, it's over!"

The Congress of the Gyorffy Collegium, May 31, 1945. The participants in the closing session included M. Rakosi, A. Kethly, J. Darras, K. Viskii, and the students. To the left of Rakosi (center) are I. Kovacs and L. Rajk.

Laszlo Rajk, as minister of the interior, was responsible for the initial Communist terror in Hungary

Imre Nagy, martyred prime minister of Hungary, led the revolutionary government in 1956 (Library of Congress)

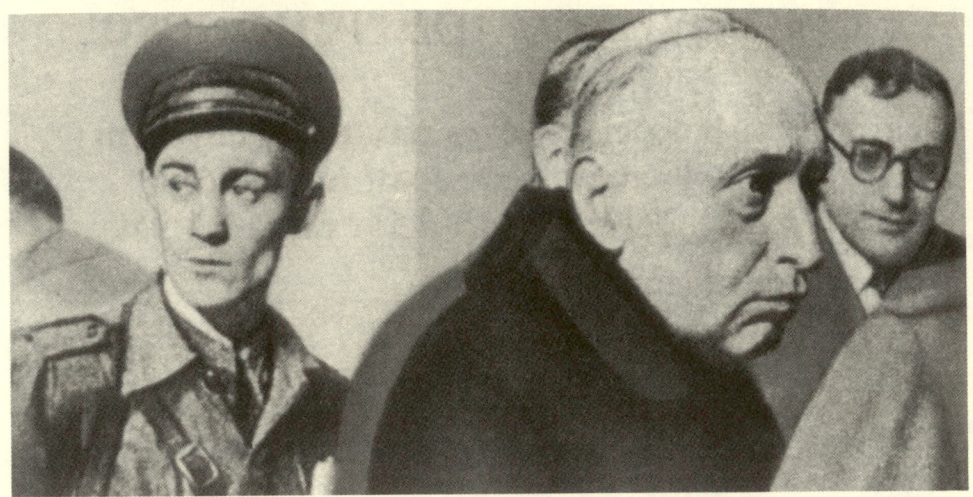

Jozef Cardinal Mindszenty being liberated by revolutionaries in October 1956

Revolutionary woman on a Budapest street in October 1956, with a destroyed Soviet tank in the background

Janos Kadar, the Hungarian Communist party secretary (in fur hat) arriving in Warsaw, Poland. On his left, Wladislaw Gomulka, his Polish counterpart. (Library of Congress)

Propaganda poster of Matyas Rakosi, the Communist dicator of Hungary between 1947 and 1956 (Library of Congress)

GERMAN DEMOCRATIC REPUBLIC (EAST GERMANY)

General Information. *Territory:* 41,610 square miles (107,771 square kilometers). *Population:* 16,641,000 in 1987. *Borders:* East Germany bordered on Czechoslovakia in the south, West Germany in the south and west, the Baltic Sea in the north, and Poland in the east. The borders were not recognized until a treaty was signed, in 1969, with the Soviet Union and then with Poland. *Major cities:* East Berlin, Magdeburg, Leipzig, Dresden. *Geography:* The land is mostly low-lying plains and mountains in the south and west. *Ethnicity:* the population was 99 percent German. Scattered groups of Poles, Czechs, and Gypsies lived within the borders of the state. *Historical background:* During most of its history, East Germany was home to over 450,000 Soviet soldiers distributed in its territory in strategic locations. The form of the state was ostensibly a parliamentary democracy. It had a president, a prime minister and a cabinet with several ministers and a state bureaucracy. In reality, the Communist party of East Germany (renamed in 1946 the Socialist Unity party) ruled the state through a parallel organization that matched state organs at every level.

Bibliography

Dennis, Mike, *German Democratic Republic: Politics, Economics, Society* (London, 1988); Krisch, Henry, *The German Democratic Republic: The Search for Identity* (Boulder, CO, 1984); Larrabee, F. Stephen, *The Two German States and European Security* (New York, 1989); Moreton, Edwina, ed. *Germany Between East and West* (Cambridge, England, 1987); Price, Arnold H., ed. *East Germany: A Select Bibliography* (Washington, DC, 1967).

CHRONOLOGY

1945 *April.* Soviet and American forces met at the Elbe river. Although the official end of the European war is listed as May 8, the Nazi state was destroyed at the Elbe river. Adolf Hitler committed suicide, and Soviet troops occupied Berlin.

June. The Allied Control Commission was established to deal with matters

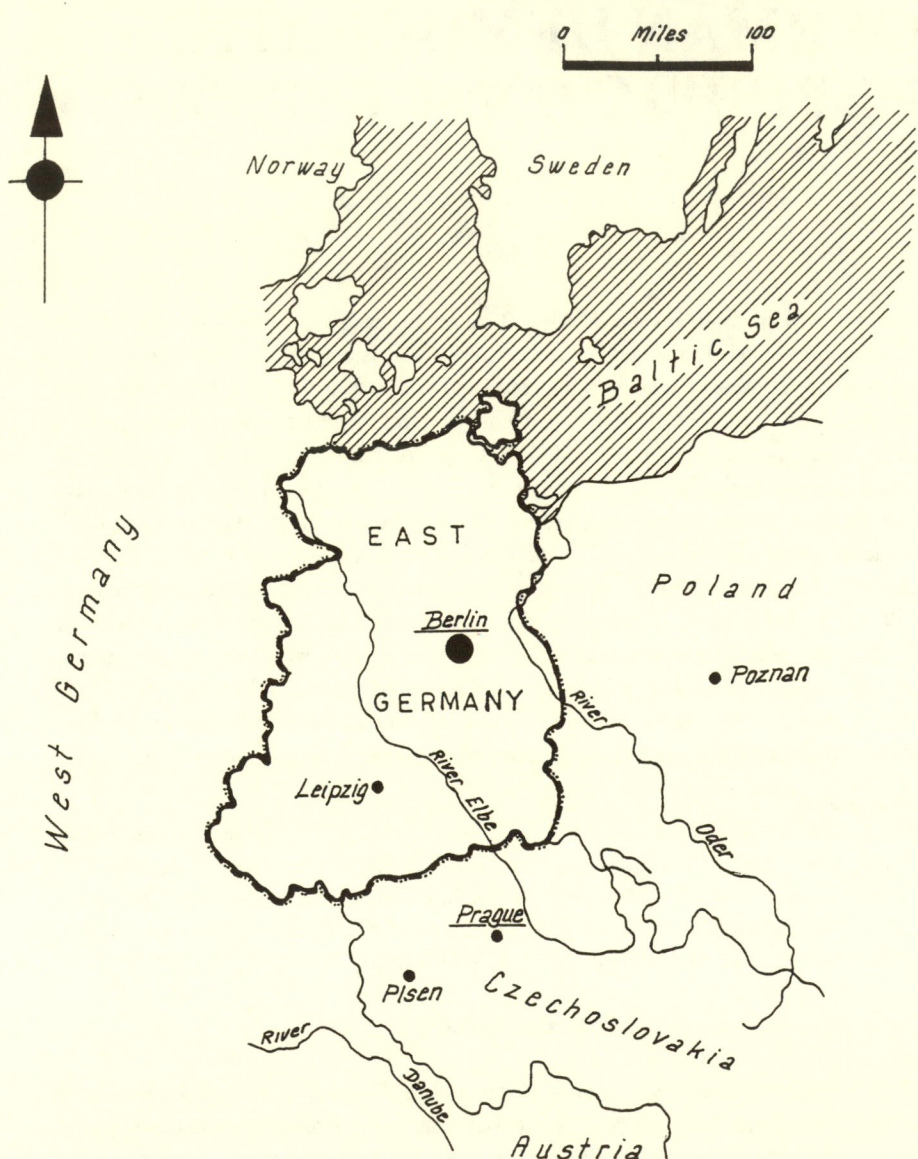

EAST GERMANY

0   Miles   100

Norway

Sweden

Baltic Sea

West Germany

EAST

Poland

Berlin

• Poznan

GERMANY

River Oder

River Elbe

Leipzig •

Prague •

Plsen •

Czechoslovakia

River Danube

Austria

concerning defeated Germany. The city of Berlin was declared a four-power occupational zone.

November. The trial of German war criminals began in Nuremberg.

1946 *April.* In the Soviet zone of occupation in Germany, the Social Democratic and Communist parties merged under pressure from the Soviet occupying authorities. The new party's name: Socialist Unity party (SED).

October. The International War Crimes Tribunal issued its verdict. Twelve Nazi leaders were sentenced to death, three were given life sentences, and nine were acquitted.

1947 *January.* The occupational zones of the three Western Allies in Germany were merged.

May. Stalinization of the Soviet zone of occupation in Germany began with the nationalization of all mines without compensation.

1948 *June.* Following a dispute over currency reform in the Western zone of Germany, the Soviet army established a blockade of the city of Berlin. Joseph Stalin's intention was to force the Western Allies out of the former German capital city. The Allies responded by an airlift of foodstuff and other necessities.

1949 *May.* The Berlin blockade ended. A new German state, the Federal Republic of Germany (West Germany), was established. Its capital: Bonn. In response, in the Soviet zone of occupation, a constitution was proclaimed for the German Democratic Republic (East Germany). Wilhelm Pieck, a communist, was named its president.

1951 *July.* East German and Polish leaders signed a declaration which proclaimed the Oder-Neisse rivers as the boundary between the two countries. The three Western Allies proclaimed the end of hostilities with Germany.

1953 *June.* The protest of construction workers in East Berlin erupted into full-scale riots in several cities in East Germany. Soviet troops put down the uprising, killing and wounding over 200 people. This threw light on the alleged sovereignty of the German Democratic Republic.

1955 *January.* The Supreme Soviet of the Soviet state declared the end of hostilities with Germany.

1960 The communist leaders ordered the full collectivization of agriculture in East Germany. More than 500,000 peasants lost their land.

1961 *August.* The Berlin Wall was erected. The work was performed by East German workers, supervised by Soviet KGB troops. The Wall effectively stopped the flow of refugees to the West from East Germany.

1966 *August.* The East German embassy in Beijing was attacked by mobs of Chinese Red Guards, whose placards declared "war on the world."

1968 *August.* East German military contingents participated in the invasion of Czechoslovakia.

1969 *June.* At a meeting of seventy-five Communist parties held in Moscow, the Soviet party leaders wanted a general condemnation of the Chinese for their "deviation" from Marxism. East German delegates strongly supported this demand, but it was denied.

1970 *March.* East German prime minister Willy Stoph and West German premier Willy Brandt met, the first time such a meeting had taken place. However, no agreement was reached.

1971 *May.* Walter Ulbricht, the communist dictator of East Germany, was replaced by Erich Honecker.

1972 *March.* West Germans were permitted to visit relatives in East Germany for the first time since the building of the Berlin Wall.

December. East and West Germany concluded a basic agreement formally recognizing each other. The agreement opened the way for the admission of both states to membership in the United Nations.

1973 *February.* Great Britain and France extended recognition to East Germany.

1974 *January.* The East German Communist party sent delegates to a meeting of European Communist parties, where the participants signed a declaration of general principles of their organizations and actions.

April. Gunther Guillaume, an East German spy, a close adviser to chancellor Willy Brandt, was arrested. This led to the resignation of Brandt.

September. The United States extended diplomatic recognition to East Germany.

1975 *July.* East Germany signed the Helsinki Accords, finalizing the post-World War II borders in Europe, and guaranteeing human rights.

1976 *June.* The conference of European Communist and Socialist parties, held in East Berlin, rejected a Soviet bid for the condemnation of the Chinese and continuing Soviet domination of the international socialist and communist movements. East German delegates strongly supported Moscow.

1980 *June.* East German athletes participated in the Moscow Olympic games, and won an unprecedented number of medals. The games were boycotted by most Western countries because of the Soviet invasion of Afghanistan.

1984 *May.* East Germany boycotted the Olympic Games held in Los Angeles as retaliation of the U.S. boycott of the Moscow games.

July. East Germany eased restrictions on travel for West Germans. In return, the West German government approved $330 million in private bank credit for East Germany.

September. Erich Honecker cancelled his planned visit to West Germany since Soviet spokesmen accused him of unilaterally trying to improve relations between the two states.

1985 *April.* East Germany signed the extension of the Warsaw Pact treaty for ten years.

1989 *February.* The Socialist Unity party of East Germany issued a statement, declaring that the party would follow its own road to socialism, and maintain its monopoly over politics, the state-control of industry, and the maintenance of a "social net," expressed in subsidies for "essential goods."

March. The East German communists prohibited the distribution of the Soviet journal, Novoie Vremia, because it published an interview with Polish Solidarity leader Lech Walesa.

June. The daily newspaper of the East German Socialist Unity party declared that the shooting of prodemocracy demonstrators at Beijing was justified.

September. Hungary announced that its border with Austria would be opened for East Germans wishing to emigrate to the West. East Germany denounced the decision but was powerless to prevent it.

October. A massive prodemocracy demonstration held in Leipzig followed, by two days, the celebration of the fortieth anniversary of East Germany's existence, an event in which Mikhail Gorbachev participated.

November. The Berlin Wall was demolished. East Germany's border with West Germany was opened.

1990 *January.* The East Berlin headquarters of the feared secret police (Stasi) was attacked by thousands of citizens, looking for files on themselves and on informers.

March. West German chancellor Helmut Kohl campaigned for Christian Democratic party candidates in East Germany. He also announced that, at reunification, the exchange rate for the East and West German Marks would be one-to-one. The election resulted in the Alliance for Democracy led by the Christian Democratic party, winning 48.1 percent of the votes. The Social Democratic Union won only 21.8 percent.

June. The West and East German parliaments ratified the declaration for the unification of Germany.

July. The parity between the East German and West German monetary units was established as chancellor Kohl had promised. President Gorbachev, at a meeting with chancellor Kohl, accepted the reunification of Germany. The latter was to pay the cost of the withdrawal of Soviet troops, provide credits for the Soviet Union, and assume East Germany's obligations to the Soviet state.

October. The East German parliament voted for unification of Germany, and the two states were merged. East Germany became five states of the German federation. The history of the East German state had come to an end.

Aufbau Verlag (Publisher). By 1950, the East German communists had gained control over society, politics, economics, and culture. One means of controlling creative people, especially writers, was to have them included (or excluded) from the state-created, and state-controlled Writers' Union, or to make sure that the publication of their works was channeled through a centralized publishing system. Aufbau Verlag, the largest and most important publishing house, was created and controlled by the state, that is, by the Communist party. There were a few exceptions to the rule, such as the small publishing houses of the Lutheran church, but even here communist censors checked their prepublication plans. The Aufbau Verlag was ostensibly owned by the so-called Kulturbund or Culture League; in reality, it was but a state-owned enterprise. This publisher issued some interesting works indeed. These included books written by Heinrich Mann and plays and novels of Bertold Brecht. However, the bulk of the firm's publishing efforts were in the various editions of Karl Marx's *Das Kapital*, and V. I. Lenin's and Joseph Stalin's "scientific" works. The publisher was heavily subsidized by the East German state, since this was the only way that the flood of propaganda works could be financed.

Bibliography

Dennis, Mike, *German Democratic Republic: Politics, Economics, Society* (London, 1988).

Baueinheiten (Construction Brigades). The brigades, set up early in the history of the East German state, served as an alternative to military service. Although the state would not recognize conscientious objectors to military service, it did introduce this concept in September 1964. Conscientious objectors were placed in quasi-military formations and were required to perform manual labor for the state. They were not required to swear military allegiance to the state. Nevertheless, they were required to state in writing that they were willing to defend the East German state if it were attacked, and they were to obey the orders of their military superiors. Their uniforms did not differ from those of ordinary soldiers. However, admission to the Construction Brigades was not automatic. If an applicant was rejected, he was required to serve in the regular army. If he refused, he faced a mandatory five-year jail term.

Bibliography

Larrabee, F. Stephen, ed. *The Two German States and European Security* (New York, 1989).

Berlin Blockade of 1948–1949. On June 11, 1948, a joint proclamation of the Western occupying powers in Berlin ushered in currency reform in their three zones. On March 20, previously Marshal Nikolai Sokolovsky walked out of a meeting of the Allied Control Commission and refused to participate in any further discussions on currency reform. Sir Bryan Robertson, the British military governor, wrote to Sokolovsky, informing the Soviet general of the decision about the new currency: The economy of the British zone is suffering acutely from the evils of inflation and of economic stagnation which our quadripartite proposals for financial reform were designed long ago to eliminate, and I feel that I am not justified in waiting any longer before taking remedial measures." Sir Robertson added that he hoped that it will soon be possible for the four occupying powers to agree to an early date to introduce currency reform for the whole of Germany. Similar letters were sent to Sokolovsky by Generals Clay and Koenig, the American and French commanders.

The city of Berlin was to exist as one according to the Allied agreements signed at Yalta and Potsdam (*see* Potsdam Declaration). However, already in April 1948 the

Soviet authorities had made an attempt to force the Western Allies out of the German capital. The occasion was provided by the municipal elections held in the Western sector of the city. Although over 85 percent of the city's population cast their votes and the Social Democrats won a majority on the new council, the Soviet commander refused to accept the results. The Soviet armed forces began to interfere with land, water, and air traffic in and out of the city. On April 5, a Soviet military aircraft collided with a British civilian airliner killing all aboard. On June 24, the Soviet army simply stopped all land traffic coming from the West into the city.

The Western response was swift. On June 26, a joint airlift of the three Western powers began to supply the city with vital necessities. The airlift, although often difficult and dangerous, was maintained until, in May 1949, the Soviet Union finally realized the futility of the blockade and lifted it. While the blockade was on, the East German communists, encouraged by their Soviet patron, attempted to take over the administration of the entire city. The Soviet commander also attempted to veto the election of Ernst Reuter, a Social Democrat, as mayor. The majority of the city council was moved to the Western sector. The minority, consisting only of members of the German Communist party, remained in East Berlin. On November 30, they established a separate city council, headed by Friedrich Ebert (*see* Ebert, Friedrich), the son of the first president of the Weimar Republic, who had long sympathized with the communists.

Although the blockade was eventually lifted, Berlin remained for a long time subject to Soviet blackmail whenever a crisis in relations between the Western Allies and the Soviet Union emerged. In each instance, the West expressed its unmistakable determination to maintain the city's status quo and invariably the Soviet Union and its East German puppets retreated.

Bibliography

Keesing Research Report, *Germany and Eastern Europe Since 1945: From the Potsdam Agreement to Chancellor Brandt's Ostpolitik* (New York, 1973); Malzahn, Manfred, *Germany 1945–1949: A Sourcebook* (London, 1991); Pittman, Avril, *From Ostpolitik to Reunification: West German-Soviet Political Relations Since 1974* (Cambridge, England, 1992).

Berlin Wall. During the 1950s, wave after wave of East Germans decided to seek a better, freer life in the West and escaped from East Germany. The confrontations between the Soviet Union and the Western Allies, as well as the obviously subordinate position of East Germany to Soviet interests, contributed to this phenomenon. Above all, continued shortages of even the simplest necessities of life and a closely regulated society, ruled by the iron fist of the German Communist party and its secret police, added to general dissatisfaction. Since East Germany's borders were closely watched, the only line of escape was through Berlin. It often meant the crossing from one side of a street to the other, or taking the subway from one part of the city to another.

On August 13, 1961, East German soldiers sealed off East Berlin from the Western sectors of the city. At first, the barricade consisted mostly of barbed wire, but soon a concrete wall was built, hermetically closing down East Berlin from the West. Subway services between the two sectors were stopped. The Western Allies did not interfere with these operations.

The Wall effectively stopped the flow of large masses of people from East Germany to the West. By the end of the year, only a handful of desperate people had been able to escape. Between 1949 and 1961, about 2.7 million East Germans sought refuge in the West, mostly young, educated people. Naturally, they had no language problem and were swiftly integrated into the economy and society of West Germany. However, between the building of the Wall and 1980, only 177,000 people succeeded in escaping from East Germany.

The Berlin Wall became a constant source of individual tragedies. Despite the well-publicized order of Walter Ulbricht, reinforced by his successor, Erich Honecker, to shoot would-be refugees, there were always some people desperate enough to take their chances. By the time the communist system had collapsed, over 300 people had been killed at the Wall. The Wall eventually became a symbol of communist oppression and brutality and the advance of the Soviet colonial empire into the heart of Europe. In 1989, it was finally dismantled.

Bibliography

Gelb, Norman, *The Berlin Wall* (London, 1986); Krisch, Henry, *German Politics Under Soviet Occupation* (New York, 1974).

Civil Defense. The East German state had a highly developed system of civil defense. Its confrontation with West Germany and the constant threat over Berlin made this state exceptionally belligerent, barely restrained by its Soviet controllers. The civil defense system consisted of full-time officers of the East German army and a large number of volunteers. The draftees of the East German armed forces had a choice of joining the ranks or the civil defense units, and a great many of them chose the latter. Women also joined the civil defense forces in large numbers. They did so because the service provided added income for them. The ministry of the interior had control over these forces. However, after 1976, jurisdiction was transferred to the ministry of defense. The civil defense troops were organized on the basis of military principles. They were required to attend regular training sessions. They also had to attend ideological training. They spent about one-third of their time studying Marxism-Leninism; the rest was filled with training and exercises.

Bibliography

Dennis, Mike, *German Democratic Republic: Politics, Economics, Society* (London, 1986); Larrabee, F. Stephen, ed. *The Two German States and European Security* (New York, 1989).

Communist Party of East Germany (Socialist Unity Party) [SED]. In 1919, radical members of the German Social Democratic party broke away from the Social Democrats under the leadership of Karl Liebknecht and the Polish-Jewish communist, Rosa Luxemburg. They formed the Communist party of Germany (KPD). They were thoroughly opposed to the Weimar Republic and were viciously attacking the Social Democratic party. Radical rightist assassins murdered Liebknecht and Luxemburg in the early 1920s. The party was thereafter thoroughly Stalinized. The party came under the indirect control of the Moscow-based COMINTERN; under the COMINTERN's orders, it cooperated with the Nazi party against the Social Democratic party, ending the Weimar Republic's existence in 1933.

When Hitler came to power, however, he banned the Communist party, and he ordered many of its members arrested; some of them were murdered. Many of the higher party functionaries escaped and went to the Soviet Union where they spent their years until the end of World War II. The hapless German communists were hit the hardest of all emigree communists by Joseph Stalin's purges. Hundreds of them were murdered by the KGB; others ended their lives in Stalin's concentrations camps.

Two of the top leaders who survived, Wilhelm Pieck (*see* Pieck, Wilhelm), and Walter Ulbricht (*see* Ulbricht, Walter), survived, and they returned to Germany in 1945, together with the other survivors. Their group functioned as advisors to the Soviet occupational authorities. On June 10, 1945, the German Communist party was revived, the first political party permitted to reemerge in the Soviet zone. Ulbricht was in charge of internal party relations while Pieck served as a contact with the outside world. Pieck was seventy years old at that time and was not in good health. Thus, Ulbricht was the real mover of party policies with the permission of the Soviet representatives, of course.

The new German Communist party courted the social democrats. Ulbricht proclaimed that his party's aim was the creation of an antifascist, democratic Germany with a fully functioning multiparty parliamentary system, free enterprise, and human rights for all citizens. However, at first, the unification of the two workers' parties was not on the agenda. Ulbricht and his Soviet masters wanted to build a solid party apparatus that was to be able to assume control in a future unified party. His efforts were also slowed by the surviving latent hostility among the communists toward the Social Democratic party. But Ulbricht, backed by Stalin, really aimed at controlling Germany as a whole. For this he needed the social democrats. However, the social democratic leaders were equally suspicious of communist intentions. They were not blind to the privileged position accorded to Ulbricht's party by the Soviet occupational authorities, and they were worried that a merger would eliminate their party from German politics.

On December 20, 1945, thirty representatives of each of the Social Democratic and Communist parties met and decided to prepare for the merger of the two organizations. The social democrats, however, insisted on consulting with their membership throughout Germany before the actual merger took place. On April 21-22, 1946, Wilhelm Pieck and Otto Grotewohl (*see* Grotewohl, Otto), the head of the Social Democratic party in the Soviet zone, signed the document for merger. About 3,000 delegates from all four occupational zones attended the meeting in Berlin.

By then, however, the reconstituted Social Democratic party enjoyed greater popular support than did the communists. The social democratic membership outside the Soviet zone refused to support the amalgamation of the two parties. Kurt Schumacher, one of the top leaders in the Western zones, refused to go along. He did not even attend the meeting.

In December 1945, the leaders of the two parties held a combined meeting of their respective Central Committees and agreed on a relatively moderate platform. They agreed to build socialism in Germany by establishing an antifascist parliamentary republic. The combined party would be Marxist but not Leninist. In other words, it would not seek a monopoly of power and would not be an elite party, but would endeavor to bring workers and peasants into the political process in a democratic way. But the opponents of the merger received support from the British and American occupational authorities. Schumacher's faction succeeded in putting through a referendum in the Western zones and 82 percent of the membership voted against the merger.

This vote was disregarded by Ulbricht and the pro-merger social democrats, who operated in the Soviet zone only. At the April 1946, meeting Otto Grotewohl and Wilhelm Pieck were elected joint chairmen of the new party, called the Socialist Unity party of Germany (in German: Socialistische Einheitspartei Deutschlands) [SED]. A joint executive committee, consisting of eighty members from each party, was appointed. The secretariat was made up of fourteen people, also equally distributed between the two parties. In the document of the merger, nothing was mentioned about the leading role of the party in German society. Many social democrats honestly believed that the new party would rebuild Germany into a democratic society. But Ulbricht and his friends wanted only to achieve a monopoly of power and used the social democrats for their own purposes, without giving them any share of that power.

Nevertheless, the membership rolls of the Socialist Unity party grew rapidly. By September 1947, there were 1.8 million members, and in 1949 the membership reached 2.5 million people. By then, the party had been thoroughly Stalinized. A central control commission was created to screen out undesirables and maintain party discipline. In 1948, territorial cells were replaced by party cells in the workplace. The following year all social democrats were excluded from the new Politburo, with the exception of Grotewohl. New party statutes were also issued, and the executive committee was replaced by a Soviet-type Central Committee. The secretariat was attached to the latter institution. Power was now in the hands of Ulbricht, first secretary of the Central Committee, although the two aging party chairmen, Pieck and Grotewohl, remained titular heads of the party.

The organizational system of the party was a copy of the Soviet Communist (bolshevik) party. Each district (*Bezirk*) had a committee consisting of sixty full- and fifteen candidate (nonvoting) members. They were elected by the district's delegate-conference held every two-and-a half years. The committee then named the members of the secretariat of the district which acted as a mini-Politburo. The dominant figure in each of these institutions was the first secretary. In the 1980s, all district first secretaries were not only members of the districts' Central Committee, but also of the Central Committee of the Socialist Unity party. They were joined in the latter office by the first secretaries of the armed forces and the political administration. Most members of the party's Central Committee were educated people and were generally in their fifties. They acted as provincial governors, and they had unlimited power in enforcing party directives. They possessed exceptional privileges and their power was supported by the local secret police apparat.

Ordinary party members belonged to a party cell wherever they worked. In the 1980s, about 79,000 such cells existed. Each had its own secretary. These were subordinated to the district secretaries. Larger cities and towns had their own party cells. At the time of the 1981, party congress the party membership stood at 2,172,000. Twenty-nine percent of the working people were, therefore, party members, and, of these, over 33 percent were females.

Allegedly, the highest organ of the party was the Central Committee. Its members had to have at least six years of service in a party cell before they became eligible for election. The committee represented the party in its relations with other Communist parties, and its members were appointed to important administrative positions. Its members approved the single list for parliamentary elections. The party's publishing houses and the Central Control Commission received their directors and membership from the Central Committee. The committee ran state enterprises and handled the party's treasury. It also ran party affairs between congresses. However, all these rights and duties existed really on paper only. The Central Committee members were conformists who willingly kowtowed to the Politburo.

This institution was a carbon copy of its Soviet counterpart. Organized in 1949, its members were ostensibly elected by the Central Committee. In reality, they were appointed directly by the Soviet leaders.

The Politburo in East Germany was a remarkably stable institution. Its membership changed little during communist rule, unless someone died. In the 1980s, the Politburo consisted of seventeen full- and five candidate (nonvoting) members. Most of the members were aging party bureaucrats, old-style, dogmatic communists, presided over in the 1970s and 1980s by Erich Honecker, himself eighty years old in 1992. The members of this body were mostly isolated from ordinary party members and citizens. They had lived in secluded compounds, guarded closely by the secret police; they had their own amusement centers and hunting lodges. They never had to face a critical electorate, nor did they owe any accounting for their actions and policies to their own people. The only body to which they were subordinated was the corresponding institution of the Soviet Communist party. Although the Socialist Unity party of Germany continuously emphasized that it was a party of workers and peasants, membership gradually shifted toward educated and professional people, most of whom assumed leading positions in the apparatus. By the mid-1980s, 45 percent of the members were declared to be working men, 28 percent were white-collar people and only 6 percent were peasants. The middle-level leaders were from academic circles. The major task of all functionaries consisted of ideological work, that is, propaganda on behalf of the party. They were also expected to execute directives issued by the higher leaders.

When Ulbricht was ousted from the Politburo, he was smoothly eased out. He remained the honorary chairman of the Socialist Unity party and continued to head the National Defense Council until 1972. He also remained chairman of the Council of State until his death in 1973. Erich Honecker's (see Honecker, Erich) supporters included Hermann Axen, Werner Filfe, Kurt Hager, Heinz Hoffmann, Erich Mielke (see Mielke, Erich) and others in the Politburo (By the 1980s, the name had been changed to the Presidium). All these men were hard-line, dogmatic communists who had considerable experience in party, state, and military administration. Willy Stoph (see Stoph, Willy), the President of East Germany, also had his own faction within the Presidium, while a small number of people who did not belong to either faction were even more dogmatic than Honecker.

Bibliography

Grote, Manfred, "The Socialist Unity Party of Germany," in Stephen Fischer-Galati, ed. *The Communist Parties of Eastern Europe* (New York, 1979); Honecker, Erich, *From My Life* (Oxford, 1981); Lipman, Heinz, *Honecker and the New Politics of Europe* (London, 1973); Wallace, Ian, *The GDR under Honecker* (Dundee, 1981).

Constitutions of East Germany. The East German state had three constitutions during its relatively short history; one was enacted in 1949, another was instituted in 1968, and a third was declared in 1974. All three documents really served the purposes of propaganda since most of their provisions existed only on paper.

The 1949 constitution was partly copied from the constitution of the Weimar Republic of 1919. It contained provisions for a People's Chamber (*Volkskammer*) whose deputies were elected from a single list statewide, and an assembly in which the five regions (*Lander*) of East Germany were represented. These two houses constituted the East German parliament. The state president was elected by the joint meeting of the parliament and could be removed by a vote of two-thirds of the deputies. Laws originated in the People's Chamber. It also elected the government on the basis of recommendations of the largest party. The Chamber's 400 members were reelected every four years. In real life, the parliament had little influence on politics. It met only a few days each year, and it simply rubber-stamped the decisions made by the party leaders. In 1952, the constitution was modified. The regions (*Lander*) were abolished and were replaced by fourteen districts (*Bezirke*). These had no legislative power even on paper. The government was now called the Council of Ministers. In 1954 and 1958, further modifications were made in the constitution. A presidency was established to head the Council of State. It carried on governmental functions between sessions of the chamber. The Council of Ministers now had the right to issue decrees with the force of law.

The 1968 constitution brought East German laws in line with Soviet law. The leadership role of the Socialist Unity party was now included in the document. It also enacted a law for state ownership of all means of production. This justified collectivization and nationalization retroactively. The right to education for all citizens, the inviolability of private dwellings, the right to health care and old-age pensions, and freedom of religion were included in the constitution. A great deal more personal human rights were also named in the document, including maternity leave, children's allowances, and financial support for expecting mothers. Prohibited were incitement to racial hatred and the promotion of war. Work was proclaimed to be a duty as well as a right. The right to strike, which was included in the 1949 constitution, was now eliminated.

The 1974 constitution was a thorough revision of the previous basic laws. The Council of State was no longer entitled to act for parliament between sessions. It could no longer issue decrees, and its right to pass judgment on the constitutionality of laws was withdrawn. Nor could it propose the person for president to parliament. It could still appoint the members of the Defense Council and organize national defense, but in all other matters its functions were reduced to those of the state president after 1949. The new document increased the authority of the Council of Ministers-at least on paper. The People's Chamber also received more authority. The examination and approval of new laws were now the task of parliament. Deputies were required to consult with their constituents. Their number was raised to 500, but their meetings continued at infrequent intervals. Deputies were not paid for their work as legislators. They were simply part-timers who received their regular salaries from the work they performed elsewhere.

Bibliography

Croan, Melvin, "Germany and Eastern Europe," in Joseph Held, ed. *The Columbia History of Eastern Europe in the Twentieth Century* (New York, 1992), pp. 345-393; Keesing's Research Report. *Germany and Eastern Europe since 1945: From the Potsdam Agreement to Chancellor Brandt's Ostpolitik* (New York, 1973); Schneider, Eberhard, *The GDR: The History, Politics, Economy, and Society of East Germany* (London, 1978); Stahl, Walter, *The Politics of Postwar Germany* (New York, 1963).

Council of Ministers. Consisting of the prime minister and his cabinet this was the government of the East German state. In reality, the first secretary (later, general secretary) of the Socialist Unity party and the members of the Presidium (formerly Politburo) ruled over the Council of Ministers. There was a closely intertwined relationship between the government and the party leadership; sometimes the two were interchangeable as had been the case with other East European countries. The state organs simply did what the party leadership told them to do. Werner Krolokowsky, a little-known apparatchik, was chairman of the Council of Ministers, and he was considered to be a confidante of the secretary general. When Erich Honecker (*see* Honecker, Erich) replaced Walter Ulbricht (*see* Ulbricht, Walter) in 1971, Honecker's wife was made a member of the Council of Ministers, strengthening her husband's hold on the government. In fact, the Council of Ministers was concerned mostly with matters of economics and left politics to the party leadership.

Bibliography

Krisch, Henry, *The German Democratic Republic: The Search for Identity* (Boulder, CO, 1985); Letgers, Lyman H, ed. *The German Democratic Republic: A Developed Socialist Society* (Boulder, CO, 1978).

Crime in East Germany. The public prosecutor of East Germany disclosed that, between 1945 and 1949, the annual number of criminal offenses was 470,000 in the country. There followed a sharp drop during the next ten years to an average of 157,000. By 1968, the rate was down to 100,000 and then picked up again to 128,000 a year after that. The Socialist Unity party's spokesmen declared that the crime rate provided evidence that, under socialism, crime diminished. There is no doubt that the high figure after 1945 was the result of the chaos and dislocations caused by the lost war, the economic difficulties, and the disappearance of social discipline. When stabilization was achieved, the crime rate slowed down. It is also likely that criminals moved to the West where there were greater opportunities for such behavior.

In 1972, the government announced a wide-ranging amnesty, allowing the liberated criminals to cross over to West Germany. Many of these "criminals" had committed political offenses and would not have been charged in a democratic society.

After 1973, the East German government simply stopped publishing statistics of criminal acts by declaring that East Germany had no criminals or organized crime. It was added that about half such acts concerned public property causing a loss of 500 million marks to the economy. The president of the supreme court, D. Toplitz, announced that there had not been an increase in crimes of violence, assault, hooliganism, rape or homicide; however, he added, there was an extra dimension of brutality in them which, he stated, was the overflow from the criminal development of the West, the capitalist world.

It seems that the relative prosperity of East Germany contributed to rising crime rates. Merchandise was available, and security in stores was not as strict as in the West. Furthermore, the population, as in other East European states, took the party's slogan, "the factory belongs to the workers," too seriously, stealing and taking home everything possible. Factory managers consistently have been caught embezzling state moneys.

Petty criminals were punished by being forced to work in work-gangs and to report regularly to the police. In 1974, and 1975, however, sentences became more severe. Petty criminals were locked up, and they lost their jobs. In the early 1970s, 30,000 petty quarrels were handled through local "disputes committees." Highly publicized drunken driving offenses, resulting in deaths, occurred. In 1975, crime preventive measures were announced. Those who were "developing attitudes to shun work"; those who tried to live in an "unworthy way"; and those who were drunkards and exhibited antisocial behavior were ordered to have extra instructions. Factory managers were to report delinquents to local authorities, who could introduce severe restrictions in a person's movements, exclude such a person from certain public places like pubs, and mete out ten days of compulsory labor. Sentences that were suspended became longer. None of these actions actually helped reduce crime, and, since official statistics were seldom published in the late 1970s and the decade of the 1980s, it is not known accurately how criminality developed before the collapse of communism.

Bibliography
Steele, Jonathan, *Inside East Germany: The State that Came in from the Cold* (New York, 1977).

Cultural Policies. From its very inception, the leaders of the East German state realized that only a complete change in attitudes among the population could gain it internal legitimacy. But the task was really impossible; it would have had to overcome hatreds of foreign suzerainty and convince the East German people that "proletarian internationalism," a euphemism for subordinating the interests of their own country to those of the Soviet Union, was legitimate. In the end, German nationalism won out, as did nationalism everywhere in Eastern Europe.

Walter Ulbricht (*see* Ulbricht, Walter) and his successor were convinced, however, that "bourgeois culture" had been so deeply imbedded in the memory of the German people that only a "new socialist man" would be able to free himself of its influence. One means by which this "new socialist man" could be created was, of course, through the educational system (*see* Educational Policies in East Germany). Another was fear of punishment. But there was, according to the communist leaders, a third way, namely, "socialist realism," a vaguely defined, amorphous notion.

According to this idea, creative people would have to be completely loyal to the ideas of Marxism-Leninism, and be devoted to the building of socialism. Their products (this term was used deliberately, as was the term "cultural workers" to signal that creative people were not superior in any way to other workers) would have to be optimistic in outlook and portray the idealism and alleged enthusiasm of the entire population for the building of socialist society. In exchange, creative people would have great privileges; their works were to be publicized by the state, and they would receive very high compensation indeed, regardless of the salability of their works.

Abstract works and concepts were not encouraged, since they did not express this realism. The party leaders reasoned that abstract works created confusion in the minds of the people who, in any case, would not understand their meaning.

Creative people who were not Marxist-Leninists would regard the struggle of the proletariat "from the outside." Consequently, they would tend to distort "proletarian culture" since they would not understand it. In the new society where the proletariat was building socialism, artists, writers, and other creative people could no longer exist as disinterested spectators. Instead, they would have to become committed cultural workers. They would have to absorb the teachings of Marxism-Leninism and then would work enthusiastically for the common goal. Those who claimed that they had a right to be detached observers of the scene were, in actuality, "enemies" of the people. Thus, socialist construction required a high level of ideological and political consciousness. Creative activity under these circumstances had to reflect the positive values of the future socialist society. Creative people would, therefore, create positive heroes in the image of the "new socialist man."

In the final count, therefore, socialist realism was a blatantly neoromantic prop to communist totalitarianism. One way to speed up the process was, as Heinz Ruhmann, a favorite comedian of the late Hitler years who became a communist after 1945, put it, to use the Soviet example. For instance, Soviet films, dubbed with German translation, were the fare in movie houses. In coffee houses "new" political cabarets were shown ridiculing Nazism and the Western ways of life. One of the most important sources of low-level cultural entertainment was sports. The revival of German football was an especially important means of establishing "socialist superiority," and the communist East German state spent enormous sums of money on this form of entertainment. When an all-German championship of European football, commonly referred to in the United States as soccer, was made impossible by political divisions, East Germany developed its own league and its own championship. The East German football team began participating in international events in 1954, and soon other sports acquired an international standing. Special training was provided for very young people to prepare them for international competition. East German athletes became world- and Olympic champions. Training regimens were supervised by a legion of physicians who worked out scientific principles for higher performances. In several international competitions, the two German states took more medals combined than most other states except the United States and the Soviet Union. The problem for the East German communist leaders was that the West German soccer teams were much better than their East German counterparts. When West Germany won the world cup in 1954 by beating a very good Hungarian team in the finals, the East German communists belittled this tremendous achievement.

While the average East German went to see his favorite soccer team, relaxed in a cabaret, or went to see a movie, the intelligentsia visited the theaters. However, even in the theaters, they were not free of the relentless propaganda churned out by the communist propaganda machine. Soviet plays were often shown in German translation, and German plays of a socialist realist content were the order of the day more often than not.

In the first few years after the end of World War II, there was a lot of soul searching, a search for explanations for the misfortunes that had befallen the nation. This did not last long, however. In literature, there were few German writers and poets who escaped the Nazi years untainted. There was, however, a great deal of demand for books and short stories that would provide an explanation for Nazism, especially works that were banned during the Nazi years. But paper supplies were scarce; the so-called Ro-Ro-Ro books (acquiring their name from Rowohlt Rotation Novels, named after their publisher Ernst Rowohlt), tried to fill the vacuum. The books were issued in paperback form, a novel idea in postwar Germany. They included translations of works previously not available in Germany. Eventually, the classics were published, including the works of Thomas Mann, Bertold Brecht and others. They were eagerly picked up by a public that was saturated by Marxist-Leninist propaganda.

The end of the Stalinist terror after the Soviet dictator's death brought some relaxation in cultural policies in East Germany. Nevertheless, the basic policies remained in force, and the communist state never gave up its efforts to control creative people and their product. Perhaps the greatest change came with the universal spread of television sets which could be directed for viewers to see programs from Western Europe, especially from West Germany. This resulted in a great emphasis being placed on reinforcing Marxist-Leninist indoctrination among the population. Anti-Western propaganda, directed especially against West Germany, was intensified. The communist leadership made a tremendous effort to contain East German cultural life within the confines of Marxist-Leninist ideology. In the end they failed.

After the Helsinki Conference on European Security and Cooperation, the East German leaders felt more secure, and there was some relaxation of censorship and other restrictions on cultural life. Nevertheless, cultural life was never completely free of the communist censors until communism as such was swept away and Germany once again became one country.

Bibliography

Held, Joseph, "Cultural Developments," in Stephen Fischer-Galati, ed. *Eastern Europe in the 1980s* (Boulder, CO, 1981); Malzahn, Manfred, *Germany 1945–1949: A Sourcebook* (London, 1991).

Democratic Peasant's Party in East Germany. Established in 1948, this party served as a communist front organization in the rural areas of East Germany. Its strength/weakness was never tested in free elections. Originally it served to split the anticommunist sentiment among the peasants and to convince nonsocialist rural folks that the Socialist Unity party was following the "correct course" from which they would eventually benefit. This institution was also set up to confuse peasant organizations in West Germany and to bring them around to support the policies of the Ulbricht regime. In the provisional parliament, the Democratic Peasant's party was given fifteen deputies, while the communists controlled 75 percent of the representatives. Yet, the Democratic Peasant's party was given representation in the government and in mass political organizations. Its leader was a member of the Council of State, "elected" by parliament.

In reality, all leaders of this party were communist collaborators or even secret members of the Socialist Unity party. They always followed communist policies obediently. The Democratic Peasant's party held its congresses, as well as other activities, on the pattern established by the communists. Their leaders even included the leading role of the Socialist Unity party in their party's statutes. With 103,000 members the Democratic Peasant's party was an important means of spreading communist propaganda among rural folks.

Bibliography
Steele, Jonathan, *Inside East Germany: The State that Came in from the Cold* (New York, 1977).

Democratic Women's Association. This major mass-organization in East Germany emerged from the communist-controlled antifascist women's committees in 1947. Although it was supposed to be neutral in politics, it was, in reality, a communist front organization, which attempted to reach women who were inactive in politics and win them over to the communist cause. The top leaders were ostensibly elected by the congress of the association; however, they were really designated by the communist Politburo. The congress met in session only every four years. While it was not in session, the leaders directed its affairs according to instructions received from the top party leadership. The key officials of the Democratic Women's Association were all members of the Socialist Unity party. Their main task was to encourage women to take jobs in industry and agriculture and to convince them that they should raise their children by observing Marxist-Leninist ideology. They were also to endeavor to impress women that the party's policies were correct and were leading East Germany in the right direction. The Association was also to convince the population that following the Soviet example in everyday life and politics was the correct way to live.

Bibliography
Lane, Christel, "Women in Socialist Society with Special References to the GDR," *Sociology,* 17.4 (1984), pp. 489-505; Steele, Jonathan, *Inside East Germany: The State that Came in from the Cold* (New York, 1977).

Demographics of East Germany. There was, at first, a considerable increase in the population of East Germany. The territory that later became the Soviet zone of occupation, then turned into the East German state, had, between 1938 and 1949, 16.5 million people. By 1949, the number increased to 19. This was the result of the expulsion of ethnic Germans from the various East European states following the war and the evacuation of Germans from lands annexed by the Soviet Union and Poland. There also must have been a moderate natural growth of the population, although this must have been balanced by the losses caused by the war.

After the establishment of East Germany, however, a new exodus began by those who refused to live under totalitarian communist rule. By 1955, the size of the population was reduced to 17.8 million, and by the time the Berlin Wall was erected, it was down to 17 million. Each time internal policies were tightened up, waves of people escaped to the West. The prosperity of the West German state also attracted large numbers in the late 1950s.

East Germany also had other demographic problems. As the result of the losses of young males during the war, the proportion of men to women was distorted. In addition, many of those who left for the West were young males. People under 24 years of age made up more than 50 percent of the refugees. In consequence, a larger ratio of dependents had to be carried by the remaining labor force than it was the case in West Germany. In both Germanies, the ratio of people over 65 years of age came to 16 percent of the total population. However, West Germany had 60 million inhabitants as opposed to the 17 million East Germans.

Not surprisingly, more women joined the labor force in the East than in the West. By 1969, almost half of all the workers in East Germany were women as compared to 36 percent in West Germany.

Before the erection of the Berlin Wall, East Germany lost about one-third of its university graduates to the West. In addition, the East German armed forces drew a disproportionately large number of skilled workers and technicians away from industrial and rural production. After 1962, service in the armed forces became compulsory, and auxiliary service organized for national emergencies also claimed many hours away from work.

During the early 1970s, East Germany began importing guest workers to make up for labor shortages. Hungarians, Bulgarians, and many other nationalities from neighboring socialist countries worked in East German factories. However, unlike their counterparts in West Germany, these workers were not permitted to bring their families with them and, therefore, their return to their homeland was ensured. Their stay was temporary, its length depending upon the contracts arranged for them by the East German authorities. The agreements had specific time limits and, after they expired, the guest workers were transported back to their home countries at government expense. Sometimes Soviet troops helped out in factories, but their wages were paid to the military authorities.

Bibliography

Leptin, Gert, and Melzer, Manfred, *Economic Reform in East German Industry* (Oxford, 1978); Schneider, Eberhard, *The GDR: The History, Politics, Economy, and Society of East Germany* (London, 1978).

East Berlin Riots of 1953. On June 16, 1953, East Berlin workers protested the work quotas that had been raised in the previous week. The following day the protest spread and became a mass riot against the Soviet occupation and the communist regime. Tens of thousands of workers took to the streets. In response, the Soviet government ordered its tanks to suppress the demonstrations. The Soviet infantry joined the tanks, and curfews and martial law were imposed on the East German sector by the Soviet command. Many people were arrested. The demonstrations in East Berlin inspired workers in other East German cities to take to the streets, demanding the end to Soviet occupation and communist totalitarian rule. Clashes with Soviet troops occurred in which there were casualties on both sides. The East German News Agency announced that 25 people were killed and 378 were injured. During the last two weeks of June, the riots were suppressed. Mass arrest of suspected opponents of the regime were made, and many people were executed. Only one execution was ever announced, that of a West Berliner, Willy Goettling. He was used to "prove" that the riots were inspired by Western agents. However, the riots served notice on the regime that popular discontent had reached a dangerously high level.

On June 24 Otto Grotewohl (*see* Grotewohl, Otto) declared that, although the riots had been instigated by "capitalist agents," they could not have happened without serious mistakes being committed by the communist authorities. He stated that serious food shortages occurred because of the flight of hundreds of thousands of peasants to West Germany. The scarcity of consumer goods, resulting from a concentration on heavy industrial development, was another factor. He said that the government had learned from its mistakes and would take prompt steps to remedy them. The Soviet role in suppressing the riots was another indication of the nature of the East German regime, of its complete dependence on Soviet tanks for survival.

The West German parliament proclaimed June 17 a day dedicated to the communist victims of the uprising. The West German government also announced that it has received information to the effect that over 25,000 people were imprisoned after the riots. The workers of East Germany were greatly disappointed by the lack of vigorous Western response to the atrocities. President Dwight Eisenhower sent a message to Chancellor Konrad Adenauer that the United States would make $15 million worth of foodstuffs available for East Germany (including grain, sugar, and other necessities). He also appealed to the Soviet occupational authorities to cooperate in the distribution of food to the population. This offer was rejected by both the East German and Soviet authorities. In spite of the rejection, Eisenhower sent large quantities of food to West Berlin where local authorities were given jurisdiction over its distribution. The people of East Berlin were then invited to pick up food at designated distribution centers. The food distribution program lasted until October 10. By then, over 3 million East Germans had obtained food. It was estimated that eighty percent of the people of East Berlin obtained at least two rations each. Sixty-eight percent of the people who crossed over to West Berlin for food came from East Germany outside of East Berlin.

Bibliography

Brant, Stefan, *The East German Rising* (London, 1955); Keesing's Research Report. *Germany and Eastern Europe Since 1945: From the Potsdam Agreement to Chancellor Brandt's Ostpolitik* (New York, 1973).

Ebert, Friedrich (1894–1979). Friedrich Ebert was the son of the first president of the Weimar Republic of Germany. His father signed the Versailles Peace Treaty with the victorious Allies in 1919. He was considered a traitor to Germany by right-wing extremists who murdered him in the early 1920s.

Friedrich, his son, became a journalist. He was also a member of the German Social Democratic party, a tradition in his family. Between 1928 and 1933, he served as a Social Democratic deputy in the Reichstag, the German parliament. When Adolf Hitler came into power, he had the Social Democratic deputies arrested, Ebert among them. Ebert was sent to a concentration camp where he survived the Hitler era and the war. In 1945, he returned to political life and had himself elected president of the Brandenburg (Prussian) branch of the German Social Democratic party. He also became president of the *Landtag* (the regional legislative assembly) of Brandenburg. He was a member of the Executive Committee of the All-German Social Democratic party. In 1946, Ebert joined the Socialist Unity party and contributed to the merger of his party with that of the communists. The following year, he was appointed to the secretariat of the party and was then appointed as a member of its Politburo. Between 1948 and 1967, Ebert was the mayor of East Berlin, and, at the same time, he was a state councillor (*Staatsrat*). Finally, he served as chairman of the election committee of the communist front organization, the National Front.

Bibliography

Moreton, Edwina, ed. *Germany Between East and West* (Cambridge, England, 1987); Schneider, Eberhard, *The GDR: The History, Politics, Economics, and Society of East Germany* (London, 1978).

Educational Policies. In July 1945, the Soviet occupational authorities set up a German administration for education. Its purpose was the complete overhauling of the educational system in the Soviet zone. On October 1, 1945, schools in the Soviet zone were opened. This was a considerable achievement since most of the school buildings and other facilities had been destroyed during the last phase of the war. Problems immediately appeared. First of all, by early 1946, the children of ethnic Germans expelled from Eastern Europe had crowded into the schools. The old textbooks were, of course, Nazi-oriented and had to be replaced. Many teachers of pre-World War II Germany had died in the war or had left for the West. They had to be replaced by others, usually less qualified. Eventually, 78 percent of the surviving teachers in the Soviet zone were replaced. Fifteen thousand new teachers were employed. During 1946 and 1947, an additional 25,000 teachers were appointed.

In 1946, a law was passed by the new parliament that stipulated that East Germany's children had to be educated in a spirit of service to their community, and they were to be taught independent thinking. The propagation of Nazism and militarism was not permitted in classrooms. The communists began to dismantle the class-based educational system of pre-World War II days, and replaced it with a Marxist-Leninist system. In line with the party's ideology, children were to be indoctrinated in "socialist thinking" in order to create a "new socialist man." Another goal of the educational system was to diminish the differences between urban and rural Germany. Last, but not least, the academic quality of education was to be reinforced.

The law of 1946 established an eight-year elementary school system, and completion of elementary education was made compulsory. The next step for children was a four-year secondary or vocational system. Teaching materials and classroom rules in these schools were homogenized. All schools were forced into the ideological mold of the Communist party, teaching in the spirit of Marxism-Leninism. In the regions (*Lander*) local administrators had authority over the school system. This authority included the right to appoint and dismiss teachers and administrators on every level. All teachers, except the first two levels of elementary schools, were required to possess a college degree. Students preparing to enter the teaching profession had to major in two related subjects (such as, for instance, History and Geography). Teachers for kindergartens (dealing with students between the ages of three and six) had to obtain a three-year degree from the school of pedagogy. Teachers who were required to conduct classes in ideological subjects had to possess a degree at least from a vocational high school or from one of the courses taught by Free German Youth (*see* Free German Youth Organization), the German equivalent of the Soviet KOMSOMOL (*see* Free German Youth Organization). In addition to their role as guardians of Marxist-Leninist ideology, these teachers had to be able to teach another subject on the lower levels of elementary school. All teachers were, of course, required to present their subjects in the spirit of the Communist party, regardless of the academic subject that they taught. This often created awkward situations, especially concerning subjects such as mathematics. Teachers educating nursery school students, as well as those who trained young people for the health-care professions, were recruited directly from schools of pedagogy. The vocational high schools, on the other hand, also produced officers for the armed forces.

The seven universities in East Germany were all subject to directions by the East German Administration for Education after 1951. Admission to any of the universities was based on high academic standards. However, students were also required to be able to convince admissions committees of their willingness to defend the East German state in an armed conflict. The most common proof of this willingness was prior service in the armed forces. This also meant that the majority of university students were older than their counterparts in the West. The economic needs of the state determined the number of students admitted to the universities and to the specific faculties. It often happened that a student interested in mechanical engineering was admitted instead to the faculty of foreign languages. Admission committees were composed of professors, representatives of the Socialist Unity party and its front organizations, and officers of the armed forces. If any industrial enterprises linked to a specific university, their representatives also participated in the admission process. During the first thirty years of communist rule, the students' class-origins were important elements for considering his admission to university studies. This requirement, however, was toned down during the 1980s. Another important consideration was the candidate's participation in the activities of Free German Youth organization.

Faculties in the natural sciences and engineering enrolled the highest number of students, with engineering leading all fields of study; education and teacher-training came next, while Economics and Management-training were third in importance. The humanities faculties admitted the fewest students. In all disciplines, the study of Marxism-Leninism as well as the Russian language, was compulsory and carried great weight.

Equally important was the student's participation in some sort of sports as a sign of his or her physical readiness to defend the East German state. Military training for men and civil defense education for women were required subjects in every faculty. Universities followed the Soviet model in their organization and award of degrees on different levels. The academic year had few breaks and most subjects were required. Tuition was subsidized by the state. The size of the subsidy was determined by such factors as the student's family income, or his or her own income. Outstanding students received the Karl Marx Award of 450 East German marks a month. Good students were given the Wilhelm Pieck Award of 400 marks a month. Not all faculty members possessed terminal degrees, since some of them were simply political appointees.

Facilities were the Achilles heel of the East German university system. Most of their buildings were old and in disrepair. Textbooks were few in numbers, and they were not always available. The use of Western texts was usually discouraged. The most consistently used textbooks were copies of Soviet publications that had been translated into German. On the other hand, often excellent technical manuals were available for students in engineering and military studies.

In 1968, all East German universities were reorganized. Some traditional disciplines were merged, and departments were consolidated. Each new department had a council composed of faculty, one or more representatives of the Socialist Unity party, and, if appropriate, representatives of respective industries. Faculty research was increasingly directed toward fulfilling the requests of industry. The ministry for universities and vocational high schools, replacing the Educational Administration, was increasingly rigid in controlling all phases of university education. It even issued directives for the faculty's daily activities and for details of the curricula.

Already in 1958, the state followed the Soviet pattern of introducing polytechnical education in the schools. Students spent a certain number of days in every month at a place of work, laboring under the supervision of master craftsmen. The theoretical justification for the system was that it allegedly introduced young people to the dignity of manual labor, so that later in their lives they would be respectful toward the workers. But there was also a practical side to the system; namely, the economy acquired free labor at a time when labor shortages were the norm.

In the last two decades of communist rule in East Germany, increasingly heavy emphasis was placed on sports and military training at every level of education. Sports-education served the interests of the state as determined by Erich Honecker (*see* Honecker, Erich) and his fellow communist leaders. A law enacted in the early 1950s stipulated the requirements for building sports facilities. It also established compulsory physical education classes from the elementary school level to the universities. An East German Sports Committee was created and was given a monopoly governing sports activities. Boarding schools for promising young athletes were established at state expense, and the College for Physical Education was raised to university status. Great emphasis was placed on participation in international competition, and this led to the relative neglect of mass sports activities.

Bibliography

Klein, Helmuth, and Zuckert, Ulrich, *Learning for Living: Education in the GDR* (East Berlin, 1979); Kohn, Erwin, and Postler, Fred, *Polytechnical Education of the German Democratic Republic* (Dresden, 1976); Schneider, Eberhard, *The GDR: The History, Politics, Economy, and Society of East Germany* (London, 1978).

Establishment of the German Democratic Republic (East Germany). The Soviet decision to establish an East German state was announced on October 5, 1949. The meeting of the Soviet-created People's Council, under the chairmanship of Wilhelm Pieck, issued the following declaration:

The formation of a separate West German state, the Occupation Statute, the dismantling operations that are contrary to international law, the refusal of (signing) a peace treaty, and the control exercised by the High Commissioners, . . . have revealed a serious national emergency brought about in Germany by the dictatorial policy of the Western Powers. To safeguard the national interests of the German people by national self-help, the German People's Council, which was elected by the German People's Congress in May 1949, is hereby requested to declare itself the Provisional People's Chamber (Volkskammer), under the articles of the constitution adopted by the People's Congress and Council, and to create a constitutional government of the German Democratic Republic. . . . On October 7 of the same year the People's Council met in East Berlin and unanimously adopted the declaration. During the next few months, rigged elections were held, and a bogus parliament was "elected" on a single list dominated by communists. Wilhelm Pieck was "elected" the first president of East Germany. The new state and the Soviet Union and its satellites soon exchanged ambassadors and established "normal" diplomatic relations.

Bibliography

Croan, Melvin, and Friedrich, Karl J., "The East German Regime and Soviet Policy in Germany," *The Journal of Politics* 20.1: (February 1958), pp. 44-63; Keesing's Research Report. *Germany and Eastern Europe Since 1945: From the Potsdam Agreement to Chancellor Brandt's Ostpolitik* (New York, 1973); Krisch, Henry, *German Politics Under Soviet Occupation* (New York, 1974); Stahl, Walter, *The Politics of Postwar Germany* (New York, 1963).

Eurocommunism and East Germany. During the mid-1970s three large European Communist parties subscribed to what they called Euro-communism. The French, the Italian, and the Spanish Communist parties adhered to this version of doctrine. Eurocommunism was interpreted by orthodox Marxist-Leninists to mean the acceptance of Western ideas on democracy, and the corresponding abandonment of the notion of the dictatorship of the proletariat as the only means of achieving socialism.

In general, the concept also meant the rejection of the assertion that the Soviet Communist (bolshevik) party was the example all Communist parties of the world should try to emulate, and the realization that each Communist party should find its own way to socialism.

The second meeting of the 29 European Communist parties was held in East Berlin in June 1976. It was called together in order to affirm the common strategy and tactics of the parties in their struggle. However, from the very beginning of the meeting, it was obvious that, with the exception of the Communist parties of the Soviet colonies in Eastern Europe, they would not sign a communique that would confirm the preeminence of the Soviet Communist party. What was worse from the point of view of the organizers of the meeting was that two Communist parties who were present, the Romanian and the Yugoslav, indicated that they, too, endorsed the concept of Eurocommunism.

By 1976, most Communist parties in Western Europe condemned the Warsaw Pact invasion of Czechoslovakia in 1968, and rejected the Soviet explanation and justification for that act. The East German communist leaders were in a quandary; they could not possibly want to join their European counterparts in criticizing the record of the Soviet communists on human rights, since they themselves were guilty of similar abuses. On the other hand, they were equally reluctant to condemn the Eurocommunists for their stand, since this would have ruined their relations which went back to the pre-Nazi period. Consequently, they were happy that the conference could not come to accept a joint, unanimous declaration.

The East Berlin conference was a spectacular affair. Leonid Brezhnev, Josip Broz Tito, Janos Kadar, the French and Spanish communist leaders, were all there. Only the Icelandic and the Albanian party leaders stayed away. The final document spoke mainly of the right of each party to its independent road to socialism. Since the East German Communist party hosted the conference, it was compelled to publish this document.

Erich Honecker (*see* Honecker, Erich), the East German communist boss, was especially troubled by the fact that there was evidence of solid support for Eurocommunism in his own party. The fact that Soviet ideologues denounced Eurocommunism as simply a Social Democratic notion, only added to its attraction in East Germany. But the attitude of Honecker was shown by the arrest of Rudy Bahro, a high-ranking official of the East German Socialist Unity party. His "crime" was that he had written a book, entitled *The Alternative in Eastern Europe*, in which he had condemned the leaders of the East German and other East European Communist parties for subjugating their organizations to their own dictatorial will. Bahro advocated the complete overhauling of communist organizations and their transformation into democratic institutions. He argued that such a process was an inevitability, and if the leaders refused to enact the changes, they would be swept away into the "garbage heap of History." Acting under strong pressure coming from the brotherly Communist parties in the West, Honecker eventually saw it expedient to release Bahro, who immediately left for West Germany. His case illustrated that Honecker was once again supporting his Soviet masters; but it also provided a glimpse of the possible opposition within the high echelons of the East German communist leadership.

Bibliography

Asmus, Ronald, "The Dialectics of Detente and Discord: The Moscow-East Berlin-Bonn Triangle," *Orbis*, 28.4 (1986), pp. 743-744; Grote, Manfred, "The Socialist Unity Party of Germany," in Stephen Fischer-Galati, *The Communist Parties of Eastern Europe* (New York, 1979).

Foreign Relations of East Germany. East Germany never really enjoyed full sovereignty during its entire existence. Consequently, its diplomacy was simply a reflection of Soviet foreign affairs. In 1949 only the Soviet satellites, plus Communist China and North Korea recognized the newly established East German state. The stream of East Germans seeking asylum in the West (over 2.5 million refugees crossed into West German between 1945 and 1961) further raised questions about the East German government's legitimacy. Through its first two decades of existence, the major aim of East Germany was to gain international recognition. In this it was aided by the Soviet leaders.

The second major issue was the relations between the two Germanies. West Germany had been recognized by most states as representing the interests of all Germans (*see* Hallstein Doctrine). On March 10, 1952, Joseph Stalin sent a note to Western statesmen, proposing the dismantling of the East German state in exchange for the unification of Germany. The former Allied Powers would then sign a peace treaty with this unified state. The government of this state would be elected through free elections, and it would then declare the neutralization of Germany and its exit from NATO. The Western Allies did not respond to the offer. They considered it to be but a propaganda ploy to fragment the Western alliance.

After the rejection of Stalin's offer the Stalinization of East Germany proceeded at a fast pace. Even the last traces of an independent East German foreign policy line were erased. The building of the Berlin Wall (*see* Berlin Wall) in August 1961, however, helped to consolidate the position of East German communists within the state. During the following decade East Germany gained increasing stature and international recognition outside the Soviet Bloc. Yet, as late as 1967, the East German regime's standing within the Soviet empire was still precarious.

The West German government initiated a new policy toward Eastern Europe (*see* Ostpolitik), and it projected a new image toward the entire East. What was even more alarming to Ulbricht (*see* Ulbricht, Walter) and his followers was that West Germany's diplomatic and political offensive was coordinated with the diplomacy of the United States and of NATO. Ulbricht's reaction was vicious, far more so than that of Moscow. He campaigned for a united offensive against the West, even at a time when Leonid Brezhnev was exploring possible cooperation with West Germany. He proposed several times that the offensive should include the severance of West Berlin.

He also endeavored to deepen the divisions between the two Germanies in order to prevent the isolation of East Germany within even the Soviet Bloc. Ulbricht's efforts were frustrated. First of all, Czechoslovakia, Hungary, and Romania were not at all enthusiastic about the anti-West German campaign, since they sorely needed improved trade relations with the West. When Ulbricht insisted at a Warsaw Pact conference that the normalization of the Soviet Bloc's relations with West Germany should have as its condition that the West recognize the East German state, he was rebuffed. The conference agreed only to urge Bonn to recognize the existence of two German states. In a new year's message to all Germans, Ulbricht simply rejected unification "under existing conditions." He announced a ten-point program that would have made even discussions on unification impossible. It seems, however, that Ulbricht had acted out of weakness. His messengers frantically tried to convince his East European and Soviet friends to support his position on West Germany, but they were reluctant to revive the darkest days of the Cold War that Ulbricht was apparently advocating. The Soviet Union simply could not permit the East German communists to take over direction of its foreign policy toward the West. Neither could an increasingly restive Eastern Europe subordinate its quasi-sovereignty to East Berlin. East Germany had a whole series of treaties with other Soviet Bloc states and the Soviet Union, but these treaties did not provide great comfort for Ulbricht.

It seemed at that time, however, that Ulbricht's counteroffensive stabilized his state's position in the face of West German moves, but within two years, the problems reemerged. In 1969, Chancellor Willy Brandt instituted his Ostpolitik toward Eastern Europe. West Germany would recognize the borders of East European states as they came to exist in 1945, and he announced his intention to seek an accord with East Germany. He gave his blessing to a conference on European security and cooperation. He formally accepted the existence of two German states and recognized the need for further four-power discussions over the status of Berlin. Ulbricht tried desperately to torpedo Brandt's policies. He worried that the Soviet Union might simply jettison East Germany.

In 1970, West Germany and the Soviet Union concluded a basic agreement, and three months later, Poland signed a treaty with Brandt's government. Ulbricht's condition that the treaties be tied to prior recognition of East Germany was not accepted. In response, he instituted unilateral action against Western access to Berlin, in an attempt to sabotage the agreements. The secretary general of the East German Communist party went too far; he had interfered with Soviet interests and jeopardized Leonid Brezhnev's aim at detente with West Germany. In May 1971, he was, therefore, replaced by Erich Honecker (*see* Honecker, Erich), a more pliable leader. However, there could hardly be a better demonstration of the limitations on East German sovereignty! In fact, Ulbricht made repeated remarks to the fact that the Germans could make even Soviet-type socialism work. Nothing could irritate his Soviet masters more than such remarks. The economic revitalization of East Germany, which was an indisputable achievement, was Ulbricht's strongest argument for Soviet support of his foreign policy objectives. Even this meant little since the Soviet Union simply wanted improved relations with the West.

In any case, by 1970, new economic problems were emerging in Eastern Europe, and the entire Soviet Bloc was entering a period of uncertain development. With Honecker at the helm, East Germany resumed its subordinate role in the foreign affairs of the Soviet Union. Yet, this very fact was to bring about real progress for the state. In September 1971, a new four-power agreement confirmed the status of West Berlin and ensured free access for Western traffic into the city. In December of the following year, the first general agreement between the two Germanys was concluded. In 1973, East and West Germany were both admitted to the United Nations. By then, sixty-eight states recognized East Germany, and a year later, the Unites States also extended recognition. Communications between the two German states as well as trade increased in volume. Through closer and more frequent contact between the two populations, it also became clear that life in general was better in the West than in the East. West Germany felt secure in the NATO alliance. Television, that important medium of communications, was eagerly watched in the East, and comparison between the two systems invariably gave the advantage to West Germany. The regime of Erich Honecker felt threatened once again by these developments. Hence the introduction of the policy of "demarcation" or "delimitation" (*Abgrenzung*). This meant, first of all, that certain categories of East Germans were forbidden to establish contact with Westerners.

Honecker's efforts were aided by the fact that international relations had become clouded once again in 1979. The Soviet Union introduced new missiles in Eastern Europe. In response, NATO decided to install its own new missiles in Western Europe. Two weeks later, Soviet troops entered Afghanistan, and the Cold War was on again. In 1980, the trade union Solidarity, which emerged in Poland, signaled renewed unrest in the Soviet Bloc. Honecker's visit to Bonn at the invitation of Chancellor Helmut Schmidt, who replaced Brandt after a scandal in Brandt's office (Brandt's chief of staff was discovered to be a spy for East Germany), planned for 1984, was postponed. By then, the Soviet leaders were opposed to further rapprochement between the two Germanys. Honecker's visit to West Germany did take place three years later. Chancellor Helmut Kohl, who had replaced Schmidt, received him as befitting a head of state.

Between 1971 and 1985, East Germany established a visible presence in the Third World, especially in Africa and Asia, as a proxy of the Soviet Union. Its agents trained Iraqi and Syrian police in techniques of crowd control and undercover work. East Germany provided support for international terrorists and gave returning terrorists safe haven in East Germany. It also provided arms and explosives for acts of terrorism against the West. East German diplomats, really intelligence agents, incited anti-Western sentiments in Third World countries. They completed the circle of organizations, directed and supervised by the Soviet KGB and GRU, for worldwide spying and subversion. When Honecker's regime had collapsed, a great deal of secret information came to light about all these activities.

Bibliography

Brandt, Willy, *A Peace Policy for Europe* (New York, 1969); Epstein, Klaus, *Germany after Adenauer* (New York, 1964); Gorgey, Laszlo, *Bonns' Eastern Policy, 1964–1971* (Hamden, CT, 1973). Honecker, Erich, *From My Life* (Oxford, 1981); Kaiser, Karl, *German Foreign Policy in Transition: Bonn Between East and West* (New York, 1968). Larrabee, F. Stephen, ed. *The Two German States and European Security* (New York, 1989); Lipman, Heinz, *Honecker and the New Politics of Europe* (London, 1973).

Free German Youth Organization. The German independent youth movement, which emerged in 1896 in Steglitz, a suburb of Berlin, developed from a hiking club of high school students. The clubs multiplied in numbers until, by 1913, they had more than 100,000 members. This was no longer a hiking association but a movement. Its chapters were, by then, spread all over the Second German empire, and their activities were varied. However, all the clubs agreed that participation in politics was not their aim.

They tried to establish a new culture, a "culture of youth," different from that of adult Germans. They had a general meeting at the Hohe Meissner in 1913 that was a memorable occasion in which they attempted to establish a unified movement. By then, each chapter went its own way, and they had not been able to act in common in the "interest of young people."

After World War I, the youth movement continued to split into several factions. One of these called itself Free German Youth. This organization was made up by veterans of the war who tried desperately to recapture their idyllic life of hiking and community action before 1914. The organization lived on until 1933. When Adolf Hitler came into power, he dissolved all independent youth organizations and had their property transferred to the Hitler Youth organization.

It was the name of Free German Youth that appealed to the East German communists in 1945. Its original groups tried to establish relations with the social democrats, but they were unsuccessful. Now the Free German Youth organization in East Germany was an equivalent of the KOMSOMOL, the youth organization of the Soviet Communist party. But the free spirit, the rejection of the direction provided by adults, and the effort to create a culture of young people, were and remained alien to this communist organization.

On March 7, 1946, when the communist youth organization was established, a great many young people living in the Soviet zone of occupation joined the organization. The organization received ample support from both the Soviet authorities and the Socialist Unity party. It supposed to be a nonparty, nonsectarian organization based on democratic ideals. The institution received ample support from both the Soviet authorities and the Socialist Unity party. But its goals became quite clear when its new leaders declared that they aimed to work in the spirit of Marxism-Leninism.

Bibliography

Dennis, Mike, *German Democratic Republic: Politics, Economics, Society* (London, 1988);
Steele, Jonathan, *Inside East Germany: The State That Came in from the Cold* (New York, 1977).

Grotewohl, Otto (1893–1964). Grotewohl, the son of a master tailor, became a book binder. He studied at the *Hochschule fur Politik,* a college maintained by the German Social Democratic party in Berlin. Between 1925 and 1933, Grotewohl was chairman of the Braunschweig branch of the German Social Democratic party and, at the same time, served as a deputy in the Reichstag. He was also president of a social democrat-run enterprise, the Land Insurance Institute. He was briefly imprisoned in 1933 after Hitler's accession to power, then he was released and worked as a tradesmen.

In 1945, he was elected chairman of the Social Democratic party in the Soviet zone. He favored close cooperation with the communists, and guided his part of the Social Democratic party to the merger with the communists in 1946. At the time of the merger, the social democrats had 620,000 members. Grotewohl expected to remain in control of the leadership of the Socialist Unity party, since he had been the leader of the Social Democratic party. This was, of course, not to be. Since the communists received close support from the Soviet occupational authorities, their dominance in the united party was assured. In 1949, the parity-principle, meaning that there was to be an equal number of social democrats and communists in the party's leadership, was shelved. This was a great disappointment to the aging social democrat Grotewohl who shared leadership with Wilhelm Pieck (*see* Pieck, Wilhelm). He was gradually pushed into the background, and real authority simply slipped out of his hands. Even the illusion of power was stripped from him.

In 1949, a new Politburo was set up with seven full-and two candidate (nonvoting) members. It created its own secretariat which was, of course, controlled by the communists. Grotewohl and Pieck were named to membership in the Politburo but Walter Ulbricht (*see* Ulbricht, Walter), the secretary general of the Communist party, had the real power.

In October 1949, the first government of the German Democratic Republic (East Germany) was created out of the Soviet occupational zone. Otto Grotewohl was named president of the republic, which was nothing more than an honorific title. He held this post until his death in 1964. His deputies included Walter Ulbricht, Otto Nuschke (of the Christian Democratic Union whose leadership had already been purged by the communists), and a Professor Kastner, a member of the Liberal party. The cabinet had a ten-to-six majority of communists. Kastner was later recruited by the West German intelligence services, and he eventually escaped to the West with his wife who was also a West German intelligence agent.

Bibliography

Dennis, Mike, *German Democratic Republic: Politics, Economics, Society* (London, 1988.);
Nettle, Jonathan P., The Eastern Zone and Soviet Policy in Germany (London, 1951);

Schneider, Eberhard, *The GDR: The History, Politics, Economy, and Society of East Germany* (London, 1978).

Gysi, Klaus (1912–). Gysi, the son of a Jewish physician in Berlin, joined the German Communist party in 1931. He studied at several European universities and worked for a time as an editor in a private publishing house. After Adolf Hitler came to power, Gysi worked in the underground Communist party and eventually escaped to France. In 1946, he returned to the Soviet zone of occupation and was immediately co-opted into the Politburo of the German Communist party. Between 1948 and 1950, Gysi was secretary general of the Communist party. In that year, however, he was removed and appointed to head the East German state publishing house (*see* Aufbau Verlag). After 1956, he was rehabilitated and served as minister of culture in Walter Ulbricht's government until 1966, when he was appointed East German ambassador to Italy. In 1980, he was recalled and appointed state secretary for religious affairs and he remained in that post until the collapse of the communist system and the reunification of Germany.

Bibliography
Krisch, Henry, *The German Democratic Republic: The Search for Identity* (Boulder, CO, 1985).

Hallstein Doctrine. In 1955, the Soviet Union recognized the Federal Republic of (West) Germany as a sovereign state. However, the West German government was not required to recognize East Germany as an equal. On September 22, 1955, Chancellor Konrad Adenauer made a statement in the West German parliament according to which the Federal Republic of Germany (West Germany) would break off diplomatic relations with any country that recognized the East German government, and would not enter into diplomatic relations with any communist state except the Soviet Union. This decision was known as the Hallstein doctrine, named after Dr. Walter Hallstein, who was foreign secretary of West Germany at that time.

This doctrine was observed by West Germany on three occasions. When Syria agreed in 1956 to the opening of an East German consulate in Damascus, West Germany recalled its ambassador from that country. When Yugoslavia extended diplomatic recognition to East Germany in 1957, West Germany withdrew its diplomatic mission from Belgrade. Finally, in 1963, when Cuba agreed to the establishment of an East German embassy in Havana, West Germany broke off all relations with that country.

Another example of the application of the Hallstein doctrine was the denial of aid to the United Arab Republic in 1965 after Walter Ulbricht (*see* Ulbricht, Walter) was received in Cairo as a head of state on official visit. When the Federal Republic of Germany decided to establish diplomatic relations with Romania in January 1967, it was the first instance of the abandonment of the Hallstein doctrine. In 1969, however, West Germany suspended diplomatic relations with Campuchea when that country received an East German ambassador, and established its own diplomatic mission in East Berlin. When the government of South Yemen extended diplomatic recognition to East Germany, relations were also suspended by West Germany. When Somalia established diplomatic relations with East Germany, West Germany simply recalled its ambassador for consultation in 1970. After this incident, however, the West German government simply ignored such recognition; in other words, West Germany abandoned the Hallstein doctrine.

Bibliography

Brandt, Willy, *A Peace Policy for Europe* (New York, 1969); Kaiser, Karl, *German Foreign Policy in Transition: Bonn Between East and West* (New York, 1968); Keesing's Research Report. *Germany and Eastern Europe Since 1945: From the Potsdam Agreement to Chancellor Brandt's Ostpolitik* (New York, 1973); Moreton, Edwina, *East Germany and the Warsaw Alliance: The Politics of Détente* (Boulder, CO, 1978).

Honecker, Erich (1912–). Honecker's father was a coal miner in Neunkirchen-Saar. He joined the Young Pioneers of the German Communist party in 1922, preparing for party membership when he came of age. Two years later, Honecker was promoted as a member of the Communist Youth Association. Three years later, he became a full-fledged member of the Communist party. In 1931, he was elected secretary of the Communist Youth Association for the Saar Valley, and in 1934, he became a member of the underground party's Central Committee. Honecker went to the Soviet Union in 1930 and spent a year in Moscow. He returned in 1931 and continued his organizational activities after Adolf Hitler came to power. In 1935, he was arrested by the Gestapo and spent ten years in a concentration camp.

After the collapse of Hitler's Third Reich, he was freed and was appointed chairman of the East German Free German Youth (*see* Free German Youth Organization). In 1956, Honecker went to the Soviet Union once again in order to study at the Marx-Engels Institute in Moscow. A year later, he returned to East Germany. In 1946, Honecker was appointed a secretary of the Socialist Unity party. Four years later he was appointed a candidate (nonvoting) member of the party's Politburo, and in 1958, he was promoted to full membership in that institution. In the same year, he was also appointed a member of the secretariat of the Central Committee. His responsibilities included the control of internal security and national defense.

In 1971, Honecker reached the highest office in his party. He replaced Walter Ulbricht (*see* Ulbricht, Walter) as secretary general. Until the collapse of the communist system in East Germany, Honecker remained the head of the party and of the government.

In 1989, Honecker was already a communist politician out of line with the rest of the statesmen of Eastern Europe. He was a hard-line, dogmatic communist. He lived in a villa reserved for high party officials and was guarded by Soviet KGB troops. In 1991, he was secreted out of East Germany by the KGB and taken to Moscow against the protestations of the government of united Germany. Mikhail Gorbachev protected him as he was protecting the Bulgarian secret service generals and other communists who had served the interests of the Soviet Union in its East European colonies. When Gorbachev was replaced by Boris Yeltsin, the new Russian government expressed its willingness to return Honecker to Germany to stand trial for ordering the shooting of refugees. Honecker sought and received asylum in the embassy of Chile in Moscow. In 1992, he decided to return to Germany and face the accusations. However, because he is suffering from terminal cancer, his trial was abruptly stopped and his case was dismissed.

Bibliography
Honecker, Eric, *From My Life* (Oxford, 1981); Lipman, Heinz, *Honecker and the New Politics of Europe* (London, 1973); Wallace, Ian, *The GDR Under Honecker, 1971–1981* (Dundee, England, 1981); Woods, Roger, *Opposition in the GDR Under Honecker* (London, 1986).

Integration of East Germany into the Soviet Bloc. In 1954, the Soviet Union announced that it recognized East Germany as a sovereign, independent state in control of its internal and external affairs. The Soviet High Commissioner's task henceforth would simply be his concern with security and with liaison with the Western Allies on questions relevant to Germany as a whole. Soviet occupation forces would remain in East Germany under the four-power agreements of Teheran, Yalta, and Potsdam. Consequently, in July 1954, a Soviet ambassador, Georgy M. Pushkin, was appointed to East Berlin. In August of the same year, the Soviet government annulled all decrees and ordinances issued by the occupational authorities between 1945 and 1953.

On April 8, 1954, the three Western High Commissioners issued a declaration, according to which the Soviet move did not change the situation, and that the so-called German Democratic Republic was simply a Soviet puppet state that would not be recognized by the international community. Britain, France, and the United States further stated that they would continue to hold the Soviet Union responsible for internal and external affairs conducted by the so-called East German government, and that they would also continue to regard the West German government as the sole legitimate representative of the German nation.

Moscow then issued invitations to twenty-three European nations and the United States to attend a conference in Moscow on "safeguarding peace and collective security in Europe." However, only the Soviet Bloc countries accepted the invitation, and sent their representatives to Moscow. At the express wish of the Soviet leaders, the meeting issued a declaration, stating that the emergence of a West German army and its inclusion in NATO represented a threat to the peace of Europe and to the eight countries that had participated in the Moscow meeting.

The participants of the conference subsequently held another meeting in the Polish capital, Warsaw, on May 11-13, 1955, where they signed a twenty-year treaty of friendship and cooperation with each other and the Soviet Union and created a unified military command, led by Soviet generals. Only East Germany was left out of this treaty with the statement that the inclusion of its armed forces would be considered later.

After the official announcement of the formation of the East German army, the East German state was admitted to the Warsaw Pact forces in 1956. With this pact and with the treaties of friendship and mutual cooperation East Germany signed with the East European communist states and the Soviet Union, East Germany was completely and thoroughly integrated into the Soviet system, and it became part of the Soviet colonial empire in Europe.

Bibliography

Keesing Research Report. *Germany and Eastern Europe Since 1945: From the Potsdam Agreement to Chancellor Brandts' Ostpolitik* (New York, 1973).

Kulturbund (Culture League). In July 1945, a Culture League for the Democratic Revival of Germany was formed in the Soviet zone of occupation. Its president was the communist poet, Johannes R. Becher. The original intention behind the establishment of this group was to propagate the works of writers, artists, and other creative people who were disliked or even banned during the Nazi era in Germany. Very soon, however, the Kulturbund became the advocate of Soviet literature and Soviet films, whose introduction into Germany it promoted.

In general, as a communist organization, it was dedicated to the propagation of "socialist realism." This organization eventually gained control of the Aufbau Verlag, the state publishing house (*see* Aufbau Verlag), that became the major source of Marxist-Leninist works in East Germany. Originally, its advocacy of Marxist-Leninist ideology was restrained. However, as time went on, and as East Germany emerged as a state, the Kulturbund no longer had to hide behind a facade, and it became an open and dogmatic advocate of socialist realism in every area of culture. It eventually became an instrument of the communist leadership to transmit cultural policies to various organizations.

As the party developed further, however, the role of the Kulturbund declined because cultural policies no longer had to be put through intermediaries but were directly dispensed by the communist leaders (*see* Cultural Policies in East Germany).

Bibliography

Krisch, Henry, *The German Democratic Republic: The Search for Identity* (Boulder, CO, 1974).

Marshall Plan and East Germany. In March 1947 the foreign ministers of the four Allied powers met in Moscow. The Soviet minister of foreign affairs presented a proposal including the following; (1) the Soviet Union should receive reparations of $10 billion at 1938 prices from the defeated nations, but mostly from Germany and Japan; (2) the German industrial heartland, the Ruhr Valley, should be placed under the control of the four powers; (3) the Oder-Neisse line should be considered definitely the border between Poland and Germany, and the former eastern territories of Poland returned to Soviet jurisdiction; (4) a provisional government for the entire German nation should be established regardless of the zones of occupation. The proposals were rejected outright by the three Western Powers.

In March 1947, President Harry Truman announced the new United States policy of containment of Soviet expansionism. In June, he introduced the Marshall Plan for the recovery of Europe and he included the three Western zones of occupation.

Joseph Stalin then decided to consolidate Soviet rule in Eastern Europe and use the states of that region as a military and economic buffer zone to isolate the Soviet Union from the West. In September 1947, he established the Communist Information Center (the COMINFORM), a successor to the Third International, which he had dissolved in 1943.

When the government of the United States issued an invitation to all European governments to participate in the Marshall Plan, several East European states indicated their interest in the Plan; however, Stalin simply issued orders against East European participation, and that was the end of it.

Bibliography

Croan, Melvin, "Germany and Eastern Europe," in Joseph Held, ed. *The Columbia History of Eastern Europe in the Twentieth Century* (New York, 1992); Keesing's Research Report. *Germany and Eastern Europe Since 1945: From the Potsdam Agreement to Chancellor Brandt's Ostpolitik* (New York, 1973); Krisch, Henry, *German Politics Under Soviet Occupation* (New York, 1974); Stahl, Walter, *The Politics of Postwar Germany* (New York, 1963).

Mass Organizations in East Germany. Mass organizations in communist-dominated societies serve two main purposes. First of all, they are transmission belts, transmitting and disseminating political directions issued by the party leadership. Second, they provide information to the leaders about public attitudes and morals. A minor role undertaken by these organizations is the training of cadres for the bureaucracy and the *nomenklatura*.

In the East German case, membership in mass organizations was voluntary. Nevertheless, the leaders of these institutions were, without exception, communists or cryptocommunists. The chairmen and secretaries of the most important such organizations were also members of the Socialist Unity party's corresponding organs. The statutes of mass organizations in East Germany included clauses about the leading role of the Socialist Unity party in society, and the organizational principles reflected those of the Communist party. Beyond being conduits for party directives, the mass organizations served as consultative groups for the party leaders in their activities in shaping policies.

The mass organizations in East Germany included the Confederation of Free German Trade Unions, the Free German Youth organization (*see* Free German Youth Organization), the Democratic Women's Association of Germany (*see* Democratic Women's Association in East Germany), the Farmers' Mutual Aid Association, consumer cooperative societies, the *Kulturbund* (*see* Kulturbund), a Society for Soviet-German Friendship, and many others.

The Confederation of Free Trade Unions, founded in February 1946, deprived the social democrats their traditional trade union-base, making it easier for the communists to absorb the Social Democratic party into their own organization. Once communist rule was unquestionably established, the "free" trade unions lost their autonomy, and they, too, became instruments of communist policies toward industrial labor.

In 1948, the independent workers' associations were transferred to the jurisdiction of the trade unions, making it easier for the party to control them. Nevertheless, industrial unrest was caused by several acts, such as the establishment of work norms that were often arbitrarily set, the imposition of trade union officials from the communist apparatus, and the annual collective agreements forced on reluctant workers by "their" trade unions. The unrest culminated in the June 1953 riots in East Berlin (see East Berlin Riots of 1953), that were matched by riots in other larger urban centers.

After the erection of the Berlin Wall, however, there developed an accommodation between communist trade union officials and the workers. In 1963, limited decentralization was introduced, and workers' rights in the factories were extended. In 1972, a new law was introduced that brought the unions into a little more independence vis-a-vis the state, enabling some activist union leaders to attempt to represent workers' interests instead of those of the communist authorities.

East Germany had 16 trade unions. Of these, 8 were concerned with industrial workers, and the rest were unions for health, education, and civilian employees of the state. But the parts did not have autonomy within the umbrella of the Confederation of Free German Trade Unions. The Presidium of the central organization instructed the leaders on the policies to be followed and could, if necessary, dissolve recalcitrant member-unions and dismiss their leaders. The Congress of the Confederation was allegedly the supreme body of the organization. However, since it met only in five-year intervals, the real power was in the hands of the Presidium.

In factories, where there were at least ten union members, branches of the unions were established. The communists simply prevented the emergence of autonomous worker-representation in the workplace. For this very reason, the Socialist Unity party exercised close supervision of the leadership of the Confederation. The organization's chairman and his deputy were party members. So were all other leaders of any significance. Their major task was to fulfill the goals of the party leadership; to achieve production targets and to raise productivity. They had no right to make economic decisions, nor could they influence the appointment of the managers of enterprises.

The trade unions did, however, administer social insurance, provide and manage health resorts and vacations spots for workers. The confederation owned over 1,600 hotels and vacation resorts where workers paid minimal sums for rent and food during their vacations. The unions also acted as arbitrators in disputes concerning the work-code and labor discipline. If an enterprise had more than fifty workers, a conflict-commission was organized to meet in open sessions and provide "popular justice" in the workplace. In the 1970s, efforts were made to raise the status of the Confederation above other mass organizations. Yet, the original role of the unions, namely their being transmission belts for the communist leadership, were not fundamentally altered.

Another mass organization was the Free German Youth, the party's copy of the Soviet KOMSOMOL. It was established in 1946 as an allegedly nonparty, nonsectarian youth association, and its name harkened back to the early years of the Weimar Republic (*see* Free German Youth Organization). By 1952, the Free German Youth association had been completely absorbed into the communist system of mass-organizations, and its twofold purpose was the indoctrination of young people in the ideology of Marxism-Leninism and preparation of them for later Communist party membership. The rules provided that young people between the ages of fourteen and twenty five could join the association and, in 1982, 2.3 million was the number of its membership. This was a typically urban group; in rural areas, fewer young people joined its ranks. Every school, university, and industrial firm had a chapter of the organization. In 1983, there were 28,191 basic organizations of this institution in East Germany. Its so-called parliament met every five years. Between sessions, the Central Council, whose members were also members of the Communist party, directed its affairs. About 650,000 officials of one sort or another worked in the organization. Most of them were, or eventually became, members of the Socialist Unity party. For instance, Egon Krenz, a former leader of the Central Council, became a full member of the Communist party's Politburo; Erich Honecker (*see* Honecker, Erich), the future secretary general of the Socialist Unity party, was the first chairman of the Free German Youth organization.

The organization was a major participant in premilitary training of young people. It also organized the Thalmann Young Pioneers Association, which recruited children for a communist equivalent of the cub scouts.

Bibliography

Dennis, Mike, *German Democratic Republic: Politics, Economics, and Society* (London, 1988); Hanke, Irma, "Rural Life under Socialism," *GDR Monitor*, 15 (1986), pp. 17-36; Lane, Christel, "Women in Socialist Society with Special Reference to the GDR," *Sociology*, 17.4 (1984), pp. 489-505.

Mielke, Erich (1907–). A native son of Berlin, Mielke joined the German Communist party in 1926 and was a member of the private army of the party. During the Spanish civil war, he joined the loyalists and was a KGB agent. As such, he participated in the persecution of Trotskyists and Anarchists. When Francisco Franco's army won the civil war, Mielke, with many others, escaped to France but was placed in a French detention camp. The Soviet secret service smuggled him out of the camp and delivered him to the Soviet Union. He spent the war years in Moscow.

In 1945, he returned to Germany's Soviet zone of occupation and organized the new political police in the service of the Communist party. In 1950, Mielke was named secretary of the Central Committee of the Socialist Unity party in charge of state security. In 1953, he moved to the ministry of the interior as deputy minister. Between 1955 and 1957, Mielke was appointed deputy minister of state security. He became minister of state security in 1957 and remained in that post until 1989. Mielke remained a member of the party's Central Committee and, in 1971, became a member of the Presidium of the party as a candidate (nonvoting) member. In 1976, he was promoted to full membership in that institution. In 1959, he was already colonel general and, in 1980, was promoted to General of the army. In 1991 he was arrested and was tried in a German court for crimes committed against the German people, especially for being responsible of shooting refugees at the East German-West German border. Originally, he was tried together with Erich Honecker (*see* Honecker, Erich), but Honecker's case was dismissed because the aging former communist leader has terminal cancer.

Bibliography

Letgers, Lyman H., ed. *The German Democratic Republic: A Developed Socialist Society* (Boulder, CO, 1978).

Ministry of State Security. The major task of the ministry was the protection of the state from internal and external "subversion," using the term in the widest sense of its meaning. General of the Army Erich Mielke (*see* Mielke, Erich) commanded the forces of the ministry throughout most of the existence of East Germany. The number of secret policemen was not known. The ministry also employed spies outside East Germany.

The Main Administration Reconnaissance, the body responsible for the direction of foreign intelligence, was especially interested in West Germany. Lieutenant General Markus Wolf headed this agency until the collapse of communism in East Germany. An extremely successful spymaster, Wolf succeeded in placing a spy even in Chancellor Willy Brandt's inner office. The unmasking of this spy led to the chancellor's resignation. But Wolf also had some spectacular failures. Defectors from the East German intelligence agencies often took reams of documents with them to the West, unmasking many operations directed by General Wolf. After the collapse of communism, Wolf sought—and received—asylum in Russia. He returned to Germany in 1992.

The security organs used large numbers of underground informers and were in constant and direct contact with the Soviet KGB. There were scores and scores of KGB agents in East Germany, and they operated as freely as if they were in their own country. In many cities during the 1989 demonstrations against communist rule, the demonstrators broke into the buildings of the security organs, ransacked their files, and took the files away. These files were freely distributed to the newspapers and the population.

Bibliography

Andrew, Christopher, and Gordievsky, Oleg, *KGB: The Inside Story of its Foreign Operations from Lenin to Gorbachev* (New York, 1990); Dennis, Mike, *German Democratic Republic: Politics, Economics, Society* (New York, 1988).

National Defense Council in East Germany. This institution was established in 1960 ostensibly by the East German parliament, but, in reality, by the Politburo of the East German Socialist Unity party. Its first chairman was Walter Ulbricht (*see* Ulbricht, Walter), to be followed by Ulbricht's successor, Erich Honecker (*see* Honecker, Erich). Twelve members of the Defense Council were officially appointed by the State Council; in reality, however, they were "recommended" by the first secretary of the Socialist Unity party and the State Council rubber-stamped the decision. The actual membership of the Defense Council was a state secret. It was known, however, that the chairman, Ulbricht and later Honecker, would become commander in chief of the armed forces in an emergency. The actual tasks of the Defense Council were never revealed to the public. Presumably, it included council of war and civil defense and the mobilization of the people in an emergency.

Bibliography

Larrabee, F. Stephen, ed. *The Two German States and European Security* (New York, 1989).

National People's Army of East Germany. In September 1947, the Soviet zone had only about 4,000 armed German security forces. Equipped mostly with outdated World War II arms, they were designated as "border police" in spite of the fact that there were no official borders as yet. By the end of 1950, almost 100,000 so-called East German policemen were under arms, constituting the kernel of the future East German armed forces. Many of the participants of these forces were former soldiers of Adolf Hitler's army. They were headed by former Wehrmacht generals Wincenz Muller and Arno von Lenski. But the commanders of the future were members of the German Communist party; these were Wilhelm Zaisser and Heinz Hoffmann, both veterans of the Spanish civil war and graduates of Soviet military academies.

On January 18, 1956, the East German parliament established the National People's Army. Its commander was the minister of defense. According to the law, the minister carried out the will of parliament. However, since the "leading force" of East Germany was designated to be the Socialist Unity party, final decisions concerning the disposition and composition of the armed forces were determined by the Politburo/Presidium of the party. There were direct communications between the People's Army and the Soviet general command in East Germany as well as the Soviet general staff in the Soviet Union. The latter provided the armaments used by the East German armed forces. A large number of Soviet military advisors were attached to the East German ministry of defense transmitting instructions on training and the use of arms. The East German minister of defense was also deputy commander in chief of the

Warsaw Pact forces. After 1960, the minister was an ex officio member of the East German Defense Council.

The relationship between the People's Army and the Soviet occupational forces was regulated by an agreement signed in March 1947. The East German state never had adequate resources to maintain the huge army it did. Therefore, its maintenance necessitated the lowering of the living standards of the population at large. The largest sums were spent on armaments and equipment. These were initially imported from Czechoslovakian armament factories and from the Soviet Union. Later, East Germany produced at least some of its military equipment. However, no tanks or airplanes were built by East German factories, probably because of Soviet fears of the Germans—even if they were communists. Small naval vessels were produced as well as small arms, antitank missiles, munitions, and explosives.

In 1980, the total strength of the People's Army was 162,000 soldiers. There were also 300,000 men in the reserves. General conscription was introduced in 1962. Women were exempted from entering the services. The People's Army was organized on the pattern of the Soviet armed forces. Each unit from the smallest to the largest had its political officer, and larger units had several security officers—some of them undercover—for counterespionage and general intelligence gathering. Each soldier was drilled not only in the use of arms, but also in Marxist-Leninist ideology. Emphasis on indoctrination was equal to that of mastering the use of armaments. The Main Political Administration of the People's Army maintained a network of Communist party cells in every unit. Some of the officers were full-time party cadres. More than 90 percent of the officers were members of the Socialist Unity party. The leadership of the People's Army maintained close communications with the ministry of state security, especially after East Germany became involved in military operations in Ethiopia and other African states. In fact, East German troops were used in combat operations in Syria, Libya, Nigeria, Congo-Brazzaville, and even in Iraq. Military advisors operated in Zimbabwe and assisted the Namibian Swapo guerrillas in fighting South Africa. The People's Army served Soviet foreign policy interests in all these adventures.

In 1990, the Peoples' Army was disbanded. Some of its officers were transferred to the armed forces of united Germany. Most of the higher officers were, however, either dismissed or pensioned.

Bibliography
Larrabee, Stephen, F., ed. *The Two German States and European Security* (New York, 1989); Schneider, Eberhard, *The GDR: The History, Politics, Economy, and Society of East Germany* (London, 1978).

Oder-Neisse Frontier of East Germany. On June 7, 1950, simultaneous announcements in East Berlin and Warsaw signaled an agreement, arrived at two days before, between Poland and East Germany. The agreement included the recognition of the Oder-Neisse line as the border between the two states. The agreement stated:

The basis of the further development and strengthening of good neighborly rela-
tions and friendship between the Polish and German peoples lies in the demarca-
tion of the inviolable frontier of peace and friendship existing between both States
along the Oder-Neisse. In this manner the German Democratic Republic confirms
the statement by prime minister Grotewohl made on October 12 1949.... Both par-
ties have decided within a space of a month to carry out the demarcation of the
frontier along the Oder-Neisse, and likewise, to regulate the question of minor fron-
tier traffic and of navigation in the waters of the frontier zone.

This agreement was further refined in January 1951, when the final frontier line
was agreed upon. In a joint statement issued on July 6, 1955, the original agreement
was reaffirmed. In 1989, the West German government, under the pressure of its
Western allies, agreed to this border.

Bibliography

Keesing's Research Report. *Germany and Eastern Europe Since 1945: From the Potsdam
agreement to Chancellor Brandt's Ostpolitik* (New York, 1973).

Ostpolitik (Policy toward the East). On January 14, 1970, Chancellor of West Germany, Willy Brandt, announced the following: "There must, there can, and, finally,
there will be negotiations between Bonn and East Berlin." Then he went on to state
that the West must take the historical perspective as the basis of its policy toward not
only East Germany, but toward Eastern Europe as a whole. He did not give up the
notion that, in the future, there would be a united Germany, but he also suggested that
the realities of great power relations did not make that possible in the short run. Then
he went on as follows:

In a future European peace arrangement, too, the national components will play
their role. But the path that leads to German self-determination within such a peace
arrangement will be a long and thorny one. Its length and labors must not restrain
us from seeking, in the present phase of history, if that is possible, regular neigh-
borly relations between the two states in Germany. The two states and social struc-
tures that have now been existing on German soil for more than two decades, re-
flect completely different and incompatible ideas of what the unity of Germany,
what a common future, should look like and how it could be reached.

Brandt offered no easy solutions and promised no quick fixes. Nevertheless, he
argued that West Germany could no longer ignore realities in Europe. He further proposed a European congress on security and common concerns and the recognition of
East Germany as a sovereign state. This declaration was followed by a lengthy exchange of letters between Willy Stoph (*see* Stoph, Willy), the East German president
and Brandt, and it led to the first visit of a West German head of state to East Germany. Brandt went to Erfurt on March 19, 1970. East Germans gave a tumultuous
welcome to Brandt, greeting him as a hero which was not to the liking of the East
German communist leaders. There was a second meeting between the two heads of
state in Kassel, West Germany, on May 21, 1970. In both these meetings Brandt

stressed that the sense of Germany's future must be preserved and that an accommodation between the two German states must be found. Important steps were taken to improve mail service and telecommunications between the two Germanys. West Germany obligated itself to pay $30 million West German marks a year to facilitate better service retroactively to 1967 and until 1973. The number of telephone lines was doubled. Steps were taken to reduce a huge West German surplus in trade with East Germany.

Finally, in August 1970, West Germany and the Soviet Union concluded a treaty on the renunciation of force in settling international disputes. The treaty contained five major provisions. These included the declaration that the relaxation of tensions in Europe was a major objective of the foreign policies of the two states; that relations between the Soviet Union and West Germany will be based on the United Nations' Charter; that the existing frontiers were inviolable; that the treaty does not affect the bilateral relations of each country with its partners; and that the ratification of the treaty accomplishes its enactment. Following this treaty, West Germany concluded another treaty, this time with Poland, on November 29, 1979. The most important provision of this treaty was the West German recognition of the Oder-Neisse line as the boundary between the two countries. In the following year, an agreement on the status of West Berlin was concluded by the four victorious powers, regulating access by mutual consent. Thus, Chancellor Brandt's *Ostpolitik* fundamentally altered relations in Europe, and it opened the doors to further relaxation of tensions between the two blocs.

Bibliography
Brandt, Willy, *A Peace Policy for Europe* (New York, 1969); *The German-Polish Dialogue* (Bonn, 1966); Griffith, William E., *The Ostpolitik of the Federal Republic of Germany* (Cambridge, MA, 1978); Keesing's Research Report, *Germany and Eastern Europe Since 1945: From the Potsdam Agreement to Chancellor Brandt's Ostpolitik* (New York, 1973); Kaiser, Karl, *German Foreign Policy in Transition: Bonn Between East and West* (New York, 1968).

People's Chamber (Volkskammer) of East Germany. Elections for this body, the lower house of the East German parliament, were held in the Soviet zone on October 15, 1950. A single list was presented to the voters who "overwhelmingly approved" it. On September 8, the West German government issued a White Paper, which pointed out the fraudulent nature of the vote. It stated that voters had no choice, since their single alternative to voting for the official list was not to drop the ballot into the voting box, which would have been observed. It also mentioned other questionable practices used in the elections.

The newly elected People's Chamber met for the first time in November and elected as its president Johann Dieckmann. Four vice presidents were also elected. It empowered Otto Grotewohl (*see* Grotewohl, Otto), one of the leaders of the Socialist Unity party, to form a government. In March 1949, the People's Chamber enacted a constitution for East Germany, changing the Soviet zone of occupation into a quasi-independent German state. It also issued a call for new elections for an East German People's Congress (*see* People's Congress of East Germany). In May 1949, the elections were held with a single list of candidates. According to official East German reports, 66 percent of the voters supported the list. The new congress created a 330-member People's Council which, in turn, named itself the People's Chamber, the lower house of parliament. Its first act was the approval of the constitution. A few days later, the five *Lander* (regions) sent their representatives to form the *Lander Kammer* (Chamber of Regions), which was intended to become a legislative body. On October 11, the two chambers met and elected Wilhelm Pieck (*see* Pieck, Wilhelm) as the first president of East Germany. The East German Christian Democratic Union and the Liberal Democratic party "accepted" the domination of the People's Chamber by the communists. A new constitution was enacted in 1974. It gave more power to the People's Chamber, at least on paper. The first discussions of drafts of proposed laws were submitted to it, providing some sort of oversight for legislation.

The People's Chamber was called to meetings infrequently during the 1950s and 1960s, and, in the 1970s, the meetings were even less frequently held. On the other hand, the parliamentary committees became more active, although the outcome of their work remained negligible. This was, of course, not accidental, since none of the deputies worked full time on legislation. In fact, the major task of the parliamentary deputies was to explain the policies of the government to the population.

The People's Chamber also maintained a facade of being a multi-party, democratic institution, but the noncommunist parties were simply transmission belts to various segments of the population not reached directly by the propaganda organs of the Socialist Unity party. All noncommunist parties were infiltrated by communist agents or cryptocommunists who ensured that the organizations adhered to the Marxist-Leninist line of the communist leadership.

On paper, seats in the People's Chamber were apportioned according to the agreements among the parties. In 1949, the number of deputies was 466. By 1963, the number had grown to 500. Elections for the chamber were held every four years until 1971. After that year, elections were held in five-year intervals to match the congresses of the Socialist Unity party. The elections were, however, meaningless affairs, and the official single list was never contested. The official elections results usually showed 99 percent of the votes cast for the list. When the communist regime collapsed, however, the People's Chamber performed an important role. In 1989, it voted for the reforms demanded by the population and, therefore, cut the legs out from under the communist hard-liners. After this vote, the chamber declared its own dissolution.

Bibliography

Keesing's Research Report. *Germany and Eastern Europe Since 1945: From the Potsdam Agreement to Chancellor Brandt's Ostpolitik* (New York, 1973); Rothschild, Joseph, *Return to Diversity: Eastern Europe since 1989* (Oxford, 1992).

People's Congress. Elections for a new People's Congress were held in December 1947, in the Soviet zone of occupation. The congress was to create a unified policy for Germany, which would then be presented for the consideration of the Allied foreign ministers scheduled to meet shortly in London. However, most of the representatives were from the Soviet zone and were acting on behalf of the communists. Characteristically, the still untamed Christian Democratic Union of the Soviet zone refused to participate in the meeting. In response, the Soviet administrators withdrew their recognition of the Christian Democratic Union whose leaders then left for the Western zones. Only one renegade Christian Democratic leader, Otto Nuschke, attended the first meeting of the People's Congress. As a reward, he was promptly appointed chairman of his now defunct party in the Soviet zone.

In March 1948, a second meeting of the People's Congress was assembled. This was better organized than the first. It proceeded to appoint 330 people to the People's Council (*Volksrat*) of whom one-hundred were ostensibly to speak for West Germans. The chairmen of the various parties and mass organizations met at the assembly and formed a presidium that was to become the executive organ of the People's Congress. However, all this was really without much substance since the communists dominated the People's Congress and they were, in turn, supported by the Soviet occupational authorities. The Congress was simply a vehicle for Joseph Stalin to use for the eventual creation of the East German state.

The presidium of the congress proceeded to write a constitution and called for elections for a new People's Congress. The elections were held with a single list of candidates in May 1949. According to official statements, 66 percent of the votes were cast for the single list. The congress in session named 330 people from the top of the list for membership in the latest People's Congress. In an abrupt change of mind, the congress then named itself a provisional People's Chamber (*Volkskammer*), the equivalent of one house of the legislature for the Soviet zone of occupation. The Chamber proceeded to approve a constitution which, at least on paper, was a rather liberal document at the time. This became the first basic law of East Germany.

Bibliography

Croan, Melvin, "Germany and Eastern Europe," in Joseph Held, ed. *The Columbia History of Eastern Europe in the Twentieth Century* (New York, 1992); Krisch, Henry, *German Politics Under Soviet Occupation* (New York, 1974); Schneider, Eberhard, *The GDR: The History, Politics, Economics, and Society of East Germany* (London, 1978); Stahl, Walter, *The Politics of Postwar Germany* (New York, 1963).

People's Police in East Germany. After the administrative machinery of Nazi Germany had been destroyed, the new police chief of Berlin was Paul Markgraf, a former prisoner of war in the Soviet Union. While in the Soviet Union, Markgraf had joined the Antifascist Alliance whose members were recruited from among German prisoners of war. On June 1, 1945, Markgraf declared the establishment of a police force in the Soviet zone of occupation. Police stations were organized and created throughout the Soviet zone, manned mostly by former prisoners of war in the Soviet Union. There were also some communist cadres who were delegated by their party for police work as well as noncommunist members of the anti-Nazi resistance.

A year later, the name of the institution was changed to that of People's Police (*Volkspolicei*, or *VoPo*). The People's Police was certainly a creation and organ of the new system established by the Soviet Union in Germany. After the creation of the East German state, it already had a ready-made police force for the enforcement of its policies. The People's Police was controlled by the East German ministry of the interior, an institution controlled by communist party members, and a subordinate of the Soviet occupational authorities. It was also a quasi-military force, and it was charged with maintaining peace and order in East Germany. In time, the People's Police became the kernel of a newly organized East German army.

Bibliography

Steele, Jonathan, *Inside East Germany: The State That Came in from the Cold* (New York, 1977).

Pieck, Wilhelm (1876–1960). Pieck was born into a poor craftsman's family and learned carpentry. He joined the German Social Democratic party at the age of nineteen in 1895. During World War I, he joined the *Spartacusbund* (League of Spartacus), a radical leftist organization. In 1918, he left the moderate German social Democratic party and threw in his lot with the newly organized German Communist party of Karl Liebknecht and Rosa Luxemburg. Immediately, he was elected a member of the new party's Central Committee. Before the end of the war he deserted the German imperial army and took refuge in Holland.

Between 1921 and 1928, he was elected a deputy to the Prussian *Landtag*, or regional assembly, on the communist ticket. He was reelected twice, the last time in 1933. He was also a deputy of the all-German parliament, the Reichstag, between 1928 and 1933. Pieck became a member of the central commission of the COMINTERN in 1928. After the appointment of Adolf Hitler as German chancellor, Pieck sought asylum at first in France, and then he found his way to the Soviet Union. In 1945, he returned to Germany with the Soviet army and immediately became chairman of the reorganized German Communist party. Between 1946 and 1954, he shared the chairmanship of the Socialist Unity party (uniting the formerly Communist and Social Democratic parties) with Otto Grotewohl (*see* Grotewohl, Otto). Between 1949 and 1960, he was the president of East Germany. He died in 1960.

Bibliography

Grote, Manfred, "The Socialist Unity party of Germany," in Stephen Fischer-Galati, ed. *The Communist Parties of Eastern Europe* (New York, 1979).

Planning in East Germany. Central planning, one of the major elements of Soviet-style economic development, was intended to provide an underpinning to the allegedly "scientific" theory of Marxism-Leninism. The first East German constitution included references to central planning as a means of control over economic life.

Planning and economic management were strictly centralized. The leading authority of the Socialist Unity party, the Presidium (formerly Politburo), determined the major targets of economic policy. Then the state's planning office worked out the details for industry and agriculture. The appropriate ministries then proceeded to implement the decisions, or at least they attempted to do so. The managers of individual enterprises had only one task, namely, the fulfillment of the targets of the plan in whose preparation they were not consulted. Great emphasis was placed on quantitative production; hardly any attention was paid to the improvement of the quality of the goods produced. Workers were laboring by piecework, and their quotas were periodically raised. All phases of economic life were under the watchful eyes of the agents of the state planning office. Up to 1959, five-year plans, after enacted, became law. Those who did not fulfill their targets were breaking the law. After 1959, a seven-year plan was introduced. In the 1970s, the state returned to the five-year plan cycles.

The East German economy—as the economies of the other East European states and of the Soviet Union—did not work well under centralized planning. Statistical information available for the planners was often incorrect. One of the reasons for this was that statistics served propaganda purposes, showing a much rosier situation than really existed. They usually exaggerated the rates of growth and productivity. Another reason was that the great stress on the quantity of production forced everyone—from wage earners, to directors, to planners—to disregard the real needs of the economy and produce goods of low quality. Instead of establishing a steady progress in economic life, central planning produced stagnation, confusion, and corruption.

The communist leaders attempted several times to tinker with the system. Between 1963 and 1969, modifications, called the New Economic System were introduced. They allowed a certain relaxation of the tempo of work. But after 1968, a new retrenchment occurred, and central direction of the system was resumed. Although the economy of East Germany did indeed experience steady growth after the building of the Berlin Wall in 1961 (see Berlin Wall), it was mainly due to massive funds provided by West Germany. The economic system hardly changed until the collapse of the communist state.

A few words about the New Economic System are due here. In 1963, the sixth congress of the Socialist Unity party of East Germany accepted a program named the New Economic System. The program introduced incentives for workers which soon resulted in increased productivity. In 1967, the five-day workweek was introduced. The lower levels of decision makers were to be given wider discretion in organizing production. Profit was no longer a dirty word, and the Association of Nationalized Enterprises was given a measure of independence. Wages were to be geared to enterprise profits, and the quality of the goods produced received primacy over quantitative production. A price reform was planned to provide a more realistic relation between wages on the one hand and materials and energy on the other. Soon prices of these necessities increased considerably. Prices of building materials, paper, and chemical products also increased. Two years later, a general price increase was introduced for industrial products. Market research was encouraged, and firms could keep some of the profit that they earned.

Before the New Economic System could gather momentum, the winds of politics had turned. Leonid Brezhnev succeeded Nikita S. Khrushchev in the Soviet Union, and Brezhnev forced an unequal trade treaty on East Germany that undermined the state's budding prosperity. On the day the agreement was signed, Dr. Erich Appel, the head of the state's planning commission, committed suicide. The treaty forced East Germany to sell its finished goods at rock-bottom prices to the Soviet Union and pay exorbitant prices for what it bought from it. One important element of the New Economic System, namely the increased quality of products that were to be sold on Western markets, was simply jettisoned. The original decentralization in the system was reversed. The New Economic System died a quiet death.

Centralization and mindless planning was resumed under the rule of Erich Honecker (see Honecker, Erich). Rigid, central planning was especially disastrous in East German automobile production. Two models, the Wartburg, produced at Eisenach, and the Trabant, manufactured at Zwickau, were produced. These firms which had originally belonged to the BMW and Audi companies, had been confiscated by the state. The major part of production consisted of the smaller Trabant which East Germany exported to the other socialist states and the Third World. The vehicles, based on outdated designs and technology, smoked, belched, and vibrated. But they were automobiles, and most East Europeans could not afford the better-built Western models, not to mention American cars. It did not matter that parts were difficult to come by and that the Trabant was built with a very thin body. It was typical that most East Germans did not—could not—buy the Trabant in great numbers, because it was hardly affordable. With the unification of Germany, both factories were closed down. They simply were not competitive with Western producers.

Perhaps the greatest harm was done by rigid, central planning to East German agriculture. The communists introduced a land reform in 1945 in the Soviet zone. It was in this zone where most of the large estates were located. The estates were confiscated and redistributed among the peasants in Mecklenburg, Brandenburg, Saxony-Anhalt, Thuringen, and Saxony. About a half million peasants received land. Almost 100,000 ethnic Germans, expelled from Eastern Europe, also received some land. However, in 1949, collectivization of the land began and was rapidly completed. As was the case in the other states of the Soviet Bloc, agriculture received a minimum of investments. The sector served as a resource to be exploited. Collectives were paid little for their produce and they had to buy expensive machinery from the state. Before the building of the Berlin Wall, the East German peasants voted with their feet and sought asylum in West Germany in droves. The planning office, however, did not relent; it demanded high quotas of food production, and when the quotas were unfulfilled, peasants were hauled off to prison or to concentration camps. By 1975, the collectives were worked mostly by older men whose physical capacity was limited. The young workers had left for West Germany or for work in the cities.

Bibliography

Croan, Melvin, "Germany and Eastern Europe," in Joseph Held, ed. *The Columbia History of Eastern Europe in the Twentieth Century* (New York, 1992); Hanke, Irma, "Rural Life under Socialism as Seen from Within: Eckart's *'So sehe Ich die Sache,' Protokolle aus der DDR*" *GDR Monitor* 15 (1986), pp. 17-36; Leptin, Gert, and Melzer, Manfred, *Economic Reform in East German Industry* (Oxford, 1978).

Potsdam Agreement (June 5, 1945). A joint statement was issued by the four victorious Allies in January 1945, concerning the zones of occupation of defeated Germany:

Germany within her frontiers of December 31, 1937, will, for the purposes of occupation, be divided into four zones, one to be allotted to each power as follows; 1. an eastern zone to the Union of Soviet Socialist Republics; a north-western zone to the United Kingdom; a south-western zone to the United States of America; and a western zone to France. 2. The area of Greater Berlin will be occupied by the forces of each of the four powers. An inter-Allied governing authority (in Russian, Kommandatura) consisting of four commandants, appointed by their respective commanders-in-chief, will be established to direct jointly its administration . . . The Allied armies are in occupation of the whole of Germany, and the German people have begun to atone for the terrible crimes committed under the leadership of those whom, in the hour of their success, they openly approved and blindly obeyed. Agreement has been reached at this conference on the political and economic principles of a coordinated Allied policy toward defeated Germany during the period of Allied control. The purpose of this agreement is to carry out the Crimean declaration on Germany (Yalta). German militarism and Nazism will be extirpated and the Allies will take, in agreement together, now and in the future, the other measures necessary to assure that Germany will never again threaten her neighbors, or the peace of the world. It is not the intention of the Allies to destroy or to enslave the German people. It is their intention that the German people be given the opportunity for the eventual reconstruction of their life on a democratic and peaceful basis. If their own efforts are steadily directed to this end, it will be possible for them, in due course, to take their place among the free and peaceful people of the world. . .

Bibliography

Keesing's Research Report. *Germany and Eastern Europe Since 1945: From the Potsdam Agreement to Chancellor Brandt's Ostpolitik* (New York, 1973); Malzahn, Manfred, *Germany, 1945–1949: A Sourcebook* (London, 1991); Nettle, Jonathan P., *The Eastern Zone and Soviet Policy in Germany* (London, 1951); Stahl, Walter, *The Politics of Postwar Germany* (New York, 1963).

Religious Policies in East Germany. Over 15 million East Germans belonged to a religious denomination, mostly Christian, and 13 million of them professed the Lutheran religion. At first, the communists handled the churches with care. They were permitted to maintain contacts with their coreligionists in West Germany. The Roman Catholics were in contact with the Vatican. As soon as the communists were in complete control, however, persecution of religion and the religious began.

By 1952, their contacts with the outside world had been completely interrupted, and the state banned all church meetings, and church authorities were forbidden to communicate with each other. The state launched an atheistic campaign among schoolchildren. The antireligious propaganda was promoted through a Society for Scientific Knowledge, established specifically for this purpose by the state. The chairman of the society was Johannes Becker, the communist minister of culture. In November 1954, the state set up substitute ceremonies for the religious rites of confirmation, baptism, and marriage. Confirmation was renamed "the consecration of youth." It prepared fourteen-year-olds for a secular ceremony centered on a young adult's duties toward the people. Other antireligious measures followed. In 1955, churches were forbidden to use educational facilities for their meetings. Church magazines were banned from book shops and street stalls. The church tax, a subsidy for religious activities, was abolished.

By 1958, there was some relaxation of these policies. East Germans were permitted to attend a German Catholic Conference in Berlin, although some police harassment of the returning people did occur. But official policies were not fundamentally altered. The communists simply could not permit religious influences to compete with Marxist-Leninist ideology. Above all, the communist state wanted to subordinate the churches completely to its purposes or, if this was not possible, eliminate their influence completely from public life. The East German communists set out to organize Christian associations that were willing to support their policies and opposed the stand of the church toward the state.

The major aim of the East German government in international relations was recognition of its legitimacy, its standing as a separate German nation, dedicated to the building of socialism. This policy, instituted in the 1960s, was called "delimitation" (*Abgrenzung*). It ran directly counter to the Lutheran church's efforts to establish a *Gemeinschaft*, or community, of all Germans. The solution for both sides was to create an image of a secular Martin Luther in order to establish a sham-connection between Marxism-Leninism and church doctrines. Friedrich Engels' criticism of Martin Luther as a servant of the ruling class, as well as the exultation of Thomas Munzer and his rebellious peasants, therefore, had to be toned down. Luther had to be connected somehow to the "progressive traditions" of Germany that, according to communist ideologues, had led directly to the establishment of the socialist state of East Germany. This was especially difficult to do, since, according to Marxism-Leninism, religion was in general, and churches were in particular, enemies of the working class that had to be suppressed.

The Socialist Unity party had already attempted to make the connection in 1967, on the 450th anniversary of Luther's nailing his ninety-five theses on the door of the church at Wittenberg. But the Lutheran church authorities had refused to participate in the official celebrations because of the generally hostile attitude of the communists toward the church. The communist efforts bore fruit in 1983 at the Luther Jubilee. The regime's spokesmen emphasized Luther's human qualities, while church authorities continued to stress the reformer's devotion to God. This eventually led to an accommodation between the two sides. After the Luther Jubilee, it was possible for an East German citizen to work for the success of socialism while, at the same time, be devoted to Martin Luther's church. The state and the church began to cooperate, and the cooperation extended to the state-sponsored peace movement that was neatly tailored to the centuries-old preaching of peace by the church.

After 1983, the communist leaders achieved a momentous breakthrough. The loyalty of Lutheran Christians was redirected toward the communist state. At the least, the two loyalties could now be merged, and through this, the state acquired a certain measure of internal legitimacy. In spite of this, the communists were unwilling to abandon their antireligious stand which they had traditionally espoused.

The balance was maintained by the Honecker regime with the cooperation of the Lutheran church leaders. The church leaders, on their part, did not have to give up their dream of creating a German *Gemeinschaft* of all religious people, regardless of their state affiliations. The communists, on the other hand, continued their efforts at delimitation. Their aim never changed; they wanted the recognition of East Germany as a separate, socialist German nation. The results were obvious in 1989, when tens of thousands of East Germans once again voted with their feet and crossed over to Czechoslovakia and then to Hungary and from there to Austria on their way to West Germany. At that time, the East German Lutheran church authorities counseled the people not to leave East Germany. Although it appeared that no one would heed this advice, the church leaders had shown how far their accommodation with the communist state had taken them. After the unification of Germany, the Lutheran church withdrew behind the bastion of its traditions and no longer participated directly in politics.

Bibliography

Ash, Garton T., "Swords into Plowshares: The Unofficial 'Peace Movement' and the Churches in East Germany," *Religion in Communist Lands* 11.3 (Winter 1983), pp. 244-250; Beck, Dan, "The Luther Revival: Aspects of National Abgrenzung and Confessional Gemeinschaft in the German Democratic Republic," in Pedro Ramet, ed. *Religion and Nationalism in Soviet and East European Politics* (Durham, NC, 1989).

Social Change in East Germany. The East German state tried to eliminate all social classes and to create the communist utopia of a classless society. The road to this goal was, according to the regime's ideological experts, through the elimination of all ownership of private property. In East Germany, the official view held that only two classes survived, namely, the working class and the peasantry. The stratum of the intelligentsia was not considered a separate class, nor were the remnants of various small groups outside the official categories. The regime was forced, by the logic of its ideology, to retain a class-based explanation of its social policies. It emphasized that the largest of all the classes was the working class, and, since the Communist party was the party of workers, it was entitled to rule the state. The discipline of sociology by which social stratifications could really be charted was handicapped by ideological blinders. There simply had to be a harmonious concept of a socialist community of the people which precluded empirical social research.

Only in the Honecker era was there a relaxation of ideological pressure, and, as a consequence, some important findings were published. According to some of the studies, the working class included manual and nonmanual employees. The size of this class was, therefore, large. In 1955, its members accounted for 78.4 percent, and in 1985, 89.0 percent, of all employees. The problem with such statistics was that they included the huge state, and party, bureaucracies as well as the officers of the police and the military. Furthermore, there was no separation between manual and nonmanual workers, which further skewed the results. The socialist sector employed most of the people. Similar to the situation in other developing societies, there was a relative stability among the industrial employees, while a considerable increase occurred in the service sectors. Furthermore, the number of the so-called core of the working class, the production workers, lost ground between 1950 and 1984. Their relative ratio declined from 72.4 percent to 62.4 percent.

The stratification of society had become more complex. Skilled workers were separated from the unskilled labor and received higher salaries. At the same time, increasing automation released large numbers of workers from heavy labor and provided for in-plant unemployment. Such a situation inevitably led to alienation and boredom at the workplace. Some of the skilled workers, however, were drawn into close collaboration with managers and engineers and gained prestige and income. The new social stratification of occupational groups had become based on skill, status, education and, ultimately, income.

In contrast, considerable leveling occurred in the peasant sector. The collectivization of land had been completed by 1960. However, as in other communist countries, agriculture was not a favored sector in terms of investment and mechanization. By 1970, however, the average income of collective farmers reached that of industrial wage earners. This did not necessarily mean actual increases, but that state wages paid to both groups were regulated in this direction.

The greatest achievement in the rural sector was in education. The professed goal of the communist regime was to eliminate wage and cultural differences between cities and rural areas, and education was one of the means by which this was to be achieved. By 1982, 90 percent of collective farm members had completed some form of vocational training. This, however, failed to create the equalization of conditions. Consequently, small rural communities were losing large numbers of collective farmers, especially the younger people, to the cities, where they entered industrial occupations. The agricultural sector suffered from these conditions until the very end of the communist regime.

Although the communist model of society did not recognize the intelligentsia as a separate social class—according to the ideology, socialism was to bring about the elimination of distinctions between manual and mental labor—the intellectuals certainly carved out for themselves a separate niche in socialist society.

In the years before and after the establishment of East Germany, the communists were compelled to use the intelligentsia who had grown up and received their education in Nazi Germany. Although all sorts of privileges were granted to these people, a yearly flow of about 5,000 of them left for West Germany between 1949 and 1961. Thus, the communist regime was forced to raise its own intelligentsia and this was gradually accomplished. People with working-class backgrounds were sent to schools and educated. Children of intellectuals, if their parents were loyal to East Germany, were also permitted to enter this social stratum. By 1964, about 80 percent of all college and university graduates had completed their education after 1951. Yet, the regime could not admit that the intelligentsia had become a new elite; this would have denigrated the party's leading role in society. Nevertheless, reality intruded in this as in other matters into ideology.

Summing it up, it seems clear that society in East Germany has undergone important changes. The industrialists who possessed immense wealth disappeared from society. Their properties were confiscated, and most of them left for West Germany. The large landowners also disappeared. Their estates were confiscated and distributed among the peasantry. In turn, the peasants were forced into the collectives and became salaried employees of their enterprises, ultimately of the state. Women were drawn in large numbers into the work force, altering traditional marriage patterns. There was a considerable leveling of incomes and, thus, differentiations based on income were lessened. At the same time, a new elite emerged from the intelligentsia loyal to the communist regime. These included not only the engineers and technicians in industry, but also creative people, writers, artists, and even sportsmen. Teachers and university instructors were also members of this stratum. Although the communist *nomenklatura* was not included among the intelligentsia, its members certainly lived like intellectuals. Many members of the state bureaucracy were also included in this stratum of society. In the final count, however, East German social developments did not greatly differ from those in other developing societies the world over, Marxist-Leninist ideology notwithstanding.

Bibliography

Dennis, Mike, *The German Democratic Republic: Politics, Economics, and Society* (London, 1988).

Soviet Policies in the Soviet Occupational Zone of Germany. The Soviet Union originally did not expect to remain in occupation of Germany for long. This was evident in the thorough looting of the zone of most of its industrial and agricultural movable resources. The dismantling and transfer of German industrial enterprises began immediately after the conquest. Machinery and equipment were removed completely from 1,900 firms and transported to the Soviet Union during the first few months of the occupation. This was done in such haste that equipment was often permitted to rust on unused railroad tracks when no appropriate buildings could be found to house it. In addition, reparations were taken out of the current production of those firms that were left behind, and these were usually declared joint Soviet-German companies. Most medium and large firms were simply stripped. At the same time, 200 large firms that were exempt were also declared joint Soviet-German companies. All these firms had Soviet directors appointed to head them who then proceeded to loot them thoroughly. The final outcome was the complete takeover of German industry in the Soviet zone. German agriculture was also looted by the Soviet occupational authorities. The huge occupational forces were fed and housed at Germany's expense. During the first two years of occupation, most choice produce went to the Soviet occupational army.

In political life, the Soviet authorities behaved somewhat differently. Once the horrors of war had subsided, they tried to promote a version of the Popular Front of the interwar years. They encouraged leftist parties and individuals to work for the elimination of Nazism from society. They quickly restored municipal services and reestablished cultural institutions. In this the Soviet authorities faced great difficulties. The infrastructures of most cities were in shambles. Drinking water, electricity, and heating fuel were not available. Epidemics threatened the physically weakened population. To ease the problems, the Soviet army helped clear the rubble from city streets and shipped some food supplies to the Germans. At the same time, the production of German agriculture had to support the huge occupying army. New organizations were encouraged to emerge after 1945. A trade union association was established with Soviet blessing, dominated mostly by German communists. The Free German Youth (*see* Free German Youth Organization) association was organized. A Cultural League for the Democratic Renewal of Germany (*see Kulturbund*) was formed. The *Aufbau Verlag*, a state publishing firm (*see Aufbau Verlag*) was also established.

Bibliography
Dennis, Mike, *German Democratic Republic: Politics, Economics, and Society* (London, 1988); Nettle, Jonathan P., *The Eastern Zone and Soviet Policy in Germany, 1945–1950* (London, 1951).

Sports. The Socialist Unity party of East Germany always considered sports a measure of a society's strength and level of development. In 1974, at the Eighth Party Congress, Erich Honecker (*see* Honecker, Erich) declared:
Our state is respected in the world today not only because of the excellent performance of our top athletes but also because of the unrelenting attention which we devote to physical culture and sports to make them an everyday need of each and every citizen.

There can be no doubt that East German sportsmen helped to break the diplomatic isolation of their state and that the best of them enjoyed unprecedented prestige and privileges in East Germany. In the Olympic games in Munich, the East Germans won unprecedented numbers of medals. In world competitions, they usually won enough medals to come in third behind the Soviet Union and the United States in medal-standing.

There were about thirty large sports clubs, where most of the talent was concentrated that received lavish state subsidies. A Sports and Physical Education College was established at Leipzig to concentrate on the scientific education of coaches. The top athletes received good jobs where they did not have to report to work, yet received high salaries. This was intended to keep up the fiction that East German athletes were amateurs when, in reality, they were professional sportsmen.

The world- and Olympic champions represented only the thin layer of the most talented sportsmen. Below them there were mass organizations dedicated to physical education. The German Gymnastics and Sports Association, a state-established body, coordinated sports activities in the entire country. It cooperated with the ministry of education and other mass organizations in organizing sports festivals and other activities. The association was established in 1957. By the mid-1980s, its membership was over 3.5 million people. It had over 10,000 sports communities, divided into subsections, that provided facilities for both the professional and the amateur sportsmen.

Sports were tremendously competitive in East Germany. Each year a so-called Spartakiad was held in schools and districts; the winners appeared in the biannual regional—and in alternate years, the national competitions. Joint sports programs were sponsored by several mass organizations to encourage the participation of casual sportsmen. Sports was, of course also a means by which military preparedness was promoted. The slogan, "ready to work and defend the homeland" was taken very seriously. The winning participants in these events were given medals recognizing their achievement; in 1983, over 4 million of these medals were awarded. The political and diplomatic rewards were important fruits of East German sports programs, but were not as important as the state's success in controlling the free time of citizens. Yet, ultimately, this success was negated by the preferences of young people to be with friends which could not always be restricted to further the communists' goals.

Several studies revealed that mass-sports activities were not as widespread among large segments of the population as had been claimed by state propaganda. Women, workers who labored in shifts, and apprentices were among those who participated less frequently in sports activities. According to one official survey, 47 percent of the citizens participated in some form of sports activity at least once a week. The rate of participation was the highest among fifteen-to-sixteen year-olds (80 percent). Among twenty-to-thirty year-olds, the percentage was down to sixty. By the time an individual reached his or her fourth decade, sports activity was reduced nearly to zero. Working women were particularly less inclined to participate even in age categories where participation was relatively high. After the collapse of communism and the unification of Germany, the East German sports apparatus fell apart. This was not surprising; state subsidies suddenly ceased, and the thousands of coaches, managers, and instructors had no more financial support. The best athletes and coaches were absorbed by the West German sports clubs, but the average sportsmen had to fend for themselves as best as they could.

Bibliography

Dennis, Mike, *German Democratic Republic: Politics, Economics, and Society* (London, 1988); Steele, Jonathan, *Inside East Germany: The State That Came in from the Cold* (New York, 1977).

Stoph, Willy (1914–). Stoph, who had been born into a worker's family, became a bricklayer. In 1931, he joined the German Communist party. He was drafted and served in the German army until the end of World War II. Between 1947 and 1948, he headed the Department of Basic Industries of the German Central Administration for Industry. In 1948, Stoph was appointed a secretary to the Central Committee of the Socialist Unity party in the Soviet zone of occupation. He was administering the section supervising the economy. In 1951, he was appointed to direct the Bureau of Economic Development, an institution subordinated to the prime minister of East Germany. He then became minister of the interior and deputy chairman of the council of ministers. He was appointed minister of defense with the rank of colonel-general of the army, and in 1959 he received promotion of the rank of army general. He was then appointed deputy chairman of the council of ministers responsible for the coordination of the policies of the Socialist Unity party with the activities of the state bureaucracy. In 1962, he became first deputy chairman of the council of ministers, replacing Otto Grotewohl (*see* Grotewohl, Otto) who was, by then, seriously ill. In 1964, he was named chairman of the council of ministers and deputy chairman of the council of state. Between 1973 and 1976, he became chairman of the council of state and, in 1976, resumed his position as chairman of the council of ministers. With the collapse of the communist regime, his political activities came to an end.

Bibliography

Dennis, Mike, *German Democratic Republic: Politics, Economics, and Society* (London, 1988).

Ulbricht, Walter (1893–1973). Ulbricht, the son of a tailor in Leipzig, was entered by his father into apprenticeship in carpentry. In 1910, he joined the youth organization of the German Social Democratic party, and, two years later, he was admitted to the party as an adult member. He served in the Kaiser's army in World War I, and he joined the *Spartacusbund*, a militant, socialist, paramilitary association. In 1919, when the Social Democratic party split between the radicals and moderates, Ulbricht joined the former and became a charter member of the German Communist party. In June 1921, Ulbricht was elected into the leadership group of the new party. Two years later, he joined the Central Committee of the party in Berlin. In 1924, he was sent by the party to the Soviet Union where he studied at the Lenin Academy for party apparatchiki in Moscow. He joined the COMINTERN as a representative of German communists and was a member of this organization between 1926 and 1927.

In the elections held in Germany in 1926, Ulbricht was elected to membership in the *Landtag* (Regional Assembly) for Saxony, and two years later he became a deputy in the national parliament, the Reichstag. From 1929 until Adolf Hitler's coming to power, Ulbricht directed the Communist party organization in the Berlin-Brandenburg-Grenzmark region. In 1933, he escaped from Germany and fled to France where he remained for five years. Then he went to the Soviet Union and spent the war years in Moscow.

In 1945, Joseph Stalin sent Ulbricht back to Germany, to the Soviet zone of occupation. He was entrusted with setting up a new German administration in East Berlin. He was elected deputy chairman of the newly established Socialist Unity party in 1946 and became a member of its secretariat and of the Politburo. In 1950, he was named secretary general of the Socialist Unity party. Between 1949 and 1960, he was also first deputy chairman of the Council of Ministers of East Germany. In July 1953, he became chairman of the Socialist Unity party and remained in that position until his death.

In the meantime, he was also chairman of the Council of State and of the National Defense Council. Toward the end of the 1960s, Ulbricht began to develop signs of megalomania. He lectured not only Western statesmen about proper international behavior, but also his Soviet mentors about Marxist-Leninist ideology. Furthermore, he began openly sabotaging Soviet efforts to establish a less tense atmosphere in Europe. He was especially obnoxious in trying to obstruct Soviet efforts to establish normal relations with West Germany. Ulbricht eventually went too far. He was quietly removed from authority in the government and the Socialist Unity party in 1971 and was replaced by Erich Honecker (*see* Honecker, Erich), a gray eminence who remained the leader of the Socialist Unity party until the collapse of communism in 1989.

Bibliography

Abusch, Alexander, ed. *Walter Ulbricht* (Berlin, 1963) (in German); Becher, Johannes R., *Walter Ulbricht: A German Worker's Son* (Berlin, 1964) (in German); Croan, Melvin, "Germany and Eastern Europe" in Joseph Held, ed. *The Columbia History of Eastern Europe in the Twentieth Century* (New York, 1992); Grote, Manfred, "The Socialist Unity Party of Germany," in Stephen Fischer-Galati, ed. *The Communist Parties of Eastern Europe* (New York, 1979).

HUNGARY

General Information. *Area:* 35,919 square miles (93,030 square kilometers). *Population:* 10,600,000. *Distribution of population:* 59.2 percent urban, 40.8 percent rural dwellers. *GNP:* 28 billion Hungarian forints. *Exchange rate:* 103:1 dollar and fluctuating. *Distribution of work force:* 41.6 percent in industry and trades, 18.8 agriculture, the rest in service industries and the bureaucracy. *Railroad network:* 8,226 kilometers; 1,290 kilometers of it is electrified. Road network: 140,000 kilometers. *Ethnicity:* 94 percent Magyars, 5 percent Gypsies, scattered groups of Slovaks, Romanians, Germans. *Major cities:* Budapest, the capital; Szeged, Kecskemet, Kiskunhalas in the south; Pecs and Kaposvar in the southwest; Gyor and Szombathely in the west; Miskolc-Diosgyor, Debrecen, Szolnok in the east. *Geography:* the center of the country consists of flatlands, the European extension of the steppes of Central Asia; the northeast and the north are mountainous, including the famous wine-producing region of Tokay; the western and southwestern parts of the country are hilly regions. *Borders:* Hungary borders on Austria in the west, on Slovakia and Carpatho-Ukraine in the north and northeast, on Romania in the southeast, and on Serbia, Croatia, and Slavonia in the south and southwest. *Communist party membership:* 800,000 card-carrying members in 1988.

Bibliography

Fejto, François, *The History of the People's Democracies* (Paris, 1979); Hanak, Peter, "Hungary on a Fixed Course: An Outline of Hungarian History," in Joseph Held, ed. *The Columbia History of Eastern Europe in the Twentieth Century* (New York, 1992); MaCartney, Carlisle, A., *A History of Hungary, 1929–1945* (New York, 1957); Seton-Watson, Hugh, *Eastern Europe Between the Wars* (London, 1945).

CHRONOLOGY

1944 *March.* The German army occupied Hungary because Adolf Hitler believed that its government was contemplating the conclusion of a separate peace. *May.* The extermination of Hungarian Jews in rural communities was begun by Adolf Eichmann's *Einsatzgruppen.* The Hungarian gendarmerie fully cooperated with Eichmann by herding Hungarian Jews into makeshift concentration camps from which they were shipped to the death camps in Poland.

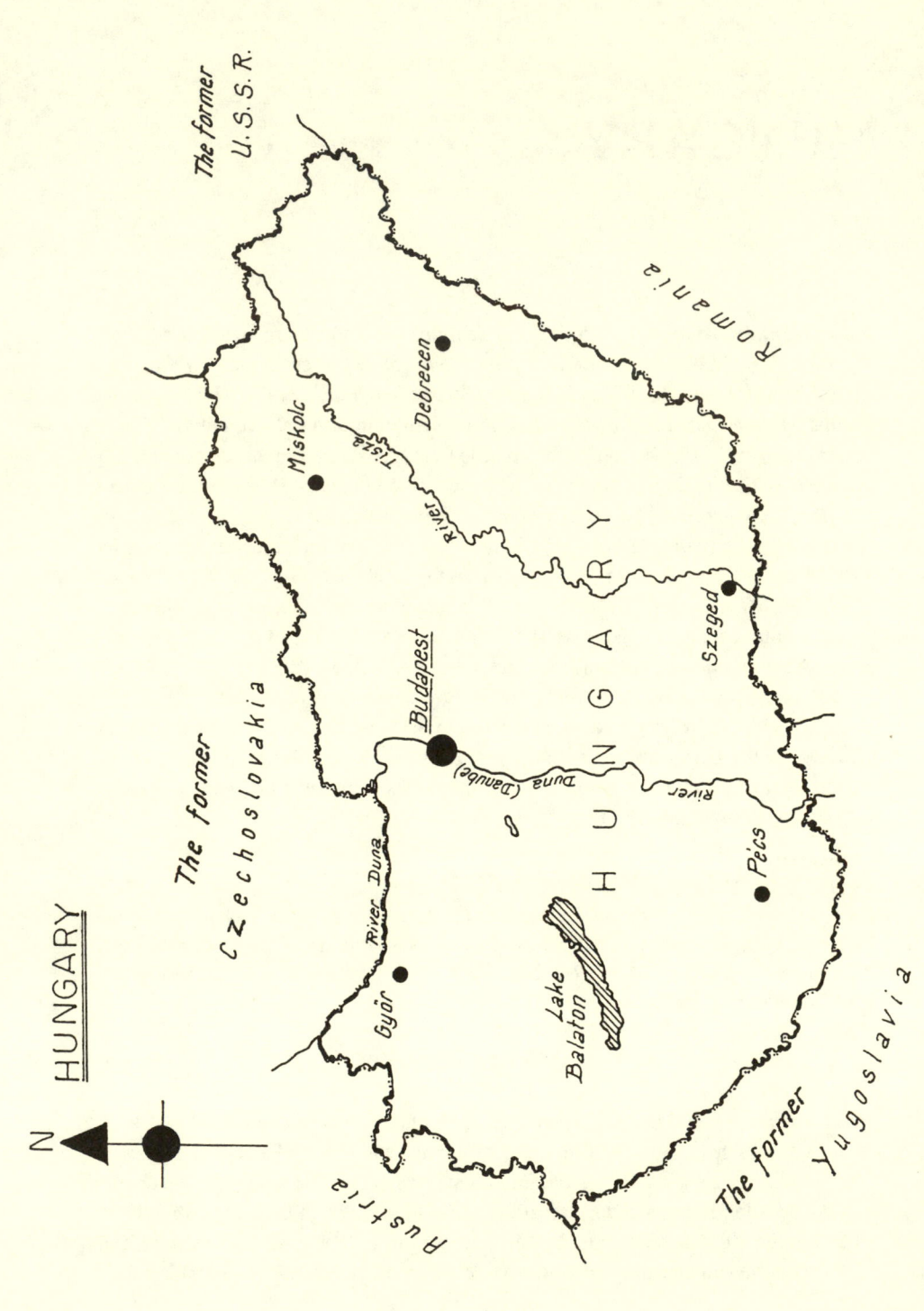

July. The deportations were stopped by the regent, Miklos Horthy, and the Jews of Budapest were saved. About 600,000 rural Hungarian Jews perished.

August. Romania surrendered to the Soviet authorities. The Soviet army reached Hungary's borders.

October. The Hungarian government made a feeble attempt to end the war by concluding a separate armistice with Soviet representatives. However, the Germans acted swiftly. They captured the regent's, family and installed Ferenc Szalasi, the head of the Hungarian Nazi party, the "Arrow Cross party" as Leader of the Nation. His reign of terror did not last long.

December. The Soviet army surrounded Budapest. A provisional Hungarian government, made up by five left-leaning parties, was installed in the eastern city of Debrecen.

1945 *April.* The last German soldiers left Hungary, carrying with them much of Hungary's wealth. The Szalasi government, as well as most members of the state bureaucracy, left the country, taking along Hungary's gold reserves and the Holy Crown of Saint Stephen.

June. Eduard Benes, Czechoslovakia's president declared that the Hungarian minority would be expelled from his country. This concerned nearly a million people.

October. In the municipal elections, the combined ticket of the Communist and Social Democratic parties received only 34 percent of the votes cast. The big winner was the Independent Smallholders party, which garnered 51 percent of the votes.

November. In the national elections, the communists received only 17 percent; the Independent Smallholders were the big winners again with 57 percent of the votes. Zoltan Tildy was named president; Ferenc Nagy was prime minister. However, the government remained a coalition of five parties, and the communists and their allies controlled the ministries of the interior and justice. Thus, they commanded the police and the quickly organized secret police organs.

1946 *February.* Hungary was declared a republic by its parliament. The exchange of Hungarians for Slovaks began, but it was stopped after a minuscule number of people volunteered for the exchange.

1947 *January.* The communist minister of the interior, Laszlo Rajk, accused the Smallholders party's leadership of harboring "enemies of state" in their ranks.

February. Hungary signed the Treaty of Paris, which revoked Hungary's territorial gains made during World War II.

May. While on vacation in Switzerland, prime minister Ferenc Nagy was accused of antistate conspiracy. He resigned with the condition that his infant son be delivered to him in Switzerland.

August. In rigged elections, the Communist party received only 27 percent of the votes cast, but the Leftist Bloc won 60.1 percent of total votes. The one-party dictatorship of the Communist party was then established.

November. The Hungarian government nationalized all banks.

1948 *February.* A Hungarian-Soviet treaty of friendship and cooperation was signed.

June. The Hungarian Social Democratic party was forced into a merger with the communists. The new name of the party: Hungarian Workers party. The new organization was completely dominated by the communists.

1949 *January.* Hungary joined the newly established Council of Mutual Economic Assistance (COMECON), Moscow's answer to the European Common Market.

September. Laszlo Rajk, the former communist minister of interior, who was named foreign minister in 1948, was subjected to a show trial. He "admitted" spying for the West and informing on his communist comrades to the interwar police. During his pre-trial detention, he was severely tortured under the supervision of Soviet KGB General Belkin. All industrial firms and trade were nationalized. A campaign began for the forced collectivization of the peasantry.

1953 *March.* Following Joseph Stalin's death, "collective leadership" was introduced in Hungary. Imre Nagy, a Muscovite communist, replaced the Stalinist Matyas Rakosi as prime minister, but Rakosi remained head of the Communist party. Nagy proclaimed the dissolution of concentration camps and the freedom of choice for peasants if they wanted to leave the collectives. He also emphasized the development of light industry instead of heavy industry.

1955 *June.* Rakosi returned to power. He wanted to undo Imre Nagy's work, but the secret police had been reduced in power, and Rakosi was no longer able to deal with his enemies in the Stalinist way.

1956 *June.* Rakosi, first secretary of the Hungarian Workers party, was removed from power and from Hungary by Nikita S. Khrushchev.

September. The rehabilitation and reburial of Laszlo Rajk attracted 200,000 Hungarians.

October. Student demonstrations in Budapest developed into a nationwide revolution against Soviet colonial oppression and its local satraps, the Hungarian communist leadership. The Hungarian Workers party dissolved in a few days and the revolution was victorious. The new prime minister was Imre Nagy.

November. Soviet negotiators lured the Hungarian minister of defense, Pal Maleter, and his aids into a trap and arrested them. The Soviet army made a massive assault on Hungary, deposed Imre Nagy, and installed Janos Kadar as both prime minister and first party secretary.

1957 *January-December.* The Kadar regime conducted a reign of terror. Participants of the revolution were hunted down and jailed. Hundreds were killed through a rigged judicial process. Thousands were jailed. 200,000 Hungarians fled to the West. The consolidation of the Kadar-regime lasted until 1963; countless thousands were victims.

1958 *June.* The Kadar-regime felt strong enough to conduct a "trial" of Imre Nagy and his associates. The charge was conspiracy against the socialist state. Nagy and four of his codefendants were condemned to death and executed. Five others were sentenced to long prison terms. Using the terror generated by the new trials and executions, Kadar ordered the swift, forcible collectivization of all lands.

1963 *May.* Janos Kadar, having consolidated his regime, and thoroughly intimidated the population, declared general amnesty for those accused of participation in the revolution. Exceptions were those who were charged with murder; many of the charges were fabrications.

July. Kadar declared "those who are not against us are with us," signaling his intention to achieve an *Ausgleich* (compromise) with the Hungarian people.

1964 *March.* Work began on a plan for economic reforms. Many of its provisions were based on Imre Nagy's program ten years before, but this aspect was hushed up.

1966 *December.* The congress of the revived Hungarian Communist party, renamed once again, this time to Hungarian Socialist Workers party (MSZMP), discussed economic reforms. However, for the time being, enemies of the reforms prevailed. Memories of the revolution were still fresh in their minds, and they feared the relaxation of controls which the reforms entailed.

1967 *April.* Hungarian communist delegates attended the Karlovy Vary, Czechoslovakia, meeting of European Communist parties where they strongly supported Leonid Brezhnev's bid for the reestablishment of Soviet domination of the international communist movement. The attempt was unsuccessful.

1968 *January.* Against strong doctrinaire opposition, the Hungarian party leaders introduced a series of economic reforms, called the New Economic Mechanism (NEM). It partially decentralized economic decision-making and freed some prices from central control. However, the central planning apparatus continued to function, negating some of the reforms.

August. Hungarian troops participated in the Warsaw Pact invasion of Czechoslovakia.

1969 *June.* At a meeting of Communist parties in Moscow, the Hungarian delegates strongly supported the efforts of the Soviet party leaders to condemn China. They did not succeed.

1970 *November.* The congress of the Hungarian Socialist Workers party declared its full agreement with the Soviet party concerning all major issues of international and national relations. It also promised the continuation of economic reforms.

1972   *February.* Janos Kadar visited Romania and signed a mutual aid and cooperation agreement with Romanian dictator Nicolae Ceausescu.

1975   *July-August.* Hungarian representatives attending the meeting of the Conference on Security and Cooperation in Europe in Helsinki signed the concluding document of the conference.

1976   *June.* Hungarian delegates attended the meeting of European Communist parties in East Berlin, witnessing the rejection of the latest Soviet bid for the domination of the European communist movements. The Hungarians supported the Soviet Union.

1978   *January.* U.S. Secretary of State Cyrus Vance headed a delegation of Americans returning the Holy Crown of Saint Stephen to Budapest.

1982   *July.* François Mitterand, prime minister of France, visited Hungary and discussed French-Hungarian relations with leading Hungarian party- and government representatives, including Janos Kadar.

1984   *February.* Margaret Thatcher visited Hungary and conferred with Janos Kadar.

         May. Hungary, following the Soviet lead, boycotted the Olympic games held in Los Angeles.

         June. West German chancellor Helmut Kohl visited Hungary.

1985   *April.* Hungary signed a ten-year extension of the Warsaw Pact.

         June. Municipal elections were conducted in Hungary with more than one candidate vying for some positions. Although these were not free elections, they did represent a change from the single-list "elections" of the past.

1986   *September.* In a small village, Lakitelek, Hungarian dissidents and reform communists met to discuss possible ways out of the economic and political crisis in which Hungary found itself in the second half of the 1980s. A leading figure of the group was Imre Pozsgay, a member of the Hungarian Politburo. The meeting criticized the party's policies concerning Hungarian minorities in neighboring states. Pozsgay subsequently published an article in a Budapest daily, rejecting the party's position that the Revolution of 1956 was a counter-revolution.

1987   *June.* Karoly Grosz, the Budapest district party secretary, replaced Gyorgy Lazar as prime minister.

1988   *May.* At the congress of the Hungarian Socialist Workers party, the ailing Janos Kadar was replaced by Karoly Grosz. Kadar was elevated to the meaningless post of party president. Reform communists were then elected to membership in the Central Committee, among them Rezso Nyers, Imre Pozsgay, and Miklos Nemeth.

         October. Miklos Nemeth was appointed prime minister of Hungary. He gradually separated his government from the Communist party.

1989   *February.* North Korea recalled its ambassador from Hungary and expelled the Hungarian ambassador in retaliation for Hungary's recognition of South

Korea. A special meeting of the Central Committee of the Hungarian Socialist Workers party discussed Pozsgay's statement that, in 1956, there was a revolution in Hungary, not a counterrevolution, as maintained by the party for 34 years. Over 13,000 refugees from Romania asked for asylum in Hungary. The Hungarian government announced that the mine fields and alarm systems that had been installed on the Hungarian-Austrian border after 1956, had been completely dismantled.

April. The Hungarian party leadership expelled four leading communists from the Central Committee, among them Janos Berecz, the most vociferous opponent of reforms.

May. Janos Kadar was relieved of his post as party chairman and Central Committee member and retired. At the last meeting he attended, Kadar broke down; he proclaimed himself a murderer and suggested that he should be shot.

June. Ferenc Glatz, minister of education and culture in the Nemeth cabinet, abolished the compulsory teaching of the Russian language in all levels of schools. He also abolished the compulsory classes in Marxism-Leninism. At the reburial of the martyred prime minister of Hungary, Imre Nagy, 200,000 people participated. Three days later, his murderer, Janos Kadar, was dead. Kadar's burial was also attended by large crowds showing the divisions in Hungarian society.

July. U.S. president George Bush visited Hungary. He was greeted by an enthusiastic crowd. He proclaimed the end of Soviet-style socialism in a speech given at Karl Marx University of Economics in Budapest.

August. The Hungarian government set up a tent city for East Germans who wanted to go to West Germany. Hungary also suspended its treaty with East Germany concerning would-be refugees from the latter country.

September. Hungary opened its border with Austria for East Germans fleeing to West Germany. A furious East German protest was rejected.

1990 *January.* The Hungarian parliament called for the complete withdrawal of Soviet troops from the country by the end of 1991. The major opposition party, the Hungarian Democratic Forum (MDF), discovered that its meetings were still being monitored by the secret (now security) police, and its mail was being opened by the same people.

March. Hungary and West Germany abolished compulsory visas for each other's citizens in transit.

April. In free elections, the Hungarian Democratic Forum and its allied parties won about 60 percent of the parliamentary seats. The coalition government was headed by Jozsef Antall.

June. the Hungarian parliament voted to withdraw from the Warsaw Pact.

July. The coalition parties proclaimed the reprivatization of farmland.

August. Arpad Goncz, a writer, was elected Hungary's new president.

October. Hungarian parties in opposition scored major victories in the municipal elections. October 23, the anniversary of the Revolution of 1956, was declared a national day of remembrance.

December. A new trade agreement was signed between the Russian Republic and Hungary. Russia owes Hungary over a billion dollars for items already delivered.

1991 *January.* Hungary's constitutional court (patterned after the Supreme Court of the United States), attained independent status. It has ten judges and has already passed judgments on several issues.

July. Parliament passed a law returning buildings confiscated by the communists to the churches. The law did not apply to land.

August. Pope John Paul II visited Hungary. The pontiff was received with great jubilation by huge crowds. Following the attempted coup d'etat in the Soviet Union, there was hope among the old-line communists that the old regime could be restored. But this was not to be the case. In Hungary, the demand for the speedy withdrawal of Soviet troops even increased.

June. The last Soviet troops left Hungary.

September. Industrial production declined in Hungary by 16.6 percent during the first nine months of the year. The inflation rate was 35 to 36 percent.

November. Hungary, along with Poland and Czechoslovakia, negotiated associate membership in the European Community. Actual membership was to begin January 1, 1992.

1992 *January.* Hungary recognized the new Commonwealth of Independent States replacing the defunct Soviet Union.

February. The national presidium of the Hungarian Democratic Forum called on Csaba Gombar and Elemer Hankiss, chairmen of national radio and television, to resign. This started a "media war" that was to last for two years.

March. A law was passed by parliament extending the statute of limitation on crimes committed by communists, if they involved murder or other capital offenses. The constitutional court declared the law unconstitutional.

May. Parliament passed a law of compensation for victims of communist oppression. Relatives of those who lost their lives for political reasons will receive a one-time payment of one million forints (about $12,000); monthly allowances were to be paid to those who had been imprisoned. Hungary was admitted to EUREKA, the high-tech research program of the European Community.

June. The constitutional court ruled that the 1974 law on the media was unconstitutional. This law was used in the dispute between prime minister Antall and president Goncz. The court ruled that the law placed the media under government control, which was a violation of the constitutionally guaranteed freedom of speech.

August. The Hungarian parliament issued a statement demanding the observance of minority rights in neighboring countries. Istvan Csurka, the leader of the extreme right wing of Hungarian populists, issued a document in which he attacked the Hungarian Democratic Forum (he is a vice president of the same party). He also questioned the health of prime minister Antall (he had brain tumors) and suggested that the party look for a successor. The document caused an uproar. The author was called a fascist by some members of his own party.

September. In an interview he gave to the German weekly, *Der Spiegel,* Csurka reiterated his views that Hungary needs more living space and that there was a Jewish conspiracy against Hungary.

October. President Arpad Goncz was prevented by a mob of skinheads and other racists from delivering his commemorative speech at a celebration of the Revolution of 1956. A demonstration, made by the same elements, in front of the building housing the national television, was prevented from entering the building and attacking the broadcasters.

November. Parliament considered a law that would classify crimes committed against Hungarians in 1956 as war crimes. A new political party, headed by Janos Palotas, emerged in Hungary. Its leader made a name for himself during the taxi-strike of 1990, and he has been consistently reported by public opinion surveys to be the most admired politician in Hungary. Boris Yeltsin, the president of Russia, visited Hungary. He signed several agreements with Jozsef Antall, settling Hungarian and Russian claims concerning the stay of Soviet troops in Hungary before 1990. They also established principles for cultural relations, for economic cooperation and for minority rights. Yeltsin apologized for the Soviet intervention in Hungary in 1956.

December. Hungary, Czechoslovakia, and Poland agreed to establish a free-trade zone which would gradually become operational, but not later than 2001. It will facilitate trade among the three participants.

1993   *January.* Hungary's police force was reorganized. The power of the minister of interior over the institution was reduced. The criminal police were separated from state security and the top police officials were replaced.

February. The congress of the Hungarian Democratic Forum affirmed the policies of the Antall government and rejected the bid of the Csurka-wing for greater power within the party and government. Although a truce had been achieved between the various factions, members of the rightist faction declared that they would not give up. Prime minister Antall then proceeded to reorganize his government, replacing some ministers with others completely loyal to him.

March. The compensation of the victims of communist confiscatory policies went slowly in Hungary, but the compensation succeeded in providing much needed capital for the private sector. Istvan Csurka launched a movement called the "Hungarian Way." His purpose was to force the MDF into more radical policies and to alter the generally centrist orientation of the party. The leaders of the MDF distanced themselves from the new movement.

April. Discussions between Hungarian and Ukrainian representatives led to a tentative agreement for further relations between the two countries. The Hungarian government, responding to a ban on Hungarian meat and livestock deliveries to the European Community, banned all imports of like products from Western Europe. Prime minister Antall met a Croatian parliamentary delegation in Budapest and declared Hungary's support for Croatia.

May. Union elections resulted in several victories for the old-style trade unions in Hungary. Thirty-eight percent of the voters chose the left-wing Hungarian National Trade Union Alliance. The others were distributed among Christian and independent trade unions. Lajos Fur, minister of defense in the Antall cabinet and executive chairman of the Hungarian Democratic Forum, abruptly resigned from his post in the party. At a meeting of the executive committee, the Hungarian Forum set itself apart from Istvan Csurka and his movement.

June. Parliament created the office of an ombudsman in Hungary. The task of the official will be the investigation of official conduct toward individuals. The ombudsman will be elected by parliament for six years with one renewable term. The person will not be able to hold any other office while serving in this capacity. The Hungarian government reported an agreement with Russia to obtain $800 million worth of military equipment in lieu of the $1.6 billion Russian debt to Hungary. The equipment will include MIG 29 aircraft. High ranking NATO officials met in Budapest for a three-day conference.

December. Jozsef Antall, Hungary's prime minister, died of brain cancer.

Action Program of 1944. Hungarian communist exiles who lived in the Soviet Union gathered in Moscow in September and October 1944 to discuss the role of the Communist party in Hungary after the conclusion of the war. The participants of this meeting consisted of about two dozen people, including the future dictator, Matyas Rakosi (*see* Rakosi, Matyas), and his close collaborators, Erno Gero (*see* Gero, Erno), Jozsef Revai (*see* Revai, Jozsef), Mihaly Farkas (*see* Farkas, Mihaly) and Zoltan Vas (*see* Vas, Zoltan), Gyorgy Lukacs (*see* Lukacs, Gyorgy), the philosopher and Imre Nagy (*see* Nagy, Imre). They were all veterans of the international communist movement, trusted by Stalin—as much as Stalin would trust anyone—and they were Hungarian in name only. Although they did speak the Hungarian language, they also spoke other languages and, above all, had Soviet citizenship. Some of them were officers of the Red Army of the Soviet Union, and at least three of them were agents of the Soviet KGB.

They composed an action program setting out the broad outlines for their individual and collective roles. This included the plan for national action against the Nazi army in Hungary and for the speedy reconstruction of the country after the war. They specifically planned for a quick solution to the peasant problem through a thorough-going land reform. Since they were as yet unsure about Stalin's plans for postwar Hungarian political life—it seems that Stalin himself did not know what he wanted to do in Hungary—the Hungarian communists did not make plans for the immediate seizure of power. However, they were ready to assume considerably more power in Hungary than the existing strength of their party would entitle them to do.

Bibliography

Fejto, François, *A History of the People's Democracies* (Paris, 1971); Kovrig, Bennett *Communism in Hungary: from Kun to Kadar* (Stanford, CA, 1979); Molnar, Miklos, *A Short History of the Hungarian Communist Party* (Boulder, CO, 1978).

Aczel, Gyorgy (1917–1992). Gyorgy Aczel was born to a middle-class Jewish family in Budapest. He studied at the Pazmany Peter—later Lorant Eotvos—University in Budapest and joined the Hungarian underground Communist party in the 1930s. During the rule of Matyas Rakosi (*see* Rakosi, Matyas) in the late 1940s and early 1950s, he was a minor functionary. After the Revolution of 1956, he became close to Janos Kadar (*see* Kadar, Janos) and was appointed secretary of the Central Committee of the Hungarian Socialist Workers party. In 1960, he was "elected" a parliamentary deputy.

In the 1970s and 1980s, Aczel was the cultural tsar of Hungary. He was responsible for the "regularization" of cultural life, and the restoration of communist control over all cultural affairs after the revolution. A skillful manipulator of people, he was responsible for the establishment of the "three categories of creative products," namely, those that were permitted, those that were tolerated, and those that were forbidden. When Kadar was deposed in 1988, Aczel himself was replaced. He retired into private life and died in 1992.

Bibliography

Konrad, Gyorgy, and Szelenyi, Ivan *The Intellectuals on the Road to Class Power* (New York, 1979); Lendvai, Paul, *Hungary: The Art of Survival* (London, 1988).

Aczel, Tamas (1921–). Aczel was born to middle-class Jewish parents, and many of the members of his family were exterminated by the Nazis. In 1945, he joined the Hungarian Communist party, and as a journalist, he became active in the Hungarian Writers' Union. Aczel was one of the young writers who honestly believed in the efforts of the communist leadership to establish progressive socialism in Hungary, and he enthusiastically supported these efforts. However, by 1955, he, together with others, had realized the dishonesty of the communist leadership and was gradually alienated from the party.

Aczel was one of the founders of the Petofi Circle in Budapest, whose meetings took on the character of an opposition to communist totalitarianism. In the summer of 1956, Tamas Aczel was on the list prepared by Matyas Rakosi (*see* Rakosi, Matyas) containing the names of intellectuals who would be arrested for antiparty agitation.

But Rakosi was deposed by the Soviet leaders, and the revolution ended an era in Hungary. Aczel was among those who supported the revolution's premier, Imre Nagy (*see* Nagy, Imre). After the revolution was suppressed, Tamas Aczel had fled to England where, in collaboration with Tibor Meray, he wrote one of the most penetrating analyses of the revolution and its causes. In the 1960s, Aczel emigrated to the United States and became a professor at the University of Massachusetts at Amherst.

Bibliography
Aczel, Tamas, and Meray, Tibor, *The Revolt of the Mind* (London, 1961).

Andics, Erzsebet (1902–1986). Andics joined the Hungarian Communist party at its inception in 1918, and she was an active party member in her teens during the first Soviet Republic in Hungary. After the suppression of the Soviet Republic by Romanian troops in August 1919, Andics escaped and went to the Soviet Union. She was sent back to Hungary by the COMINTERN but was caught quickly, arrested, and tried. She received a sentence of fifteen years in prison. However, she spent only one year in jail: she was exchanged for some Hungarian military officers who had been captured during World War I, and kept in the Soviet Union after the Russian Revolution.

She spent the rest of the interwar and World War II years in the Soviet Union. After 1945, she returned to Hungary and served in various party- and government posts. Between 1948 and 1956, she was a member of the Politburo. After the Hungarian Revolution of 1956, Andics became a departmental chairperson of the Humanities at Eotvos Lorant University in Budapest. She was a rabid communist, who had rigidly adhered to Marxism-Leninism-Stalinism both as a functionary and as a teacher.

Bibliography
Aczel, Tamas, and Meray, Tibor, *The Revolt of the Mind* (London, 1961).

Antall, Jozsef (1930–1994). Antall was born to a family of civil servants and attended Lorant Eotvos University in Budapest. He never joined the Communist party. In the 1980s, Antall was the director of a museum in Budapest. He had splendid family traditions. His father was active in the antifascist movement during World War II and was successful in saving several Jewish families from the Nazi extermination camps. He was a member of the Smallholders party and, after 1945, a member of the democratic coalition government that existed all too briefly in Hungary. He was the minister of reconstruction, an important post in war-ravaged Hungary. With the victory of the communists, Antall's father was, of course, cashiered, but his antifascist past probably saved him from persecution.

The younger Antall joined the Smallholders party when the communist system was beginning to totter in Hungary in 1988, but eventually he chose the Hungarian Democratic Forum. When the Democratic Forum, together with its coalition partners, the Smallholders party and the Christian Democratic People's party, won a parliamentary majority in the first free elections held after communist rule in 1990, Antall was chosen prime minister of Hungary. He created his cabinet by appointing eight ministers from the ranks of the Democratic Forum—some of them his personal friends and relatives—four from the Smallholders party, one from the Christian Democrats, and two independents.

His government reflected the party alignments; it was center-right with a good dose of nationalist, some anti-Semitic, and populist sentiments. Antall's governing style, as he had defined it, was that of "the calm power." In real life, however, this had meant procrastination and the inability to put through his government program in parliament. He suffered from brain cancer and the continuous treatments that he had received, obviously affected his performance. He had attempted to unite the three major trends in the Democratic Forum, namely, the populist, the nationalist, and the liberal, but without much success. The popularity of the Antall-government after the 1990 elections had taken a nose dive. In December, 1993, Antall suddenly died. He left behind a demoralized party who is unlikely to succeed in the upcoming elections in May, 1994.

Bibliography

Pataki, Judith, "Hungarian Government Midway through its First Term," *Radio Free Europe Research Report* 1.24 (June 12, 1992), pp. 18-24; Racz, Barnabas, "The Hungarian Parliament's Rise and Challenges," *Radio Free Europe Research Report* 1.7 (February 14, 1992), pp. 22-26;. Reisch, Alfred. "Roundtable: Hungary's Parliament in Transition," *Radio Free Europe Research Report* 1.48 (December 4, 1992), pp. 27-35.

Bata, Istvan (1910–). Bata was a manual worker in a ship-building factory in Budapest. A skilled craftsman, he was involved with trade union activities during the interwar years, and he joined the Hungarian Communist party in 1945. In 1953, during Imre Nagy's (*see* Nagy, Imre) first premiership, Bata was appointed minister of defense. In October 1956, he escaped from the revolution and took refuge in the Soviet Union. In 1958, he returned to Hungary but no longer participated in political activities. In 1959, he was appointed chief of a railroad station.

Bibliography

Aczel, Tamas, and Meray, Tibor, *The Revolt of the Mind* (London, 1961).

"B" Lists in Post-World War II Hungary. In 1945 and 1946, the provisional government of Hungary intended to exclude from the state bureaucracy the fascist sympathizers and others who had served the interwar regime all too willingly. Thus, the government devised a method, the so-called "B" list, to weed out undesirables from public offices. However, it soon became obvious that the system was being used by the communists, who increasingly dominated politics, simply to get rid of people who were not supportive of the Communist party. According to first estimates, about 100,000 people were to be discharged. However, no provision was made for their reemployment, and most of them were simply put out on the streets. In time, the "B" list became a weapon against the enemies of the communists, and only affiliating with the Communist or Social Democratic party could save the job of a person singled out.

The "B" list was administered by committees composed of representatives of all the coalition parties, but the noncommunist members of these committees were usually intimidated to go along with communist-inspired decisions. The "B" list was ended in 1947 when it was obvious that the communists would come into power regardless of the list.

Bibliography

Hanak, Peter, "Hungary on a Fixed Course: An Outline of Hungarian History," in Joseph Held, ed. *The Columbia History of Eastern Europe in the Twentieth Century* (New York, 1992), pp. 164-229.

Beginning of the Collapse of Communism. In May 1988, a conference of the Hungarian Socialist Workers party and its Central Committee ended in the change of the guard of the leadership. Not only was Janos Kadar, (*see* Kadar, Janos) the dictator of Hungary since 1956, removed, but 37 new members joined the Central Committee. Most of the new members had joined the party since 1985. The members of the Central Committee who were replaced by the newcomers included most of Kadar's cronies and supporters. The changes did not yet affect the party's position in society. It was, in 1988, still the dominant political group with 800,000 card-carrying members. But party discipline was breaking down. The reformists were out in the open and vigorously supported the necessary changes obstructed by the hard-liners. What was even more important, the political agenda was being set by forces outside the party's control. In July, the party accepted the economic program of the reformists. Yet, in June, a demonstration commemorating the murder of Imre Nagy (*see* Nagy, Imre) was broken up with great brutality.

On September 5, the Hungarian Democratic Forum, established by oppositional forces in 1985 at their meeting at Monor, transformed the organization into a quasi-political party. The Central Committee of the Communist party then declared its readiness to talk to the opposition. At the end of September, another opposition group, the Alliance of Free Democrats, was established. In early November, the Smallholders party reemerged, and in January 1989, the Social Democratic party was reestablished. In March 1989, the Opposition Roundtable was created.

At first, the communist leadership was willing to talk only on its own terms with this group. Specifically, they wanted to pack the meeting with representatives of the communist front organizations. Finally, after protracted discussions, a formal meeting was announced on June 10. In the meantime, reform circles were formed within the Hungarian Socialist Workers party. They openly proclaimed that they had formed a faction, an act severely forbidden by Communist party traditions. In May, finally, the Central Committee declared it would hold a special congress in October.

In the meantime, another important movement was created, the Alliance of Young Democrats. The Endre Bajcsy-Zsilinszky Fraternal Society added color to the emerging new political landscape. Several independent trade unions made their appearance, and other groupings were also in the process of establishing themselves. In September 1989, prime minister Miklos Nemeth made the decision to permit the East German "tourists," who were pouring into Hungary in ever increasing numbers, to cross the border into Austria on their way to West Germany. This decision contributed to the collapse of the Honecker regime, followed by the end of the Czechoslovak communist system.

The Opposition and the communists in Hungary finally came to an agreement about the elections to be held in March 1990 and, if needed, runoff balloting a week later. In the elections, the Democratic Forum and its coalition partners, the Smallholders party, and the Christian Democrats, received 58 percent of the votes cast. Jozsef Antall (*see* Antall, Jozsef) of the Democratic Forum formed a coalition government with a platform of establishing institutions of a multiparty democratic political system and a market economy. The Communist party, which split at its October meeting into two new parties, one the Socialist party, and the other, comprising the hard-liners of the old Hungarian Socialist Workers party, received minimal support. The hard liners did not even succeed in placing their own deputies in the new parliament. The new regime moved slowly, however. At the time of this writing (1993), it has not yet completed its program of privatization of the economy.

Bibliography
Rothschild, Joseph, *Return to Diversity: A Political History of East Central Europe Since World War II* (Oxford, 1992); Swain, Nigel, *Hungary: The Rise and Fall of Feasible Socialism* (London, 1992).

Benke, Valeria (1920–). She was educated as an elementary school teacher, and in 1941, she joined the illegal Hungarian Communist party. Between 1945 and 1946, she was an instructor in the Central Party School in Budapest, while serving at the same time as secretary of the Hungarian Democratic Women's Association. Between 1954 and 1958, Benke was director of Hungarian National Radio, and she refused, on October 23, 1956, to broadcast the demands of students and workers. This led to the outbreak of street fighting in Budapest, and the shooting of unarmed students and workers in front of the radio's building by the secret police.

Bibliography
Aczel, Tamas, and Meray, Tibor, *The Revolt of the Mind* (London, 1961).

Berend, T. Ivan (1930–). Berend was born to a middle-class family. He studied at Lorant Eotvos University in Budapest and joined the Hungarian Communist party while still a young university student. After graduation he became a member of the faculty of his alma mater and was appointed to the Historical Institute of the Hungarian Academy of Sciences. In the 1960s, he became president of Karl Marx University of Economic Sciences in Budapest.

Berend became a prolific historian. He worked with Gyorgy Ranki, a contemporary of his, who became deputy director of the Historical Institute. Their joint works received wide publicity and gained them both a well-deserved international reputation. Berend lectured at most of the European universities, including Oxford and Cambridge. He was also a frequent guest at conferences in the United States and taught as a guest professor at the University of California at Los Angeles, Columbia University, and elsewhere. In 1984, Berend was appointed president of the Hungarian Academy of Sciences, and became vice president of the International Association of Historians. He chaired the committee of the academy that reexamined the data of the Hungarian Revolution of 1956, and declared that it was not a counter revolution, but a popular uprising against tyranny. In 1990, Berend left Hungary, and accepted a distinguished professorship at UCLA.

Bibliography

Berend, Ivan, T., *Decades of Crisis: Central and East Europe between the two World Wars* (in Hungarian and English) (Budapest, Hungary, 1982); Berend, Ivan, T., and Gyorgy Ranki, *The Economy of Eastern Europe between the World Wars* (New York, 1980).

Bibo, Istvan (1911–1967). Bibo received an excellent education in a gymnasium (a German-style High School) in Budapest. He attended the University of Szeged and earned a doctorate in political science. He also studied in Geneva, Switzerland. After his return to Hungary, he was appointed a judge in Budapest. In the early 1930s, Bibo became interested in the fledgling populist movement in Hungary. What attracted him to this movement was that it promoted a popular front movement in opposition to the conservative-dominated political life in the country without succumbing to radical Marxist ideology. In fact, he considered Marxism an ideology not suitable for Hungarian conditions.

Bibo's sympathy for the populists did not translate into political action. Nevertheless, after World War II, he joined the National Peasant party which was the gathering place for most of his populist friends. He was promptly appointed under secretary in the ministry of the interior, headed at that time by the Peasant party leader, Ferenc Erdei (*see* Erdei, Ferenc). Bibo worked out a plan for reforming the state bureaucracy; however, when the communists took over in 1948, Bibo's plan was shelved.

While working as under secretary, he wrote a study entitled, "The Crisis of Hungarian Democracy." In this work he analyzed the dangers of the extreme right and of the left. He also worked on a draft for a new constitution for Hungary. In 1946, Bibo wrote another study, about the "Misery of the Small States of Eastern Europe," with which he intended to educate the Hungarian public. He was a bit naive, however, because the Communist party had already secured the bases on which it was to build its monopoly of power.

In 1949, following the show trials of Laszlo Rajk (*see* Rajk, Laszlo) and Jozsef Cardinal Mindszenty (*see* Mindszenty, Jozsef Cardinal), Bibo no longer was active. He was transferred from the ministry of the interior to a chair at the University of Szeged. He lasted in that position for a little over a year. Then he accepted another transfer, this time back to the capital city, as a clerk working in the National Szechenyi library. In the library, Bibo worked at his assigned tasks and occasionally wrote studies for his desk drawer.

The Revolution of 1956, however, brought him back to political life. During the first few days of the revolution, he joined the leadership of the reorganized Peasant party, now renamed the Petofi party (after the revolutionary poet of the Revolution of 1848). On November 3, the day before the commencement of the Soviet army's attack on Hungary, Bibo was asked to join Imre Nagy's (*see* Nagy, Imre) government as a minister without portfolio.

When Soviet tanks reached the Hungarian parliament building the following day, they found the huge complex empty of people. The cabinet had fled, some of them, including Imre Nagy, to the Yugoslavian embassy. Only Istvan Bibo remained at his post, calmly typing his suggested solution to end Soviet-Hungarian confrontations. His memorandum, addressed to the United Nations, was widely published in the West and created a tremendous sympathy in Western public opinion for the aims of the Hungarian Revolution.

On May 27, 1957, the reorganized Hungarian secret police arrested Istvan Bibo. He was kept in prison without a trial until September 1958. He was then charged and tried at a secret court and sentenced to life imprisonment. In 1963, he was freed by a general amnesty, but he never returned to public life.

Bibliography

Nagy, Karoly, ed. *Istvan Bibo, Democracy, Revolution, Self-Determination: Selected Writings* (Boulder, CO, 1991).

Communist Party of Hungary. The Hungarian Communist party was established by former prisoners of war who were converted to bolshevism while in Russia in 1917. The group was led by Bela Kun, a former journalist, who was instrumental in creating the first communist state outside the Soviet Union in March 1919. The first Soviet Republic of Hungary was short lived; it lasted 133 days and was crushed by invading Romanian troops. The atrocities committed by the communists, especially against the rural population, were then used by the regime of Nicholas Horthy to outlaw the communist party in 1920.

The leaders of the Soviet Republic, including Matyas Rakosi (*see* Rakosi, Matyas), fled to Vienna, Austria, and eventually to the Soviet Union. When some of them returned clandestinely, they were captured, tried, and were kept in prison during most of the interwar years. Some others remained in the Soviet Union. During the second half of the 1930s Joseph Stalin's purges caught up with the Hungarians, and many perished, including Bela Kun.

In late 1944, the exiles returned to Hungary with the Soviet army. Five of them, Matyas Rakosi, Erno Gero (*see* Gero, Erno), Jozsef Revai (*see* Revai, Jozsef), Mihaly Farkas (*see* Farkas, Mihaly), and Zoltan Vas (*see* Vas, Zoltan), became leaders of the revived Communist party immediately upon their return. They had plans for their participation in political life, but were not yet sure that they would gain a monopoly of power (*see* Action Program of 1944). In 1944, the Hungarian Communist party had perhaps a few thousand members. Opinions vary on the numbers, ranging from 1,000 to 4,000. However, the numbers increased rapidly as soon as it became obvious that membership had its privileges.

Rakosi was the real leader of the party. He had Stalin's support, and he was intelligent, cunning, and well-versed in intrigues. He inspired fear in most people around him. When it became clear that Stalin would support a communist takeover of Hungary, the Muscovites divided the tasks among themselves. Gero became the czar of economic life; Revai became the Hungarian Andrey Zhdanov; Farkas, the most brutal of them, headed the secret police, then became minister of defense; Vas, the least influential among the Muscovites, was entrusted with various organizational tasks as the mayor of Budapest. By the end of 1948, the communists were in complete control of Hungary. Their rule was enforced by the brutal methods of the secret police. Rakosi and his friends were determined to transform Hungarian society by building Soviet-style socialism. In the process, the party was declared to be "all-knowing," a version of infallibility.

In 1948, the Hungarian Communist party enforced a merger with the old Social Democratic party organization. It changed its name to the Hungarian Workers party. The membership rolls swelled to 1.2 million. The organization of the party followed the Soviet pattern; starting with local cells in the work places and villages and towns, continuing in regional organs, the party was nominally headed by the Central Committee. It "elected" members for the Political Committee, referred to as the Politburo, the real possessor of power.

Matyas Rakosi was first secretary and, at the same time, he was prime minister. He ensured the development of parallel bureaucracies of the state and the party. He had personal control over the dreaded secret police, the AVO, later AVH, meaning Department of State Security and Section of State Security, through Mihaly Farkas.

During the anti-Tito campaign in 1949–1953, the prominent leader, Laszlo Rajk (*see* Rajk, Laszlo), was executed together with others after a show trial. A wave of purges followed, "cleansing" the party of social democrats who were coopted after the enforced merger of the two parties. Further show trials were conducted against prominent church leaders and noncommunist organizations. However, some leading communists, who remained in Hungary in the underground party, were also subjected to the horrors of torture and show trials. These included Janos Kadar (*see* Kadar, Janos) and Gyorgy Marosan (*see* Marosan, Gyorgy). About 7,500 communists fell victim to the purges, of whom about 2,000 were killed. Altogether, almost 750,000 Hungarians were investigated for possible political opposition. Many thousands were expelled from their homes, and about 250,000 were placed in concentration camps. There was hardly a family in Hungary who escaped persecution. By 1953, it was clear that the terror had failed to transform Hungary into a socialist state. Furthermore, the power struggle that followed Stalin's death in the Soviet Union had its reverberations in Hungary.

In 1953, Rakosi was replaced by Imre Nagy (*see* Nagy, Imre), another Muscovite who sincerely believed in the ideas of socialism but was also a moderate person. What was most important was that Imre Nagy was not tainted by the horrors of Rakosi's rule, since he was kept in the background by the other Muscovites. He ordered the dissolution of the concentration camps and the release of political prisoners. He eased the harsh agricultural policies of his predecessor, reduced compulsory delivery quotas of foodstuffs, and permitted the voluntary dissolution of collective farms.

Imre Nagy did not last long in power. Rakosi regained the support of the leadership in Moscow and soon replaced Nagy in the premiership and as head of the Communist party. He even succeeded in expelling Nagy from the party altogether as a "rightist deviationist." In 1955 Nikita S. Khrushchev wanted to ease tensions with Yugoslavia. Tito's conditions included the ousting of Rakosi, who was the leading spokesman of Stalin in the anti-Tito campaign. In the summer of 1956, this was accomplished, but Rakosi was simply replaced with his alter-ego, Eron Gero. Gero was an arrogant, aloof man, an agent of the KGB, who acted as a political commissar in Spain during the Spanish civil war; he was known for his unquestioning loyalty to Rakosi and the Soviet Union. He was deeply disliked by most Hungarians.

In October 1956, the long-simmering tensions erupted into a revolution. Early in that month, the exhumed body of Laszlo Rajk was given a state funeral, which was attended by an estimated 200,000 people. On October 23, a demonstration by university students provided the spark for the revolution (*see* Revolution of 1956). In three days, the Communist party and its dreaded instrument, the secret police, simply disintegrated. Imre Nagy became prime minister once again, and on October 30, he declared Hungary's neutrality and its exit from the Warsaw Pact alliance.

Only a large-scale intervention by the Soviet armed forces, beginning on November 4, could reverse the situation and restore communist rule in Hungary. A counter-revolutionary government, headed by the traitor, Janos Kadar, was established. Kadar extracted a terrible vengeance from the population. Thousands of people were accused of crimes against the state and jailed. Many were summarily tried and executed. A terrorized people watched helplessly while teenagers were kept in prison until they reached legal age and then executed. In June 1958, Imre Nagy and ten of his supporters were also tried at a secret court. Their death sentences were predetermined in Moscow, and they were executed on June 18th.

The new Communist party was once again renamed the Hungarian Socialist Workers party. It attracted only die-hard communists at first but, with the passage of time, opportunists also joined its ranks. By 1963, the party had again become a mass organization; its 800,000 card-carrying members had special privileges. The top echelons were able to shop in special stores reserved for them, packed with goods not available to the rest of the population. A party militia was recruited from former officers of the armed forces, the secret police, and other organizations. These made sure that the last sparks of 1956 were extinguished.

By 1963, Kadar felt secure enough to issue a general amnesty for those who survived the inhuman conditions in his prisons. He also proposed a compromise to the population by declaring; "He who is not against us is with us." The regime, however, refused to cut its ties with the past. It continued many of the policies of the previous regime albeit at a slower pace. It renewed the collectivization drive with great vigor and did not permit private ownership of the means of production. Above all, it continued to insist on the monopoly of power by the communists. After 1963, however, the government did not renew the terror of the Rakosi years. There were no more show trials. Instead, it attempted to establish its internal legitimacy by improving living conditions for the population at large. It also sought peace in the rural communities and reduced interference in the daily lives of ordinary citizens. More toleration was shown for unconventional cultural creations.

By the end of the 1970s, Kadar's communist party simply represented just another version of "conventional" dictatorship, using much of the ideological paraphernalia of Marxism-Leninism as a camouflage of its activities. These policies brought about a measure of social peace and prosperity for Hungarians. However, the Kadar-regime would constantly rub salt into the wounds of patriots by demeaning the revolution as "counterrevolution," a "crime against socialism."

By 1985, serious problems emerged in the Hungarian Socialist Workers party. The regime's leaders had grown old. Their ideas and convictions no longer suited the era of *glasnost* and *perestroika*, propagated by Mikhail Gorbachev. It was also increasingly clear that, in case of trouble, the Soviet tanks would not roll in defense of the Kadar regime.

There was also a group of young reformists who were quite willing to challenge the ossified leadership and propagate changes in politics. They were justified by the deteriorating economic conditions in the country. Hungary faced severe economic problems. The country was deeply in debt, (although the extent of indebtedness was kept secret by the regime) and prosperity, the basis of Kadar's compromise with the people, was disappearing.

Kadar, however, did not see the crisis. He proclaimed repeatedly in his public speeches that everything was going on as scheduled; any "temporary difficulties" would soon be ironed out. He believed that a little more emphasis on discipline would do the trick. By 1989, however, the Hungarian Socialist Workers party had split between reformers and hard-liners. Kadar was forced out of the leadership together with most of his supporters. In October, the split was made official; there emerged a Socialist party and an old-style Hungarian Socialist Workers party, each taking a different road. By 1990, the communist system was finished. It was replaced by a multiparty pluralistic democracy. The original Communist party continued to exist, but it had became a minuscule organization playing no longer any role in Hungary's political life.

Bibliography

Aczel, Tamas, and Meray, Tibor, *The Revolt of the Mind* (London, 1961); Bruszt, Laszlo, and Stark, David, "Remaking the Political Field in Hungary: From the Politics of Confrontation to the Politics of Competition," in Ivo Banac, ed. *Eastern Europe in Revolution* (Ithaca, NY, 1992); Fejto, François, *A History of the People's Democracies* (Paris, 1971); Kovrig, Bennett, *Communism in Hungary from Kun to Kadar* (Stanford, CA, 1979); Molnar, Miklos, *A Short History of the Hungarian Communist Party* (Boulder, CO, 1978); Rothschild, Joseph, *Return to Diversity: A Political History of East Central Europe Since World War II* (Oxford, 1992); Swain, Nigel, *Hungary: The Rise and Fall of Feasible Socialism* (London, 1992).

Csoori, Sandor (1930–). Csoori, born of peasant ancestry, became a poet and writer. In 1954, he was appointed a journalist to *Szabad Ifjusag* (Free Youth), the journal of Hungarian Democratic Youth Association, a communist front organization. Three years later, he became a journalist for the *Irodalmi Ujsag* (Literary Journal), the official organ of the Writers Union. In 1956, he became a contributor to *Uj Hang* (New Voice), a journal supportive of Imre Nagy (*see* Nagy, Imre) and the revolution. He was a close friend of Gyula Illyes (*see* Illyes, Gyula), one of the great Hungarian poets of the twentieth century. Csoori aspired to succeed Illyes upon his death, but his talents did not measure up to those of the great poet. In 1987, Csoori was among the founders of the Hungarian Democratic Forum. Two years later, he was appointed president of the World Association of Hungarians.

Bibliography

Aczel, Tamas, and Meray, Tibor, *The Revolt of the Mind* (London, 1961).

Csurka, Istvan (1934–). Csurka was born to Calvinist parents, and his formative years were spent under the influence of his father who had strong rightist views. He studied at the College for Drama and Film in Budapest, but his career was slow to develop. In 1956, Csurka supported the revolution and was, therefore, forbidden to publish his writings. During the 1960s and 1970s, however, officialdom forgave him, and Csurka published several novels and wrote plays. The communist regime rewarded him with the prestigious Jozsef Attila Prize twice. The awards were given to him by Gyorgy Aczel (*see* Aczel, Gyorgy), the communist party's overseer of Hungarian cultural life. Csurka was later to denounce Aczel as a Jewish conspirator against Hungary, but Csurka was a born rebel.

During the 1970s and 1980s, his work was banned several times, and he was silenced for short periods. In 1983, he resigned from the leadership of the Hungarian Writers' Union after yet another brush with authorities, when some of his works were published in the West without official permission. In 1987, Csurka was one of the instigators of the first meeting of the opposition at the village of Monor, and later at Lakitelek, which resulted in the establishment of the Hungarian Democratic Forum.

In the free elections held in March 1990, he was elected a parliamentary deputy on the party's list. Simultaneously, he became deputy chairman of the Democratic Forum. In August 1992, Csurka issued a document in which he condemned the slow pace of transition from communism to a democratic society. At the same time, however, he also declared that Hungary needed more "living space" (presumably at the expense of its neighbors), and that Hungary was being dominated by Jews who obeyed instructions from New York and Tel Aviv.

In 1993, Csurka was expelled from the Hungarian Democratic Forum and from the party's parliamentary caucus. He established a new movement called *Magyar Ut* (Hungarian Way), and appealed to right-wing sentiments in the country. His isolation from the mainstream of politics, however, was accomplished. His newspaper, *Magyar Forum* (Hungarian Forum), continues to publish his views. In July 1993, he admitted that he had signed a promise to be an informer for the communist secret police during the 1960s. Surprisingly, the admission did not diminish Csurka's popularity in right-wing circles.

Bibliography

Oltay, Edith, "Hungary: Csurka Launches 'National Movement,'" *Radio Free Europe Research Report* 2.13 (March 26, 1993), pp 25-31.

Cultural Policies in Communist Hungary. Immediately after the conquest of power by the Hungarian Communist party, Jozsef Revai (*see* Revai, Jozsef), aspiring to the position of the "Hungarian Zhdanov," declared the commencement of a cultural revolution. This concept had nothing in common with the later developments in communist China. In the Hungarian case, it meant that "appropriate" cultural activities and creative work would be heavily subsidized by the state. It also meant wide publicity for works supporting the Marxist-Leninist view of social and political processes. Naturally, subsidies meant state—that is, Communist party—control, and the state demanded works in the spirit of "socialist realism." The concept of socialist realism was difficult to define. In the interpretation of the communist leaders, it meant that "cultural workers," that is, writers, actors, painters, and others, would produce creative works that were geared to supporting the "building of socialism." They were to portray happy people in work, proletarians, peasants and intellectuals, with some soldiers thrown in, and they would show them in their struggle against the "enemies of socialism." Since History was believed to be working for socialism as well, creative people would have to show permanent optimism even under the most difficult of circumstances. They would have to create the images of "socialist men"—and women—utterly and totally dedicated to bringing about the victory of socialism against the wicked enemies of the people. Socialist realism also meant abject humility in the face of the great geniuses of mankind, above all, V.I. Lenin, but also of Karl Marx and Friedrich Engels, with Joseph Stalin thrown in for good measure, at least until the famous speech of Nikita S. Khrushchev detailing Stalin's crimes.

The Hungarian version of socialist realism was different from other East European versions in the sense that it was more rigorous in enforcing communist standards and more ruthless in pursuing deviations. In fact, the Soviet example of the concept was placed above all Hungarian cultural endeavors, and the heroic struggle of the Soviet peoples for socialist realism was one of the central themes to be pursued. In consequence, often mediocre Soviet books were translated into Hungarian and widely disseminated. Large quantities of Lenin's and Stalin's works were printed and distributed to every library. Party apparatchiki felt an obligation to obtain these multivolume sets and proudly—or opportunistically—display them in the most visible places in their homes, together with the busts of the "leaders of mankind," Lenin, Stalin, Rakosi (*see* Rakosi, Matyas) and, occasionally, Karl Marx. The other side of the coin was that Western cultures and their products were ridiculed and excluded from libraries and bookshelves. The Hungarian communists went so far as to cull the libraries for works of "bourgeois" writers and remove them from the shelves. They excluded the works of entire generations of Hungarian and foreign writers as if they had never existed. In no other East European country did communists act with greater zeal in attempting to destroy the past.

At the same time, great stress was placed on literacy and education in general. Within five years of the conquest of power, the communist party succeeded in practically eliminating illiteracy. In every village a cultural center was established. It had a small library—stacked with appropriate works—and a reading room. They served, above all, as centers of indoctrination in Marxism-Leninism. Newspapers were widely disseminated, and the party's daily, *Szabad Nep* (Free People), was required reading in every workplace. The communists succeeded in bringing large strata of society into cultural life, people who would not have picked up a book in the past. In addition, the cultural centers usually had a small stage that was used for the performance of plays by a local cultural society or by visiting artists. Socialist realist writers and artists gave readings in rural areas from their works, visiting villages in the most remote areas of the country. This was part of their efforts to keep in touch with the people, to learn from them and then include the lessons in their next works. The only problem was that many of the manifestations of this sort of culture were, and remained, alien to Hungarians.

After the death of Stalin, slow changes began to take place in cultural policies. Conformity was required less, although Marxist-Leninist ideology remained in force. In 1956, the revolutionary ferment was begun by the protests of young communist writers and students who felt that they had been lied to by the party leaders. They demanded the freedom of expression that had been denied to them for long years.

After the suppression of the revolution, the Kadar regime continued the repressive policies of its predecessor, at least for a time. However, in the mid-1960s, the regime felt sufficiently safe to permit some relaxation in cultural policies. The demand for conformity with Marxism-Leninism was not abandoned, but it was more muted. Writers such as Tibor Dery, who was jailed after the revolution, and Gyula Illyes (*see* Illyes, Gyula), as well as others whose works were not published before, reappeared in bookstores and library shelves. Istvan Fekete and Aron Tamasi were working again, and their writings came out of their desk drawers. Criticism of the policies of the Rakosi regime was permitted, but Kadar and his system had to be left alone.

Above all, works critical of the Soviet Union were tabu. In addition, writers who knew better, left subjects dealing with the Communist party severely alone.

Gyorgy Aczel (*see* Aczel, Gyorgy), the successor to Jozsef Revai (*see* Revai, Jozsef), let it be known that there were three kinds of subjects; those supported by the party, those that were tolerated and those that were forbidden. Subsidies went invariably to those who published in the first category; those whose work were in the second category, were sold in large quantities to an eager reading public.

Hungarian intellectuals eventually made their own deal with the Kadar regime. They wrote socialist realist books and refrained from discussing subjects in the third category. In turn, the cultural policies of the Hungarian party became the most relaxed in the Soviet Bloc. Aczel was less dogmatic than was Revai, and he treated intellectuals less brutally; however, this did not mean that the few creative people who went beyond the permissible were treated kindly.

In the early 1980s, a group of sociologists began discussing Marxism in a critical way, and the party came down hard on them. Andras Hegedus, a former prime minister-turned-scholar, head of the Sociology Institute, Mihaly Vajda, Janos Kis, Agnes Heller, and others were dismissed from their jobs, and their works were banned by Aczel. Ivan Szelenyi, and Gyorgy Konrad, who discussed the road of the intellectuals to a compromise with the regime, and Istvan Kemeny, who examined the real situation of industrial workers in the dictatorship of the proletariat, were advised to leave Hungary. Their works were banned. For a considerable time after that, most intellectuals submitted to the demands of the Kadar regime. In exchange, they received honors and prizes not to speak of considerably more money than outstanding engineers or professors. Not surprisingly, dissidence had less importance in Hungary than in other East European states.

Bibliography

Aczel, Tamas, and Meray, Tibor, *The Revolt of the Mind* (London, 1961); Held, Joseph, "Cultural Developments," in Stephen Fischer-Galati, ed. *Eastern Europe in the 1980s* (Boulder, CO, 1981); Konrad, Gyorgy, and Szelenyi, Ivan, *The Intellectuals on the Road to Class Power* (New York, 1979); Revai, Jozsef, "On the Character of Our People's Democracy," *Foreign Affairs* 28 (1949), pp. 143-152.

Demeny, Pal (1901–1990). Demeny was a writer who became involved in left-wing causes. He was among the illegal communists in Hungary who succeeded in evading the police. But he and his organization were independent from the COMINTERN. In fact, Demeny and his faction separated themselves from the illegal Hungarian Communist party in the 1930s, and severely criticized it for its mistaken policies and its subordination to the Soviet Communist party and Soviet national interests. Demeny was among the first communists to be arrested by his communist rivals in 1945. He was subjected to a show trial and sentenced to prison. In 1957, he was freed and made his living as a translator. In 1990, he joined the newly formed Hungarian Socialist party and was elected to parliament on the party's ticket.

Bibliography
Demeny, Pal, *My Prison-Mate, Spinoza* (In Hungarian) (Budapest, 1989).

Economic Policies in Communist Hungary. Immediately following World War II, the Hungarian Provisional Government (*see* Provisional Government of Hungary in 1944) ordered the nationalization of all large private enterprises. Hungary had a tradition of state ownership of public works, such as railroads and gas- and electric services. The new nationalization was, however, mostly a symbolic gesture, since most of the industrial firms had been thoroughly destroyed during the war. The Allied bombing campaign damaged 60 percent of the factory buildings. The retreating Germans took away a great deal of industrial equipment, and what was left was thoroughly looted by the Soviet occupying army.

The rebuilding of Hungarian industry began even while fighting was still going on in the western parts of the country. By the time the communists came into power in 1948, the factory buildings had been mostly restored, and some plant equipment had been returned to Hungary by the Western Allies.

In 1949, the nationalization of all firms employing more than nine workers was declared. By 1950, no private enterprises were in existence. By then, even newspaper vendors were state employees; they sold papers and magazines produced by printing shops owned by the state. Matyas Rakosi (*see* Rakosi, Matyas), the Communist party chief, declared in 1949 that Hungary was on its way to being turned into a country of iron and steel. This statement was in line with Stalinist policies of creating a new heavy industrial sector in Hungary, serving the interests of Soviet military plans.

The first five-year plan, introduced in 1949, set production targets for heavy industry 200 percent higher than they were in 1949. Two years later, the targets were increased to 380 percent! All sorts of unnecessary projects were built. For instance, the City of Stalin (*Stalinvaros*) was constructed under extraordinarily difficult circumstances in a small rural town in southern Hungary with the expectation that this industrial giant would be fueled by Yugoslav coal. When Josip Broz Tito was expelled from the socialist bloc, however, coal from the city of Komlo was substituted. This was a lower grade coal than that of Yugoslavia, necessitating the replacement of machinery already installed. To transport Komlo's coal to the City of Stalin, a new railroad line had to be built in great haste. The new steel works were to start production on Rakosi's birthday, and the hastily constructed railroad tracks sank into the muddy ground under the weight of the second train load of coal. The blueprints for the steel mill of the City of Stalin turned out to have been pilfered from steel mills, originating in the late 1920s, from Pittsburgh, Pennsylvania. The huge plant was, therefore, already outdated when it started production.

Similar practices were followed everywhere. Hungary lacked the essential raw materials for the development of heavy industry, and these had to be imported mostly from the Soviet Union or other Soviet Bloc countries, strengthening the economic hold of the Soviet Union over the country.

By 1953, the Hungarian economy exhibited signs of overexpansion. The new industries were so inefficient that they had to be heavily subsidized. Subsidies, and new investments, were taken out of social income which resulted in lowering living standards.

After the death of Stalin, some important changes were introduced in industrial policies. In 1954, investments in heavy industry was lowered by 40 percent. In 1956, the revolution in Hungary swept the Communist party out of power, but only for a short time (*see* Revolution of 1956). But the Soviet-installed Kadar government realized that the Stalinist methods of economic development did not work. In spite of this, rapid industrialization acquired its own momentum. The government raised wages by 20 percent in 1963 while maintaining tight control over consumer prices. Consumer goods were also becoming more available. By 1968, the gross national product had increased by 6 percent, and this rate of increase continued, with minor fluctuations, during the 1970s.

By the end of that decade, the government was pursuing a different industrial policy. Rapid industrialization was not entirely shelved, but its speed was slowed. Autarky, the aim of the Stalinist regime, was still the aim, but it was now pursued with less vigor than before. Metallurgy, a preferred sector, was replaced by the chemical industry. Plastics, artificial fertilizers, and pharmaceutical products became important. Instead of importing huge quantities of iron ores and coal from the Soviet Union and Poland, the country used increasing amounts of oil. As long as the Soviet Union was able to deliver adequate oil supplies, Hungarian industry survived. But it was clear that Hungary's economy was so tightly integrated into that of the Soviet Union, that any decline of the latter would result in a serious crisis.

By the mid-1960s, Hungary had become primarily an industrialized state without, however, possessing the necessary resources for further progress. Labor resources had been exhausted. Serious imbalances emerged, and the New Economic Mechanism (NEM), introduced in 1968, failed to eliminate them. At first, the oil price increases, following the crisis of 1972, did not affect Hungary. Soviet oil prices were averaged on a five-year basis. When the increases finally impacted Hungary in early 1980, only huge subsidies for industrial firms could balance their results. Most of Hungary's industrial firms were producing for the COMECON market, including producing armaments and spare parts for the Soviet Bloc. For a time, Hungary paid for the subsidies through loans from Western banks. By the early 1980s, however, no more loans were forthcoming, and the country had to pay huge interests on an accumulated debt of $20 billion. The legitimacy of the Kadar government, built upon the promise of a better life for the people, vanished. When Soviet tanks were no longer used on behalf of the regime, the Kadar government collapsed.

In 1990, the Communist party was swept away in the first free elections in Hungary held since 1945. The economic policies of the Antall government were hesitant. The government and the parliament have struggled with the issues of reprivatization and the establishment of a market economy. Efforts have been made to attract Western investment, and these efforts have been fairly successful. General Electric and General Motors have bought into Hungarian firms, and the Japanese firm, Suzuki, has established local factories in the country.

The agricultural policies of the Hungarian regimes have varied from time to time. In the summer of 1945, the provisional government introduced land reform on a large scale, righting the historical injustice that had deprived the peasants of land. But the reform was based on the confiscation of estates over 1,000 "holds," or 1,420 acres in size. These estates were distributed in small parcels among the peasants. However, when the Stalinization of Hungary began, the Hungarian communists began a vicious drive to force peasants into agricultural collectives. They were classified according to the size of their possessions, and those who had more that twenty-five "holds" were declared to be kulaks. Until then, this Russian term, designating a tight-fisted, well to do peasant, was unknown in Hungary. In communist parlance, the term actually meant enemy of the people. Kulaks were harassed, imprisoned, and sent to concentration camps with their families. They were accused of all sorts of crimes against the state, including sabotage of planting and harvesting of crops. The campaign had a great many casualties, reaching mostly the best experts in agriculture. The aim of the communists with collectivization was to drive as many peasants off the land and into industrial occupations as possible. Those who stayed in the villages became agrarian workers employed by the collectives—that is, the state.

The collectives did not work well. As in other East European countries where collectivization was pursued, the sullen peasants felt betrayed by the communists who gave them land in 1945 and then took it away. The collectives lacked essential machinery. There were state-owned tractor stations whose machines often broke down because spare parts were not available. The Central Planning Office established impossibly high compulsory delivery quotas for food products. It also determined the kinds of plants to be planted and the amounts to be harvested! Rice was planted in areas totally unsuitable for its production, and citrus fruits were introduced in Hungary with a climate unfavorable for them. Few collectives were able to pay decent wages. Thievery became endemic, and work quotas were falsified on a large scale.

Not surprisingly, food production plummeted. So did rural incomes. The average income of peasant families was in 1952 only 30 percent of that of 1949. Hungary, a food exporter until 1944, was forced to import food in order to feed the population. Changes in these policies came after the death of Stalin.

In 1953, Imre Nagy (*see* Nagy, Imre), a Muscovite communist who was not tainted with the policies of the Rakosi regime, became prime minister, and he announced a new course. However, Rakosi, who remained secretary general of the Communist party, still wielded considerable power, and he tried to sabotage Nagy's policies. By then, the villages had little food, and the cities were threatened by famine. Nagy decreed that the peasants were free to leave the collective farms if they so desired. Compulsory deliveries were reduced in size. He also proposed to increase investments in agriculture. Many collectives were dissolved, and the peasants began to produce more food.

In 1955, however, Rakosi returned to power with Soviet support, and he promptly reestablished the previous quota system for food deliveries. After the Revolution of 1956, the regime of Janos Kadar (*see* Kadar, Janos) renewed a vicious drive for the collectivization of the land. By 1963, 93 percent of all lands were controlled by collectives, but this did not solve Hungary's food problems.

The government, against considerable opposition by old-style Stalinists, permitted the peasants to work small, private plots of their own and to sell their products on the open market. The peasants immediately responded. On less than 3.5 percent of the land, they produced over 33 percent of the country's food. Suddenly, the cities were receiving enough food. Since open market food prices were not controlled, they became higher than prices in state-owned stores, but the products were of better quality than those in the controlled market. Individual peasants began to prosper, and even the collective farms were showing increases in their productivity. Soon, there emerged a stratum of peasant entrepreneurs who built new houses in their villages and were increasingly prosperous.

In 1968, a new course, called the New Economic Mechanism (NEM), was introduced. It permitted a certain fluctuation of prices except in essential foodstuffs. The NEM retained the functions of the Central Planning Office and the huge subsidies paid to heavy industrial firms. The system was slowed down in 1972. The dogmatists in the Communist party argued that the system established preferential conditions for the peasants while the alleged "ruling class," the proletariat, did not fare so well. Thus, Kadar slowed down the reforms. Once again, however, food production also slowed. Soon, there were empty shelves in grocery stores in the cities, and the regime beat a hasty retreat.

In the mid-1970s and 1980s, Hungarian agriculture was the only system in the Soviet Bloc that functioned well. It provided more than adequate food supplies for the population and demonstrated the wisdom of permitting a mixture of private and collective enterprises to function side by side. The essential ingredient in this mixture was a set of private incentives without which the peasants would not work.

With the collapse of the communist system in Hungary in 1989, agriculture became a large question mark. The issues of land ownership, the possible redistribution of the lands of the collective farms, and compensation to be paid for those whose land had been confiscated, engendered long debates in parliament. It seems certain that some sort of privatization is in the works, and laws to that effect will probably be enacted after the next round of elections in the spring of 1994. It is likely that most collective farms will be dissolved, and their lands will be returned to the former owners. However, it is unlikely that large estates will be reestablished. The fact that the churches were not permitted to reclaim their lands, is a good indication of the direction the new system is taking.

Bibliography

Adam, John, *Economic Reforms in the Soviet Union and Eastern Europe Since the 1960s* (London, 1989); Hare, P.G. et al., eds. *Hungary: A Decade of Economic Reform* (London, 1981); Kornai, Janos, *The Economics of Shortage* (Amsterdam, Holland, 1980); Richet, Xavier, *The Hungarian Model: Markets and Planning in a Socialist Economy* (Cambridge, England, 1989); Swain, Nigel, *Hungary: The Rise and Fall of Feasible Socialism* (London, 1992); Szelenyi, Ivan, *Urban Inequalities Under State Socialism* (Oxford, 1983); Volgyes, Ivan, "Dynamic Change: Rural Transformation, 1945–1975," in Joseph Held, ed. *The Modernization of Agriculture: Rural Transformation in Hungary, 1848-1975* (New York, 1980), pp. 351-500.

Educational Policies in Communist Hungary. In communist dictatorships, the schools are considered a major means for the creation of the much-desired "socialist man"—and woman—whose dedication to the building of socialism is guaranteed. Therefore, all influences that were not of the Marxist-Leninist variety were excluded and severely forbidden in the curricula.

These policies inevitably created conflicts with churches throughout Eastern Europe, especially in Hungary, where the churches traditionally performed teaching functions in their own schools. In fact, before World War II, Hungarian elementary education was dominated by schools run by the churches. They also had a strong presence in secondary education. The Roman Catholic church maintained 1,706 elementary schools before 1948, 1,205 general education schools, 52 gymnasia (secondary schools whose quality was, in general, higher than those of American high schools), 38 trade schools, and 27 secondary schools for adults. The Calvinist church was also deeply involved in education. It maintained 1,029 elementary and 52 secondary schools. In addition, it sponsored two colleges of great traditions and reputations, one in the famous town of Sarospatak, and the other in Papa. The churches were able to maintain their schools because they had huge land holdings and received ample donations. They were also closely identified with the ideology of the interwar state and received moral and financial support from it. When the large estates were nationalized in 1945, the churches were deprived of the means to maintain their schools. This, in itself, would have been a major source of conflict between them and the communist state even if the ideological conflict had not existed.

On June 16, 1948, a law ordered the confiscation of all schools not sponsored by state institutions. The law affected 436,000 students and nearly 12,600 teacher-instructors in the Roman Catholic institutions alone. Altogether, nearly 1 million students were involved. Teachers were particularly hit hard by nationalization if they belonged to religious orders. Thousands of highly educated monks and nuns, many of them schooled at universities in Italy, France, and Germany, were suddenly expelled from the schools and were forbidden to teach. Only nonreligiously affiliated teachers were permitted to stay at the schools. In 1950, an agreement between the communist leadership and the churches resulted in the reopening of a few elementary and secondary schools by the churches, but no real teaching functions by the religious were permitted. By then, religious orders had been disbanded by order of the state, and many of their former members had been herded into concentration camps or to prison. In the camps, they could employ their intellect and knowledge by quarrying stones or building roads for the greater glory of socialism.

Once the schools had been nationalized, all instruction was delivered in terms of Marxist-Leninist ideology. The curricula were slavishly copied from those of Soviet schools. Technical education had priority, and the humanities and social sciences were transformed into the tools of propaganda. History was heavily laced with the story of the Hungarian Communist party and its sister institution, the Soviet Communist party. Much of what went on in history classes was simply falsified history. Students could not advance in their classes without knowledge of Marxism-Leninism. However, since the teachers were themselves often ignorant of the finer points of ideology, "teaching" usually consisted of the recital of Joseph Stalin's, less often of Lenin's, sayings. The once proud, and eminently successful, Hungarian secondary education which produced such Nobel Laureates as Eugene Wigner, Edward Teller, John Neuman, Otto Szilard, Albert Szentgyorgyi, and other eminent scientists, sank into abject mediocrity.

The universities fared no better. University students were subjected to the same pressures as their lower-level fellow students. They had to learn Marxism-Leninism before they could graduate in their subjects. Their admission to university studies was skewed by the feudal notion, so well taken over from a long-gone era, that gave advantages to students who were born into certain social strata. This was affirmative action, Stalinist style. University professors were well paid, indeed. Yet, they were isolated from advances in their fields in the West by the fact that few Western scientific journals were permitted to enter Hungary. During the 1950s and 1960s, travel to the West was forbidden; no one was to be contaminated by bourgeois ideas. The Academy of Sciences maintained several research institutions. These employed an intellectual elite that was as well trained and informed as any in Western countries. They were the cultural ambassadors of communist Hungary and deservedly received accolades when they performed in their fields in Western countries. The institutions received all relevant scientific literature after the Revolution of 1956.

A meeting organized by Ferenc Donath and others in 1985, at the small town of Monor, opened the way to the solution of the crisis. The significance of the meeting was that it had taken place at all. In addition, it was the first postwar effort to find a way of understanding between the democratic opposition centered on the samizdat publication, *Beszelo* (Speaker), and the populist writers, the spiritual descendants of the earlier populist movement of the 1930s. This was a preliminary meeting whose participants were at pains to dispel the notion that they were gathering to form a party for the overthrow of the Kadar regime. That would have resulted in the arrest of the leaders and certain jail terms for most participants. What the meeting achieved was an understanding among leading intellectuals and reform communists, such as Imre Pozsgay (*see* Pozsgay, Imre), chairman of the communist front organization, the Patriotic People's Front, that the system had to be changed. What they did not realize, however, was that the Kadar regime could not be reformed. It was from this meeting that the Hungarian Democratic Forum eventually emerged two years later.

Bibliography

Bruszt, Laszlo, and Stark, David, "Remaking the Political Field in Hungary: From the Politics of Confrontation to the Politics of Competition," in Ivo Banac, ed. *Eastern Europe in Revolution* (Ithaca, NY, 1992); Swain, Nigel, *Hungary: The Rise and Fall of Feasible Socialism* (London, 1992).

Elections of 1945. During the autumn of 1945, elections were to be held in Hungary. At the insistence of the Communist and Social Democratic parties, municipal elections were to be held first. These two parties reasoned that the city workers would vote for them, and they would gain the majority in the industrial centers. The national elections would, therefore, be influenced by the municipal elections, providing a good chance for the two parties to gain a majority in parliament. But the leaders of the two parties were disappointed.

The Smallholders party, considered by the majority of the population to be the strongest bulwark against communism, won 51 percent of the votes in the municipal elections. The Social Democratic party and the Communist party, running on a joint ticket, won only 39 percent of the votes cast. The National Peasant party, a surrogate for the communists in the countryside, received 7.1 percent, and the rest of the ballots were shared by smaller parties.

Before the elections, the Soviet chairman of the Allied Control Commission in Hungary, Kliment Voroshilov, pressured the leaders of the Smallholders party to agree to the continuation of the coalition government regardless of the outcome of the elections. The Smallholders agreed. In the national elections, the Smallholders received the absolute majority of the votes, 57 percent. The Communist party, now running on its own, received seventeen percent. The Social Democratic party gained 17.1 percent, and the National Peasant party received 6.8 percent. In the new government, 50 percent of the ministerial posts were given to the Smallholders party, but the ministries of the interior and of justice came into communist hands. This ensured the eventual Stalinization of Hungary.

Bibliography

Fejto, François, *A History of the People's Democracies* (London, 1971); Nagy, Ferenc, *The Struggle Behind the Iron Curtain* (New York, 1948).

Erdei, Ferenc (1910–1971). Erdei was born into a peasant family and he absorbed his father's political ideas. He grew up in opposition to the interwar Hungarian regime and acquired an innate hatred for middle-class society. He was able to attend university studies and grow into a scholar. His books about the history of peasant society became standard works on the subject.

In 1939, Erdei was among the founders of the National Peasant party. He gravitated to the radical wing of the party and established close relations with the underground Communist party of Hungary, led by Ferenc Donath. In 1944, in Debrecen, Erdei was present at the establishment of the Provisional Government under Soviet auspices. The following year he had a brief stint as minister of the interior, a sign of his close affiliation with the communists. It was during his tenure as interior minister that the communists took control of the regular police apparatus and began building the dreaded secret police with Soviet KGB advisers. In 1948, when the Stalinization of Hungary began, the Erdei-led National Peasant party simply became a front organization for the Communist party. It remained in existence throughout the communist era as a transmission belt of communist policies toward the rural population.

Erdei was an eager collaborator with Matyas Rakosi (*see* Rakosi, Matyas) and his entourage in turning Hungary into a Soviet colony. During the height of the Stalinist terror, Erdei was minister of state without portfolio. He retained his post during the first premiership of Imre Nagy from 1953 to 1955 (*see* Nagy, Imre). By then, Erdei had changed his views and supported the moderate course embraced by the Imre Nagy government (*see* Nagy, Imre). When Nagy was ousted and Rakosi returned to power in 1955, Erdei was elevated to the vice presidency of the council of ministers. He remained in that post for one year.

After the Revolution of 1956 (*see* Revolution of 1956), Erdei was a completely discredited politician. Although he once again became a turncoat and pledged his allegiance to the counterrevolutionary government of Janos Kadar (*see* Kadar, Janos), the new dictator wanted nothing to do with Erdei. In 1964, however, he was appointed president of the Hungarian Academy of Sciences, a highly politicized post, and he remained in office until 1970.

Bibliography

Aczel, Tamas, and Meray, Tibor, *The Revolt of the Mind* (London, 1961); Held, Joseph, "Hungary on a Fixed Course," in Joseph Held, ed. *The Columbia History of Eastern Europe in the Twentieth Century* (New York, 1992), pp. 204-228; Kovrig, Bennett, *Communism in Hungary from Kun to Kadar* (Stanford, CA, 1979).

Expulsion of Ethnic Germans. Ethnic Germans living in Hungary were collectively made responsible for the excesses of the German Nazis. The truth was that some of them did collaborate with Adolf Hitler's minions, but the majority of them had remained passive. The Allies nevertheless agreed that the ethnic Germans would be removed from Eastern Europe after the war.

In 1945, after the war was over, Hungarian authorities collaborated with the Red Army in rounding up about 65,000 ethnic German civilians, mostly young men and women, who were then deported to the Soviet Union for "reparation works." More than half of the ethnic Germans never returned; they died of starvation and ill treatment in Soviet concentration camps. The survivors were permitted to return to Hungary in 1950 and were promptly arrested by the Hungarian secret police. They were interned until 1956.

In the meantime, a campaign was started by a minor figure in the National Peasant party, Imre Kovacs (*see* Kovacs, Imre), for the expulsion of all ethnic Germans from Hungary. Kovacs was a populist in the 1930s, and he hated the Germans with a passion. In the National Peasant party's newspaper Kovacs wrote that "they (the Germans) arrived in Hungary (in the seventeenth century) with a backpack: now let them leave the same way."

The fact was that ethnic Germans went to Hungary in waves, starting after the expulsion of the Ottoman Turks from the country in 1699 and again during the nineteenth century, at the invitation of various governments and high noblemen. Most of them became assimilated, but they kept their German language. The elite of these people participated in Hungarian politics. Many of them fought in the various wars of independence against Habsburg dominance. Now they were made collectively responsible for Nazi atrocities in Hungary.

The Hungarian communists were reluctant at first to embrace the cause of expulsion. However, they soon perceived advantages in making the Germans scapegoats for the excesses committed by Hungarians against the Jews and against the Soviet people during the war. In 1947, therefore, between 170,000 and 250,000 ethnic Germans were rounded up. They were mostly rural folks who tilled the land or were small craftsmen. They were permitted to carry twenty kilograms of their belongings with them. They were herded into cattle cars with great brutality and deported to Germany. The lucky ones ended up in the Western occupational zones, but many of them arrived in the Soviet zone and remained in East Germany. Their absence certainly made it more difficult to rebuild war-torn Hungary.

Bibliography

Nagy, Ferenc, *The Struggle Behind the Iron Curtain* (New York, 1948).

Farkas, Mihaly (1904–1965). The least talented, most brutal member of the Hungarian Muscovites who returned to Hungary in 1944, Farkas was born and raised in Czechoslovakia. Born a Jew, he renounced his religion and Jewishness and embraced Marxism-Leninism at an early age.

In the 1930s, he emigrated to the Soviet Union, where he joined the group of Hungarian exiles. During World War II, Farkas was a Soviet officer. When he returned to Hungary, he was one of the "four horsemen of the Apocalypse," including Rakosi (*see* Rakosi, Matyas), Gero (*see* Gero, Erno), and Revai (*see* Revai, Jozsef). (The fifth member of the group, Zoltan Vas, was not included by the public in the group.) Farkas became the head of the Hungarian secret police, the AVO-AVH (*Allamvedelmi Osztaly* and *Allamvedelmi Hivatal*), and supervised the Stalinist terror of the late 1940s and early 1950s. Although, ultimately, Rakosi was responsible for the terror, Farkas overfilled Rakosi's orders, and his brutality in dealing with alleged enemies of the communist regime became the norm in the secret police. In 1949, Farkas was appointed minister of defense, but he maintained his relations with the secret police. He participated in the transformation of the Hungarian army on the pattern of the Red Army, including Russian uniforms and training manuals. Before assuming his ministerial post, Farkas participated in the "preparation" of Laszlo Rajk (*see* Rajk, Laszlo) for his show trial by personally supervising Rajk's torture.

In 1954, knowing that Rakosi's days were numbered, Farkas sided with Imre Nagy (*see* Nagy, Imre) and became a member of Nagy's first cabinet. When Rakosi returned to power, Farkas was removed from the Politburo of the Communist party, and he was made a scapegoat for the atrocities committed by Rakosi's regime. Ironically, he was tried on trumped-up charges and imprisoned. He died in obscurity in 1965. His son, Vladimir, a former colonel of the secret police, has since undertaken the task of whitewashing his father's crimes.

Bibliography

Aczel, Tamas, and Meray, Tibor, *The Revolt of the Mind* (London, 1961); Kovrig, Bennett, *Communism in Hungary from Kun to Kadar* (Stanford, CA, 1979); Farkas, Vladimir, *No Excuses* (Budapest, 1990) (in Hungarian).

Foreign Relations of Communist Hungary. Hungarian foreign relations may be divided into three distinct phases. The first of these, extending from 1945 to 1948, was characterized by the government's efforts to rebuild relations with the Western countries while, at the same time, maintaining a working relationship with the Soviet Union. Hungary was required to pay reparations to the Soviet Union, Yugoslavia, and Czechoslovakia. The Hungarian economy was, however, so depleted by the war, and the Red Army's occupation of Hungary was so oppressive, that no reparations were paid to Yugoslavia or Czechoslovakia. Relations with these two countries did not get off to a good start. The Czechoslovaks wanted to expel all Hungarian minorities. When this was vetoed by the Allies, president Eduard Benes resorted to large-scale deportations of Hungarians to western Czechoslovakia. The Hungarian government was powerless to prevent this action. The period was ended by the peace treaties of Paris, concluded in 1947, which declared Hungary's pre-World War II borders as final, depriving about three million Hungarians of the opportunity to live within an ethnically Hungarian state.

The second phase of Hungarian foreign affairs began with the conquest of power by the communists. After the Stalinization of Hungarian society was completed, Hungarian foreign affairs simply mirrored Soviet policies. Hungary's role in the United Nations was simply to support whatever the Soviet representatives proposed and oppose what they disliked. The situation changed briefly in 1956. In 1955, Hungary had joined the Warsaw Pact alliance, integrating the Hungarian armed forces under Soviet leadership. When the Revolution of 1956 (*see* Revolution of 1956) broke out and, in a few days, it defeated the secret police and the Soviet garrison in Hungary, the new Hungarian government attempted to create an independent, neutral foreign policy. It did not succeed because the Red Army suppressed the Revolution in November 1956.

The third phase of Hungary's foreign relations began at that time. For more than three decades afterward, the counterrevolutionary government of Janos Kadar simply followed the lead of the Soviet Union in most foreign policy decisions. For example, Hungary supported the Soviet invasion of Afghanistan, boycotted the Los Angeles Olympic Games, and fought vigorously against the installation of American missiles in Western Europe. This period ended with the last communist government Hungary and the exit of the Hungarian state from the Warsaw Pact alliance.

Bibliography

Fejto, François, *A History of the People's Democracies* (London, 1971); Gati, Charles, *Hungary and the Soviet Bloc* (Durham, NC, 1986); Kertesz, Stephen D., *Diplomacy in a Whirlpool: Hungary Between Nazi Germany and Soviet Russia* (Notre Dame, IN, 1953); Kiraly, Bela K., *The First War Between Socialist States: The Hungarian Revolution of 1956 and its Impact* (New York, 1984).

Gero, Erno (1898–1980). Gero was the highest ranking Hungarian member of the COMINTERN. He spent the interwar years in the Soviet Union and was an early recruit of the Cheka (later the NKVD and the KGB). He was a commissar in the Spanish civil war and was reported to have been responsible for the persecution of Anarchists and Trotskyists fighting alongside the communists.

He spoke several languages, including Russian and German. He was a typical apparatchik who obeyed the orders of higher party organs unquestioningly. Rigidly dogmatic, he was one of the few communist leaders in Hungary who spurned a luxurious life-style. He was an aloof man who inspired fear even among his closest collaborators. He had no friends, only coworkers.

In 1944, Gero expected to be named the first secretary of the Hungarian Communist party. However, when Joseph Stalin's choice was Matyas Rakosi (*see* Rakosi, Matyas), he accepted this without a murmur and served Rakosi loyally. In 1948, he was entrusted with the supervision of the Stalinization of Hungary's economy. He acted with great zeal even when it became obvious that forced industrialization was harming the country's economy. In June 1956, Rakosi was removed from power and sent to exile in the Soviet Union by Nikita Khrushchev. Gero was the Soviet leadership's choice to replace the fallen dictator.

At the outbreak of the revolution in October (*see* Hungarian Revolution of 1956), Gero hastily returned to Hungary from a fence-mending visit with Yugoslavia's Josip Broz Tito. He declared martial law and asked for Soviet military assistance to subdue the revolutionary students, workers, and intellectuals. Five days later, he was removed from the leadership of the Hungarian Communist party and was replaced by Janos Kadar (*see* Kadar, Janos). Gero then fled to the Soviet Union. In 1961, he was permitted to return to Hungary and worked as a translator, until his death in 1980.

Bibliography

Aczel, Tamas, and Meray, Tibor, *The Revolt of the Mind* (London, 1961); Fejto, François, *Behind the Rape of Hungary* (New York, 1957); Molnar, Miklos, *A Short History of the Hun-*

garian Communist Party (Boulder, CO, 1978); Vali, Ferenc, *Rift and Revolt in Hungary* (Cambridge, MA, 1961).

Glatz, Ferenc (1941–). Glatz was born into a worker's family who lived in one of the workers' suburbs in Budapest. He was educated at Lorant Eotvos University in Budapest, and after graduation, he became a member of the Historical Institute of the Hungarian Academy of Sciences. He joined the Hungarian Socialist Workers party and was, for a short time, secretary of the party cell at the Historical Institute. He was gradually entrusted with administrative tasks under the direction of Zsigmond Pal Pach, the director of the Institute, and later by Gyorgy Ranki, who succeeded Pach. Upon the death of Ranki in 1988, Glatz was appointed to succeed him. In 1989, he became a member of the cabinet of Miklos Nemeth as minister of education and culture.

In a short time, Glatz became one of the most popular cabinet members. He reorganized the ministry and started a process of reforms. He abolished the compulsory teaching of the Russian language in Hungarian schools, colleges, and universities. He established an organization, called the Europe Institute, that became the center of graduate-level instructions for students from the countries of Eastern Europe. Next, he abolished the compulsory teaching of Marxism-Leninism in the schools. He began the process of creating a new curriculum for the schools, and he ordered the democratization of the administration of the universities.

After the elections of 1990, Glatz returned to the Historical Institute, where he continues his work as director. The journal that he established in 1986, called *Historia*, has become the source of unorthodox articles. His journal was the first to reexamine many of the policies and events of the communist era in Hungary, breaking new ground in informing the public of controversial historical events. He was elected a member of the Hungarian Academy of Sciences in 1992, and he became deputy president of the organization. A prolific writer, Glatz has become a leading historian of Hungary. He has traveled extensively in Europe, the United States, and the Soviet Union, lecturing at various international conferences and universities.

Bibliography
Glatz, Ferenc, *Historical Writing at the Time of Changing Ages* (In Hungarian) (Budapest, 1990); ——, *National Culture–Cultured Nation* (In Hungarian) (Budapest, 1988). Kulcsar, Kalman, and Szelenyi, Ivan, *The Road of the Intelligentsia to Class Power* (In Hungarian) (Budapest, 1989).

Goncz, Arpad (1922–). Goncz received his education in agricultural science and also obtained a degree in law. He was one of the relatively few intellectuals who participated in the armed resistance to the Germans in Hungary. Between 1945 and 1957, he was a member of the Independent Smallholders party. After the demise of his party, Goncz worked as an agricultural expert. In 1956, he was a participant of the Revolution (*see* Revolution of 1956) and, as a consequence, was tried and sentenced to life in prison in the same trial that resulted in the jail term for Istvan Bibo (*see* Bibo, Istvan).

Goncz was freed by the general amnesty in 1963 and found work at first as a translator, then as a writer. He participated in the democratic opposition during the 1970s and 1980s. Goncz was among the founding members of the Committee for Historical Justice and the Alliance of Free Democrats. In 1989, he was elected president of the Hungarian Writers' Union. A year later, the Hungarian parliament elected Goncz president of the republic.

Bibliography

Hegedus, Andras, *Life in the Shadow of an Ideology* (In Hungarian) (Munich, 1985); Ministry of Education, *The Hungarian Revolution of 1956: Reform, Uprising, Fight for Freedom, and Vengeance* (In Hungarian) (Budapest, 1991).

Hanak, Peter (1921–). Hanak was born to a middle class Jewish family. He keenly felt the persecution of the late 1930s and early 1940s; most of his family perished in the German death camps in 1944. After World War II, Hanak joined the Hungarian Communist party and became an ardent believer in the ideals of Marxism-Leninism. In the early 1950s, he became a member of the Historical Institute of the Hungarian Academy of Sciences, where he soon rose to the post of department chairman.

The Revolution of 1956 (*see* Revolution of 1956) changed Hanak's outlook on politics. He was a supporter of Imre Nagy (*see* Nagy, Imre), and, when the Revolution was suppressed by Soviet tanks, Hanak refused to join the reconstituted Hungarian Socialist Workers party, as the Communist party was renamed. Instead, he concentrated his energies on raising the next generation of historians. In 1980, he was invited to become a professor of history at Eotvos Lorant University in Budapest while remaining a member of the Historical Institute. He was long bypassed for membership in the Academy of Sciences for less prolific and lesser known historians because of his withdrawal from politics.

Finally, in 1986, Hanak was elected to that institution. He traveled widely in the West, taught as a guest professor at various universities in the United States and Europe, and contributed to various historical projects in Hungary and abroad. He interested himself mainly in the last period of the history of the Habsburg empire and its successor states in the nineteenth and twentieth centuries. He has been a prolific writer whose contributions to history will be long lasting. In the 1990s, Hanak became the director of the Central European University, established through support by private funds, whose headquarters in Prague and Budapest are aimed at providing graduate-level education for East European as well as Russian students. In 1992, Peter Hanak retired from the Institute of History of the Hungarian Academy of Sciences.

Bibliography

Hanak, Peter, *Hungary in the Monarchy; Studies* (in Hungarian) (Budapest, 1975); ———, *The Garden and the Shop* (In Hungarian) (Budapest, 1988); Kulcsar, Kalman, and Szelenyi, Ivan, *The Road of the Intelligentsia to Class Power* (In Hungarian) (Budapest, 1989).

Hegedus, Andras (1925–). Hegedus was the son of a poor sharecropper and a wealthier peasant woman. He received a good education and he became acquainted with leftist ideas. He joined the Communist party in 1945 and participated in the distribution of land to poor peasants. He was a minor official in the party's youth organization. He rose gradually in the ranks and, by 1953, when Joseph Stalin died, Hegedus was a member of the highest organ of the party, the Politburo. He was a protege of Erno Gero (*see* Gero, Erno).

In June 1953, Hegedus was a member of the Hungarian government delegation that visited the Soviet Union, and here he listened to the chastisement meted out to the delegation by Lavrenty Beria, Georgy Malenkov, and Nikita Khrushchev.

In April 1955, Hegedus became the prime minister of Hungary. When the Revolution of 1956 (*see* Revolution of 1956) broke out, Hegedus signed the request for the Soviet authorities to activate the Red Army garrison in Hungary to suppress the Revolution. When the revolution was temporarily victorious, Hegedus fled to Moscow. After the revolution was suppressed, he returned to Hungary, but he was a disillusioned, broken man. Appointed by Janos Kadar (*see* Kadar, Janos) director of the new Institute of Sociology of the Academy of Sciences, he began to gather around himself scholars who were not afraid of exploring the ills of Hungary's socialist system. When Hegedus condemned the invasion of Czechoslovakia by the Warsaw Pact in August 1968, he was removed from the Institute and expelled from the Communist party. He is now living in retirement.

Bibliography

Hegedus, Andras, *Life in the Shadow of an Ideal* (in Hungarian): Interview with Zoltan Zsille (Vienna, Austria, 1985); Konrad, Gyorgy, and Szelenyi, Ivan, *The Intellectuals on the Road to Class Power* (New York, 1979); Kovago, Jozsef, *You Are All Alone* (New York, 1959).

Hungarian Democratic Forum. The *Magyar Demokrata Forum* (MDF) was established in the small village of Monor in 1986 by 160 intellectuals, many of whom were populist writers. The organizers were encouraged by Imre Pozsgay (*see* Pozsgay, Imre), a member of the reformist wing of the leadership of the Hungarian Socialist Workers party, the name the communists adopted in 1956. The group was an amorphous gathering whose members declared that they were not an oppositional movement. They wanted to reform the Kadar regime and move it toward internal legitimacy. The movement crystallized at another meeting held in the house of Sandor Lezsak in the small village of Lakitelek near Budapest in 1988. The movement changed into a political party in 1989. The party never became the representative of any specific social group. It was a genuine national liberation movement whose leading aim was the independence of Hungary in parallel with the removal of Soviet occupational forces from the country.

In 1989, together with other oppositional groups, the leaders of the MDF began a series of discussions with the reformist wing of the communist leadership, and this led to the free elections of 1990. In the elections, the MDF received 43 percent of the seats in parliament and, its allies won another 16 percent. The second largest party, the Alliance of Free Democrats (*Szabad Demokratak Szovetsege,* or SZDSZ), won 24 percent. The Alliance of Young Democrats (*Fiatal Demokratak Szovetsege,* or Fidesz) received 10 percent of the votes cast.

The president of the MDF, Jozsef Antall (*see* Antall, Jozsef), formed the new government in coalition with the Smallholders and National Christian Democratic parties. His government had a solid parliamentary majority. In 1991, however, internal disputes undermined the effectiveness of the Antall government. By then, the Hungarian Democratic Forum consisted of three wings with mutually irreconcilable political ideologies and motives. The right wing was led by Istvan Csurka, a populist writer who, in June 1993, admitted to having been an informer of the communist secret police. The center clustered around Antall and his immediate supporters, such as Lajos Fur, the minister of defense, and Sandor Lezsak, the moving force behind the establishment of the MDF. The left, or what was named the liberal wing, was represented by Janos Debreczeni and Istvan Elek. These three strains could not easily get along with each other.

Csurka made the first move to capture the MDF and change its center-right orientation into a radical rightist movement. In August 1992, he published an article in his newspaper *Demokrata Forum,* in which he demanded that the prime minister institute harsh measures against the oppositional parties and use the police in removing the heads of Hungarian national radio and television, who were considered by him "enemies of the Hungarian people." Csurka also declared that Hungary was allegedly a victim of a century-old Jewish conspiracy, directed from New York and Tel Aviv. This created a storm of criticism, directed at Csurka as well as at Antall, who was unwilling to dissociate his party from the demagogue.

In January 1993, the national representatives of the party met and decided to support Antall against Csurka. In June, Csurka was removed from the leaders (he was vice president of the MDF) as well as from the parliamentary fraction of the party. He formed his own group, named the Hungarian Way, and his followers created the Hungarian Truth party with about ten parliamentary deputies. At the same time, the party rid itself of its liberal wing, expelling Debreczeni and Elek from its membership. All these moves were made with a view to the upcoming elections. The fact is that the Hungarian Democratic Forum has lost much of its appeal among the voters, and it will probably go down to defeat in the next elections in May, 1994.

Bibliography

Oltay, Edith, "Hungary: Csurka Launches 'National Movement,'" *Radio Free Europe Research Report* 2.13 (March 26, 1993), pp. 25-31; Pataki, Judith, "Hungary Makes Slow but Steady Progress," *Radio Free Europe Research Report* 2.1 (January 3, 1993), pp. 87-90; ———, "Hungary: Domestic Political Stalemate," *Radio Free Europe Research Report* 2.1 (January 1, 1993), pp. 92-95; ———, "Hungarian Youth Party Comes of Age," *Radio Free Europe Research Report* 2.21 (May 21, 1993), pp. 42-45; Reisch, Alfred, "Hungary Pursues Integration with the West," *Radio Free Europe Research Report* 2.13 (March 26, 1993), pp. 32-38.

Illyes, Gyula (1902–1983). Born into a sharecropper peasant's family, Illyes knew great privation as a child. His parents sent him to school at great sacrifice, and he justified their effort. He became a leading intellectual during the 1930s, an advocate of the exploration of village life, an effort to show the people of Hungary how poor people really lived. His best-known documentary work, entitled *Pusztak nepe* (People of the Puszta), was published in several languages and countries.

During the 1930s, Illyes visited the Soviet Union as a guest of the Soviet government. When he returned to Hungary, however, he published critical notes on Soviet agricultural practices, and of the kolhoz-system.

Illyes stayed out of politics in general, except for his advocacy of the peasants' cause. As a consequence, every regime in Hungary paid tribute to his talent as a writer. He was indeed the best-known representative of Hungarian literary life in much of the twentieth century.

In 1955, however, Illyes broke with his stand on politics and wrote a poem that became the rallying cry a year later for the revolution. Entitled *Egy mondat a zsarnoksagrol* (One Sentence on Tyranny), he painted a terrible picture of oppression that was immediately understood as describing the Rakosi-regime in Hungary. Nevertheless, after the suppression of the revolution, Illyes was left alone by the regime of Janos Kadar (*see* Kadar, Janos). In the 1960s and 1970s, he continued to be regarded as the grand old man of Hungarian literature.

Bibliography

Illyes, Gyula, *People of the Puszta* (Budapest, 1967); Aczel, Tamas, and Tibor, Meray, *The Revolt of the Mind* (London, 1961).

Kadar, Janos (Original name: Cservenka) (1912–1989). The illegitimate son of a very poor servant woman, Cservenka joined the underground Hungarian Communist party in 1932 and took the conspiratorial name of Kadar. In 1942, he was made a member of the party's Central Committee and became its first secretary in 1943. In the following year, the German Gestapo arrested him in Hungary, but he survived the war as the highest ranking member of the local communists in Hungary. In the national elections held in 1945, Kadar was elected parliamentary deputy. The following year, he became a member of the Politburo. He was also a deputy secretary of the Central Committee. In 1948, he was appointed minister of the interior, replacing Laszlo Rajk (*see* Rajk, Laszlo) who was, by then, being singled out for a show trial without his suspecting it. Kadar took an active part in the "preparation" of Rajk after he was arrested, trying to convince Rajk to accept the role of a traitor in the interests of the party. In 1951, however, Kadar himself was arrested and brutally beaten by Mihaly Farkas (*see* Farkas, Mihaly) and his son, Vladimir. However, Kadar was freed in 1953 and rehabilitated.

In 1956, Kadar was a member of the party's Central Committee and its secretariat. In late October, he replaced Erno Gero (*see* Gero, Erno) as the general secretary of the Hungarian Communist party. In a speech, he welcomed the revolution and declared that it was the result of accumulated resentment Hungarians felt toward communist policies. Kadar became a member of Imre Nagy's (*see* Nagy, Imre) revolutionary government; however, he betrayed Nagy. He fled to join the Red Army which was then preparing to invade the revolutionary Hungary, and he formed a counterrevolutionary government under Soviet auspices. After the revolution was suppressed, Kadar became the head of a Soviet puppet government.

With the approval of his Soviet masters, Kadar pursued a terrible vengeance against the population. Hundreds were murdered by his people's courts, really kangaroo courts manned by vicious communists, and thousands were imprisoned. Kadar's revenge lasted until 1963. By then, it was obvious that the country had been subdued and was sullenly obeying the communists' orders. In that year, Kadar decreed general amnesty except for those who were charged with capital offenses during the revolution. The reorganized Communist party took the name of Hungarian Socialist Workers party, but the name change did not mean the renunciation of previous communist practices.

Kadar gradually relaxed the terror and, in 1968, his government introduced the New Economic Mechanism (NEM), whose basic principles had been laid down in 1954 by Imre Nagy's government. By this time, Imre Nagy and Pal Maleter (*see* Maleter, Pal), the two best known leaders of the revolution, were dead. They had been tried in secret and executed on Kadar's orders in 1958. But the economic changes ushered in by the new policies were beneficial for Hungary. They relaxed central controls and permitted private initiative, especially in agriculture, but also in industry. In the 1970s, after some setbacks, the economy functioned relatively well and Hungary was able to feed its population, alone among the members of the Soviet bloc. Consumer goods were also available, even if their price was often too high.

Hungary began to show a certain level of prosperity, unknown in the other Soviet colonies in Eastern Europe. There was also a relaxation in communications. Western visitors were permitted to enter the country and Western newspaper reporters gave glowing reports of the policies of the Kadar regime. The most often voiced opinion was that Kadar would be elected head of the government in a free election. Such a step, of course, was never tried.

By the mid-1980s, however, prosperity had vanished. Hungary borrowed heavily from Western sources, and the bills came due. It turned out that Kadar had used the borrowed funds not for investments, but for subsidies for inefficient and unprofitable firms. There was also a continuous shipment of cash directly to the Soviet Communist party. This brought about the revolt of the younger, reformist members of the Hungarian Socialist Workers party in 1988. In May of that year, Kadar was removed from the post of general secretary and was named to the meaningless office of president of the party. In 1989, he was removed even from that post and was forced to resign.

Kadar lived to see the rehabilitation and reburial of Imre Nagy, his most prominent victim. Two days later, on June 18, 1989, he was dead. Kadar's legacy was an economic system that was on the verge of collapse. His ideology was discredited and rejected by most Hungarians. Not surprisingly, his party received less than 4 percent of the votes cast in the national elections in 1990.

Bibliography

Kovrig, Bennett, *Communism in Hungary from Kun to Kadar* (Stanford, CA, 1979); Molnar, Miklos, *A Short History of the Hungarian Communist Party* (Boulder, CO, 1978).

Kallai, Gyula (1910–1986). Kallai, a journalist, joined the illegal Hungarian Communist party in the 1930s. During World War II, he participated in the resistance movement against the Germans, although he did not bear arms. In 1949, he was appointed minister of foreign affairs in Matyas Rakosi's (*see* Rakosi, Matyas) government. However, in 1951, he was put through a show trial and sentenced to a long prison term. In 1954, Kallai was rehabilitated, and in 1955 he was appointed minister of people's education. After 1956, he joined the newly formed Hungarian Socialist Workers party, the new organization replacing the old Communist party, and was appointed a member of the party's Politburo. In 1965, he replaced Janos Kadar (*see* Kadar, Janos) as prime minister of Hungary, but real power remained with Kadar, who retained the post of secretary general of the party.

Bibliography

Kovrig, Bennett, *Communism in Hungary from Kun to Kadar* (Stanford, CA, 1979).

Kardos, Laszlo (1920–1980). The child of a middle-class family, Kardos studied at Budapest University and came into contact with the populist movement in the 1930s. He became director of the *Gyorffy Collegium*, a dormitory established for students who came from rural areas, in 1942. Kardos participated in the youth movement of the underground resistance. In 1945, he was appointed to the commission distributing land for poor peasants. He was also first secretary of the national committee of the people's colleges, an organization helping peasant youth to obtain a higher education.

In 1956, Kardos was among the organizers of the Petofi Circle, which consisted of intellectuals, many of them young party officials, who openly questioned the dictatorship of Matyas Rakosi (*see* Rakosi, Matyas). When the counterrevolutionary Kadar government came into power, Kardos was arrested. He was accused of smuggling the works of Imre Nagy (*see* Nagy, Imre), the prime minister of the Revolution, to Western countries. He received a sentence of death, but it was changed into life imprisonment. In 1963, he was freed under the general amnesty. After he was released from jail, Kardos continued his sociological research.

Bibliography

Aczel, Tamas, and Meray, Tibor, *The Revolt of the Mind* (London, 1961).

Kethly, Anna (1889–1976). Kethly, a leading social democratic politician during the years between the two World Wars, was a member of her party's parliamentary delegation. In 1944, she was imprisoned by the Germans, but survived and returned to Hungary in 1945. After 1945, she opposed the merger of her party with that of the communists. When the merger was nevertheless accomplished, Kethly was arrested by the secret police, put through a show trial, and she was given a long prison term.

In 1954, she was released. During the Hungarian Revolution of 1956 (*see* Revolution of 1956), Kethly was instrumental in reestablishing the Hungarian Social Democratic party as a separate entity from the communists. She was appointed minister of state by Imre Nagy (*see* Nagy, Imre), the revolution's prime minister. When the revolution was suppressed by the Soviet army, Kethly sought refuge in the West. She was instrumental in establishing the Imre Nagy Institute in Brussels, Belgium, which issued studies on Hungary and the revolution. In 1957, Kethly was elected chairman of the Hungarian Revolutionary Council in exile in Strasbourg, France.

Bibliography

Aczel, Tamas, and Meray, Tibor, *The Revolt of the Mind* (London, 1961); Kovrig, Bennett, *Communism in Hungary from Kun to Kadar* (Stanford, CA, 1979).

Kopacsi, Sandor (1915–). Kopacsi, the son of a worker in the Diosgyor factory of ironworks, became involved with the labor movement early in his life and was a member of the anti-Nazi resistance who actually fought against the Germans. After 1945, he joined the Communist party and became a policeman. Rapidly rising in rank, he was brought to Budapest in the early 1950s and became a police administrator. In 1954, he was appointed police chief of the capital city, Budapest.

During the Revolution of 1956 (*see* Revolution of 1956), Kopacsi gradually became convinced of the validity of the cause for which the revolutionaries were willing to risk their lives, namely the independence of Hungary. When the Imre Nagy (*see* Nagy, Imre) government was formed, Kopacsi was appointed, jointly with General Bela Kiraly, to head the newly formed national guard. When the Revolution was suppressed by Soviet forces, Kopacsi was arrested and imprisoned. He became a defendant in the Imre Nagy trial in 1958. He was found guilty of conspiracy for the destruction of the communist regime, falsely, of course, and sentenced to life imprisonment. In 1963, he was freed by the general amnesty. In 1966, he was permitted to emigrate to Canada, where his daughter had received asylum after 1956. He worked as a janitor in a Canadian factory. After the collapse of the communist system in Hungary, he returned to Budapest and he is currently living in retirement.

Bibliography

Donath, Ferenc, *Reform and Revolution.* (In Hungarian) (Budapest, 1980); Molnar, Miklos, *Budapest 1956: A History of the Hungarian Revolution* (London, 1971).

Kosary, Domokos (1913–). A well-known historian, Kosary was the director of the Historical Institute of the Hungarian Academy of Sciences until 1949. He was ousted in that year in favor of the communist Erik Molnar. Kosary was sent to work as a librarian at the Agrarian Sciences University in Godollo. Kosary participated in the revolution (*see* Revolution of 1956) and, as a consequence, he was tried and sentenced to five years in jail. He was freed in 1960 and worked as an archivist in Budapest. In 1963, Kosary became a member of the Historical Institute of the Hungarian Academy of Sciences, now under the direction of another communist apparatchik, Zsigmond Pal Pach. In 1990, Kosary was elected president of the Hungarian Academy of Sciences.

Bibliography
Kosary, Domokos, *Hungarians in Europe: Reconstruction and Bourgeois Development, 1711–1867* (In Hungarian) (Budapest, 1990); ——, *Bibliography of Hungarian History* (Budpest, 1943), 3 vols.

Kovacs, Bela (1908–1959). One of the outstanding leaders of the Smallholders party and the Peasant Alliance in Hungary, Kovacs was appointed first secretary of the Smallholders party in 1945. He was an outspoken critic of the Hungarian communists, especially of Matyas Rakosi (*see* Rakosi, Matyas). In 1947, in spite of his parliamentary immunity, Kovacs was arrested by members of the Soviet secret police in the Hungarian parliament building and was deported to a Soviet concentration camp. He was permitted to return to Hungary in 1956, before the outbreak of the revolution. However, by then, Kovacs was seriously ill. He was appointed minister of state in the revolutionary Imre Nagy (*see* Nagy, Imre) government. When the revolution was suppressed, Kovacs was in a hospital, and was, therefore, left alone by the Kadar regime.

Bibliography
Aczel, Tamas, and Meray, Tibor, *The Revolt of the Mind*. (London, 1961); Fejto, François, *Behind the Rape of Hungary* (New York, 1957); Nagy, Ferenc, *The Struggle Behind the Iron Curtain* (New York, 1948).

Kovacs, Imre (1913–1980). Peasant origin, Kovacs was an outspoken critic of the interwar Hungarian governments. He was a populist, a writer who explored the conditions of the Hungarian countryside. He was also a student at Peter Pazmany University in Budapest, favored by Count Pal Teleki, former prime minister and chair holder in geography at the university. He was instrumental in the establishment of the March Front in 1937, and for the formation of the National Peasant party in 1939.

After 1945, Kovacs worked in the National Peasant party's organization and was better noted for his articles demanding the expulsion of ethnic Germans from Hungary. He deplored the increasing subjection of the Peasant party to communist domination, and he eventually broke his relations with Ferenc Erdei (*see* Erdei, Ferenc) who favored close collaboration with the communists. In 1947, Kovacs left Hungary. At first, he worked for Radio Free Europe, later he retired and lived in New York until his death.

Bibliography
Nagy, Ferenc, *The Struggle Behind the Iron Curtain* (New York, 1948).

Losonczy, Geza (1917–1958). The son of a Calvinist minister, Losonczy was educated at the Calvinist College in the city of Debrecen, where he majored in French language and Hungarian literature. Before graduating, Losonczy visited Paris and attended several courses taught at the Sorbonne. While in Paris, he came across a pamphlet written by an obscure communist writer, the later culture czar, Jozsef Revai (*see* Revai, Jozsef), and Losonczy had the pamphlet smuggled into Hungary.

When he returned to Hungary, he participated in leftist causes. He eventually joined the underground organization of young communists, where he met many of the future functionaries of the Hungarian Communist party. Losonczy was soon jailed for illegal activities. After 1945, Losonczy became an important leader in the youth section of the Communist party. He was deputy editor of the party's daily newspaper and a parliamentary deputy. In 1949, he became secretary to Matyas Rakosi (*see* Rakosi, Matyas), the head of the party in Hungary. Nevertheless, Losonczy was suspect in the eyes of the ever vigilant secret police. His time spent in Western Europe was held against him. Soon he was transferred to a meaningless job in the National Szechenyi Library.

In 1951, he was arrested with other leading members of the party, including Janos Kadar (*see* Kadar, Janos). He spent three years in prison where he contracted tuberculosis. After he was freed, he went through a series of treatments, but his lungs remained weak. Imre Nagy appointed Losonczy editor-in-chief of *Magyar Nemzet*, the official journal of the government, during his first prime ministership. Two years later, Losonczy joined a group who wrote a memorandum demanding the democratization of Hungarian politics. He was also a leader of the Petofi Circle, the group of young communist writers who demanded reforms. Losonczy traveled all over Hungary, carrying the message of reform and of a new patriotism to the people. At the outbreak of the revolution, Losonczy joined the group that gathered around Imre Nagy. He was appointed in Nagy's government minister without portfolio. When Soviet tanks rolled into Budapest, Losonczy took refuge in the Yugoslav embassy with Nagy and other government members, and he was detained with them when they left the embassy under the promise of safe conduct.

During the autumn of 1957, Losonczy was brought to Budapest from a Romanian detention camp where the Hungarian officials had been incarcerated and he had been subjected to prolonged torture. Protesting the absurdity of charges, Losonczy began a hunger strike. The secret police tried to force-feed him, but the tube they were using was pushed into his lungs, and he died of suffocation. His murderers have never been punished.

Bibliography

Aczel, Tamas, and Meray, Tibor, *The Revolt of the Mind* (London, 1961); Kovrig, Bennett, *Communism in Hungary from Kun to Kadar* (Stanford, CA, 1979).

Lukacs, Gyorgy (1885–1971). Lukacs was the son of wealthy, middle-class Jewish parents who participated in the intellectual movements of the early twentieth century. He was a member of the early liberal societies such as the *Huszadik Szazad* (Twentieth Century) *Tarsadalomtudomanyi Tarsasag* (Association for Social Science), and others. In 1918, he joined a circle of progressive intellectuals, which gathered around Count Mihaly Karolyi. Karolyi led the first revolution after World War I. However, Lukacs changed sides; he joined the Hungarian Communist party.

During the first Hungarian Soviet Republic in 1919, Lukacs was commissar for culture. After the destruction of the first communist regime, Lukacs asked for and received asylum in Austria, then moved to Weimar Germany. Finally, he went to the Soviet Union, where he was severely criticized by Soviet ideologues for his efforts to seek a democratic way to socialism, but in each case he practiced self-criticism and survived Stalin's times.

In 1944, he returned to Hungary with Matyas Rakosi (*see* Rakosi, Matyas) and other Muscovites, and he became a leading source of ideological purity in the Hungarian Communist party. In 1949, his speculations were condemned by Jozsef Revai (*see* Revai, Jozsef) and Laszlo Rudas, his competitors for the position of the "Hungarian Zhdanov." In 1956, Lukacs was appointed minister of education in the revolutionary government of Imre Nagy (*see* Nagy, Imre), and he was deported to Romania with the members of Nagy's government after the suppression of the Revolution. However, for some unknown reason, he was not charged in the trial of Imre Nagy and his supporters. In 1967, he was rehabilitated and readmitted to the Communist party. His disciples formed the Lukacs School of Marxist Thought.

Bibliography
Kovrig, Bennett, *Communism in Hungary from Kun to Kadar* (Stanford, CA, 1979); Molnar, Miklos, *A Short History of the Hungarian Communist Party* (Boulder, CO, 1978).

Magyar Kozosseg (Hungarian Community). This organization originally established as a resistance group against the Nazi domination of Hungary. Its membership came from various colleges and Peter Pazmany University in Budapest. In January 1947, however, the organization was unmasked by minister of the interior, Laszlo Rajks's (*see* Rajk, Lszlo) secret police. Seven leaders were captured and tried, including Gyorgy Donath; Domonkos Szentivanyi, who signed the armistice with the Soviet Union in October 1944; Istvan Szentmiklosi, a former officer of the general staff, a member of the anti-Nazi resistance; Balint Arany; Dr. Janos Heder; General Lajos Dalnoki-Veres; and Dr. Kalman Salata, a parliamentary deputy. Three members were condemned to death by the communist court, which charged that they led a conspiracy for the overthrow of the government. Only Donath was executed; the others were sent to prison for decades. This was the first show trial in which the techniques of torture were used in Hungary. Ironically, the minister of the interior, Laszlo Rajk, who personally supervised the "preparations" for the trial, was himself to fall a victim in 1949.

Bibliography
Nagy, Ferenc, *The Struggle Behind the Iron Curtain* (New York, 1948).

Maleter, Pal (1917–1958). Maleter became one of the martyr heroes of the Revolution of 1956 (*see* Revolution of 1956). He was born in a small town in Czechoslovakia. His father, a teacher in a local school, was an ardent Hungarian patriot. Maleter wanted to be a professional soldier, but not in Czechoslovakia. But this was not possible. Therefore, he went to Charles University in Prague and studied medicine. When Hungary regained parts of Slovakia in 1940, Maleter went to Budapest where he joined the officers' training academy. He studied military science for three more years. In 1942, he graduated valedictorian of his class and received his commission as lieutenant in the Hungarian army. When the First Hungarian Army was mobilized to fight against the Soviet Union in 1944, Maleter was sent to the front. In May, he was captured. While in a prisoner of war camp, he was persuaded by a Hungarian exile communist leader to become a Soviet officer.

Maleter received further training at the Soviet military academy at Kiev and, during the second half of 1944, he fought in Transylvania. He received medals for bravery from the front commander, General R. Ia. Malinovski. After the war had ended, Maleter remained a professional soldier. He was stationed at Balassagyarmat with the rank of captain of the border guards. In 1948, he was already a member of the Republican Guard entrusted with the security of the country's leaders. As a major, he also served as a liaison officer in the ministry of defense. But his new masters did not fully trust the lanky soldier. Although he was promoted to colonel, he was moved to a group entrusted with formulating the training manual of the Hungarian infantry. In 1953, his private life was also disturbed; he was divorced from his wife.

During the first prime ministership of Imre Nagy (*see* Nagy, Imre), Maleter's fortunes began to change. He was appointed commander of the army's labor service battalions. Maleter remained in this position until 1956. During the revolution (*see* Revolution of 1956) in October, Maleter was sent by his communist minister to the Kilian barracks in Budapest in order to maintain order. When Maleter entered the barracks, the revolution was already in full swing, and Maleter experienced the enthusiasm of the people of the capital for change. Maleter followed his conscience. He joined the revolutionaries and defended the Kilian barracks against Soviet attacks. On October 31, Maleter was appointed deputy minister of defense in Imre Nagy's revolutionary government. He was also promoted to the rank of colonel general. On November 3, he led a high-level Hungarian delegation to the town of Tokol, where they were to meet Soviet government representatives to discuss the withdrawal of Soviet forces from Hungary. Instead, the delegation was treacherously arrested by Soviet KGB General S. Serov, acting on Nikita Khrushchev's orders.

In January 1958, Maleter was tried by a secret tribunal of the Kadar regime, separately from other members of Imre Nagy's cabinet. Maleter was sentenced to death, and he was executed following day. He was rehabilitated and reburied in 1989.

Bibliography

Kiraly, Bela K., *The First War Between Socialist States: The Hungarian Revolution of 1956 and its Impact* (New York, 1984); Meray, Tibor, *Thirteen Days That Shook the Kremlin*

(New York, 1959); Molnar, Miklos, *Budapest in 1956: A History of the Hungarian Revolution* (London, 1971).

Marosan, Gyorgy (1908–). Marosan, of workingman origin, was trained as a baker and was active in the labor union movement in Hungary before World War II. He also joined the Social Democratic party. He was a man of limited intelligence who compensated for this lack by the use of extremely vulgar language. Marosan was appointed secretary of the Social Democratic party and, between 1945 and 1947, he was first secretary of his party's organization. He was one of the major promoters of the merger of the Social Democratic party with the Communist party. After the merger, he became first secretary of the Budapest organization of the Hungarian Workers party, as the new association was called. In 1950, however, Marosan was arrested on trumped-up charges. He was tortured and kept in prison until 1956. In 1956, he was freed and rehabilitated. He was also appointed deputy prime minister and a member of the leadership of the Communist party.

After the revolution (*see* Revolution of 1956), Marosan was the most vicious supporter of vengeance on the population. He was appointed a member of the Politburo and the Central Committee, and he also became first secretary of the Budapest organization of the Communist party. In 1962, however, he became a liability for Janos Kadar (*see* Kadar, Janos) who wanted to effect some sort of accommodation with the population. Therefore, Marosan was expelled from the Politburo. In 1965, Marosan withdrew from the party, but in 1972, he asked for reinstatement. He remained, to this day, a dogmatic, radical, vulgar Marxist.

Bibliography
Aczel, Tamas, and Meray, Tibor, *The Revolt of the Mind* (London, 1961); Kovrig, Bennett, *Communism in Hungary from Kun to Kadar* (Stanford, CA, 1979); Nagy, Ferenc, *The Struggle Behind the Iron Curtain* (New York, 1948).

Mindszenty, Jozsef Cardinal (original name: Pehm) (1899–1975). In the late 1930s and early 1940s, Mindszenty was bishop of Veszprem. He was an outspoken critic of Nazism, and he spoke out courageously against the deportation of Hungarian Jews to the death camps in 1944. He was persecuted by the Hungarian Nazis.

In 1945, Mindszenty was appointed bishop of Esztergom, an office that usually carried the title of cardinal. From his pulpit, Mindszenty continued his crusade against barbarity, this time of the Stalinist variety. He declared that Marxism-Leninism was incompatible with Christian beliefs. He was especially vehement in opposing the state's takeover of the schools of the churches. Mindszenty was undoubtedly courageous and a man of deep convictions, but he was also belligerent and it appeared that he was seeking martyrdom.

In 1949, the cardinal was arrested by the secret police. He was accused of illegal foreign currency manipulations, because his church received donations from Western religious institutions, and he used the funds to strengthen his church. He was tortured and put through a show trial on trumped-up charges. He was broken (some said that he was also drugged) at his trial, and he confessed to the charges. He was sentenced to life in prison.

During the revolution (*see* Revolution of 1956), Cardinal Mindszenty was freed by the revolutionaries. He immediately appealed to the nation over the national radio for an end to the bloodshed. When Soviet troops crushed the revolution, Mindszenty was given asylum in the embassy building of the United States in Budapest. He lived in the embassy building for nearly twenty years, walking in the garden, and celebrating mass for the embassy personnel in his quarters. In 1984, the Kadar government finally concluded an agreement with the Vatican that included a provision for the release of the cardinal from the American embassy and his emigration to the West. He left the country. Thereafter Mindszenty visited Hungarian exile groups in Europe and in the United States, encouraging them to remain faithful to Roman Catholicism and to their Hungarian heritage. He died in 1975.

Bibliography
Lendvai, Paul, *Hungary: The Art of Survival* (London, 1988); Vali, Ferenc, *Rift and Revolt in Hungary* (Cambridge, MA, 1961).

Munich, Ferenc (1886–1967). Munich, of Jewish descent, served in the Habsburg army in World War I. He was captured in 1916 and, in 1917, joined the Soviet communists. He participated in the Russian revolution, and returned to Hungary in 1919. He was appointed military commander of the Hungarian Soviet Republic in March 1919. After the destruction of the Bela Kun regime by the Romanian army (*see* Communist party of Hungary), Munich emigrated first to Vienna, then to the Soviet Union. He acquired Soviet citizenship. Munich participated in the Spanish civil war. During World War II, he served in the Red Army.

In 1945, Munich returned to Hungary and was immediately appointed a high official of the Communist party. Between 1946 and 1949, he was the police chief of Budapest and was responsible for the excesses committed against the opposition. Between 1950 and 1956, Munich served as a diplomat in Soviet Bloc countries and in Western Europe. When Soviet tanks crushed the Hungarian revolution in November 1956, Munich sided with Janos Kadar (*see* Kadar, Janos), and he was appointed minister of the interior with control over the reorganized secret- and regular police. Between 1958 and 1961, Munich was prime minister of Hungary, and from 1961 to 1966, he served as minister of state in the Kadar regime.

Munich was a dogmatic Marxist who, together with the other Muscovites, was a rigid supporter of Soviet colonialism. He spoke Hungarian, but he was really a loyal Soviet subject who always placed Soviet interests above those of Hungary.

Bibliography
Hegedus, Andras, *In the Shadow of an Ideology*. (In Hungarian) (Vienna, 1980); Kopacsi, Sandor, *In the Name of the Working Class* (Toronto, Canada, 1986).

Nagy, Ferenc (1903–1979). Ferenc Nagy was a leading member of the Smallholders party before, during, and after World War II. He opposed the Horthy-regime before the war and demanded land reform to create a strong peasant stratum in Hungary. During the last year of the war, especially during the German occupation of Hungary beginning in March 1944, Nagy went into hiding. He survived the war and was invited by the Russian occupational authorities to participate in the formation of the provisional government for Hungary on December 21, 1944. He was also a member of the provisional parliament formed at the same time. He was minister of reconstruction in 1945. He was the leader of his party during and after the first elections when his party won absolute majorities in both the municipal-and the national elections. Nagy was then elected president of the new parliament. In February 1946, he was appointed prime minister of Hungary.

Nagy was under great pressure by the communists to cooperate with them in Stalinizing Hungarian politics. He proved to be too weak to withstand the pressure and gradually gave in to every demand made by Matyas Rakosi (*see* Rakosi, Matyas). Nagy would have had difficulty in openly opposing the communists, however, because they were increasingly supported by the Soviet army occupying Hungary.

Nagy sacrificed many parliamentary deputies in order to stay in power. He even accepted the arrest of Bela Kovacs (*see* Kovacs, Bela), first secretary of the Smallholders party, a parliamentary deputy, who was charged by the Soviet KGB of antistate activities. In 1947, Nagy was on vacation in Switzerland, when he received notice that he was to be investigated for oppositional activities. He resigned on condition that his four-year-old son be delivered to him in Switzerland. His condition was fulfilled. He ended his life in exile in the United States.

Bibliography
Aczel, Tamas, and Meray, Tibor, *The Revolt of the Mind* (London, 1961); Nagy, Ferenc, *The Struggle Behind the Iron Curtain* (New York, 1948); Ferenc Vali, *Rift and Revolt in Hungary* (Cambridge, MA, 1061).

Nagy, Imre (1896–1958). Nagy was born into a poor peasant's family. His father found occasional work on large estates and was also the blacksmith of his village. Nagy left his family's home in his early teens and found work in Budapest at the Hungarian Railroad Carriage Works. In 1914 he was drafted and sent to the Russian front during World War I. In 1916, he was captured. A year later, he joined the Bolsheviks and participated in the establishment of V.I. Lenin's regime in the newly formed Soviet Union.

In 1921, Nagy returned to Hungary upon instructions of the COMINTERN. He worked as an underground organizer of poor peasants in southwestern Hungary. He was about to be arrested, but learned of the police plans and fled to Vienna, Austria in 1928. By then, he was married and his wife and daughter accompanied him in his flight.

From Austria he returned to the Soviet Union. He worked at first at the Institute of

Agricultural Sciences in Moscow, then transferred to the Central Statistical Office. None of these positions was important enough to arouse the envy of the quarrelsome members of the exiled Hungarian communist group. Nagy refused to participate in their disputes in any case. Fortunately for him, Joseph Stalin did not consider Nagy important enough to get rid of him, as he did with most of the original leaders of the Hungarian exiles, including Bela Kun. During World War II, Imre Nagy served in a special unit of the Red Army, then was transferred to the broadcasting studio of Kossuth Radio, the propaganda arm of the Soviet Union, that broadcast propaganda programs to Hungary.

In December 1944, Nagy returned to Hungary with the other Muscovites and became minister of agriculture in the provisional government. On March 17, 1945, Nagy spoke for the government in introducing the most thoroughgoing land reform ever enacted in the country. However, in November he was removed from the ministry of agriculture and was appointed the first communist minister of the interior. But Nagy was not the ruthless, hard-hearted communist demanded by this post. He was replaced by Laszlo Rajk (*see* Rajk, Laszlo) on March 23, 1946. Two years later, Imre Nagy was named president of the parliament. By then, this institution had been thoroughly purged of the opposition. In 1951, he was appointed professor at Karl Marx University of Economics in Budapest, a post for which he was utterly unqualified. He had no university education at all, but he studied Marxism-Leninism in the Soviet Union and this was judged sufficient for a professorship.

After 1949, Nagy no longer participated in the activities of the communist leadership. He deeply disagreed with the forced collectivization then being pursued by his party. This was, of course, surprising, since he could not fail to observe the same process in the Soviet Union in the 1930s. He never openly criticized Matyas Rakosi (*see* Rakosi, Matyas) and the other Muscovite leaders and, thus, avoided the "unpleasantness" that those who did encountered.

In 1951, he was recalled from obscurity and was appointed a member of the Political Committee (Politburo) of the Communist party. After Stalin's death in 1953, the surviving successors of the dictator decided that Hungary needed a new government, less tainted by the Stalinist past than was Rakosi's. They decided that Imre Nagy should become prime minister of the country but that Rakosi should remain head of the Communist party. The problem with this arrangement was that the state and party bureaucracies were so closely intertwined that neither of them could function independently of the other. The party's apparatus was already a solidified bureaucracy that did not trust Imre Nagy. He was not implicated in the murderous purges of the 1940s and 1950s, as were the higher echelons of the *nomenklatura*, and they were afraid of Nagy's intentions in exposing their activities. Nagy believed, on the other hand, that only fundamental changes could save the tottering regime, and he did his best to bring these changes about. However, by then it was already evident that the system could not really be reformed. It could only be abolished.

But Imre Nagy was a convinced Marxist-Leninist; he believed that the Communist party was destined to save mankind, and he revered the process that had brought the party into power. Although he ordered a review of all show trials and the rehabilitation of the unjustly accused, he was unwilling to break with the system that had made the trials possible in the first place. He ordered the dissolution of the Hungarian Gulag. He ordered that investments in heavy industry be reduced and investments in light industry and agriculture increased. He reduced compulsory deliveries of foodstuffs by the collectives and announced that the peasants were free to leave the collectives if they wanted to. He also ordered the destruction of the notorious "kulak lists" in the villages, which were instruments of the persecution of wealthier rural folks. Nagy's first government lasted for twenty months.

Changes in the Soviet leadership, with the emergence of Nikita S. Khrushchev as the dominant leader and the execution of Lavrenty Beria, favored Rakosi over Imre Nagy. In February 1955, Rakosi was reappointed prime minister while retaining his post as first secretary of the Communist party. In turn, Nagy was excluded from the Political Committee as well as from the Central Committee of the party. Nagy had suffered a mild heart attack; the strains of his constant struggle with the party bureaucracy and with the other Muscovites must have affected him. Rakosi took advantage of Nagy's incapacity. He had the veteran communist expelled from the party. But times had changed by then; Stalin's best pupil, as Rakosi liked to be called, no longer had authority to have Nagy imprisoned. Nagy protested his expulsion and provided a focus for disgruntled young communist intellectuals to resist Rakosi and his supporters.

On November 10, 1955, at a meeting of the Writers' Union, the first voices were heard by communists who compared the tenets of Marxism-Leninism with the real situation in Hungary. Rakosi tried to suppress the questioning, but he could no longer use the secret police without restraint. In March 1956, the Political Committee decided to rehabilitate Laszlo Rajk, one of Rakosi's victims, and this did not bode well for the dictator. Even his closest collaborators, such as Erno Gero (*see* Gero, Erno), turned against Rakosi. In June, the Soviet leadership decided to get rid of Rakosi for good since he was an obstacle in their efforts to bring Yugoslavia back to the Soviet Bloc. They turned to Gero as Rakosi's replacement, which proved to be unsatisfactory for Hungarian communists. Gero was too closely identified with Rakosi, and he was known to be a ruthless, dogmatic person. Matters came to ahead on October 23, 1956, when university students, young communist intellectuals, and workers demonstrated in Budapest, leading to the outbreak of the revolution.

Already, in early October, Nagy had been readmitted to the party. His name was being mentioned more and more often as a replacement for the discredited Gero. Nagy spoke to the demonstrators from the balcony of the parliament's building, but he was unwilling to repudiate the previous regime as they demanded. By October 30, however, the revolution was victorious, and Imre Nagy was its premier. On November 1, Soviet armored and motorized troops began arriving in Hungary in large numbers, an ominous sign of the real intentions of Khrushchev. Nagy declared Hungary's neutrality and the country's withdrawal from the Warsaw Pact. On November 4, a massive Soviet attack of 2,000 tanks and 150,000 infantrymen stifled the revolution. Nagy and most of his cabinet sought refuge in the Yugoslav embassy. However, they were offered safe conduct to return to their homes and they left the embassy. As soon as Nagy and his friends were on the street, they were surrounded by Soviet KGB troops who forced them into closed vans, and they were all flown to Romanian exile.

In 1958, Nagy and several of his cabinet members were returned to Hungary, tried in secret, and found guilty of crimes against the socialist state. Seven of them were executed, including the rightful president of Hungary. After the executions, they were secretly buried, face down in an unmarked grave, showing that Janos Kadar (*see* Kadar, Janos) wanted to express his hatred for the martyred premier even after his death. However, Imre Nagy's story did not end there. On the anniversary of his death on June 16, 1990, he was rehabilitated and reburied with great pomp and ceremony with the attendance of about 200,000 people. Two days after Imre Nagy's reburial, his executioner, Janos Kadar, was dead.

Bibliography

Gati, Charles, *Hungary and the Soviet Bloc* (Durham NC, 1986); Peter Hanak and Held, Joseph, "Hungary on a Fixed Course: An Outline of Hungarian History," in Joseph Held, ed. *The Columbia History of Eastern Europe in the Twentieth Century* (New York, 1992); Meray, Tibor, *The Life and Death of Imre Nagy* (in Hungarian) Paris, 1972); Rothschild, Joseph, *Return to Diversity: A Political History of East Central Europe Since World War II* (Oxford, 1992).

Nemeth, Laszlo (1901–1975). A true polyhistor, in the best sense of the term, Nemeth fulfilled several roles as a writer, physician, and teacher. He became in the 1930s the leading ideologue of the Hungarian populist movement. His writings and lectures aroused great interest among young people in the country. He established a journal, called *Tanu* (Witness), which had only a limited circulation and a relatively short life, whose influence among the populists became decisive.

Nemeth had called for Hungarians to reject capitalism and communism, both of which, he judged, were incompatible with the national character. He advocated the establishment of a Garden Hungary, based on scientific agriculture, which would have created, according to him, a better life for the vast majority of the population. Nemeth never understood urban civilization; he opposed the cities as incompatible with the Hungarian national character at a time when urbanization was proceeding with leaps and bounds in Hungary.

In 1943, at a conference of the populists held at the village of Szarszo, Nemeth voiced his concern that, with the end of the war approaching, Hungarians would become involved in a fratricidal struggle from which no victors would emerge. Nemeth was a humanitarian: his works were banned by the communists, and some appeared in print only after his death.

Bibliography
Borbandi, Gyula, *Der Ungarische Populismus* (Mainz, Germany, 1976); Nemeth, Laszlo, *The Destiny of the Intelligentsia* (Budapest, 1944) (in Hungarian); ——, *Preparations: Before the Witness* (Budapest, 1941) (in Hungarian).

Nyers, Rezso (1923–). Nyers, a printer before World War II, joined the Hungarian Social Democratic party. After the merger of the social democrats and communists, Nyers was appointed a member of the central apparatus of the Hungarian Socialist Workers party. He attended the Karl Marx Economic University in Budapest and received his diploma in 1956. In June 1956, he was appointed minister of food industry, and he remained at that post even during Imre Nagy's brief premiership during the revolution. When Janos Kadar (*see* Kadar, Janos) became Hungary's dictator, Nyers was appointed secretary for food supplies. Between 1957 and 1960, he was director of the Alliance of Trade Unions. He was then appointed minister of finance and held this office until 1962. For the next twelve years, Nyers was working as a secretary of the Political Committee, the Politburo of the Hungarian Socialist Workers party was called.

During this time, he was one of the architects of the reforms of the New Economic Mechanism (NEM), introduced in 1968. The reforms created a prosperous peasantry and a working agricultural system. In 1972, however, the hard-liners of the party leadership succeeded in slowing down the reforms since, according to them, it provided too much prosperity for the peasantry. Nyers was entrusted with cleansing the economic leadership of the advocates of reform. After he completed this task, he himself was removed from the leadership and was appointed director of the Economics Institute of the Hungarian Academy of Sciences. He remained in that post until 1981. However, he did not earn the gratitude of the leaders since he continued his advocacy of reforms.

In the mid-1980s, Nyers joined the group of reformists who were increasingly restive and demanded the complete overhaul of Hungary's political and economic systems. He was used by the leadership in various capacities but was not given support for the reforms. In 1988, Nyers was one of the spokesmen of the reformists who removed Kadar from the head of the party, and he was a member of the group that formed the Socialist party of Hungary in 1989. In the 1990 elections, Nyers was elected a parliamentary deputy, and he is currently the most important member of the Socialist party in parliament.

Bibliography
Swain, Nigel, Hungary: *The Rise and Fall of Feasible Socialism* (Oxford, 1992).

Patriotic People's Front. This organization emerged in 1944 at the insistence of the communists. It included the major political parties who had resisted the Germans, and it provided the basis for a provisional government and provisional parliament, established in the city of Debrecen in December 1944. After the conquest of power by the communists, however, the People's Front simply became a front organization. It was a mass group whose tasks included the fostering of "proletarian internationalism," that is, the dedication of Hungarians to the cause of world revolution led by the Soviet Union.

When Imre Nagy (*see* Nagy, Imre) came into power in 1954, he was able to use the National People's Front as an instrument in trying to curb the powers of the state and party bureaucracies. He was not successful because the front's leaders were communist bureaucrats who were loyal to Nagy's opponents. Yet the National People's Front eventually served as a forum for outspoken communist reformers during the mid- and late 1980s. By then, the president of the front was Imre Pozsgay (*see* Pozsgay, Imre) and he skillfully used his organization to prod the leadership toward reform. When the communist system collapsed, however, the Patriotic People's Front disappeared together with the other communist front organizations.

Bibliography

Kovrig, Bennett, *Communism in Hungary from Kun to Kadar* (Stanford, CA, 1979).

Peace Treaty of 1947 with Hungary. A Hungarian state delegation was summoned to Paris in the summer of 1947 to sign a peace treaty with the victorious Allies; however, the "treaty" that was presented to the Hungarians was not a treaty at all. It was the collection of decisions that had been arrived at by the four Allies after they had listened to spokesmen of the Successor States for advice. The Hungarians tried to challenge some of the harsher provisions of the proposal but in vain. The peace treaty returned all territories awarded by Germany and Italy to Hungary in 1938–1941 to their previous states. This meant the restoration of the Trianon borders of Hungary with the loss of about 3 million ethnic Hungarians. Hungary was also required to pay hundreds of millions of dollars worth of future products in reparations to the Soviet Union, Czechoslovakia, and Yugoslavia; with the dismantled factories and other equipment carried away by the Soviet army, the peace treaty presented a tremendous burden for the postwar Hungarian state.

Bibliography

Kertesz, Stephen D., *Between Russia and the West: Hungary and The Illusion of Peacemaking, 1945–1947* (Notre Dame, IN, 1993); Romsics, Ignac, *Wartime American Plans for a New Hungary: Documents from the U.S. Department of State, 1942–1944* (New York, 1992).

Pocspetri Case in Hungary (1949). When the newly established communist government ordered the confiscation and nationalization of all church schools, there were some open expressions of discontent with the decree. In the village of Pocspetri in southern Hungary, several hundred citizens demonstrated against the decree. The mob surrounded a policeman whose gun was accidentally fired and he shot himself. The policeman in question was a communist. Next day, several hundred police, led by Laszlo Rajk (*see* Rajk, Laszlo), then minister of the interior, surrounded the village and arrested about a hundred inhabitants. These were brutally tortured, until they "admitted" conspiring for the murder of the victim. The organizer of the demonstration, a young clerk in the council house, was charged with murder and executed. The leadership of the village, including the local teacher, the parish priest, and some wealthier peasants were also tried, and sentenced to long imprisonment. The local teacher, called Som, spent twenty-four years in jail. The case was used by Rakosi (*see* Rakosi, Matyas) and his supporters to intensify their campaign against what they called the clerical reaction, and was a preliminary for the persecution of church leaders.

Bibliography
Aczel, Tamas, and Meray, Tibor, *The Revolt of the Mind* (London, 1960).

Populist Movement in Hungary. Hungarian populism emerged in the early and mid-1930s, when a group of young intellectuals, university students, and writers began to survey the rural communities. Their purpose was to provide an accurate measure of the people's living conditions as well as social habits and customs in the rural areas. These young people, called the "village explorers," were excellent writers and propagandists of their cause. In countless monographs, they detailed life in the villages on the pattern of Gyula Illyes' (*see* Illyes, Gyula) book, *People of the Puszta*. Jozsef Darvas, Imre Kovacs (*see* Kovacs, Imre), Tibor Tardos, and many others opened the eyes of the public to the often miserable and brutal life led by the poor peasants. They were soon joined by Laszlo Nemeth (*see* Nemeth, Laszlo) a schoolteacher, and ideologue of a so-called Third Road for Hungarian society. Nemeth proposed that Hungary should not follow either the socialist or the capitalist model of development, but a third road between the two, one that would preserve the essentially "Hungarian" characteristics of society. The populists believed that the Hungarian peasantry, long the so-called backbone of the nation, must be provided with a decent standard of living, and that they should not be exploited in the interests of the urban centers. For most of them, Budapest was "sin city," in that it was dominated by "aliens," namely, ethnic Germans and Jews who allegedly ran a conspiracy to keep the peasants ignorant, uneducated subjects, not citizens of a free Hungary.

The populists were unable to attract a mass audience before World War II. They remained a small, but dedicated group of people working hard for the realization of their aims. Since the Horthy regime, according to the populists, catered to the sin cities, they were in opposition to it. They also disliked the Germans and were willing to cooperate with anyone of the same persuasion, including the illegal Communist party.

However, some members of the populist movement went in different directions. While Imre Kovacs, Jozsef Darvas, and others proceeded to establish the March Front in 1937 as a vehicle of political opposition to the regime and, two years later, founded the National Peasant party, others moved to join the political right. The populist movement was, thus, split, and it became even less influential in Hungarian society.

In 1943, a meeting was organized for the populists at the village of Szarszo, near Lake Balaton in western Hungary, where they exchanged views and predictions about the future of Hungary. This meeting represented a catharsis for the movement, similar to what happened to another populist movement, the German Independent Youth movement in 1913 at the Hohe Meisner. In both cases, a lot of talk led to no action. During World War II, especially after Hungary was occupied by the Germans in March 1944, young populists joined the resistance. They were led by brave young men such as Sandor Kis and Pal Jonas, both of whom were to play major roles immediately after the end of the war in Hungarian politics. Both were eventually forced to leave Hungary by the communists. The populists' program was used to some extent by the communists after 1945, to win the peasantry over to their side. But the populists were simply brushed aside and were not given leading roles in politics and society.

After 1989, the populists reemerged and moved more to the right of the political spectrum. Some of their leaders, such as, for instance, Istvan Csurka, became outspoken, racist-nationalists with a large following. They represent an extreme that threatens Hungary's progress toward democracy.

Bibliography
Borbandi, Gyula, *Der Ungarische Populismus* (Mainz, 1976); Oltay, Edith, "Hungary: Csurka Launches National Movement," *Radio Free Europe Research Report* 2.13 (March 26, 1993), pp. 25-31.

Pozsgay, Imre (1933–). Pozsgay was of the generation that hardly knew any system but socialism. He grew up in Somogy county where he joined the Hungarian Socialist Workers party and became a small time apparatchik. In 1970, he began his rise in the communist apparatus. In that year, he was appointed a member of the party's Central Committee, in charge of the operations of the Patriotic People's Front. Two years later, he joined Janos Kadar's (*see* Kadar, Janos) cabinet as minister of education and immediately introduced a series of reforms in the stagnant educational system.

Pozsgay soon sought contact with the populist writers who had been relegated to the background by the regime. He also became friendly with intellectuals who were chafing under the restrictive policies of the regime. Pozsgay used the front as a shield for nonconformist intellectuals and encouraged them to step over the limits set by Gyorgy Aczel (*see* Aczel, Gyorgy), the ideological guru of the Kadar government.

By the mid-1980s, Pozsgay had become the spokesman for reform communists. In 1988, he shocked the Kadar regime when he declared that the "events" of 1956 represented a genuine popular uprising against an oppressive system.

By the end of the 1980s, Pozsgay was in the forefront of reform communists, urging the party leaders to abandon their monopoly of political power and to move toward the establishment of a pluralistic democracy. In 1989, Pozsgay was one of those who engineered the dissolution of the Hungarian Socialist Workers party. He became a leading spokesman for the new Hungarian Socialist party that separated from the hard-liners.

Pozsgay ran for the presidency of the new Hungarian republic; however, he was defeated by the successful efforts of the Alliance of Free Democrats, who obtained a sufficient number of signatures for a referendum that placed the right of electing the president in parliament. The parliament then proceeded to elect a member of the Alliance of Free Democrats for the presidency, Arpad Goncz (*see* Goncz, Arpad). After his failure, Pozsgay semi-retired from politics. In 1992, however, he participated in the establishment of a new party, called the Democratic party, that is preparing for the new elections due in 1994.

Bibliography
Pataki, Judith, "Hungary: Domestic Political Stalemate," *Radio Free Europe Research Report* 2.1 January 1, 1992), pp. 92-95; Swain, Nigel, *Hungary: The Rise and Fall of Feasible Socialism* (Oxford, 1992).

Provisional Government of Hungary in 1944. Formed on December 21, 1944, in the east Hungarian city of Debrecen (by then under Soviet occupation), the provisional government was established through sponsorship by the Soviet government. Its members were recruited from the Hungarian Communist party, the Independent Smallholders party, the Social Democratic party, the National Peasant party, and the Civic Democratic party. Heading the government was General Bela Miklos, a soldier from the Horthy regime who changed sides during the last months of the war.

The authority of this government was limited. At the time of its formation, the western part of Hungary was still occupied by the Germans who were fighting a bitter rearguard actions against the Soviet army. One of the first acts of the new government was the establishment of a political police, that soon came under the control of the communists. It would have been easy for the communists to seize power right after World War II, but they were restrained by Joseph Stalin, who was not yet sure of the extent of Soviet power in Eastern Europe.

The provisional government proved itself to be extraordinarily effective in restoring essential services for the population. By mid-1945, the cities were being supplied with essential foodstuffs, even if these were less than plentiful. The bridges connecting the two halves of the capital city over the Danube river, destroyed by the retreating Germans, were being rebuilt, and the recovery of the economy was on its way. The provisional government also introduced land reform, providing incentives for the peasants to increase their production. By the time the elections took place, the foundations for Hungary's recovery from the devastations of the war were well in place.

Bibliography
Fejto, François, *The History of the People's Democracies* (Paris, 1971); Nagy, Ferenc, *The Struggle Behind the Iron Curtain* (New York, 1948).

Rajk, Laszlo (1909–1949). Rajk was a university student in Budapest in 1930 when he joined the underground Communist party. In 1936, he was sent to Spain to fight in the civil war and, at the end of the war, he ended up in a French prisoner of war camp. He escaped from the camp in 1941 with the help of an American, Noel Field, who worked for the Unitarian Services Commission in Europe. Rajk returned to Hungary and was named secretary of the illegal Communist party. He was one of the leaders of the resistance against the Germans in 1944 and was captured. He was saved from harm by his brother, a high-ranking official in the Hungarian fascist party, the Arrow Cross. Rajk was taken to a German concentration camp from which he returned to Hungary in May 1945. He was soon appointed minister of the interior, and he directed the terror against the opponents of the communists.

In the summer of 1948, Matyas Rakosi (*see* Rakosi, Matyas), the chief Hungarian communist, was summoned to Moscow where he was informed that Rajk was an agent of various Western intelligence services and that he maintained his connections with them through Noel Field, who was still active in humanitarian services in Western Europe. Upon his return to Budapest, Rakosi removed Rajk from the ministry of the interior and appointed him minister of foreign affairs. Rajk's successor in the interior ministry was Janos Kadar (*see* Kadar, Janos). Preparations for Rajk's arrest and show trial began immediately. Soviet KGB generals Likacsev and Makarov were sent to Budapest to supervise the preparations. General Bielkin (real name: Abakumov, the deputy commander of the KGB) personally arrested several coworkers of Rajk and subjected them to inhuman tortures. They extorted "confessions" from them concerning Rajk's alleged treasonous activities. Noel Field was lured to Prague with the promise of a teaching position at Charles University and was arrested. He was transferred to Budapest and made to "confess" his own intelligence activities, implicating Rajk.

On May 19, 1949, Rajk was arrested together with his wife. Their one-year-old son was taken from them and placed in an orphanage under a different name. Rajk was tortured for several weeks, but he did not break. Finally, Rakosi sent Kadar to Rajk to convince him that he should admit his alleged crimes as a service to the party. Rajk was to serve as an example of "rampant Titoism" and to show that Titoism was the equivalent of Western imperialism.

In September, Rajk and his fellow conspirators were tried in a Budapest court. They confessed to everything with which they had been charged. They admitted the absurd charge that they served the CIA and the British and French intelligence services, and they had conspired with Josip Broz Tito for the overthrow of the East European People's Democracies. Rajk and seven of his alleged collaborators were convicted of all charges. Lazar Brankovic, a Yugoslav intelligence officer attached to the Yugoslav embassy in Budapest, received a sentence of life imprisonment. Rajk, general Gyorgy Palffy (Oesterreicher), and two other defendants were sentenced to death and executed. Two others received long prison terms. After this, other show trials were conducted, spreading terror on all levels of Hungarian society, especially among the members of the Communist party.

On October 6, 1956, Rajk was rehabilitated. The party officials admitted that he had been innocent of the charges, and they held a lavish funeral for him, which was attended by almost 200,000 people. This proved to be the preliminary skirmish of the Hungarian Revolution of 1956.

Bibliography

Fejto, François, *The History of the Peoples Democracies* (Paris, 1971); Gati, Charles *Hungary and the Soviet Bloc* (Durham, NC, 1986).

Rakosi, Matyas (1892–1971). Rakosi was one of the founding members of the Hungarian Communist party in 1918 and was a commissar in Bela Kun's first communist government in March-August, 1919. After the collapse of the Hungarian Soviet Republic, Rakosi fled to the Soviet Union. He became a member of the Soviet Communist party. However, he had no talent for learning languages and spoke a broken Russian. In 1924, he was sent back to Hungary by the COMINTERN to bring the moribund underground Communist party back to life. He lasted for about a year. In 1925, he was arrested and sentenced to eight years in prison. When his term expired, he was retried and convicted of crimes that he had committed in 1919. This time, his sentence was life imprisonment. In 1940, however, Rakosi, together with other communists, was sent to the Soviet Union. He lived there through World War II as the first secretary of the Hungarian Communist party. By then, the original leaders of the Hungarian Soviet Republic were mostly dead. They had been killed in Joseph Stalin's purges of the 1930s.

Rakosi returned to Hungary in December 1944 as the leader of the reorganized Hungarian Communist party. He engineered the communist takeover of 1948. He liked to be called the "best pupil of Comrade Stalin," and he did indeed copy Stalin's terroristic methods completely. After 1949, he became the most outspoken, often vulgar opponent of Titoism and repeatedly denounced Josip Broz Tito and his entourage as the "chained dogs of the imperialists."

After Stalin's death, Rakosi's excesses were too much even for his Soviet patrons. In June 1953, he was summoned to Moscow with other Hungarian communist leaders and was ordered to pass the premiership to Imre Nagy (*see* Nagy, Imre), who had not been implicated in Rakosi's reign of terror. In 1955, however, Rakosi succeeded in maneuvering himself back to power and had Nagy expelled from the leadership and eventually from the party. He reversed Nagy's policies and threatened the population with the return of Stalinist terror. In the summer of 1956, however, he was finally ousted by the Soviet leaders and sent to the Soviet Union into exile. He died there in 1971.

Bibliography

Aczel, Tamas, and Meray, Tibor, *The Revolt of the Mind* (London, 1961); Fejto, François, *The History of the People's Democracies* (Paris, 1971); Gati, Charles, *Hungary and the Soviet Bloc* (Durham, NC, 1986); Kovrig, Bennett, *Communism in Hungary from Kun to Kadar* (Stanford, CA, 1979).

Ranki, Gyorgy (1930–1988). Ranki came from a prosperous, middle class Jewish family. During 1944, he was taken to a concentration camp in Hungary and transported to Auschwitz together with his parents. They all perished, except the fourteen-year-old Gyorgy. After World War II, Ranki returned to Hungary and was educated at the Jewish High School and Eotvos Lorant University. While at the university, he joined the Hungarian Communist party. After graduation, Ranki became a member of the Historical Institute of the Hungarian Academy of Sciences. In 1976, he was named deputy director of the institute. He worked together with Ivan T. Berend, and many of their works were published under their joint imprint. In 1982, Ranki succeeded Zsigmond Pal Pach as the director of the Historical Institute. He was an excellent organizer and had a good judgment of human nature. His closest coworkers were Berend (*see* Berend, Ivan T.), Peter Hanak (*see* Hanak, Peter), and Ferenc Glatz (*see* Glatz, Ferenc). Ranki traveled extensively abroad. He was elected honorary member of the faculty of Oxford University, and he taught at Cambridge University as a guest professor. He was elected vice president of the World Historical Association. In the early 1980s, Ranki was invited as a guest professor to the University of Indiana at Bloomington, Indiana, where he spent one semester a year thereafter. He established a Hungarian Studies program at that university which, continues to function today. Ranki became very ill in 1988, and he died of cancer that year. His legacy includes voluminous works on Hungarian history, dealing with the period of the twentieth century. Some of his books were translated into English and were published in the United States.

Bibliography

Glatz, Ferenc, ed. *Modern Age—Modern Historian: In Memoriam of Gyorgy Ranki, (1930–1988)* (Budapest, 1990).

Religious Policies in Communist Hungary. The religious allegiances of Hungary's population were not uniform. About 60 percent of the population belonged to the Roman Catholic church; the majority of the rest belonged to various Protestant churches. About 80,000 Jews live in Hungary today, evenly distributed among conservative and reform Judaism. Regardless of religious affiliations, most of the people identified themselves with Western cultural and religious traditions, sharply separated from those confessing Orthodox Christianity in the southern belt of Eastern Europe. Religion in general and religious institutions in particular have always represented a serious obstacle to Marxist-Leninists whose ideology took on a distinctly Russian, that is eastern, character in Hungary. Jozsef Cardinal Mindszenty (*see* Mindszenty, Cardinal Jozsef), the archbishop of Esztergom in the years immediately following World War II, was considered by most Roman Catholic Hungarians as a courageous prelate, an inheritor of the mantle of leadership of his statesmen-churchmen predecessors. By 1948, Cardinal Mindszenty was the last outspoken critic of the communist system being imposed on Hungary. In spite of constant threats and efforts at intimidation, he spoke out for legality and respect for basic human rights. He was also a vociferous defender of religious education in the schools and of his church's right to maintain a large educational establishment in Hungary. This position had, as its logical consequence, the necessity for Mindszenti to defend the huge land holdings of the church that were included in the land reform and distributed among the peasants in 1945.

The Hungarian communists simply could not afford to let the outspoken cardinal become the focus of opposition. His defense of Hungarian national interests in the face of Soviet pressures was especially unwelcome. His frequent pastoral letters, read in the churches, warned people about the incompatibility of Marxism-Leninism and religious beliefs. All this enraged Matyas Rakosi (*see* Rakosi, Matyas) and the rest of the Muscovites. Communist propaganda took an ever harsher tone toward Mindszenty and the religious institution he represented. He was smeared as a Nazi and a reactionary, intent on the prevention of socialist construction. Finally, the cardinal was arrested, subjected to torture, and sentenced to life imprisonment in a show trial.

Between 1949 and 1956, the communist regime exerted brutal pressure on all religious institutions in Hungary. Priests and ministers were jailed or sent to concentration camps. Some of them were simply murdered. Religious orders were dissolved, their houses and other properties were confiscated, and their members were imprisoned. Nuns who served as teachers in schools and nurses in hospitals were driven out of their institutions. Religious instruction, even in the churches, was forbidden. The state conducted a vicious atheistic propaganda campaign through the schools and its mass organizations. Church officials were intimidated, and religious people were dismissed from their jobs. The remaining practicing priests and ministers were closely watched by the secret police, their sermons often censored before delivery. In this atmosphere, the Protestant churches fared somewhat better than the Catholic church. Their laymen-presbyteries were more easily infiltrated by the secret police, and some of their leaders were crypto-communists in any case. In 1948, the leaders of the Calvinist and Lutheran churches signed agreements with the state formally agreeing to support the building of socialism in Hungary. The Catholic episcopate found it hard to hold out alone. In 1950, it was also compelled to sign an agreement with the communist government in which it promised to support government policies.

In spite (or, perhaps, because) of oppression and persecution, the loyalty of religious people to their churches had hardly diminished. Many of the disrobed priests and ministers continued to receive help from their parishioners. In 1956, during the Revolution, Jozsef Cardinal Mindszenti was liberated from prison, but after the Soviet reimposition of communist rule, he found asylum in the embassy of the United States in Budapest.

After the severe retribution meted out to the Hungarian people, the Soviet-installed Kadar regime began to relax its religious policies. In the mid-1960s, the state began to seek the voluntary cooperation of the Christian churches in building socialism. It initiated a discussion between Marxists and Christians. It joined in the celebration of the four-hundredth anniversary of the establishment of the Calvinist church in

Hungary in 1967. Three years later, it also supported the celebration of the millennial anniversary of the conversion of the first Christian king of Hungary, Saint Stephen. Church leaders were invited to participate in the activities of the National People's Front. The party leaders were even issuing praises for the churches' role in inculcating citizens with their moral teachings. The churches were encouraged to establish relations with Hungarian exiles abroad, including ethnic Hungarian minorities in the surrounding communist states of Eastern Europe.

After the collapse of the communist regime in 1989, the freely elected Hungarian parliament expressed its support for religion in general and for individual churches in particular. However, in line with the rules of democracy, church and state remained separate institutions. The new law of compensations enabled churches to apply for the restitution of confiscated buildings—although not landed properties—including monasteries and convents. Over 10,000 requests for buildings were received. The new government of Jozsef Antall (*see* Antall, Jozsef) removed all state restrictions on religious practices. Freedom of religion and of conscience were fully restored.

Bibliography
Laszlo, Leslie, "Religion and Nationality in Hungary," in Pedro Ramet, ed. *Religion and Nationalism in Soviet and East European Politics* (Durham, NC, 1989).

Revai, Jozsef (1889–1959). Revai was a true intellectual, a gifted writer and essayist of considerable talent. He was born into a middle-class Jewish family and received a university education. In 1919, he was a minor functionary in the first communist government in Hungary headed by Bela Kun. After the fall of the Soviet Republic, Revai found asylum in the Soviet Union. During the 1920s and 1930s, Revai worked for the COMINTERN. He kept a low profile, and escaped the bloody purges that decimated the Hungarian exile community in the Soviet Union.

In 1944, Revai returned to Hungary as a member of Matyas Rakosi's (*see* Rakosi, Matyas) inner circle and became, in 1948, minister of culture and education. He was responsible for the Stalinization of Hungarian cultural life. Revai tried hard to imitate the behavior of his Soviet example, the Russian ideologue Andrey Zhdanov. He ordered the changing of curricula at every level of schooling to include heavy doses of Marxism-Leninism. He forced Hungarian writers and artists to conform to the tenets of "socialist realism," portraying the allegedly eager cooperation of all the people in the building of Stalinist-style socialism. As the result of Revai's dogmatism and rigidity in directing cultural policies, followed by the enforcement efforts of the secret police, Hungarian cultural life was saturated by propaganda. It extolled the "achievements" of Soviet "socialist men" and denigrated Western culture as decadent, being on the verge of collapse.

In October 1956, Revai once again took refuge in the Soviet Union. In 1957, however, he was permitted to return to Hungary. He died two years later, a discredited, obscure man.

Bibliography

Held, Joseph, "Cultural Developments," in Stephen Fischer-Galati, ed. *Eastern Europe in the 1980s* (Boulder, CO, 1981); Aczel, Tamas, and Meray, Tibor, *The Revolt of the Mind* (London, 1961).

Revolution of 1956. On October 23, 1956, University students demonstrated in Budapest in front of the statue of General Joseph Bem. Bem was a Polish officer who had joined the Hungarians in 1848 in their revolt against Habsburg domination. The students were expressing their solidarity with the Polish uprising in Gdansk a few weeks before. They demanded the democratization of Hungarian life and the appointment of the communist Imre Nagy (*see* Nagy, Imre) to head the government. They marched to the National Broadcasting studio and demanded that their twelve-point program be broadcast to the nation by the station. Secret policemen, stationed inside the building, opened fire on the unarmed demonstrators. Seeing the outrage, soldiers and regular policemen gave their arms to the students who then besieged the building. In another part of the city, at Heroes' square, a crowd of workers and ordinary citizens began dismantling a giant statue of Joseph Stalin. They had to use welding torches, but they cut down the bronze dictator at his boots.

Erno Gero (*see* Gero, Erno), who replaced the discredited dictator, Rakosi (*see* Rakosi, Matyas), just returned from the island of Brioni, where he visited Josip Broz Tito, mending fences with the Yugoslav dictator. He ordered the introduction of martial law and asked for the intervention of Soviet troops stationed in Hungary. By midnight, Soviet tanks were on the streets of Budapest. They turned the fighting into a national revolution against Soviet colonialism. The fighting increased in ferocity through the next few days. The Hungarian army remained neutral, some of its units disintegrated. The secret police disappeared. Imre Nagy finally became prime minister and Gero left for the Soviet Union. Fighting spread to other cities, and the revolutionaries began to hunt down the hated secret police. On October 28, a new government was formed. The Communist party also disintegrated, but its skeletal higher leadership remained in existence. Janos Kadar was the new first secretary, and he endorsed the revolution.

On October 25, a terrible massacre took place. A crowd of thousands gathered in front of parliament, and secret police troops stationed on the roof of an adjacent building opened fire on them. Some Soviet tanks, whose crews befriended the demonstrators, eventually silenced the gunners. By then, about 300 people were dead and hundreds were injured. This aroused such ire in the population that a large crowd besieged the Communist party headquarters, which was defended by low-level secret police men. They were routed, and several were murdered by the mob. By October 28, the fighting had quieted down. A cease-fire came into effect and Soviet tanks were being withdrawn from the streets of Budapest. Independent worker's councils were being established in factories, and similar councils took over the municipal governments. The government announced the dissolution of the secret police. By October

30, fighting had stopped and the revolution was victorious, but the Soviet leadership decided to send in huge reinforcements to subdue the Hungarians.

Imre Nagy declared the abolition of the one-party state. A new coalition government was formed under his leadership that included representatives of former political parties that had been suppressed by the communists. General Pal Maleter (*see* Maleter, Pal) was appointed minister of defense, and Miklos Vasarhelyi was named minister of information. General Bela K. Kiraly, freshly out of hospital and prison, was appointed to head the new national guard, composed of soldiers, policemen and revolutionaries. Sandor Kopacsi (*see* Kopacsi, Sandor) was appointed deputy commander of the guard. By November 3, the government was in complete control of the situation. On November 3, Janos Kadar fled to the city of Szolnok on a Soviet tank, where, on the following day, he declared the formation of a new government under Soviet auspices. Simultaneously, huge Soviet forces attacked the city of Budapest and other centers of the revolution. The Soviet Union sent 2,000 tanks and 150,000 motorized infantry to subdue the Hungarians. Fighting continued until December. By January, about 200,000 Hungarians had fled to Austria. The revolution was over.

Kadar's counterrevolutionary government took over and, for a time, reestablished the Stalinist system in Hungary. His vengeance against the population was terrible. Hundreds were executed with or without trial, and tens of thousands were incarcerated. The terror lasted until 1963, when the regime felt secure enough to relax its pressure on the population.

Bibliography

Arendt, Hanna, "Reflections on the Hungarian Revolution," *Journal of Politics* 20.1 (February 1958); Fejto, François, *Behind the Rape of Hungary* (New York, 1957); Kecskemeti, Paul, *The Unexpected Revolution: Social Forces in the Hungarian Uprising* (Stanford, CA, 1961); Kiraly, Bela K., *The First War Between Socialist States* (New York, 1984); Lasky, Melvin J., ed. *The Hungarian Revolution* (New York, 1957); Lomax, Bill, *Hungary 1956* (London, 1976). Meray, Tibor, *Thirteen Days That Shook the Kremlin* (New York, 1959); Molnar, Miklos, *Budapest, 1956: A History of the Hungarian Revolution* (London, 1971); *United Nations Report of the Special Committee on the Problem of Hungary* (New York, 1957); Vali, Ferenc, *Rift and Revolt in Hungary* (Cambridge, MA, 1961).

Salami Tactics. Between 1945 and 1947, the Hungarian communists conducted a relentless campaign for the dismemberment of the moderate government coalition, led by the Smallholders party. Popular politicians of that party were singled out one by one, and they were relentlessly assailed as "reactionaries" or "enemies of the people." This was the infamous salami tactics boasted about by Matyas Rakosi (*see* Rakosi, Matyas). By mid-1945, the politicians of the pre-World War II regime were either in jail or in exile in the West. Many of them were anti-Nazi, but they were also anticommunist. Many of them were charged with crimes they never committed.

The tactics worked. In 1946, the moderate right of the Smallholders party, led by Dezso Sulyok, Sandor Kis, and others, was eliminated. They were charged with the "crime" of insufficient enthusiasm for "Soviet help" in restoring Hungary's "sovereignty." In the same year, Karoly Peyer and Anna Kethly (*see* Kethly, Anna), leaders of the Social Democratic party were eliminated, because they opposed the cooperation of their party with the communists.

In 1947, the turn of the other leaders of the Smallholders party arrived. First, Bela Kovacs (*see* Kovacs, Bela), the first secretary of the party, was arrested by Soviet KGB agents in the Hungarian parliament's building, since he was a deputy elected by the people. Then twenty-two other deputies were forced out of the Smallholders party, including Kalman Salata and others, charged with conspiracy against the state. Finally, Ferenc Nagy (*see* Nagy, Ferenc), the prime minister, was charged with being involved in an antistate conspiracy. He was, however, out of the country and he resigned after his son was delivered to him in Switzerland.

By 1948, the salami tactics had worked and the oppositional parties were destroyed piecemeal.

Bibliography

Kovago, Jozsef, *You Are All Alone* (New York, 1969); Nagy, Ferenc, *The Struggle Behind the Iron Curtain* (New York, 1948).

Social Changes in Communist Hungary. Society has undergone substantial alterations during forty-four years of Communist rule in Hungary. The former middle class, small as it was, completely destroyed. It was replaced by the class of party-and state bureaucrats, privileged intellectuals, industrial managers, whose numbers swelled during these decades, and collective farm managers. The *apparatchiki*, that is, members of the apparatus, were stratified according to their position in the hierarchy. The upper echelons had access to special stores where they could buy consumer goods not available to the general public at reasonable prices. In the 1980s, the apparat was rejuvenated with economic, and other experts, whose living did not entirely depend upon the party. This group was better educated than the rest of society and, toward the end of communist rule, were approaching a dominant position in society. At the lower ends, one could find the pensioners and the unskilled workers, especially in the collective farms. They lived in poverty well below minimum standards of living.

The communists proclaimed the equality of the sexes and, because of the enormous demand on labor for the expanding industries, women entered the labor force in large numbers. This had a serious effect on traditional family life. The state provided child care in state nursing homes, giving itself yet another opportunity to indoctrinate the next generations in communist teachings.

At the same time, large numbers of peasants were forced off the land and entered the industrial labor force. By the mid-1970s, a large number of villages had few people left residing in them, mostly old women and men who continued to work in the collective farms. The government introduced policies for villages which unified school systems, and students were often bused for long distances, or were provided boarding schools. Villages whose population included few children were often completely abandoned. By the end of the communist era, the ratio of people living from agricultural labor was reduced from 55 percent in 1945 to about 18 percent in 1990.

The peasantry was, however, increasingly stratified as the years went by. Because of the economic reforms of the late 1960s, there emerged a group of well-to-do peasant entrepreneurs who worked their household plots and sold their produce in the markets of nearby cities. They were increasingly prosperous, and they practically rebuilt the villages. By the end of the 1970s, the typical peasant house was a thing of the past in Hungary. Villages were paved, they had electricity, and the roofs of new houses sprouted television antennas. Most of the new houses were built with indoor pluming, running water, and indoor toilets. Visitors were struck not only by the changed villages, but also by the cemeteries; they were full of elaborately carved monuments, showing that peasants now even had money to spend on unnecessary consumption.

At the other end of the scale, one could find the ordinary collective farm workers who were either unable or unwilling to work two shifts (one at home, one at the job). They were generally poor, although few of them starved.

The largest group of society, and the stratum in whose name the communists ruled, was the least powerful and the most exploited, namely, the industrial workers. They had some opportunity to work extra hours and participate in the second economy, but not many of them were in the position to work for themselves. Not surprisingly, industrial workers were the most alienated segment of the population.

Bibliography

Konrad, Gyorgy, and Szelenyi, Ivan, *The Intelligentsia on the Road to Class Power* (New York, 1979); Lendvai, Paul, *Hungary: The Art of Survival* (London, 1988); Szelenyi, Ivan, *Urban Inequalities Under State Socialism* (Oxford, 1983).

Szakasits, Arpad (1888–1965). Szakasits, born to a working class family, joined the Hungarian Social Democratic party in 1903. He was a member of the first Soviet government in Hungary in 1919 as a member of the ministry of the interior. After 1920, he was imprisoned and spent three years in jail. Between 1925 and 1948, he was a member of the leadership of the Social Democratic party. In 1948, he was one of the signers of the document that united the Social Democratic and Communist parties in a Hungarian Worker's party. He was a member of the provisional, then the first coalition government of Hungary. After the merger of the two parties, he was one of the presidents of the new united party.

In 1949, he was appointed president of the Hungarian Republic. The following year, however, Szakasits fell victim to the purges and spent the next six years in prison. In 1956, he was released and rehabilitated. He did not participate in the Revolution of 1956 (*see* Revolution of 1956). In 1958, he was appointed by Kadar president of the Union of Journalists. A year later, he was the new president of another communist front organization, the Alliance of Hungarians of the World. He held the position until his death in 1965.

Bibliography
Aczel, Tamas, and Meray, Tibor, *The Revolt of the Mind* (London, 1961): Kovrig, Bennett, *Communism in Hungary from Kun to Kadar* (Stanford, CA, 1979).

Szucs, Jeno (1930–1988). Szucs was born into a family whose traditions included memories of lesser nobility in Hungary. He received his education at Eotvos Lorant University in Budapest and, after graduation, he joined the Historical Institute of the Hungarian Academy of Sciences. In spite of his "class alien" family background, he was accepted at the institute. Early in his career, it became obvious that he would become one of the best historians of his generation. He was a political outsider; the more remarkable is, therefore, his rapid advance in the ranks of the institute. He specialized in late-medieval history, and his works were of a path-breaking nature.

He broke into the limelight with the publication of a study on the fifteenth-century development of market towns in Hungary. He was not a prolific writer, but his works exhibited thoroughness of research and a clarity of mind characteristic of the best historians. His studies of early nationalism in Eastern Europe and of the retarded development of peripheral societies raised the attention of historians everywhere. Szucs traveled extensively, and lectured at most of the great universities of Europe and the United States. In 1988, despondent over the death of his close friend, Gyorgy Ranki (*see* Ranki, Gyorgy), and his personal problems, Szucs committed suicide.

Bibliography
Szucs, Jeno, *Towns and Handicrafts in Fifteenth-Century Hungary* (Budapest, 1955) (in Hungarian).

Tildy, Zoltan (1889–1961). Tildy, a Calvinist minister, was a small-time politician with little practical experience in running a government. After the elections of the autumn of 1945, Tildy suddenly found himself the leader of the largest political party of Hungary, the Smallholders party. In 1946, he was elected the first president of the Hungarian Republic. In 1947, when Ferenc Nagy (*see* Nagy, Ferenc) was driven out of his office as prime minister by false charges, Tildy resigned the presidency and was held under house arrest. During the Revolution of 1956 (*see* Revolution of 1956), Tildy once again came into the limelight and was appointed a member of Imre Nagy's (*see* Nagy, Imre) cabinet. However, he played no part in the major decisions made by his colleagues. In 1958, as part of the Kadar regime's terrorist campaign, Tildy was sentenced to six years imprisonment. He was freed in 1959 and died as a private citizen.

Bibliography
Nagy, Ferenc, *The Struggle Behind the Iron Curtain* (New York, 1948).

Vas, Zoltan (1903–1983). Vas was among the first members of the Hungarian Communist party. He joined Bela Kun's group in 1919 and was, after the collapse of the first Hungarian Soviet Republic, sentenced to sixteen years in prison. In 1940, the

Soviet government obtained his freedom on condition that he would emigrate to the Soviet Union. In 1945, Vas returned to Hungary as a member of the highest level of the party's leadership. He was appointed secretary of public supplies, then he became the mayor of the capital city, Budapest. He was then appointed head secretary of the Economic Council of State, and finally, he became the head of the State Planning Office.

In 1951, however, Vas was expelled from the Communist party and became a victim of the purges. In 1955, he joined Imre Nagy's (*see* Nagy, Imre) circle and became a close friend of the communist politician. In 1956, Vas was deported to Romania together with the Imre Nagy group. When he was permitted to return, he was not indicted and was permitted to live as a private citizen. He never again participated in politics. Toward the end of his life, he was busy writing his autobiography which was not permitted to be published for years. Only after the collapse of communism could his widow finally publish his work.

Bibliography

Fejto, François, *The History of the People's Democracies* Paris-(London, 1971); Vas, Zoltan, *Sixteen Years in Prison* (Budapest, 1953) (in Hungarian); ———, *My Forbidden Book* (Budapest, 1990) (in Hungarian).

Veres, Peter (1897–1970). Veres, born into a very poor peasant family, starved more often than not. He was a self-educated man. He wrote about the life of the peasants, and early in his life he became involved with politics in the Smallholders party. He became a member of the group of populist writers (*see* Populist Movement in Hungary) who considered him a genuine peasant intellectual (most of the others were at least two generations removed from peasant life).

In 1945, Veres became a member of the leadership of the National Peasant party and, together with Ferenc Erdei (*see* Erdei, Ferenc), favored close cooperation with the communists. In 1946, he was appointed minister of agriculture, and, in 1947, he became minister of defense. He was also a parliamentary deputy.

He was considered by most people to be a strange man. Many of his colleagues regarded him as a buffoon. He appeared in parliament and in the ministry in traditional peasant dress, in a black suit with high boots, and no necktie. He was a willing tool of Matyas Rakosi (*see* Rakosi, Matyas), not because he was evil, but because he had little inkling of politics.

In the early 1950s, he was slowly eased out of office. Between 1954 and 1956, he was president of the Writers' Union. As such, he supported the rebellious young writers and demanded the appointment of Imre Nagy (*see* Nagy, Imre) to the premiership. He was a member of the reorganized National Peasant party during the revolution (*see* Revolution of 1956). With the establishment of the Kadar regime, Peter Veres retired from politics. He died in obscurity in 1970.

Bibliography
Aczel, Tamas, and Meray, Tibor, *The Revolt of the Mind* (London, 1961); Ferenc Nagy, *The Struggle behind the Iron Curtain* (New York, 1948).

Year of Great Change in Hungary, 1948. The year of 1948 was significant for Eastern Europe and for Hungary for more than one reason. This was the year of the Berlin Blockade, and the overthrow of the democratic government in Czechoslovakia. It was also the year in which the first signs of a rupture in Joseph Stalin's empire had appeared, in the dispute between Josip Broz Tito and Stalin.

In Hungary, this was the year in which the communists completed the conquest of power in every sphere of national life and when Stalinization began in earnest. The leaders of the opposition either were under arrest, or, like Ferenc Nagy (*see* Nagy, Ferenc), Dezso Sulyok, and Zoltan Pfeiffer, had been driven out of Hungary. The most forceful Smallholders leader, Bela Kovacs (*see* Kovacs, Bela), was carted off by the KGB to the Soviet Gulag.

Terror was institutionalized. Any citizen suspected of having the wrong attitude toward the Soviet Union and the Communist party could find himself in prison or in a concentration camp. The nationalization of industry was completed in 1948, and the Communist party began discussing forcible collectivization of land. The Social Democratic party and the Communist party merged in a Hungarian Workers party with Matyas Rakosi (*see* Rakosi, Matyas) having unquestioned authority over the new party. Hungary was forced into establishing a series of bilateral treaties with the Soviet Union, tying its economy to that of the Soviet state. Finally, this was also the year in which the Central Planning Office became the sole authority for directing the Hungarian economy.

The National Front policy was abandoned; the Communist party acquired a monopoly of power and would not permit any deviations from its policies. The oppositional political parties were dissolved. Only the communist stooge, the National Peasant party, survived in a nominal form, but its only independent-minded leader, Imre Kovacs (*see* Kovacs, Imre), was now in exile.

In January 1949, Hungary became a member of the Council of Mutual Economic Assistance (KGST), the Soviet response to economic integration in Western Europe. Zoltan Vas (*see* Vas, Zoltan), a member of the Muscovite group of communists, was appointed head of the National Planning Office. By mid-1949, a new constitution was passed by a subservient parliament solidifying the communist gains; the last private industrial enterprises were nationalized, and Stalinist methods of production, the Stachanovite method, was being pushed on the workers. A "kulak list" was established in the villages to single out wealthier peasants for despoliation, and compulsory delivery of food at confiscatory prices was the law. The managers of companies owned by Western firms were arrested and put on trial for alleged sabotage, and relations with the Western democracies were frozen.

Bibliography
Nagy, Ferenc, *The Struggle Behind the Iron Curtain* (New York, 1948); Swain, Nigel, *Hungary: The Rise and Fall of Feasible Socialism* (London, 1992).

СССР

**НАРОДНЫЙ КОМИССАРИАТ
ВНУТРЕННИХ ДЕЛ**

" марта _ 1940 г.
№ 794/Б

г. Москва

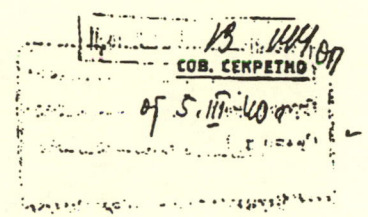
СОВ. СЕКРЕТНО

от 5.III.40

ЦК ВКП(б)

товарищу СТАЛИНУ

В лагерях для военнопленных НКВД СССР и в тюрьмах западных областей Украины и Белоруссии в настоящее время содержится большое количество бывших офицеров польской армии, бывших работников польской полиции и разведывательных органов, членов польских националистических к-р партий, участников вскрытых к-р повстанческих организаций, перебежчиков и др. Все они являются заклятыми врагами советской власти, преисполненными ненависти к советскому строю.

Военнопленные офицеры и полицейские, находясь в лагерях, пытаются продолжать к-р работу, ведут антисоветскую агитацию. Каждый из них только и ждет освобождения, чтобы иметь возможность активно включиться в борьбу против советской власти.

Органами НКВД в западных областях Украины и Белоруссии вскрыт ряд к-р повстанческих организаций. Во всех этих к-р организациях активную руководящую роль играли бывшие офицеры бывшей польской армии, бывшие полицейские и жандармы.

т. Калинин - за.
7 Чагакович - за

The first page of Beria's March 5, 1940 memorandum to Stalin proposing that the Polish prisoners be shot. The first signature is Stalin's.

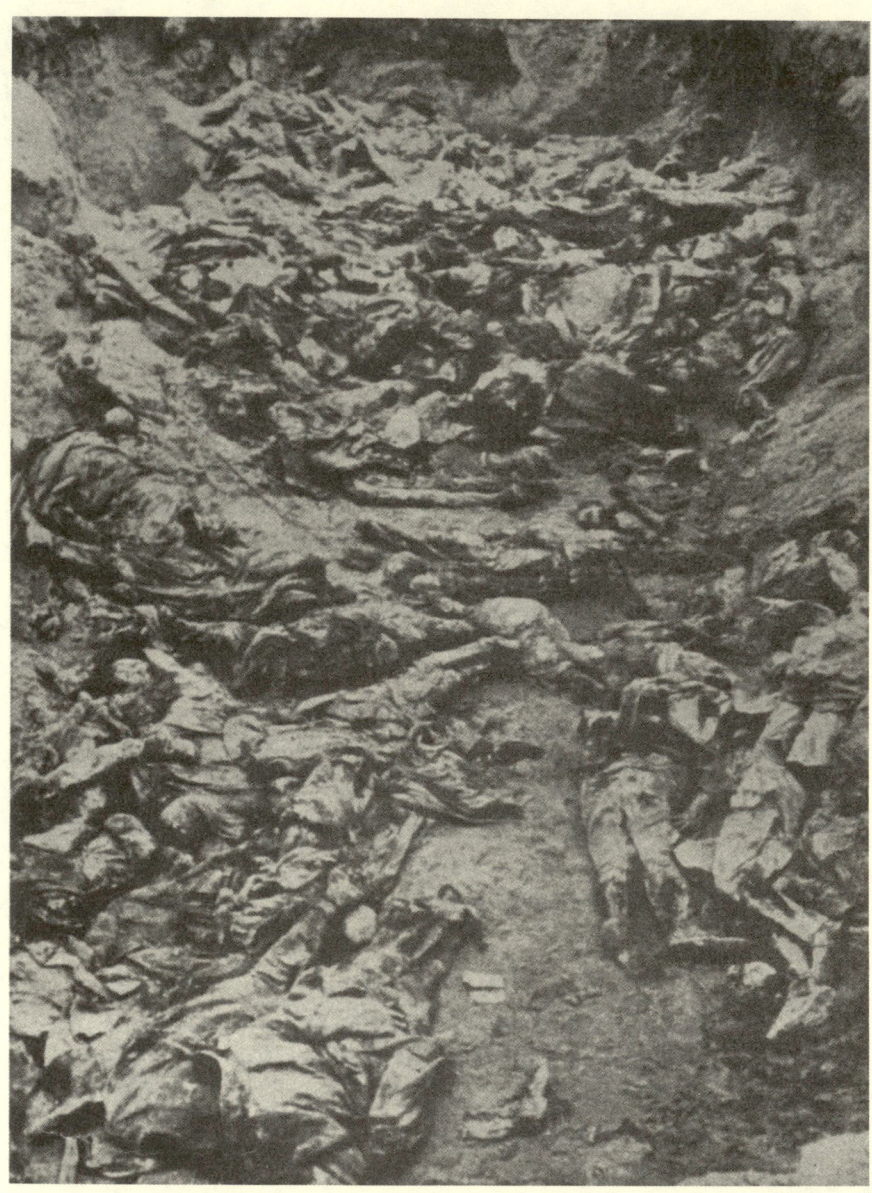
One of the mass graves of the murdered Polish officers unearthed by the Germans in the Katyn Forest near Smolensk

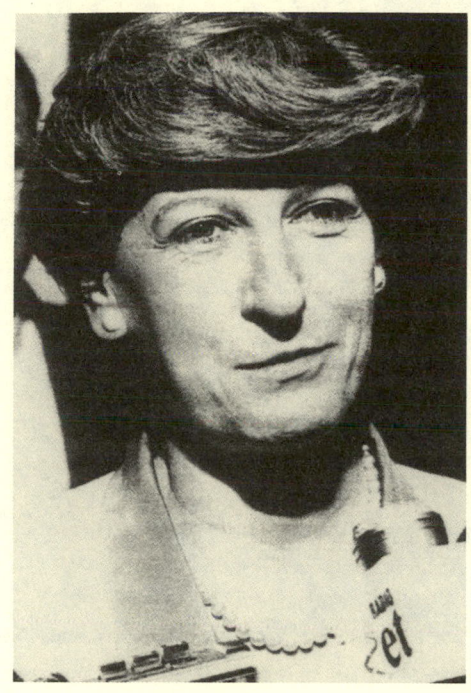

Hanna Suchocka, prime minister of Poland in 1993

Boleslaw Bierut, Polish party chief and prime minister (Library of Congress)

Konstanty Rokossowski, Soviet army general, appointed Polish minister of defense. He was sent home in 1956 by Wladislaw Gomulka. (Library of Congress)

Wladislaw Gomulka, Polish party chief between 1945 and 1951, when he was ousted. Brought back to power in 1956, he was ousted again in 1970. (Library of Congress)

The meeting of the heads of state and Communist parties participating in the Warsaw Pact Alliance in Warsaw, Poland (Library of Congress)

Leonid Brezhnev (on left), Todor Zhivkov, Bulgarian party leader and Josef Cyrankiewicz of Poland at a meeting of the leaders of the Warsaw Pact (Library of Congress)

Todor Zhivkov of Bulgaria (on left), Josef Cyrankiewicz and Wladislaw Gomulka in Warsaw, Poland (Library of Congress)

Standing in line for food in Bucharest, in socialist Romania (Library of Congress)

Going for milk in Bucharest (Library of Congress)

Entrance to the V.I. Lenin Collective farm in Romania (Library of Congress)

Street scene in the ancient Transylvanian city of Brasov, Romania (Library of Congress)

Nicolae Ceausescu, secretary general of the Romanian Communist party, president of the Socialist Republic of Romania

Petru Groza, prime minister of Romania in 1946, transferred power to the Communists

Gheorghe Gheorghiu-Dej, secretary general of the Romanian
Communist party

Tito at his headquarters in 1944

Edward Kardelj, a close aide to Tito

Alexander Rankovic, minister of the interior and head of the secret police

Koca Popovic, an important aide to Tito

Roduljob Colakovic, an important aide to Tito

Peasants in the countryside in the former Yugoslavia (Library of Congress)

POLAND

General Information. *Area:* 312,677 square kilometers (120,725 square miles). *Population:* 37,811,000 in 1988. *Urban dwellers:* 60 percent of the people; 40 percent live in rural areas. *GNP:* $65 billion. *Railroad network:* 23,707 kilometers in 1985. *Road network:* 153,000 kilometers. *Ethnicity:* 98 percent Polish, 35,000 Jews, 300,000 Belorussians, 25,000 Gypsies. *Borders:* In the north, Poland sits on the Baltic sea; in the east, it borders on Latvia, Lithuania, and Russia: in the west, the Oder-Neisse line separates Poland from Germany; in the south, Poland borders on Slovakia and the Czech Republic. *Major cities:* Warsaw, the capital city, Lodz, Cracow, Wroclaw, Poznan, Gdansk. *Geography:* The land is mostly flat, except in the southwest where the Carpathian Mountains separate Poland from Slovakia and the Czech republic.

Bibliography

Korbonski, Andrzej, "Poland, 1918–1990," in Joseph Held, ed. *The Columbia History of Eastern Europe in the Twentieth Century* (New York, 1992), pp. 229–276; Halecki, Oscar, *Poland* (New York, 1955); Heymann, Frederick, G., *Poland and Czechoslovakia* (New York, 1965); Morrison, James, F., *The Polish People's Republic* (Baltimore, MD, 1968).

CHRONOLOGY

1944   *August.* After encouraging the Polish Home Army to begin its uprising against the Germans in Warsaw, the Red Army stopped its advance and permitted the Germans to destroy the Home Army in addition to leveling the Polish capital.

1945   *January.* Soviet troops entered what was left of Warsaw.

April. The Lublin Committee of National Liberation, a group of Polish communists who were in the Soviet Union during the war, signed a treaty of friendship and cooperation with the Soviet Union. The Soviet government gave its recognition to the Lublin Committee as the provisional government of Poland.

June. The provisional government of Poland formed a cabinet with twenty-one ministers. Sixteen ministers came from the Lublin Committee; five from the Polish government in exile in London.

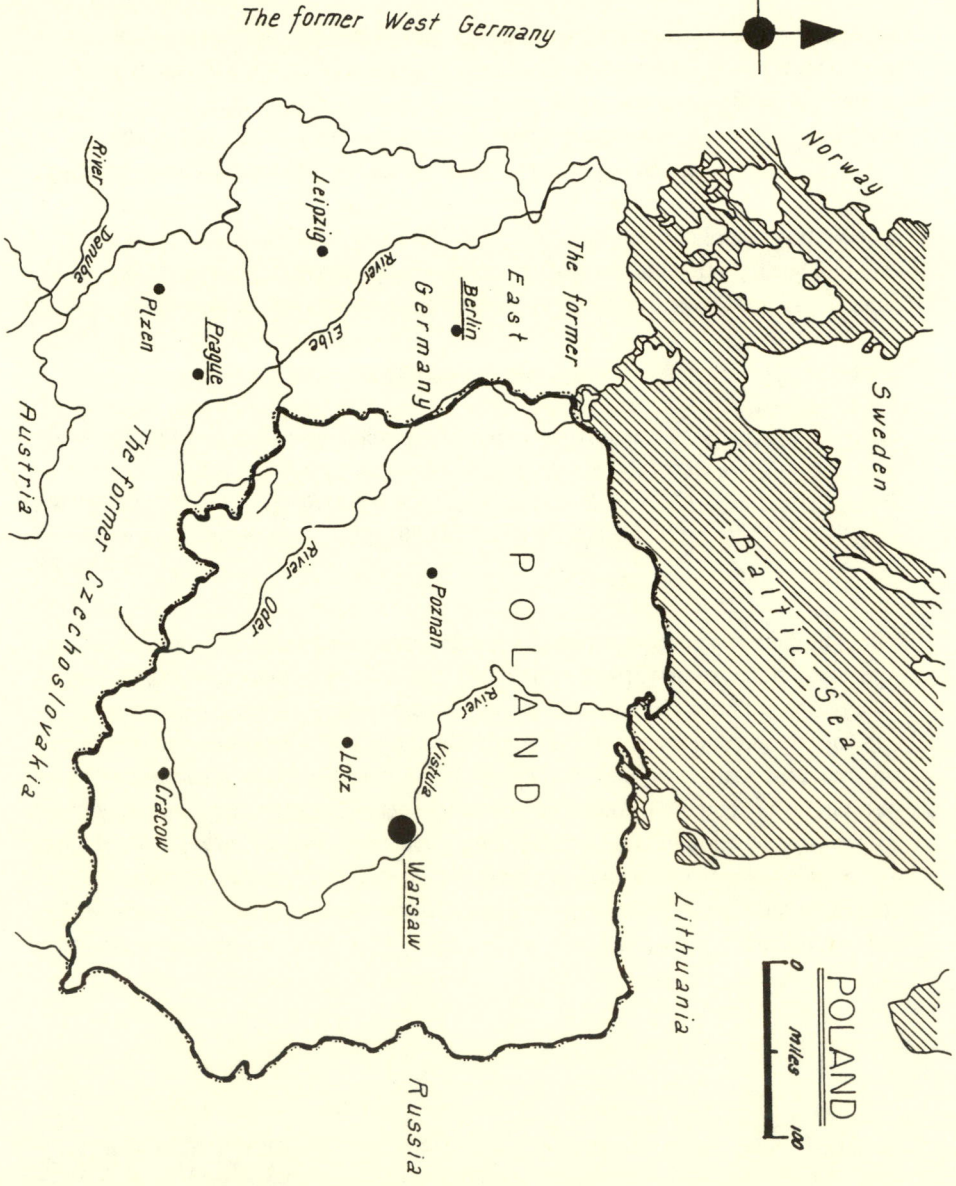

The former West Germany

Norway

River Danube

Leipzig

Plzen

Prague

River Elbe

East

Germany

Berlin

The former

Austria

The former Czechoslovakia

River Oder

Poznan

P O L A N D

Lotz

Vistula River

Sweden

Baltic Sea

Lithuania

Cracow

Warsaw

Russia

POLAND

0 miles 100

1947 *January.* In rigged elections, the Polish Socialist Workers party (a name the communists adopted), participating in a so-called Democratic Bloc, won 384 seats in a 444-seat parliament. Stanislaw Mikolajczyk, head of the London-Poles, remained prime minister for only eight more months; then he was hounded out of the country. The new prime minister was Wladislaw Gomulka, a Muscovite communist, also the first secretary of the Polish Socialist Workers party.

1948 *December.* The Polish communists forced a merger of their party with the Polish Socialist (Social Democratic) party, creating the Polish United Workers party and, incidentally, eliminating their competition in the workers' movement.

1949 *January.* Poland joined the newly formed Council of Mutual Economic Assistance, an organization intended to match the European Common Market.

1950 *July.* Poland signed an agreement with East Germany according to which the border between the two states would be the Oder-Neisse line, as it was established by Soviet pressure in 1945.

1953 *September.* Polish secret police arrested Stefan Cardinal Wyszynsky, head of the Polish Roman Catholic hierarchy, and interned him in a monastery.

1955 *May.* Poland signed the Warsaw Pact Treaty, integrating the armed forces of the Soviet bloc countries under Soviet command. The commanding general of the Warsaw Pact forces was always to be a Soviet general.

1956 *April.* Wladislaw Gomulka, former first secretary of the Polish United Workers party, who had been arrested in 1951 on charges of nationalist deviation, was rehabilitated and freed from prison.

June. The Polish government announced sudden price increases for essential food products. In response, rioting broke out in the city of Poznan. The Polish army was ordered to fire on the workers demonstrating against the increases. More than 50 were killed and 300 were wounded. This brought down the regime.

October. Against some Soviet opposition, Gomulka was reappointed to head the Polish government as well as the Polish United Workers party. He immediately eased some restrictions on the people and rescinded the price increases.

1966 *April.* Foreign visitors who had planned to attend the celebrations of 1,000 years of Polish Christianity, were refused permission to enter the country.

1967 *April.* Twenty-four European Communist parties attended a meeting held at Karlovy Vary, Czechoslovakia. Polish delegates supported the Soviet Communist Party's bid for reasserting Soviet domination. The bid was unsuccessful.

1968. *August.* Polish troops joined the Soviet Union and three other Warsaw Pact countries in the invasion of Czechoslovakia, ending the experiment of "Socialism with a human face."

November. At the Polish United Workers party's congress, Soviet communist boss Leonid Brezhnev announced the so-called Brezhnev doctrine. According to this doctrine, a threat to socialism in any socialist country would be considered a threat to the entire Soviet Bloc, and would bring on a response by the Warsaw Pact.

1969   *June.* A meeting of seventy-five Communist and Socialist parties was held in Moscow. The Polish delegates strongly supported the Soviet demand for the condemnation of the Chinese, but they did not achieve their aim.

1970   *December.* The Polish government once again raised consumer prices suddenly, without prior notice. A repetition of the riots of 1956 occurred, this time beginning in the city of Gdansk. Edward Gierek replaced Gomulka as head of the Polish government and party. He immediately rescinded the increases and raised the wages of industrial workers.

1975   *July.* The Helsinki Accords were signed by delegates of the Polish government. The accords declared the security of European state borders and guaranteed basic human rights for the people.

1978   *October.* Karol Cardinal Woytila, elected the new pope, took the name of Pope John Paul II. By then, Cardinal Wyszynsky had been released from detention, and some cooperation between the Roman Catholic hierarchy and the Polish government was worked out.

1979   *June.* Pope John Paul II visited his homeland. Huge crowds greeted him everywhere, greatly embarrassing the atheistic Polish communist government.

1980   *August.* Gierek's government ordered sudden increases for consumer goods. The usual response resulted: A wave of strikes hit the industrial centers. By August 20, over 120,000 workers were on strike in the city of Gdansk alone. The strikes resulted in the emergence of a new, free trade union, Solidarity, led by electrician Lech Walesa. The government accepted Solidarity and recognized the workers' right to strike.

September. Striking Polish workers returned to work. Stanislaw Kania replaced Edward Gierek as the Polish leader. The Soviet Union provided $260 million for aid to Poland. The United States provided aid to the amount of $670 million in the form of food deliveries.

October. The communist Polish government officially recognized the legality of Solidarity. Sporadic broadcasts of Roman Catholic church services became more frequent in Poland.

December. Several communist members of the Polish parliament resigned, among them Edward Gierek.

1981   *January.* The Polish government, in discussions with Solidarity, agreed to the establishment of a 41.5-hour workweek and the publication of a newspaper by the trade union.

February. General Wojciech Jaruzelski was appointed new prime minister.

For the first time in the history of the communist movement, a military man replaced the party secretary as head of government.

April. The Polish government accepted the right of farmers to form their own union.

June. A struggle in the Polish party leadership resulted in victory of general secretary Kania.

August. A general strike was proclaimed in Poland in response to the government's new price increases and cuts in food rations. Prices of bread and cereals were tripled.

September. The first national congress of the Solidarity trade union was held in the city of Gdansk, and its leaders announced that membership had reached 9 million.

October. General Jaruzelski replaced Kania as general secretary of the Polish United Workers party.

December. General Jaruzelski declared martial law in Poland. The leaders of Solidarity were arrested and detained. The trade union was declared outside the law.

1982 *January.* The Common Market declared restrictions on trade with Poland and the Soviet Union. NATO members also introduced sanctions.

May. Huge demonstrations occurred in Warsaw. Mass arrests of men, women, and even children followed.

October. Jaruzelski ordered the dissolution of all trade union organizations. New laws restricted the right to strike for political reasons.

November. Lech Walesa and members of the leadership of Solidarity were released from prison.

December. Martial law was suspended in Poland.

1983 *June.* Pope John Paul II visited Poland for the second time. He discussed the situation in Poland with both General Jaruzelski and Lech Walesa.

July. President Stanislaw Jablonski declared that the emergency in Poland was over. An amnesty was proposed, but members of Solidarity's leadership were not included.

October. Solidarity leader Lech Walesa received the Nobel Peace Prize. The Soviet Union announced that new missile bases were being established in Poland.

1984 *July.* Six-hundred-fifty-two political prisoners in Poland received amnesty.

October. Father Jerzy Popieluszko, an adviser to Solidarity, was kidnapped and murdered by four secret police officers. The minister of the interior reported that members of his organization confessed to murdering the Roman Catholic priest.

1985 *February.* A secret police colonel and a captain received jail sentences of twenty-five years each for the murder of Father Popieluszko. Two lieutenants, who participated in the atrocity, were sentenced to fifteen years each.

April. Poland signed a ten-year extension of the Warsaw Pact Alliance.

November. General Jaruzelski was ousted as Polish prime minister. His replacement was Zbigniew Messner, a professor of economics. Jaruzelski remained first secretary of the Communist party and president of the state.

1986 *January.* Jaruzelski, still in power, appointed a new Polish ambassador to the Soviet Union as part of his efforts to get rid of hard-line communists in important positions.

1987 *February.* President Ronald Reagan lifted the remaining sanctions on U.S.-Polish relations.

November. A referendum proposing severe austerity measures was defeated. Solidarity, still illegal, urged rejection of the proposal.

1988 *January.* The Polish government announced its intention to eliminate most state subsidies in order to create a market-based economic system. Price increases were to be offset by wage increases.

April. Workers in the city of Bydgoszcz held a wildcat strike lasting twelve hours. At the end of the strike, the government granted a 63 percent wage increase to the workers. The strike was organized by an official transport workers' union. By the end of the month, labor unrest had spread throughout the country.

August. Upper Silesian miners struck for higher wages and the legalization of Solidarity. Lech Walesa called for discussions with the government. As a result, most strikers returned to work by September.

1989 *February.* Discussions between Solidarity leaders and the government were finally under way. The opposition journal *Odrodzanie* published a report on the Katyn massacre of 14,000 Polish officers and intellectuals by the Soviet KGB. Myeczislaw Rakowski, the Polish prime minister, attended a play by Vaclav Havel, the Czech playwright, in Warsaw. He deplored the imprisonment of Havel for political reasons in Czechoslovakia.

May. Lech Walesa received the Human Rights Prize of the Council of Europe.

June. In the national elections, Solidarity candidates won 92 seats out of 100 in the Senate and 160 of 161 seats in the lower house (Sejm).

July. U.S. president George Bush arrived on a visit to Warsaw. He lunched with the Walesa family and laid a wreath for the memory of workers killed during the strikes of 1970. The Polish Citizen's Parliamentary Caucus refused to join a communist-led government. Members of Solidarity followed their lead.

August. The Polish senate declared that the invasion of Czechoslovakia by Warsaw Pact armies in 1968 should be condemned. Walesa announced that Solidarity was ready to form a government of its own without the communists. President Jaruzelski nominated Tadeusz Mazowieczki for the post of prime minister. The senate approved the appointment.

1990 *January.* The Polish United Workers party announced the dissolution of its organization. Its members formed a new party, the Polish Social Democratic party.

March. Polish government sources reported that inflation had dropped to the 10 percent level the previous month.

April. All censorship was abolished by the Polish parliament.

May. Lech Walesa acknowledged the growing split between the blue-collar and intellectual wings of Solidarity. The latter was headed by prime minister Mazowieczki.

July. Jaruzelski announced that he would make room for an elected president for Poland by the end of the year. Soviet oil deliveries to Poland were reduced by 30 percent.

September. General Jaruzelski resigned as president of Poland by asking parliament for a date to end his service.

November. West German diplomats in Warsaw signed an agreement recognizing the existing frontiers between Poland and Germany as permanent. Lech Walesa won the national elections for the presidency of Poland. General Jaruzelski, on leaving office, apologized for all the misdeeds committed by the communists against the Polish citizens during the four decades of their rule.

December. Walesa appointed Jan Krysztof Bielecki as the new prime minister of Poland. Free elections resulted in the entrance of ten major and eleven minor parties into parliament, fragmenting the political process.

1991 *January.* Bielecki was not accepted as prime minister. In his place, Walesa was compelled to appoint Jan Olszewski.

February. Trade with the former Soviet Union virtually collapsed. This caused a crisis of the budget, and many firms were threatened by bankruptcy. In contrast, private economic activity increased.

August. The new electoral law, proposed by the lower house of parliament (Sejm), created a large number of minuscule parties that lacked cohesion, further fragmenting politics.

September. Private firms accounted for 19.1 percent of industrial production, 43 percent of construction, and 70 percent of sales. They created 1.6 million new jobs altogether.

October. Share trading began in a new stock market, ironically located in the former communist Central Committee building in Warsaw.

November. In spite of increased privatization, industrial production declined by 14 percent in the first nine months of the year. Unemployment was at 11 percent.

December. After a two-month stalemate, the Sejm approved a new cabinet headed by Jan Olszewski. Poland established diplomatic relations with South Africa.

1992 *March.* The parliament rejected the economic plan introduced by prime minister Olszewski. He announced that, if the redrawn budget were also rejected, he would resign. Discussions about broadening the coalition government commenced.

May. Three former members of the riot police (Zomo) of the communist era were arrested and charged with causing eleven deaths during the period of martial law. The prime minister dismissed the heads of national radio and television. Many opposition politicians perceived the move as a return to government control of the media. Calls for the resignation of government in the Sejm were heard. Finally, Walesa asked parliament to replace Olszewski as prime minister.

June. Parliament approved a law that excludes all former police agents from public life. It also declared no-confidence in the Olszewski government. Waldemar Pawlak, chairman of the Polish Peasant party, was his replacement. A list of suspected former secret police collaborators was distributed in parliament by the ministry of internal affairs.

July. Two secret police generals, accused of organizing and approving the murder of Father Jerzy Popieluszko, were indicted and put on trial. They both pleaded not guilty. Parliament finally approved Pawlak's new cabinet, but the government did not last long. Hanna Suchocka, the first woman prime minister, was finally approved by parliament.

August. Thousands of veterans converged on Warsaw to celebrate the Polish victory over the Soviet army in 1920. Various independent trade unions threatened strikes if the workers' living conditions did not improve. Solidarity was skeptical about a new wave of strikes. A new presidential-parliamentary system of government was approved by the Sejm. The strikes called by six radical unions fizzled out.

September. Former prime minister Piotr Jaroszewicz and his wife, a former communist journalist, were found murdered at their home. A "little constitution," providing enlarged powers for the president, was approved by a narrow vote.

October. Former interior minister Jozef Kiszczak testified at the trial of two secret police generals that the KGB had been behind the murder of Father Popieluszko.

November. Prime minister Suchocka visited Pope John Paul II in Rome. Discussions began between government and trade union representatives about a new social compact. President Walesa signed little constitution, enhancing his powers.

December. Disputes ranged about the interference of the Roman Catholic church in Polish politics. Most public opinion polls reported opposition to an enhanced role of the church.

1993 *January.* Polish diplomacy began to focus on three major goals; securing Poland's borders, insuring cooperation with Poland's neighbors, and impeding international crime and drug trafficking. The second goal was helped by the formation of the Visegrad Triangle, a cooperative association with Hungary and Czecho-Slovakia, named after the town where it was formed. The release of the Katyn documents by Boris Yeltsin, proving that Stalin and the Soviet Politburo had personally approved the KGB murder of 26,000 Polish officers and other members of the Polish intelligentsia, had a cathartic effect in Poland.

February. Discoveries that some arms dealings by individual firms were illegal created an effort in the Sejm to bring the armament industry under close supervision. The 1993 state budget was approved by parliament.

March. Poland's relations with its eastern neighbors began to focus on economic issues, showing that preoccupation with security had become unnecessary. Nevertheless, Poland intends to pursue admission to NATO. Zbigniew Dyka, minister of justice, resigned because of indiscretions committed during an investigation. Gabriel Janowski, Poland's minister of agriculture, resigned. His resignation was a protest against the setting of minimum prices for food products lower than he recommended. Polish agriculture has been stagnating during the three years following the collapse of communism.

May. A strike by 600,000 teachers and health workers issued a challenge to the government of Hanna Suchocka. Solidarity's participation in the strike added special significance to it. The government considered the strike a sign of irresponsibility on the part of the unions. The fiftieth anniversary of the Warsaw ghetto uprising was commemorated in Poland. The Sejm issued a no-confidence vote in the government. President Walesa then decided to dissolve parliament and schedule new parliamentary elections. Germany and Poland signed an agreement concerning asylum-seekers from the east.

June. New elections were scheduled for September. The new electoral law, signed by Lech Walesa after the Sejm passed it a few hours before the no-confidence vote, stipulated that a minimum of 5 percent of the votes was necessary for parliamentary representation, and 8 percent for coalitions. President Walesa vetoed a bill that would have increased pensions but would also have destroyed the budget. A concordat was signed between Poland and the Vatican. It regulated state-church relations and created a special commission to regulate the financial conditions of the church in Poland. The prime minister announced in a speech that the government had no choice but to continue the economic reforms, painful as they might be.

Baginski, Kazimierz (1910–). Baginski was an active member of the Polish Peasant party during the interwar years. After the German and Soviet occupation of Poland in 1938, he was a leader of the underground organization of the Peasant party, heading the organizational department. He escaped in 1942 and became the director of the interior department of the Polish government in exile in London. He was entrusted with maintaining relations with the Polish Workers party, organized by the "Initiative Group" of Polish communists, headed by Marceli Nowotko, in 1941 (Among the secretaries of the Polish Workers party was Wladislaw Gomulka (*see* Gomulka, Wladislaw), who later became the communist leader).

In 1945, Baginski was arrested by the Soviet KGB, along with fifteen other members of the underground, controlled by the London-based Polish government. He was released, but soon afterward, in 1946, he was arrested again. In April 1947, he was tried and sentenced for 8 years in prison on trumped-up charges, among which collaboration with the Germans was the most ridiculous. However, later in the same year, he was pardoned by Boleslaw Bierut (*see* Bierut, Boleslaw), the communist chief and prime minister. In November 1947, he escaped to the West and spent the rest of his life in exile.

Bibliography

Polonsky, Antony, and Druiker, Boleslaw, *The Beginnings of Communist Rule in Poland* (London, 1980); Staar, Richard F., *Poland, 1944–1962: The Sovietization of a Captive People* (New Orleans, LA, 1962).

Bierut, Boleslaw (1892–1956). Bierut joined the Polish Communist party in 1933. It is likely that he was also an agent of the Soviet KGB, at least after 1936. In 1943, he was chosen by Joseph Stalin to head the newly organized Polish Workers party. He was then sent to Nazi-occupied Poland to direct guerrilla warfare directed by the underground communist organization. Jointly with Edward Osobka-Morawski and Marshall Rola-Zimierski, Bierut chaired the Polish Committee for National Liberation (the so-called Lublin Poles). This was a group of communists and fellow travelers directed by Moscow.

In June 1945, the legislative branch of the Polish national government, called the National Council of the Homeland, was formed under the presidency of Boleslaw Bierut. This appointed body was under the domination of the Muscovite Polish communists. Bierut remained president of the Polish legislature. First secretary of the Polish Workers party, Wladislaw Gomulka (*see* Gomulka, Wladislaw), was its vice-premier. After the fraudulent elections of 1947, conducted under the watchful eyes of the Soviet army command and the Soviet KGB, Bierut was confirmed as president of the Polish republic. When attending the Twentieth-Congress of the Soviet Communist party in the spring of 1956, he died unexpectedly.

Bierut had modest talents as a leader. However, while he was in office, he managed to spare Poland the show-trials that racked the other East European countries. His policies toward the Polish peasants were, however, as ruthlessly exploitative as those of Stalin. He was also an anti-intellectual, which attitude often manifested itself in the decisions he made. His successor, Edward Ochab (*see* Ochab, Edward) was only an interim leader who paved the way for the return of Wladislaw Gomulka, purged in 1950, to power.

Bibliography
Bain, Leslie B., *The Reluctant Satellites* (New York, 1960); Korbonski, Andrzej, "The Polish Communist Party, 1938–1942," *Slavic Review* 16.3 (September 1967), pp. 436-444; Mikolajczik, Stanislaw, *The Rape of Poland: Patterns of Soviet Aggression* (New York, 1948).

Brystygierowa, Julia (1902–1980). She was an early member of the Polish Communist party and, at the same time, was active in the Ukrainian Communist party during the interwar years. During World War II, she lived in Lvov and worked on the editorial board of the underground paper of the Lvov section of the party. She was a member of the executive committee of the Union of Polish Patriots, a communist front-organization and between June and September 1944, she was a secretary of its presidium. She was also deputy secretary of the executive committee of the Union and directed the work of its organizational department. Between 1948 and 1954, Brysty-gierowa was a member of the Polish United Workers party's central control commission. Between 1944 and 1956, she was also a director of a department in the Ministry of Public Security and a member of the supersecret Committee for Public Security. In September 1956, she was removed and retired to private life.

Bibliography
Polonsky, Antony, and Druiker, Boleslaw, *The Beginnings of Communist Rule in Poland* (London, 1980).

Caritas in Communist Poland. Jan Frankowski, a shrewd Catholic layman, led this political group in communist Poland. Its origin went back to the Christian Social Society established in 1945, whose self-assigned task was to help victims of World War II. The Communist party tolerated the organization and, after the 1961 elections, permitted it to have three parliamentary deputies.

Caritas closely collaborated with the Communist party. For instance, Frankowski delivered a speech in parliament (the Sejm) in 1961, strongly supporting the elimination of two Catholic holidays from paid days of rest. He sided with the communists against the other Catholic lay organizations, PAX (*see* PAX) and ZNAK (*see* ZNAK), speaking of "uniformism" in the Catholic camp, when the church's hierarchy accused the communists of "ideological uniformism." Frankowski was revealed to have been involved in a scheme when, as vice-chairman of Caritas, he sold its subsidiary, Ars Christiana, to himself.

In 1950, the Catholic church was forced by the state to agree to the transfer of Caritas which was, until then, under church jurisdiction, to a so-called "union of Catholics," a state-controlled front organization. In turn, the state paid 243 million zlotys a year to Caritas from which 40 million went to nuns working for the organization. In 1962, the communists removed 300 kindergartens and 60 children's homes from the jurisdiction of Caritas. It still maintained hundreds of institutions for crippled children, for mentally retarded people, and for old people, cared for by nuns. About

13,000 individuals were under the care of Caritas. About 400 physicians and un-counted nuns and priests also worked for the organization. The church was worried that priests who worked for Caritas might become allies of the communist authorities just as many of those who worked for PAX and ZNAK eventually did. But the num-bers of collaborators were, in both of these cases, relatively small, and the state, al-though it would have liked to use Caritas for its own purposes, did not succeed in the effort.

Bibliography

Bromke, Adam, *Poland's Politics: Idealism vs Realism* (Cambridge, MA, 1967); Simon, Maurice D., and Kanet, Roger E., eds. *Background to Crisis* (New York, 1982).

Committee for the Defense of Workers (KOR). This oppositional organization was established in 1976 by volunteer intellectuals attempting to assist workers who had been arrested by the communist authorities in Radom during a strike as well as workers in other cities who had supported their fellow workers' movement. The com-mittee provided lawyers for the accused workers who had been charged with crimes against the state. It organized support for their families and petition drives for the reinstatement of those who had been fired because of their participation in the strikes.

The committee also organized campaigns for the dismissal of corrupt officials and factory managers and demanded an investigation of police brutality against the strik-ing students and other young people. The committee demanded the release of those who had been arrested for their political activity, and a general amnesty for the dem-onstrators. Its members informed foreign journalists of the abuses of human rights committed by communist officials and the police. The problem of the committee was that most of its members were intellectuals, and that they had few direct contacts with other social groups. The workers were wary of the committee until its intentions be-came quite clear.

After Poland signed the Helsinki Final Act of the Conference on Security and Co-operation in Europe, KOR was succeeded by the Committee for Self-Defense and other oppositional groups. All of them functioned openly in accord with the Polish constitution. The authors whose works were published by the opposition wrote under their real names. They published uncensored newspapers that were ostensibly under-ground publications, but were openly promoted.

Bibliography

Andrews, Nicholas G., *Poland 1980–1981: Solidarity Versus the Party* (Washington, DC, 1985); Misztal, Bronislaw, *Poland After Solidarity: Social Movements Versus the State* (New Brunswick, NJ, 1985).

Communist Front Organizations. Communist parties everywhere favored setting up so-called mass-organizations in order to provide the appearance of mass public support for their policies. These organizations were used in countries where the Com-munist parties succeeded in acquiring a monopoly of political control in order to mask the basic illegitimacy of the regimes, especially toward left-leaning Western intellectuals.

In Poland, such mass-organizations included the League of Soldiers' Friends, the League of Democratic Women, the Polish-Soviet Friendship Society, the League of Communist Youth, the Patriot Priests, the Association of Children's Friends, the Association of Atheists and Free Thinkers, and the Union of Fighters for Freedom. Some political parties served the same purpose, such as the Democratic party and the Polish Peasant party, whose membership consisted of cryptocommunists and whose leaders were approved in advance of their appointment by the Politburo of the Polish United Workers party. Many of these organizations also served the domestic needs of the communist leadership and were used for the mobilization of certain segments of the population for specific tasks designated by the communists. This was especially the case with two Catholic laymen's organizations, Caritas (*see* Caritas in Communist Poland) and PAX. These two groups were used to weaken the hold of the episcopate on the believers. Most mass-organizations were supervised by the secret police. In many ways, the establishment of these organizations was the substitute of the communists for a nonexistent civil society.

Bibliography

Blit, Lucjan, *Gomulka's Poland* (New York, 1968); Polonsky, Antony, and Druiker, Boleslaw, *The Beginnings of Communist Rule in Poland* (London, 1980); Staar, Richard F., *Poland, 1944–1962: The Sovietization of a Captive People* (New Orleans, LA, 1962).

Communist Information Bureau (COMINFORM). Delegates from nine Communist parties attended a meeting held at Szklarska Poreba, in Poland, on September 22–27, 1947, to establish this organization. A successor to the Third International (COMINTERN), so brilliantly used for subversion in the interwar years by the Soviet Union, the new institution was expected to be a similar tool for the post-World War II Soviet leadership. The COMINFORM rejected the notion of separate, national ways to communism, deplored the failure of the Czechoslovak Communist party to conquer power, and scolded the French and Italian Communist parties for "permitting" their exclusion from their respective governments without resorting to civil war.

Following this meeting, the consolidation and/or the conquest of communist power in East European countries was speeded up. Czechoslovakia and Hungary were brought tightly into the fold of the developing, new Soviet colonial empire, and a series of strikes and labor unrest was initiated in Western European countries. The COMINFORM helped the Soviet leadership to enforce discipline in Eastern Europe, and linked closely the countries of the region to the Soviet Union through their economies, communist parties and secret police organizations.

At its June 28, 1948, meeting, from which the Yugoslav communist delegates were absent, the COMINFORM discussed the so-called Yugoslav deviation from Marxist-Leninist doctrines and condemned Josip Broz Tito for his allegedly nationalistic actions. On May 22, 1949, the COMINFORM condemned Tito and his supporters as agents of capitalist imperialism and called on "true Yugoslav communists" to oust "Tito and his gang" from power.

Bibliography
Mosely, Philip E., *The Kremlin and World Politics: Studies in Soviet Policy and Action* (New York, 1960).

Communist Party of Poland. In December 1918, two left-wing parties, the Social Democracy of the Kingdom of Poland and the Polish Socialist, party merged and formed the Communist party of Poland. The goal of the party was to establish the "dictatorship of the proletariat" on the Leninist pattern. In twenty years' time, the party never came even close to fulfilling its goal. Following the conclusion of the Soviet-Polish war in 1920, the Communist party of Poland was declared illegal, and its leaders and membership went underground. It instigated a few minor strikes in the 1920s, and this just about exhausted its activities. The number of members remained small throughout the interwar years.

The major reason for the party's failure was its position on Polish independence. It claimed that the survival of an independent Poland not only was impossible in the long run, but also undesirable. An independent Polish state was, according to the leaders, a transitional phenomenon, a state that would soon be absorbed in the coming international socialist world. The Polish communists, therefore, wanted nothing to do with an independent Poland, and this position suited V. I. Lenin and Joseph Stalin just fine. The Polish communists also opposed the establishment and maintenance of the Polish armed forces, and they boycotted the first elections held in 1919. They wanted, above all, the absorption of Poland into the Soviet Union and were, therefore, totally alienated from the large masses of nationalistic Polish population. When, in the Soviet-Polish war, the Polish proletariat stood solidly behind its bourgeois leadership, this stand made the position of communists untenable in Poland. They were simply regarded as Russian agents—which they were—who were advancing Soviet interests under the guise of advocating social revolution. The less support the Polish communists received at home, the more they were forced to rely on the Soviet Union; thus, a vicious circle was created, depriving them of any meaningful authority.

During the 1930s, therefore, the Polish Communist party was totally subordinated to Stalin's whims. Since the Communist party of Poland had so few native followers, Stalin had decided in 1938 to dissolve the party. His reasoning was that the party harbored only spies and saboteurs. Stalin then ordered the murder of several hundred Polish communists living in exile in the Soviet Union. Ironically, the only survivors were those who were imprisoned in Poland proper. One of these was Wladislaw Gomulka (*see* Gomulka, Wladislaw).

After the German attack on the Soviet Union in 1941, Stalin declared that the Soviet Union would like to see the reemergence of a "free and independent Polish state" after the war. There was a significant cooperation between the Soviet government and the Polish government in exile, stationed in London. However, when the Polish victims of the Katyn massacre were discovered in 1943 (*see* Katyn Woods Massacre), relations between Moscow and the London Poles deteriorated and eventually ended. A small Polish contingent was formed in the Soviet Union in order to help fight the Germans, and a new Communist party, called the Polish Workers party, was formed. Gomulka, who continued to live in Nazi-occupied Poland, became the acknowledged leader of the new party. There were a few resistance fighters who proclaimed themselves communists, but their numbers were negligible when compared to those of the underground Home Army supported by the London Poles.

In 1944, the Muscovites (the surviving communists in the Soviet Union) and the home-grown communists, together with some left-wing groups, formed the Committee for National Liberation which, in time, became a Soviet-sponsored polish provisional government. The new Polish Workers party repeatedly dissociated itself from the policies of its predecessor. It rejected union with the Soviet Union and proclaimed its goal as the independence of Poland. In spite of this, the new party did not succeed in becoming popular among the masses of people. Most Poles remained loyal to the government in exile in London, and supported the Polish Peasant party at home.

The change in Soviet policies toward conquered Poland came in 1947. In September, the COMINFORM was established to coordinate the policies of all East European Communist parties with those of the Soviet Union. Gomulka, who genuinely believed in Polish independence, resisted the Stalinization of the party. The following year, the Stalin-Tito controversy came into the open, and Gomulka followed the Soviet line reluctantly. He continued to stress the Polish way to socialism as separate from those of other countries, including the Soviet Union. He stood up against the forced collectivization of Poland's agricultural sector. He was removed from the leadership in 1950 and was arrested and imprisoned in 1951. His followers were also purged from the party. But there were no show-trials in Poland, unlike in Bulgaria, Hungary, Czechoslovakia, Romania, and Albania. This was a clear sign of the fact that, although the leadership did buckle under to Stalin's demands, it did so reluctantly. Boleslaw Bierut (*see* Bierut, Boleslaw) took over from Gomulka as first secretary of the party and prime minister of Poland. Eventually, one-fourth of the party membership was purged. Although, at that time, most ordinary noncommunist Poles considered the Gomulka affair not their own, and did not care about who came out on top among the squabbling communists, the popular image of Wladis-law Gomulka changed with time. Communism was still considered "bad" per se, but Gomulka was one of its victims. His often vicious denunciation by the Stalinists increased his importance in the eyes of ordinary people.

After Gomulka's removal, the Polish Workers party and the Polish Socialist party merged to form the Polish United Workers party. The "new" organization, led, of course, by Bierut, declared its strict adherence to Marxist-Leninist doctrines and to "proletarian internationalism," that is, Soviet leadership. At least until 1954, the party accepted its subordinate role to Soviet interests. Bierut brought Poland's economic and social systems into line with Stalinist practices. In 1952, the new Polish constitution was a virtually complete copy of the Stalinist Soviet constitution of 1936. Several Polish institutions came under direct Soviet control. In 1949, Soviet Marshal Rokossowski (*see* Rokossowski, Konstanty) was appointed Polish minister of defense. The Polish secret police acquired Soviet KGB supervisors. The Soviet ambassador oversaw the affairs of the Polish state and directly intervened in everyday affairs.

In the 1950s, the changes that occurred in the Soviet leadership had their repercussions in Poland. In parallel with the fall of Lavrenty Beria, the weight of the Polish secret police in affairs of state and party was reduced, but not eliminated. Some of the victims of the Stalinist terror were released, among them was Wladislaw Gomulka. There came some relaxation over cultural life. However, there was no improvement in a mismanaged Stalinist economy that was not subject to reforms. As a consequence, discontent soon emerged among the population.

In the spring of 1956, Nikita Khrushchev decided to disband the COMINFORM and establish a new relationship with the Communist parties of Eastern Europe. Polish communists also began to speak once again of a Polish road to socialism. Stalin was roundly denounced and, in June 1956, workers' demonstrations in the city of Poznan turned into open revolt against the communists. The Polish army was ordered to fire on the demonstrators; it did and scores were killed and hundreds were wounded. This event demoralized the Polish army to such an extent that it could never again be used in such action. In March, Bierut attended the Twentieth Congress of the Soviet Communist party in Moscow and listened to Khrushchev's denunciation of Stalin's crimes. His heart had given out, and he died in the Soviet Union.

His successor was Edward Ochab (*see* Ochab, Edward), a colorless apparatchik, who tried to steer a middle-course between oppression and concessions, but was unwilling to commit the party to fundamental reforms. Gomulka was cleared of the previous charges, but his alleged "nationalist deviation" was still being condemned. Thee Poznan revolt ended Ochab's career.

The leadership of the Polish United Workers party split into two opposing factions. One of these, the so-called Natoli-faction, wanted the introduction of harsh measures, even a return to Stalinist terror, in order to end expressions of discontent. The other faction consisted of more moderate communists who wanted fundamental reforms. In July, the second faction won out, but the promised reforms did not calm the situation. The people on the streets demanded a change in leadership and, above all, they wanted Gomulka in power.

Early in August, Gomulka was readmitted to the party and was soon promoted to the Politburo. This signaled an important shift within the leadership of the party. For the first time since World War II, a group of communist leaders seemed genuinely interested in public opinion and were willing to act against Soviet advice. In late July, Nikolay Bulganin visited Warsaw and explicitly warned the Poles about taking de-Stalinization too far, perhaps even undermining the socialist system. Nevertheless, the Polish communist leaders went ahead with the formulation of extensive reform proposals.

On October 19, an uninvited Soviet government delegation, led by Khrushchev himself, appeared in Warsaw. Soviet troop movements on or near the Polish borders accompanied the visit. But the Polish army was ready to fight if necessary; General Waclaw Komar's special troops ringed the Polish capital city ready for any eventuality. Workers and students in Warsaw were now armed. The Soviet delegation stayed for one day only, it had enough time to become convinced of Polish determination. The following day, Soviet troops were ordered to return to their bases and the crisis was over. The party's Central Committee was called into session, and it approved the reforms and Gomulka's return to power.

For the next decade and a half, Polish society quieted down somewhat. The overwhelming power of the Soviet Union was acknowledged. Gomulka turned out to be a disappointment for most people. At the same time, a strong anti-Western feeling emerged among the ordinary people, most of whom believed that they had been abandoned by the Western powers. There was also rising concern with the reemergence of West Germany as a first-rate military power. The danger was, of course, exaggerated by communist propaganda, but memories of German aggression continued to linger in the public mind. Nor did German noises about the Oder-Neisse border (*see* Oder-Neisse Line) help assuage Polish fears. This played into the hands of the communist regime, since virtually the entire population supported Gomulka's policies toward West Germany. There continued to be Soviet pressure for Polish adherence to Soviet interests. Gomulka's program was relatively simple; he wanted to preserve the relative independence of the Polish United Workers party. In this, he was increasingly forced to disregard public opinion. In addition, the execution of economic reforms was sabotaged by a bureaucracy that feared the loss of its privileges. Gomulka had to satisfy Soviet demands. The ambiguities of his position eventually led Gomulka and his party into another crisis situation.

At the congress of the Polish United Workers party held in 1968, economic reforms were once again being discussed. The plan's projection included an increase in industrial production of 47 percent between 1971 and 1975, and an increase in real per capita income of 20 to 22 percent. Early in 1969, the people were told by the party that a small Polish automobile would be produced, based on plans provided by the Italian Fiat firm, that would sell for about 40,000 zlotys and would, therefore, be affordable by ordinary people. But the party leaders backed off this promise. It seems that Gomulka, quite out of touch with his people by then, considered it "too bourgeois-like" to own an automobile! The party chiefs concluded that real economic progress could be achieved only through more efficient management or more capital investments. But investments could be increased only by cutting back on consumption, especially of food, leaving more money available for the import of Western technology.

Gomulka chose the latter course. The cost of building materials was increased at first, and this simply infuriated the rural population. Consequently, production of foodstuffs was reduced. Queues before food stores began to grow in length. Gomulka became a very unpopular leader indeed. On December 7, 1970, West Germany and Poland signed a treaty, removing the threat of German designs on Polish territory. Five days later, the government announced sudden price increases of food and food products. The Baltic port cities of Gdansk, Gdynia, and Szczecin revolted. Several hundred people were killed by the secret police, and Gomulka was replaced by the Silesian communist, Edward Gierek (*see* Gierek, Edward).

The price increases were canceled. A Soviet loan was obtained to tide the economy over the crisis. The party announced a more consumer-oriented economic policy. Gierek started out the same way as his predecessor had, and, ironically, he was to end his rule in almost the same way. He listened to complaints and showed respect for ordinary people. His solution for the economic crisis was to obtain Western loans in order to import modern technology. The loans would be repaid by increased exports derived from the new technology. By 1973, Gierek felt strong enough to amend the constitution, declaring the Polish United Workers party the "leading force" in Poland and including in the documents declarations of "eternal friendship" and cooperation with the Soviet Union. When several organizations, including the Roman Catholic hierarchy raised objections to the language of the document, however, Gierek backed down and a milder version of the document was proclaimed. Gierek also changed the agrarian policies of the party. He emphasized support for state farms once again. This was shown by the fact that 70 percent of the investments in the agrarian sector went to state farms. Overall investment in agriculture was reduced. The result was a familiar one; by 1980, there were food shortages once again further undermining the party's and Gierek's prestige. In June 1976, sudden price increases were once again announced. There were renewed protests by workers, students, and intellectuals. A day after the announcement was made, the party canceled the increases; this did not mitigate crisis conditions that had emerged in every sector of the economy.

The problems had indigenous origins, yet the world recession following the oil crisis of 1973 certainly aggravated the economic conditions in Poland. In February 1980, the eighth congress of the Polish United Workers party was held. Gierek delivered a tough speech, and he did not promise improvements in the living standards of the population. On July 1, the government did it again. Meat prices were increased without prior notice. Strikes broke out in major cities, and in the Baltic ports of Gdansk, Gdynia, and Szczecin, demonstrations took place against the communist regime. Soon, Gierek was ousted.

A new phenomenon in communist Eastern Europe emerged; the free trade union of Solidarity. Although it took nearly nine years, Solidarity and the Polish people ended the rule of the Communist party in 1989 and established a freely elected government. After that, the Communist party simply withered away, and it no longer plays a decisive role in Polish politics.

Bibliography
Andrews, Nicholas G., *Poland 1980–1981: Solidarity Versus the Party* (Washington, DC, 1985); Bromke, Adam, *Poland's Politics: Idealism vs Realism* (Cambridge, MA, 1967): Dziewanowski, M.K., *The Communist Party of Poland* (Cambridge, MA, 1976), 2nd ed.; Jan T. Gross, "Poland: from Civil Society to Political Nation," in Ivo Banac, ed. *Eastern Europe in Revolution* (Ithaca, NY, 1992), pp. 57-71; Korbonski, Andrzej, "Poland 1918–1990," in Joseph Held, ed. *The Columbia History of Eastern Europe in the Twentieth Century* (New York, 1992); Stehle, Hans, Jakob, *The Independent Satellite: Society and Politics in Poland Since 1945* (New York, 1965); Syrop, Konrad, *Spring in October: The Story of the Polish Revolution of 1956* (London, 1958); Woodall, Jean, *Politics and Policy in Contemporary Poland* (London, 1982).

Communist Seizure of Power in Poland. When the Soviet Red Army crossed the Bug river (better known as the Curzon-line) in January 1944, Moscow introduced a so-called Polish Committee of National Liberation, made up mostly of formerly underground communist leaders. The committee also included members of the Union of Polish Patriots, as well as individual members of the Socialist and Peasant parties who were willing to cooperate with the communists. On January 1, 1945, the Committee declared itself the provisional government of Poland. At the same time, resistance leaders loyal to the Polish government in exile in London were arrested or were drafted into the Kosciuszko division of the Soviet-led Polish army in the eastern front.

At the Yalta and Potsdam conferences, Poland's eastern borders were modified according to Joseph Stalin's wishes. Poland was "compensated" for the losses by receiving German lands up to the Oder-Neisse rivers and the southern parts of East Prussia, the northern part of which was absorbed into the Soviet Union. The German population of the western territories was expelled and deported to defeated Germany. The same thing happened to the Polish population that came into Soviet hands.

The provisional government was accepted as the legal government of Poland after some hesitation by the Western Allies. Their objections were alleviated by the addition of some members of the exile government in London, including Stanislaw Mikolajczyk (*see* Mikolajczyk, Stanislaw). The Peasant party, led by Mikolajczyk, had 600,000 members by 1945, more than the Communist party. Nevertheless, the communists, who controlled only six of the cabinet posts, dominated the other sixteen through communist under secretaries and the secret and not-so-secret collaborators from other parties, including those from the Peasant party. They were also able to create an atmosphere of terror and intimidation with the help of the occupying Red Army and the ever-present Soviet KGB.

In 1944, the Polish Workers party, the communists, had only about 20,000 dues-paying members. This was mainly the result of their identification with Poland's traditional enemy, the successor to the empire of the tsars, the Soviet Union. However, this was mitigated to some extent by the fact that the Soviet Union unconditionally guaranteed Poland's new borders in the west, gaining some support for the communists among the population. The traditional opponents of communism, the prewar middle classes, the army officers, the Roman Catholic clergy, and the intelligentsia, had been partly exterminated by the Germans, partly by the Soviet KGB.

Prospects of advancement soon drew many more people into the Communist party. Between January 1945 and January 1946, the membership of the party increased to 210,000 and by January 1947, there were more than a half million card-carrying members of the Polish Workers party. The party, however, had no charismatic leadership, and its major enemies were not former Nazi collaborators, but the anti-Nazi underground resistance leaders. The advantages of the communists were, however, overwhelming. Stalin was determined to draw Poland into the Soviet orbit. First of all, he wanted the Soviet Union to keep the former Polish eastern territories, and only the communists could be relied on to accept this. Second, he wanted to make sure that Poland would be an active, not a passive, buffer zone between Germany and the Soviet Union. He considered Poland to be a pivotal region in the projected Soviet domination of Eastern Europe. Therefore, he supported the Polish Workers party's efforts to gain a monopoly of political power unconditionally. Since the Soviet Red Army occupied Poland, it exercised an unmatched political and economic influence. Communists were also in control of the Polish ministry of the interior, the defense ministry, and the ministry of the western territories. Thus, they had vast areas in which they could control patronage. In 1945, they quickly redistributed the large estates in Poland, giving the land mostly to poor peasants and they did the same in the newly acquired territories. This way they succeeded in undermining rural support for the Polish Peasant party.

The communists were not keen on having elections in 1945 and 1946, as the Yalta and Potsdam agreements stipulated. Instead, they had their Socialist ally propose a referendum on the abolition of the interwar bicameral legislature, the distribution of land, the nationalization of heavy industry, and the ratification of the treaty securing Poland's western borders. Mikolajczyk recommended to the Peasant party to oppose the first of the recommendations, but support the others. When the votes were counted, the Polish Workers party was "victorious." It is known that large-scale fraud was committed when the ballots were counted. This was a test of how well elections can be manipulated; thereafter, the communists no longer worried about the possible outcome of elections.

In January 1947, the national elections were finally held. The communists organized the so-called Democratic Bloc. It was composed of the socialists, the communists, and two other smaller parties. The campaign was conducted under the constant threat of terror. No wonder that the Democratic Bloc won 80.1 percent of the votes. The Peasant party received only 10.3 percent; and small parties, 1.4 percent. The Peasant party, therefore, received only 27 deputies out of a possible 444 in the Polish Sejm (parliament). The Democratic Bloc gained 394 deputies and its small allies won 7 and 12, respectively. This meant the end of any meaningful activity for Mikolajczyk and the London Poles. Mikolajczyk fled to England on October 21, 1947, and several of his followers also went into exile.

Next came the turn of the Polish socialists. The party's membership temporarily increased to 800,000, because masses of former Peasant party supporters now saw the Socialists as the only choice after the failure of the Peasant party. Soon the communists prevailed over the leaders of the Socialist party to purge their membership of "rightist" elements, and about 150,000 people were expelled from the party. Over 200 members of the middle-level leadership of the Socialist party were arrested and falsely charged with collaboration with the anti-communist resistance. The socialists had to acquiesce in the rejection of the Marshall Plan by Poland and were forced to withdraw from the Socialist International in March 1948. Finally, in December 1948, the Socialist party was forced to merge with the Polish Workers party, and the new party assumed the name of the Polish United Workers party. Power was, therefore, securely in communist hands by the end of 1948.

Bibliography

Bain, Leslie, *The Reluctant Satellites* (New York, 1960); Bliss, Lane A.., *I Saw Poland Betrayed* (New York, 1948); Bregman, Aleksander, ed. *Faked Elections in Poland as Reported by Foreign Observers* (London, 1947); Gross, Jan T., "Poland: from Civil Society to Political Nation," in Ivo Banac, ed. *Eastern Europe in Revolution* (Ithaca, NY, 1992), pp. 56-71; Lewis, Flora, *The Polish Volcano* (London, 1959); Mikolajczyk, Stanislaw, *The Rape of Poland: Patterns of Soviet Aggression* (New York, 1948); Rothschild, Joseph, *The Return to Diversity. A Political History of Eastern Europe* (Oxford, 1992); Staar, Richard F., *Poland 1944–1962: The Sovietization of a Captive People* (New Orleans, LA, 1962).

Cultural Policies in Communist Poland. When the communists came into power in Poland, they considered their tasks to be twofold. They had to destroy a class-society based on precommunist values, and they had to create the proper conditions to mold a new generation of "socialist men," whose sole aim in life would be the building of a Soviet-style socialist society. Throughout four and a half decades of communist rule, these basic goals never changed, although tactics were adjusted to the changing situations.

Cultural policies were subordinated to these fundamental goals. The old values dominant in Polish society were diametrically opposite to Marxist-Leninist values. First among the old values was Polish nationalism. This was rooted in the centuries of struggles for Polish independence against the two great empires on Poland's borders, Germany and tsarist Russia. Other values included a highly developed sense of individualism and close identification with the Roman Catholic religion. All these values were underscored by the Western orientation of the Polish people, which was anathema to communists in Warsaw and Moscow. The memories of World War II that began with the Hitler-Stalin pact at the expense of Poland, the occupation of the country by the two powers in 1939, the Katyn massacre (*see* Katyn Woods Massacre) of Polish officers by the Soviet KGB, and the negative role of the Soviet army in the destruction of Warsaw in 1944 made the Soviet orientation of the Polish United Workers party suspect in the eyes of most Polish people.

In order to combat and, if possible, destroy these values, the communists promoted

Marxism-Leninism above all else. This ideology was taught in every school from kindergarten to university, in factory seminars, and in study circles in the villages. Collectivism was stressed above individualism. Without schooling in Marxism-Leninism, no student was admitted to university studies, and all party- and government functionaries had to be knowledgeable in this ideology. The state did everything possible to curtail and, if possible, eliminate religious influences from society. Atheism was the official position of the communists, and they endeavored to impose this on the people in lieu of religion. The Catholic church, however, proved to be more resilient than the communists believed, and they were eventually forced to tone down their antireligious propaganda.

The communist apparatus spent a great deal of time and effort in promoting the "correct" ideology in every sphere of the nation's cultural life. Books approved by censors were heavily subsidized. These included a flood of books translated from the Russian, produced mostly by mediocre Soviet writers. Plays, and the cinema of the "socialist realist" variety were widely disseminated. All these efforts focused on Marxist-Leninist indoctrination and on the alleged superiority of Soviet culture over that of the West.

In line with these policies, concerted efforts were made at Russification. Russian language courses were made compulsory in secondary and higher education. Proficiency in the Russian language and literature was, with Marxism-Leninism, a major criterion for university admissions.

The state-sponsored mass organizations, such as the Association of Polish Youth, the Young Pioneers, the Democratic Women's Alliance, had as their main task the indoctrination of their membership in the party's ideology. Special attention was paid to young people. The Youth Association served as a school for preparing young people for membership in the communist party. The trade unions were strictly controlled by the communists. They also had a special cultural role to play. These institutions intended to supervise leisure time; they were in control of vacation spots and resorts, and rewarded workers with space for their vacations if they conformed to party strictures.

In the 1970s, cultural policies became somewhat more relaxed,. however, this did not mean that the communist leaders had given up their efforts to create a "new socialist man." The major vehicle to reach the goal remained the educational system. School curricula continued to focus on Marxism-Leninism and a materialist view of life. Atheism remained the official line toward religion. Nevertheless, the authorities seemed to have realized that Polish society would not be changed drastically, and that they would have to identify to some extent with Polish national pride to become halfway legitimate. Jon Szczepanski, a party-spokesman, asserted that great strides were being made in changing the intelligentsia's thinking along "scientific and rationalistic" lines which, in the party's thinking meant away from religion. The election of Polish Cardinal Woytila (*see* Woytila, Karol, Cardinal) as Pope John Paul II and his visit to his native country in 1978, where he was greeted by hundreds of thousands of people at open-air masses, provided an example of the continued power of religion in Poland. The dangers of a diluted Marxist-Leninist ideology was countered by the order of the communist leadership in 1978, tightening control over the nation's university system.

In spite of all these efforts, the most articulate, most efficient dissident movement of all the East European satellites of the Soviet Union emerged in Poland. In the 1970s, dissidents established an entire network of underground publishing houses, issuing newspapers and even magazines. The Polish communist government was powerless to stop the dissidents without resorting to outright terror. Unwilling to do this, the government resorted to periodic arrests of intellectuals and the confiscation of underground presses. It wanted to remind the dissidents that the government still had the power to act against them. Such arrests were invariably followed by protests, reminding the government that public opinion was not on its side. Nevertheless, the tone of vituperation that characterized Czechoslovak cultural life after the Warsaw Pact invasion of that country in 1968 was completely absent in Poland. The Polish dissidents (and, sometimes, the communist government), acted with prudence and circumspection.

After 1985, when Mikhail Gorbachev made it quite clear to all Soviet Bloc leaders that Soviet tanks would no longer come to their aid in domestic matters, the Polish government gradually retreated and provided greater latitude for dissident cultural activities. With the beginning of the Round-table discussions (*see* Roundtable talks in Poland) between the dissident movement and the government in 1986, all censorship was finally abolished. The press was freed of official restraints, and the compulsory teaching of Marxism-Leninism and the Russian language in schools was discontinued. The postcommunist governments ended government subsidies of cultural life which, at times, presented hardships for creative people. The rule of the market place was established in cultural life, and the Polish economy will not be able to do much for culture at least in the short run.

Bibliography

Czarnecka, Ewa, and Fiut, Aleksander, *Conversations with Czeslaw Milosz* (San Diego, 1987); Held, Joseph, "Cultural Policies," in Stephen Fischer-Galati, ed. *Eastern Europe in the 1980s* (Boulder, CO, 1981); Kridl, Manfred, *A Survey of Polish Literature and Culture* (New York, 1966); Michnik, Adam, *Letters from Prison and Other Essays* (Berkeley, CA, 1985); Milosz, Czeslaw, *The Captive Mind* (New York, 1953).

Demographic Changes in Communist Poland. The war-related losses came to over 11.5 million people, including the Jews who were exterminated by the Nazis, the Poles who were lost as a consequence of the German occupation, the people who died following the Soviet occupation of Poland, and the Germans who were expelled from the country after 1945. Nearly 6 million ethnic Poles were killed. Almost 2 million new settlers, expelled from the Soviet-absorbed eastern territories, were moved in to replace the expelled Germans. Before World War II, the Jewish population of

Poland came to about 3.5 million people. This number was reduced to 100,000 in 1945. The missing millions were burned in the crematoria of Auschwitz and other death-camps. On the other hand, Poland had lost almost all of its Ukrainian, Belorussian, and Great Russian minorities.

After the war, the Polish state emerged as an ethnically almost homogeneous state. Ninety-eight percent of the population were Roman Catholic and were ethnically Polish. There were about 250,000 Germans left in Silezia (a fact not admitted by the Polish government until 1989). There was a tremendous upsurge in the birth rate in the new Poland after 1945, especially in the former German lands. By 1961, nearly 8 million people lived in western Poland, including 1.5 million indigenous Poles. Of the Jews, about 95,000 left Poland for Israel or other western countries. Scattered groups of Gypsies and other minorities added up to about 35,000 People.

Bibliography
Bethell, Nicholas, *Gomulka, His Poland and His Communism* (London, 1972); Gruchman, Bohdan, et al., eds. *Polish Western Territories* (Poznan, 1959).

Economic Policies in Communist Poland. In 1946, the nationalization of large-scale enterprises was ordered in Poland. In theory, the former owners of these firms were to receive compensation in some form. In fact, they were lucky if they did not end up in jail or in concentration camps. The nationalization decree also ended foreign property ownership in Poland. The economy, or what was left of it after five years of occupation and war, was, by then, under complete state control. The first postwar years were spent in rebuilding the shattered system. This was helped by aid from the United Nations, which came to about $500 million between 1945 and 1947. Between 1946 and 1949, another $675 million was received, some of it from the Soviet Union. In 1947, the Polish government expressed its interest in participating in the Marshall Plan, but it was forced to withdraw on Soviet insistence. Although the Potsdam agreements stipulated that Poland should receive 15 percent of the reparations going to the Soviet Union, this paragraph of the agreement was forgotten. In addition, the Soviet army looted everything of value in the formerly German territories, removing $500 million worth of equipment and goods, leaving the lands devastated. After the expulsion of the Germans, the new Polish settlers found nothing of value in the territories except abandoned German houses. These were, however, completely empty. Most of Poland's oil resources were located in the eastern territories taken by the Soviet Union. Chemical fertilizers and other industrial needs of the agrarian sector of the country could not be supplied.

A whole new set of industries was established after 1946. These consisted mostly of heavy industrial firms, geared to the production of military hardware. Since the raw materials needed by this huge, new industrial sector had to be imported, mostly from the Soviet Union, economic dependence on the Soviet Union became overwhelming. Accordingly, most Polish trade was conducted with the Soviet Union and the other Soviet Bloc countries after 1946. Trade with western nations was reduced to a minimum. The trade agreements that Poland was forced to conclude with the Soviet Union were often unfavorable. For example, one of these agreements stipulated the delivery of large shipments of Polish coal to the Soviet Union at prices that were 80 percent lower than what Poland could have received for them on the world market. Poland also had to pay for the maintenance of Soviet troops on its territory as required, including rail and bus services.

In March 1947, however, the Soviet Union provided loans for Poland in the amount of $28.85 million. Included in the loans were blueprints for factories and other economic projects as well as for Soviet advisers. A series of technical assistance agreements were also signed in 1947 with the Soviet Union. These provided for the exchange of technical information for a nominal charge. During the period of reconstruction, these agreements contributed considerably to the Polish economic recovery.

After 1948, Poland embarked on a twofold economic policy whose parts often contradicted each other. On the one hand, the government tried to achieve self-sufficiency in industrial development; on the other, it tried a limited cooperation with the other East European states, but mainly with the Soviet Union. The government shunned western contacts, and as a corollary, tried to expand exchanges of goods with the other Soviet satellites. The confused policy resulted in an ever growing dependence on the Soviet Union for raw materials and trade. Self-sufficiency was, thus, eventually abandoned. As a consequence of this policy, all remaining enterprises were nationalized. Even individual craftsmen were forced to join collectives licensed by the state.

In 1950, a six-year plan was introduced whose aim was to make Poland into an industrialized country. The emphasis was on heavy industrial developments, and the production of consumer goods was kept at a minimum. Strict labor discipline was introduced in the factories, and work norms were gradually increased. Large numbers of former peasants entered the industrial labor force, and women were also actively encouraged to do so. Special emphasis was placed on shipbuilding together with machine and tool production. Almost all the industrial enterprises were heavily subsidized by the state.

Great stress was placed on the quantity of goods produced. In this, the Soviet Stachanovite method was introduced. The method involved the singling out of exceptional workers, providing them with all the assistance they needed in overfilling the work norms several times, then setting them up as examples for the average workers to follow. Work norms were adjusted accordingly, although the average worker was not provided with assistance similar to that received by the Stachanovites. This crass exploitation of labor created a great deal of resentment among the factory workers, but the workers did not have trade unions to defend their interests. The so-called trade unions in industrializing Poland were state controlled. Their task was to support state policies in setting work norms, on the one hand, and to reinforce labor discipline, on the other.

Nevertheless, there were visible results of the great efforts put into industrialization. New firms emerged such as the Zeran automobile factory in Warsaw and a giant steel production firm at Nova Huta. New shipyards were created at Gdansk (the former Danzig) and Gdynia on the Baltic cost. Soviet production standards were adopted in all Polish factories that helped further to remove them from Western practices. After the outbreak of the Korean war, the six-year plan was revised upward. The Polish industrial firms began producing jet fighter planes, radar equipment, and other sophisticated war machines. All military equipment was inspected by Soviet technicians, and most of the equipment was shipped to the Soviet Union. Incidentally, the prices were set by the Soviet government. All this led to still higher levels of delivery of Soviet raw materials.

In the early 1950s, Polish industry gradually changed over to oil as its main energy source, and the oil was obtained exclusively from the Soviet Union. Prices of oil deliveries were, for a time, kept below world market prices, and this was the only real advantage that the Polish economy enjoyed in its relations with the Soviet Union.

In January 1949, the Council for Mutual Economic Assistance was established (COMECON). It was envisaged at first that this organization would become a counterpart to the emerging West European Common Market. However, Joseph Stalin and later his successors were wary of creating any close economic cooperation among their East European satellites. They preferred Soviet control and supervision over voluntarism. The organization standardized and coordinated bilateral agreements among Soviet Bloc countries. It was so heavily dominated by Soviet personnel that the "mutual" in its name was a misnomer.

Throughout the communist period, Polish coal deliveries, as well as of other goods, went to the Soviet Union at prices well below those on the world markets. Soviet deliveries, on the other hand, were more highly priced and were lower in quality. Only oil prices were consistently lower than those charged by OPEC, and this was undoubtedly an important element in the Polish economy. However, this did not mean that the Soviet Union had suddenly turned altruistic and was providing genuine economic help for Poland. At times of crises, such as in 1956, 1970, 1976 and 1980, the Soviet Union did indeed provide some economic assistance, but this was in the form of loans that Poland had to repay with hefty interests.

There were some important setbacks because of changing Soviet plans. For instance, in the late 1960s, an entire shipyard was built for the Soviet Union according to Soviet specifications. When the work was completed, however, the order was canceled retroactively and the enormous costs had to be absorbed by Poland. Poland had concluded an agreement with the Italian automobile firm, Fiat, for building low-cost cars to be sold mainly in Eastern Europe and the Soviet Union, perhaps in Third World countries. The initial price of the small automobile was to be affordable for average Polish workers. However, the agreement had to be canceled in 1969 because the Soviet leadership insisted that the Poles buy a Soviet license instead, producing Soviet-style automobiles that were inferior in quality and were largely unsuitable for

Polish roads. In addition, the prices of Soviet models would be too high for the average worker. Military expenditures were especially onerous and difficult for the Polish economy to absorb. What was more, the enormous expenditures were kept secret even from most party leaders except the members of the Politburo.

Even after the turmoil of 1956, the rapid development of heavy industry continued. The only concession made concerned the introduction of more relaxed work norms. Central planning, however, the cancer of economic life in all East European countries and, incidentally, in the Soviet Union, was continued. It was the means by which tight communist control over the economy was maintained.

Pressure for change emerged in the spring of 1956. At that time, spontaneous workers' councils emerged, demanding that fundamental changes be made in the direction of the economy. The communist government eventually had to increase the production of consumer goods. At the same time, small private enterprises emerged spontaneously, and the state quietly acceded to their activities. Already, in 1955, the Soviet Union had provided Poland with a nuclear reactor. Following this, a series of technical collaboration-agreements were signed between the two countries. Similar agreements were concluded among the members of COMECON. An organization for regulating railway traffic was set up in 1957, and a multilateral clearing house was established. An agreement for establishing an East European-Soviet power grid was signed in 1958, and work on the project was completed in 1962. An agreement for laying an oil pipeline through Poland, Czechoslovakia and East Germany was signed in 1959, and the work was completed in 1965.

The Polish communist government was strongly supportive of expanding COMECON and making it into a real East European-Soviet common market. This was vital for the further development of the Polish economy, since the West European Common Market had gradually eliminated much of Poland's exports, little as it was. Poland was especially interested in spreading investment costs among COMECON members, especially in the areas of mineral resources. East Germany was first to accede to Polish needs; its government invested $25 million in Polish coal mines that was to be repaid with coal deliveries. Czechoslovakia joined East Germany in 1966 by providing another $25 million for the modernization of Polish sulphur production. Yet the very nature of Polish industrialization continued to increase Polish dependence on the Soviet Union for raw material deliveries. Many Polish plants produced exclusively for the Soviet market, a fact that was to cause grave problems for Poland after the collapse of the Soviet economy in the late 1980s.

After the troubles of 1956, export prices paid for Polish goods by the Soviet Union were slightly increased. In the same year, compulsory deliveries of coal to the Soviet Union were discontinued. The Soviet leadership canceled a Polish debt of $525 million in exchange for Polish claims for uncollected German reparations and unfair prices for coal deliveries. Poland also received credit to the amount of 700 million rubles and an additional credit for 1.4 million tons of wheat that had to be repaid two years later.

In the 1960s, the production of consumer goods was increased. Polish trade with Western states also began to increase, since this was the only way to correct Poland's chronic shortage of hard currency. Private enterprise was no longer categorically forbidden, although the high taxes levied by the state and the generally uncertain climate retarded their normal development.

From 1963 to 1973, a considerable slowdown occurred in industrial development. This was only natural, since the initial phase of explosive growth had reached a diminishing return. Until 1963, the Polish economy made up for the destruction caused by the war and added new enterprises. By 1973, labor reserves were exhausted, and raw material prices began to increase substantially. The worldwide recession of the early 1970s, caused by the sudden doubling of oil prices, had its repercussions in the Soviet Bloc. Although the communists insisted that their centrally-planned economies were immune to recession, this was obviously not true. The Soviet Union was instrumental in maintaining this fiction; its leaders concluded five year agreements with their East European satellites, maintaining steady prices for energy deliveries at considerable expense for the Soviet economy. But sharp price increases for all consumer products were unavoidable.

In Poland, this necessity led to repeated crises, in which workers, students, and intellectuals took to the streets. The regime's initial response was to call out the troops and fire on the demonstrators as happened in 1970 and 1976. However, repression did not end the crises. In the meantime, real wages continued to decrease, and inflation further reduced the purchasing power of the population. Under these circumstances, an inevitable second economy developed. Black markets in food and other consumer goods thrived in parallel with long lines in front stores.

Poland resorted, in the 1970s and 1980s, to borrowing enormous sums of money from Western creditors. The plan was that the new technologies purchased through the loans would increase the quality of Polish goods and, thus, increase Polish exports to the West. However, these plans did not materialize. Eventually, much of the funds were spent on subsidizing inefficient firms. Full employment was a sacred cow, and this created a great deal of in-plant idleness among huge numbers of workers. The streamlining of industries was hardly possible because of ideological considerations. Central planning was maintained, although it increasingly relied on doctored statistics that hid the real situation even from the leaders of the Polish Workers party. The nationalized firms were producing inefficiently, using outdated technologies. The electronic revolution that began to change Western capitalist production methods, had hardly penetrated the Polish economy.

By the early 1980s, the signs of economic breakdown appeared. This was accompanied by unrest, strikes, and the emergence of the Solidarity trade union. By 1988, the communist economic methods proved to be a resounding failure, and Poland embarked on the restoration of a free market economy. The transformation, however, proved to be difficult.

The eastern market for Polish goods collapsed. The new East European countries were suffering from the same illnesses of over-centralization, outdated smokestack industries, management inefficiency, and huge foreign debts. In addition, the Polish economy faced a difficult time because of chaotic political conditions. Yet, the economic performance in Poland was better than in the rest of Eastern Europe.

After February 1992, industrial production showed a strong trend of recovery. The construction industry revived. Inflation fell from 70 percent in 1991 to about 45 percent. Surpluses were recorded on merchandise trade accounts and in export balances. The private sector grew with great rapidity in spite of the failure of parliament to pass laws on privatization. Almost half of domestic production was provided by private firms in 1992.

The Polish economy, however, has not yet been able to get out of the woods entirely. The state budget deficit was larger in 1992 than anticipated, preventing an agreement with the International Monetary Fund. This prevented the London Club of creditor banks to agree to a restructuring of the Polish national debt. Problems with the harvest dampened hopes for further reduction of inflation.

Communist agricultural policies reflected the anti-peasant bias inherent in Marxism-Leninism. Karl Marx considered the peasant to be a stubborn, small-time capitalist whose support for a worker-led revolution was uncertain. Lenin himself introduced policies of confiscation of peasant properties during the Russian Revolution and civil war, and Stalin's policy of forced collectivization of all peasant properties followed in the Marxist-Leninist trends. Yet, Polish communists could not hope to maintain power long if some sort of accommodation was not reached with the people of the countryside.

In September 1944 the provisional government enacted a comprehensive land reform law that served two purposes. One of these was the elimination of large land holdings, and the other was to provide land for the millions of Polish citizens expelled from the eastern lands by the Soviet Union. Landed properties over 100 hectares (a hectare consists of 100 square meters), of which at least 50 hectares were arable, were confiscated without compensation. German-owned properties, as well as land owned by alleged or real collaborators was also taken away. The state acquired about 9.8 million hectares of land by these measures, of which about 60 percent was redistributed: the rest were retained for the establishment of state farms. The managers of the state farms were newly appointed communist functionaries: most of them knew little about agriculture. General collectivization on the Stalinist pattern was not stressed immediately after the war, and most lands remained in the hands of private farmers. A decree issued in 1946, however, changed the situation. It proclaimed the nationalization of all means of production, including land. This was the first step toward collectivization.

By 1948, the communist leaders felt secure enough in power to begin the establishment of "socialist modes of production" in agriculture. An intensive propaganda campaign was begun to convince skeptical peasants of the alleged advantages of collective farming. The campaign was accompanied by a concerted effort to ruin wealthier peasants, the so-called kulaks, many of whom were jailed or sent to concentration camps.

But the hearts of the leaders were not in this campaign. They were quite aware of the pervasive terror that accompanied collectivization in the Soviet Union, and of the atrocities committed against the industrious people of the Russian countryside by Stalin's minions. Perhaps, not surprisingly, the first collectivization drive in Poland proved less than successful. Only about 10 percent of the lands came into the possession of collectives. Most of these were located in the former German lands. The total land area controlled by state farms came to 13 percent of all farmlands in Poland. All in all, only 26 percent of land was collectively farmed.

With or without collectivization, Polish agriculture did not work well. When the state established unfairly high compulsory delivery quotas for foodstuffs, it dampened peasant initiative. Prices paid for food products were kept artificially low, adding to disincentives for increases in production. Farmers, collectivized or private, had hardly any incentives to produce more than needed by their immediate families. In the 1950s, some delivery quotas were, therefore, lowered. However, without fundamental price reform, this alone had little impact. The fact was that the infrastructure of Polish agriculture had been damaged, and quick solutions would not fix it. The necessities of increased production; small agricultural machinery, chemical fertilizers, and low-interest loans were simply not available. In the state farms, even large tractors were few in numbers.

Agricultural policies were reversed after 1956. The compulsory delivery of foodstuffs was not eliminated, but the quotas were further reduced. Prices paid to farmers were increased, and new state investments were introduced in the agrarian sector. Once again, however, the reforms were severely restricted; 70 percent of the new investment was directed into the collective-and state sectors. On the other hand, the state acquiesced in the decision of collective farm members if they chose to dissolve their collective.

In 1955, the collectives employed 189,000 people; as the result of the new policies, this number had dropped to 37,000 by December 1956. Nevertheless, agricultural production did not expand as fast and at a volume desirable for feeding the expanding population. The main reason was that agricultural prices were still too low in comparison with the prices of industrial products.

In 1957, a new campaign was begun by the communists to establish "agricultural circles." These organizations were similar to the voluntary collectives that had been sponsored by the Polish Peasant party during the interwar years. Their functions included advice to farmers concerning better methods of production; they provided rental machinery and sold supplies to the rural population. But these circles were not what Polish agriculture needed for its development.

In 1958, prices paid for foodstuffs were increased once again, this time accompanied by the introduction of higher agricultural taxes, further discouraging farmer initiatives. This was done at a time when agricultural exports had become important sources of hard currency revenues for Poland. In 1958, 58 percent of meat exports went to Great Britain. Three years later, 100 percent of bacon exports went to the same country. In 1963, frozen meat exports went almost exclusively to Italy and Spain, and canned meat to West Germany, Great Britain, and the United States.

Polish agricultural policies did not change much until the communist regime collapsed at the end of the 1980s. During the last two decades, the communist regime was forced to import huge quantities of food from Western states. Between 1969 and 1975, 2.4 million tons of bread grains alone were imported. When the communist system collapsed, food prices were gradually freed, and government intervention in the agrarian sector was reduced. There was little need for reprivatization in this sector, since most agricultural land was already in private hands.

Bibliography

Alton, Paul T., *The Polish Postwar Economy* (New York, 1955); Blazyca, George, and Rapacki, Ryszard, eds. *Poland Into the 1990s: Economy and Society in Transition* (New York, 1991); Charemza, Wojciech, *Plans and Disequilibria in Centrally Planned Economies: Empirical Investigation in Poland* (New York, 1988); Karpinski, Andrzej, *Poland and the World Economy* (Warsaw, 1960); Kolaja, Jiri, *A Polish Factory: A Case Study* (Lexington, KY, 1960); Korbonski, Andrzej, *Politics of Socialist Agriculture in Poland* (New York, 1960); Landau, Zbigniew, *The Polish Economy in the Twentieth Century* (New York, 1988); Lange, Oscar, *Some Problems Relating to the Polish Road to Socialism* (Warsaw, 1957); Marer, Paul, *Creditworthiness and Reform in Poland* (Bloomington, IN, 1988); Montias, John M., *Central Planning in Poland* (New Haven, CT, 1962).

Gdansk Riots. Originally an ancient Slav settlement, located on a branch of the Vistula river at the Gulf of Gdansk, the city was a member of the Hanseatic League in the course of the thirteenth century. Since that time, the majority of the population consisted of German craftsmen and merchants. The city was also a point at which German and Polish nationalism collided, and it provided the spark for the outbreak of World War II.

During the communist era, Gdansk was a busy Polish port on the Baltic sea. Its huge shipyard, one of the largest in the world, served as a source of shipbuilding for the Soviet Union and other East European countries. The shipyard workers included some of the best-known people in Poland in the 1970s and 1980s, among them Lech Walesa (*see* Walesa, Lech) and Anna Walentynowicz (*see* Walentynowicz, Anna). In 1970, when riots broke out in Poznan and the Polish army fired on the demonstrating workers, the unrest spread to Gdansk, where it eventually led to the formation of an Inter-factory Strike Committee, a forerunner of the Solidarity trade union. Disturbances occurred in Gdansk in 1976 and 1980; the 1980 disturbances led to the building of Solidarity. This organization was eventually instrumental in the destruction of the communist regime and the transformation of Poland into a democratic society.

Bibliography

Andrews, Nicholas G., *Poland 1980–1981: Solidarity Versus the Party* (Washington, DC,

1985); Zinner, Paul E., *National Communism and Popular Revolt in Eastern Europe: A Selection of Documents on Events in Poland and Hungary* (New York, 1956).

Geremek, Bronislaw (1932–). A young intellectual who had received his doctorate from Warsaw University, Geremek studied History and was employed as a researcher at the Historical Institute of the Polish Academy of Sciences. He joined the intellectuals who founded the Committee for the Defense of Workers (KOR) (*see* Committee for the Defense of Workers), and in 1981, he became an advisor to Lech Walesa (*see* Walesa, Lech) and the Solidarity trade Union movement (*see* Solidarity Trade Union of Poland). When the communist government, headed by General Wojciech Jaruzelski (*see* Jaruzelski, Wijciech), declared martial law in December 1981, Geremek was arrested together with other members and leaders of Solidarity. He spent years in jail. Upon his release in 1985, he continued his oppositional activities. He remained an important member of the advisory group around Lech Walesa until the elections that brought Solidarity into the government.

Bibliography
Perski, Stanislaw, and Flam, H., eds. *The Solidarity Sourcebook* (Vancouver, 1982); Rosenbrink, John, *Poland Challenges a Divided World* (Baton Rouge, LA, 1988).

Gierek, Edward (1913–). Gierek began his career as a minor apparatchik in Silezia. By 1970, he had moved up the ladder of the *nomenklatura* and was appointed party leader of the region. He drew attention to himself by his relentless energy and organizational activity.

In 1970, he was chosen to replace Wladislaw Gomulka (*see* Gomulka, Wladislaw) as secretary general of the Polish United Workers party. Gierek's elevation was a maneuver on the part of the party leadership to appease a restive population, angered over sudden price increases. Gierek immediately rescinded the price increases and made other concessions. He crisscrossed the country, listening to complaints by the population and showing respect for simple people. He succeeded in calming down the people. Gierek reshuffled the communist leadership, enlarged the Central Committee of the Communist party and changed the personnel of the party secretariat and the Politburo.

The essential elements of communist dictatorship, however, remained unchanged. Central planning of the economy continued; the party's monopoly of political power remained intact, and intellectual life remained in bondage to Marxism-Leninism. The concept of class-struggle was not abandoned, but it was somewhat toned down. The party had made an effort to improve living standards without instituting major reforms in the economy but this just did not work. Gierek was intent on tightening discipline in the communist party. In the name of efficiency, some bureaucrats were removed from their posts. Higher industrial wages were introduced, food prices were lowered, and the compulsory delivery of foodstuffs was reduced to a minimum. Gierek also attempted to reach a modus vivendi with the Polish Catholic church. But those who participated in the riots and demonstrations, had received harsh sentences.

With all the changes, however, the situation basically remained the same. The economic priorities, centering on the development of heavy industry, remained in force. The production of consumer goods was not sufficiently expanded. The tax system was changed for the worse, and the leadership did not break with the official policy of "socialized agriculture," frightening peasants with the specter of forced collectivization. A new economic plan, introduced in 1971, promised 1.8 million new jobs and the building of 1.08 million new housing units. It also projected the production of 600,000 small automobiles whose price was to make them affordable for the average worker. On the other hand, Gierek rejected workers' demand for a greater voice in the management of industrial enterprises.

Gierek attempted to solve Poland's chronic economic problems by obtaining large loans from Western banks and governments. The purpose behind the loans was to modernize Polish industry and agriculture and to make them competitive on the world markets. However, most of the funds were not spent productively. They were used, instead, for subsidies for inefficient enterprises, mostly producing for the Soviet and East European market. They also served the purpose of financing a temporary improvement in the living standards. However, the growing indebtedness eventually led to a need to tighten expenditures, and this had an adverse effect on living standards.

In September 1980, Gierek's rule came crashing down. He was dismissed and his policies were repudiated. Only a military dictatorship could have saved the rule of the Communist party, and even then only for a short time. Gierek has retired to private life.

Bibliography

Barker, Colin, *Festival of the Oppressed: Solidarity, Reform and Revolution in Poland 1980–1981* (London, 1986); Gross, Jan T., "Poland: From Civil Society to Political Nation," in Ivo Banac, ed. *Eastern Europe in Revolution* (Ithaca, NY, 1992); Simon, Maurice D., and Kanet, Roger E., eds. *Background to Crisis* (New York, 1982).

Glemp, Jozef, Cardinal (1929–). Born to a peasant family, the future cardinal graduated from high school in 1950, entered Warsaw University, then transferred to Torun before entering the seminary for the priesthood. He was ordained a priest in 1956 and did graduate studies at Lateran and Gregorian Universities in Rome. He received doctorates in canon and civil law.

Glemp returned to Poland in 1964 and was appointed to the secretariat for Higher Priest's Seminary and to the secretariat of the metropolitan Curia. In 1967, he became secretary to Cardinal Wyszynski (*see* Wyszynski, Cardinal, Stefan) and accompanied the cardinal on his foreign visits. He was also a lecturer at the Catholic theological seminary in Warsaw. At Wyszynski's suggestion, the pope appointed Glemp Bishop of Warmia in 1979. Glemp participated in the work of a commission of government and the episcopate of Poland, considering the granting of legal status to the church. Upon the death of his mentor, Wyszynski, the pope appointed Glemp cardinal and primate of Poland.

In July 1981, after his return from a pilgrimage to the shrine of Czestochova, offering a mass at the national shrine, Glemp conferred with general and prime minister Wojciech Jaruzelski (*see* Jaruzelski, Wojciech), then followed this up with consultations with the leaders of Solidarity (*see* Solidarity Trade Union of Poland). Glemp made it clear from the very beginning that he considered mediating between the communist government and Solidarity one of his major tasks. The regime did not make a secret out of its satisfaction that the new cardinal wanted to smooth things over in Poland. It was rather desperate for the good services of the Catholic church and hoped that Glemp would play a stabilizing role similar to that played by Cardinal Wyszynski. Glemp, on his part, declared that the church wanted better ties with lay Catholic organizations. In line with this, the cardinal began criticizing both Solidarity and the government for their uncompromising attitudes and appealed for reconciliation. In a pastoral letter that was sent to all parishes, Glemp declared his intention of keeping the church out of everyday politics. He said that he believed the declarations of the authorities that their aim was renewal of society through democracy.

In July 1981, a papal encyclical warned Solidarity not to challenge the government but to concentrate on the improvement of conditions in Poland. Glemp saw this as a justification of his own position. This was, of course, wishful thinking. The hard-liners in the Communist party were already working on the ouster of the premier, Stanislaw Kania (*see* Kania, Stanislaw), and were putting pressure on Solidarity. Within Solidarity, there was an atmosphere of disillusionment with the negotiations, since the government seemed bent on destroying the organization. On November 4, 1981, joint talks were held with Lech Walesa, head of the Solidarity trade union; Cardinal Glemp; and General Jaruzelski, by then head of the government.

On November 26, during a session of the hierarchy of the church, the bishops declared that they hoped that some sort of national accord could be reached to rescue Poland from its economic difficulties. Glemp once again tried to intervene in politics by urging Solidarity and the government to end their conflict. Rather naively, he recommended to parliament, ruled by communist deputies, not to vote for a law enabling the government to govern by emergency decrees, since this would lead to the restriction of civil rights. He sent letters to Solidarity and the Students Union urging both to stop their protests. When the Jaruzelski government declared martial law on December 13 and arrested the leaders and supporters of Solidarity, Glemp suddenly retreated. The government, however, did not impose new restrictions on the church. It did not need any more complications.

Glemp tried to revive talks between the workers and the government, but he was unsuccessful. In fact, his urging had the opposite effect; they contributed to a deterioration of relations between state and church. He tried to minimize the importance of the events sweeping the country, and he urged the people not to oppose the government. However, in a pastoral letter issued on December 16, he condemned the arrest and jailing of Solidarity leaders and their sympathizers. Typical was a letter to be read in the churches on December 20, in which the episcopate endorsed the movement for the self-organization of society as a balancing factor. Glemp had the letter withdrawn at the last moment. The church set up an aid program to help the families of those who had been arrested. In January 1982, Glemp once again appealed for restraint and peace. He agreed with Jaruzelski by declaring that Western sanctions made it more difficult to overcome the crisis. On January 21, a joint letter of the bishops were issued with Glemp's approval, demanding freedom for the entire nation. It asserted that peace and freedom are inseparable and demanded the freeing of all those who had been arrested.

There was, at the same time, a growing breach between the episcopate and the ordinary priests. Many of the priests sided with Solidarity from the beginning and were disappointed in the stand taken by Glemp and the bishops. Glemp, however, kept to the line he had originally introduced throughout martial law and even afterward. He had, therefore, lost a great deal of support in society.

After the collapse of the communist regime, the episcopate withdrew from politics, except for occasional forays into legislation concerning issues in which it was interested. These included efforts to make abortion illegal and plans for a convent to be built in the former concentration camp of Auschwitz. The latter brought Glemp into open conflict with Jewish organizations the world over. Pope John Paul II ordered the nuns to abandon the site, closing the conflict over the head of Glemp in 1993.

Bibliography

Monticone, Ronald C., *The Catholic Church in Communist Poland 1945–1985: Forty Years of Church-State Relations* (Boulder, CO, 1986); Ramet, Pedro, *Religion and Nationalism in the Soviet Union and Eastern Europe* (New York, 1991).

Gomulka, Wladislaw (1905–1982). Gomulka was born to peasant parents. At the age of sixteen, he worked as a locksmith journeyman in the Polish oil industry. He became active in his trade union and soon joined the underground Communist party. In the 1930s, he worked as a professional union organizer. In 1932, during a minor strike in the city of Lodz, he was shot and severely wounded. After he recovered, he was tried and sentenced to four years in prison for subversion. He was released after two years and then traveled to Moscow where he studied at the International Lenin Institute. In 1936, he was sent to Poland where he was promptly arrested and sent back to prison on a four-and-a-half-year sentence.

Gomulka was released from prison when World War II broke out. He fought against the Germans in Warsaw and, after the defeat, went to southern Poland where he remained until 1941. In 1942, he joined the revived Polish Workers party (a new name for the Communist party) and was named secretary of its Warsaw branch. In December, he became a member of the party's Central Committee. In 1943, he became secretary general of the party in the German occupational area of Poland. He remained at that post until 1948.

He was resentful of the Polish communists who spent the war years in the Soviet Union, while he and his comrades risked their lives daily in Poland. He was sympathetic to the Polish Social Democratic party, which was considered by Joseph Stalin to be a traitor to socialism. Gomulka was not a strong supporter of the collectivization of agriculture.

By the end of the 1940s, Stalin considered Gomulka too independent. When the Yugoslav communists broke with Stalin, Gomulka came under suspicion of being a Titoist, that is, a nationalist communist. When the COMINFORM condemned Marshal Tito, Gomulka's position became untenable. The Central Committee of the Polish Workers party declared, on September 3, 1948, that Gomulka was a rightist-nationalist and removed him from his party posts. On January 21, 1949, he was removed from his position in government. On August 21, 1951, Gomulka was arrested; however, he was not tortured and put through the ordeal of a show trial as were the Hungarian Laszlo Rajk, the Czech Rudolf Slanski or the Bulgarian Traicho Kostov. After Stalin's death, Gomulka was released and he was rehabilitated in 1955.

In February 1956, Nikita S. Khrushchev made his memorable speech condemning Stalin's crimes. Within a few weeks, Boleslaw Bierut (*see* Bierut, Boleslaw), who replaced Gomulka at the head of the Communist party, died in Moscow. Political ferment ensued in Poland. In June, workers in the city of Poznan protested increased work norms, and the Polish army was ordered to fire on the demonstrators. Over fifty workers were killed and 300 were severely wounded. The incident created general revulsion and demoralized the Polish army. There was a threat of revolt in the army possibly leading to a national uprising of unforeseeable consequences.

In October, the communist leadership turned to Gomulka in order to avoid civil war and a possible revolutionary war against the Soviet Union. The Soviet leadership had little choice; either it accepted Gomulka, or it had to send the Red Army to suppress the Poles. Gomulka began his activities by sending the host of Soviet technical and military advisors packing. But he was no flaming liberal. He reasserted the party's control over society. The workers' councils, organized spontaneously by workers during the spring, were brought under government control. Compulsory deliveries of foodstuffs were reduced, but not eliminated, and the party once again declared itself in favor of collectivization. Relations with the Roman Catholic church were relaxed, but the state's official atheism was not rescinded. The system was tinkered with, but major reforms were not introduced. Relations with the United States were somewhat improved, but West Germany continued to be considered an enemy of Poland.

A new crisis came in 1968, when Myeczislaw Moczar (*see* Moczar, Myeczislaw), the minister of internal affairs, challenged Gomulka's authority (*see* Moczar, Myeczislaw). But Gomulka successfully fought Moczar off and retained his control over the party and government.

During the 1960s, Polish economists put forward several proposals for economic reform, similar to those proposed by the Czech Ota Sik and the Hungarian Rezso

Nyers. But Gomulka refused to entertain the proposals seriously, since he considered them ill-concealed efforts to smuggle capitalism back into Poland. On December 13, 1970, he finally decided to make his move for the improvement of the Polish economy. He ordered a broad range of price increases for the next day, without any prior notice to the population. His intention was to prevent a run on the stores. The workers in the Baltic port of Gdansk demonstrated against the increases in front of the local party headquarters. They were fired on by the secret police. Similar confrontations occurred in other cities, and hundreds of workers were killed and wounded. There was a danger of civil war once again, and the leadership of the party decided to oust Gomulka. They replaced him with Edward Gierek, a Silezian leader. (*see* Gierek, Edward). Gomulka retired to private life and never again participated in politics.

Bibliography
Bethell, Nicholas, *Gomulka: His Poland and His Communism* (London, 1972); Blit, Lucjan, *Gomulka's Poland* (New York, 1968); Groth, A.J., *People's Poland: Government and Politics* (Scranton, PA, 1972); Korbonski, Andrzej, "Poland 1918–1990," in Joseph Held, ed. *The Columbia History of Eastern Europe in the Twentieth Century* (New York, 1992), pp. 229-276; Morrison, J.F., *The Polish People's Republic* (Baltimore, MD, 1968); Syrop, Konrad, *Spring in October: The Story of the Polish Revolution of 1956* (London, 1958).

Grabski, Stanislaw (1871–1949). Grabski was born and educated in Warsaw. He received a degree in economics from Warsaw University. Between 1910 and 1939, he was a professor at the University of Lvov. Between 1919 and 1927, he served as a deputy in parliament as a member of the National Democratic party. In 1923, and again between 1925 and 1926, he was minister of religious cults and public education. Between 1942 and 1945, Grabski was the chairman of the National Council that served as the parliament of the Polish government-in-exile in London. In July 1945, he returned to Poland with Stanislaw Mikolajczyk (*see* Mikolajczyk, Stanislaw) and became deputy chairman of the National Council for the Homeland. After 1947, he was a professor of economics at the University of Warsaw, until his death two years later.

Bibliography
Polonsky, Antony, and Druiker, Boleslaw, *The Beginnings of Communist Rule in Poland* (London, 1980).

Inter-Factory Strike Committee (1980–1981). In August 1980, a wave of new strikes hit Poland's industrial regions, in response to the government's announcement of sudden price increases of food staples. By then, Lech Walesa (*see* Walesa, Lech), a former electrician in the shipyards at Gdansk, a leader of the newly formed Solidarity trade union (*see* Solidarity Trade Union of Poland), came into contact with members of the Committee for the Defense of Workers (KOR), and the Young Poland movement. These consisted of students and intellectual dissenters.

On August 15, Prime Minister Jozef Babiuch addressed the country on television and admitted that the Polish United Workers party had neglected to inform the population fully of actual economic conditions. He contended that the solution to the shortage of meat could be found only in the future, but he promised that the party leaders would make great efforts to solve the problem. He also declared that wage increases, demanded by the striking workers, could be granted only if productivity increased; otherwise, the economy would simply collapse. He appealed to the workers to return to work.

On August 16, negotiations between the Gdansk shipyard workers and the government representatives seemed to have been concluded with the victory of the workers. However, when workers at other factories in the city heard about this, they complained that they had not even begun negotiations with their managements. They pleaded with Walesa not to agree to the resumption of work until their cases had been settled.

Walesa immediately recognized the merit of joint action. He also observed that this was the moment to achieve at least some of the goals of the democratic opposition. Solidarity's advisors also urged him to consider the request of the workers of other factories. Walesa convinced the nucleus of the strikers at the shipyard to continue their strike.

The next day, on August 17, an Interfactory Strike Committee of thirteen persons was established. It had representatives of the workers from three Baltic cities; Gdansk, Gdynia, and Sopot. They drew up a list of sixteen demands. This extended to some extent the original points that the government had already agreed to. The communist leadership was appalled by the fact that, beyond the original demands of the shipyard workers of Gdansk, the workers were now demanding the recognition of free trade unions nationwide. They demanded economic reforms, and began suggesting that the role of the security forces be restricted and democratic changes be introduced into Poland's political life.

The Polish communist leaders were frightened. Their representatives made further concessions to the workers and continued negotiations now with the Inter-Factory Strike Committee. Deputy Prime Minister Stanislaw Jagielski led the negotiating team for the government. By then, other intellectuals from the writers union came to help the workers. At hand were Tadeusz Mazowieczki, editor-in-chief of the Catholic monthly, *Wiez*, and Dr. Bronis-law Geremek (*see* Geremek, Bronislaw), a medievalist historian and a member of the Historical Institute of the Polish Academy of Science. Five other intellectuals joined them in helping the workers. For the first time, an alliance of workers and intellectuals was forged.

On August 20, the government began a campaign against so-called antisocialist forces, and arrested fourteen members of (KOR). By then, almost every factory on the Baltic coast had stopped working in support of the Interfactory Strike Committee, and strikes had also begun in Wroclaw, Lodz, Nowa Huta near Cracow, Kielce, Rzeszov, and other cities. Local branches of the Interfactory Strike Committee were formed in the huge steel plant at Nowa Huta and in Wroclaw.

On August 30, the committee reached an agreement with a government delegation led by Deputy Premier Barcikowski. On the same day, Jagielski initialed an agreement with Walesa. The following day, the party's Politburo approved both agreements, and Walesa signed the famous text to be known afterward as the Agreement of Gdansk.

Bibliography

Andrews, Nicholas G., *Poland 1980–1981: Solidarity Versus the Party* (Washington, DC, 1985); Barker, Colin, *Festival of the Oppressed: Solidarity, Reform and Revolution in Poland, 1980–1981* (London, 1986); Misztal, Bronislaw, *Poland after Solidarity: Social Movements Versus the State* (New Brunswick, NJ, 1985).

Jaroszewicz, Piotr (1909–1993). Jaroszewicz was a primary school teacher before World War II. He joined the underground Communist party, and when the war broke out, he fled to the Soviet Union. In 1943, he joined the Koszciuszko Brigade, a Soviet-organized Polish contingent fighting the Germans. Jaroszewicz became a political officer. He was a deputy commander of the 2nd Infantry Division, responsible for political education. He soon became deputy commander of the 1st Polish army for political education.

From 1945 on, Jaroszewicz rose steadily in the party's ranks. First, he was appointed deputy director of the main office of the Polish armed forces, dealing with political education. In 1946, he was promoted to the rank of general. Simultaneously, he was appointed quartermaster of the Polish army, and deputy minister of national defense. Between 1950 and 1952, Jaroszewicz became the deputy chairman of the state planning commission. In 1952, he also became deputy prime minister to Jozef Babiuch. In 1957, he was promoted to the post of vice chairman of the council of ministers, heading the committee on the economy. In 1958, he became permanent Polish representative to the COMECON and, in 1970, he was appointed prime minister. In 1980, however, Jaroszewicz was ousted. In 1993, he and his wife were found murdered in their home.

Bibliography

Polonsky, Antony, and Druiker, Boleslaw, *The Beginning of Communist Rule in Poland* (London, 1980).

Jaruzelski, Wojciech (1923–). Jaruzelski has been a military officer most of his life. He fought against the Germans in World War II and survived the war. He joined the Polish communist party in 1944 and, in 1956, rose to the rank of general. In 1960, he became the armed forces' representative in the Central Committee of the Polish United Workers party. He was, thus, a political general. At one point in his career, he was appointed to membership in the military command of the Warsaw Pact forces. He was a fully convinced Marxist-Leninist, and, accordingly, the Soviet leaders completely trusted the Polish general.

On December 13, 1981, Jaruzelski took over the government of a Poland torn by strife between striking workers and the communist regime. Jaruzelski, arguing that if he had not acted, the Soviet army would have marched into Poland, declared martial law, outlawed the Solidarity trade union and, had its leaders and supporters arrested and thrown into jail. He also took control over the secret police and used it for the restoration of calm in Poland. Jaruzelski was fully supported by Leonid Brezhnev and his Soviet colleagues.

In 1982, new demonstrations erupted in Poland against martial law, and these were put down with great brutality on Jaruzelski's orders by the secret police. The Western powers introduced an embargo on Polish goods. In 1983, therefore, Jaruzelski was forced to lift martial law, but this did not bring about the end of general repression of the dissenters.

Two years later, Jaruzelski stepped down from the post of prime minister, but he remained head of the Polish United Workers party. An obedient parliament, filled with communist deputies, elected him president of the republic, so that he retained considerable power. In 1989, when the communist regime collapsed, the opposition agreed to Jaruzelski's continued presidency. However, in the free elections of 1990, Jaruzelski was replaced by Lech Walesa (*see* Walesa, Lech), his former Solidarity opponent as president of Poland.

Bibliography

Ash, Timothy, Garton, *The Polish Revolution* (London, 1985); Koralewicz, J., I. Bialecki, and M. Watson, eds. *Crisis and Transition: Polish Society in the 1980s* (London, 1987); Malcher, George, *Poland's Politicized Army* (New York, 1984); Misztal, Bronislaw, *Poland after Solidarity: Social Movements Versus the State* (New Brunswick, NJ, 1985).

Kania, Stanislaw (1927–). Kania's father was a peasant who owned a small parcel of land. Stanislaw worked for two years before World War II as a laborer, then he joined the Communist Peasant Battalions for one year. In April 1945, he joined the Polish Workers party. He was soon sent to a party school attached to the party's Central Committee. He was then sent, in 1958, as a party functionary to work in the Polish Youth Association, a front organization of the Communist party. In the same year, Kania was adopted by the party apparatus in Warsaw province. He became the director of the agricultural department of the provincial party committee. In 1964, he became a candidate (nonvoting) member of the party's Central Committee. Four years later, Kania became a full member of the same committee. He was appointed director of the Central Committee's administrative department. In April 1971, he was elected secretary to the Central Committee. In December, he was promoted candidate (nonvoting) member of the Polish United Workers party's Politburo while remaining a member of the Central Committee's secretariat. In 1975, he was promoted to full membership in the Politburo.

Kania, an ordinary apparatchik, worked his way up the hierarchy's ranks by conforming to party rules and regulations. During his last year as Central Committee secretary, Kania was responsible for military and internal security, a position of great power. When he became successor to the ousted Edward Gierek (*see* Gierek, Edward) in September 1980, Kania was largely unknown to most of the Polish people. Yet, he was a key member of Gierek's government, and Gierek sponsored Kania during the 1970s. When the time was right, Kania jettisoned his benefactor. In October 1981, however, Kania himself was ousted by General Wojciech Jaruzelski (*see* Jaruzelski, Wojciech), who considered Kania too soft in dealing with the Solidarity trade union.

Bibliography
Andrews, Nicholas G., *Poland 1980–1981: Solidarity Versus the Party* (Washington, DC, 1985); Taras, Ray, *Poland: Socialist State, Rebellious Nation* (Boulder, CO, 1986).

Katyn Woods Massacre. In 1939, when the Soviet Union joined Nazi Germany in the attack on Poland, about 14,000 officers of the Polish armed forces were captured by, or gave themselves up to, the Red Army. This was the last time most of them were ever heard from; aside from a few postcards, their families received no further news of their fate. A clue to their treatment was provided by a Soviet NKVD-KGB decree, issued in 1940, according to which fourteen categories of people were to be deported from the Soviet-occupied areas of Poland. One of the categories was membership in the officer corps of the Polish armed forces. Altogether, about 1.5 million Polish citizens were declared "class enemies" by the Soviet secret police and were transported to Kazakhstan and Siberia. After the German attack on the Soviet Union, an amnesty was declared for the deportees but, by then, barely half of them were still alive.

The 14,000 officers were, however, murdered closer to home. The victims included not only the professional soldiers, but also intellectuals, scientists, and other culturally important people who served as reserve officers in the Polish armed forces.

They were deposited in three prisoner-of-war camps. The first, in Kozelsk, was located along the railway line connecting the city of Smolensk with Tula. Here they were placed in an abandoned old monastery. The camp consisted of two hermetically isolated compounds; one for officers who originally were stationed in territories now in German hands, and the other for those captured on Soviet-occupied Polish lands.

The second camp was established at Starobelsk, south of Kharkov in eastern Ukraine. All the officers who defended the region around the city of Lvov were brought here. Among them were about twenty university professors, about four hundred physicians, and hundreds of engineers, teachers, lawyers, and pilots of the Polish air force.

The third camp was at Ostashkov, southwest of the city of Tver. Altogether, there were 14,300 prisoners of war in the three camps.

The murder of the prisoners of the three camps began just before Christmas 1939. On Christmas eve, all the priests were collected from the three camps (they numbered about 200), and secret policemen murdered them. The location of their graves is still not known. The next wave of murders began on April 3, 4, and 5. Groups of from 50 to 250 prisoners were sent, sometimes on foot, sometimes by train, other times by trucks, to their places of death. Of the 14,300 prisoners, only 449 were spared (it is not known why they were not killed), and these eventually became the most important eye witnesses to the calamity. The prisoners were sent to Gniezdovo railroad station, three kilometers from the mass graves that were later found.

On June 22, Nazi Germany attacked the Soviet Union. Joseph Stalin decided to establish a Polish army, and the Western Allies also organized a Polish legion. When the Polish government in exile inquired about the missing officers, it received evasive answers from Moscow.

In the winter of 1942, some Polish laborers, who were working in forced labor gangs under Nazi supervision at the Smolensk railroad junction, heard from local peasants about Polish officers shot by the NKVD-KGB in the forests of Katyn, near the Dnieper river, fifteen kilometers to the west of Smolensk. The Poles dug up one of the small humps in the reported area and found the skeleton of a man dressed in a Polish uniform. The workers simply reburied the skeleton, and placed a crude cross on the grave. There was a cold winter, and no further searches were made then.

When the Germans learned about the alleged graves in the Katyn woods, they did not think much of them, but in March and April, 1943, they began serious exhumations in the area.

The news broke like lightning out of the blue sky. The officers wore Polish uniforms. Every one of them had been shot in the back of the head. The Germans, naturally, wanted to derive the maximum propaganda advantage from the gruesome discovery. They collected a group of Polish intellectuals and political personalities in April 1943, and transported them to Katyn where they could see the tragedy with their own eyes. On April 15, Radio Moscow countered by asserting that the Polish officers had fallen into German hands when the Soviet army retreated and that they were massacred by the Nazis.

In 1943, the world had not yet learned of the existence of Nazi death camps and the mass extermination of Jews and other subjects of the Nazi totalitarian machine. Nevertheless, the Western Allies and the neutral countries were inclined to believe anything about the brutality of the Nazi machine. The Polish government in exile then sent an envoy to the Red Cross headquarters in Switzerland, asking for its representatives to visit the scene of the horrible crime. The Germans welcomed the creation of an international commission to examine the Katyn graves. This, in itself, indicated that they had nothing to fear. On April 20, the Polish government in exile in London sent a note to Stalin, demanding information about the officers. The next day, the Soviet government accused the Poles of cooperating with the German enemy. The Red Cross refused the Polish request, and the Soviet government broke off relations with the London Poles. On April 19, the Polish Red Cross sent several of its representatives to Katyn and began the exhumation of the graves. The Germans left them alone to their terrible task. Another group of observers, some from the countries allied to Germany, others from neutral countries, also visited Katyn.

The two groups exhumed 982 corpses and came to the following conclusions. (1)

The bodies were in the ground for about three years; therefore, they were buried before the German army reached the area; (2) The bodies were those of the missing Polish officers; (3) Notes and diaries found on the bodies generally provided the exact dates of execution because they ended abruptly between April and May, 1940.

For half a century, the Soviet government denied its responsibility for the Katyn massacre. It accused the Nazis of killing the Polish officers and then trying to make the Soviet Union the culprit in the case. Western public opinion—and Western governments as well—were inclined to believe the Soviet government. Only in 1991 did the new Russian government confess that it was the KGB whose murderers had committed the massacre on Stalin's direct orders. It seems that the groups to be killed were put together on each occasion on the basis of lists received directly from Moscow. The Russian government of Boris Yeltsin finally apologized to Poland for the terrible deed. In 1993, the Russians sent a record of a Soviet Politburo meeting, initialed by Stalin, Vyacheslav Molotov, Anastas Mikoyan, Lazar Kaganoyich, and Lavrenty Beria, approving of the murder of the officers and intellectuals, altogether numbering 26,000 men.

Bibliography

Jerzewski, Leopold, *Katyn, 1940* (New York, 1987); Zawodny, J.K., *Death in the Forest: The Story of the Katyn Forest Massacre* (South Bend, IN, 1962).

Kiernik, Wladislaw (1879–1971). Kiernik was a peasant politician from Galicia who was very active in the Polish Peasant party during the interwar years. During World War II, he opposed the tactics followed by the Peasant party's resistance against the Nazis, since he did not believe that it was effective enough. In June 1945, he went to Moscow to participate in the discussions, initiated by Joseph Stalin, for the formation of a provisional government with the participation of the Peasant party.

Between 1945 and 1947, Kiernik was minister of public administration. After 1945, he became more and more critical of the policies of Stanislaw Mikolajczyk (*see* Mikolajczyk, Stanislaw), the former head of the Polish government-in-exile, the London Poles, who had returned to Poland and simply was being pushed out of the government by the communists. In 1946 and 1947, Kiernik was a member of the National Council of the Homeland. He cooperated with Stanislaw Gomulka (*see* Gomulka, Stanislaw), the secretary general of the Polish Workers party, successor to the Polish Communist party. Kiernik was also a parliamentary deputy until 1952. He was second to Mikolajczyk in the Peasant party, quite well known among the general population.

After the referendum, which was rigged and ended with communist victory, Kiernik supported a Peasant party compromise with the communist-social democratic alliance. He was in a minority in his own party, most of whose members and leaders backed Mikolajczyk.

After the elections of 1947, Kiernik became openly hostile to Mikolajczyk. When the latter fled to England, Kiernik, who was then in the United States, returned to

Poland to salvage the organization of the Peasant party, as he later claimed. In fact, he collaborated with the communists to subordinate his party to communist domination. However, in October 1948, he was ousted as president of the Peasant party. His removal corresponded to the first drive of the communists for collectivization of agriculture.

Bibliography
Polonsky, Antony, and Druiker, Boleslaw, *The Beginnings of Communist Rule in Poland* (London, 1980).

Kowalski, Aleksander (real name: Czarny, Olek) (1908–1951). Kowalski joined the League of Young Communists in 1927, and the following year he became a member of the Communist party of Poland. Between 1936 and 1937, he was the secretary of the underground communist youth organization and several times he suffered prison terms. When World War II broke out, Kowalski fled to the Soviet Union. In May 1942, he was sent back to Poland as a member of the revived Communist party, the Polish Workers party, and was appointed secretary for the Warsaw region. After the war, he became chairman of the Young Fighters Union, a communist front organization, while remaining a member of the Central Committee of the Polish Workers party. In 1948, he was removed from the leadership, because he was a supporter of Wladislaw Gomulka (*see* Gomulka, Wladislaw) who was accused of nationalist deviation. Kowalski died in 1951.

Bibliography
Dziewanowski, M.K., *The Communist Party of Poland* (Cambridge, MA, 1976); Staar, Richard F., *Poland 1944–1962: The Sovietization of a Captive People* (New Orleans, LA, 1962).

Kozlowska, Helena (1906–1967). Kozlowska joined the Polish Communist party in 1929. She was imprisoned several times for illegal activities. After the reemergence of the communists under the name of the Polish Workers party in 1942, Kozlowska was one of the organizers of the party's guerrilla group, the Fighting Youth of Poland. In July 1944, she was a member of the reserve leadership after the Politburo was transferred to German-occupied Poland. During the Warsaw uprising, Kozlowska participated in the communist wing of the People's Army. After the war, she was a member of the communist leadership who organized the Warsaw City Council. From 1944 to 1959, she was a member of the Central Committee of the Communist party. Between 1945 and 1947, she was the deputy director, then director, of the propaganda department of the Central Committee. In 1954 she became the director of the Central Committee's department educating party members in Marxism-Leninism. In 1954, she was appointed to direct the organizational department of the Central Committee of the party. She was then moved to the revisions committee of the central party apparatus.

Bibliography
Dziewanowski, M.K., *The Communist Party of Poland* (Cambridge, MA, 1976).

Kuron, Jacek (1936–). Kuron was the son of an intellectual. He attended Warsaw University and was one of the organizers of the student revolt of 1968. Together with Adam Michnik (*see* Michnik, Adam), Kuron headed the group calling itself the Young Commandoes, a youth organization that included many members whose parents were active in the Polish United Workers party. Kuron was one of the founders of the Committee for the Defense of Workers (KOR) (see Committee for Defense of Workers) and, as such, was one of the young rebels watched by the Polish secret police.

In 1976, Kuron and Karol Modzelewski wrote "An Open Letter to the Party," in which they demanded democratization and reform of the economy. Both of them were jailed for their courageous action. When the strike of the Gdansk shipyards began in 1980, Kuron was already advising Lech Walesa (*see* Walesa, Lech) and became, with Tadeusz Mazowyeczki and Bronislaw Geremek (*see* Geremek, Bronislaw), the principal adviser to the Solidarity trade union (*see* Solidarity Trade Union of Poland). In September 1980, following the Gdansk agreement between Solidarity and the government, he declared:

"Something extraordinary happened in the life of the nation. Now we have an organized society within a communist regime."

When martial law was declared in December 1981, Kuron, together with other opposition and trade union leaders, was arrested. He was kept in jail until 1983. Nevertheless, he continued to be an active dissenter after his release and greatly contributed to the organization of the Roundtable talks between the government and Solidarity, which brought an end to communism in Poland.

Bibliography
Craig, Mary, *Lech Walesa and His Poland* (New York, 1987); Taylor, John, *Five Months with Solidarity* (New York, 1981); Tischner, Jozef, *The Spirit of Solidarity* (New York, 1982).

Michnik, Adam (1946–). Michnik's father was a pre-World War II communist militant. He raised his son in the spirit of Marxism-Leninism, and Adam was, indeed, a zealous Marxist in his early youth. During his university studies, however, the young communist discovered great discrepancies between life in contemporary Poland and Marxist theories. As a student at Warsaw University, Michnik became more and more outspoken about social injustice perpetrated by the communist *nomenklatura*. At fifteen years of age, Michnik established a club for his peers called Seekers of Contradictions, known by their friends as the Revisionist Toddlers' Club. At the age of eighteen, he was arrested for the first time for disseminating "An Open Letter to the Party," written by Jacek Kuron (*see* Kuron, Jacek) and Karol Modzelewski, which was critical of the regime and demanded democratic reforms.

Kuron and Modzelewski were given a sentence of three and a half years in prison; Michnik was sent to jail for two months.

After his release, Michnik alternated between prison terms and oppositional political activities. In 1964, he enrolled at Warsaw University to study history. Two years later, he was suspended for participating in a discussion led by Leszek Kolakowski, during which the well-known philosopher criticized the communist regime. In 1968, he collaborated with others in organizing a protest against the censor's closing of a play, *Forefathers' Eve*, by Adam Mickiewicz. He was expelled from the university on the orders of the ministry of higher education.

He went to work as an unskilled factory worker, while his fellow students protested his expulsion. An official campaign was organized against the protesters and, as part of the process, Michnik was again arrested and sentenced to a three-year prison term for allegedly planning to overthrow the communist regime. He was freed after spending a year and a half in jail, and took a job in a factory once more.

In 1971, he left the factory and enrolled at Poznan University as an extension student. In 1975, he received the equivalent of an MA degree in history. In May 1977, he was again arrested, but when widespread protests erupted in the intellectual community against his imprisonment, he was freed after two months. In 1979, he was among the founders of an independent publishing house, and the so-called Flying University, a study-group meeting at private homes, offering lectures by well-known scholars and dissidents. In August 1980, following the strikes in the cities on the Baltic coast, Michnik was arrested once again. The workers of the Interfactory Strike Committee (*see* Interfactory Strike Committee) made his release one of the conditions of the famous Gdansk agreement. After martial law was declared in December 1981, Michnik found himself in jail again, this time for 30 months. Six months of freedom was followed by another jail term for three years. After the collapse of communism in Poland, Michnik, now a completely free man, remained an advisor to Lech Walesa (*see* Walesa, Lech) and the Solidarity movement (*see* Solidarity Trade Union of Poland).

Bibliography

Schell, Jonathan, "Introduction to Adam Michnik," *Letters from Prison and Other Essays* (Berkeley, CA, 1985).

Mikolajczyk, Stanislaw (1901–1966). Mikolajczyk was an active member of the Peasant party during the 1930s; in 1931, he was deputy chairman of the party. Between 1928 and 1939, he was a Peasant party deputy in the Polish parliament (Sejm). During the exile of Andrzej Witos, Mikolajczyk directed the affairs of the Peasant party. Between 1939 and 1940, he was chairman of the National Council. When Germany attacked Poland in September 1939, Mikolajczyk escaped and went into exile in London.

After the Teheran conference, Winston Churchill informed Mikolajczyk of the Allied decision concerning Poland's eastern and western frontiers, including the transfer of the Polish population from the east and the expulsion of Germans from the western lands. Mikolajczyk argued that, although he was head of the government-in-exile, he had no authority to agree to any such resolution, since it would have to be approved by the postwar Polish parliament. He also pointed out that the proposed new borders would make Poland utterly dependent on the Soviet Union for its future security. However, after his visit to Moscow, Mikolajczyk became convinced that Poland had no other choice except to acquiesce in the proposal.

In April 1943, after the discovery of the graves of massacred Polish officers in the Katyn woods (*see* Katyn Woods Massacre), the London Poles were denounced by Joseph Stalin, and relations with the Soviet government were broken off. When three out of the four parties participating in the London-based Polish government-in-exile rejected the new borders on November 24, 1944, Mikolajczyk resigned as prime minister.

In June 1945, Mikolajczyk returned to Warsaw and was named copremier with the communist Wladislaw Gomulka (*see* Gomulka, Wladislaw) in the provisional Polish government, but he was soon outmaneuvered by the communists and received a barrage of false accusations. In the 1947 elections, conducted under great communist terror, the Peasant party was a loser. When the attacks on Mikolajczyk's person were renewed, he fled to the West once again.

Bibliography

Bregman, Aleksander, ed. *Faked Elections in Poland as Reported by Foreign Observers* (London, 1947); Bliss, Lane A., *I Saw Poland Betrayed* (New York, 1948); Korbonski, Andrzej, "Poland 1918–1990," in Joseph Held, ed. *The Columbia History of Eastern Europe in the Twentieth Century* (New York, 1992); Mikolaj-czyk, Stanislaw, *The Rape of Poland: Patterns of Soviet Aggression* (New York, 1948).

Military Policies in Communist Poland. Nowhere in Eastern Europe was Soviet intrusion into society as open and as brutal as it was in the Polish military establishment. Most Polish officers and noncommissioned officers remained loyal to the exiled government in London after the defeat by Germany. About 14,000 regular and reservist officers were captured by the Soviet army in 1939, and most of them were massacred in the Katyn woods in 1940 (*see* Katyn Woods Massacre).

In 1943, Polish communists in exile in the Soviet Union formed the Kosciuszko division and recruited former prisoners of war into the ranks. The division was eventually joined by various communist guerrilla bands who were fighting the Germans within Poland. When the war ended, Soviet officers, who commanded all the Polish forces, were recalled to the Soviet Union and were replaced by reliable communist cadres.

After the establishment of the North Atlantic Treaty Organization (NATO) on April 4, 1949, Joseph Stalin decided to strengthen his hold on the Polish armed forces. On November 6, Marshal Konstanty K. Rokossowski (*see* Rokossowski, Konstanty), a Soviet officer of Polish ancestry who had spent four years in the Soviet

Gulag on false charges, but was freed at the outbreak of the German-Soviet war, was appointed minister of defense for Poland. A large number of Soviet officers were also transferred to Poland to command the various Polish military formations. Rokossowski was a member of the Polish Politburo. He started the purges in the armed forces on Stalin's orders, replacing unreliable Polish officers with Soviet nationals. The size of the Polish army was expanded, and it received modern arms from the Soviet Union.

In 1950, universal conscription was introduced, and the training of new officers was directed by the establishment of a Soviet-style institution for staff officers. Special attention was paid to the political indoctrination of the recruits. Rokossowski's role made his presence in Poland deeply resented by the population. He was the epitome of the arrogant Soviet military commander. Although the Polish soldiers were still dressed in the traditional uniforms, Rokossowski's army was hardly considered by the population as their own. Nevertheless, the reliance of the Polish state on Soviet security arrangements was not totally artificial.

The Federal German Republic (West Germany) was rapidly recovering from the damages of the war, and it was soon integrated into the NATO organization. Its armed forces were trained by old-style officers who were outstanding experts in military affairs, and its armaments were ultramodern equipment provided by the United States. Furthermore, the West German government was not willing to declare its acceptance of Poland's western borders. This made Poland's reliance on Soviet military support unavoidable. After the outbreak of the Korean war, this reliance was a reciprocal one. Poland made serious contributions to the North Korean and Chinese military efforts.

By 1953, the Polish army consisted of about 400,000 men, mostly draftees, as well as large numbers in the border guards formations and in the secret police. In 1950, a paramilitary formation was also created in which membership was made compulsory for young people between the ages of thirteen and eighteen. To begin with, the service cooperated in seasonal and construction works, but it soon became an important means of paramilitary training and Marxist-Leninist indoctrination. After 1953, the Polish military budget was moderated somewhat with the accompanying reduction in the number of soldiers.

Until 1956, however, when Wladislaw Gomulka (*see* Gomulka, Wladislaw) came into power the second time, the Polish armed forces remained under strict Soviet control. In October 1956, Polish officers and soldiers simply refused to obey the commands of their Soviet officers. The Soviet personnel, including Marshal Rokossowski, were sent packing when Gomulka solidified his position.

Throughout the communist period, Polish military policies were heavily complicated by the need to protect the newly acquired German lands in the west. Thus, resentment of Soviet military presence in the country was somewhat mitigated by the need for Soviet support. In 1980, Poland's politicized army took over the government. For the first time in the history of communist movements, a communist country was placed under martial law, military personnel were directed to perform police duties, and a general of the army, Wojciech Jaruzelski (*see* Jaruzelski, Wojciech), assumed the post of head of the communist party and prime minister of Poland. He was even elected president of the republic but was eventually brushed aside after the collapse of the communist system.

Bibliography

Johnson, Ross A., *The Warsaw Pact: Soviet Military Policy in Eastern Europe* (New Haven, CT, 1984); Malcher, George, *Poland's Politicized Army* (New York, 1984); Sanford, George, *Military Rule in Poland* (London, 1986).

Milosz, Czeslaw (1911–). Born of professional parents in Lithuania, Milosz received his education in Vilnius, then he moved to Paris where he attended university studies. Already in his early twenties, Milosz began publishing his poems and essays and aroused the interest of Western intellectuals.

In 1939, when Poland was attacked first by Nazi Germany and then by the Soviet Union, Milosz went back to Warsaw and joined the underground resistance. He wrote and edited the underground publications issued by the resistance.

In 1946, he was appointed a member of the Polish diplomatic service. Until 1950, he was stationed at the Polish embassy in Washington, D.C. Then he was transferred to Paris as first secretary for cultural affairs. In February 1951, however, Milosz broke off his relations with the communist government of Poland and went into exile. He stayed in France for a time, but he was subjected to vicious attacks by the French communists. Milosz decided to move to the United States. Since 1960, he has been professor of Slavic languages and literatures at the University of California at Berkeley. He has written volumes of poetry and has published several collections of essays, two books of fiction, and an autobiography. In 1978, Milosz received the Neustadt International Prize for Literature. In 1980, he was awarded the highest literary distinction in the world when he won the Nobel Prize for literature.

Bibliography

Czarnecka, Ewa, and Fiut, Aleksander, *Conversations with Czeslaw Milosz* (San Diego, CA, 1981); Milosz, Czeslaw, *The Captive Mind* (New York, 1981).

Moczar, Myeczislaw (real name: Mietek) (1913–). Moczar joined the illegal Polish Communist party in 1937, one year before Joseph Stalin ordered its dissolution. In 1938, he was arrested and put in prison. When the war broke out, he was freed and became one of the leading commanders of the People's Army and the People's Guard, both communist guerrilla bands. He successively commanded the guerrillas in Lodz, Lublin, and Kielce.

After the war, he was appointed a member of the security bureau of the Polish state. Following 1948, he occupied various party and government posts. He was a member of the Polish United Workers party's Central Committee. In 1948, he was purged with Gomulka (*see* Gomulka, Wladis-law). After Gomulka's return to power in 1956, Moczar was appointed deputy minister of the interior. In 1964, he became the minister of the interior.

In 1967, the Jewish members of the Polish United Workers party were pleased when Israel defeated its Arab adversaries in a lightning fast war. The problem was that the Soviet Union supported the Arabs, and the Soviet leaders instructed Gomulka to dampen Jewish enthusiasm in his party. Gomulka declared that Jewish communists cannot have two homelands. He used the anti-Zionist argument, invented by the Soviet leaders, against Polish Jews. Moczar may or may not have received encouragement from the Soviet leadership, but he used the incident to challenge Gomulka. When, in 1968, students and intellectuals openly challenged the party's cultural policies, Moczar did not wait for Gomulka's approval; he stepped in and ordered the secret police to round up the discontented elements.

There were three days of demonstrations in Warsaw over the closing of a play that contained some antitsarist statements that had brought the audiences to their feet each night. Moczar ordered the mass arrest of the students and professors who had demonstrated against the closing.

Moczar was a controversial fellow. He never kept his scorn hidden about the Muscovites who had spent their time in comfortable offices in Moscow during the war. Many of these Muscovites were Jewish. Moczar, an anti-Semite, conducted a vicious anti-Semitic campaign against Jews in Polish cultural life, in the sciences, in education, and, especially, in the state and party bureaucracies. It was quite obvious that Moczar and his supporters used official anti-Semitism as a pretext to vent their personal biases, but also to challenge Gomulka's leadership in the party. Moczar wanted to show that he was tougher than Gomulka, therefore, better suited to lead Poland than his rival. Ironically, there were few Jews left in Poland by that time. The remaining ones then decided to apply for emigrants' visas, since the atmosphere in Poland was just too hostile to Jews.

However, Moczar's campaign backfired; Poles had their fill of anti-Semitism, and Moczar's support fizzled. Party members were especially appalled by the brutality with which Moczar's secret police treated Jewish students and intellectuals. Yet, Moczar survived the removal of Gomulka. However, when the time came in 1970, the party leaders, supported by their Soviet colleagues, did not choose him, but settled on Edward Gierek (*see* Gierek, Edward), a Silezian communist, to head the Polish United Workers party. In 1971, Moczar was finally ousted, and he retired from politics.

Bibliography
Blit, Lucjan, *Gomulka's Poland* (New York, 1968); Stehle, Hans Jakob, *The Independent Satellite: Society and Politics in Poland Since 1945* (New York, 1965).

National Council of the Homeland. This organization, created by the Soviet leadership in 1944, was controlled through the Polish Workers party, organized in 1942. On July 22, 1944, the council declared itself the only Polish governing authority and, on December 31, was proclaimed the provisional national government of the country. In January 1945, the Soviet Union recognized this government as the legitimate authority in Poland. However, at the Yalta meeting, the Western Allies insisted that the provisional government include members of the London-based Polish exile government if it wanted Western recognition. There were already some ostensibly noncommunist members of this government, but they were, in reality, crypto-communists. In 1945, therefore, several members of the "London Poles" were included in the new government. They lasted until 1947 when, after the rigged elections, they were forced to flee the country or were arrested and jailed.

Bibliography

Bain, Leslie, *The Reluctant Satellites* (New York, 1960); Staar, Richard F., *Poland, 1944–1962: The Sovietization of a Captive People* (New Orleans, LA, 1962).

Ochab, Edward (1906–). Ochab joined the underground Polish Communist party in 1929. In 1936, he was arrested and spent two years in prison. When Germany attacked Poland in 1939, Ochab fled to the Soviet Union. In the German-Soviet war, he served as deputy chief of indoctrination of the troops of the Polish Kosciuszko division under Soviet command. After the war, he worked in various positions in the apparatus of the Polish United Workers party. In 1950, he was appointed a member of the secretariat of the Central Committee of the party. Already in 1948, he was a candidate (nonvoting) member of the party's Politburo, and in 1951 he was promoted to full membership in that body. When Boleslaw Bierut (*see* Bierut, Boles-law) who replaced Gomulka (*see* Gomulka, Wladislaw) in 1948 died in 1956, his successor was Edward Ochab.

Ochab was a reformer, within limits, of course, who somewhat reduced the role of the secret police in Poland, shifted some investments away from heavy industry, and sought some accommodation with the Roman Catholic church. On June 28-29, the workers in the city of Poznan revolted. They had enough of food shortages, the lack of adequate housing, constantly increasing work norms, and decreasing living standards. They openly deplored the uneven trade with the Soviet Union and denounced the communist bureaucracy.

Ochab ordered the Polish army to suppress the disturbances; over fifty workers were killed, and hundreds were wounded in the skirmishes. This act so demoralized the Polish army that Ochab and his supporters feared a soldiers' revolt. Ochab blamed "imperialist agents" for the workers' uprising at first, using the standard communist propaganda slogans. Then he was forced by circumstances to shift his position and admit that the workers' grievances were real. In spite of strong opposition from the Muscovites, Ochab continued his reformist course. He removed some of the hard-line Stalinists from the communist leadership, and he ordered the exploration of the reasons for the failure of economic policies.

In the meantime, the workers were not intimidated. They proceeded to elect independent workers councils and were becoming increasingly vocal in demanding honest political reforms. On August 25-26 1956, nearly a million people traveled to the monastery of Jasna Gora at Czestochowa to commemorate the liberation of Poland from the Tatar armies three hundred years before. They demanded a similar liberation from Soviet domination.

The party leadership offered the chance to Wladislaw Gomulka to return to power (he had been released from prison in 1955 and was living in retirement), but with all sorts of restrictions. Gomulka knew that he was the people's choice, and he refused to accept the conditions. He insisted on a free hand. He declared the collectivization of the land to be a costly failure, and announced that he would insist on the primacy of Polish national interests in Poland's relations with other states.

Ochab had little choice, and he finally acceded to Gomulka's demands. He realized that only Gomulka could still save Soviet-style socialism in Poland. The Soviet leaders who were opposed to the reemergence of Gomulka as Poland's communist chief were finally convinced that they, too, had little choice. They realized that the choice was civil war, which could turn into a national uprising against the Soviet Union. Ochab was, therefore, replaced by Gomulka in October 1956, and he retired from political life.

Bibliography

Bethell, Nicholas, *Gomulka: His Poland and His Communism* (London, 1972); Syrop, Konrad, *Spring in October: The Story of the Polish Revolution of 1956* (London, 1958); Rothschild, Joseph, *Return to Diversity. A Political History of Eastern Europe since 1945* (Oxford, 1992).

Oder-Neisse Line. At the conferences of the Allied leaders at Teheran, Yalta, and Potsdam, there were many discussions of Poland's postwar borders. Joseph Stalin insisted that the country's boundaries in the east with the Soviet Union should be moved to the west, since Poland had acquired the eastern territories in the war with the Soviet Union in 1920. Furthermore, the eastern lands of Poland contained large Great Russian, White Russian, and Ukrainian populations. The territory in question amounted to 180,000 square kilometers or 69,479 square miles. In order to compensate Poland for the loss, about 103,000 square kilometers of German lands in the western part of Poland were to be ceded to the postwar Polish state, up to the line of the Oder-Neisse rivers. The Allied leaders eventually accepted these proposals, and Poland was "moved to the west."

According to the agreement, Polish citizens living in the eastern lands were to be removed. More than 3 million Germans were expelled and settled in the Allied occupational zones of Germany. Polish-German national antagonisms were, thus, ensured, and Poland's reliance on Soviet guarantees of its security was made a necessity. The newly acquired territories, officially called the "recovered lands" by the successive Polish governments, included the cities of Gdansk (Danzig), Wroclaw (Breslau), Szczeczin (Stettin), and parts of East Prussia, as well as the entire industrial basin of Silesia.

Bibliography

Gotthold, Rhode, ed. *The Genesis of the Oder-Neisse Line in Diplomatic Negotiations During World War II: Sources and Documents* (New York, 1962); Gruchman, Bochdan, et al., eds. *Polish Western Territories* (Poznan, 1959); Jordan, Zbigniew, *Oder-Neisse Line: A Study of the Political, Economic and European Significance of Poland's Western Frontiers* (London, 1952); Kruszewski, Anthony Z., *The Oder-Neisse Boundary and Poland's Modernization: The Socioeconomic and Political Impact* (New York, 1972); Sword, Keith, *The Soviet Take-over of the Polish Eastern Provinces, 1939–1941* (New York, 1991); Wagner, Wolfgang, *The Genesis of the Oder-Neisse Line* (Stuttgart, 1957).

Pawlak, Waldemar (1959–). Pawlak was born into a peasant family. He graduated from the automotive and agricultural machinery department of Warsaw Polytechnic Academy, and, in 1984, he took over the family farm of forty-two acres. He also joined the United Peasant party the following year. This party was the rural satellite of the Polish United Workers party. He became a member of the Rural Youth Union, a mass-organization sponsored by the communists. In the 1989 elections, Pawlak won one of the seventy-six seats preserved for his party. However, he enjoyed the endorsement of Rural Solidarity. He was one of the members of the United Peasant party who revolted against the satellite status of their organization and joined Solidarity (*see* Solidarity Trade Union of Poland). Their joint effort brought Tadeusz Mazowieczki to the prime ministership. In this struggle, the discredited leadership of the Peasant party was ousted. The party then changed its name to the Polish Peasant party-Renewal, and it was determined to recapture its precommunist past.

In May 1990, the Peasant party merged with the Polish Peasant party, Wilanow, the largest rural organization growing out of the opposition movement. The chairman of the new organization, Roman Bartoszcze, proved to be an erratic leader and the following year, he was ousted. He was charged with slowness in dealing with the members of the former rural *nomenklatura*, that is, the rural communist functionaries who had joined the Peasant party after 1989. Pawlak was elected to replace Bartoszcze as party leader.

Many in the party considered Pawlak's ascent the restoration of the old Peasant party apparatus. This was, however, not really the case. In the elections of 1991, the alliance of the two wings of the Peasant party dissolved. Pawlak's faction won forty-two seats in parliament (Sejm), and its representatives aggressively defended rural interests. They demanded that the state guarantee minimum purchase prices for agrarian goods, which was the continuation of some sort of subsidy for food producers, and provide more credit to farmers. They also demanded that restrictions be placed on food imports.

After the October 1991 elections, however, the party's stance became more conciliatory. In mid-December, Pawlak provided crucial support for the Olszewski government during a debate where a no-confidence vote was taken. In exchange, the party received several administrative posts, although it refused to join the government. Pawlak then formed a tentative and, as it turned out, unstable alliance with the

Christian National Union and the Peasant Alliance. Yet, in June, 1992, it voted to support the no-confidence vote which ended the rule of the Olszewszki government.

After this, Pawlak was elected prime minister by a coalition of oppositional parties. He was the fourth prime minister of Poland since the collapse of the communist regime, the youngest man at the age of thirty-three ever to occupy the post of prime minister. His opponents charged that the Pawlak government was tainted by its past, namely, that the party of the prime minister had been a communist satellite and that many of the party's leaders were really communists before 1989. Although some of the charges are obviously true, Pawlak himself was certainly not tainted by collaboration, since he is too young for such a charge. In 1993, the Pawlak government was replaced by another cabinet, headed by Hanna Suchocka (*see* Suchocka, Hanna).

Bibliography
Vinton, Louisa, "Olszewski's Ouster Leaves Poland Polarized," *Radio Free Europe Research Report* 1.25 (June 19, 1992), pp. 1-10.

PAX (A Catholic Lay Organization in Communist Poland). This tightly-knit, Warsaw-based group, organized around a weekly journal, was ostensibly Roman Catholic. Most of the leaders of the group came from an organization called FALANGA, a radical rightist splinter group of the National Democratic party of the interwar years. The leader of PAX during the 1930s was Boleslaw Piasecki, whose ideas came close to those of the fascists. The organization was anticommunist and anti-Semitic and was strongly nationalistic.

The FALANGA had few followers in pre-World War II Poland. It survived the war as an underground organization fighting against both the Germans and the communists. In 1944, Piasecki fell into the hands of the Soviet Army. In spite of his past, he soon reemerged on the political scene. It has been rumored that he became an agent of the Soviet KGB. Piasecki established the so-called Progressive Catholics movement, or PAX, with its own publishing house. According to some sources, including Jozef Swiatlo, a Polish security officer who defected to the West, Piasecki saved himself by agreeing to "subvert the Catholic church from within."

Piasecki, having been a right-wing radical, was naturally closer to left-wing radicals in his ideology than to moderates. He was certainly an opportunist who was eagerly embraced by the early communist leadership in their march to totalitarian power. Piasecki himself had a strong drive to succeed in politics, and the circumstances gave him an opportunity by making a deal with the communists. He was also a realist, and cooperation with the Soviet KGB may have seemed a realistic choice. He was convinced that the next global conflict would be fought between the Soviet Union and the United States, and that the U.S. would be the winner. For the communists, Piasecki was an ally who was eager to help them while the communist organization was still weak.

In the late 1940s, when the first great conflict between the communists and the Catholic church began, PAX sided with the state. In the disputes over the charitable activities of the church, over the confiscation of the church's lands and other properties, over the removal of religious instruction from the schools, PAX invariably opposed the hierarchy of the church. Its leaders incessantly declared their loyalty to the church as an institution with the qualification that they opposed the political stance of the episcopate.

By 1953, when church and state were locked in seemingly insoluble conflicts, PAX was at the height of its activities. It was then that Piasecki, who had no theological training, began disputing the doctrines of the church. He published a book entitled *The Essential Problems*, which was condemned by the Holy Office in Rome together with his journal. This only encouraged the Progressive Catholics to intensify their activities. The communists rewarded Piasecki handsomely.

PAX actually worked almost as a capitalist enterprise. It was involved not only in commercial but also in industrial production almost like a privileged nationalized firm. PAX hardly paid any taxes. In 1956, the organization showed a profit of over 100 million zlotys. Thirty-eight million of this money paid for the deficits by PAX's so-called socio-political enterprises, that is, political propaganda against the church's leadership. The communist state suppressed most other Catholic lay organizations except ZNAK (*see* ZNAK), giving PAX an open field for its activities. While more and more clergymen loyal to the episcopate found themselves under arrest, PAX established an alliance with the so-called priest-patriots, a group of renegade clergy organized by the secret police.

The year 1956, however, brought some reverses for PAX. Wladislaw Gomulka (*see* Gomulka, Wladislaw) came back to power. Cardinal Wyszynski was released from confinement (*see* Wyszynski, Cardinal, Stefan), and there were open allegations about the connections between Piasecki and the Polish secret police. Gomulka needed the support of the Catholic hierarchy to calm the rebellious nation. In addition, PAX and Piasecki were never liked much by ordinary Communist party members. Piasecki's attempt to reconcile Catholic theology with Marxism-Leninism was frowned upon.

During the crisis of 1956, Piasecki declared that force was necessary to prevent democratization. In November, many leading members of PAX withdrew from the organization. Piasecki saw it necessary to apologize to the church and pledge his cooperation to the hierarchy. Yet, PAX was not dissolved, nor were its enterprises closed down. Gomulka was obviously thinking of using it as insurance against possible recalcitrance by the church's hierarchy.

In the spring of 1957, Piasecki renewed his activities. Consequently, Cardinal Wyszynski forbade Catholics to cooperate with the publications of PAX, and the communist censors promptly prevented the dissemination of his message. The alliance between Piasecki and the communists was, therefore, restored.

In 1958, the progressive Catholics began a campaign for "moral renovation," hoping to increase their meager membership rolls. They made a special effort to recruit young people. They also tried to gain international recognition. In the local elections held in 1958, PAX was allowed to run candidates in 300 districts. Piasecki issued two ideological statements under the titles of *Polish patriotism* and *An Ideological guide*. His proposal amounted to communism without Marxism. He emphasized the socialist character of PAX and stressed the alliance with the Communist party, but he rejected materialism as the guide to his ideology and declared that PAX was continuing Polish national traditions. He called on the communists to broaden the base of the dictatorship of the proletariat by including the "progressive Catholic movement" in the governing alliance. He promised that PAX would continue doing all it could to become a formal ally of the Communist party. In short, he wanted to be included in the government.

In 1961, however, the winds changed once again. The government began to restrict the economic activities of PAX. Its tax privileges were withdrawn reducing its profits by half. Its political activities were also curtailed and only three PAX deputies were seated in parliament. There were several reasons for these steps. A strong group within the Communist party's highest leadership disliked Piasecki and his organization. They observed that Piasecki's frantic efforts to expand the membership rolls of PAX had failed. Cardinal Wyszynski refused to have anything to do with the group, and the Catholic masses followed the cardinal's directions. Piasecki himself became an irritant from an asset for Gomulka, and his high aspirations were not supported by a sizable following. All this, however, did not dampen Piasecki's zeal. He continued to issue statements attacking Cardinal Wyszynski's position in almost anything and blamed the Polish episcopate for the lack of cooperation between the church and the communists.

In the fall of 1964, there was a new crisis between state and church in Poland. PAX attacked the Cardinal once again, accusing him of confusing his position of bishop with that of a politician. It demanded that the Catholic hierarchy recognize the benefits of the communist economic system for the country. In consequence, PAX was able to seat five deputies in parliament the following year. However, Piasecki lost much of his value for the communists. PAX was, therefore, quietly relegated to the background. Piasecki, the realist, went too far in appeasing the Soviet leaders, and he eventually endangered Polish national interests. He was being considered by most people as a Quisling. After 1965, his political ambitions and participation in political life in Poland had come to an end.

Bibliography
Bromke, Adam, *Poland's Politics: Idealism vs Realism* (Cambridge, MA, 1967); Ramet, Pedro, ed. *Religion and Nationalism in the Soviet Union and Eastern Europe* (New York, 1990); Shneiderman, Stephen L., *The Warsaw Heresy* (New York, 1959).

Polish Elections in 1989. The Polish political situation in 1989 was unsettled. The communist leadership was aware that something fundamentally important had happened but insisted that the communist system could still be saved if reforms were introduced. They were ensured of a majority of 65 percent in parliament (Sejm) and were in control of most of society's infrastructures. But the results of the elections of June disabused the communists of their illusions. Their party suffered a staggering defeat while the Solidarity-led opposition (*see* Solidarity Trade Union of Poland) proved that it did, indeed, represent the will of the majority of the people. Long-time communist allies, the United Peasant party and the Democratic party abandoned the alliance and joined the Solidarity deputies in parliament. The communists had to give up their control of the government if they did not want civil war.

The new prime minister was Tadeusz Mazowieczki, one of the founders of Solidarity. His cabinet was composed mostly of members of Solidarity with a few additions from other parties. Although the communists were still in control of the ministries of the interior and defense, they no longer had the power to impose their will on their opponents. As a concession to the communists, General Wojciech Jaruzelski (*see* Jaruzelski, Wojciech) was named president of the republic.

The new government began its work promptly. In January 1990, a new economic system, based on a free-market mechanism, was established. The new government started Poland on the road to economic recovery. A policy of privatization was introduced. State monopolies were to be abolished and foreign investments encouraged. Efforts were started to replace communist party apparatchiki with officials who had not been compromised during the communist regime. At the same time, centuries-old Polish political traditions reasserted themselves. Political parties and other political organizations proliferated. The Mazowieczki government replaced the communist ministers of the interior and defense with its own choices.

In November 1990, new presidential elections were held. After a runoff, Lech Walcsa (*see* Walesa, Lech) emerged victorious. But opposition to what was perceived as his authoritarian disposition soon emerged. Walesa's authority has been repeatedly challenged, and the new prime minister, Jan Olszewski, eventually became his rival for power. The Olszewski government was eventually replaced in the summer of 1992, and a new government under the prime ministership of Hanna Suchocka (*see* Suchocka, Hanna), the first woman prime minister in Poland, emerged.

Bibliography

Vinton, Louisa, "Poland's Government Crisis: an End is in Sight?" *Radio Free Europe Research Report*. 1.30 (July 24, 1992), pp. 15-25.

Popieluszko Murder. Father Jerzy Popieluszko was an outspoken supporter of the Solidarity trade union movement. (*see* Solidarity Trade Union of Poland) In 1980, he had been attached to the Saint Stanislaw Kostka church in Warsaw, in a predominantly working-class neighborhood. Starting in February 1982, he celebrated mass on the last Sunday each month for Poland, during which he prayed with the parishioners for the release of political prisoners. Everyone knew, of course, that he meant especially Lech Walesa (*see* Walesa, Lech). In July 1984, the deputy prosecutor of Warsaw filed an indictment against Father Popieluszko for allegedly working against Poland's interests from the pulpit. At the same time, fearful of providing an excuse for the communists to clamp down on the church, Cardinal Glemp (*see* Glemp, Cardinal Jozef) ordered Popieluszko to tone down his sermons which he judged to be too political in character. On July 22, 1984, however, a general amnesty was issued and the indictment was dropped.

In October, Father Popieluszko was abducted by officers of the ministry of the interior, that is, the Polish secret police. He was tortured and then murdered by these brutal thugs. The barbarous act created a general revulsion against the communists throughout Poland. His funeral services were conducted in front of his church on November 3, 1984 (with the attendance of a quarter of a million mourners) by Cardinal Glemp himself. The cardinal referred to Popieluszko as a martyr and a missionary for the people and for truth. The cardinal also took the opportunity to appeal for national reconciliation. Lech Walesa, freed by the amnesty, placed a wreath on Popieluszko's coffin. Solidarity leaders from the Mazowsze region held three minutes of silence in the priest's honor.

The autopsy report, released by the government, showed that he had been tortured and beaten before he was thrown into the river with his hands and feet bound. The government realized that an enraged people could burst into revolution if the murderers were not brought to justice. It also wanted to show the world that it was not a totalitarian state and that it would observe its own laws. The Politburo therefore announced that the secretary general of the Polish United Workers party, Wojciech Jaruzelski (*see* Jaruzelski, Wojciech) himself would take control over the ministry of internal affairs. General Czeslaw Kiszczak, the minister of internal affairs whose troops had committed the murder, told parliament that three officers of the ministry had been formally charged with the murder of the priest, and two others who had been implicated in the crime had been detained. Kiszczak asserted that the murder of Father Popieluszko was a provocation and called its perpetrators "politicians and enemies of socialism."

The trial began on December 11, 1984, and it lasted until February 7, 1985. It resulted in the conviction of four officers of the security services. A Colonel Adam Pietruszka was convicted of instigating the priest's murder and was sentenced to twenty-five years in prison. Captain Grzegorz Piotrowski, who led the murder squad, also received twenty-five years in jail, although the prosecutor asked for death for both men. Lieutenant Leszek Pekala and Lieutenant Waldemar Chmielewski were sentenced to fifteen and fourteen years imprisonment, respectively. Jaruzelski then declared that there was no proof that the murderers were directed to do their deed by higher authorities.

At the trial, the church was accused of tolerating priests who used the pulpit as a forum for agitation against the socialist state. The state prosecutor went so far as to state that Father Jerzy Popieluszko was the incarnation of hatred for Polish socialism and the state. He was accused of storing underground newspapers as well as tear grenades and ammunition in his apartment. The prosecutor tried to blacken the reputation of the dead man and excuse the murderers as outraged defenders of socialism.

The prosecutor, Leszek Pietrasinski, named other priests as following Popieluszko's example in inciting hatred against the state. He also presented Popieluszko's murder as a provocation by counterrevolutionaries. He stated that the act was designed to discredit the Polish socialist system in the eyes of the public and of the world. At the same time, Jaruzelski's henchmen began suggesting to Western diplomats that the murder was really instigated by hard-liners in the communist party leadership as a way to scuttle Jaruzelski's "conciliatory efforts" toward the Catholic church.

Bibliography

Monticone, Ronald C., *The Catholic Church in Communist Poland 1945–1985: Forty Years of Church-State Relations* (Boulder, CO, 1986); Moody, John, *The Priest Who Had to Die: The Case of Jerzy Popieluszko* (New York, 1987); Sanford, George, *Military Rule in Poland* (London, 1986).

Poznan Riots of June 1956. Poznan is located in central Poland on the Warta river. The city developed rapidly during the twentieth century, and its port has become a major point of embarkation for the Polish export-import trade. It also became a center of the machine tool and chemical industries. In June 1956, the workers of the city responded to sudden price increases of food and other consumer goods by strikes, demonstrations, and riots. The communist government ordered the army and the secret police to suppress the riots by any means necessary. The troops fired on the demonstrators killing over 50 people and wounding more than 300. This action raised general indignation throughout Poland. The People's Army, so called, killing ordinary people! The army was deeply shaken by its role in Poznan. Its officers and recruits were on the verge of mutiny. The generals declared that, in case of a Soviet invasion, they would order the troops to fight.

Nikita Khrushchev, who was first secretary of the Soviet Communist party at that time, backed off. He did not want to risk a war with Poland, since it could have led to a general conflagration in Eastern Europe. He consented to the installation of Wladislaw Gomulka (*see* Gomulka, Wladislaw) as secretary general of the Polish United Workers party. Gomulka immediately rescinded the price increases and introduced several reforms, but he refused to alter the system in any fundamental way. The victims of the Poznan riots received a memorial in 1980.

Bibliography

Lewis, Flora, *The Polish Volcano* (London, 1959); Korbonski, Andrzej, "Poland, 1918–1990," in Joseph Held, ed. *The Columbia History of Eastern Europe in the Twentieth Century* (New York, 1992); Syrop, Konrad, *Spring in October: The Story of the Polish Revolution of 1956* (London, 1958).

Rapacki Plan. Adam Rapacki (1909–) was born in the city of Lvov, which is part of Ukraine today. His father, a professor, was killed during the Warsaw uprising in 1944. Rapacki studied in France and Italy. He was an active member of Socialist Youth, the youth wing of the Polish Social Democratic party. Rapacki spent five years in a German prison camp during World War II, where he was befriended by the communist writer, Woldenberg, and was converted to Marxism-Leninism.

After the war, he discovered that Jozef Cyrankiewicz, the head of the Polish social democrats, was enthusiastic about merging his organization with that of the communists. When the Polish United Workers party was established by the merger of the two parties, Rapacki became a member of the first joint Politburo. In rapid succession, he was minister for shipping, and minister of higher education and culture; in 1956, he became foreign minister of Poland.

In the spring of 1957, Rapacki introduced a plan for a nuclear-free zone in Europe in a speech delivered at the general assembly of the United Nations. The zone was to include both Germanies, Poland, Czechoslovakia, Hungary, and Holland. At first, the plan elicited no reaction in the West. It was generally considered one more Soviet effort to divide and neutralize NATO. The Rapacki-plan, as it became known, found enthusiastic acceptance only among members of the Soviet Bloc.

The author described his plan as part of "constructive coexistence," an effort to develop better relations with the West after the brutal military suppression of the Hungarian Revolution by Soviet troops the year before led to the worsening of relations. But the December 1956 declaration issued in Moscow, signed by Rapacki himself, contradicted these aims. That declaration was a program for world revolution and the destruction of Western democracies. When the Rapacki plan was discussed by Western statesmen, this contradiction was repeatedly pointed out. Rapacki's counterargument was that Poland was inexorably bound to the Soviet Bloc. Although, he argued, the unification of Germany (which his plan also envisaged) would present a danger for Eastern Europe, the continuing stalemate between the Western alliance and the Soviet Bloc represented an even greater danger. German unification was, therefore, necessary, but only in the framework of the disarmament of both Germanies. The best way to begin this would be, according to him, by not introducing nuclear arms into Central and Eastern Europe.

The West disagreed. Heinrich von Brentano, West Germany's foreign minister, observed that, if the Rapacki plan were implemented, this would mean de-facto recognition of the East German state. He further argued that the plan would leave Western Europe at the mercy of the Soviet Union, whose overwhelming superiority in conventional armaments was balanced by the nuclear forces of the Western nations. He also pointed out that, in a war in Europe, nuclear-free zones would not be immune to a nuclear exchange.

Rapacki attempted to meet Western objections to his plan by working closely with Soviet leaders. They agreed that conventional arms reduction should become part of the plan. A number of control points would be established, and land and air supervision would be introduced. Moreover, West Germany would not have to negotiate directly with East Germany, thus, avoiding the divisive issue of recognition. German unification was then lifted out of the plan.

Rapacki now proposed a two-stage process. During the first phase, the great powers would agree not to introduce nuclear weapons beyond existing levels. This would have meant, of course, the exclusion of the territory of West Germany from stationing nuclear weapons. In the second stage, nuclear arms would be removed simultaneously together with some reductions in conventional arms.

In 1958, a few weeks after this proposal was made, Nikita Khrushchev torpedoed the Rapacki plan. He proposed the settling of problems between the two superpowers, if need be at the expense of their allies. This, of course, included Poland. Several times after the fiasco, the Polish government tried to resuscitate the Rapacki plan, but its time had passed. Another version of the plan was submitted to the eighteen members of the Disarmament Conference meeting in Geneva in February 1962. According to this version, the nuclear-free zone would include only states that wanted to be included. This was, however, no longer being seriously considered. It eventually disappeared quietly from the diplomatic scene.

Bibliography
Keesing's Research Report, *Germany and Eastern Europe Since 1945: From the Potsdam Agreement to Chancellor Brandt's Ostpolitik* (New York, 1973); Stehle, Hans Jakob, *The Independent Satellite: Society and Politics in Poland Since 1945* (New York, 1965).

Religious Policies in Communist Poland. The communist leaders never really understood the relationship between Polish Catholicism and nationalism. They were dogmatic Marxist-Leninists who considered religion a tool of the ruling classes and a distinctly bourgeois ideology. When both the ruling classes and the bourgeoisie were eliminated, religion and nationalism would become irrelevant. They were unwilling to admit the historical fact that the Catholic church was instrumental in preserving Polish nationality and culture at the time when Poland was divided among three great empires, and at the time when Joseph Stalin made great efforts to turn Poles into Russians after World War II.

The church also took on the role of encouraging the integration of the western territories by Poland, lands that were acquired from Germany after the war. The Polish emigrants who were transferred from the east when they were expelled from eastern Poland by the Soviet authorities to the west, faced chaotic conditions. The Catholic church not only provided food for them, but also helped them in rebuilding an almost completely destroyed economy. It provided health services and started up new schools. The Catholic organization, Caritas, supervised by a committee of bishops, performed all these services (*see* Caritas in Communist Poland). Collections were taken up in every church in Poland to support the people in the western lands, and the Catholic church made great efforts to convince the United Nations' relief organization (UNRRA) to contribute its share to the solution of problems.

Polish society was undoubtedly shaped by Catholicism. The church was an especially important institution for the peasantry. During dismemberment, the church provided the links between Poles living under German, Habsburg, or Russian occupation. It upheld national traditions, inspired Polish literature and the arts, and played a major role in all levels of education.

It was in the system of education that the communists began their attack against the Catholic church. Their attacks eventually reached every area of church life. The curricula of the schools were "purified" of church teachings, religious instruction was excluded, and Polish history was modified to suit Marxist-Leninist ideology. The historical role of the Catholic church was simply left out from official textbooks, and Polish history was simply taught as the product of materialism and class struggle. Marxism-Leninism was made a compulsory subject in all schools and universities together with the Russian language. Clergymen were expelled from the schools. Stefan Cardinal Wyszynski (*see* Wyszynski, Cardinal Stefan) issued several pastoral letters. He protested the imposition of materialism on school children and the falsification of Polish history. He was eventually forcibly removed from his office and kept under arrest in a monastery.

The struggle between the communist state and the Catholic church was especially acute around the Catholic University of Lublin. This institution was established by the church in 1918, was closed by the Nazis, and was reopened in 1944. The communists interfered with the operations of the university on every possible occasion. In 1951 and 1965, they imposed their own selection as rector. The admission of students was severely curtailed, and in 1952, the university's law school was closed. The faculty of socioeconomic sciences was disbanded in the same year. Several clergymen-professors were dismissed. The construction of new buildings was prohibited. The state made an effort to force the introduction of a new curriculum based on atheism at the Catholic university. Thanks to the almost superhuman efforts of the church's hierarchy, the university nevertheless survived. Five times a year, Sunday collections in the parishes were dedicated to the maintenance of the institution. About two-thirds of the university's expenses were covered by these funds.

The church never missed an opportunity to remind the people of their religious past. In 1966, it celebrated Poland's millennium as a Roman Catholic nation; it celebrated the contribution to science of such great Polish Catholics as Nicholas Copernicus and Johannes Comnenus. It also celebrated nonreligious national holidays that had been abolished by the communists, including the reestablishment of an independent Polish state in 1918 and the victory over the Soviet armies in 1920. The dioceses organized "days of national culture," under the sponsorship of Tadeusz Uszinski, the chaplain of Warsaw University, for the first time in 1975, which turned out to be a huge success. In Cracow, Karol Cardinal Woytila (*see* Woytila, Karol Cardinal), the later Pope John Paul II, was a strong supporter of the "days of national culture" movement. It became an annual celebration of the survival of the Polish nation. The festivities provided an opportunity for writers, actors, painters, and other creative people who were ostracized by the communists to show their talents.

Another initiative originated from the Reverend Jan Palusinski of Lodz in 1968. This was the so-called sacro-songs movement. This was an effort to adapt the church's work to new social relations and to attract young people to its ranks. Each year, huge crowds were attracted by the festivities. They listened to music and poetry composed and presented by their authors who contributed lasting works to Polish culture. The church was, therefore, able to counter the communists' efforts to impose their ideology on the nation without choice. Alone among the churches in the Soviet Bloc, the Polish Catholic church managed not only to survive the great pressure of the communist authorities, but was also to advance its own brand of "Polishness" in the face of a hostile government.

During the 1950s and 1960s, the methods the Polish communists used were the same as those used throughout the Soviet Bloc against the church. The most important means used were terror and intimidation in restricting the work of the church in Poland. They eliminated Sundays as a universal day of rest; they discriminated against religious people in employment and promotion; they made university admissions dependent upon the knowledge and acceptance of Marxist-Leninist ideology. They also closed seminaries, jailed priests, and persecuted the episcopate.

Stefan Cardinal Wyszynski was in the forefront of countering the communist pressure. As bishop of Lublin before he became cardinal, he issued several pastoral letters, the most famous of which was entitled "On the Christian Liberation of Man." Later as primate of Poland, (1949–1981), he continued the struggle even while he was under arrest.

The communists used all sorts of methods to divide the hierarchy. Two Catholic laymen's organizations, PAX (*see* PAX) and ZNAK (*see* ZNAK) were under their control. But the people saw through these chicaneries and did not support the "peace priests" who were often agents of the secret police.

In 1978, the church's prestige was strengthened immensely when Karol Cardinal Woytila was elected Pope John Paul II. He did not make a secret of his sympathies and issued several encyclicals critical of Marxism in general and the communist application of this ideology in particular. His visit to his homeland in 1979 was a huge success; millions went to see him and hear him deliver his message.

When the free trade union Solidarity (*see* Solidarity Trade Union of Poland) was established, the Polish church hierarchy did not know at first how to relate to the new organization. Wyszynski soon realized that Solidarity offered an opportunity to strengthen the relations between the Catholic church and the working people of Poland. Thus, the episcopate provided church services and advice to the leaders of Solidarity, but priests were generally forbidden to participate in the activities of the organization. The episcopate, soon headed by Jozef Cardinal Glemp (*see* Glemp, Jozef Cardinal) (Wyszynski died in June 1981), feared the revolutionary potential of the workers' organization. It feared direct Soviet intervention even more, and it abhorred the possibility of the recurrence of the terror of the 1950s. The caution which the hierarchy espoused created the first open conflict between the church and large masses of the people. Cardinal Glemp kept his distance and this provided the first words of satisfaction that the communist authorities ever expressed in their relation with the Catholic church.

When martial law was imposed on the country, the church began to change its stand. It supported Lech Walesa (*see* Walesa, Lech), and the other imprisoned leaders and supporters of Solidarity, and it permitted some priests to participate in helping their families. When the outspoken priest, Jerzy Popieluszko (*see* Popieluszko murder) was murdered by secret policemen, Cardinal Glemp himself conducted his funeral service and spoke out against the lawlessness of the government. With the collapse of the communist system in 1989, the Polish Roman Catholic church assumed a "new" role. Freed of interference by governmental authorities, the church began concentrating once again on its spiritual and cultural role in Polish society.

Bibliography

Chrypinski, Vincent C., "Church and Nationality in Postwar Poland," in Pedro Ramet, ed. *Religion and Nationalism in Soviet and East European Politics* 2nd ed. (Durham, NC, 1989), pp. 241-263; Krzywicki, Herbert, and Ziemba, Walter Z., trans. *The Prison Notes of Stefan Cardinal Wyszynszki* (London, 1985). Monticone, Ronald C., *The Catholic Church in Communist Poland, 1945–1985* (New York, 1986); Wyszynski, Stefan Cardinal, *A Strong Man Armed: Speeches* (New York, 1968); Zmijewski, Norbert A., *The Catholic-Marxist Ideological Dialogue in Poland, 1945–1980* (Aldershot, Great Britain, 1991).

Rokossowski, Konstanty (1896–1968). Rokossowski joined the Soviet Red Army in 1917. In the purges of Joseph Stalin during the late 1930s, he was tried and sentenced to twenty-five years in prison together with other high-ranking Soviet officers. He could consider himself lucky, because general M. N. Tukhachewsky and other high-ranking generals were executed in the same purges.

At the outbreak of the Nazi-Soviet war, however, Rokossowski was released from the Soviet Gulag and given a division to command. He acquitted himself brilliantly and, in 1944, he was promoted to the rank of marshal. In November 1944, he was appointed commander of the second Belorussian front.

In November 1949, Stalin sent Rokossowski to Poland to assume the post of minister of defense of the Polish state. He was also named deputy prime minister, member of the Central Committee of the Polish United Workers party, and a full member of the party's Politburo. Although Rokossowski was instrumental in Sovietizing the Polish army in the 1950s, he remained in the background and did not attempt to cause harm to the Polish people. This was evident in 1956, when he did not prevent the return of Wladislaw Gomulka (*see* Gomulka, Wladislaw) to power. Nevertheless, his presence in Poland was resented because he was a symbol of Soviet domination. When Gomulka assumed the prime ministership, and the post of first secretary of the party, he sent Rokossowski home to the Soviet Union.

Bibliography

Malcher, George, *Poland's Politicized Army* (New York, 1984).

Roundtable Talks in Poland. In the late 1980s, popular anger was becoming ever more visible in Polish society, and social and political tensions were reaching a dangerous point. This atmosphere threatened the communist government with the complete collapse of its policies and the repudiation of the communist system. The leaders of the armed forces, except General Wojciech Jaruzelski (*see* Jaruzelski, Wojciech), declared that they were not willing to repeat the experience of the Poznan riots of 1956, or the firing on the people in 1976. In addition, the Soviet leader, Mikhail Gorbachev, made it quite clear that Soviet tanks would not be given orders to save the communist regimes in Eastern Europe.

The communists were left to their own devices, and they had no choice but to try to make peace with their own people. The result in Poland was that the government was forced to sit down with the opposition in order to work out some form of consensus and to settle the future of the Polish republic. This was an unprecedented development in the history of Polish communism.

The Roundtable discussions, as the negotiations were called, began in 1989. The talks centered at first on the status of the Polish economy and the steps needed to make it work again. This time, the discussants included the best economic experts that could be found in Poland regardless of their political views. The discussion, however, led to agreements only on short-term economic measures, not to the acceptance of fundamental reforms. The creation of a new economic system was postponed until after the elections to be held in June 1989. The elections resulted in an overwhelming victory for the Solidarity party, and, when a new Polish government was formed, it included noncommunist ministers, for the first time since 1948.

The Roundtable discussions also dealt with the new electoral law and the distribution of parliamentary mandates. The communists still hoped to be able to salvage the system, but the elections ended their illusions. In the final count, the Roundtable discussions did not accomplish much; however, they did contribute to a peaceful transition of power from the communists to the opposition, a process that would have been unthinkable only a few years before.

Bibliography

Sabbat-Swidlicka, Anna, "Poland: A Year of Three Governments," *Radio Free Europe Research Report*. 1.1 (January 1, 1993), pp. 102-107; Vinton, Louisa, "Poland: The Anguish of Transition," *Radio Free Europe Research Report* 1.1 (January 3, 1991), pp. 91-95.

Solidarity Trade Union. On July 1, 1980, the Polish government increased the prices of some consumer goods, including food, without advanced notice. The following day, workers who demanded compensatory wage increases held short work stoppages in factories. There were strikes in the area of Lublin. On August 14, workers in the shipyards of the Baltic port, Gdansk, went on strike. Two days later, led by the electrician Lech Walesa (*see* Walesa, Lech), and a 48-year old crane operator, Anna Walentynowicz (*see* Walentynowicz, Anna), they formed an Interfactory Strike Committee (*see* Interfactory Strike Committee) in order to coordinate the strikes in all

Gdansk factories. Soon the strikes spread to Gdynia and the shipyards of Szczecin as well as to other industrial cities in the north of Poland.

The communist leaders responded slowly to the challenge. In July, when the workers in Lublin struck, a deputy prime minister, Myeczislaw Jagielski, was sent to negotiate with the strikers, but the talks dragged on without results. At the end of July, Edward Gierek (*see* Gierek, Edward), the leader of the Polish state and Communist party, traveled to Moscow and discussed the situation with Leonid Brezhnev. Toward the end of August, negotiations with the workers at Gdansk began, and on August 31, a far-reaching agreement was reached with them. Prime Minister Jozef Babiuch was then dismissed, and a settlement was reached with the workers at Szczecin.

However, this was only the beginning. The strikes were spreading to Silesia, the most highly industrialized region of Poland. On September 6, Gierek, who was ill, was dismissed. He was replaced by Stanislaw Kania (*see* Kania, Stanislaw) as first secretary of the Polish United Workers party. Eighteen days later, Lech Walesa, now chairman of the newly formed Self-Governing Trade Union, Solidarity (*see* Solidarity Trade Union of Poland), applied for official recognition of the organization.

The new prime minister, Jozef Pinkowski, and the Communist party's leader, Kania, visited Brezhnev in Moscow, where they were pressured to suppress Solidarity by force, and Brezhnev offered the "fraternal help" of the Soviet army to do so. East German leader Erich Honecker advised Brezhnev to take strong measures against the Poles lest the contagion spread to the rest of the Soviet Bloc nations. Gustav Husak, the Czechoslovak communist leader, made representations similar to Honecker's. Kania and Pinkowski declined the offered Soviet help. While they were in Moscow, the Polish courts decided that Solidarity's registration was not against the law.

In January, the idea of the establishment of an independent trade union for farmers began to spread far and wide. In Bielsko Biala province, workers struck in 110 industrial plants demanding to join Solidarity. Students at Lodz University followed suit. In January 1981, Lech Walesa led a delegation to Rome, to visit the former Karol Woytila, now Pope John Paul II (*see* Woytila, Karol Cardinal). Their meeting with the pope provided a powerful image of Solidarity as a new force in the communist bloc. The hard-liners among the Polish communist leaders demanded harsh measures against the workers by the "workers' state." Kania and Pinkowski tried to moderate the party's actions.

In early February, the hard-liners seemed to have won the day. Pinkowski was replaced by the communist general Wojciech Jaruzelski (*see* Jaruzelski, Wojciech). The new prime minister asked for ninety days without strikes and promised to institute reforms that were widely demanded by the workers. The strikes by farmers and students were, by then, settled with the government agreeing to most of the workers' demands.

In March, Kania and Jaruzelski went to Moscow, and the conclusion of the Soviet leadership after the meeting was that "the Poles have the ability and the strength to reverse the course of events." The Polish hard-liners and their Soviet mentors were fully justified in their fears. By the spring of 1981, the Solidarity organization had become a genuine national liberation movement, a focus for hope of the Polish people.

However, an incident in the city of Bydgoszcz showed that the hard-liners had not given up the fight. There was a meeting in that city between the local Solidarity leaders in the provincial assembly's building and the local assembly leaders. After the meeting, two Solidarity leaders and one member of the farmers' union were beaten by plainclothes secret policemen. The communist Politburo immediately condemned Solidarity, accusing it of provoking the incident even before it received an official report of the case. In response, the national coordinating committee of Solidarity called for a four-hour warning strike on March 27 and for a general strike on March 31 if the government did not punish the culprits. A day before the scheduled general strike, however, the government admitted its error, and the strike was canceled.

On May 28, 1981, Stefan Cardinal Wyszynski (*see* Wyszynszki, Cardinal Stefan) died. He was a moderating influence on both the government and Solidarity. He was soon replaced by Jozef Glemp (*see* Glemp, Cardinal Jozef), archbishop of Warnia, who proved himself more cautious than his predecessor. Walesa led Solidarity delegations to Japan and to Switzerland, establishing contacts with international labor organizations. All this time the internal struggle of the communist leadership continued; the hard-liners were encouraged by Brezhnev.

In July, an extraordinary congress of the Polish United Workers party was called to Warsaw. It reelected Kania first secretary and introduced important changes in party procedures. The congress endorsed multiple candidates for party offices to be elected by secret ballot. This brought new people into the party's leadership. Gierek and his former supporters were expelled from the party. The leaders appealed for a unified national effort to end the crisis, but they were unable to provide a detailed plan for the solution of the crisis. Tensions continued, however, mainly because the country's food supply did not increase. Truck drivers blocked traffic at one point in Warsaw.

The coordinating committee of Solidarity appealed to the government urging the introduction of fundamental economic reforms. The committee also recommended that future elections to parliament and other representative bodies of state be based on democratic principles. It demanded government acquiescence in the establishment of self-managing workers' associations and, almost as an afterthought, that only voluntary work should be a rule on the eight remaining free Saturdays in 1981. Caught between increasing Soviet interference and the pressure of hard-liners in the communist leadership for action against Solidarity, Kania and Jaruzelski used increasingly tougher language in their messages to striking workers. In September, the first national congress of Solidarity convened in Gdansk. It sent a greeting and a message of support to all East European and Soviet workers struggling for their own independent trade unions.

The Soviet government became increasingly impatient with Poland. On September 16, the Polish Politburo declared that Solidarity had violated the Gdansk Agreement of August 31 and had become the spearhead of political opposition in the country. At the end of the month, a six-men Committee for National Salvation was set up by the communist leaders. It was headed by generals Jaruzelski and Czeszlaw Kiszczak, the minister of the interior. Special police and security units were set up in order to deal with possible political disturbances. On October 18, Kania resigned. Jaruzelski now united both party and government positions in his person. At the same time, he began accusing Solidarity of planning to seize the state. All Communist party members who held simultaneous membership in Solidarity were now ordered to withdraw from one or the other.

On November 4, General Jaruzelski, Jozef Cardinal Glemp, and Lech Walesa met in order to discuss the possible formation of a national front for reconciliation. They agreed to discuss four topics: the economy, preparations for the coming winter season, Solidarity's access to the mass media and the creation of a mechanism to settle local conflicts. The discussions were getting nowhere.

The government increasingly resorted to the use of force when confronted by workers or students and asked parliament to grant it extraordinary powers to protect the state. On December 13, Jaruzelski imposed martial law on the country. He set up a Military Council for National Salvation, consisting of twenty-one members; travel by the population was curtailed; public meetings were banned. Trade unions were suspended for the duration of martial law, and a curfew was established throughout the country. All leaders of Solidarity, including Lech Walesa, were arrested, together with intellectuals and others opposed to the regime. The following year, Jaruzelski declared the dissolution of Solidarity.

All these acts notwithstanding, general support for Solidarity did not slacken among the population. It was equally high in Western countries. The United States declared an embargo of all Polish goods, and Great Britain and France concurred. Only West Germany was lukewarm to sanctions, and it continued economic relations with the military junta in Poland. When it became obvious that repression had not eased social and political tensions in the country, Jaruzelski ordered the release of imprisoned Solidarity leaders in 1983 and 1984. The union reemerged as a force in Poland.

In 1984, four secret police officers murdered Father Jerzy Popieluszko (*see* Popieluszko murder), an outspoken priest, whose sermons in support of Solidarity made him a hated symbol of resistance to the communist government. The revulsion following the murder shook not only the government, but also a reluctant church hierarchy, whose leaders were previously cautious in endorsing the efforts of Solidarity.

After 1985, when Mikhail Gorbachev came into power in the Soviet Union, it became increasingly clear to the Polish regime that the Soviet army would not come to its aid in the event of a major revolution in the country. In 1988, therefore, Jaruzelski was forced into a series of talks with the opposition, symbolically called the Roundtable (*see* Roundtable Talks in Poland) discussions. In 1988, Solidarity was reinstated with full rights, and, in a semi-free election held in June 1989, its candidates won every contest against communist representatives. After the elections, the first government, dominated by Solidarity members, was formed under the prime ministership of Tadeusz Mazowiecki. In the presidential elections of 1990, Walesa won after a runoff. He is now the president of the Polish republic.

Bibliography

Andrews, Nicholas G., *Poland, 1980–1981: Solidarity Versus the Party*. (Washington, DC, 1985); Ash, Timothy Garton, *The Polish Revolution: Solidarity, 1980–1982* (London, 1983); Barker, Colin, *Festival of the Oppressed: Solidarity, Reform, and Revolution in Poland 1980–1981* (London, 1986); Blazyca, George, and Rapacki, Ryszard, eds. *Poland into the 1990s: Economy and Society in Transition* (New York, 1991); Brandys, Kazimierz, *A Warsaw Diary, 1978–1981* (London, 1984); Kemp-Welch, Anthony, *The Birth of Solidarity: The Gdansk Negotiations, 1980* (London, 1983); Misztal, Bronislaw, *Poland after Solidarity: Social Movements Versus the State* (New Brunswick, NJ, 1985); Persky, Stanislaw, and Flam, H., eds. *The Solidarity Sourcebook* (Vancouver, 1982); Potel, Jean Y., *The Promise of Solidarity* (New York, 1982).

Strzelecki, Ryszard (1907–1982). The son of an industrial worker who studied and became a mechanical engineer, Strzelecki joined the communist guerrilla army in Poland in 1944, and he became its chief of staff. After 1945, he served in various governmental and party posts. When Wladislaw Gomulka (*see* Gomulka, Wladislaw) was arrested in 1951, Strzelecki adopted the fallen leader's son as his own, earning Gomulka's gratitude. In January 1960, he was appointed a member of the Central Committee of the Polish United Workers party. In 1956, he became minister of railways. In the late 1970s, however, Strzelecki became seriously ill and could no longer participate in political or governmental activities.

Bibliography

Polonsky, Antony, and Druiker, Boleslaw, *The Beginnings of Communist Rule in Poland* (London, 1980).

Suchocka, Hanna (1946–). Suchocka's parents inherited a pharmacy from their parents in Pleszew, near Poznan. The pharmacy was nationalized in 1951. Suchocka graduated in law at Adam Mickiewicz University in Poznan in 1968. She taught for one year in the school's constitutional law department but she was pressured to join the Communist party. Instead, she joined the Democratic party, a communist satellite, designed to draw middle-class intellectuals into politics on behalf of the communist ideology. In 1972, she was appointed a full-time lecturer at the university. She completed her doctorate in 1975. She was elected to membership in the Polish Academy of Sciences, and she has been lecturing regularly at the Catholic University of Lublin.

Between 1980 and 1985, Suchocka was a parliamentary deputy for the Democratic party. She joined Solidarity (*see* Solidarity Trade Union of Poland) in 1980. In

June 1982, she refused to vote for the retroactive confirmation of martial law. Her membership in the Democratic party was then suspended, and she resigned from parliament in 1984.

In 1989, Suchocka was the choice of Solidarity for membership in the group participating in the Roundtable discussions (*see* Roundtable talks in Poland) with the government. When the citizen's parliamentary caucus disbanded, she joined the new Democratic Union and, in the October 1991 free elections, she ran on the union's list for parliament. She was elected deputy and served as chairman of the parliament's committee on legislation. She has been an ardent supporter of antiabortion legislation, but she has opposed the criminalization of abortions. She has also supported the inclusion of "Christian values" in the new curricula of the schools; however, she opposed religious indoctrination as a means of education.

On July 6 1992 a new coalition of various streams of the Solidarity movement was formed in parliament, and it elected Suchocka Prime Minister of Poland. She was the first woman to head any Polish government and was only the second woman to do so in Europe, after Margaret Thatcher. Suchocka was ousted from the government after the elections of 1993.

Bibliography
Vinton, Louisa, "Poland's Government Crisis: An End is in Sight?" *Radio Free Europe Research Report* 1.30 (July 24, 1992), pp. 15-25.

Walentynowicz, Anna (1930–). Walentynowicz, a shipyard worker, a crane operator in Gdansk, was dismissed by the factory manager in August 1980 for union activities. Her dismissal brought on the famous strike that led to the creation of the Solidarity Trade Union (*see* Solidarity Trade Union of Poland). She had been a member of the Trade Union of the Baltic Coast between 1978 and 1980. When the strike began at the Gdansk shipyard, Walentynowicz and Lech Walesa (*see* Walesa, Lech) were its leaders. When martial law was declared in December 1981, she was arrested with the other Solidarity leaders. After the collapse of the communist regime, Walentynowicz consistently argued for more democracy in politics and opposed Walesa's presidency.

Bibliography
Andrews, Nicholas G., *Poland 1980–1981: Solidarity Versus the Party* (Washington, DC, 1985).

Walesa, Lech (1943–). Walesa was born during World War II, while his father was in a German labor camp, from which he never came out alive. The young Walesa was apprenticed to become an electrician and was employed by the Lenin shipyards at Gdansk. In 1970, when he was twenty-seven years old, he participated in the riots that ended with the shooting death of over fifty workers by the hands of the Polish People's Army. This left such an impression on him that, from then on, Walesa became a dissident among the workers.

In April 1978, Walesa was among the group of people who announced the formation of the Baltic Committee for Free and Independent Trade Unions. In Gdansk, the group was first instructed by Andrzej Gwiazda, an engineer; he was joined by Alina Pienkowska, a nurse in the shipyard, and Bogdan Lis, a young riveter. Their spokeswoman was Anna Walentynowicz (*see* Walentynowicz), a widowed crane operator. The group worked hard to convince the workers that, by acting together, they were stronger than the secret police. Walesa was a member of the group that decided to issue a newspaper, *Worker of the Coast*. The title reflected the newspaper of the Committee for the Defense of Workers (KOR) (*see* Committee for the Defense of Workers), called *Worker*. At this time, Walesa was not yet considered a potential leader. He remained in the background, observing and learning from the others. After 1976, Walesa worked in the transport section of the factory. He made his name by being a first-class mechanic. His boss told him that, if he just did his job well, he did not care about Walesa's other activities.

In the meantime, Walesa was distributing the *Worker of the Coast*, and other clandestine leaflets in the factory. He soon aroused the interest of the secret police and was frequently interrogated. At the end of December 1978, he was fired from his job for his political activity. He found a new job in the Gdansk shipyards as an electrician. However, he continued his clandestine activities, and he was, once again, fired. When new protests erupted in the factories in Gdansk after the sudden price increases in the summer of 1980, the workers demanded not only that they be withdrawn but also that Walesa be reinstated.

He was instrumental in the establishment of Solidarity (*see* Solidarity Trade Union of Poland), and became its most articulate spokesman. On December 31, 1981, he was arrested when martial law was imposed on Poland, together with other leaders of Solidarity and their supporters. Walesa was kept in confinement until 1983 when he was conditionally released. During the Roundtable (*see* Roundtable Talks in Poland) negotiations in 1988, he was one of the leaders of the workers' representatives. In the presidential elections of 1990, Walesa won the presidency after a runoff. He continues to head the Polish republic as its president.

Bibliography
Brolewicz, Walter, *My Brother Walesa* (New York, 1984); Craig, Mary, *Lech Walesa and His Poland* (New York, 1987); Walesa, Lech, *A Way of Hope: An Autobiography* (New York, 1987).

Warsaw Pact. Created in May 1955, the Warsaw Pact was named after the city where it was established. It was an alliance, joining the armies of the countries of Eastern Europe under Soviet control. Yugoslavia was excluded, and Albania opted out of the alliance in 1961.

The organizational principle of the Warsaw Pact was the integration of the armed forces of the Soviet Bloc under a unified Soviet command. The commanding general of the Warsaw Pact forces has always been a Soviet citizen. The training manuals, the tactics, and the strategic concepts to be followed in a war with the West were all developed by Soviet general staff officers. Military equipment used by the Warsaw Pact armies was also provided by the Soviet Union, although some of the heavy tanks and artillery were produced in East European factories. Their production was, however, usually supervised by Soviet technicians, mostly officers of the Soviet armed forces. Soviet garrisons were stationed in member countries with the exception of Romania. They assured the obedience of the military of these countries to Soviet command decisions. In case of war, each national component of the Warsaw Pact forces was assigned specific tasks according to the general strategy developed in Moscow.

In August 1968, Warsaw Pact forces were used by Leonid Brezhnev's government to intervene in Czechoslovakia, ending the Prague Spring of reforms. The subsequent declaration of the infamous Brezhnev doctrine proclaimed the right of the Soviet Union to intervene wherever "socialism was being threatened." In 1988, this doctrine was renounced by Brezhnev's successors.

After the collapse of communism in Eastern Europe and the Soviet Union, the military organization of the Warsaw Pact was dissolved in March 1991. The political organization was turned into a consultative body, and even this was abandoned in 1992.

Bibliography

Johnson, Ross A., *The Warsaw Pact: Soviet Military Policy in Eastern Europe* (New Haven, CT, 1984).

Woytila, Karol, Cardinal (Pope John Paul II) (1920–). Woytila was born in Wadowicze, a town near Cracow, and completed high school there in 1938. He then entered the Jagellonian University of Cracow and studied Polish literature. During the Nazi occupation of Poland, Woytila worked at the Solvay Chemical factory in Cracow. In 1942, the future pope began his theological studies in a clandestine seminary (all schools and universities in Poland had been closed by the Nazis). At that point, he was sent to Rome to do studies there for two years. In 1948, he returned to Poland and was appointed an auxiliary priest in a small town. Between 1949 and 1951, he served at Saint Florian church in Cracow. Woytila then continued his studies in theology at the Jagellonian University and received his doctorate in 1953. He began lecturing at the theological seminary in Cracow. In 1954, he received a chair in social ethics at the Catholic University of Lublin. In 1958, Woytila became acting bishop of Ombi and auxiliary bishop of Cracow. Four years later, he became vicar capitular, or acting head of the diocese of Cracow. In 1963, he rose to the post of archbishop of Cracow, and in 1967 he was appointed cardinal by the pope. Between 1969 and 1978, Woytila was the deputy chairman of the conference of the Polish episcopate.

Woytila was one of the most active members of the Church Council Vatican I; he also visited the United States in 1969 and 1976. Woytila was often at odds with Cardinal Wyszynski (*see* Wyszynski, Cardinal Stefan) over issues of church government and relations with the communist state. He accepted the decisions of Vatican II unconditionally and became a mentor of ZNAK (*see* ZNAK) and its Catholic laymen's periodicals. He was also much more critical of the social policies of the communist Polish government than was Wyszynski. He was known by the government as the real patron of dissidents.

Upon the death of Pope John Paul I, a most beloved pontiff who reigned for only a short time, the College of Cardinals elected Woytila the new pope. He took the name John Paul II. His election helped to raise the prestige of the Catholic church in Poland, and it provided renewed hope for believers and nonbelievers alike. The communist leaders were quite conscious of his impact on Polish politics, and when he visited Poland on two occasions, they cringed at the millions who greeted the pope as their own. It is possible that the assassination attempt made by Ali Agca, a Turkish national, on Pope John Paul II was secretly organized by the Soviet KGB, and the cooperation of the Bulgarian secret police. However, this has never been proven.

Bibliography

Monticone, Ronald C., *The Catholic Church in Communist Poland, 1945–1985: Forty Years of Church-State Relations* (Boulder, CO, 1986).

Wyszynski, Stefan, Cardinal (1901–1980). The son of a sacristan and an organist in Zuzela, in northeastern Poland, Wyszynszki was ordained a priest in 1924 and was sent to study at the Catholic University of Lublin. After graduation, he spent two years in Rome, and then he went to Paris and Brussels. After his return to Poland, Wyszynski taught at a seminary at Woclawek and edited a theological review, *Ateneum Koplansie*. The higher clergy of Poland was very conservative at that time and they considered Wyszynszki a leftist. When the Germans occupied Poland, Wyszynski went underground and administered to his flock in secret. The diocese where he served was terribly affected by the war; it lost nearly half of its priests to Nazi and Soviet murderers. After 1945, Wyszynski was appointed bishop of Lublin. He also became the chancellor of the Catholic University of Lublin. By then, he was inclined toward mysticism. Two years later, he was appointed bishop of Warsaw and cardinal of the Catholic church.

In 1950, he signed an agreement with Poland's communist government regulating religious teachings in schools and churches and declared that the church would help build socialism. But the continuous harassment by the government resulted in Wyszynski's becoming more and more outspoken, and his pastoral letters became harsher in criticizing the state's record on civil rights. In 1951, therefore, he was arrested and confined to a monastery. In 1956, he was released and resumed his post as primate of Poland. In 1957, the communist authorities decided to accelerate the secularization of Polish society. However, it became obvious that some sort of modus vivendi must be reached with the Catholic hierarchy, since the influence of the church had not been diminished among the people. In 1966, therefore, the state reluctantly joined the church in the celebration of the millennium of Polish Christianity. Wyszynski proposed a plan for the following nine years with a message for each year with binding rules for practicing catholics and the preaching clergy. These messages included "national revival through God and Fatherland," "protection for the unborn, marriage and the family," "the education of youth in the Christian spirit," "the cultivation of national virtues of patriotism, courage and loyalty." The communist government did not challenge Wyszynski directly after the celebrations. Both the state and the church were concerned by growing public indifference to ideological messages. Thus, an understanding between state and church developed. Although the communists did not give up their efforts to turn society into supporters of Marxism-Leninism, they accepted the fact that the church would remain an important part of Polish everyday life. In the early 1960s, Gomulka's government began a subtle effort to divide the church from within. It encouraged laymen's associations such as PAX (*see* PAX) to challenge the hierarchy and created an Association of Atheists that sponsored sessions for children in the schools. It also organized a group called "peace priests," who were openly antagonistic to the hierarchy and preached cooperation with the communist party. Eventually, all these efforts were relegated to the background. Wyszynski died in peace and was replaced by Jozef Glemp (*see* Glemp, Jozef Cardinal) as primate of Poland.

Bibliography

Krziwicki, Herbert, and Ziemba, Walter J., trans. *The Prison Notes of Stefan Cardinal Wyszynszki* (London, 1985); Monticone, Roland C., *The Catholic Church in Communist Poland, 1945–1985: Forty Years of Church-State Relations* (Boulder, CO, 1986); Wyszynski, Stefan Cardinal, *A Strong Man Armed: Speeches* (New York, 1968).

ZNAK (A Catholic Organization in Communist Poland). This group emerged in Cracow in 1945–1946. It gathered around a sophisticated monthly publication called *ZNAK*. It cooperated with another periodical, *Tygodnik Powszechny*, and the two journals became a source of orientation for Catholic intellectuals. In time, the contributors and editors developed a common political outlook. This included the conviction that the communists were in Poland indefinitely, and some form of accommodation would have to be found with them in order to preserve Polish Catholicism. In 1951, *ZNAK* was closed down by the censors. In 1953, *Tygodnik Powszechny* followed.

After Wladislaw Gomulka's (*see* Gomulka, Wladislaw) return to power in December 1956, both periodicals were revived. Five members of their editorial boards were "elected" as parliamentary deputies. In exchange, the episcopate gave lukewarm support for the election of the candidates of the Polish United Workers party. ZNAK was accepted by the communists as one of the laymen's groups representing Catholics, but the rival PAX organization (*see* PAX) also enjoyed Communist acceptance.

ZNAK's ideology was based on an unconditional acceptance of the doctrines of the church, and there was no doubt in the minds of the members that Marxism and Catholicism could never be compatible. This, however, did not exclude the possibility of cooperation in practical matters if it could be achieved without compromising

Catholic teachings. ZNAK was concerned with Polish national interests; in fact, one of its tenets on cooperation with the communists was based on this principle. The leaders were convinced that Polish national interests coincided with Catholic doctrines, and the only way both could be served was by a compromise with the communists. ZNAK approached each communist policy decision with this in mind. It succeeded in participating in national policies without becoming a satellite of the Communist party.

ZNAK's stand on foreign policy was determined by the leaders' conviction that Poland had been abandoned by the Western Allies in 1945. They also feared the revival of West Germany. They saw the Polish-Soviet alliance as the only guarantee of Polish security. These leaders did not accept Soviet-style socialism on an ideological basis, and they did not openly reject capitalism. They supported the communist policies on industrialization as a way to increase national wealth. Ultimately, of course, ZNAK could not achieve the compromise with the communists its leaders sought, because the communist state simply could not accept Catholicism on an equal footing.

Bibliography
Bromke, Adam, *Poland's Politics: Idealism vs Realism* (Cambridge, MA, 1967).

ROMANIA

General Information. *Area:* 237,500 square kilometers (140,000 square miles). *Population:* 22,760,449. *Road network:* 76,598 kilometers (46,158 miles). *Railroad network:* 11,007 kilometers (4,404 miles). *Major cities:* Bucuresti (Bucharest), the capital (2.64 million people), Brasov, Cluj, Constanta, Iasi, Timisoara, Ploiesti. *Distribution of the population:* 37 percent urban, 63 percent rural inhabitants. *Total school enrollments:* 4,270,877; *in higher educational institutions:* 137,677. *National income:* industry, 49.7 percent; agriculture and forestry, 29 percent; transport and communications, 4.1 percent; building trades, 8 percent; trade, 6 percent; other branches, 3.2 percent. *Major natural resources:* oil, copper, coal, gold, uranium, timber, bauxite, salt, water power. *Major products:* refined petroleum and derivatives, meat, bread grains, vegetables, fodder, lumber, machinery. The economy uses the metric system. *Currency:* lei. Geography: the land is varied. In the center of the country, the Carpathian mountains divide its territory into two segments; to the south of the mountains, the land is mostly flat; to the north of the Carpathians, the province of Transylvania is mostly mountainous and hilly country with good, fertile soil in the river valleys. The southern provinces are watered by the Danube river, which is a natural boundary separating Romania from the former Yugoslavia and Bulgaria.

Bibliography
Cretianu, Alexandre, *Captive Romania: A Decade of Soviet Rule* (New York, 1959); Fischer-Galati, Stephen, *The Socialist Republic of Romania* (Baltimore, MD, 1969); ———, *Twentieth Century Romania* (New York, 1970); Ratiu, Ion, *Contemporary Romania: Her Place in World Affairs* (Richmond, Gr. Britain, 1957).

CHRONOLOGY

1944 *August.* King Michael had General Ion Antonescu arrested, and he surrendered Romania to the Allies. The Red Army promptly occupied Bucharest, outflanking the Carpathian mountains.

1945 *March.* A coalition government, headed by Petru Groza, was established in Bucharest. It included the communists who controlled the ministries of the interior and justice.

September. At the first meeting of Allied foreign ministers, the U.S. representative demanded the dismantling of the communist-dominated government in Romania, without result.

1946 *November.* Elections were held in Romania under the shadow of the Red Army and the Soviet KGB. The communist-dominated coalition of parties received 91 percent of the votes cast.

1947 *February.* Romania signed the peace treaty with the Allies. The Romanian state lost Bessarabia once again to the Soviet Union but regained all of Transylvania.

October. Romania joined the newly established Communist Information Bureau (COMINFORM).

November. Ion Maniu, head of the Peasant party, was tried and sentenced to life in prison on trumped-up charges.

December. King Michael of Romania was forced to abdicate his throne and leave Romania.

1948 *April.* The Romanian Communist party formed a new government. The prime minister was Gheorghe Gheorghiu-Dej, a former railroad worker. The government included Ana Pauker and Vasile Luca, two Muscovites who pressed on for the Stalinization of Romanian society.

1949 *January.* Romania joined the newly established Council of Mutual Economic Assistance (COMECON), a counterpart to the European Common Market.

1950 *March.* The collectivization of all farmlands was ordered in Romania. It was pursued with great brutality, and resisting peasants were either killed or sent to concentration camps.

April. The building of the Danube-Black sea canal commenced.

1952 *April.* A series of purges consolidated the position of Gheorghiu-Dej as Romania's dictator. Ana Pauker and Vasile Luca were ousted, and Lucretiu Patrascanu, a wartime communist leader, was jailed.

1955 *May.* Romania joined the Warsaw Pact alliance.

December. Romania, together with some other East European states, was admitted to the United Nations.

1956 *April.* The COMINFORM was disbanded.

October. Following the Polish lead of resistance to Soviet domination, national revolution broke out in Hungary. The Romanian communist leaders worried about the spillover to the Transylvanian Hungarian minority population.

November. Romania provided support and safe passage for Soviet armored divisions on their way to Hungary to suppress the revolution. Imre Nagy, Hungary's prime minister, was treacherously captured and interned in Romania. Romanian security personnel supervised his and his supporters' detention.

1958 *May.* The Warsaw Pact withdrew its Soviet armed forces from Romania. This was a reward for Romania's loyal service to the Soviet Union during the Hungarian Revolution of 1956.

1959 *April.* The new oil pipeline that was being built was to carry oil to Eastern and Western Europe from the Soviet Union. The pipeline was to cross Romanian territory.

1965 *March.* Romania's communist dictator, Gheorghe Gheorghiu-Dej, died of cancer. His replacement was the liberal-appearing Nicolae Ceausescu. The youngest member of the top echelons of the communist leadership, Ceausescu promised a moderate course for Romania.

1968 *May.* Romania began gradually to distance itself from Soviet politics. The Communist party's leaders, especially Ceausescu, began to identify the party with Romanian nationalism.

August. Romania refused to participate in the invasion of Czechoslovakia. Ceausescu denounced the invasion as an unwarranted intervention in the internal affairs of a socialist country. The Romanian leader attempted to become a mediator in the Sino-Soviet dispute but his efforts were rejected.

1975 *July.* Romania signed the Helsinki Accord, finalizing the borders of the European states and guaranteeing human rights. However, Nicolae Ceausescu, firmly in power by then, had no intention of abiding by the agreement.

1976 *June.* Romanian delegates attended the meeting of European Communist and Socialist parties in East Berlin. Romania abstained from supporting the Soviet bid for reestablishing its supremacy in the international communist movement.

1981 *October.* Romanian dictator Ceausescu issued severe decrees against hoarding food. The decrees stipulated that citizens could buy food only in state-owned stores. Private food trade was considered a crime against the state.

December. The Ceausescu regime ordered the confiscation of all private typewriters in order to stop citizens' complaints against the regime sent to foreign embassies and radio stations.

1982 *May.* Elena Ceausescu, wife of dictator Nicolae Ceausescu, declared that each Romanian woman must bear five children in order to increase the population of Romania to 30 by the year 2000.

1985 *April.* Romanian delegates to the Warsaw Pact meeting signed a ten-year extension of the treaty. Romania, however, refused to participate in the military exercises of the pact, and refused to permit the entry of even skeletal exercise crews into Romanian territory.

1987 *November.* Violent protests broke out in the city of Brasov. Tens of thousands of angry workers wrecked the city hall and attacked party headquarters. They protested the austerity program of the Ceausescu regime and the likelihood of shortages of heating fuel for the third consecutive winter.

1989 *February.* Hungary permitted the entry of over 13,000 refugees from Romania. This was, however, only the first wave of people escaping the dreadful conditions in Romania. More than twice this number was to enter Hungary during the following year. Sayed Ali Khameini, the Iranian president, visited

Romania. He concluded an agreement with the Ceausescu regime, envisaging trade relations between the two countries to reach $1 billion a year.

March. The official newspaper of the Romanian Communist party declared that criticism of the socialist Romanian government was tantamount to spying and treason.

April. Dictator Ceausescu declared that Romania was capable of producing nuclear weapons and would not hesitate to use them if its survival was threatened. A discussion about a new economic agreement between Romania and the European Community was suspended—the reason: the dismal Romanian record on human rights and the inadequate treatment of minorities in Romania.

May. Romanian delegates to the Warsaw Pact meeting suggested that an emergency meeting be convened to "restore unity" to the alliance, meaning that it should suppress dissenting governments.

December. A revolution, sparked by an unlikely Protestant pastor, Laszlo Tokes of Timisoara, spread into the major cities and ended with the overthrow of the Ceausescu regime. The dictator and his wife fled from Bucharest but were arrested. An extraordinary court found them guilty of corruption and other crimes and sentenced them to death. They were both executed.

1990 *January-February.* The members of the Ceausescu clan, most of whom were placed in important positions by the now dead dictator, were taken into protective custody.

March. Nicu Ceausescu, son of the dictator who was head of the communist organization in Transylvania, was tried and found guilty of the abuse of power. He was sentenced to twenty years in prison, but he was hospitalized before his incarceration. The new Romanian government, many of whose members were employed by the Ceausescu regime, issued a decree permitting Romanians to obtain passports and travel abroad. The Romanian government placed the Communist party outside the law.

May. Elections were held in Romania. The National Salvation Front, whose leaders were accused by their opponents of continuing many former communist leaders in office, won the elections. The president of the new state was Ion Iliescu; the prime minister; Petru Roman.

June. The Council of Europe denied Romania observer status in the organization, because of Romania's continuing abuse of minority rights. Miners from the Jiu Valley, allegedly encouraged by the Roman government, descended on Bucharest and attacked demonstrators against government policies with staves and axes. The police did not intervene in the atrocities.

October. After uncovering horrendous conditions in Romanian orphanages and hospitals, where children had been abandoned by their parents by the thousands, some of them sick with the AIDS virus, the European Community offered $7.7 million to help the orphans. The latest counts discovered at least

100,000 children living under unspeakably filthy and miserable conditions without medicines and adequate care.

November. The Romanian Communist party, banned by the government, was reorganized under the name of Socialist party of Romania.

December. Former King Michael arrived in Bucharest unexpectedly. Within twelve hours, he was declared persona non grata and expelled from the country for the second time in his life.

1991 *April.* The Petru Roman government introduced price liberalization on a large scale. It was expected to improve economic conditions in the country, opening the way to the formation of a market economy.

September. The miners were back in Bucharest once again. However, this time they went too far. Not only did they beat up the opposition, they caused havoc on their way to the capital. This, and personality conflicts between president Iliescu and Petru Roman, led to the dismissal of the Roman cabinet.

October. President Iliescu appointed Todor Stolojan as the new prime minister for Romania. Inflation in Romania reached 220 percent a year. Crime rates doubled, and unemployment appeared for the first time as a major problem.

1992 *January.* Iliescu declared that the unification of Moldavia (formerly Bessarabia) with Romania should follow the pattern of German unification. The Democratic Convention, a coalition of opposition parties, organized a giant rally in Bucharest, demanding the resignation of Iliescu.

February. The Vatra Romaneasca, an ultra-nationalist organization, held its conference in Lugoj. Josif Constantin Dragan, a wealthy former exile, was the guest of honor. Nicolae Andruta Ceausescu, younger brother of the dead dictator Nicolae, was temporarily released from prison for medical treatment. He has been serving a sentence of twenty years. In local elections, the National Salvation Front won about 45 percent of the votes.

March. A protest rally of 6,000 ethnic Hungarians demanded the observation of minority rights.

May. Defense Minister Alexander Spiroiu reported that 19,000 secret police files had been taken out of the country after the revolution. A report issued by the Romanian senate concluded that the Petru Roman government had disposed of hundreds of mansions confiscated from their previous owners by the communists. These buildings and estates were given to friends and relatives of the cabinet members.

June. Tirgu Mures, the scene of fierce violence against ethnic Hungarians by the Vatra Romaneasca in March 1991, elected Gyozo Nagy, an ethnic Hungarian, its mayor. Nagy announced that he wanted to shift the focus of politics from ethnic rivalry to economic reconstruction. King Michael urged Romanians to restore him to the throne as a step toward reconstruction.

July. New national and presidential elections were scheduled for September.

Petru Roman announced that he would not seek the presidency. Iliescu will be the candidate of the National Salvation Front once again. Ex-king Michael planned to visit Romania in August, but his visa request was denied. The government argued that his visit would disrupt the elections scheduled for September 27.

August. Hungarian prefects of Covasna and Harghita counties, whose population is mostly ethnic Hungarian, were dismissed. They were replaced by one Hungarian and one Romanian each.

September. In the national elections the Democratic National Salvation Front received 47 percent of the votes, and Ion Iliescu was elected president.

October. Since none of the parties won an absolute majority of parliamentary seats, a coalition government was to be established. Nicolae Vacaroiu was appointed prime minister. A former communist official in Ceausescu's planning office, he is an economist.

November. Parliament confirmed the new government of Vacaroiu.

December. Mayor Funar, an ultra-nationalist of Cluj, ordered the changing of Hungarian street names in his city. Funar had been bent on provoking the 2 Hungarians in Transylvania by his chauvinistic policies in his city.

1993   *January.* The Vacaroiu government's stop-gap measures aimed at ensuring enough food and heating fuel for the population for the winter. The sputtering Romanian economy would need infusion of capital from abroad that is not available.

February. Severe winter weather caused conditions reminiscent of the Ceausescu-era. There was a shortage of heating fuels, and water was unavailable in the cities often for weeks. The opposition accused Vacaroiu of inaction and charged that he was using the economic difficulties to slow down reforms. Meanwhile, ethnic tensions continued in Transylvania.

March. The Romanian government tried to mediate the conflict in the former Yugoslavia without success, while adhering to the UN sanctions against Belgrade. Rump-Yugoslavia blocked the flow of traffic on its share of the Danube river, causing difficulties for Romania.

April. Widespread labor unrest and a wave of strikes hit Romanian industries. In Bucharest, over 15,000 workers marched and denounced the government's economic policies. King Michael canceled a planned visit for the Orthodox Easter, because the government insisted that it had to be strictly private.

May. The Ukraine accused Romania of observing UN sanctions against the former Yugoslavia only in order to hold up Ukraine's trade with the West. The Romanians denied the accusation. President Iliescu met with Alija Izetbegovic and Franjo Tudjman, presidents of Bosnia-Herzegovina and Croatia respectively. The purpose of the meeting was to mediate the dispute in former Yugoslavia. Iliescu travelled to Belgrade where he talked to the politicians of rump-Yugoslavia, offering his "good services" to solve the murderous conflict.

June. Ian Van der Stoel, high commissioner for the Council of Europe, visited Romania to investigate the ethnic situation in the country; however, he was not scheduled to talk with ethnic representatives. The Romanian parliament established a special commission to investigate allegations of new corruption in the ministries. A Romanian military delegation visited Washington, D.C. and conferred with General Colin Powell. Two major trade unions merged, with a combined membership of 3 million. Romanian foreign minister Teodor Melescanu visited Budapest and held discussions with Geza Jeszenszky, his Hungarian counterpart. Afterward he travelled to Holland on an official visit. Mihai Botez, a former Romanian dissident who received asylum in the United States during the Ceausescu regime, was named Romania's ambassador to the United Nations.

Apostol, Gheorghe (1912–). Apostol's father was a railroad worker, and he found employment at the Romanian railways. He joined the illegal Communist party in 1930, and spread the party's message while traveling throughout the country. Apostol was discovered and arrested by the royal police, and he spent the rest of the interwar years in prison. Most of the local leaders of the Communist party were incarcerated in that same jail, and, therefore, they had ample opportunity to communicate with each other. It is likely that Apostol, together with other leaders, taught Marxism-Leninism to a young man, really a boy, who was locked up with them for acting as a courier for the party. He was Nicolae Ceausescu (*see* Ceausescu, Nicolae), nineteen years old at that time. The communist leaders in prison included Gheorghe Gheorghiu-Dej (*see* Gheorghiu-Dej, Gheorghe), the later leader of the party after the Stalinization of Romania; Chivu Stoica; Alexandru Moghioros; and others. They were destined to play important roles in the Stalinization of Romania after 1944.

When Gheorghiu-Dej died of cancer in 1965, the candidates for the succession included Apostol. The struggle was won by Ceausescu who gradually reduced his competitors to impotence. In 1968, the new leader ordered the rehabilitation of several of the former leaders who had been purged and executed in the 1950s, including Lucretiu Patrascanu (*see* Patrascanu, Lucretiu) and Stefan Foris. Apostol's complicity in these judicial murders was revealed. He was discredited and eventually removed from the Communist party's highest organ, the Politburo (renamed the Presidium). He was shunted off to Brazil as Romanian ambassador and later sent to represent the Romanian state in Argentina. He survived the Ceausescus and is currently living in retirement.

Bibliography

Graham, Lawrence S., *Romania: A Developing Socialist State* (Boulder, CO, 1982); Shafir, Michael, *Romania: Politics, Economics and Society* (Boulder, CO, 1985).

Bobu, Emil (?–). Prime minister of the Ceausescu-clan, Bobu was a true sycophant, readily feeding the leader's latent megalomania in the 1980s. He was left behind with Elena Ceausescu and Manea Manescu (*see* Manescu, Manea) as a committee of three when Nicolae Ceausescu (*see* Ceausescu, Nicolae) left for a state visit to Teheran, Iran, on December 17, 1989, two weeks before his overthrow. Therefore, Bobu was partially responsible for the committee's order to the secret police and the regular police forces to fire on demonstrators in Timisoara (*see* Timisoara revolt). The order resulted in a massacre of civilians whose bodies were secretly cremated by the secret police.

Bobu then accompanied the fleeing Ceausescu couple in their last fateful helicopter ride from the roof of the Communist party's Central Committee building on December 22, 1989, and he was left behind by the couple in Snagov. Bobu was tried in late January 1990, together with three others, the closest confidantes of Ceausescu, and was convicted for crimes against the Romanian people. During the trial, only Bobu was willing to defend himself vigorously against the accusations. When the presiding judge asked him why he obeyed the obviously insane orders of the tyrant, Bobu's answer was that he did not want to face the consequences of a refusal. He was eventually sentenced to life in prison, a sentence which he currently is serving.

Bibliography

Almond, Mark, *The Rise and Fall of Nicolae and Elena Ceausescu* (London, 1992). Behr, Edward, *Kiss the Hand You Cannot Bite* (New York, 1991). Pacepa, Ion Mihai, *Red Horizons* (Washington, DC-New York, 1987).

Bodnaras, Emil (1904–). Born of a Ukrainian father and a German mother in a prosperous middle-class family in Bukovina, Bodnaras attended the Romanian Cavalry School in the early 1930s and graduated at the top of his class in 1933 as a second lieutenant. He almost immediately deserted and appeared in the Soviet Union where he underwent training by the NKVD-KGB. In 1935, Bodnaras returned to Romania under false identity; however, a chance encounter with a former classmate led to his arrest. He was sent to Doftana prison, where all the communist leaders were kept. Bodnaras acted as a mentor to young Ceausescu (*see* Ceausescu, Nicolae and Elena) who arrived in the same prison.

In 1943, Bodnaras's sentence ended and he was released. He was set up, probably with the help of the Soviet NKVD-KGB, as a lumber salesman in Braila, where his brother had a photographic studio. Bodnaras was soon in touch with the titular head of the underground Romanian Communist party, Stefan Foris, and he urged Foris to organize armed action against the Germans and the Romanian army, engaged at that time in the battle for Stalingrad. However, Foris knew how weak the communist organization was and he was slow to act.

Bodnaras then visited the imprisoned Gheorghe Gheorghiu-Dej (*see* Gheorghiu-Dej, Gheorghe) who violently opposed Foris and accused Foris of being a police informer. This accusation had no real basis; nevertheless, when Gheorghiu-Dej became the ruler of communist Romania, he ordered the arrest of Foris and had him beaten to death by Vasile Posteacu, with an iron pipe. Posteacu was then awarded the post of deputy minister of the interior. He even received the Order of Tudor Vladimirescu from Ceausescu in 1968.

In August 1944, Bodnaras cooperated with King Michael in the arrest of General Ion Antonescu and the changing of sides by Romania during the war. The king turned Antonescu over to Bodnaras and Lucretiu Patrascanu (*see* Patrascanu, Lucretiu), another communist leader, who spirited the Romanian general out of Bucharest and delivered him to the Red Army.

When the Groza-government was formed in 1945, Bodnaras served as a top aid for the prime minister. When the king was sent into exile, the new government included Bodnaras as minister of defense. In 1950, Bodnaras used Nicolae Ceausescu as his deputy. By then, Bodnaras was a member of the Politburo of the Communist party, one of the most powerful men after Gheorghiu-Dej in Romania. Upon the death of Gheorghiu-Dej in 1965, Bodnaras was one of the sponsors of Ceausescu for the post of first secretary of the Communist party. In turn, Ceausescu included Bodnaras in the new Politburo (now called the Presidium) of the Communist party. However, when Ceausescu ordered the rehabilitation of Patrascanu and Foris, and revealed that the charges against them had been false, and that they had been tortured, Bodnaras, who was a member of the Politburo, was discredited. Nevertheless, Bodnaras survived Ceausescu, and when the revolution broke out in December 1989, he fled to the Soviet Union.

Bibliography

Fischer-Galati, Stephen, *The Socialist Republic of Romania* (Baltimore, MD, 1969); Floyd, David, *Rumania: Russia's Dissident Ally* (New York, 1965); Ionescu, Ghita, *Communism in Romania, 1944–1962* (New York, 1964).

Brasov Strike. The city of Brasov is an old city, established by German settlers in the twelfth century. It was part of Siebenburgen (seven cities) in Transylvania. The city was an important center of the Levantine trade in the later Middle Ages, long before Romanians appeared in the northern reaches of the Carpathian mountains. The city became part of Romania in 1918 as a reward for Romania's participation in World War I on the side of the Western Allies. It is located 150 miles north of Bucharest.

November 15, 1987, was local election day. Crowds took to the streets, however, for other reasons. They demonstrated for economic and political changes. The demonstrations began at a large truck factory in the suburbs where negotiations between management and workers were stalemated. Several hundred workers then marched toward the center of the city. Voting, that is, confirming the Communist party's choices for local offices, was the last thing on their minds. By the time they reached the city center, the crowd had grown to 15,000. They chanted, "Down with the dictator!" "Down with communism!" The crowd stormed the local party headquarters and burned Nicolae Ceausescu's portraits and pamphlets. At first, the secret police did not intervene. Then special troops were trucked into the city and these troops beat hundreds of people. Some leaders of the demonstration were killed outright. Others were put on trial in December and sent to prison. Silviu Brucan (*see* Brucan, Silviu), an old party member and a Marxist theoretician-turned-dissident, noted that the Brasov riots signaled the anger of working people no longer willing to tolerate being treated as servants by the Ceausescus (*see* Ceausescu, Nicolae and Elena).

Bibliography

Galloway, George, *Downfall: The Ceausescus and the Romanian Revolution* (London, 1991); Gilberg, Trond, *Nationalism and Communism in Romania: The Rise and Fall of the Ceausescus' Personal Dictatorship* (Boulder, CO, 1990); Ratesh, Nestor, *Romania: The Entangled Revolution* (Washington, DC, 1989).

Brucan, Silviu (1920–). Brucan joined the Romanian Communist party as a teenager in the late 1930s, and he became a Marxist theoretician. In 1944, when World War II had ended for Romania, Brucan was appointed editor-in-chief of the communist daily newspaper, *Scinteia*, and was an ardent propagandist for the dictatorship of the Communist party. In 1956, he was appointed Romanian ambassador to the United States and remained in Washington, D.C. until 1961. When he returned to Bucharest, he was appointed chairman of the state radio and television stations.

When Nicolae Ceausescu (*see* Ceausescu, Nicolae and Elena) was appointed general secretary of the Communist party, Brucan's political career was over. Presumably, the dictator did not trust him. He was then appointed professor at Bucharest University where he taught Marxism-Leninism. He wrote several books on Marxist theory and was permitted to travel abroad, including several visits to the United States. He lectured and taught at several American universities and published books in the United States by the approval of the Romanian government. However, when Brucan's books began to include several critical remarks about Romanian socialism, his travels were restricted.

In 1986, he contacted Radio Free Europe and received its help for travel. His direct, open criticisms of the Ceausescu regime came after the suppression of the Brasov riots in 1987 (*see* Brasov Strike). Less than a year later, however, he was once again permitted to visit the United States. He was in New York in 1988, when he gave a long and wide-ranging interview to Radio Free Europe. He roundly criticized the policies of the Ceausescu regime. He denounced the leader's "sectarianism" and his intolerance. He proclaimed that Ceausescu stifled creative thinking among Romanian intellectuals and condemned true Marxist thought to stagnation. He said that, if the regime continued on its current course, then Romania would be the first country in the world to plan deliberately its own underdevelopment for the year 2,000. He asserted that the Romanian government had become an obstacle to progress. Concluding the interview, Brucan stated that economic reforms must be accompanied by the democratization of politics in Romania.

This interview was broadcast to Romania. An open defiance of the Ceausescu-dictatorship, it required considerable courage. Nevertheless, Brucan returned to Romania and, although he became the subject of vilification and the secret police kept constant watch on him, he survived the Ceausescu regime.

He was to become the author of the famous "Letter of the Six" (*see* Letter of the Six), signed by six senior members of the Romanian Communist party, demanding reform and the end of the rule of the Ceausescu clan. He was probably under Soviet protection. After the publication of the letter, a Soviet journalist, probably a KGB agent, visited him every day to make sure of his welfare. After the overthrow of the Ceausescus in December 1989, Brucan declared that communism was dead in Romania. By 1990, he no longer considered himself to be a Marxist. In the post-Ceausescu government of the National Salvation Front, Brucan was named chairman of the Committee on Foreign Policy. He was an ardent defender of the National Salvation Front, but he also quarreled with president Ion Iliescu (*see* Iliescu, Ion) and the prime minister. A few months into the new regime, Brucan was dismissed from the government. Currently, he continues to defend the policies of the National Salvation Front.

Bibliography
Almond, Mark, *The Rise and Fall of Nicolae and Elena Ceausescu* (London, 1992); Behr, Edward, *Kiss the Hand You Cannot Bite* (New York, 1991); Fischer, Mary Ellen, *Nicolae Ceausescu: A Study in Political Leadership* (Boulder, CO, 1989).

Ceausescu, Ilie (1912–). One of the older brothers of Nicolae (*see* Ceausescu, Nicolae and Elena), Ilie resembled his sibling the most in his physical appearance. When Nicolae consolidated his hold on power, he drew his relatives into the ruling circle, since he could not trust outsiders. As time went on, he trusted his colleagues in the party and government leadership even less and relied more and more on his clan. However, none of his and his wife's relatives were permitted to share the limelight with him. Nicolae was so jealous of his power that the only person he permitted to share in it was his wife, Elena (nee Petrescu).

Ilie was appointed deputy minister of defense with the rank of lieutenant general. He pretended to be a military historian, but his "works" were written by members of the Historical Institute in Bucharest. (He never attended a university and had no professional training as a historian.) Ilie often visited Western countries, including the United States, attending scholarly conferences on history. At these meetings, he read "his" papers which were rather crude by Western scholarly standards. Mostly they extolled the achievements of socialist Romania.

As deputy minister of defense, his major task was to ensure that appointees to the officer corps of the armed forces were completely loyal to his younger brother. During the revolution of 1989, Ilie Ceausescu panicked, took on a disguise of ordinary workingman's clothes, and attempted to escape from Bucharest in a cheap automobile. He was caught by a group of revolutionaries, and was taken into custody. One of the revelations made in Ion Mihai Pacepa's book (*see* Pacepa, Ion Mihai) was that

Ilie was involved in passing Soviet military secrets and technology to the United States and, at the same time, passing American secrets to the Soviet Union. After the revolution, he disappeared into protective custody.

Bibliography
Almond, Mark, *The Rise and Fall of Nicolae and Elena Ceausescu* (London, 1992); Georgescu, Vlad, *Romania: 40 Years (1944–1984)* (New York, 1985); Pacepa, Ion Mihai, *Red Horizons* (Washington, DC, 1987).

Ceausescu, Marin (1910–1989). The oldest sibling of Nicolae (*see* Ceausescu, Nicolae and Elena), he went with his sister, Maria, to Bucharest in the 1930s in search of work. A year later, he took his youngest brother, Nicolae, with him and found work for him as an apprentice shoemaker. Marin had been on the fringes of the Romanian Communist party, and he introduced Nicolae to his friends in the organization when Nicolae was only fourteen. Maria was probably acquainted with Gheorghe Petrescu, another former peasant lad, now living in the capital city. Petrescu's sister, Elena, eventually became Nicolae's wife and political associate.

In the late 1970s, Marin Ceausescu was appointed deputy minister of foreign affairs by his brother Nicolae and became permanent Romanian representative of trade in Vienna, Austria. He received millions in foreign currencies from Romania, which were used to satisfy the earthly needs of the Ceausescu family. He acted as a procurer of Western television sets, video cameras, VCRs, and other goods not available to ordinary Romanians. When he learned about the overthrow of his brother, Marin Ceausescu committed suicide.

Bibliography
Behr, Edward, *Kiss the Hand You Cannot Bite* (New York, 1991).

Ceausescu, Nicolae and Elena (1918–1989; 1918–1989). Nicolae Ceausescu was born into a typical peasant family in the Regat (the former Vallachia). His father was a brutal, self-centered drunkard. His mother, Alexandra, was a deeply religious, but contentious, woman who raised a brood of eleven children under very difficult circumstances. Nicolae left school at the age of eleven. By then, his older brother, Marin (*see* Ceausescu, Marin) and his sister, Maria, were living in Bucharest, and they took young Nicolae with them. They found work for him as an apprentice shoemaker. Nicolae lived with his brother and sister, and increased his income by petty theft.

By the time he was sixteen, Nicolae was involved with a communist front organization, the Romanian Antifascist Committee, headed by Gheorghe Apostol (*see* Apostol, Gheorghe). Nicolae acted as one of the organization's carriers. In December 1935, he was arrested for the first time for the possession of antigovernment pamphlets. He was freed after two months. In two years, however, he found himself in jail once again for a similar offense. While in prison, he joined the Romanian Communist party, whose leaders were locked up in the same building. He met Gheorghe Gheorghiu-Dej, (*see* Gheorghiu-Dej, Gheorghe) and became a protege of the much older man. He was a reliable aid and messenger and earned Gheorghiu-Dej's gratitude.

Elena Petrescu's father was a village innkeeper, and the family lived above the inn. She attended a one room village school and had difficulties learning to read and write. She had to repeat a grade. She moved to Bucharest with her older brother and met Nicolae Ceausescu in 1939. By then, her brother Gheorghe Petrescu was a member of the underground Communist party. While Nicolae was in prison in the late 1930s, they did not see each other. In 1945, however, they were married.

Between 1945 and 1965, the Ceausescu couple worked in the communist apparatus, and Nicolae made his way into the highest party organ, the Politburo. They also had three children, Valentin, the oldest, Zoia, and Nicu (*see* Ceausescu, Valentin; Ceausescu, Zoja; Ceausescu, Nicu). By 1965, Nicolae was able to gain the post of first secretary of the Communist party (the title changed thereafter to secretary general). With great cunning, he gradually eliminated his competitors for power and, by 1974, he was the undisputed leader, the *Conducator* of Romania. Already in 1967, Nicolae had united the posts of party leader and head of government in his own person, and ordered the creation of a new constitution proclaiming Romania a socialist state, not a people's democracy.

At first, Ceausescu wanted to appear more liberal than his predecessor. He ordered the rehabilitation of several victims of the show-trials of the 1950s. Because he was basically an arrogant, rude man, it did not take him long to treat everyone around him with disdain. After 1974, there was unprecedented terror in Romania. Ceausescu ruled by relying on the Securitate, as the secret police was called, and he succeeded in intimidating most everyone in society. He eventually resembled an oriental despot, and nepotism, the hallmark of oriental despotism, became a means through which he conducted his everyday business. He appointed his wife, Elena, deputy prime minister; his brother, Ilie (*see* Ceausescu, Ilie), was deputy minister of defense. His older brother, Marin, was a trade representative in Vienna, and supplied the family with capitalist goods. Other relatives were placed in positions where they could keep an eye on officials, ensuring their loyalty to the leader.

At the same time, Ceausescu tried to make his regime internally legitimate. The worn-out Marxist-Leninist baggage of the Communist party survived, but the regime increasingly stressed its identification with old-fashioned Romanian chauvinistic nationalism. The idea of *Romania Mare* (Great Romania) made a new appearance in official communications, and cautious announcements were made about Romanian Bessarabia (the Moldavian Soviet Republic).

After 1974, the *Conducator* was exalted above everyone else. Ceausescu's family was declared to have descended from ancient Dacian stock, embodying the strength and survival instincts of the ancient "Romanian" people. The regime could not decide whether to declare Romanians the descendants of Dacians or of the Roman soldiers stationed on the Danubian borders of the empire during Emperor Traian's time. Archaeologists made a "great discovery" in Ceausescu's native village, unearthing bones of early men, suggesting that the *Conducator's* roots went even deeper than those of most other Europeans. He was proclaimed to be the best hunter of wild beasts, having shot a world-record brown bear in the Carpathians (what was not said was that the bear had been drugged by forest rangers). With all the hoopla of a never-ending election campaign, Ceausescu advanced the half-truth of protecting the interests of the Romanian people against Soviet pressure and exploitation. It is now known, however, that he also assured Leonid Brezhnev that all this was done to deceive the West. He also proved to the Soviet leaders that, despite his "opening to the West," the essential one-party state was to be maintained.

In the mid-1970s, Romania did make economic progress. It paid off all its Western creditors. Industrialization continued, albeit at a slower pace than before. Huge projects were undertaken, including the rebuilding of an earthquake-shattered Bucharest (1977), and the construction of the Danube-Black Sea canal was restarted. However, agricultural production stagnated. Collectivized Romanian agriculture had all the shortages of machinery and spare parts that plagued other socialist agrarian systems. There was no incentive for collective farm workers to produce more, since their salaries were kept artificially low.

Elena Ceausescu was appointed minister of culture in 1974 by her husband. Simultaneously, she was proclaimed to be a great scientist. Her doctoral dissertation in chemistry was produced by a collective of university professors, and her published works were also done by others. She was now presented to the public as a great supporter of Romanian culture. As a politician, she was working feverishly behind the scenes, urging the secret police to invent ever new ways to control the population. Her most memorable decree was to order the confiscation of all typewriters in the country to prevent clandestine publications. She also decreed that every Romanian woman must bear five children, in order to expand the population of Great Romania. Her megalomania matched that of her husband. Romanian ambassadors in Western countries and in the Third World were instructed to approach universities and academies of science to solicit honorary doctorates and membership in their institutions for Elena Ceausescu.

The foreign policies of Nicolae Ceausescu had a double purpose. On the one hand, he intended to become a power-broker between the West and the Soviet Bloc serving and deceiving both at the same time. His diplomats made great efforts to convince Western statesmen and their public to consider Romania an East European maverick, protecting itself against the Soviet Union. At the same time, a huge organization of intelligence agents worked at stealing Western military and industrial technology. While he maintained correct diplomatic relations with Israel, when the rest of the Soviet Bloc refused even to have diplomats in Tel Aviv, Ceausescu plotted with his best friend, Yassir Arafat, against the Jewish nation. It was characteristic of this sinister tyrant that, a few days before his overthrow, he ordered the closing of Romania's borders to all visitors except those from Castro's Cuba, Kim Il Sung's North Korea, the Palestinians, and China.

When viewed in retrospect and in the perspective of twentieth century dictatorships, Ceausescu's Romania shows the classic pattern of a man and woman slowly losing touch with reality. The cruelty that the Ceausescus imposed on their Romanian subjects, the humiliation of a public subjected to the stage-managed adulation of the "hero of heroes" and his wife, created resentments that the couple's execution on Christmas day in 1989 will not assuage. The terror that compelled neighbor to inform on neighbor, the requirement to be a stool pigeon to obtain promotions, a comfortable apartment, or a half-way decent job, led not only to general hatred but also to contempt for the Ceausescus and their brood. Yet, this was the same couple that was received with near-adulation in the West. Queen Elizabeth II made Nicolae a British knight. Elena was given membership in various Western academies and scientific societies. They received presents royal indeed, and they were hailed as modern-day heroes.

At home, however, all the twists and turns of the Ceausescu clan failed to create permanent conditions for "dynastic socialism." The country's economy followed those of other East European nations in the 1980s, and it plunged into a deep depression. The regime's prestige at home went down with the economy. There were riots and unrest throughout the country, especially in the urban centers. Although the disturbances were quelled with great brutality, the underlying tensions were not lessened. In December 1989, the discontent erupted into a revolution that overthrew the dictator. Nicolae and Elena Ceausescu fled their capital but were captured, tried by a hastily convened court, and executed. This marked the end of "socialism in one family" and the communist system in Romania.

Bibliography

Deletant, Andrea, *Romania* (Santa Barbara, CA, 1985); Fischer, Mary Ellen, *Nicolae Ceausescu: A Study in Political Leadership* (Boulder, CO, 1989); Funderburk, David, *Pinstripes and Reds: An American Ambassador Caught Between the State Department and Romanian Communists, 1981–1985* (Washington, DC, 1987); ——, *Nationalism and Communism in Romania: The Rise and Fall of Ceausescu's Personal Dictatorship* (Boulder, CO, 1990); Gilberg, Trond, *Modernization in Romania Since World War II* (New York, 1975); Pacepa, Ion Mihai, *Red Horizons* (New York, 1987); Shafir, Michael, *Romania: Politics, Economics and Society* (Boulder, CO, 1985).

Ceausescu, Nicu (1955–). Nicu Ceausescu came into his teens while his father and mother (*see* Ceausescu, Nicolae and Elena) were already the rulers of communist Romania. An unstable young man, he was unable to relate to normal, everyday people. Early in his life, he became an alcoholic, and his escapades with women became the talk of the country. His mother, Elena, doted on him, and indulged his every whim. His father often protected him from criminal charges. Nicu's political activities were fostered by his parents. Since his older brother wanted to be left alone, Nicu was considered by his parents their natural successor. In the early 1980s, however, Nicu made some critical remarks about his father's economic policies, and he was sent to the Transylvanian city of Sibiu to head the local party organization.

Nicu Ceausescu had all the characteristics of a spoiled child. Although he did show early promise in mathematics, and his mother tried to encourage his interest in nuclear physics, he was too spoiled to stick with a subject for long. Ion Mihai Pacepa, the chronicler of the saga of the Ceausescus, mentioned several instances of Nicu's drunken escapades.

After the revolution of December 1989, Nicu Ceausescu was arrested, more to protect him from the crowd than to punish him. At his trial held in January 1990, he used his reputation as a permanently drunk man who had never really grown out of the mentality of his teens. He claimed that he was drunk when he ordered the secret police in Sibiu to fire on crowds and that when he sobered up he withdrew the order. By then, of course, many people were dead or wounded. He also stated that he had given up trying to stop his parents from taking their insane course. The court sentenced him to twenty years in jail, but his liver condition, the result of his alcoholism, landed him in a hospital at least for the time being.

Bibliography
Almond, Mark, *The Rise and Fall of Nicolae and Elena Ceausescu* (London, 1992); Behr, Edward, *Kiss the Hand You Cannot Bite* (New York, 1991); Pacepa, Ion Mihai, *Red Horizons* (New York, 1987).

Ceausescu, Valentin (1952–). Valentin Ceausescu was educated in London at the Imperial College and received a BA degree there. He had the relatively best reputation within Romania of the Ceausescu family. A quiet, retiring man, he incurred his parents' displeasure because he showed no interest in politics. He professed to pursue his professional scientific interests with greater pleasure and he had shown little interest in the youth association of the Romanian Communist party, to whose leadership his mother tried to direct him. In addition, he married the daughter of a rival of his father, Iordana Borila, whose father was critical of the Ceausescu clan's policies.

Valentin found it difficult to escape his mother's ambitions for him. In November 1988, probably without his consent, he was added to the Central Committee of the Communist party. This was understood in December 1989, and Valentin was not prosecuted by the new government. Not surprisingly, he was the best-balanced member of the Ceausescu family. Although he was taken into protective custody in December 1989, together with his sister Zoia and younger brother Nicu, he was soon freed and is living quietly in Bucharest today.

Bibliography
Galloway, George, *Downfall: The Ceausescus and the Romanian Revolution* (London, 1991); Pacepa, Ion Mihai, *Red Horizons* (Washington DC, 1987); Ratesh, Nestor, *Romania: The Entangled Revolution* (Washington, DC, 1989).

Ceausescu, Zoia (?–). Rumor has it that Zoia was an adopted daughter of the Ceausescus, but this has never been confirmed. She was a student of mathematics who had shown some promise. However, she had an unhappy private life and, like her younger brother Nicu, she, too, became a heavy drinker. Eventually she retreated into her private world, gathering pets and bottles in her home. She was pushed through her university studies but did not have the ability nor the inclination to complete her studies abroad. Her exams and written class work were usually done by tutors, and professors had to give her good grades if they wanted to keep their jobs.

In December 1989, she, too, was taken into protective custody together with her uncles, aunts and siblings, but only one of her pet dogs was mistreated. She was eventually released. Although she lost her job at the Institute of Nuclear Energy, where her mother placed her, she was not otherwise taken to task for her family's crimes.

Bibliography

Almond, Mark, *The Rise and Fall of Nicolae and Elena Ceausescu* (London, 1992); Galloway, George, *Downfall: The Ceausescus and the Romanian Revolution* (London, 1991).

Central Planning in Communist Romania. By 1949, the communist government, headed by Gheorghe Gheorghiu-Dej (*see* Gheorghiu-Dej, Gheorghe), was in complete control of all political processes in Romania, but in other areas of life many of the old ways continued to prevail. This was especially true in economics where the nationalization of private property was completed, but agriculture, in spite of the collectivization drive that began in that year, was still outside the control of the Communist party.

In order to tighten control over every phase of social existence, a central planning office was set up under the direction of the Muscovite Vasile Luca (*see* Luca, Vasile) with orders to coordinate and centralize all economic activities. The office of planning received broad powers. Its orders carried the weight of law. It appointed industrial and collective farm managers, after approval by the appropriate party organs. It set work norms in industry for individual firms and compulsory delivery quotas for collective and surviving private peasants.

Copying Soviet methods, the central planning office introduced two one-year plans and a five-year plan that began in 1951. In the first two years of the five-year plan, investments grew by 34 percent of the national income, over 90 percent of which was spent in industrial development. Only 10 percent of the total was spent in agriculture, and minuscule amounts were devoted to new housing.

The dislocations caused by the investment policies threatened society with chaos. The ongoing collectivization drive forced large numbers of the rural folks to abandon their villages, and seek work in the new industries. However, apartments in the cities, where industry was located, were scarce. Commuting was hardly possible since the road system was not developed, and trains and buses were inadequate for the purpose. Thus, the industrial workers were housed in barracks and dormitories, hastily thrown together in the outskirts of cities, without the most elementary hygienic services. They usually travelled home once a month, but their wages often precluded even such pleasures.

In 1953, the first five-year plan was abandoned. In March of that year, Joseph Stalin had died. His successors abandoned some of the shibboleths of Stalinist times. The Romanian communists dutifully followed the Soviet example and introduced their own "new course," but the central planning of the economy was not abandoned. Industrial expansion was, for a time, slowed down. Between 1956 and 1958, the central planning office abolished the system of compulsory deliveries of food by the collectives and increased the wages of industrial workers by 15 percent. Nevertheless, the central planning office continued to micro- and macromanage the Romanian economy. After 1959, the office played a major role in the renewed drive for industrialization and assumed an even more important position during the Ceausescu years after 1965. The central planning office was finally abolished in 1990 after the completion of the revolution that overthrew the communist regime.

Bibliography

Gilberg, Trond, *Modernization in Romania Since World War II* (New York, 1975); Montias, John M., *Economic Development in Communist Romania* (Cambridge, MA, 1967); Turnock, David, *The Economic Geography of Romania* (London, 1974).

Communist Party of Romania. The Romanian Communist party was founded in 1921. It was a small, insignificant organization that could not become a major force in Romanian national life without heavy outside support. The party began a series of terrorist actions in the early 1920s and was, therefore, declared illegal in 1924. Further repressive action was taken by the government in 1936, when all the known leaders of the party were imprisoned. By then, the Romanian Communist party was directed by the COMINTERN, which also provided funds for its operations. The jailing of the leaders eliminated the party as a political force in Romanian society.

In 1944, when the party was revived, it had less than 1,000 members. Some of its leaders, who had fled to the Soviet Union, or were exchanged for Romanian officers after 1940, returned. At first, party membership consisted mostly of ethnic minorities who were persecuted during the interwar years. This was reflected in the leadership that consisted of three factions: the Muscovites (leaders who spent the war years in Moscow), including Vasile Luca (*see* Luca, Vasile) and Ana Pauker (*see* Pauker, Ana); the local communists who were in jail, headed by Gheorghe Gheorghiu-Dej (*see* Gheorghiu-Dej, Gheorghe) and Lucretiu Patrascanu (*see* Patrascanu, Lucretiu); and "free floaters," such as Emil Bodnaras (*see* Bodnaras, Emil), who were jailed at first but were freed after spending their allotted time in prison. The Muscovites were the dominant faction in 1944, and they remained in this position until 1952.

In 1952, Ana Pauker and Vasile Luca were eliminated. Gheorghiu-Dej became the undisputed leader, and he eliminated his opposition one by one. He also began cautiously to distance Romania from the Soviet Union, and he appealed more and more to national sentiment. Gheorghiu-Dej was a Stalinist; he accepted the Stalinist method of modernization, and the party that he led organized the rapid industrialization of Romania. He also believed that the process had to be accompanied by the collectivization of the peasantry, and the drive for this began in 1949. He also enforced the monopoly of the Communist party in every sphere of national endeavors. Gheorghiu-Dej died of cancer in 1965.

His successor, Nicolae Ceausescu (*see* Ceausescu, Nicolae and Elena), showed a relatively liberal disposition in the first years of his rule. However, he, too, followed the well-known Stalinist recipe and eliminated his rivals for power. In time, Ceausescu turned the Communist party into his personal fiefdom. He placed his brothers and sisters, uncles and aunts in responsible positions where they could keep an eye on the party and on the government leaders to ensure their loyalty. Ceausescu also turned the secret police, which was enormously strengthened during his rule, into the real instrument of government. He instituted a reign of terror that lasted until his overthrow in 1989.

The Romanian communists took control of the government between 1945 and 1948. In 1948, they forced through a merger with the Romanian Social Democratic party, giving a new name to the organization: the Romanian Workers party. The name was changed back to Communist party in 1965, when Ceausescu took power.

The highest organ of the Romanian Communist party, as was the case in other communist states, was the congress. It was to meet every five years; its delegates were elected at regional meetings. The work of the party organs that went on when congress was not in session had to be approved, retroactively most of the time, by the congress. This body was also to approve the party's program, and elect the members of the Central Committee and the members of the central auditing commission. When it went into recess, the Central Committee was to function as its executive body.

The Central Committee, therefore, was the supposedly dominant body of the party. It supervised the work of the government by establishing parallel party offices that were located next to local government bodies, and it administered the growing financial empire of the party organizations. The differences between party and government purses gradually disappeared, however, and the party leaders freely used the moneys of the state for their own personal needs. The Central Committee was also to elect the members of the Politburo (later changed to Presidium, and again to the Political Executive Committee) and the secretariat. In reality, the party leader made all the choices, which were then rubber-stamped by the Central Committee and eventually by the congress. The Central Committee included not only the highest party leaders but also members of the government. Of the forty-six members of the council of ministers (the cabinet), all held seats in the Central Committee in 1988.

The real power rested with the Political Executive Committee or Politburo. It supervised the work of the secretariat and the party's control commission (later renamed the central collegium). The permanent bureau, elected by the Political Executive Committee consisted of seven members. This small group, however, never became a major political force because power remained in the Politburo. The Central Committee was empowered to review the decisions made by the Political Executive Committee in plenary session, but this was only a pro forma action that never challenged the leaders.

The next level of organization was in the counties. The county committees and other party organizations were carbon copies of the higher party organs. The first secretary of the county party committee was also a member of the Central Committee. Party cells in the lower levels were to meet once every two months to approve the directives of the county authorities, but the actual meetings simply approved actions without debate. There were 40 county organizations, 237 city and municipal party sections, and 2705 cells in village communities. In addition, 8,500 cells operated in factories and other places of work in 1987. The basic cells existed in every institution, factory, collective farm, and mass organization. Their size varied between 3 and 300 members. Each cell had a secretary and a deputy secretary; the larger cells had a secretariat. These groups supervised the activities of local government organs or managements.

The communist apparatus, therefore, reached into practically every segment of Romanian society. From the initial membership of 1,000 in 1944, the party had grown to 2 million by 1948. In 1988, party statistics had shown a membership list of 3,709,000 people, or about 15.8 percent of the total population of the country. Its mass organizations included the Communist Youth of Romania (an imitation of the Soviet KOMSOMOL), the Pioneers for smaller youngsters, organizations for women, and so on. They all served the role of disseminating party directives and mobilizing the populations for the party's purposes.

All this disappeared in the revolution of December 1989. The Communist party disintegrated; its membership disappeared. In the 1992 elections, however, the party reappeared in two new incarnations, one bearing the name, Romanian Socialist party, the other running under its old designation. Neither of them succeeded in gaining substantial voter support.

Bibliography

Gilberg, Trond, "Multiple Legacies of History: Romania in 1990," in Joseph Held, ed. *The Columbia History of Eastern Europe in the Twentieth Century* (New York, 1992); King, Robert R., *History of the Romanian Communist Party* (Stanford, CA, 1980); Nelson, Daniel N., *Romania in the 1980s* (Boulder, CO, 1981); Tismaneanu, Vladimir, *Personal Power and Elite Change in Romania* (Philadelphia, PA, 1989).

Cornea, Doina (?–). Cornea has been one of the bravest, most active and incisive critics of the Ceausescu regime. A teacher of the French language in the Transylvanian city of Cluj, she denounced the economic and moral disaster that Romania had become in the late 1970s and 1980s. She sent letters abroad, to Radio Free Europe and to prominent Western statesmen and governments. Radio Free Europe immediately broadcast the letters in its Romanian language programs, but governments and individual statesmen did not take her letters seriously.

The Ceausescu clan took personal affront at her criticisms. She was treated harshly; she was insulted and even beaten by the thugs of the secret police. Eventually, she was confined to her house and was not permitted to have visitors. The American consul tried to see her in 1986 but was rudely shoved away from her door, creating a minor diplomatic incident. Cornea never yielded an inch and bravely bore all efforts to silence her. It was Cornea who brought the horrors of systematization, that is the destruction of villages, to the attention of the world (*see* Systematization). Eventually her letters brought protests and helped world public opinion understand the nature of the Ceausescu regime. In December 22, 1989, Cornea was included among the leadership of the National Salvation Front that took over government affairs from the defunct Communist party. However, she soon left the front and once again became a severe critic, this time of the front's authoritarian practices.

Bibliography
Ratesh, Nestor, *Romania: The Entangled Revolution* (Washington, DC, 1989).

Danube-Black Sea Canal. The Romanian communist leaders were always awed by the monumental scale of construction that took place during Joseph Stalin's rule in the Soviet Union. They, too, had to have monumental projects that were to symbolize the "magnificence" of the Romanian communist system. For Gheorghe Gheorghiu-Dej (*see* Gheorghiu-Dej, Gheorghe), the project that was to be the mother of all projects, the monument to his leadership, was the Danube-Black sea canal. He gained COMECON support for this project. Work on the canal began in 1949. Using mostly slave labor on the pattern of the Soviet Gulag, the canal was supposed to eliminate the uncertainty of navigation at the great river's delta. It was also supposed to connect the southern regions of Romania with Soviet commerce on the Black sea and with Western Europe. However, the canal's ecological impact, was never ascertained and this was to cause tremendous problems.

By 1952, only three kilometers of the projected seventy-five had been fully excavated. Enormous investments, thousands of lives, and tremendous amounts of labor were wasted on the next seven kilometers, started but not finished. Swamp drainage and irrigation was completed in some sections but left unfinished in others. A cement factory, two thermoelectric plants, and seventy-eight kilometers of road that led to nowhere were constructed. Immediately after the death of Gheorghiu-Dej, the project was abandoned.

When Nicolae Ceausescu (*see* Ceausescu, Nicolae and Elena) established his control over Romania, however, he, too, was looking for some would-be monument that would survive his rule. The Danube-Black sea canal was an obvious choice. Thus, the construction recommenced in the early 1970s. The old method of using slave labor was revived. Thousands more innocent political prisoners died while building the great canal. The project's progress was now ensured because the secret police had no difficulty in identifying new victims.

The canal was finally completed in 1984. Week-long celebrations followed, glorifying the "great builder of the century," Nicolae Ceausescu. Poems and songs were composed in his honor; his adulation exceeded even that of Stalin at the height of the Soviet dictator's power. Romanian television spent most of its programs celebrating the "monumental achievement of the Communist party and Comrade Ceausescu."

But the canal proved to be economically unsuccessful. Instead of the increase of trade expected, only a trickle of it came through the new waterway. This was partly the result of the collapse of the Soviet economy and the diminishing volume of Soviet trade. But the Balkan states, including Greece and Bulgaria, shipped their exports through the traditional routes leading through the Mediterranean and Aegean seas. The Iran-Iraq war did not help Romania either. The crude oil that was to be shipped through terminals in Turkey never materialized.

At the present time, the great Danube-Black sea canal is just another project that seems to have been unnecessary. It certainly contributed its share to the exhaustion of the Romanian economy in the 1980s. It is undoubtedly possible that the Danube-Black sea canal might eventually become a regular trade route. For that to happen, however, first the shattered Russian and other economies in the successor states of the former Soviet Union would have to be revived. There is a good possibility that this will happen but it will be in the future.

Bibliography
Georgescu, Vlad, ed. *Romania: 40 Years (1944–1984)* (New York, 1985); Ionescu, Ghita, *Communism in Romania 1944–1962* (New York, 1964); Jowitt, Kenneth, *Revolutionary Breakthroughs and National Development: The Case of Romania, 1945–1965* (Berkeley, CA, 1971); Shafir, Michael, *Romania: Politics, Economics, and Society* (Boulder, CO, 1985); Zissu, Iancu, *The Regime of Forced Labor in Romania* (Washington, DC, 1952).

"Declaration of Independence" (1964). By the mid-1960s, Nikita Khrushchev and the Soviet leadership had become deeply concerned about the developing integration of the economies of the West European countries. The visibly growing gap between the Common Market and that of the Soviet Bloc countries was considered by the Soviet leaders a threat to their quest for world domination. This development also promised long-range consequences for Soviet military power on the European continent. The solution, as Khrushchev saw it, was the closer integration of the economies of Soviet Bloc nations with that of the Soviet Union. The vehicle for this integration was to be COMECON, the intended equivalent of the Soviet bloc with the Common Market. However, it was easier said than done.

When COMECON was originally established by Joseph Stalin, it was not intended to be an inter-bloc economic organization. Its members were bound together economically by a series of bilateral treaties, not by a general agreement on trade, tariffs, and production target-and distribution. Each country also had its own agreements with the Soviet Union. Khrushchev was not really interested in changing the guiding principles of the organization; he simply wanted the Soviet Union to be able to coordinate economic activities within the bloc.

Thus, the Soviet representatives in COMECON simply forced through a system for the division of labor among the states of the bloc. According to this division, the less developed Balkan countries, except Bulgaria, were to concentrate on developing their agricultural production and related industries. This included Romania. As a secondary goal, Romanian oil and petrochemical industries were also emphasized.

In the reasoning of the Romanian communist leaders, however, such a role would have relegated Romania to the status of a permanently backward country and would have called into question all the sacrifices that they asked from their people in the interest of industrialization. Furthermore, since, until that time, industrialization concentrated on heavy industry, with the corresponding neglect of consumer goods production, Romania did not have the resources for the mechanization of its agriculture, a sine qua non of modernization. The infrastructure for such a policy was also missing; there were no warehouses to store food, and the secondary road and railway network was nonexistent. In 1964, therefore, Gheorghe Gheorghiu-Dej (*see* Gheorghiu-Dej, Gheorghe) followed the earlier example set by Albania; Romania refused to participate in the new division of labor but with more caution than Enver Hoxha exercised. He knew that open defiance of Khrushchev might bring about unforeseen consequences.

By the mid-1960s, Romania's economy was fundamentally changed. The agrarian labor force was reduced from 76.4 percent in 1950 to closer to 30 percent. The ratio of industrial wage earners increased from 10.5 percent to nearly 40 percent. The former large landowners had disappeared. All industrial enterprises were state-owned, and only about 2 percent of the land was still in private hands. If agricultural production were to be reemphasized, this would be such a radical change that it would have required the repudiation of everything that the Communist party stressed in the previous two decades. What made the situation easier for the Romanians was the fact that no Soviet troops had been stationed on Romanian soil since 1958, and the usual coercive method would, thus, not be immediately available to Khrushchev and his colleagues.

The opposition of Gheorghiu-Dej to integration into COMECON suddenly made the Communist party more legitimate in the eyes of the Romanian people. He appeared to be a genuine Romanian, one who was unwilling to subordinate the country's interests to those of the Soviet Bloc.

To reinforce this view, the regime began to loosen its political ties with the Soviet leadership. The most visible sign of this effort appeared in cultural life. Streets bearing Soviet names were renamed; Soviet cultural centers were taken over and turned into Romanian institutions. There was also more open talk in party circles about Soviet encroachments on Romanian sovereignty. Nationalism in Romania, as elsewhere in Eastern Europe, eventually proved to be a much stronger force than Marxist-Leninist ideology.

In April 1964, the Central Committee of the Romanian Communist party issued a declaration. According to this note which was later called "Romania's Declaration of Independence," Romania did recognize the need for closer economic cooperation within the socialist bloc. However, such cooperation had to be conducted on the basis of the principle of nonintervention in the internal affairs of each country. In October

1964, after Khrushchev had been removed from office, his successors signed an agreement with Romania for providing considerable technical and economic assistance for Romania's developing industries. This step implicitly recognized Romania's right to economic independence.

Bibliography
Matley, Ian M., *Romania: A Profile* (New York, 1970); Montias, John M., *Economic Development in Communist Romania* (Cambridge, MA, 1967).

De-Stalinization in Romania. Joseph Stalin's death in March 1953 was followed by a period of uncertainty in Eastern Europe and the Soviet Union. The Soviet leaders were jockeying for power and issued often contradictory orders to their East European satraps. When Nikita Khrushchev finally emerged as the Soviet leader, he began to air the crimes committed by Stalin.

The Romanian communists saw no need to follow Khrushchev's lead. Even before Stalin's death, Ana Pauker (*see* Pauker, Ana) and Vasile Luca (*see* Luca, Vasile), the two most distasteful Stalinists had been removed from the party's leadership. But a discussion of Stalin's crimes and their effects in Romania would have compromised Gheorghe Gheorghiu-Dej (*see* Gheor-ghiu-Dej, Gheorghe) and his followers.

Although the terror by which the communists ruled the country was somewhat relaxed, it was not completely eliminated. Nor were economic policies of the party changed. The Stalinist method of rapid industrialization accompanied by centralized planning and a collectivized agriculture remained in effect. The standard of living for most of the population remained low.

Gheorghiu-Dej sought other means to establish the party's internal legitimacy. The major means was an old-fashioned Romanian nationalism. This was something that everyone in Romania could understand and even approve: the liberation of the country from the Soviet yoke. The communist leaders accomplished their purpose without, however, relaxing their control over the population. The teaching of nationalist Romanian history, albeit in a distorted version, and the recall of Romanian historical traditions replaced the emphasis on Marxism-Leninism-Stalinism in schools and party propaganda. In the late 1960s, the trend continued; Ceausescu (*see* Ceausescu, Nicolae and Elena) began to stress that he was leading Romania to a more prestigious position in the world.

In 1963, Gheorghiu-Dej declared that every socialist state had the right to pursue its own way to socialism. He added that relations among socialist states must be based on equality and mutual advantage. Finally, he emphasized that noninterference in the internal affairs of states must be a guiding principle even within the socialist bloc. In other words, Gheorghiu-Dej reinvented the normal principles of international relations. When the Brezhnev-doctrine was announced in 1968, Romanian leaders vehemently denounced it as an imperialist design. After 1974, the Romanian communist regime placed increasing emphasis on nationalism, but it was combined with a terrorist regime that resembled Stalin's.

Bibliography
Fischer-Galati, Stephen, *The New Romania: From People's Democracy to Socialist Republic* (Cambridge, MA, 1967); Gilberg, Trond, *Nationalism and Communism in Romania: The Rise and Fall of Ceausescu's Personal Dictatorship* (Boulder, CO, 1990).

Draghici, Alexandru (1917–). Draghici was a member of the leadership of the illegal Communist party in Romania during the 1930s, and he spent time in prison with the other leaders after 1936. When Gheorghe Gheorghiu-Dej (*see* Gheorghiu-Dej, Gheorghe) came into power in the late 1940s, he appointed Draghici minister of the interior, which controlled the regular and the secret police organizations. He was a close friend of Gheorghiu-Dej and was a frequent companion to the leader when Gheorghiu-Dej became ill with cancer.

When the first secretary was on the verge of death in 1965, Draghici became a compromise candidate to succeed him. His competitors were Gheorghe Apostol (*see* Apostol, Gheorghe), and Nicolae Ceausescu (*see* Ceausescu, Nicolae and Elena). Draghici was a formidable opponent since his control of the police forces gave him almost unlimited power, but Ceausescu skillfully outmaneuvered both him and Apostol and obtained the post of head of the Communist party.

In July 1965, at the ninth congress of the Romanian Communist party, Ceausescu succeeded in increasing the membership of the Central Committee of the party where his power base was. At the same time, he reduced the number of the members of the Politburo, where Draghici and Apostol had the most support. Finally, Draghici was removed as minister of the interior, losing control of his most powerful instrument. But this was not enough for the new leader. At a meeting of the Central Committee, Ceausescu openly criticized Draghici as the man directly responsible for the torture and show trials of the interwar leadership of the Communist party, especially Lucretiu Patrascanu (*see* Patrascanu, Lucretiu) and Stefan Foris. (Patrascanu was executed in 1954; Foris was beaten to death by a secret police thug in 1949). For good measure, Ceausescu added that the Politburo also knew about the fabricated charges and approved the death sentence of Patrascanu in spite of this knowledge. Draghici was removed from the leadership because of these charges, but he survived Ceausescu and the revolution.

Bibliography
Almond, Mark, *The Rise and Fall of Nicolae and Elena Ceausescu* (London, 1992).

Economic Policies in Communist Romania. The aim of the communist government in Romania was, as elsewhere in the East European countries, to nationalize all industry, banking, and their auxiliary services and then to use the system to serve as an instrument for socialist construction. By June 1948, most privately owned firms and banks had been taken over by the government without compensation to their former owners. Foreign-owned companies shared in this process. By 1960, over 98 percent of all firms were nationalized.

The leaders then began a drive for rapid industrialization of the Stalinist-type. Most investments were poured into heavy industry. The policy continued in effect with minor slowdowns into the 1970s and the 1980s. For instance, between 1970 and 1975, 57 percent of all investments went to heavy industry. However, Romania did not have the necessary raw material base for such a development. Consequently, large amounts of iron ore, rolled metals, and even fuel had to be imported, in spite of the fact that Romania did have considerable oil reserves.

In 1962, free of the Soviet occupational forces which had been were withdrawn in 1958, Romania embarked, albeit cautiously, on a separate foreign policy. It gradually turned to the West for financial support. In 1963, Romania bought the largest steel mill in the world; it also acquired a complete rubber tire-making factory and a paper mill from Great Britain. The Soviet Union had also sold Romania a large steel mill. In time, West Germany became Romania's next largest trading partner after the Soviet Union. The latter had also sold Romania a large steel mill. French firms built a large winery and a sugar beat-processing plant. The Soviet share in Romania's trade was perceptibly declining.

In the early 1980s, still more than half of Romania's investments went into heavy industrial development. After 1985, however, some change occurred in agricultural investment, but not enough to raise the agricultural sector out of its stagnation. The Romanian economy was seriously effected by the decline in the world economy following the steep increases of oil prices. By 1985, Romanian oil reserves were exhausted, and the country had to import most of its oil. Deeper and deeper did Romania go into debt. In the end, $12 billion were owed to various Western banks and governments. Romania also acquired nuclear energy plants from the Soviet Union, but even these could not satisfy the energy needs of the economy. Since agriculture was still stagnating, food rationing had to be introduced in 1982. Finally, in order to end the chronic problems, the Ceausescu government decided to repay all loans at any price.

This necessitated the further lowering of the living standards of the population. Long lines in front of food and other stores, dimly lit apartments, and electric-current blackouts several times daily were the results. The patience of the population was eventually exhausted. In 1977, a strike was held by miners in the Jiu Valley (*see* Jiu Valley Strike). In 1987, the Brasov workers rioted (*see* Brasov Strike). In December 1989, the tensions erupted into open defiance of the regime, and the overthrow of the Ceausescu clan.

Agricultural policies were also organized on the Stalinist patterns. In 1945, the communist government introduced land reform. Holdings exceeding fifty hectares of arable land and the lands possessed by the so-called war criminals were confiscated. The lands of most of the German and Hungarian minorities were also nationalized. About 1 million Romanian peasant families were given the confiscated properties. At the same time, compulsory deliveries of foodstuffs from individual peasant families were required. Since the quotas were high to begin with and were constantly changed, peasants were eventually driven into the collective farmers since they could not fulfill the delivery requirements.

In 1949, the drive for collectivization began in earnest. The scant agricultural machinery in possession of the peasants was confiscated. Small rural credit institutions were nationalized and closed down. Mills and oil presses also became state property. Monetary "reform," introduced in 1950, confiscated the savings of peasant families. In spite of all the pressure, only 2.5 percent of the lands were in the hands of collective farmers by 1950. By 1957, however, 13,065 collective farmers existed. Surprisingly, they controlled only about 25 percent of the arable lands. By 1960, however, about 80 percent of the lands were cultivated by collective farms. In 1962, the government announced that the goal of collectivization had been achieved and that 96.5 percent of the lands were now worked collectively.

But collectivization by itself did not help the Romanian economy. Although about one-third of the working population was still engaged in agricultural production, they produced only 14 percent of the national income. The peasants hated the collectives, they considered the loss of their implements and animals to the state as robbery, and they worked as little as possible. In addition, the state levied heavy taxes even on the collective farms, syphoning off the resources for the benefit of industries.

Since the peasants hated the collectives so much, the government tried to assuage their hostility by establishing several types of collective farms. The state-owned collectives were usually large and were directly administered by the ministry of agriculture. They were, on the whole, better supplied with instruments than other collectives. But most of these farms were located in hilly regions, and their aggregate size came to about 5 percent of the arable lands. Most of them were farmed extensively, producing bread grains. During the 1970s and 1980s, there was a constant drive to turn collectives into state farms. But the numbers of these farms increased slowly, and they did not affect production volumes in a major way.

In 1970, a new law on agriculture was passed. Collective farm members were permitted to have small private plots. They were allowed to sell their produce from these plots on the open market. Even this did not solve the problem of the food supply. In 1981, agricultural councils were created in order to control land in parcels of 20,000 acres each. In the next year, investments in agriculture were increased. The International Monetary Fund helped out with a $75 million loan for agricultural machinery, and the following year another loan in the amount of $80 million was issued for the development of Romanian animal husbandry. All this was to no avail. The interests and needs of individual peasant families continued to be neglected. By the early 1980s, the collective farms were worked mostly by old men and women, under such conditions that even increased mechanization would have been ineffective.

Bibliography

Crowther, William E., *The Political Economy of Romanian Socialism* (New York, 1988); Montias, John M., *Economic Development in Communist Romania* (Cambridge, MA, 1967); Shafir, Michael, *Romania: Politics, Economics and Society* (Boulder, CO, 1985); Stahl,

Henry, *Traditional Romanian Village Communities* (London, 1980); Tsantis, Andreas C., *Romania: The Industrialization of an Agrarian Economy Under Socialist Planning* (Baltimore, MD, 1974); Turnock, David, *An Economic Geography of Romania* (London, 1974).

Gheorghiu-Dej, Gheorghe (1901–1965). Born in Barlad, Moldavia, to a workingman's family, he became an electrician and started working at the Danubian port of Galat. Soon, however, Gheorghiu-Dej was employed by the Romanian National Railways. He became a member of the railroad worker's union and, in 1930, joined the underground Communist party. By then, he had accumulated some political experience, having flirted with the Romanian Social Democratic and the Peasant parties. Because of his illegal union activities, he was transferred to the Transylvanian village of Dej (originally, Des) in 1931. He then added Dej to his original name.

In 1931, Gheorghiu-Dej became secretary to the "action committee" of railwaymen. The following year, he may or may not have been a leading figure in organizing the railroad strike that paralyzed the repair yards near Bucharest. He was then arrested, tried, and sentenced to twelve years of forced labor; however, he never had to do a day's work. In prison, he was locked up with most of the other local leaders of the Romanian Communist party, who had all been rounded up and imprisoned. A young man who was a courier for one of the illegal party's front organizations was also locked up with him. The young man's name was Nicolae Ceausescu see Ceausescu, Nicolae and Elena). In April 1944, when the Soviet army was approaching Romania's borders, the jailed local communist leaders held a "reorganization meeting" in the prison hospital. At this meeting, a new provisional leadership emerged. It included Gheorghiu-Dej as first secretary, Emil Bodnaras (*see* Bodnaras, Emil) and young Nicolae Ceausescu.

Gheorghiu-Dej was accepted by Joseph Stalin as the future Romanian leader with the provision that exiled Romanian communists living in the Soviet Union during the war, should be included in the leadership when they returned to Romania. These Muscovites included Vasile Luca (*see* Luca, Vasile) and Ana Pauker (*see* Pauker, Ana). In the mid- and late 1940s, Gheorghiu-Dej successfully led the Communist party, with Soviet support, of course, to the dictatorship in Romania. He skillfully used the secret police, organized with the help of the Soviet NKVD-KGB, to terrorize and eliminate his party's opponents. By 1948, he was the ruler of Romania, but he still had to face the challenge of the Muscovites. In 1952, he eliminated his rivals, taking advantage of Stalin's latent anti-Semitism. He succeeded in this because he could prove to Stalin that he, Gheorghiu-Dej, was more trustworthy than his rivals.

By then, the Stalinization of Romanian society was in full swing. The Politburo, organized by Gheorghiu-Dej, was now composed only of "local" communists, cronies of the leader, most of whom had been in prison with him before and during World War II. In 1952, following Stalin's example, Gheorghiu-Dej added the post of prime minister to his title of party leader. Yet another show trial eliminated Lucretiu Patrascanu (*see* Patrascanu, Lucretiu), a "local" rival of Gheorghiu-Dej for the control of the party. Five years later, he eliminated two more of the survivors of the old party leadership, Gheorghe Cicinevci and Alexander Constantinescu. He purged Constantin Parvulescu in 1961.

During the Hungarian Revolution of 1956, Gheorghiu-Dej earned special gratitude of Nikita S. Khrushchev. He contributed to the suppression of the Hungarians by facilitating the movement of Soviet troops and tank divisions through Romania into Hungary. He also provided a detention center for Imre Nagy, prime minister of revolutionary Hungary, after he and his cabinet members were treacherously captured by the Soviet KGB. Romanian diplomats defended vigorously the brutal Soviet action against Hungary in international forums. As a reward, Khrushchev withdrew the Soviet occupational forces from Romania in 1958, to the later regret of the Soviet leadership.

The Romanians then began a cautious, slow opening to the West. In 1959, trade with Western countries slightly increased (imports by 7.8 percent and exports by 6.3 percent). By then, the conflict between China and the Soviet Union was looming over the horizon, and Gheorghiu-Dej skillfully exploited the conflict to assume the position of an honest broker between the two communist giants. In 1960, he attended the meeting of Communist party leaders in Moscow and in exchange for his support of the Soviet line, he received substantial economic aid for Romania. When the COMECON (that is, Khrushchev) demanded that Romania slow down her industrialization and concentrate on agricultural development instead, Gheorghiu-Dej demurred. Conflicts emerged also around the Romanian collectivization of agriculture, opposed by Khrushchev, who was worried about the deterioration in food production within the Soviet bloc. By 1962, relations between the Soviet and Romanian leaders were at a low point.

Gheorghiu-Dej began to flirt with the Chinese, and he refused to submit to further COMECON decisions about East European-Soviet economic integration. A series of conflicts followed between Romania and its East European allies. The Romanians complained about the low quality of the machinery delivered by the East Germans and the Czechoslovaks, of the lack of spare parts, and of the often delayed deliveries. The East Europeans retorted that Romania was sending its food exports to the West, instead of helping them out of their food shortages. They deplored the Romanian decision to establish a huge steel mill at Galat, arguing that the country had no raw material resources for its operation. Gheorghiu-Dej responded by pointing out that neither did France.

In 1963, the Romanian government signed a trade agreement with China. At the same time, it renewed diplomatic relations with Albania, interrupted in 1961. Gheorghiu-Dej argued that China and Albania were two socialist states and that trade was a natural expression of common interests. Gheorghiu-Dej was conspicuously absent from the meeting of communist leaders held in East Berlin in June 1963, a meeting that was intended to reaffirm European support for the Soviet Union in its dispute with China. In November, he visited Marshal Tito in Yugoslavia for nine days, and he concluded an agreement with the Yugoslavs for the joint construction of a hydroelectric power station on the Danube river at the Iron Gate. The joint investment was to come to $400 million.

In the general assembly of the United Nations, Romania voted a few times against the Soviet Union, when it was safe and was not against direct Soviet interests. In response, the British and the French governments upgraded their diplomatic missions to embassies in Bucharest. Gheorghiu-Dej, therefore, gradually assumed the stance of a "national" communist and, in the process, he gained in popularity not only among Romanians but also among foreign governments. He took further steps to reduce Soviet influence in Romania. The Maxim Gorky Institute in Bucharest was closed down. The compulsory teaching of the Russian language in Romanian schools was discontinued. Streets named after the "Soviet liberators" reverted to their original Romanian names. He even released some political prisoners. This development, however, did not last long. In late 1964, Gheorghiu-Dej suddenly became ill. His illness was diagnosed as terminal cancer. In a few months, he was dead. He left behind a leadership whose members were engaged in a struggle over the succession. Gheorghe Apostol (*see* Apostol, Gheorghe), Alexandru Draghici (*see* Draghici, Alexandru), and Nicolae Ceausescu were the contenders. Eventually, Ceausescu came out the victor.

Bibliography

Cretianu, Alexandru, *Captive Romania: A Decade of Soviet Rule* (New York, 1956); Fischer-Galati, Stephen, *The Socialist Republic of Romania* (Baltimore, MD, 1962); Georgescu, Vlad, ed. *Romania: 40 Years (1944–1984)* (New York, 1985); Gilberg, Trond, "The Multiple Legacies of History: Romania in 1990," in Joseph Held, ed. *The Columbia History of Eastern Europe in the Twentieth Century* (New York, 1992); Ionescu, Ghita, *Communism in Romania 1944–1962* (Cambridge, MA, 1967); Markham, Reuben, *Romania Under the Soviet Yoke* (Boston, MA, 1949); Matley, Ian M., *Romania: A Profile* (New York, 1970).

Goma, Paul (1930–). In 1977, following the publication of the declaration of human rights activists in Communist Czechoslovakia, the Charter 77, Paul Goma wrote an open letter to Romanian party leader Nicolae Ceausescu (*see* Ceausescu, Nicolae and Elena). He complained about the suppression of human rights in Romania, in spite of the fact that Ceausescu had signed the Helsinki Final Act, guaranteeing civil and human rights for all citizens. Goma, a well-known writer, had been jailed in the 1950s for his human rights activities, and his contempt for the communist dictatorship, masquerading as a democracy, was public knowledge. Between January and April 1977, Goma had written several letters and appeals, and he had obtained the signatures of some 200 intellectuals in support of his views. Goma was persecuted in every possible way, but he was not jailed.

Ceausescu was enraged by his letters; he personally ordered the secret police to have the writer severely beaten by a former boxer. None of this silenced the courageous writer. On April 1, he was finally arrested, but an aroused Western public opinion saved Goma's life. He was allowed to leave Romania. He settled in Paris, and continued his criticism of the Ceausescu regime from abroad. Finally, the dictator ordered his assassination, but the man sent to arrange Goma's death gave himself up to the French police. He gave a detailed description of his instructions and turned the poison that was to kill Goma over to the French. Thus, Goma survived the collapse of communism in Romania.

Bibliography
Hajducu, Matei, *I Refused to Kill* (In French) (Paris, 1984); Pacepa, Ion Mihai, *Red Horizons* (Washington DC, 1987); Ratesh, Nestor, *Romania: The Entangled Revolution* (Washington DC, 1989).

Groza, Petru (?–1958). Groza was originally a leader of the Plowmen's Front, a radical populist organization in interwar Romania. He was a prosperous Transylvanian landowner, a lawyer by profession. He was fluent in both the Hungarian and Romanian languages. He was the head of a coalition government established in 1945 whose main purpose was the enactment of radical land reforms. Groza's government was also determined to end the traditional hostility between Romanians and Hungarians. Above all, he wanted to accommodate the interests of the Soviet Union with those of Romania. On March 25, 1945, the land reform law was introduced. Groza's government also established a Hungarian-language administrative area in Transylvania with far-reaching autonomy. However, Groza did not realize that Joseph Stalin would not be satisfied until a communist government was established in Romania and considered any other government only a temporary one.

In November 1946, elections were held. By then, the communists had succeeded completely in intimidating the opposition. They split the Social Democratic party, inducing its left wing to run on a joint ticket with the communists. Groza went along with the communist demands. In fact, he had little choice. In the summer of that same year, the upper house of parliament, traditionally the power-base of the aristocracy, was abolished. The media were strictly censored, and the participation of the "nondemocratic" that is, oppositional parties, in the elections was prohibited. The victory of the coalition government was taken for granted. According to the official reports, the coalition, which included the Communist party, received 5 million votes. In contrast, the opposition received a very few number of seats in the new parliament.

On February 10, 1947, Groza signed the peace treaties in Paris. Considering Romania's eager participation in the war against the Soviet Union on the side of Nazi Germany, the treaty was not harsh. Romania received the entire territory of Transylvania with its nearly 3 million ethnic Hungarians and half a million Saxons (Germans) and lost only Bessarabia which had been in Soviet hands since 1940 in any case. What helped the Groza government was that, in Hungary, the communists had a much more difficult time in gaining total power than they did in Romania. Thus, they gained Stalin's support, although the Soviet leader also demanded $300 million worth of reparations from Romania. This was not accepted by the Western Allies, and Romania was not obligated to pay any reparations.

Bibliography
Cretianu, Alexandru, *Captive Romania: A Decade of Soviet Rule* (Baltimore, MD, 1969);
Georgescu, Vlad, *Romania: 40 Years (1944–1984)* (New York, 1985); Ionescu, Ghita, *Communism in Romania, 1944–1962* (New York, 1964); Shafir, Michael, *Romania: Politics, Economics and Society* (Boulder, CO, 1985).

Iliescu, Ion (1930–). For many years before 1985, Ion Iliescu was considered, in well-informed Romanian circles, to be the likely successor to Nicolae Ceausescu (*see* Ceausescu, Nicolae). His father, a railroad worker, had joined the illegal Communist party in the 1930s. In 1945, young Ion joined the Union of Communist Youth and soon rose to leadership in the organization. In 1950, he was sent to the Soviet Union where he studied to become a hydroelectric engineer. In Moscow, he was appointed secretary to the Communist Youth of Romanian University Students.

In 1954, Iliescu returned home and became a party apparatchik. For three years, he was the full-time chairman of the Communist Federation of Romanian University Students. In 1966, he was promoted to membership in the propaganda and ideology department of the Central Committee of the Communist party. He was still only thirty-five years old when he reached that prestigious position. By then, Ceausescu was the general secretary of the party. Iliescu next became minister of youth affairs and the leader of the Union of Communist Youth. In 1971, he was again promoted, this time to the secretariat of the Central Committee of the party in charge of ideology. In that year, he accompanied Ceausescu on his official visit to Beijing and Pyongyang. However, when Ceausescu, upon their return, drew up plans for a Chinese-style Romanian cultural revolution, Iliescu demurred. In consequence, he lost the leader's favor and was sent to the county of Timisoara as party secretary of the region in charge of propaganda. But he also became a candidate (nonvoting) member of the Political Executive Committee, as the Politburo was then called.

In 1979, Iliescu was recalled to Bucharest as head of the National Water Council. He also became a member of the Council of State, headed by Nicolae Ceausescu himself. By 1984, however, Ceausescu once again considered him unreliable. He was then deprived of all his posts and appointed director of the state technical publishing house in Bucharest, a politically meaningless appointment.

Iliescu acquired a reputation as a moderate even in the Ceausescu circles, and his personable ways endeared him to many in the administration. On December 22, 1989, Iliescu resurfaced and was immediately included in the leadership of the National Salvation Front. The front won the elections in 1990, and Iliescu became head of the government. When the opposition became vocal, because the old *nomenklatura* remained basically in power after the revolution, Iliescu invited the miners of the Jiu Valley "to clear the square before parliament," occupied by antigovernment demonstrators. His government provided buses and trains for the miners who had done a thorough job of intimidating the opposition, beating them up and wrecking their party offices. Through such undemocratic means, Iliescu and his

National Salvation Front won the 1992 elections and Iliescu became the president of the republic. He is still occupying that position.

Bibliography
Almond, Mark, *The Rise and Fall of Nicolae and Elena Ceausescu* (London, 1992); Galloway, George, *Downfall: The Ceausescus and the Romanian Revolution* (London, 1991); Gilberg, Trond, *Nationalism and Communism in Romania: The Rise and Fall of Ceausescu's Personal Dictatorship* (Boulder, CO, 1989); Tismaneanu, Vladimir, *Personal Power and Elite Change in Romania* (Philadelphia, PA, 1989).

Jiu Valley Strike (1977). The most spectacular action taken against the excesses of the Ceausescu regime occurred in the Jiu Valley. In August 1977, 30,000 miners simply walked out of the mines. They demanded higher wages and other improvements in their living conditions. They refused to talk to any emissaries of the government and demanded to see the leader, Nicolae Ceausescu (*see* Ceausescu, Nicolae and Elena) himself.

The Conducator was unwilling to oblige them at first. He sent members of the Politburo, Ilie Verdet and Constantin Babalu, the minister of mining, to negotiate with the miners. But the miners at Lupeni pushed Verdet and Babalu into the porter's shack at the mine's entrance, and they had to telephone Bucharest transmitting the miners' demands. For three days, the miners held the officials hostage. They explained to the frightened apparatchiki what would happen to them if the government used force. They also told them that the miners would blow up the mines if Ceausescu tried to force them back to work without fulfilling their demands.

After a standoff of three days, Ceausescu finally gave in and went to talk to the strikers. When he attempted to speak to the miners and their assembled families in the dilapidated soccer field at Lupeni, he was received with catcalls. He spoke, nevertheless, in a way to placate the crowd and recalled his own background as a worker. He announced that the pay cuts that were scheduled—actually, the miners were supposed to work at the same pay for higher work norms—and the rules that would have reduced the pensions of retired miners were all rescinded. He also promised to meet the miners' other demands.

Ceausescu had no intention of fulfilling his promises. After his return to Bucharest, he instructed the managers to keep the new production norms as high as they were set since they were necessary to meet the needs. He also ordered Ilie Verdet to find some way around his other promises.

The miners had actually struck for better living conditions; and they had made no political demands. Nor were they interested in the establishment of a free trade union as were their Polish counterparts were later. Their leader, Costica Dobre, unlike Lech Walesa, lacked the political savvy and natural charisma of a people's tribune. He was talked into leaving the mine by Ceausescu himself, and he let himself be persuaded to follow his own personal interests by attending the Academy Stefan Gheorghe, the party's higher ideological school in Bucharest. There he studied for a while and was eventually made into a low-level party official.

But this was not the end of the story. The secret police saturated the Jiu Valley with a wave of terror. Some strikers were forcibly moved to mines in other parts of the country, and they were replaced by other miners from different regions. Several leaders of the workers, not as obedient and meek as Dobre, were killed in "accidents." The strikers were, thus, thoroughly cowed. The tragedy of this was that the outside world hardly learned about the affair and, therefore, had no chance to voice its protests.

Bibliography
Almond, Mark, *The Rise and Fall of Nicolae and Elena Ceausescu* (London, 1992); Ratesh, Nestor, *Romania: The Entangled Revolution* (Washington, DC, 1989).

Letter of the Six (1989). During the spring of 1989, Romania's international isolation was becoming apparent. In March, even the Soviet Union supported a United Nations resolution ordering a commission to investigate human rights abuses in Romania. This was the moment taken by six former leaders of the Romanian Communist party to publish an open letter calling for the replacement of Nicolae Ceausescu (*see* Ceausescu, Nicolae and Elena) as head of the party and government.

All six of them were older comrades who had lost the power struggle won by the younger Ceausescu. They proclaimed that the leader discredited socialism with his policies. They attacked "systematization" (*see* Systematization) as a means of destroying Romanian historical traditions. They stated that the building of the huge and hideous Palace of the People in the center of Bucharest was a crime and that the law forbidding Romanians to meet and converse with foreigners was an abomination. They criticized Ceausescu for "discrediting" the security services by using their personnel against workers who demanded their rights, and against old party members like themselves. They demanded that Ceausescu stop exporting food, abandon "systematization," renew Romania's traditional relations with the European nations and abide by the Helsinki agreements that he signed.

The oldest signer of the letter was Constantin Pirvulescu, ninety-four years old at the time, a founding member of the Romanian Communist party. Another was Alexandru Barladeanu, also a veteran communist. Gheorghe Apostol (*see* Apostol, Gheorghe), another signer of the letter, was a former contestant for power with Ceausescu. Corneliu Manescu, who joined the dissenters, was an early favorite of Ceausescu and, until 1974, he was foreign minister of Romania. Grigore Ratianu, another signer, shared a fate similar to that of Manescu.

The actual writer of the letter was Silviu Brucan (*see* Brucan, Silviu), one of the most persistent Marxist critics of Ceausescu. In the late 1960s, he, too, was ousted from power and was relegated to the academic world. Some observers of the Romanian scene asserted that Brucan was trying to obtain Soviet help for an internal putsch. According to this version, he approached the KGB for support, but the uncertainty that surrounded Mikhail Gorbachev's accession to power made the Soviet leader cautious even after the publication of the "Letter of the Six" and Brucan was declined. The fact that Brucan was allowed to travel abroad, is proof that he had protection on the highest levels.

Ceausescu's sycophants assured the leader that the letter was proof positive of the demise of the opposition. But the signatories were the most senior communists in Romania, and Barladeanu and Brucan were well known for their Soviet connections. But none of them could conceivably be a competitor to replace Ceausescu at the helm. They were a nuisance, especially because they sent copies of the letter to Western embassies.

Ceausescu's main concern was to deter other possible opponents to imitate the old-timers. Consequently, the signatories were accused of spying for various Western intelligence services. The secret police pulled them all in and tried to pressure them to admit their guilt. Together with their elderly wives, they were removed from their comfortable homes in Bucharest and were transferred to the city's slums into dingy apartments without running water and electricity. They were told that, if they did not retract the letter, they would be facing the possibility of being tried for treason. Only Gheorghe Apostol caved in to the pressure. He signed a confession implicating Brucan as the ringleader in a plot hatched by the CIA. But it seems that someone intervened, possibly Gorbachev, because there was no trial. Thereafter, each week, a "TASS correspondent," Nikolai Morozov, visited the Brucans to make sure of their well-being. During the 16th party congress in November 1989, Brucan quietly disappeared from Bucharest and turned up in Moscow. He and the other signers of the "Letter of the Six" survived the ouster and execution of the Ceausescu couple.

Bibliography
Almond, Mark, *The Rise and Fall of Nicolae and Elena Ceausescu* (London, 1992); Behr, Edward, *Kiss the Hand You Cannot Bite* (New York, 1991).

Luca, Vasile (1898–?). Luca was an ethnic Hungarian from Transylvania, whose original given name was Vazul. He joined the Romanian Communist party in the 1930s, was arrested in Bessarabia by the Romanian police, tried, and sentenced to a long prison term. In 1940, when the Soviet Union regained Bessarabia, following the Nazi-Soviet pact, Luca was liberated by Russian soldiers from his jail cell. He spent the war years in the Soviet Union and acquired Soviet citizenship. In 1944, he returned to Romania with the Red Army, together with Ana Pauker (*see* Pauker, Ana) and Emil Bodnaras (*see* Bodnaras, Emil) as Joseph Stalin's Romanian emissaries. Immediately after his return, Luca became a member of the Politburo of the Romanian Communist party and assumed control over the party's affairs. In 1947, in the first purely communist government, he was minister of finance. But his authority went way beyond his ministry. In 1952, however, Gheorghe Gheorghiu-Dej (*see* Gheorghiu-Dej, Gheorghe) won the internal struggle for power, and Luca, together with Pauker and Bodnaras, was expelled from the leadership.

Bibliography
Ionescu, Ghita, *Communism in Romania, 1944–1962* (New York, 1964).

Manescu, Manea (1924–). Manescu, the brother-in-law of Nicolae Ceausescu (*see* Ceausescu, Nicolae and Elena), was, in the 1980s, a deputy prime minister of Romania. He was a member of the "committee of three" on December 16, 1989, entrusted by Ceausescu to deal with the uprising in the city of Timisoara (*see* Timisoara Revolt), during the visit of the leader to Teheran, Iran. The other members of the committee were Elena Ceausescu and Emil Bobu (*see* Bobu, Emil). Most likely, it was Elena Ceausescu who gave the order to the police to fire on the demonstrators, but Manescu certainly shared in that decision.

Together with Bobu, Manescu fled with the Ceausescus in a helicopter from the roof of the Communist Party's Central Committee building on December 22, 1989, escaping from the crowd surging into the building on the first day of the revolution. Manescu took the ride to Snagov, where he and Bobu were left behind. It was reported by the helicopter pilot that Manescu knelt and kissed the hand of Ceausescu before parting from him. This was the perfect expression of the nature of the relationship that Ceausescu's collaborators had with their leader. Manescu returned to Bucharest where he was arrested and tried for his crimes in late January 1990. He is currently serving a life sentence in prison.

Bibliography
Almond, Mark, *The Rise and Fall of Nicolae and Elena Ceausescu* (London, 1992); Behr, Edward, *Kiss the Hand You Cannot Bite* (New York, 1991); Galloway, George, *Downfall: The Ceausescus and the Romanian Revolution* (London, 1991).

Maurer, Ion Gheorghe (1910–). Maurer who was born to a Transylvanian Saxon family, received a university education. Since the mid-1930s, he had been a close personal friend of Gheorghe Gheorghiu-Dej (*see* Gheorghiu-Dej, Gheorghe) and a member of the Romanian Communist party. In 1944, he organized the release of Gheorghiu-Dej from prison, earning further credits with the party leader. During the early 1950s, Maurer filled various cabinet posts. However, during the ascendancy of the Muscovites, Maurer was frequently criticized. In 1956, he was once again included in the highest party leadership, and he became active in the Romanian diplomatic service. In 1957, Maurer was appointed minister of foreign affairs. Upon the death of Petru Groza (*see* Groza, Petru) a year later, Maurer became president of the republic. He was also included in the Central Committee of the Communist party. In June 1960, he became a voting member of the Politburo. A year later he was prime minister, replacing the purged Chivu Stoica. His post of president was assumed by Gheorghiu-Dej.

In the 1960s, Maurer accompanied Gheorghiu-Dej to India and Indonesia on state visits. In 1964, he led a Romanian delegation to Beijing. The aim of the delegation was to attempt to mediate in the dispute between China and the Soviet Union. As such, the mission was a failure.

Back in Bucharest, a meeting of the Central Committee of the party listened to the report of the delegation. The outcome of the meeting was a declaration, later referred to as the "Romanian Declaration of Independence" (*see* "Declaration of Independence"), a lengthy document of 16,000 words. It reaffirmed the faith of the party leaders in the communist movement, and it condemned Western capitalism. It declared Romania's support for the so-called national liberation movements, and its adherence to the concept of peaceful coexistence. (The contradiction between these two aims escaped the Romanian communists.) The most important part of the declaration discussed the nature of relations among Communist parties. It also described Romania's problems with COMECON.

Maurer had an important role to play when, upon the death of Gheorghiu-Dej, a successor was selected. He agreed with Bodnaras (*see* Bodnaras, Emil), that Nicolae Ceausescu (*see* Ceausescu, Nicolae and Elena) should be the chosen one, at least until the next meeting of the Central Committee. It is possible that he believed that the older members of the party leadership would be able to manipulate the young Ceausescu. During Ceausescu's years, Maurer had been an influential advisor. During the later 1960s, he supported Ceausescu's stand against the Warsaw Pact invasion of Czechoslovakia, and in the 1970s, he advised Ceausescu on foreign relations. Eventually, however, he fell out of favor. Even then, he was appointed honorary chairman of the International Law and International Relations Association and survived the overthrow of the Ceausescu regime.

Bibliography

Behr, Edward, *Kiss the Hand You Cannot Bite* (New York, 1991); Floyd, Davis, *Romania; Russia's Dissident Ally* (New York, 1965).

Milea, Vasile (?–1989). As the chief military officer of the Ceausescu (*see* Ceausescu, Nicolae and Elena) regime in the late 1980s, he was ordered by Elena Ceausescu (left behind by her husband to manage affairs during his state visit to Iran on December 17, 1989) to order the army to fire on demonstrators in Timisoara (*see* Timisoara Revolt). The minister submitted to the raving tyrant but refused to issue the order. The secret police, not under his direction, did the firing. They killed 40 people and wounded many others.

For disobeying the order, Ceausescu reprimanded the minister in the vilest language. By the morning of December 22, Milea was dead. The circumstances of his death remain unclear to this day. It was announced that he committed suicide; some people claim, however, that he was murdered on orders of Ceausescu. His death, however, did not benefit the dictator. It simply convinced the senior commanders of the armed forces, including the chief of the secret police, General Iulian Vlad, that the Ceausescus had lost touch with reality and that they would have to be disposed of, which is exactly what happened.

Bibliography
Behr, Edward, *Kiss the Hand You Cannot Bite*. (New York, 1991). Almond, Mark, *The Rise and Fall of Nicolae and Elena Ceausescu* (London, 1992).

Multilateral Development in Romania. With the ascendance of Nicolae Ceausescu (*see* Ceausescu, Nicolae and Elena) to the leadership of the Romanian Communist party in 1965, the party's goals were not changed. However, the control of society was intensified through the extensive use of the secret police. At the same time, Ceausescu announced the "multilateral development" of Romanian society. This concept originally meant that every section and structure of society, including the economy, cultural life, and social institutions would be developed at the same speed. It turned out, however, that the investment policies did not change; this meant that the agricultural sector did not develop at the same speed as industry.

At the same time, the party increased its propaganda efforts to convince Romanians that they were better off under the Ceausescu regime than at any other time in Romanian history. If one sector was developed faster than any other, it was the institution entrusted with ideology and propaganda. New seminars were established in factories, offices, and collective farms, as well as in schools, with the intention of indoctrinating the entire population in Marxism-Leninism. Censorship was strengthened in cultural life. Periodic purges in cultural institutions served the purpose of tightening discipline. Even the Bucharest opera company was subjected to close supervision by the secret police. Only creative people willing and able to conform to the principles of "socialist realism" could publish or have their works exhibited.

Life on every level became saturated with politics. "Voluntary" weekend work was encouraged, and those who refused became marked. Material incentives were scarce, and the intensified propaganda campaign was intended to offset their absence. Special titles, medals, and certificates were given to workers who exceeded the work norms in lieu of higher wages. The propaganda organs also made great efforts to root out old values, such as religious convictions and individualism. Love of private property was especially singled out for scorn. The establishment of circles of friends was discouraged. Multilateral development, thus, ended as a propaganda effort by the party leaders that justified itself in their eyes by its very existence.

Bibliography
Gilberg, Trond, "The Multiple Legacies of History: Romania in 1990," in Joseph Held, ed., *The Columbia History of Eastern Europe in the Twentieth Century* (New York, 1992); Graham, Lawrence S., *Romania: A Developing Socialist State* (Boulder, 1982).

National Democratic Front in Romania. Created in October 1944, the purpose of this communist front organization was to help the Communist party gain a monopoly of political power. The front included the Communist and Social Democratic parties, the Plowmen's Front, the Union of Patriots, and the Trade Union Alliance.

In January 1945, the front began its campaign for total control of Romania. The first task was to enact a radical land reform. This was intended to allay the fear of the peasantry of communist plans for collectivization. At the same time, the front began a noisy campaign for the elimination of "reactionaries" from public life, that is, the opponents of communism. The front also appealed to latent Romanian nationalism by insinuating that, as the result of its activities, Stalin promised the return of the entire area of Transylvania, part of which was awarded to Hungary in 1940, to the Romanian state.

The propaganda of the front was reinforced by violent demonstrations held in major cities. Strikes in privately-owned firms, seizure of land by indigent peasants (all secretly and, sometimes, openly advocated by the front), and the arrest of opponents by the newly organized secret police added to the front's tactics. Premier Nicolae Radescu was finally provoked into an intemperate outburst on Romanian national radio, calling the communists "venal foreign beasts," referring to the Jewish and Hungarian backgrounds of some of the leading party officials. Three days after this statement, Soviet army units occupied the headquarters of the Romanian armed forces, and the Soviet representative, who happened to be Andrei Y. Wyshinski of Stalinist show-trials fame, forced King Michael to dismiss Radescu. The king held out for a while but, on March 5, he had to give in. He appointed Petru Groza (*see* Groza, Petru) to replace Radescu, and Groza eventually paved the way for the communist takeover of Romania.

Bibliography
Fischer-Galati, Stephen, *Twentieth Century Romania* 2nd ed. (New York, 1991); Gilberg, Trond, "The Multiple Legacies of History: Romania in 1990," in Joseph Held, ed. *The Columbia History of Eastern Europe in the Twentieth Century* (New York, 1992), pp. 277-305.

National Minorities in Romania. A little over 10 percent of the population of Romania consists of ethnic minorities. At least, this is the percentage given by Romanian statistics. However, the number of ethnic Hungarians alone is probably more like 15 percent of the total population. According to some information, the number of ethnic Hungarians in Romania is about 2.5 million. The German minority, located mostly in Transylvania, number about 350,000 people. Other groups, including Gypsies, Jews, Russians, Bulgarians, Turks, Tatars, and others can also be found in the country. The largest minority of the latter are the Gypsies, but their number has never been fully ascertained.

During the interwar years, there were schools where children were taught in their mother tongue. There were ethnic theaters and even a Hungarian language university at Cluj. The Romanian constitution, accepted in 1952, created a Hungarian Autonomous Region in Transylvania.

However, after the impact of the Hungarian Revolution of 1956 reached Romania, the communist authorities resorted to coercion, more and more curtailing the rights of ethnic Hungarians and Germans. In 1959, the Hungarian Bolyai University of Cluj was merged with the Romanian Babes University in the same city. Hungarian language instructions were practically abolished. The Hungarian Autonomous Region was reduced in size, and thousands of ethnic Hungarians were now living outside its boundaries, subject to Romanization pressures. Hungarian archives and libraries, some of them centuries old, were simply destroyed. Eventually, Hungarian language classes in schools were merged with those of Romanian instruction, and the Hungarian curriculum was simply eliminated. Similar tactics were used against the German minority. In addition, the communists encouraged the ethnic Germans to leave Romania. West Germany actually paid for every emigrant who wanted to leave Romania, and this provided a handsome profit for the Ceausescu regime.

During the 1970s and 1980s, the situation concerning ethnic and human rights continued to deteriorate. The Ceausescu regime proclaimed Romania to be a unitary national state, refusing even to acknowledge the existence of national minorities. Since the overthrow of the communist regime, the situation has changed somewhat, and a Hungarian political party has emerged, but pressure for the assimilation of ethnic minorities has not stopped.

Bibliography

Fischer-Galati, Stephen, *Twentieth Century Romania*, 2nd ed. (New York, 1992); King, Robert R., *Minorities Under Communism* (Cambridge, England, 1973).

Oil Production in Romania. Romania has had tremendous oil reserves. The German, and Soviet, interest in the Ploiesti oil fields has been the cause of much misery for the Romanians. However, by the time the Romanian Communist party had gained power, the reserves had gone into a decline. The emergence of OPEC and the oil embargo against the West in 1973 changed the situation. By then, Romania was an oil-importing country. But the Ceausescu government did not give up its effort to remain in the forefront of oil production. It concentrated on building a first-class oil refinery system, with capacities far beyond those needed by Romania. The country began to import cheap oil, refine it, and sell the product for good prices to Western and other customers. But crude oil was available only for hard currency. Even the Soviet Union began to insist on charging dollars for oil delivered to Romania. Romania simply did not have the hard currency for this purpose. The further jump in oil prices in 1978 was not followed by a corresponding increase in prices for refined oil on the world markets. This created imbalances in Romania's economy.

The Iranian revolution created more problems for the Romanians. Before the revolution, Ceausescu signed a very favorable agreement with the Shah. But the Ayatollahs repudiated all previous agreements whether they were signed with Western or Eastern governments. The Iraq-Iran war further complicated the situation. The Romanian economy was then squeezed between high crude oil prices, inadequate levels of domestic crude oil production, and idle refining capacities.

At first, the regime tried to solve the problem by severely restricting domestic energy consumption. Private automobile travel was reduced to every second day regulated by the odd and even numbers of license plates. Automobile travel on Sundays was altogether banned. The lighting of homes was restricted to two hours a day, and the use of light bulbs of higher than forty Volts was prohibited. Fuel for home heating was also severely restricted. Cold apartments and even colder workplaces in winter were becoming the norm. Workers in factories and offices labored with their over-coats and gloves on, which certainly did not increase their productivity. The domestic energy crisis became a permanent feature of Romanian life, and it led to a serious decline in the standard of living. The Western loans obtained by the government were not used to change the nature of the crisis. They were swallowed up by projects inspired by Ceausescu's gigan-tomania. The economic decline that began with the oil crisis undermined whatever prestige the regime had at home and abroad and contributed to its overthrow in 1989.

Bibliography

Jordan, Constantine, *The Romanian Oil Industry* (New York, 1955); Shafir, Michael, *Romania: Politics, Economics and Society* (Boulder, CO, 1985); Turnock, David, *The Economic Geography of Romania* (London, 1974).

Pacepa, Ion, Mihai (1930–). Pacepa was a trusted adviser of the Ceausescus (*see* Ceausescu, Nicolae and Elena) in the 1970s, completely familiar with the inner workings of the Ceausescu clan and the highest echelons of the Romanian Communist party. He was also familiar with the operations of the Romanian secret service, especially its spying in Western countries. He directed operations of influence in the United States, Great Britain, and West Germany. Pacepa was present in the secret discussions that Ceausescu held with Yassir Arafat, chairman of the Palestinian Liberation Organization, whose purpose was to find means to have the PLO accepted as a legitimate representative of the Palestinian people. Pacepa knew about the operations directed against Western firms for the illegal acquisition of technology, both civilian and military. He also knew about Ceausescu's double dealings with the West and the Soviet Union.

By 1978, Pacepa had enough. His carefully planned defection to the United States had dramatic results. Hundreds of East European secret agents operating in the West were withdrawn. The Romanian agency for foreign influence was disbanded. When Pacepa's memoires, entitled *Red Horizons*, were published in 1987, the book became an instant sensation. It provided an insight for the Western public into the manipulations used by the Ceausescus for Western acceptance. Pacepa, now a U.S. citizen, resides in the United States under an assumed identity.

Bibliography

Pacepa, Ion Mihai, *Red Horizons* (New York, 1987).

Patrascanu, Lucretiu (?–1954). The son of a wealthy Moldavian landowner, Patrascanu attended university studies and became a lawyer. His wife was a well-known interior decorator. In the late 1930s, he joined the underground Communist party. He was skilled in avoiding arrest and, while the entire leadership of the Communist party was in jail, Patrascanu directed the party's affairs from outside.

After August 23, 1944, when Romania changed sides in the war, Patrascanu was the first communist to become a member of the Sanatescu government. He led the Romanian delegation at the armistice negotiations held in Moscow. However, it soon became apparent that both the Muscovites, as well as the Gheorghiu-Dej-led "local" communists, considered Patrascanu a rival. His impeccable credentials made him a difficult target indeed; nevertheless, he was excluded from the post-1944 Politburo.

When the Tito-Stalin conflict came out into the open, Patrascanu became an obvious candidate for the role of a nationalist, a "Tito-deviationist" in Romania. He was singled out for criticism by the Muscovites in 1948 and was expelled from the Central Committee of the Communist party. It is most likely that he was imprisoned, although he was not put to a show trial as yet. However, Gheorghiu-Dej's (*see* Gheorghiu-Dej, Gheorghe) victory over the Muscovites in 1952, and Joseph Stalin's death a year later did not result in Patrascanu's release and rehabilitation. Instead, he was tried in April 1954, including former Stalinists Stefan Foris and Remus Koffler. Patrascanu was sentenced to death and executed. It seems that there were some old scores left unsettled between himself and Gheorghiu-Dej, and Patrascanu, although no longer representing a challenge, could not be trusted to remain passive. In 1968, however, Patrascanu's case was reopened at the orders of Nicolae Ceausescu (*see* Ceausescu, Nicolae and Elena). The Central Committee investigated the charges against him and found no evidence to support them. It was proven that Patrascanu had been interrogated on and off for two years and that he had been severely mistreated. It was found out that Gheorghiu-Dej was behind the events and that Alexandru Draghici (*see* Draghici, Alexandru), the secret police chief, personally assembled the false charges against Patrascanu. It was also shown that not only Draghici and Gheorghiu-Dej, but also the entire Politburo at the time, were aware of the falseness of the charges and of the tortures that Patrascanu was subjected to. Similar findings were announced in the cases of Foris and Koffler. Patrascanu was, therefore, posthumously rehabilitated, something that was not unusual among East European communists.

Bibliography

Behr, Edward, *Kiss the Hand You Cannot Bite* (New York, 1991); Floyd, David, *Romania: Russia's Dissident Ally* (New York, 1965); Ionescu, Ghita, *Communism in Romania, 1944–1962* (New York, 1964).

Pauker, Ana (1902–1960). Pauker was born to a kosher butcher in the city of Iasi, but later she altered this fact by asserting that her father was a rabbi. In her youth, Pauker, a strictly orthodox young woman, was a teacher in an orthodox Jewish school. She visited Paris where she was converted to atheism and Marxism-Leninism. After her return to Romania, she became active in the underground Romanian Communist party. In 1935, she was arrested and sentenced to ten years in prison. In 1940, Pauker was exchanged by the Soviet Union for a captured Bessarabian nationalist army officer. Pauker spent the war years in the Soviet Union and returned to Romania in 1944 with the Soviet army.

On Joseph Stalin's insistence, she immediately became a member of the party's Politburo, responsible for the organization of the party. She was eminently successful in the recruitment of new party members, although much of her success was undoubtedly due to help she received from the Red Army. She was also instrumental in the organization of the Tudor Vladimirescu division that eventually fought alongside the Soviet army against the Germans, suffering horrendous casualties. The surviving members of this division were later to become the core of the communist police forces, and increased the membership of the Communist party.

From the very beginning, there was a conflict and rivalry between the Muscovites and the "local" communists. The Muscovites were, in fact, Joseph Stalin's representatives; they held Soviet citizenship, and they could count on the support of the Soviet dictator. In November 1947, Pauker was appointed minister of foreign affairs. She directed Romanian foreign policies in the interests of the Soviet Union. By then, the Soviet KGB representatives were present in every Romanian government and party organ, including the police and the military. They received their orders directly from Moscow and were, in fact, the true rulers of Romania.

The conflict between Pauker and the Muscovites, on the one hand, and the "local" communists headed by Gheorghe Gheorghiu-Dej (*see* Gheorghiu-Dej, Gheorghe) on the other, simmered under the surface. The party's Politburo dominated by Pauker, Vasile Luca (*see* Luca, Vasile) and Teohari Georgescu, was under the complete control of Pauker. The Muscovites were also members of the secretariat of the Central Committee, and their influence outweighed all of the others. They were, in general, arrogant and overbearing. Pauker, with the help of the KGB, also dominated the secret police, the most important means of communist power. She had the telephones of the leaders tapped and simply intimidated all of them.

Gheorghiu-Dej remained first secretary of the party throughout the Muscovites' reign, and was not inclined to dispute Pauker's dominance openly. He worked slowly and gradually; he succeeded in convincing Stalin that Soviet interests would be better served if he were given control. Thus, by 1952, he was ready to act. He removed Pauker and the other Muscovites from the party's leadership. Pauker was not subjected to a show trial and was permitted to live out her days in Bucharest. She died of cancer in 1960.

Bibliography
Floyd, David, *Rumania: Russia's Dissident Ally* (New York, 1965); Ionescu, Ghita, *Communism in Romania 1944–1962* (New York, 1964).

Post-Communist Romania. The overthrow of the regime of the Ceausescus (*see* Ceausescu, Nicolae and Elena) did not mean the ouster of the communist *nomenklatura* from the administration of the country. Although the most compromised leaders, the minions of the dictator, are gone, the rest of the administration remain in place. Characteristically, the former secret police now provides security and protection for the new government.

In May 1990, the National Salvation Front won the elections, but many of its promises are still awaiting practical application. The government, headed by Petru Roman, attempted to shepherd genuine economic reforms through parliament, but it was frustrated by conservatives in the front. Democratization was a very slow process, and it often appeared that the front was mostly intent on perpetuating itself in government. In September 1991, the Roman cabinet was forced to resign. It was replaced by one headed by Todor Stolojan on October 1. The new prime minister announced that the enactment of economic reforms was his first priority.

The year of 1990 had seen considerable unrest. The miners of the Jiu Valley, the same people who stood up to Ceausescu in 1977, descended on Bucharest three times during the year and a fourth time in September 1991. The first three times, they were "invited" by the Roman government as a means to suppress the opposition. With cudgels and truncheons, the miners beat demonstrating students, putting some of them into hospitals, and they ransacked the offices of oppositional parties. They were provided with buses and special trains for their forays at government expense. The fourth time the miners "visited" the capital, however, they got out of hand. They caused a great deal of damage in Bucharest as well as on their way to the city, providing plenty of proof of the dangers of a crowd getting out of control. After this "visit," the Roman government could not stay in office any longer.

Another problem hastened the demise of the Roman cabinet. There were strikes in various industries, causing slowdowns in production. This led to shortages once again and long lines in front of stores causing a lot of discontent. When Roman resigned, inflation was 220 percent in comparison to October 1990, and industrial production had declined by 30 percent. Although unemployment was low at 2 percent, it was expected to increase. The government seems determined to close down unproductive enterprises, and this will certainly contribute to more unemployment.

The opposition has been split into many factions making it powerless in face of a determined government. Realizing this, an umbrella organization for oppositional parties was created in December 1990; the National Convention for the Establishment of Democracy. Originally, the convention included the National Liberal, the National Peasant, and the Social Democratic parties. It also included the Democratic Association of Romanian-Hungarians, the Romanian Ecological party, and the Party of Civic Alliance.

There are extremist parties both on the right and on the left. On the right, one finds the Romanian National Unity party, a racist, anti-Hungarian movement, and the Great Romania movement, an outright fascist organization. Both of these parties would like to repeat the Romanian version of Serb "ethnic cleansing." The left consists of the Socialist Labor party, the self-proclaimed successor to the communists, and the unreformed Romanian Communist party which reappeared in July 1991. In November, a

Union of the Democratic Left was organized, and it attempts to exploit the unrest in society for some sort of restoration of the communist regime.

One of Stolojan's major tasks was the organization of new elections scheduled for February-March 1992. The new elections changed the political landscape. The National Salvation Front won only 33.6 percent of the local votes as opposed to 66.3 percent two years before. The Democratic Convention, on the other hand, received 24.3 percent, becoming the second strongest party in Romania. The results were followed by a split in the National Salvation Front. The two leading personalities of the leadership, Ion Iliescu (*see* Iliescu, Ion) and Petru Roman (*see* Roman, Petru), took their personal followers and established two versions of the original organization. Iliescu's group took the name, Democratic National Salvation Front, while Roman's retained the organization's original name. But the opposition could not take advantage of the split, since it could not maintain its unity.

The National Liberals withdrew from the convention, and their leader, Radu Campeanu, suddenly came out for the restoration of the kingship of King Michael. He declared his support for the possible candidacy of King Michael for the presidency of the republic as a preliminary step toward restoration. But Michael declined the offer. In the general elections held in September 1992, Campeanu's party received less than 3 percent of the votes and was, therefore, excluded from parliament.

In the general and presidential elections held on September 27, Iliescu was the strongest candidate for the presidency. He did not win in the first round and had to face a runoff against Emil Constantinescu, the candidate of the Democratic Convention. Iliescu won the runoff with 61.4 percent of the votes. The Democratic National Salvation Front once again became the strongest party in parliament, but it did not gain enough votes to form a government alone. The convention strengthened its positions, but the extremists also gained support.

The new government is headed by Nicolae Vacaroiu. His cabinet is made up by technocrats, members of the Democratic National Salvation Front, and some who had been in government offices during the Ceausescu era. The cabinet is, however, based on a minority of deputies and could be voted out of office.

The greatest problem facing the new government continues to be the declining economy. Industrial production continued to drop throughout the year (by 23.5 percent), and unemployment increased to 9 percent of the work force. On the other hand, about 6 million peasants had regained their collectivized lands, and the development of the private sector accelerated. The number of new private businesses was 362,000, a phenomenal growth, and joint Western-Romanian ventures also gained. Social tensions were low and ethnic conflicts decreased, until the election of a new mayor for Cluj, a character called Funar, whose racist policies are aimed at the suppression of the large Hungarian minority in the city.

Romania has had some foreign policy successes. It was accepted as an associate member of the European Community, the fourth East European state after Poland, Hungary, and Czechoslovakia to be accepted. Relations with the United States, however, hardly improved. A bilateral trade agreement was rejected by the U.S. House of Representatives, and most-favored nation status in trade was denied. Romania, being caught between the two conflicts in the former Yugoslavia and in Moldova, and beset by a resurgence of racist sentiments toward ethnic minorities domestically, is in a difficult situation. Relations with Turkey and Bulgaria were better than during Ceausescu's rule, but Romanian-Hungarian relations are stagnant.

Bibliography
Shafir, Michael, and Ionescu, Dan, "Political Change and Economic Malaise in Romania "*Radio Free Europe Research Report*,1.1 (January 1, 1993), pp. 108-112; Shafir, Michael, "The New Romanian Government," *Radio Free Europe Research Report*, 1.2 (January 12, 1992), pp. 35-38; ——, "Romania's Torturous Road to Reform," *Radio Free Europe Research Report*, 1.1 (January 3, 1992), pp. 96-104; Socor, Vladimir, "Romania: Political Parties Emerging," *Radio Free Europe Research Report*, 1.7 (February 16, 1990), pp. 28-35.

Postelnicu, Tudor (?–). A typical representative of the corrupt elite of the Ceausescu era (*see* Ceausescu, Nicolae and Elena), whose petty pilfering generated so much hatred for the regime among the population, Postelnicu climbed steadily in the ranks of the apparatchiki, to minister of state in the early 1980s, to the post of the minister of the interior, and finally to that of chief of the state security department. It was reported that, as minister of the interior, Postelnicu demanded that a "dead-letter box" be maintained in his office in the toilet, regularly supplied with Scotch whisky. It was well known that promotion in his ministry could be obtained through personal favors for the minister.

After the overthrow of the Ceausescu regime in 1989, Postelnicu, together with other members of the Politburo, were tried in January 1990. Although he was not responsible for the shooting at Timisoara (Elena Ceausescu and the "committee of three" had given the order to fire on the crowds), he did give the order for the secret cremation of the victims. It was revealed at the trial that, upon his arrest, eleven radio sets, sixty-six cartons of Western cigarettes (each was worth a week's salary for ordinary Romanians), 400 bars of soap (a commodity for which Romanians stood countless hours in lines before stores), twenty-two pounds of gold, and 440 pounds of meat were found in his house. (Most Romanians were given meat on rare occasions at exorbitant prices, and only a precious few had freezers outside the highest echelons of the communist hierarchy.) Postelnicu was found guilty of abuse of power and was sentenced to life in prison.

Bibliography
Almond, Mark, *The Rise and Fall of Nicolae and Elena Ceausescu* (London, 1992); Behr, Edward, *Kiss the Hand You Cannot Bite* (New York, 1991).

Post-Stalin Changes in Romania. On August 19, 1953, Gheorghiu-Dej (*see* Gheorghiu-Dej, Gheorghe), the Romanian communist leader, declared that the Romanian Communist party had made mistakes in the past and that the leadership would make sure that mistakes in the future were avoided. This declaration foreshadowed Nikita Khrushchev's coming denunciations of Joseph Stalin. In Romania, the admission did not result in the repudiation of the system of Stalinism. Although Gheorghiu-Dej also proclaimed that the party would henceforth be led by a collective, this did not mean the reduction of power of the secretary general of the party. The leader admitted, albeit carefully, that the party's emphasis on rapid industrialization, based on the development of heavy industry, was probably a mistake. In parallel with this, the neglect of the development of consumer industries was a blunder.

The following year, the camps of the Romanian Gulag, including the one that held prisoners building the Danube-Black sea canal, were dissolved. Georgy Malenkov and Nikita Khrushchev supported the Romanian reforms. They agreed that the joint Soviet-Romanian companies, one of the means by which the Soviet Union had exploited Romania, should be dissolved. On October 5, 1955, however, new decrees were issued that tightened party control over Romanian cultural life, and destalinization came to an abrupt halt. In December 1965, following the death of Gheorghe Gheorghiu-Dej, the Romanian party's Central Committee elected a new leadership. Heading the party was the new secretary general, Nicolae Ceausescu (*see* Ceausescu, Nicolae and Elena). His elevation to the highest party post signaled a new wave of repressions, creating a system of personal rule and a personality cult that went beyond anything Stalin had ever enjoyed in the Soviet Union.

Bibliography
Berciu, Dumitru, *Romania* (New York, 1967). Cretzianu, Alexandru, *Captive Romania: A Decade of Soviet Rule* (New York, 1956); Gilberg, Trond, *Modernization in Romania Since World War II* (New York, 1975).

"Rebuilding" Bucharest. Dictator Nicolae Ceausescu (*see* Ceausescu, Nicolae and Elena) was determined to leave behind for posterity some monument reminding future generations of the magnificence of his rule. This monument was to be the House of the People, sometimes also called the Palace of the People, now dominating the center of the capital city, Bucharest. This huge building is seven times the size of the Palace of Versailles, and Buckingham Palace could be fitted into the underground parking garage at its rear. Another huge complex built to the south of the House of the People, the House (or Palace) of Science, was to commemorate the achievements of Elena Ceausescu (nee Petrescu), the so-called world renowned scientist of Romania.

In the 1960s, Bucharest was a city of mixed architectural styles, carrying the memories of several historical periods. This was not suitable for the Ceausescus. The opportunity to remodel the city came in 1977, when a terrible earthquake destroyed parts of the city. Ceausescu, deeply impressed by the gigantomania of Stalinist architecture in the Soviet Union, and even more so by the Palace of the People built by Kim Il Sung, the North Korean dictator, ordered the monumental palace to be built. The palace required 30 percent of national resources. In addition, further sums had to be spent to provide new housing for people displaced from the center of Bucharest by the building. In the end, the monstrous projects remained empty; but, after all, they were built to exclude the people. This was typical of the dictator who seems to have lost all sense of reality. He also ordered the resumption of the construction of the Danube-Black sea canal (*see* Danube-Black Sea Canal). That project, finished in 1984, was empty of traffic. The power stations that were built along the new canal had no fuel to run them; the new apartment houses built in Bucharest had no electricity and running water.

The people of Bucharest suffered greatly for the dictator's excesses. The streets leading to the House of People and the House of Science were straightened, and old houses, many of historical significance, were destroyed. Historical churches were moved and, in the process, their structures were damaged. People in the old houses were usually given only a few hours to pack their belongings, while the bulldozers were already idling outside their homes. The old city center was practically emptied; in 1988 alone over 40,000 people were removed. But the imperial couple did not have the time to move into their new lodgings; the revolution ended their rule and, incidentally, their lives.

Bibliography

Almond, Mark, *The Rise and Fall of Nicolae and Elena Ceausescu* (London, 1992); Galloway, George, *Downfall: The Ceausescus and the Romanian Revolution* (London, 1991).

Religious Policies in Communist Romania. Romania's population belonged to a variety of religious denominations. As in the case of other East European nations, religion often defined nationality, and it was an important factor in preserving ethnicity and national cultures. Romanians, living under the control of two great empires for most of the last 500 years of their history, adhered to Orthodox Christianity as a defense of their nationality.

With the establishment of communist rule in 1945, and the return of northern Transylvania under Romanian administration, ethnic diversity was paralleled by religious diversity. Romanians were mostly Orthodox Christians, although there were also followers of Greek Catholicism among them. Hungarians were mainly Calvinists, but there were also Roman Catholics among them in Transylvania. The Germans adhered to Lutheran Protestantism. There were also Jews in Romania who survived the Holocaust.

The initial approach of the communists to religious issues was harsh. In 1948, a government decree simply abolished the Uniate (Unitarian) church, a denomination of Protestantism that originated in the sixteenth century. Harsh repression was used against Roman Catholics and Protestants alike. Small Protestant denominations, such as the Baptists, suffered greatly. The communists were determined to wipe out all ideological competitors. They pursued openly atheistic policies in schools and work places. Even some elements of the Orthodox church were persecuted. Priests and ministers of the Orthodox church were jailed or killed outright. Many religious people were sent to concentration camps; many of them died building the Danube-Black sea canal (*see* Danube-Black Sea Canal).

After the death of Joseph Stalin, some relaxation in religious policies was introduced. The regime increasingly resorted to using Orthodox church leaders to initiate contacts with religious institutions abroad. When Gheorghe Gheorghiu-Dej died in 1965 (*see* Gheorghiu-Dej, Gheorghe), his successor, Nicolae Ceausescu (*see* Ceausescu, Nicolae and Elena) took three years to establish his unquestioned control over Romania. During this time, and the following years of the Ceausescu regime, there was no uniform policy toward religion and religious institutions. The state approached the churches on a case-by-case basis, suiting its decisions to the personal whims of the leader. Between 1965 and 1968, Ceausescu frequently consulted with the Orthodox hierarchy. This was especially true in 1968 when, after the Warsaw Pact invasion of Czechoslovakia, there was fear of possible Soviet intervention in Romania, and the leadership wanted to use Romanian nationalism to resist any possible invasion.

By 1969, however, relative tolerance of the Orthodox church had come to an end. (The other denominations never really enjoyed a respite from persecution.) The saturation of every sphere of society with Marxist-Leninist ideology brought a more systematic campaign against organized religion. Atheistic propaganda increased in volume and intensity, especially in the educational system. The media conducted relentless "exposures" of religious "mysticism" and "superstitions." Yet the campaign was less successful than the ideological saturation of society.

In the 1980s, the anti-religious campaign slowed down once again. By then, Ceausescu realized that his brand of "socialism in one family," buttressed by old-fashioned Romanian chauvinistic nationalism, could not endure without coopting the Orthodox Christian church and its hierarchy. He permitted intermittent contacts between the Orthodox leaders and churchmen abroad. He even welcomed the American Baptist preacher, Billy Graham, to come to Romania, where he was feted and permitted to preach to the local congregations. He went so far as to permit the renewal of contacts between the Vatican and Roman Catholic bishops in Transylvania. Some old church buildings were restored at state expense, and bishoprics were upgraded.

This trend did not last long. By the second half of the 1980s, church buildings in the countryside were being razed in line with Ceausescu's policy of "systematization," a euphemism for strengthening communist control over the people of the countryside (*see* "Systematization"). Historical church edifices in the capital city were demolished during the building of the House of the People and the House of Science in the center of Bucharest. Tighter controls were placed on all religious activities, signaling the renewed effort to weaken them in their relations to the state. The Orthodox church leaders became subservient to the government and the Communist party. Often they acted in an overzealous way in fulfilling state demands. The Roman Catholic and Protestant churches were under especially heavy pressure, because of their identification with ethnic minorities. Ceausescu was determined to force them into becoming Romanians.

In November 1989, the courageous stand of one Protestant clergyman, Laszlo Tokes (*see* Tokes, Laszlo) of Timisoara, started the avalanche that was to bury the communist regime in Romania. Tokes openly defied the regime, calling on religious people everywhere to raise their voices against persecution in Romania. His anguished cry against injustice aroused not only Hungarians but also the Romanian people against Ceausescu. After the successful revolution, restrictions on religious activities were removed, and a new relationship is being built between the government and religious institutions.

Bibliography

Gilberg, Trond, "Religion and Nationalism in Romania," in Pedro Ramet, ed. *Religion and Nationalism in Soviet and East European Politics* (Durham, NC, 1989).

Roman, Petru (1930–). Roman's father was a communist official, and he received a university education. After graduation, he became a party apparatchik. After the revolution of 1989, Roman was elected Prime Minister of Romania. However, he and President Ion Iliescu did not agree on the necessity of the rapid transformation of Romania's economy. They also disagreed on the pace political reforms should follow. Roman was involved in the government's effort to suppress the opposition, and he, together with President Iliescu, provided the troop of miners of the Jiu Valley, who rampaged through the capital city, Bucharest, four times during 1990, destroying printing shops and newspapers of the opposition parties. They also beat up antigovernment demonstrators, and some leaders of the opposition parties.

When the miners returned to Bucharest for the fourth time in September 1990, they had done great harm not only in the capital city, but also in the countryside while they were under way. As a consequence, President Iliescu dismissed Petru Roman's government, accusing the Prime Minister of complicity in the events. Roman then split the governing coalition, the National Salvation Front, and took some of its parliamentary deputies with him, forming a new party. However, they were not able to prevent the reelection of Ion Iliescu as President of Romania.

Bibliography

Shafir, Michael, and Ionescu, Don, "Political Change and Economic Malaise in Romania," *Radio Free Europe Research Report,* 1.1 (January 3, 1992), pp. 108-112; Shafir, Michael, "The New Romanian Government," *Radio Free Europe Research Report,* 1.2 (January 12, 1992), pp. 35-38.

Romanian-Soviet Relations in the Post-Stalin Era. While Soviet dictates forced all East European countries to embark on a rapid, forced industrialization based on the development of heavy industry in the 1960s, Soviet policies dictated a change of directions in economic policies. Joseph Stalin prevented multilateral economic relations among the Soviet Bloc countries. He insisted on the conclusion of bilateral agreements between each of these states and the Soviet Union. In 1947, when COMECON was established, it only permitted bilateral agreements between individual countries, but no general economic treaties were concluded to parallel the Common Market. The reason for this was that Stalin was suspicious of any common initiative on the part of his satellites, fearing that their joint efforts might turn them against Soviet interests. As a consequence, COMECON never developed into a viable economic organization.

In June 1962, Nikita Khrushchev decided that COMECON should become a means of economic integration in the Soviet Bloc. The new Soviet plan envisaged the division of labor by the satellites, each state concentrating on a form of economic activity best suited to its resources and manpower.

First the Albanians, then the Romanians refused to accept their place in the new system. The Romanians believed that their assigned role (to become a major agricultural producer country with the addition of developing their oil refining capacities) would relegate Romania to perpetual backwardness. The Romanian leaders took advantage of the emerging Sino-Soviet dispute to carve a special role for their country among the Soviet Bloc nations. They skillfully maneuvered between the two communist giants. Traditional Romanian nationalism came to their aid. Since Soviet troops had been withdrawn from Romania in 1958 as a reward for Romania's part in the suppression of the Hungarian Revolution, the communist leaders of the country had more room to maneuver than other Soviet satellites. The Chinese were delighted by the opportunity to weaken Soviet influence in Eastern Europe, and they were quite willing to help the Romanian drive for independence. The Western powers saw an opportunity to do the same and were also willing to help.

After the overthrow of Khrushchev, the Soviet leadership accepted Romania's semi-independent economic orientation. They concluded an agreement to provide Romania with more resources in furthering its industrialization drive. Relations during the Ceausescu era were cordial, but not subservient. Although the regime liked to emphasize that it was acting independently of the Soviet Union, and indeed it made some unilateral moves such as the establishment of diplomatic relations with Israel, it was also careful not to injure Soviet interests.

Above all, the Ceausescu regime carefully maintained the monopoly of power for the Communist party. With the accession of Mikhail Gorbachev to power, relations began to deteriorate more seriously. The Soviet leader visited Bucharest and had to listen to a lecture by Ceausescu about "real" socialism. When the Soviet Union remained inactive during the collapse of its satellite empire in Eastern Europe, the Romanian leader urged joint action against the "capitalists." He even proposed a Warsaw Pact intervention in Poland when the first Solidarity government was formed in that country.

By 1989, the Romanian regime was becoming an anachronism in Europe, and its overthrow opened the way for a new relationship with the successor states of the former Soviet Union.

Bibliography

Basic Principles of Romania's Foreign Policy: Joint Meeting of the Central Committee of the Romanian Communist Party, the State Council, and the Romanian Government (Bucharest, 1968); Floyd, David, *Romania: Russia's Dissident Ally* (New York, 1965). Shafir, Michael, *Romania: Politics, Economics and Society* (Boulder, CO, 1985).

Royal Coup D'Etat (1944). Until the Soviet army approached Romania's borders in 1944, the Romanian government, headed by General Ion Antonescu, was quite subservient to Nazi Germany. Romania shipped a great deal of foodstuffs and oil to the German war machine, and it sent an army to fight against the Soviet Union. It also cooperated in the extermination of hundreds of thousands of Romanian Jews. In the summer of 1944, the Soviet army's drive against the Germans grew in intensity. On August 4, 1944, Adolf Hitler summoned Antonescu to Berlin and attempted to extract a promise from him to the effect that Romania would stand by Germany under any circumstances. Antonescu gave an ambiguous response because he had already contacted the Allies for a possible separate peace, but the Romanians continued to support the German war effort.

King Michael prepared carefully to end Romania's participation in the war on Germany's side. The most powerful politician next to Antonescu, the National Peasant party's leader, Iuliu Maniu, supported the king. The young king wanted to forestall the exposure of Romania to an assault by the Red Army and hoped to save the old regime, or as much of it as possible. Thus, he summoned trustworthy politicians and army officers to the palace on August 23, 1944, and invited General Antonescu to be present.

When Antonescu arrived, he was arrested and was handed over to the communist leaders. The general was then spirited out of Bucharest and delivered to the Soviet army. In 1945, he was tried in Bucharest as a war criminal and shot. The king who had shared in Antonescu's decisions before and during World War II, was not touched.

The new government installed by Soviet assistance, consisted mostly of army generals. Only one member of the Communist party, Lucretiu Patrascanu (*see* Patrascanu, Lucretiu), was added to the cabinet as minister of justice and of state. The four civilians came from the National Peasant party, the Social Democratic party, and the Liberal party. Within two years after the royal coup d'etat, the king was forced to abdicate and consider himself lucky to be able to leave Romania as a penniless refugee.

Bibliography

Cretzianu, Alexandru, *Captive Romania: A Decade of Soviet Rule* (New York, 1956); Ionescu, Ghita, *Communism in Romania 1944–1962* (New York, 1964).

Sanatescu Government. Following the royal coup d'etat on August 23, 1944, General Constantin Sanatescu was called to form a new government for Romania.

Sanatescu served before as a liaison between King Michael and the armed forces. The Sanatescu government consisted mostly of generals. Only four civilians were included, one of whom was a communist.

The first act of this government was to restore the constitution of 1923—suspended by King Carol, Michael's father—legitimizing the revival of political parties. The Sanatescu government was also expected to mobilize Romanians against the expected response of Germany. When the German attack did not materialize, the government was reorganized. Sanatescu remained prime minister and he added that of the post of minister of defense to his titles. All other cabinet posts were given to civilians of the coalition, including the communists, the liberals, the social democrats, and the peasants. Two additional communist ministers were appointed, increasing their number to three in the new government; Gheorghe Gheorghiu-Dej (*see* Gheorghiu-Dej, Gheorghe), who took over the ministry of transportation and communications; Vlad Rakoasa, who gained the post of minister of minority affairs; and Lucretiu Patrascanu (*see* Patrascanu, Lucretiu) who retained his earlier assignment. The leading communists who had spent the war years in the Soviet Union, the Muscovites, included Ana Pauker (*see* Pauker, Ana), Vasile Luca (*see* Luca, Vasile) and Emil Bodnaras (*see* Bodnaras, Emil). They returned to Bucharest but remained in the background for the time being. They spent their time in reorganizing the almost defunct Communist party, which had less than 1,000 members.

The second Sanatescu government lasted for only a month. Its minister of the interior, a member of the Plowmen's Front, a radical peasant organization that was infiltrated by the communists, could be counted on to support communist policies.

At this point, Joseph Stalin used blackmail to change the Romanian political scene. He declared that Romania was in default in the obligations its government undertook when it signed the armistice in Moscow. The government allegedly did not supply the Soviet occupying armies with the necessities agreed upon. Therefore, the transfer of the administration of Transylvania, promised to the Romanians, was delayed.

At this, King Michael replaced Sanatescu with another military man, General Nicolae Radescu, as prime minister. Radescu reorganized the government. He had good credentials in the new situation; originally, he was opposed to Romania's participation in the war against the Soviet Union and was consequently imprisoned. Now he combined the prime ministership with the post of minister of the interior and replaced the communist minister of the minorities with a non-party man. But his government, also, lasted for only a short time, since Stalin was determined to turn Romania into a Soviet satellite.

Bibliography

Markham, Reuben, *Romania Under the Soviet Yoke* (Boston, MA, 1949); Fischer-Galati, Stephen, *The Socialist Republic of Romania* (Baltimore, MD, 1969); Berciu, Dumitru, *Romania* (New York, 1967); Deletant, Andrea, *Romania* (Santa Barbara, CA, 1985).

Socialist Unity Front of Romania. This mass organization was ostensibly the directing force of all other mass organizations in communist Romania, such as the labor unions, the National Union of Agricultural Cooperatives, the Union of Communist Youth, the National Women's Council, and the Writers' Union. The representatives of the Socialist Unity Front were also present in every organization in Romanian society. They were involved in the elections on the national and the local levels, and named candidates for all elective offices. Since all these elections were conducted by single lists of candidates, approved by the Communist party, being placed on one of these lists meant an "election" to office. The Socialist Unity Front was, of course, simply an arm of the Romanian Communist party. Its creation was intended to reach social strata not directly affected by party decisions. Their leaders were usually also members of the Communist party subject to party discipline. Their major task was to convince the citizenry that the party line was "correct" and that party policies were the only way to achieve prosperity for the population.

Bibliography

Fischer-Galati, Stephen, *The New Rumania: From People's Democracy to Socialist Republic* (Cambridge, MA, 1967); Graham, Lawrence S., *Romania: A Developing Socialist State* (Boulder, CO, 1982); Shafir, Michael, *Romania: Politics, Economics, and Society* (Boulder, CO, 1985).

Stalinist Terror in Romania (1947–1953). The Romanian secret police, organized and directed by the Soviet NKVD-KGB, began a series of arrests in 1947, usually executed during the night hours. From the spring of 1945 to 1947, the opponents of the communists were terrorized. In those years, the leaders of the National Peasant party, including Iuliu Maniu and Ion Michalache, were taken into custody. In October and November, 1947, they were tried on false charges and sentenced to life imprisonment. By the end of that year noncommunist politicians had been intimidated to such a degree that they no longer offered any resistance to the communists. Ion Tatarescu and his fellow Liberal party ministers were removed from the cabinet and replaced by communists. The new minister of foreign affairs was Ana Pauker (*see* Pauker, Ana), a Muscovite; Vasili Luca (*see* Luca, Vasile), another Muscovite communist, took over the ministry of finance; the third member of the trio, Emil Bodnaras (*see* Bodnaras, Emil), was named minister of defense. On December 30, King Michael was forced to abdicate and leave the country. On April 13, 1948, a new constitution was introduced which proclaimed Romania a People's Democracy. There were further arrests and show trials, this time of "local" communists who were charged with Titoist deviation.

In February 1948, the Social Democratic party was forced into a merger with the communists. The united party took on a new name; the Romanian Workers party. The remnants of the National Peasant party and the Plowmen's Front, whose leadership cooperated with the communists in destroying their own organizations, joined the "new" party. A semi-independent Hungarian party was also absorbed into the communist organization. The Romanian Workers party was declared to be a member of the United Democratic Popular Front of Romania. Elections were held on March 28, 1948, and, predictably, the front's single list candidates won an overwhelming victory. During the year, arrests of suspected opponents of communism continued, and victims disappeared into prisons and concentration camps. In 1954, Lucretiu Patrascanu (*see* Patrascanu, Lucretiu), the minister of justice in the Sanatescu government after August 23, 1944, was tried, together with several local communist leaders, and he was executed. Others received long prison terms or were killed. The terror slackened somewhat after the death of Joseph Stalin, but it never disappeared completely from Romanian society. It was the only means that could secure the rule of the communists.

Bibliography
Georgescu, Vlad, *Romania: 40 Years, 1944–1984* (New York, 1985); Ionescu, Ghita, *Communism in Romania 1944–1962* (New York, 1964); Jowitt, Kenneth, *Revolutionary Breakthroughs and National Development: The Case of Romania, 1945–1965* (Berkeley, CA, 1971); King, Robert, *History of the Romanian Communist Party* (Stanford, CA, 1980).

Stalinization of Romania. During 1948, Romanian society was forced into the Stalinist pattern of development. All major enterprises in banking, industry, mining, transportation, and communications were confiscated from their previous owners without compensation. A long list of joint Romanian-Soviet enterprises was created, headed by Soviet directors who set the price of their products and organized their activities under Soviet personnel. At the same time, the state began to establish machine- and tractor stations in the countryside, a preliminary step before the collectivization of land began. A central planning office was created with the task of setting up a plan for the socialization of the national economy. The Romanian army was reorganized. Its soldiers received Soviet-style uniforms, and were equipped with outdated Soviet arms. A system of political commissars was introduced. In 1948, after the break between Joseph Stalin and Marshal Tito occurred, Romania, together with other satellites, was assigned a special role in the expected military conflict with Yugoslavia. The headquarters of the Communist Information Bureau (COMINFORM) was transplanted to Bucharest from its previous location in Belgrade. In a few short years, therefore, Romania was transformed into a Soviet satellite, with all the characteristics shared by the other colonies of the Soviet Union's East European empire.

Bibliography
Cretzianu, Alexandru, *Captive Romania: A Decade of Soviet Rule* (New York, 1956); Georgescu, Vlad, *Romania: 40 Years 1944–1984* (New York, 1985); Graham, Lawrence S., *Romania: A Developing Socialist State* (Boulder, CO, 1982).

"Systematization" in Romania. This scheme was initiated by Nicolae Ceausescu (*see* Ceausescu, Nicolae and Elena) ostensibly to equalize conditions in the rural and urban areas of Romania and, incidentally, to increase agricultural production by providing better living conditions for the peasantry. However, the program had more sinister purposes as well. It was aimed at gaining full control over the lives of the rural folk, a goal that even full collectivization of the land had failed to achieve. It was also a means for the drastic "solution" to the existence of Hungarian and German minorities in Transylvania. In this sense, this was a traditional goal of chauvinistic Romanian nationalism.

The plan was introduced soon after Ceausescu gained complete control of the Romanian Communist party. According to the plan, the peasants in a given area were to be concentrated in new, high-rise apartments, and their old dwellings were to be bulldozed into the ground. The high-rises would become the nuclei of new urban concentrations from which farm workers would travel to the fields of their collective farms. After the completion of their day's work, they would return to their new homes which would be equipped with modern amenities and cultural opportunities.

However, the plan, fit for a Corbousier, turned out differently in real life. The simple country folks affected by "systematization," had to be driven by force to abandon their homes which had been in their family's possession often for many generations. The process also meant that they had to abandon hope to ever regaining their lands from the collectives into which they were being driven by force. The modern conveniences promised them turned out to be electricity which could be used for only two hours a day; running water which was not running for weeks on occasion; and heat which was simply not available for the long months of winter. They had to spend inordinately long hours each day commuting between their collectives and their homes. Agricultural production in the "systematized" villages actually declined. But the government's purposes were achieved at least in one sense. The apartments were equipped with listening devices, enabling the secret police to monitor conversations and "ferret out" people's secret thoughts. Thus, the control of the population was "modernized" and made more complete.

Systematization was especially vicious in the areas occupied by ethnic minorities. Villages with their ancient churches and cemeteries were razed to the ground. All memories that would remind people of their ethnic and cultural heritages were eliminated. This was a giant step toward creating a Romanian national state indeed by methods sinister enough to raise an outcry in Western public opinion when they became known. Fortunately, the lack of gasoline and other instruments of destruction limited the systematization process, and it was still in its early stages when the Ceausescu clan was overthrown.

Bibliography
Giurescu, Dinu, *The Razing of Romania's Past* (New York, 1989); Sampson, Steven L., *National Integration Through Socialist Planning* (Boulder, CO, 1984); Shafir, Michael, "The Historical Background of Rural Resettlement," *Radio Free Europe Research Report: Romanian Situation Report*, No.10 (August 23, 1988).

Timisoara Revolt (1989). On December 20, 1989, Nicolae Ceausescu (*see*

Ceausescu, Nicolae and Elena) was due to arrive in Teheran for a state visit with the Iranian government. He was to arrange for new oil deliveries for Romania and renew friendship between the two governments. The Communist party congress, concluded a few weeks before, had awarded the leader the title, "hero of heroes of Romanian history," and he received sixty-seven standing ovations during his five-hour long introductory speech. However, every member of the congress knew that this was just a facade. By then, the Berlin Wall had fallen, and the communist regimes in most East European countries had been swept away. Equally important, Soviet tanks were no longer threatening to roll in the defense of socialism. Only Romania and Yugoslavia still kept the old faith. Nicolae and Elena Ceausescu were unanimously reelected to their party and government posts, and even their elder son, Valentin (*see* Ceausescu, Valentin), was added to the membership of the Central Committee of the party. But the process was nothing more than a stage-managed ritual, and the country was seething with discontent, ready to explode at the first opportunity.

The trouble started in the unlikely city of Timisoara. The immediate cause of the explosion was the attempt of the security police to remove a popular Calvinist minister, Laszlo Tokes (*see* Tokes, Laszlo), from his congregation. The Calvinist church in Transylvania has an exclusively Hungarian character. It has over 600,000 members and is governed by bishops. The communists controlled the church through its hierarchy. The Reverend Tokes was not only an electrifying preacher, but he was also a brave defender of the human and ethnic rights of the Hungarian minority. The Calvinist bishop of Oradea county, who had religious authority in Timisoara, was another ethnic Hungarian, Laszlo Pap, an ardent and willing collaborator with the communist regime. In the summer of 1989, the bishop was instructed to remove Tokes from Timisoara. By then, he was a highly respected man in the city. Pap ordered him to take over a parish in a remote village, but Tokes simply refused to move. A stalemate developed. By the end of August, Ceausescu was alone as a communist tyrant in Eastern Europe. There was a rising tide of Romanian refugees escaping across the border into Hungary. In the meantime, Tokes continued preaching and revealed more human rights abuses in Transylvania.

On December 16, the secret police in Timisoara decided to remove him from the city by force, using a court decree that was obtained by Bishop Pap for the purpose. But the parish house was surrounded by a human chain, including Hungarians and Romanians, and the crowds began to demonstrate in the city against the government. Bookstores filled with books containing Ceausescu's speeches were broken into, and their contents were burned on the streets. Placards praising the leader were stripped from the walls.

Ceausescu did not want to postpone his Iranian trip and left his wife and two of his sycophants in charge of the situation. Elena Ceausescu ordered the police to fire on the demonstrators. More than forty people were killed (the exact number was never revealed), and hundreds were wounded. The bodies of the dead were spirited out of the city and secretly cremated. But the people were no longer intimidated. They continued to protest, especially after Tokes was whisked out of Timisoara. The unrest soon spread to other cities and the revolution was on.

Bibliography

Almond, Mark, *The Rise and Fall of Nicolae and Elena Ceausescu* (London, 1992); Behr, Edward, *Kiss the Hand You Cannot Bite* (New York, 1991); Galloway, George, *Downfall: The Ceausescus and the Romanian Revolution* (London, 1991).

Tokes, Laszlo (1946–). In the province of the Banat lies the city of Timisoara, an urban center that was given to Romania by the peace treaties of 1918. The province and the city have always had a large ethnic Hungarian population. The Calvinist church, established by Calvinist preachers in the course of the sixteenth century, was almost exclusively Hungarian in character. It was the center of resistance to the Catholic Habsburgs during and following the Catholic Reformation of subsequent centuries.

In the 1980s, a young Calvinist minister, Laszlo Tokes, was elected pastor of one of Timisoara's Calvinist congregations. In a short time, he became a popular man in the city. He was a vigorous preacher who did not mind offending the communist authorities with his open criticism of the abuse of human and ethnic rights and of the general mistreatment of the minorities in communist Romania. The superior of Tokes in the county of Oradea was Bishop Laszlo Pap, another ethnic Hungarian, who was an ardent and willing servant of the communist authorities. By the summer of 1989, the activities of the Reverend Tokes had become too much for the regime, and Bishop Pap was ordered to remove him from the city.

Accordingly, the bishop instructed Tokes immediately to take up a new ministry in a godforsaken little village far from Timisoara. Tokes simply refused to go, and he was supported by his congregation. Non-Calvinist ethnic Romanians also came to his support because, by then, he was a symbol of resistance to the regime. Bishop Pap, desperate to obtain the required transfer, took his case to the communist courts, where it was a foregone conclusion that Tokes would be transferred. However, against all expectations, the case dragged on all late summer and early autumn, and it rapidly developed into a case of mighty mouse versus the almighty giant of the state.

An interesting episode was provided by the visit of the American Baptist preacher, Billy Graham, to Romania in the summer of 1989. He was wined and dined by the party leaders, and so, he did not take the time or trouble to inquire about the fate of a fellow Protestant minister whose case was becoming widely known. When, upon arriving in Hungary from Romania, he was interviewed by Hungarian radio reporters about this strange omission, Graham responded that he did not want to meddle in Romanian politics.

By the fall of that year, communism had disappeared from most East European countries and, in November, even the Berlin Wall had fallen. In October, the Hungarian government opened its western borders to East German refugees which brought down the Honecker regime. On December 16, the authorities in Timisoara enforced the order to remove Tokes from the city. This created disorders and demonstrations, and the police fired on the crowd, killing forty and wounding several hundred people. The disorders spread to other cities, including Bucharest, and the Ceausescu clan was overthrown on December 22.

The Reverend Tokes returned to his congregation, and he became an important leader of a new political party, the Democratic Association of Romanian-Hungarians. His party became the second strongest party in the elections of 1991, and it joined the Democratic Convention in 1992.

Bibliography

Nelson, Daniel N., ed. *Romania after Tyranny* (Boulder, CO, 1992); Pacepa, Ion Mihai, *Red Horizons* (Washington, DC, 1987).

Urban Development in Romania. Various efforts were made in Romania during the interwar decades by various governments to expand the number of industries and, parallel with it, to help urbanization. Many of the processes that the communists claimed to have originated with their rule, had actually began during the old regime. However, it was the speed and depth of industrialization initiated by the communist government that was new in Romanian history. In the process of creating a Soviet-style command economy, based on long-range central planning, all productive forces and the overwhelming majority of investments were concentrated in industrial expansion. Since most industries were located in urban areas, there was a corresponding movement of the population to these regions. By 1972, 8.5 million Romanians, out of a total population of 22 million, were living in urban centers. Of these people 6.9 million lived in 77 cities and towns with populations of less than 20,000 but more than 5,000 people each. Thirty-eight towns were declared to have become cities.

Bibliography

Constantinescu, Miron, Henry H. Stahl, and Ion Dragan, et al. eds. *Urban Growth Processes in Romania* (Bucharest, 1974); Tsantis, Andreas C., and Pepper, Roy, *Romania: The Industrialization of an Agrarian Economy Under Socialist Planning* (Baltimore, MD, 1979).

Warsaw Pact and Romania. Romania was among the founding members of the Warsaw Pact when the alliance was formed in 1955. According to the charter, Soviet troops were stationed in each of the participating countries as a defensive force against the so-called "revanchist" forces of West Germany, the United States, and NATO. However, in 1956, the Romanian government was able to extract a statement from Nikita Khrushchev to the effect that Soviet troops were in Romania only on a temporary basis. As soon as Romania's own army was able to secure the integrity of the socialist state, the Soviet troops were to be withdrawn. In 1958, the promise of withdrawal was fulfilled. Romania had facilitated the suppression of the Hungarian Revolution two years before and, therefore, had earned the gratitude of the Soviet leaders.

This was also part of the effect of the Sino-Soviet dispute. In that year, Chinese troops were withdrawn from North Korea and the Soviet leaders wanted to demonstrate that they were no worse than the Chinese comrades. This provided the Romanian communist leaders with an opportunity to initiate a quasi-independent foreign policy. However, they were extremely cautious not to offend the Soviet Union. Romania remained a member of the Warsaw Pact throughout its communist era, but Romanian troops did not participate in joint military exercises. Nor did the Romanian government permit Warsaw Pact forces to exercise on Romanian soil. In August 1968, Romania simply refused to join in the Warsaw Pact invasion of Czechoslovakia. President Nicolae Ceausescu (*see* Ceausescu, Nicolae and Elena), in fact, roundly condemned the invasion as an act of aggression. The Romanian leaders also rejected the Brezhnev doctrine as simply a means of intervention in the internal affairs of allied countries. However, when the Polish and Hungarian peoples ousted their communist governments, Ceausescu attempted to have Mikhail Gorbachev intervene in these two countries. The Warsaw Pact's military section was disbanded in 1990. The political section survived until the dissolution of the Soviet Union in 1991.

Bibliography

Alexiev, Alex, *Party-Military Relations in Eastern Europe: The Case of Romania* (Los Angeles, CA, 1979).

YUGOSLAVIA

General Information. *Area:* 255,804 square kilometers (98,766 square miles). *Population:* 20,000,000 (in 1976). *Major cities:* Belgrade (Beograde), the capital; Zagreb, capital of the Croatian Republic; Skopje; Sarajevo, capital of Bosnia-Herzegovina; Ljubljana, capital of Slovenia; Novi Sad, Rijeka, Subotica. *Literacy:* 80.3 percent (10 years or older) (in 1976). Borders; Austria and Hungary on the north and northwest, Romania and Bulgaria in the east, Greece in the south and Albania in the southwest; the Adriatic sea on the west was Yugoslavia's border. *Distribution of work force:* 22.4 percent in industry, 7.1 percent in trade and handicrafts, 50.6 percent in agriculture and forestry, 5.9 percent in education and cultural activities, 6.2 percent with private incomes, and 7.8 percent other. *Religious denominations:* Orthodox Christians, 41.2 percent; Roman Catholics, 31.3 percent; Protestants 0.93 percent; Moslems, 12.31 percent; other Christians 0.4 percent; Jews, 0.01 percent; Nonbelievers, 12.45 percent; unknown, 1.4 percent. *Ethnicity:* Serbs, 41.7 percent; Croats, 23.5 percent; Slovenes, 8.8 percent; Macedonians, 5.3 percent; Montenegrines, 2.7 percent; Moslem Slavs, 5.9 percent; Albanians, 4.5 percent; Hungarians, 3 percent; Turks, 1.5 percent; others, 3.1 percent.

Bibliography

Byrnes, Robert F., *Yugoslavia* (New York, 1957); Djordjevic, Dimitrije, "The Yugoslav Experiment," in Joseph Held, ed. *The Columbia History of Eastern Europe in the Twentieth Century* (New York, 1992), pp. 305-344; Radulovic, Milan, *Tito's Republic* (Wrotham, England, 1951); Vucinich, Wayne, ed. *Contemporary Yugoslavia* (Berkeley, CA, 1969).

CHRONOLOGY

1944 *September.* Josip Broz Tito's partisan army, in cooperation with contingents of the Soviet armed forces, liberated Belgrade. Tito became the undisputed ruler of Yugoslavia.

December. The Yugoslav army entered Trieste and immediately ran into a conflict with the Western occupying forces. Joseph Stalin refused to support Tito's claim to Trieste and he was forced to retreat.

1945 *February.* Yugoslav gunners shot down three American airplanes, followed by protests by the U.S. government.

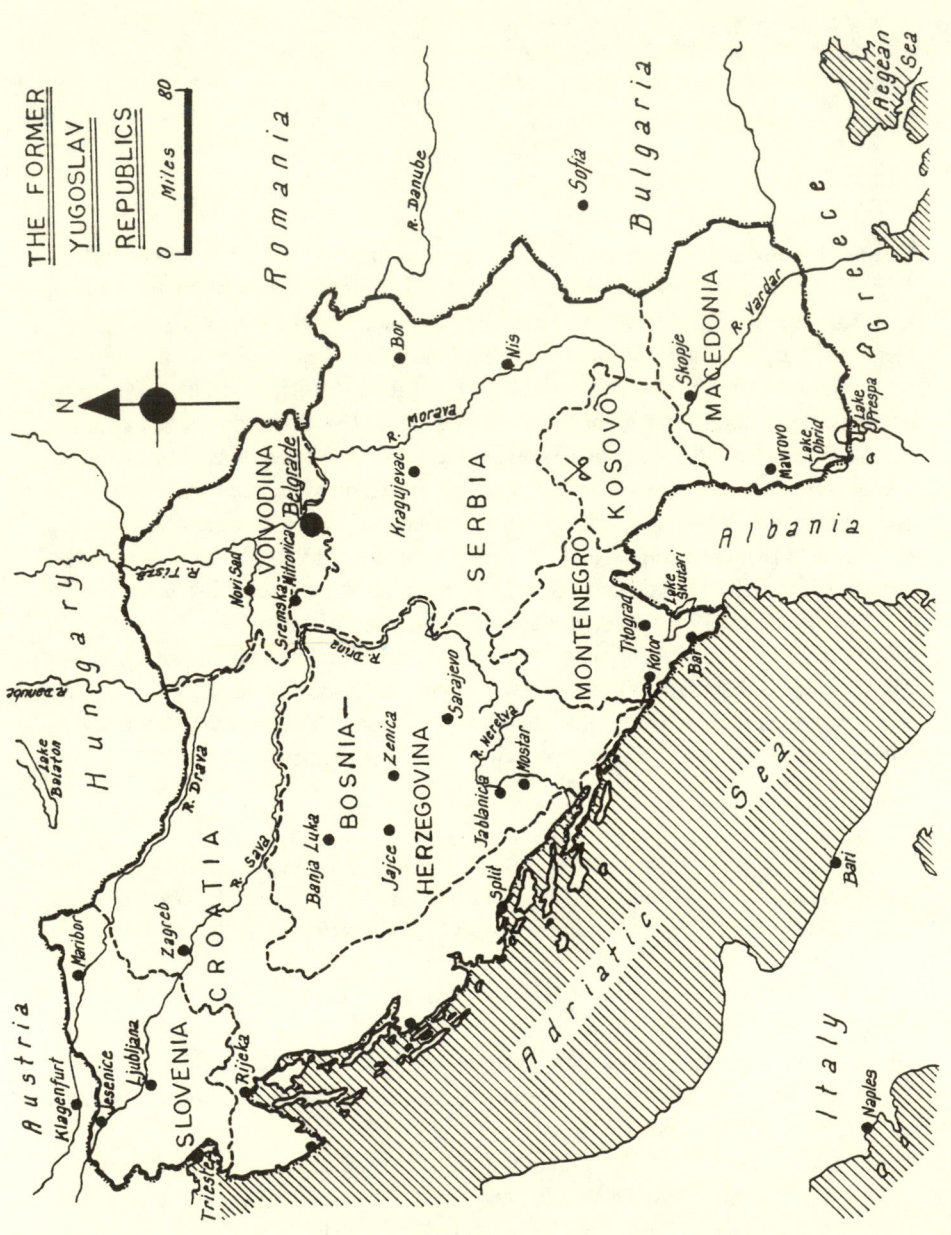

March. Tito's government was finally formed. It consisted mostly of Partisan fighters, but, at Stalin's insistence, five former exiles were also included.

November. Elections were held in Yugoslavia with a single list of Tito's party. The two houses of the Yugoslav parliament received an overwhelmingly large number of deputies from Tito's Communist party.

1947 *February.* The Allied governments signed the peace treaties with Germany's former allies. Yugoslavia was to receive reparations from Hungary and Bulgaria.

October. A new organization, called the Communist Information Bureau, or COMINFORM, was established with headquarters in Belgrade.

1948 *March.* Soviet proposals for a Yugoslav-Bulgarian federation were rejected by the Yugoslav government. Tito wanted a federation of all Slavic Balkan states, and Stalin was unwilling to support this idea.

June. Yugoslavia was expelled from the COMINFORM and the headquarters of the organization were removed from Belgrade. Soviet propaganda began a vicious campaign against Tito, proclaiming that he had always been an "imperialist spy." The rest of the leadership of the East European communist countries echoed the Soviet charges. One of the side effects of the campaign was that Yugoslavia ended the clandestine support of the Greek communist insurgency. Tito's government slaughtered about 50,000 Yugoslav citizens in "cleansing" the party of the supporters of Stalin.

1950 *June.* Workers' self-management was introduced in Yugoslavian factories along with a certain economic decentralization. However, no parallel political decentralization was permitted.

1951 *November.* Yugoslavia, fearing a Soviet invasion, lodged a complaint in the United Nations against the Soviet Union. The Yugoslavs complained about the openly hostile attitude the Soviet government exhibited toward their country.

1954 *January.* Rifts within the top Yugoslav leadership were shown when Milovan Djilas was ousted from all his state and party offices. He was charged with antiparty activities for publishing a book abroad on the "new class" in communist-dominated societies. He was not yet expelled from the Yugoslav Communist party because of his wartime activities.

1955 *May-June.* Nikita Khrushchev and Nikolay Bulganin traveled to Belgrade in order to restore amicable relations between the Soviet Bloc and Yugoslavia. The two Soviet statesmen openly acknowledged Yugoslavia's independence and unique "road to socialism." Tito's demands included the replacement of Matyas Rakosi as head of the Hungarian Communist party for his incredibly vicious attacks on Yugoslavia during the conflict.

1956 *June.* Tito returned Khrushchev's and Bulganin's visit by visiting Moscow.

July. In line with Tito's condition, Rakosi was removed from the leadership of the Hungarian Communist party. He was exiled to the Soviet Union and never returned to Hungary.

October. Khrushchev paid a second visit to Yugoslavia after the outbreak of the Hungarian Revolution. He received Tito's agreement for the suppression of the revolution by Soviet tanks.

November. After Soviet armed forces attacked Hungary, Imre Nagy, the prime minister, sought refuge in the Yugoslav embassy in Budapest, together with some members of his cabinet and their families. They were induced to leave by the promise of safe conduct, but they were arrested immediately after leaving the embassy building. Their arrest was supported by Tito.

1968 *September.* Tito criticized the Warsaw Pact nations for their intervention in Czechoslovakia.

December. Tito denounced the Brezhnev doctrine as a justification for intervention in the internal affairs of socialist countries.

1971 *March-April.* The twenty-fourth congress of the Soviet Communist party, held in Moscow, was attended by Yugoslav delegates.

1974 *March.* A new federal constitution was proclaimed for Yugoslavia. It provided for the recognition of six republics as components of the Yugoslav state (Croatia, Serbia, Slovenia, Montenegro, Macedonia, and Bosnia-Herzegovina) while granting autonomous province-status to Vojvodina and Kosovo. The new arrangement was to be overseen by the unitary League of Yugoslav Communists, a name given to the Communist party. However, this provided for the fragmentation of the party into republican components.

1975 *July.* Yugoslavia signed the Helsinki Accords, finalizing Europe's post-World War II borders and obligating the signatories to observe the human rights of their states' citizens.

1976 *June.* Yugoslav delegates attended the gathering of Communist party representatives held in East Berlin. The delegates refused to condemn the Chinese and reestablish Soviet supremacy in the European communist movement.

1980 *May.* Tito, head of the Yugoslav League of Communists, president of Yugoslavia, died at the age of eighty-eight. His legacy included a collective presidency rotating every year among leaders of constituent republics, and a staggering foreign debt of $21 billion.

1988 *May.* Wage controls were introduced in Yugoslavia. This was a condition set by the International Monetary Fund for the approval of a new loan of $430 million. Yugoslavia's foreign debt was rescheduled.

November. All public meetings and demonstrations were banned in the autonomous province of Kosovo. The Albanians, who make up about 90 percent of the population of the province, protested the proposed changes in the status of the province that were scheduled to take away its autonomy.

1990 *January.* The growth of inflation in Yugoslavia was matched by a decline of industrial production. The government tried to introduce austerity measures to stop these trends. A special meeting of the Yugoslav League of Communists was called, and its delegates agreed to abolish the party's monopoly of power. However, when the Slovenian delegate walked out in response to the refusal of the meeting to grant greater autonomy to the Slovenian Communist party, the meeting ended in recriminations.

February. The Slovenian Communist party declared its independence from the Yugoslav League of Communists.

July. The Slovenian parliament declared that its laws had priority over the laws of the Yugoslav federation. Serbia dissolved the parliament of Kosovo. The Serb government also withdrew the autonomy of the province, illegally altering its 1974 constitution.

August. The Serb minority in the Croatian republic began voting in an unofficial referendum about autonomy for the 11 percent ethnic Serbs in Croatia.

September. The presidents of Slovenia and Croatia met in the Croatian capital and agreed on the dissolution of the Yugoslav federation.

October. Amidst increasing tensions, the Croatian and Slovene governments demanded the alteration of the Yugoslav federation, transforming it into a loose confederation. If their demands were not met, they threatened the secession of their republics. The Serb government made threatening noises using the Serb-dominated army as a guarantee of the unity of the state. Slovenia imposed tariffs on transiting Serbian goods. This was a response to earlier Serb pressure against Slovenian trade.

December. General Veljko Kadijevic warned Croatia and Slovenia that the Yugoslav army was prepared to defend the unity of Yugoslavia against antisocialist and anti-Serbian elements. Croatian president Franjo Tudjman rejected Kadijevic's statement as totally inappropriate for a military officer to make. A popular referendum in Slovenia overwhelmingly approved secession if the efforts to establish a confederation in Yugoslavia failed.

1991 *May.* The rotation of the federal presidency was held up for six weeks by Serbia, and Stipe Mesic of Croatia started his presidency late. Serbia, Montenegro, and the Serb administration of Kosovo and the Vojvodina completely ignored Mesic. Serbian irregulars in Croatia were being heavily armed by the former Yugoslav army.

June. The federal army, commanded mostly by Serbian officers, began an unauthorized war against Slovenia.

July. Slovenian territorial defense forces defeated the Serb army. The Serbians left Slovenia. The war in Croatia raged on. The Serb army intervened more and more openly. Its heavy artillery devastated towns and cities, especially Vukovar. Over 40,000 refugees entered Hungary.

September. Serbian newspapers and other media asserted that Germany and Austria were trying to establish a Fourth Empire in the Balkans with Italy,

Hungary, the Vatican and the Habsburg family. Croatia and Slovenia were, according to this propaganda machine, the tools of the Germans.

December. Macedonia and Bosnia-Herzegovina declared their secession from rump-Yugoslavia. The European Community recognized the independence of Slovenia and Croatia. Ante Markovic, prime minister of Yugoslavia, resigned. He declared that as long as 80 percent of the budget of the state was earmarked for the armed forces, no peace initiatives could succeed. Bosnia-Herzegovina requested recognition by the European Community as an independent state.

1992 *February.* A UN peace plan was worked out between Croatia and Serbia. 11,500 peacekeeping soldiers were to be sent in to enforce a cease-fire. Macedonia arranged the withdrawal of the Yugoslav army from its territory. The independence of Macedonia was imminent.

March. The shelling of the Bosnian city of Sarajevo by the Serb insurgents intensified. Croatian and Serb commanders agreed on an exchange of prisoners.

April. Bosnia's Serb minority declared independence. The fighting continued and intensified. Senseless killing of Muslims, regardless of age or gender, was perpetrated by the Serbians.

May. Serbian units continued the shelling of Sarajevo. The devastation was intensive. At least six cease-fires had been agreed upon by Bosnian Muslims and Serbs, yet each was broken in a short time. The Serbian Orthodox church proclaimed that Slobodan Milosevic should resign in the interests of peace.

June. Fighting continued in and around Sarajevo. Serb snipers shot children, women, and the elderly without discrimination.

July. American businessman Milan Panic was sworn in as prime minister of rump-Yugoslavia. He declared that no idea was worth fighting for at the end of the twentieth century.

August. In the Croatian elections, the Croatian Democratic Community and Franjo Tudjman were leading for legislative seats and the presidency, respectively.

September. A mass grave, containing over 200 bodies of Muslims, killed by the Serbs, was found in the Mostar region.

October. Mass protests broke out in the province of Kosovo. Albanians resented the constant Serbian terror against the Albanian people, the closing of their schools, and the persecution of their politicians. Another mass grave was found, this time near Vukovar, containing the bodies of 170 Croatian soldiers murdered by the Serbs.

November. Macedonia and rump Yugoslavia agreed on mutual recognition. In the national elections seven parties earned representation in the Slovenian parliament.

1993 *January.* The UN High Commission reported that about 2 million people had become homeless as the result of Serbian aggression in the territory of the former Yugoslavia. Fighting resumed in Croatia. Croatian forces reopened a highway connecting Zadar with the rest of the country that was being blocked by irregular Serb forces. They drove the Serbs back, but the fighting only slowed down; it did not completely stop. The Serbs had tried to blow up a dam that would have flooded civilian areas, but Croatian engineers soon had matters under control and prevented an ecological disaster. In the elections, Milosevic won against Panic, and his party became the strongest group in parliament.

April. A plan was presented to the fighting groups in Bosnia-Herzegovina by Cyrus Vance and Lord Owen. According to this plan, the territory of Bosnia-Herzegovina would be divided into ten regions based on the ethnic distribution of the population. The Serbs would have to give up some lands that they had conquered.

May. Vojislav Seselj, chairman of the Serb Radical party, said on Italian television that missiles would be launched against Austria, Italy, and all other countries that served as staging areas for UN aircraft if Serb positions were attacked. He specifically stated that only civilian targets would be attacked.

June. Vuk Draskovic, the leader of the Serbian opposition to Milosevic, was severely beaten and tortured by the Serb police. His wife was also beaten. It has been reported that six areas were to be set aside for safety zones for Bosnian Muslims. The areas would be secured by United Nations forces. Macedonia accepted troops from the United States as part of a UN contingent serving as observers of the peace. Croatia now houses 250,000 Muslim refugees. The Vance-Owen plan was rejected by both sides and it is now considered dead.

Andrejev, Bane (1905–?). He attended the University of Belgrade but did not graduate. In 1927, Andrejev joined the Yugoslav Communist party. He also was a member of the Macedonian Revolutionary Committee. He was captured, tried, and sentenced to fifteen years of hard labor. During World War II, Andrejev became a member of the Partisans in Macedonia, and he was captured by the Bulgarian occupiers. In 1943, he was freed and was elected a member of the presidium of the Yugoslav Anti-Fascist People's Liberation Council. In 1945, Andrejev became a member of the Constituent Assembly, and he was appointed minister of mining. In 1948, he supported Joseph Stalin in his conflict with Marshal Tito (*see* Tito, Josip Broz). He was, therefore, expelled from the Communist party and lost all his posts. He was arrested with Andrej Hebrang (*see* Hebrang, Andrej), but his fate is unknown, because he did not go through a public trial. It is most likely that Andrejev died in jail.

Bibliography

Clissold, Stephen, *Yugoslavia and the Soviet Union* (London, 1975); Hoffman, George, and Neal, F. Warner, *Tito's Yugoslavia* (Berkeley, CA, 1960); Rudzinski, Alexander, "Politics and Political Organizations," in Robert F. Byrnes, ed. *Yugoslavia* (New York, 1957).

Anti-Fascist Council for National Liberation. In November 1943, this Council was formed to unify Yugoslav resistance to the German occupiers. It was dominated by the communists. Wherever the Partisan army established control, the council was called on to establish local government, also communist controlled.

In 1944, the council proclaimed itself the supreme legislative body of Yugoslavia, and it announced the establishment of a federal state of Yugoslavia. It also proclaimed itself the provisional government of the country and announced that King Peter II had been deposed. It prohibited the former king to return to Yugoslavia. At the end of the year, the council elected a national committee and transferred to it the power to govern the country.

Bibliography
Avakumovic, Ivan, *History of the Communist Party of Yugoslavia* (Aberdeen, England, 1964); Denich, Bogdan D., *The Legitimization of a Revolution: The Yugoslav Case* (New Haven, CN, 1976).

Bakaric, Vladimir (1912–). Bakaric was born into a middle-class family; his father was a judge. He attended Zagreb University and received a degree of doctor of law. In 1933, Bakaric, while still in a secondary school, joined the underground Communist party. During his university days, he was president of the Law Students Association. In 1934, Bakaric was arrested and sent to prison for three years. After his release in 1937, he began practicing law and continued his illegal activities. Bakaric joined Tito's (*see* Tito, Josip Broz) partisan army in 1941, and he was named secretary to the Antifascist People's Liberation Council for Croatia.

In 1944, he was appointed minister without portfolio in the federal government and deputy minister for foreign affairs. In 1945, he was prime minister for the federal republic of Croatia. In the same year, he was a member of the Constituent Assembly of Yugoslavia and also of Croatia. The following year, Bakaric was a member of the Yugoslav delegation at the Paris peace conference. Tito's supporter in the Soviet-Yugoslav dispute, he led a delegation to Moscow after Nikita Khrushchev tried to patch up the relationship in 1955. In time, Bakaric filled important government and party posts in Croatia and the federal government, and he was considered an influential advisor to Tito on agricultural matters. It is possible that he was responsible in 1952 for stopping the drive to collectivize the land.

Bibliography
Byrnes, Robert F., ed. *Yugoslavia* (New York, 1957).

Bosnia-Herzegovina. *Population:* 4,365,000. *Area:* 51,129 square kilometers (31,960 square miles). *Capital city:* Sarajevo (475,000 people). *Major ethnic groups:* Muslim Slavs 43.7 percent; Serbs 31.4 percent; Croatians 17.3 percent; others 7.6 percent. *Major religions:* Orthodox Christian, Muslim, Roman Catholic. *President:* Alia Izetbegovic.

The medieval state of Bosnia, which included present-day Bosnia-Herzegovina, struggled constantly for independence. In 1463, however, the Ottoman armies invaded the country and subjected it to the sultan's sovereignty. Subjection lasted until 1878. In that year, the Habsburg empire occupied the land and, in 1908, it formally annexed it to the empire. Following World War I, Bosnia was included first in the Kingdom of Serbs, Croats and Slovenes, then, in 1926, it became part of the Yugoslav kingdom. In 1941, Yugoslavia was occupied by Nazi Germany, in alliance with Hungary, Italy and Bulgaria. After the war, Bosnia-Herzegovina was one of the six republics created by Josip Broz Tito's communist government (*see* Tito, Josip Broz). Following the death of Tito in 1980, disputes within the Yugoslav federations began over ethnic and national power.

In November 1990, the Muslim Party for Democratic Action won a plurality of the seats in parliament. In June 1991, Yugoslavia began to disintegrate, first with the declaration of independence by Croatia and Slovenia, then by Bosnia-Herzegovina. The republic's parliament declared its sovereignty in a memorandum on October 15, 1991. A referendum on independence, held on February 29 and March 1 1992, was supported by the majority of the population. The fact that the local Serbs boycotted the referendum foreshadowed trouble. On April 7, 1992, Bosnia-Herzegovina was recognized as an independent, sovereign state by the European Community and the United States.

The state had a strong agriculture and mining industry. In 1990, Bosnia produced about 85 percent of the iron ore of the former Yugoslavia, and 40 percent of its lignite and coal. It also has lead, zinc, manganese and bauxite resources.

The civil war that broke out in late 1991, was still raging in 1994 with minor interruptions. The ethnic Serbs, supported at first clandestinely by the federal Yugoslav army, then openly by the government of Slobodan Milosevic (*see* Milosevic, Slobodan), attacked in Bosnia-Herzegovina with the openly admitted purpose of "ethnic cleansing," namely, the elimination of Muslim Slavs from territories claimed by them. The Serbs indiscriminately slaughtered women, children, and old men, as well as all adult males that they could. Their argument was that they did not want to live as a minority in their own country because the Muslims would do the same to them.

The United Nations organized a relief effort to provide food and medicine to besieged towns and cities, such as Sarajevo and Gorazda, and it attempted to arrange at least a truce, but the Serbs stopped relief convoys and continued their attacks. The European community and NATO were unwilling to send troops to the former Yugoslavia to stop the obvious genocide. The United Nations organized a commission to look into war crimes committed by the Serbs. It also ordered a no-fly zone over Bosnia-Herzegovina and a general economic blockade of Serbia-Montenegro, now calling themselves Yugoslavia. All these actions were only partially effective. Romania was reluctant to join the embargo, and Russia even permitted volunteers to join the Serbs in fighting against Muslim Slavs. The Muslim world has also been reluctant to intervene. At the present writing, thousands of innocent people are dying in

Bosnia-Herzegovina, and the outside world looks on with sympathy for the sufferers but is unwilling to act.

The United Nations (represented by an American diplomat, Cyrus Vance, and a British statesman, Lord Owen) worked out a precarious peace proposal at Geneva, according to which Bosnia-Herzegovina would be carved up into ten autonomous provinces, each with ethnically as pure a population as possible. But the plan was unsatisfactory for the Bosnian-Herzegovinian Muslin Slavs as well as for the Serbs. In addition, the new American administration of President William Clinton objected to the plan as giving the aggressor Serbs what they wanted. The war, therefore, continues as intensely as before.

Bibliography

Andrejevich, Milan, "Bosnia-Herzegovina: A Precarious Peace," *Radio Free Europe Research Report*, 1.9 (February 28, 1992), pp. 6-14; ———, "Bosnia-Herzegovina in Search of Peace," *Radio Free Europe Research Report*, 1.23 (June 5, 1992), pp. 1-11; Dyker, Davis, and Bojicic, Vesna, "The Impact of Sanctions on the Serbian Economy," *Radio Free Europe Research Report*, 2.21 (May 21, 1993), pp. 50-54; Moore, Patrick, "Islamic Aspects of the Yugoslav Crisis," *Radio Free Europe Research Report*, 1.28 (July 10, 1992), pp. 37-42; ———, "Ethnic Cleansing in Bosnia: Outrage but Little Action," *Radio Free Europe Research Report*, 1.34 (August 28, 1992), pp. 1-7; ———, "The London Conference on the Bosnian Crisis," *Radio Free Europe Research Report*, 1.36 (September 11, 1992), pp. 1-6; ———, "The Widening Warfare in the Former Yugoslavia," *Radio Free Europe Research Report*, 1.1 (January 1, 1992), pp. 1-11.

Civil War in Post-Communist Yugoslavia. In its seven decades of existence, the Yugoslav state has not been able to create a single nation out of the many ethnic groups and nations living within its borders. The imposition of communist rule and the prestige of Tito (*see* Tito, Josip Broz), himself a mixture of Croatian and Sloven ancestry, kept the lid on the long-standing resentments and hostility that existed among the ethnic groups.

Four factors were instrumental in keeping peace in Tito's Yugoslavia: Tito's personal prestige as a statesman of international stature, the federal nature of the League of Communists of Yugoslavia, the large federal bureaucracy, and the federal army. An added factor whose weight, however, cannot be ascertained was the secret police under the personal command of Tito. President Tito had died in 1980. His legacy was a collective leadership whose members had been selected from among the various ethnic groups, but who were also all communists. A rotating presidency was intended to prevent any one individual from gaining sole control over the federal government. But there were signs that the long-suppressed nationalism of the Croats and Slovenes was about to burst through the confines of communist federalism.

The collapse of communism in the Soviet Union and the other East European countries shook the Yugoslav system also, but the communist successors to Tito succeeded in evading major changes in their system. They changed the name of the party from "communist" to "socialist," but the same personnel continued to direct the affairs of state.

However, the federal communist bureaucracy became more and more fragmented as the latent nationalism of its members came to the fore. Only the federal army remained intact, since the overwhelming majority of its officers were made up by Serbian nationals.

The Serbs moved first. In 1986, the Serbian Academy of Sciences published a list of grievances against Titoism, that is, the equality of all republics and provinces in federated Yugoslavia. The following year, a former communist apparatchik, Slobodan Milosevic (*see* Milosevic, Slobodan), who turned his talents as a member of the communist nomenklatura to banking, appeared on the political scene. He is an outstanding orator who has appealed to Serbian nationalism. He has repeatedly asserted that the Serbs had been cheated and oppressed by the "Croatian Tito," a charge that would hardly stand up to closer examination. Nevertheless, he was elected Serbia's president in 1990. He immediately moved to force through changes in parliament amending the Yugoslav federal constitution. The autonomy of the provinces of Vojvodina and Kosovo was withdrawn. Coercive Serbian rule was reintroduced in both regions. But Milosevic did not have all he wanted.

The democratization process proceeded in Yugoslavia. All the constituent republics held open and free elections in which the local nationalist parties won convincing victories. The Slovenes elected Milan Kucan as their president. A former communist, Kucan formed a center-right coalition government that decided to work for Slovene independence. In Croatia, the elections resulted in a broad coalition government headed by Franjo Tudjman, a former general officer of the federal army who was imprisoned at one time for his "nationalist" orientation. In Bosnia-Herzegovina, three parties formed a coalition: Serb, Muslim-Slav and Croatian parties, representing the religious and national divisions in the two provinces. The government was headed by Alija Izetbegovic, a prominent Muslim lawyer. In Macedonia, nationalist parties also gained the upper hand and began working for independence from Yugoslavia. In Serbia, the largest republic with about 9.5 million people, Milosevic won the elections. He was also head of the Socialist party. In Montenegro, Momir Bulatovic, a supporter of Milosevic, was elected president.

On June 25, 1991, Slovenia and Croatia declared their independence. Two days later, the federal army attacked in both republics. The Slovenes were well prepared. They took over the arms depots of the territorial defense forces and successfully repelled the attack. The situation in Croatia was, however, different. The large Serb communities who live in that republic demanded autonomy that the Tudjman (*see* Tudjman, Franjo) government was slow to grant. The Serb communities formed irregular bands—they called themselves Chetniks in memory of old—and they turned to the federal army for help. The army obliged. It provided arms and equipment for the insurrectionists.

The ensuing war was fought with great brutality. It also generated a flood of refugees and resulted in tremendous destruction of property. About half a million people were forced out of their homes. More than 10,000 were killed and 15,000 wounded. The Serbs succeeded in linking up all Serb populated areas with their brethren in Greater Serbia. Croatia lost about half of its original territory. The cities of Vukovar and Dubrovnik were practically destroyed. In turn, the former Yugoslavia's economy simply collapsed. Serb and Croatian foreign trade, Croatian tourism, and Slovene commerce ground to a halt. The conflict was soon expanded to include Bosnia-Herzegovina.

In the meantime, Macedonia also declared its independence. The conflict could grow even wider, if the Serbs attempt "ethnic cleansing," that is, genocide in Kosovo, and if Macedonia is attacked. This would certainly bring Bulgaria, Greece, Turkey, and Albania into war with Serbia.

Bibliography

Gow, James, "Military-Political Affiliations in the Yugoslav Conflict," *Radio Free Europe Research Report*, 1.20 (May 15, 1992), pp. 16-25; Hayden, Robert M., "The Partition of Bosnia-Herzegovina, 1990–1993," *Radio Free Europe Research Report*, 2.22 (May 28, 1993), pp. 1-18; Moore, Patrick, "Yugoslav Ethnic Tension Erupts into Civil War," *Radio Free Europe Research Report*, 2.1 (January 3, 1993), pp. 68-73.

Colakovic, Radoljub (1900–?). Colakovic was born into a well-to-do family and attended secondary school in Sarajevo. He also attended the University of Belgrade, but never completed his studies. In 1919, Colakovic was among the first members of the Communist party of Yugoslavia. In 1922, he was arrested for subversion and sentenced to fifteen years in prison. He was released in 1932 and went to France and then to the Soviet Union. In 1936, he was sent to Spain to fight in the civil war and returned to Yugoslavia in 1939.

In 1941, he immediately joined the partisan forces and organized the resistance in Bosnia-Herzegovina. Between 1942 and 1945, he was a member of the supreme headquarters of the Partisan Army of Liberation and secretary of the presidium of the Antifascist Council of National Liberation. Between March 1945 and February 1946, Colakovic was prime minister of the government of the republic of Bosnia-Herzegovina and a member of the presidium of the Constituent Assembly. He headed the Federal Board of Science and Culture and the ministry of education. From 1945 to 1948, he was the president of the Yugoslav Society for Cultural Collaboration with the Soviet Union. In 1947, Colakovic was a member of the Yugoslav delegation sent to the Paris peace conference and was one of the three Yugoslav signatories of the Italian peace treaty. In 1953, he became one of the four vice presidents of the federal government and was also appointed chairman of the committee for cultural relations with foreign countries. He was a member of the Central Committee of the League of Yugoslav Communists and a member of the presidium of the Socialist Alliance of the Working People of Yugoslavia, a communist front organization. In 1955, Colakovic was entrusted with creating a reform proposal for the Yugoslav educational system.

The proposal, ready by 1956, was, as Colakovic announced, based on the principles of Marxism-Leninism. Colakovic continued to be politically active until the death of Marshal Tito (*see* Tito, Josip Broz), when he retired from political life.

Bibliography

Byrnes, Robert F., Yugoslavia (New York, 1957); Rusinow, Denison, *The Yugoslav Experiment, 1948–1974* (Berkeley, CA, 1977).

Communist Party of Yugoslavia. During the election campaign of 1920, a new party emerged on the Yugoslav political scene. This party was not about to wait patiently for the "inevitable collapse" of bourgeois society. It was to hasten the process through a series of terrorist actions. Consequently, the Communist party was declared illegal in 1921, and its leaders and few members went underground. From 1924 on, the Yugoslav Communist party was the willing instrument of Soviet foreign policies through the COMINTERN. The Yugoslav party followed faithfully all directions from the Soviet leadership. It declared that the Kingdom of Serbs, Croats and Slovenes, as the state was called until 1926, was illegitimate because it was the product of a capitalist conspiracy called the Versailles treaty. It declared that the government of the kingdom was an agent of French imperialism and it would have to be destroyed.

Until 1928, the Communist party of Yugoslavia worked hard and diligently for this purpose. The party found it convenient to collaborate with the Croatian fascists, the Ustashi, and the Bulgarian-Macedonian Internal Macedonian Revolutionary Organization (IMRO), another terrorist group, since all these groups shared the same purpose. From 1935, however, the tactics of the COMINTERN had changed. Fearing the rise of Nazism and Adolf Hitler into power in Germany, communists throughout Europe switched to support coalitions of center-right parties, the so-called popular fronts, and the Yugoslav communists followed suit.

By 1937, most Yugoslav communist exiles in the Soviet Union were dead. They had been killed in Joseph Stalin's purges of foreign communists. A new man emerged on the scene, Josip Broz, who took the conspiratorial name of Tito (*see* Tito, Josip Broz). He was sent back to Yugoslavia by the COMINTERN to reorganize the dispirited remnants of the illegal Communist party and to appoint people who were unquestionably loyal to him and to the Soviet Union, into leadership positions. In 1939, the Yugoslav Communist party had about 1,000 members. By 1941, the membership had increased to 12,000. In 1946, 258,000 people joined the Yugoslav Communist party and this number had increased to 482,000 by 1948.

The Yugoslav Communist party directed part of the resistance to the German occupiers (the other part was organized by Dragoljub-Draza Mihajlovich and his Chetnicks) (*see* Mihajlovich Dragoljub, Draza), and it fought a war on two fronts. One was against the Germans, the other, against other resistance groups. The seasoned core of the party, having spent most of its time in underground activities where conspiracy was a way of life, quickly adapted to the new situation after 1941.

In 1942, the party leaders established an underground government. Tito, who was the commander of the communist army, succeeded in expanding its size. Wherever the Partisan army went, it established local governments staffed by communist cadres. It succeeded in combining Yugoslav nationalism with its Marxist-Leninist ideology and focusing its efforts on national liberation. Toward the end of the war, the Soviet Red army arrived in Yugoslavia, and helped in the final act of liberation. Stalin advised Tito to share power, at least for a time, with noncommunist left-wingers. Tito refused. He also refused to spare his rival, Mihailovich, who was dragged before a "people's court" and sentenced to death in 1946.

The Communist party recruited a great many young peasant fighters, who were bursting with energy and enthusiasm for the new government. They were not about to support power-sharing with anybody. They all stood behind Tito who was, in any case, a convinced Stalinist at the time, albeit with a strong sense of Yugoslavia's national interests. In 1945, therefore, the popular front coalition was jettisoned. The most popular noncommunist parties, the Democrats led by Milan Grol, and Jasa Prodanovic's Republicans, were hounded out of existence; their leaders and cadres were charged with treason or other capital offenses, and were imprisoned or murdered outright.

In the immediate post-World War II period, the Communist party of Yugoslavia was considered to be the most radical of all East European Communist parties. But reality was something else again. There existed tensions and a growing friction between Stalin and Tito, which, in 1948, ended with the expulsion of the Yugoslavs from the Soviet Bloc. But Stalin's expectation that the Yugoslav communists would get rid of Tito ("I have only to shake my little finger," Stalin allegedly said, "and Tito will disappear") did not materialize. The conflict actually helped to shore up the organization of the party and tighten discipline. The supporters of Stalin were "unmasked" and jailed or murdered. The situation was ripe for Tito and his followers to develop their own brand of socialism, changing the character of the Communist party in the process.

To begin with, Tito introduced reforms, separating the state and party administrations. Collectivization of agriculture was eventually abandoned. The position of political commissars in the armed forces was abolished. In 1952, the party's sixth congress approved of the reforms. Milovan Djilas (*see* Djilas, Milovan) urged further reforms. In 1953, he even proposed that the party give up its monopoly of power, but his suggestions were brushed aside. The following year, Djilas was disciplined for "rightist deviation." The party bureaucrats, however, felt the impact of reforms; many of them left their posts and became managers of firms that were nationalized in 1945 and were under state control. By the end of the 1950s, the Yugoslav communists faced as many problems as other states.

The situation was further aggravated by the uneven development of the constituent republics. There was a growing conflict between reformists and conservative communists over the proper role of the party in society and politics. Alexandar-Marko

Rankovic (*see* Rankovic, Alexandar-Marko), the heir apparent to Tito, led the conservative camp. He represented the vested interests of the bureaucracy and the secret police, and he was set against the lowering of the profile of the party in Yugoslavian affairs. There was apprehension in party circles when it became more and more apparent that Rankovic was advocating the return of Stalinism. He was also a Serb, and many reformists, who were not Serbian, feared the establishment of Serbian hegemony in the Yugoslav federation. Rankovic started a campaign for what he termed the curbing of corruption, but it was really directed against his possible rivals for power. Although corruption was not eliminated, the campaign did shed light on the fact that the bureaucracy was overblown and that its members enjoyed undeserved privileges. What Rankovic missed was that uncovering the misdeeds did not improve the general economic conditions of the country.

By 1964, the failure of the conservative course was apparent, but Rankovic did not give up easily. It is likely that he planned to stage a coup d'etat and intended to replace Tito as head of the Communist party and of the Yugoslav state. Tito, however, was not to be so easily pushed aside. In 1966, the Executive Committee of the party's Presidium (the former Politburo) removed Rankovic from all his party- and government posts. This was confirmed by the party's Central Committee in July of that same year.

This was an important turning point in the history of the Yugoslav League of Communists, as the Communist party was now called. Although the internal struggles over power did not end with the fall of Rankovic, the party seemed to embark on a road of renewal. A series of student demonstrations held in Belgrade and Zagreb and the Warsaw Pact invasion of Czechoslovakia in 1968, provided further impetus for change. The ninth congress of the party in March 1969 adopted new party statutes. These statutes not only changed the structure of the party; they all but gave up on the concept of "democratic centralism," the Leninist concoction that was a means of one-man control of the party apparatus. The rights of individual party members were restored, and a greater voice was granted for party organizations in the individual republics for party affairs on the federal level. This latest rule was the beginning of the fragmentation of the party, an unintended consequence of the reorganization.

By the summer of 1969, there were signs of further problems. The Slovenian party leaders attempted to gain control of part of a Western loan intended for road construction on the federal level. Their efforts were rejected. Thereupon they protested and muttered about discrimination and possible movements for secession from Yugoslavia. Tito was not about to tolerate such disobedience, but his action did not stop the growing rivalries that were happening among the constituent republics.

The struggle soon assumed nationalist overtones. Slovene and Croatian communist leaders protested against large federal projects which, they contended, were financed at the expense of their republics. It was becoming ever more difficult to come to agreements over common economic policies. The party organizations in the republics more and more identified themselves with local interests. In the process, they became separate Communist parties in fact, if not yet in name.

The ninth congress of the Yugoslav League of Communists held in the summer of 1969 charged the republican parties with the selection of members for the party's Presidium. In January 1970, at the plenum of the Central Committee of the Croatian part of the Communist party, the participants enumerated reasons for the redistribution of economic decision-making from federal authorities to the republican ones. This was the beginning of the Croatian party's drive for autonomy. The constitution adopted in 1974 strengthened the fragmentation of the party. It recognized six constituent republics and two autonomous provinces and granted them autonomy in ordering their own affairs. Tito believed that he had succeeded in calming nationalist passions in 1971 and 1972. In 1975, a new campaign was launched against pro-Soviet elements in the Communist party, a cover-word for conservatives.

Before his death, Tito devised a scheme to prevent nationalist squabbles by creating a collective presidency that would come into being following his death. However, even this scheme could not save the unity of the League of Communists of Yugoslavia. The collective presidency did not last very long. Its breakdown and the collapse of communism in Eastern Europe and the Soviet Union actually ended communist rule on the federal level and, incidentally, it also ended a unified federal Yugoslavia. In the Serb republic, where the party changed its name to that of "socialist," the leaders identified their party with chauvinistic Serb nationalism and initiated civil war with the breakaway republics. Former party leaders elsewhere jettisoned their Marxism-Leninism and adopted unabashed national garbs.

Bibliography

Avakumovich, Ivan, *History of the Communist Party of Yugoslavia* (Aberdeen, England, 1964); Djilas, Milovan, *The New Class: An Analysis of the Communist System* (New York, 1957); Korbel, Josef, *Tito's Communism* (Denver, CO, 1961); Lukic, R., *The State Organization of Yugoslavia* (Belgrade, 1955); Neal, F. Warner, *Titoism in Action: The Reforms in Yugoslavia after 1948* (Berkeley, CA, 1958); Radulovic, Monty, *Tito's Republic* (London, 1948); Shoup, Paul, "The League of Communists of Yugoslavia," in Stephen Fischer-Galati, ed. *The Communist Parties of Eastern Europe* (New York, 1979); Zaninovic, George M., *The Development of Socialist Yugoslavia* (Baltimore, MD, 1968).

Cosic, Dobrica (1921–). Born in Central Serbia near Krusevac, Cosic joined the Yugoslav Communist party in 1939 while a journalism student at the University of Belgrade. He was a political commissar in Tito's (*see* Tito, Josip Broz) Partisan army in 1941 and fought through the war. In 1945, he was appointed a member of the Central Committee of the Communist party. However, in May 1968, he was expelled from the Central Committee on the charge of Serbian chauvinism.

Thereafter, he became an outspoken advocate of Serbian interests. He always protested the charge that Serbs oppressed other nationalities in Yugoslavia stating, instead, that it was the Serbs who were being exploited by the other nationalities. He was particularly vehement in supporting the suppression of Kosovo Albanians. In

1968, Cosic quit the League of Communists of Yugoslavia. He continued his harsh criticism of the communists and was coauthor of the infamous memorandum of the Serbian Academy of Sciences in 1986, which argued that the Serbs were the most persecuted people of Yugoslavia. He also advocated a multiparty political system. Cosic is considered to be the political godfather of Slobodan Milosevic (*see* Milosevic, Slobodan). He was elected president of the Federal Republic of Yugoslavia, the remnant of the old Yugoslavia, on June 15, 1992.

Cosic is the author of fifteen books. He concerns himself mostly with Serbia's struggles for nationhood and Serbians in World War II. He has been twice nominated for the Nobel Prize for literature but has so far been unsuccessful.

Bibliography

Andrejevich, Milan, "What Future for Serbia?" *Radio Free Europe Research Report*, 1.50 (December 18, 1992), pp. 7-17; ———, "Serbia's Bosnian Dilemma," *Radio Free Europe Research Report*, 2.23 (June 4, 1993), pp. 14-21; Byrnes, Robert F., *Yugoslavia* (New York, 1957).

Croatia. *Area:* 56,538 square kilometers (35,340 square miles). *Population:* 4,760,300. *Capital city:* Zagreb (900,000 people). *Major ethnic groups:* Croats 77.9 percent; Serbs 12.2 percent; *Major religions:* Roman Catholicism, Eastern Orthodox Christianity. *President:* Franjo Tudjman. *Prime minister:* Hrvoje Sarinis.

Croatians are Slavs who arrived in their present territory sometime during the sixth-seventh century A.D. They were converted to Roman Catholicism in the seventh century by missionaries from Rome. The arrival of the Hungarians in the Danube basin meant the end of the Croatian kingdom in the eleventh century. In 1526, following the defeat of the Hungarians by the armies of the Ottoman Sultan, Croatia became an Ottoman dependency. The Habsburg empire's armies pushed the Ottomans out of Croatia in 1699, when most of the territory became part of the military border region separating the Ottoman and Habsburg empires. Croatian nationalists initiated the unification of the southern Slav peoples in 1918, when Croatia became part of the Kingdom of Serbs, Croats, and Slovenes; however, the unification did not work well. The different religious, national, and historical traditions of the nations and ethnic minorities included in the mini-multinational state by the Treaty of Trianon in 1919 worked against the creation of a unified nation. The Slavic language did not become the great unifying force either. Croats always considered themselves more sophisticated and cultured than Serbs and resented the domination of the state by Serbians. In turn, the Serbs were the ones who had sacrificed the most for the unification in terms of soldiers lost and property destroyed in World War I, and they resented Croatian airs of alleged superiority.

Tito's Yugoslavia was only a temporary solution; it did suppress national feelings for a while, but eventually these feelings triumphed over communist ideology. In the elections held in April and May 1990, the Croatian Democratic Community party, headed by Franjo Tudjman, became the majority party in parliament. On June 25,

1991, Croatia declared its dissociation and, on October 7, its independence from Yugoslavia. The state quickly received recognition from most major countries.

Bibliography
Bicanic, Ivo, and Domicis, Iva, "Tudjman Remains Dominant After Croatian Elections," *Radio Free Europe Research Report,* 1.37 (September 18, 1992), pp. 20-26; Bonifacic, Antun F., and Mihanovic, Clements, eds. *The Croatian Nation* (Chicago, IL, 1955); Borowiec, Andrew, *Yugoslavia after Tito* (New York, 1977); Crnja, Z., *Cultural History of Croatia* (Zagreb, 1962); Johnson, Ross A., *Yugoslavia: In the Twilight of Tito* (Beverly Hills, CA, 1974);. Moore, Patrick, "Issues in Croatian Politics," *Radio Free Europe Research Report,* 1.44 (November 6, 1992), pp. 9-12; ———, "War Returns to Croatia," *Radio Free Europe Research Report* 2.9 (February 26, 1993), pp. 40-43; Shoup, Paul, *Communism and the Yugoslav National Question* (New York, 1968); Stojkovic, Ljubisa, and Martic, Milos, *National Minorities in Yugoslavia* (Belgrade, 1952).

Dapcevic, Peko, General (1913–). General Dapcevic was born in Montenegro and attended the University of Belgrade where he joined the Communist party in 1933. Dapcevic fought in the Spanish civil war and became the first Yugoslav commander of a brigade. After his return to Yugoslavia, he was arrested and jailed. During the German occupation of Yugoslavia, he was in charge of organizing the resistance in Montenegro. In 1942, he was commander of the fourth, then the second partisan division. In 1943, he commanded the second corps of the Partisan Liberation Army. In 1944, he was the commander of the Partisan Liberation Army in Serbia. In 1946, he was commander of the Fourth Yugoslav Army in the Yugoslav zone of Trieste. In the same year, Dapcevic was appointed commander of an army corps at Skoplje, and he directed guerrilla actions in northern Greece.

Between 1953 and 1955, Dapcevic was chief of staff of the Yugoslav armed forces. He was also a member of the Central Committee of the Communist party and of the People's Front. However, in 1953, he became indirectly involved in the Djilas affair (*see* Djilas, Milovan). It seems that his wife mistreated Djilas' spouse, which the latter used to argue for the establishment of a second political party. Soon thereafter, Dapcevic was removed from his commanding position in the army and was relegated to an obscure position.

Bibliography
Avakumovic, Ivan, *History of the Communist Party of Yugoslavia* (Aberdeen, England, 1964); Byrnes, Robert F., *Yugoslavia* (New York, 1957).

Dedijer, Vladimir (1914–?). Dedijer was born into a well-to-do family and attended the University of Belgrade. In 1939, he joined the illegal Communist party and became a close collaborator of Tito (*see* Tito, Josip Broz). For two years he was a correspondent for the Belgrade newspaper *Politika* and was stationed in London. In July 1941, after the German attack on Yugoslavia, he returned home and became chief of propaganda for Tito's Partisan army. In 1944, the British Mediterranean Command invited Tito to establish a mission in Bari, Italy. Dedijer was appointed chief of this mission. In 1945, he was elected to the Constituent Assembly. He was also appointed director of the information and propaganda department of the federal government and editor-in-chief of the Communist party's official newspaper, *Borba*. In 1952, he became a member of the Central Committee of the League of Communists of Yugoslavia (the new name for the Communist party). However, in 1954, Dedijer sided with Milovan Djilas (*see* Djilas, Milovan) in the latter's efforts to expose the bureaucratization of the Communist party. He was dismissed from all his public functions and relegated to obscurity. Before his dismissal, Dedijer was the official biographer of Tito; his works have been translated into many languages, and they are still the fundamental works on the Yugoslav leader.

Bibliography

Armstrong, Hamilton F., *Tito and Goliath* (New York, 1951); Dedijer, Vladimir, *Tito* (New York, 1953); ——, *With Tito Through the War: A Partisan Diary* (London, 1951); Vucinich, Wayne, ed., *Contemporary Yugoslavia* (Berkeley, CA, 1969).

Demography in Yugoslavia. Some of the most troubling problems of interwar in Yugoslavia concerned the large ethnic groups, some minorities, others entire nations, that were included in the new state at its inception in 1918. Some of these nations, such as the Croatians and the Slovenes, joined Yugoslavia on their own account. Other ethnic groups, such as the Albanians, Hungarians, Germans, and others, were included in the new state with a total disregard for the principles of national self-determination. In the case of Hungarians and Albanians, the conationals of these ethnic groups lived in their own states just across the Yugoslav borders. Their inclusion in the south Slavic state was justified on strategic grounds, or on the simple ground of brutal force.

World War II "solved" this problem to some extent. First, the Jews of Yugoslavia were exterminated by the German Nazis. Then came the turn of half a million Germans; some of them left Yugoslavia with the retreating German army, others were massacred by Tito's partisans. Croatians had their own fascist movement, the Ustashi, and they did their own killing of Serbs and Montenegrines. Then came the Partisan army, which massacred the Ustashi and large numbers of Hungarian civilians. Yugoslav losses came to about 1.7 million people in World War II, including civilians and military men. The largest part of these losses were the result of a brutal civil war fought by the communists against their opponents alongside the war of liberation. By 1944, the population of the country had been reduced to about 15 million people. After the war, however, the birthrate suddenly increased and, by 1953, the losses had largely been replaced.

By the mid-1950s, large-scale industrialization and the effects of forced collectivization of agriculture drove people into the cities. Zagreb and Belgrade attracted the largest number of people. By 1955, Belgrade added some 400,000 new inhabitants. However, there continued to exist some troubling problems. Croats numbered about

4.5 million by 1990; Serbs increased to nearly 9.5 million. The number of Macedonians and Montenegrines also increased. The Muslim Slavs of Bosnia-Herzegovina
came to close to a million. There were about 500,000 Hungarians and nearly 2 million Albanians in the Yugoslav state. About 100,000 ethnic Turks and about the same
number of ethnic Romanians also lived within the state's borders. Jews numbered
only a few, but there were large numbers of Gypsies, although they were not counted
by Yugoslav officials. The mini-multinational state of Yugoslavia succeeded in post-
poning the struggles over nationality and ethnic rights until well after the death of Tito
(*see* Tito, Josip Broz), but, in 1991, civil war broke out and, it continued with great
ferocity well into 1994.

During the 1960s, the birth rate in the federal Yugoslav state was still 20.2 per
1,000, and the death rate was 8.0 per 1,000. This was one of the highest rates of increase and lowest of decrease in Europe. Marriages came to 8.5 per 1,000. Such a
high expansion of the population was somewhat balanced by a high rate of emigration
from the country (about 10,000 in 1966). In the 1970s and 1980s, the birthrate declined somewhat, and the latest Serb policy of "ethnic cleansing" has resulted in the
violent deaths of tens of thousands of citizens (some estimates put the death-toll at
200,000). It seems clear that nation-building has never been very successful in Yugoslavia. This mini-multinational state seems to be following the pattern set by the great
multinational empires of the Habsburgs, the Romanovs, and the Ottoman sultans,
where nationalism ultimately led to the destruction of unified state organizations.

Bibliography
Hoffman, George W., and Neal, F. Warner, *Yugoslavia and the New Communism* (New York,
1962); Johnson, Ross A., *Yugoslavia in the Twilight of Tito* (Beverly Hills, CA, 1974).

Djilas, Milovan (1914–1992). True intellectuals, although they do fall captive to
totalitarian ideologies, seldom remain long in their embrace. This was exactly the
case with the Serb thinker, Milovan Djilas. He was born in Montenegro to middle-
class parents. At the age of eighteen, he was admitted to Belgrade University where
he soon became known for his short stories and poetry. He also acquired a reputation
as an enfant terrible for championing the cause of the poor of the capital city and his
rebellion against the abuse of social privileges.

In 1932, he joined the illegal Communist party. Government agents quickly discovered and arrested him, and he was put on trial and sentenced to three years in
prison. But jail did not stop Djilas. After his release, he continued his illegal activities. By 1938, when Tito (*see* Tito, Josip Broz) had reorganized the Communist party,
Djilas was already considered an important party leader. He was unwaveringly loyal
to Tito, who used Djilas' organizing ability in attracting new members to the party.
By 1940, just before the German invasion of Yugoslavia, Djilas was included in the
Politburo, the highest organ of the Communist party of Yugoslavia.

During the Second World War, Djilas fought in Tito's Partisan army as a high-
ranking officer. He demonstrated great savagery against the communists' opponents.

He participated in several massacres of his own countrymen. By the end of the war, he was promoted to general in the Partisan army.

In 1944, Djilas was sent to Moscow as head of the Yugoslav military mission. He met Joseph Stalin for the first time, and it seems that the Soviet dictator liked the upstart Yugoslav communist. Always an observer, Djilas noted the life-style of the Soviet elite, the unprecedented privileges they enjoyed even during the scarcities of the post-war times, and the great contrasts between their propaganda and everyday Soviet realities. He began to have doubts about Soviet-style socialism. Later he was to describe the vast Soviet bureaucracy as a parasitic "new class," with all the faults of the old Tsarist administration. But that was still to come ten years later.

In 1945, Djilas was a member of the first Yugoslav federal government. He was sent to Moscow once again in order to smooth out relations between the two countries which were already becoming strained by Tito's actions that went against the "advice" of Stalin. It was, by then, obvious to Djilas that the Soviet Union had become, in spite of all propaganda to the contrary, a great imperialist power intent on solidifying a colonial empire in Eastern Europe. Yet, in 1947, he still participated in the establishment of the Communist Information Bureau (COMINFORM), which was fast becoming a Soviet instrument of colonization. Ironically, this organization, controlled by Stalin through the NKVD-KGB, was located in Belgrade.

In 1948, Djilas went to Moscow again. This time his task was to convince Stalin that Tito wanted to maintain "brotherly" relations with the Soviet leadership. His trip was a complete failure. Yugoslavia was ostracized and excluded from the Soviet Bloc. Tito and his supporters then embarked on a close examination of their policies, and blamed the plight of Yugoslavia on Stalinist methods in establishing socialism.

Djilas came into conflict with some of his colleagues and with Tito himself. He argued that the Communist party's monopoly of power bred arrogance in the leaders, as the case of his wife's clash with General Dapcevic's wife has shown. He criticized certain aspects of Marxism-Leninism and its Yugoslav practitioners. He contended that the communist federal bureaucracy had become a new class that monopolized power and subjected the rest of the population to its uncontested rule. For this criticism, he was expelled from the Politburo of the Communist party in 1954.

His first book, entitled *The New Class*, was published abroad in 1955, and it earned him a jail sentence in Tito's "democratic" Yugoslavia. He published another volume soon thereafter, entitled *The Land Without Justice*, which was followed by his expulsion from the Communist party of Yugoslavia. When he gave an interview to a reporter of the *New York Times* in 1955, he was taken to court and charged with "hostile propaganda against the Yugoslav government." His "crime" was that he exposed the anomalies of the Tito regime. He received a three-year suspended sentence.

In 1956, Djilas openly criticized the Tito-government for its betrayal of the Hungarian Revolution; this time, he was jailed for three years. When *The New Class* was widely disseminated in the West, Djilas received an additional sentence of seven years in prison. In 1961, Djilas was released; however, when his latest book, *Conver-*

sations With Stalin was published in Great Britain in 1962, he was rearrested.

After spending four more years in prison, Djilas was released, but his passport was revoked, and he was ostracized by his former friends and comrades. In his autobiography, published in 1978, Djilas talks frankly about his life and struggles. He was finally permitted to travel in the early 1980s, and he was received in universities in the United States and Western Europe as a hero. He died in 1992 in Belgrade.

Bibliography

Djilas, Milovan, *My Life* (New York, 1978), 2 volumes.

Economic Policies in Communist Yugoslavia. In 1945, the communist government followed the Stalinist pattern of building socialism in Yugoslavia. This pattern was based on the wholesale nationalization of industrial enterprises, central planning for the entire economy, and the beginning of collectivization of agriculture. The devastations caused by World War II, as well as the death or emigration of owners of private businesses, contributed to a relatively smooth takeover of industrial properties by the communist government. The Germans confiscated many firms during the war, and these were now proclaimed to be state property. Collaborators with the enemy, as well as "war profiteers," also lost their properties to the state. The latter term was, of course, broad enough to include any one who opposed the communist government. But there was practically no resistance to nationalization. The law of December 1946 made the process legal. It declared the nationalization of all significant industrial enterprises and banks. A five-year plan, adopted and started in 1947, was based on plans developed by the federal planning office. It envisaged the transfer of over 1 million people from agriculture to urban-based industries.

Industrialization completely changed Yugoslavia's social structure. In 1948, 67.2 percent of the population made their living from agriculture. By 1981, only 19.9 percent did so. The tremendous influx of rural folks into the cities created the region-wide problem of inadequate infrastructures. Housing, food supplies, transportation, and communications were all overburdened and inadequate. All sorts of tensions emerged as a result. After the break with Joseph Stalin, Tito (*see* Tito, Josip Broz) ordered a review of all previous socialist policies. At the same time, travel restrictions were eased, and thousands left for various Western countries in search of work. The Yugoslav economy benefited from the exodus in several ways. First of all, a safety valve was opened and excess population was drawn off. Second the income that the Yugoslav guest workers sent home in hard currency helped those who stayed home and, indirectly, the economy as a whole.

The great innovation introduced into the Yugoslav economy was worker self-management. Edvard Kardelj (*see* Kardelj, Edward) was the ideological "father" of worker self-management. This provided workers in industrial firms a voice in running their factories and made management accountable for profitability. Part of the profits were then retained by the firms in question, providing further incentives to all concerned. This worked quite well in the case of small– and medium–sized enterprises.

In large firms, however, self-management proved less efficient than expected. It undermined the authority of managers and placed too much emphasis on equality instead of the quality of products. The greatest, and entirely unexpected, consequence of worker self-management was that people soon began to think in terms of extending it to the political sphere, and the communists were naturally unwilling to do this. In addition, self-management produced even larger bureaucratic organizations than had already existed.

In spite of all the handicaps, however, Yugoslavia could show some impressive results in industrialization. Between 1948 and 1970, industrial production increased by over 400 percent. Electric energy, coal, and crude iron production were taking the lead. Construction increased by nearly six times in value.

The sudden increase of oil prices in the early 1970s caught the Yugoslavian communist government off guard. The following readjustment of nearly all commodity prices required a flexibility that the communist system simply did not have. The Yugoslav economy entered a period of stagnation. Tito's death in 1980 further undermined stability. By the mid-1980s, the burden of foreign debt had increased to a crushing level, and the Yugoslav economy rapidly declined. Industrial production was the hardest hit; outdated plants were producing goods that could be sold only to the Soviet Bloc nations or Third World countries, and none of these states could pay with hard currency. Eventually, the Soviet market collapsed, followed by the collapse of the trade of most East European countries including Yugoslavia. This time, Western help was not forthcoming. The Yugoslav civil war that broke out in 1991 did not help the economy, and the United Nations-imposed general blockade of Serbia only aggravated the situation. It is not very likely that the successors of the former Yugoslavia will be able to attract Western investments without which the rebuilding of industry will be almost impossible.

In agriculture, the communist regime did an almost complete about-face from its earlier policies. After gaining power, Tito's government immediately began a collectivization drive, forcing the peasants into Soviet-type kolk-hozes. But the Yugoslav agricultural system had very few large estates that could be confiscated, and the small peasant farmers resisted collectivization which they viewed as theft of their land. Complicating the situation was the fact that a substantial part of the support the communists had received during the war had come from among the peasantry. Although many of the leaders around Tito wanted to speed up collectivization on the Stalinist model, Tito himself disagreed with them.

By 1960, only about 15 percent of the lands were the property of collectives; the rest was still owned by private farmers. The state levied heavy taxes on the independent producers and interfered with their work in other ways as well. The greatest burden was provided by compulsory deliveries which were based on the size of land possessed, not on fertility and the availability of chemical fertilizers.

Two major types of collectives were promoted; one in which the land was completely given up by individual members when they joined; the other was a combination of producers-consumers cooperative, based on similar organizations during the interwar years. A combination of several bad harvests due to drought and the lack of incentives forced the government not only to reconsider its agricultural policies, but also to import huge amounts of bread grains to avert famine. By 1965, even the dogmatists realized that the Stalinist system of agriculture was unworkable, and not only in Yugoslavia.

The communist government began to promote close cooperation between collectives and independent farmers. It also permitted the dissolution of collectives and even demanded their disbandment if they operated in the red. Compulsory deliveries of foodstuff were abandoned. The fixed prices for most agricultural products were abolished. The new prices were based on world-market prices. Some essential goods, such as dairy products, pork, bread, and vegetables, were among the few commodities that still received state subsidies.

Investments in agriculture, however, remained at a steady 14 percent, although private farmers were no longer excluded from the subsidies. As a consequence, the socialist sector began to show a respectable growth rate of 4.9 percent between 1965 and 1975, while the growth of the private sector came to 2.3 percent. Only Hungary among the socialist states in Eastern Europe was able to surpass these rates in the same period. The growth of agricultural prices, however, did not keep up with soaring industrial prices. Industrial machinery registered price increases of 70 percent between 1964 and 1967 alone. Land prices also skyrocketed. Using 1963 as a base, an acre of land cost 369 percent more in 1967.

After 1975, Yugoslav agriculture could no longer sustain its previous rate of growth. The purchasing power of agrarian workers declined, and the market for foodstuffs became uncertain. Exports for Yugoslav food products found it more and more difficult to enter the Common Market, because West European governments had introduced high tariffs that were accompanied with subsidies for their own farmers. The collapse of the communist system in the Soviet Union and the other East European countries also dealt a heavy blow to Yugoslav agriculture. The eastern markets disappeared so swiftly that collective and individual producers were left with a lot of unsold and unsalable goods. There were efforts in 1993 in the remnants of the former Yugoslav state to dismantle the entire collective sector, but final decisions will not be rendered until the end of the civil war.

The foreign trade orientation of Yugoslavia experienced several changes of direction during communist rule. Following World War II, Yugoslavia's exports and imports were heavily eastern-oriented. Over 50 percent of foreign trade went to the Soviet Union and the members of the Soviet Bloc, and only a little less of the imports arrived from that direction. After 1948, however, economic assistance from the United States and other Western countries increased to the point where Yugoslavia was able to maintain its independence from the Soviet Bloc. Foreign trade with the West simply replaced the previous trade with the East. This situation lasted until 1954, then Yugoslav trade with the Eastern Bloc increased once again. Economic agreements provided for small barter deals amounting to $5 million, and a new agreement in 1955 doubled this amount. Later, the limit was raised twice, until it reached $30 million. In 1956, Yugoslav exports to the Soviet Bloc amounted to 22.8 percent of the total, and imports came to 22 percent. In later years, Yugoslav exports as well as imports increased, but there were wide fluctuations from year to year. The increases enabled the Yugoslav government to continue its trade relations with Western countries even when it normalized its economic relations with the Soviet Bloc. Only in the mid-1970s did Yugoslavia's trade balance turn decisively negative, which presaged the economic problems of the 1980s. At the present time, rump-Yugoslavia's foreign trade is at a standstill, and it will not be revived until the civil war comes to an end.

Bibliography

Bicanic, Ivo, "Privatization in Yugoslavia's Successor States," *Radio Free Europe Research Report*, 1.22 (May 29, 1992), pp. 43-49; Milenkovic, Deborah, *Plan and Market in Yugoslav Economic Thought* (New Haven, CT, 1971); Pejovich, Svetozar, *The Market-Planned Economy of Yugoslavia* (Minneapolis, MN, 1966); Prout, Christopher, *Market Socialism in Yugoslavia* (Oxford, 1985); Remington, Robin A., "Self-Management and Development Strategies in Socialist Yugoslavia.," in Augustinos Gerasimos, ed. *Diverse Paths to Modernity in Southeastern Europe* (New York, 1991); Sirc, Ljubo, *The Yugoslav Economy Under Self-Management* (London, 1979); Tyson, Laura A., *The Yugoslav Economic System and its Performance in the 1970s* (Berkeley, CA, 1980); Vojnic, D., R. Lang, and B. Marendic, "The Socioeconomic Model in Socialist Self-Management," in George Masesich, ed. *Essays on the Yugoslav Economic Model* (New York, 1989).

Foreign Policy of Communist Yugoslavia. Until 1948, Yugoslavia's foreign policies were, by and large, similar to those of the Soviet Union. However, Tito (*see* Tito, Josip Broz) was belligerent in regard to his conception of Yugoslavia's interests.

Yugoslavia almost went to war with Italy over the question of Trieste. Tito's belligerent statements against the Western Allies went farther than those of Joseph Stalin. His forces fired on and shot down American airplanes that strayed over Yugoslavia. Above all, he was actively involved in the communist insurrection and the civil war in Greece by providing arms and food for the communist guerrillas. Tito and his cabinet members made violent speeches against the West, repeating the well-known slogans about the demise of capitalism.

All this changed abruptly after 1948. Yugoslavia was isolated from the Soviet Bloc when the COMINFORM expelled the Communist party of Yugoslavia from the community of "fraternal parties." However, this isolation did not mean that Tito would suddenly become a friend of the West. On the contrary. While receiving enormous amounts of American aid (over $2.5 billion in food, military, and direct financial assistance during the 1950s) and similar amounts from the Allies, Tito continued to revile the "imperialist" powers, but action was better than talk.

Yugoslavia withdrew its help from the Greek guerrillas, and their movement collapsed. The defiance of Tito had become an example for the other East European communists, some of whom looked to Yugoslavia as an alternative to Soviet-style socialism. They observed that the Yugoslav government had signed a mutual defense and assistance agreement with the United States in 1951, providing some measure of security for Yugoslavia in the face of constant Soviet pressures. Yugoslavia also terminated its long dispute with Italy over Trieste and exchanged diplomats with Turkey and Greece in 1953 and 1954, respectively. However, there could not exist real, long-term friendship between the West and Yugoslavia as long as Tito and his supporters continued to follow Marxism-Leninism, even if this ideology received a distinct Yugoslav tint.

When Nikita Khrushchev and Nikolay Bulganin visited Yugoslavia in 1955, Tito readily agreed to the resumption of "fraternal" relations with the Soviet Union. At the least, this removed the threat of direct Soviet intervention. Yet, Tito was never really reconciled with his Soviet counterparts. The rift was renewed in 1958. Yugoslavia refused to sign a declaration of thirteen European Communist parties meeting in East Berlin, acknowledging the primacy of the Soviet Communist party in the "struggle for socialism." This created further recriminations and, at this time, the Chinese leaders joined in the condemnation of Yugoslavia in the strongest terms. When the Warsaw Pact intervened in Czechoslovakia in 1968, relations deteriorated further. The proclamation of the Brezhnev-doctrine as a justification of intervention was considered a naked imperialist design by the Yugoslav leaders. The intervention heightened Yugoslav apprehension about Soviet aims in the Balkans.

Eventually, Tito turned to the Third World for support. He was received with open arms and soon became a dominant statesman in the international meetings of the non-aligned nations organization. Yugoslav diplomacy subtly supported the aims of the Socialist Bloc in encouraging and exploiting the often violent nationalism of the emerging nations. This process was distinctly anti-Western, and it fit Tito's Marxist convictions. The nonaligned movement, allegedly neutral between the Soviet and Western alliances, proved to be an excellent theater for the aging but vain Tito in his personal quest for recognition as a leader of world-stature. The Arab nationalist Gamal Abdel Nasser, the Indian Jawaharlal Nehru, Ethiopia's Haile Selassie could safely include Tito in their company. By the early 1980s, the group included some 100 countries, among them such "nonaligned heroes" of the Third World as Cuban dictator Fidel Castro and Idi Amin Dada of Uganda.

Given its diversity of needs and orientations, however, the nonaligned world was not always able to present a united front in international disputes. Many of its leaders were very much aligned with the Soviet Bloc. Others, like India's Nehru, opted to depend upon Soviet military hardware and advisers in their disputes and wars with their neighbors. Most wars of the 1950s, 1960s, and 1970s were fought among the members of the nonaligned nations. Yugoslavia undoubtedly benefited from its membership in the nonaligned movement. It was the only European country accepted by the group, and Tito assumed a role in international diplomacy way out of proportion to his country's economic, military, and industrial power. Above all, Tito's increasing egotism and venality was greatly bolstered by his standing in the movement, where his "moral authority" was widely recognized.

At the same time, the membership in the group could not alleviate Yugoslavia's increasing isolation in Europe, where economic power was shifting more and more to the Common Market. Tito's unconditional support for Arab extremists against Israel, created revulsion even within his own country. As a consequence, Yugoslavia found itself increasingly handicapped in its efforts to capitalize on its standing in the Third World for economic development. Tito's diplomacy simply could not be backed up by his country's resources. The Federal Republic of Germany (West Germany) broke off diplomatic relations with Yugoslavia over Tito's recognition of the German Democratic Republic (East Germany) as a legitimate state of Germans, cutting off an important source of foreign investments.

Tito died in 1980, leaving behind a collective presidency. By then, Yugoslavia's foreign policy orientation, and the posturing of the new leaders who inherited Tito's ambition but not his international standing, had become obsolete. Diplomatically, economically, and politically, therefore, the Yugoslav state was completely unprepared for the breakup of the Soviet Union and the demise of communism in Eastern Europe. These leaders operated on the basis to which they had become accustomed during Tito's dictatorship. Disregarding public opinion at home and abroad, they began a devastating civil war in 1991, for which the entire world community condemned them. Yugoslavia is isolated, it is suffering under a total embargo imposed on it by the United Nations. Even this could not compel its leaders to change their policies.

Bibliography

Djordjevic, Dimitrije, "The Yugoslav Experiment," in Joseph Held, ed. *The Columbia History of Eastern Europe in the Twentieth Century* (New York, 1992); Kardelj, Edvard, *Yugoslavia in International Relations and in the Nonaligned World* (Belgrade, 1979); McVicker, Charles P., *Titoism, Pattern for International Communism* (New York, 1957); Royal Institute for International Affairs, Soviet-Yugoslav Dispute (London, 1948); Rubinstein, Alvin Z., *Yugoslavia and the Nonaligned World* (Princeton, NJ, 1970).

Gligorov, Kiro (1917–). Born to middle-class parents, Gligorov attended the University of Belgrade where he studied law. After the German invasion of Yugoslavia, Gligorov joined Tito's (*see* Tito, Josip Broz) Partisan army. A Macedonian by birth, he was delegated by Tito to serve as a member of the Antifascist Assembly for the People's Liberation of Macedonia, a communist cover group.

Gligorov was appointed a member of the provisional government of Yugoslavia in 1945. In that same year, he joined the Yugoslav Communist party, and was appointed assistant to the secretary-general of the Federal government of Yugoslavia. Two years later, he served as assistant to the minister of finance. In 1952, he became deputy director of the Federal Administration for Economic Planning and Development. Three years later, he moved to the post of secretary, for economic affairs of the Federal Executive Council, and, in 1962, he became a member of the Federal Executive Council. In 1974, Gligorov became the president of the federal parliament of Yugoslavia. He was also a professor at the University of Belgrade.

Gligorov served as a member of the Central Committee of the League of Yugoslav Communists. In 1991, he became the president of the Republic of Macedonia, and directed the country to its independence.

Bibliography
Perry, Duncan M., "Politics in the Republic of Macedonia: Issues and Parties," *Radio Free Europe Research Report* 2.23 (June 4, 1993), pp. 31-37.

Hebrang, Andrej (1899–1948). Hebrang was born in Croatia and his family background is unknown. He became a communist activist in the Yugoslav trade union movement. In 1928, he was arrested, tried, and sentenced to twelve years in prison. Released in 1940, he rejoined the Communist party and, in 1941, he joined Tito's (*see* Tito, Josip Broz) partisans as the secretary of the Croatian branch of the Yugoslav Communist party. During World War II, Hebrang was a constant member of Tito's headquarters, participating in the presidium of the Partisan Army of Liberation Council. In the first federal government, Hebrang was appointed minister of industry, a key area of Yugoslavia's development. In 1945, he was also a member of the Constituent Assembly and the Croatian Constitutional Assembly. In 1946, he participated in the Stalinization of Yugoslavia as the chairman of the federal planning board.

Later in the year, however, he took over the federal ministry of light industry, and his post in the planning apparatus was given to Boris Kidric (*see* Kidric, Boris).

By that time, Hebrang had lost favor with Tito. A special commission, set up to investigate his wartime activities, found that he had shown cowardice during the war. He was also charged with collaborating with the Croatian Ustashi, a charge that was patently false. He was also charged with being a "fractionalist" and an individualist who refused to follow the party line. The Central Committee of the Communist party severely reprimanded Hebrang and stripped him of his post as minister of light industry. In 1948, Hebrang was probably against the break with the Soviet Union. He was allegedly arrested while trying to flee the country through Romania. An official statement announced that he had committed suicide; however, it is more than likely that he was murdered in prison.

Bibliography
Avakumovic, Ivan, *History of the Communist Party of Yugoslavia* (Aberdeen, England, 1964); Byrnes, Robert F., *Yugoslavia* (New York, 1957).

Jovanovic, Blaza (1907–). A Montenegrine, Jovanovic was born into a family of intellectuals. He was a noted Communist party activist in Montenegro during the interwar years, and he was involved with the organization of the local partisan resistance during the German occupation. In 1952, Jovanovic was elected to membership in the Central Committee of the Yugoslav Communist party, then renamed the League of Communists of Yugoslavia, and to the presidium of the Socialist Alliance of the Working People of Yugoslavia, a grand-sounding group that was a mass-organization dominated by communists. In 1953, he became the president of the Executive Council of the People's Assembly of Montenegro, and ex officio member of the Federal Executive Council, that is, the government. When Vladimir Dedijer (*see* Dedijer, Vladimir) was dismissed for his support of Milovan Djilas (*see* Djilas, Milovan) in 1954, Jovanovic took Djilas' post and became director of the information and propaganda department of the federal government, and editor-in-chief of *Borba*, the party's daily newspaper. He retired to private life in the late 1970s.

Bibliography
Byrnes, Robert F., *Yugoslavia* (New York, 1957); Ramet, Pedro, ed. *Yugoslavia in the 1980s* (Boulder, CO, 1985).

Karadzic, Radovan (1926–). Karadzic, a Serb, spent his life fighting for Serb supremacy in the territory of Bosnia-Herzegovina. When Yugoslavia fell apart to its constituent states, Karadzic met his Croatian counterpart, a member of the Croatian Democratic Alliance's leadership, at the Austrian city of Graz. The result was an unwritten agreement to divide Bosnia-Herzegovina between Croatia and Serbia. Karadzic proclaimed that an independent Bosnia-Herzegovina would provide no guarantees for the survival of ethnic Serbs, since a central government dominated by Muslims would repress the Orthodox Christian Serbs. When the Bosnian government refused to accept Serb autonomy, Karadzic led the Bosnian Serb forces in a war of "ethnic cleansing."

The war was fought with great ferocity on both sides. The Serbs had the upper hand, because they received armament and supplies from the Serb government and the army. They besieged the major Bosnian cities, indiscriminately shelling and sniping at the population. Their aim was to force the Moslems to leave Bosnia-Herzegovina or be killed. They did not distinguish among children, women and the old; they were all targets for Serb gunners. Tens of thousands of people were killed in the carnage.

In January, 1993, Croatia made an agreement with the Bosnian Muslims, which provided for joint action against the Serbs. At the same time, Cyrus Vance and Lord David Owen, two statesmen from the United States and Great Britain, respectively, presented a peace plan for the settling of the Bosnian crisis. Their proposal included the establishment of ten ethnically pure regions that would be parts of a new Bosnian state. They also called for a meeting of the warring parties to Geneva to refine the proposal. Karadzic disliked the proposal, because it meant that the Serbs would have to give up some of their territorial gains. Karadzic's purpose continued to be to conquer enough land in order to connect Bosnian Serb territories with those of Serbia proper. The Geneva meeting ended with the signatures of Karadzic and Alija Izetbegovic. However, the war did not stop. It continues to take thousands of lives in Bosnia-Herzegovina.

Bibliography
Cohen, Lenard, J., *Broken Bonds: The Disintegration of Yugoslavia* (Boulder, CO, 1993).

Kardelj, Edvard (1910–). A Slovenian by birth, Kardelj received a diploma from the Teacher's College of Ljubljana. When he was only twelve years old, he joined the Communist party, and in 1928, he became a regular member. He was arrested for subversive activities in 1930 and was put into prison for two years. In 1934, Kardelj left Yugoslavia. For a short time he lived in Paris, then traveled to Moscow. He attended the Communist party school where foreign communists received training in party organization and clandestine activities.

Kardelj returned to Yugoslavia with Tito (*see* Tito, Josip Broz) in 1937, and became one of the most trusted friends of the Yugoslav communist leader. His excellent training in Marxism-Leninism made him invaluable to Tito. He was the chief theoretician of the Yugoslav Communist party. He wrote many articles for Slovenian leftist newspapers and periodicals under the name of "Sperans," that is, the Hopeful. He acquired a reputation as a commentator on international affairs. He remained at Tito's side during the war of liberation against the Germans. He wrote various ideological instruction for the partisan commissars and prepared legislative texts that the partisan government of Tito issued.

Beginning in 1943, Kardelj was vice president of the Liberation Council. He was appointed deputy prime minister in the first Yugoslav government after World War II. He was also head of the Communist party's control commission and was in charge of the ministry in preparation for the Constituent Assembly. He headed the Yugoslav delegation at the Paris Peace Conference in 1946 and was one of the signers of the peace treaty with Italy. He was appointed head of the Yugoslav delegation to the United Nations Assembly in 1945, and again in 1948, 1949, 1950 and 1951.

In 1953, after the reform of the constitution, Kardelj was appointed first vice president of the government. He was mainly responsible for the text of the new constitution and the other basic laws that decentralized the federal administration and the management of the economy. He was then appointed secretary of the Executive Committee of the Communist party (the name for the Politburo), and of the Socialist Alliance of the Working People of Yugoslavia. He was politically active throughout the 1960s but retired at the end of the period into private life.

Bibliography
Byrnes, Robert F., *Yugoslavia* (New York, 1957); Denitch, Bogdan D., *The Legitimation of a Revolution: The Yugoslav Case* (New Haven, CT, 1976); Kardelj, Edvard, *The Communist Party of Yugoslavia in the Struggle for New Yugoslavia, for People's Authority and for Socialism* (Belgrade, 1948); Neal, F. Warner, *Titoism in Action: The Reforms in Yugoslavia after 1948* (Berkeley, 1958); Rusinow, Dennison, *The Yugoslav Experiment 1948–1977* (London, 1977).

Kidric, Boris (1919–1952). One of the most brutal, ruthless communist leaders in Tito's (*see* Tito, Josip Broz) Yugoslavia, Kidric was born in Vienna, Austria, where his father was the assistant librarian at the University of Vienna. His family moved to the University of Ljubljana where his father became a professor of Slavistics. He graduated from secondary school and went to Charles University in Prague to study chemistry, but he did not graduate.

In 1928, Kidric joined the Communist party and performed various tasks at the party's behest in Slovenia. He was a member of Tito's Partisan army from its beginning. He was appointed political commissar for Slovenia, where he is remembered for the brutality with which communism was imposed on the population. In 1945, he was appointed premier for Slovenia. His administration was marked by its special brutality and bloodshed. In 1946, Kidric was sent to the Soviet Union to study the Soviet economy, especially the organization of the Soviet five-year plans. He returned the same year and was appointed chairman of the Central Economic Council and minister of the federal ministry of industry. He became chairman of the Central Commission for Planning in 1948, replacing Andrej Hebrang (*see* Hebrand, Andrej) in the post.

He had great power; he controlled not only the Planning Commission, but also the ministries of finance, agriculture, and foreign trade. He was the organizer of the first-five year plan and the ruthless collectivization drive. He was also the architect of the organization of compulsory deliveries. He was a member of the Politburo of the Communist party from 1944. In 1952, when the collectivization drive collapsed, Kidric died of leukemia.

Bibliography

Burns, Robert F., *Yugoslavia* (New York, 1957); Djilas, Aleksa, *The Contested Country: Yugoslav Unity and the Communist Revolution* (Cambridge, MA, 1991); Zaninovic, M. George, *The Development of Socialist Yugoslavia* (Baltimore, MD, 1968).

Kolisevski, Lazar (1914–). Born in Skoplje, Macedonia, Kolisevski joined the Communist party in 1932. He was a worker at the state arms factory at Kragujevac, where he performed clandestine work for the party. He joined the partisan army in 1941 and became secretary to the Macedonian Communist party. He organized several partisan groups in Macedonia. He was arrested in 1942 by the Bulgarians, who occupied Macedonia at that time, and he was sent to prison on a fifteen-year sentence. In 1945, the Soviet Red Army liberated him from jail. After 1945, he became premier of the Macedonian republic. In 1953, Kolisevski was appointed a member of the federal government. He was also a member of the Politburo of the Communist party of Yugoslavia.

Bibliography

Byrnes, Robert F., *Yugoslavia* (New York, 1957); Hoffman, George W., and Neal, F. Warner, *Yugoslavia and the New Communism* (New York, 1962); Pavlowitch, Stevan K., *The Improbable Survivor: Yugoslavia and its Problems 1918–1988* (London, 1988).

Kosovo, the Intractable Yugoslav Problem. The destabilization of Yugoslavia in the late 1980s actually began in the south, not in the north. The province of Kosovo, which received considerable autonomy in the 1974 constitution, has an overwhelmingly large Albanian population; over 90 percent of the people. Serbia conquered Kosovo before World War I, and the conquest was approved by the victorious Allies after the war. Kosovo was returned to Albania by Benito Mussolini in 1939, when Italy established a foothold in the Balkans. The local Albanians promptly chased the Serb population out of Kosovo. After World War II, Kosovo was given to communist Yugoslavia.

Historical traditions make Kosovo an important territory for both Serbs and Albanians. The province was the birthplace of Serbian culture and of the first independent Serbian state in the Middle Ages. It was also the location of the great battle of Kosovo Polje (Field of Blackbirds), where the Ottoman army of Sultan Murad I destroyed a combined army of Serbs, Albanians, and Bulgarians on June 28, 1389, ending Serbian independence for the next 400 years. Kosovo served as a base of operations for the great Albanian hero, the fifteenth-century general Skanderbeg (George Kastriota) who checked the advance of the Ottoman armies during the first half of the fifteenth century. Skanderbeg, and the equally heroic Hungarian general, Janos Hunyadi, the regent of the Hungarian Kingdom, were instrumental in stopping Ottoman advances into Central Europe.

After World War II, Tito's (see Tito, Josip Broz) government treated the Albanians of Kosovo relatively well. Tito dreamed of establishing a Balkan federation of all south Slavs, including Yugoslavia and Bulgaria, to which the non-Slavic Albanians would have been joined. This dream ended with the Stalin-Tito break in 1948. By 1949, Tito's government had begun using strong measures to curb Albanian desires for joining Kosovo with Albania. In 1966, when the dreaded minister of the interior, Alexandar-Marko Rankovic (see Rankovic, Alexandar-Marko) was ousted, the grip of the Yugoslav secret police on Kosovo was loosened. In 1974, the new constitution gave wide-reaching autonomy to the province. After Tito's death, however, further restrictions were enacted, and, in 1989, a revised Yugoslav constitution abolished Kosovar autonomy altogether.

Between 1966 and 1980, the Kosovar Albanians enjoyed few restrictions on their rights. Education was mostly conducted in the Albanian language. They had their own Academy of Sciences, a university, and other cultural institutions. The Yugoslav federal fund for underdeveloped regions spent considerable amounts of money in Kosovo. Albanian representatives worked in several federal institutions. In spite of the best intentions, Kosovo province remained the poorest of the regions of Yugoslavia. One reason for this was the corruption of federal officials; investments usually went into their own pockets. At the same time, Kosovo experienced an unprecedented growth of the Albanian population. In 1948, their number was only 733,000; in 1981, this number was 1,730,000 people. By 1990, there were 2 million Albanians in the province. The ratio of Serb inhabitants in the province dropped considerably. In 1953, they still constituted 27 percent of the total population; by 1987, they accounted for less than 10 percent. Part of this decline resulted from the emigration of Serbs from the province. There was also an Albanian national revival, fueled by the unemployed native intelligentsia who, trained only in its own language, could not find jobs outside the province. The local Serbs, on the other hand, were frustrated by the fact that they could hardly conduct business in the province because they did not want to learn Albanian.

In 1981, there were mass demonstrations all over Kosovo province against Serbian oppression. The federal government responded by force. The Albanians demanded the establishment of their own republic; the Serb authorities feared for the lives of the Serbian minority. If such a republic were established, the Serbs feared, it would eventually merge with Albania. The Albanians, on the other hand, demanded that the principle of national self-determination be recognized. The Albanians of Kosovo are, at the time of this writing (1993) waiting for the end of the civil war in the former Yugoslavia. If the Serb nationalists decide to "cleanse" Kosovo of its Albanian population, this might result in a general Balkan war in which besides Serbia, Greece, Bulgaria, Romania, and Albania would all participate. Such a war would dwarf the Bosnian conflict in bitterness and casualties.

Bibliography
Adrejevich, Milan, "The Radioalization of Serbian Politics," *Radio Free Europe Research Report* 2.13 (March 26, 1993), pp. 14-24; Lydell, Harold, *Yugoslavia in Crisis* (Oxford, 1989); Shoup, Paul S., *Communism and the Yugoslav National Question* (New York, 1968); Stojkovic, Ljubisa, and Martic, Milos, *National Minorities in Yugoslavia* (Belgrade, 1952); Zanga, Louis, "The Question of Kosovar Sovereignty," *Radio Free Europe Research Report,* 1.43 (October 30, 1992), pp. 21-26.

Kreacic, Otmar (1913–). Colonel General Kreacic was born a Croat and attended elementary and some secondary schooling in Zagreb. In 1937, Kreacic joined the Communist party and went to Spain to fight in the Spanish civil war. In 1941, he joined Tito's Partisan army and had various command assignments. By 1945, he had risen to the rank of colonel general. In 1946, Kreacic became a member of the general staff of the Yugoslav army. In the same year, he attended the Frunze Military Academy in the Soviet Union.

When he returned, he was put in charge of the political department of the general staff. In 1948, when Tito (*see* Tito, Josip Broz) was reviled by the Soviet and East European communist leadership, Kreacic was Tito's most vocal defender. He made sure that the COMINFORM could never seriously penetrate the Yugoslav armed forces. In 1952, he was appointed a member of the Central Committee of the League of Communists of Yugoslavia (the new name for the Communist party) as well as of the People's Front. He remained in active service until the death of Tito, when he retired to private life.

Bibliography
Byrnes, Robert F., *Yugoslavia* (New York, 1957); Gow, James, *Legitimacy and the Military:*

The Yugoslav Crisis (London, 1991); Hoffman George W., and Neal, F. Warner, *Yugoslavia and the New Communism* (New York, 1962).

Macedonia in Communist Yugoslavia. *Area:* 25,713 square kilometers (16,070 square miles). *Population:* 2,038,847. *Capital city:* Skopje (600,000 people). *Major ethnic groups:* Macedonians 64.5 percent; Albanians 21.1 percent; Turks 4.8 percent; Gypsies 2.7 percent; Muslims of undetermined ethnicity 2.5 percent; Serbs 2.2 percent; Others 2.2 percent. *Major religions:* Macedonian Eastern Orthodoxy, Islam. *President:* Kiro Gligorov. *Prime minister:* Branko Crvenkovski.

Macedonia emerged into the limelight of history in the fourth century BC, when a native son, Alexander the Great, son of Philip, conquered most of the known world of the Mediterranean and Indian oceans. The land was part of the Ottoman empire from the late fourteenth century until 1913, when, after the Second Balkan War, it was divided among Serbia, Bulgaria, and Greece. The land has been a bone of contention among these nations since the early nineteenth century. It has been variously argued that the majority of the population was Serb, Greek, or Bulgarian. The peace treaties of 1919 gave Macedonia to the Kingdom of Serbs, Croats and Slovenes (later named Yugoslavia). In 1941, the province was given to Bulgaria by Italy and Germany, but after the defeat of the Central Powers, Yugoslavia regained its share of Macedonia.

In the 1974 Yugoslav constitution, Macedonia was named a republic with considerable autonomy. In the first multiparty elections held in December 1990, a multitude of parties gained parliamentary representation. On November 20 1991, a new constitution was promulgated which proclaimed Macedonia an independent republic.

Macedonia is rich in mineral resources. It possesses iron ore, lead, zinc, nickel, mercury and gold in good quantities. It also has a well-developed agriculture, including grapes, tobacco, apples, rice, and livestocks. A major producer of wines, Macedonia has the economic resources for independent survival.

Bibliography
Barker, Elizabeth, *Macedonia: Its Place in Balkan Politics* (London, 1950); Kolisevski, Lazar, *Macedonian National Question* (Belgrade, 1959); Perry, Duncan M., "Macedonia: A Balkan Problem and a European Dilemma," *Radio Free Europe Research Report*, 1.25 (June 19,1992), pp. 35-45; ——, "The Republic of Macedonia and the Odds of Survival," *Radio Free Europe Research Report*, 1.46 (November 20, 1992), pp. 12-19; Poulton, Hugh, "The Republic of Macedonia after United Nations Recognition," *Radio Free Europe Research Report*, 2.23 (June 4, 1993), pp. 22-30; Shoup, Paul S., *Communism and the Yugoslav National Question* (New York, 1968).

Mihajlovic, Dragoljub-Draza (1912–1946). Mihajlovic, a Serb, attended the royal military academy in Belgrade. At the outbreak of World War II, Mihajlovic was already a general staff colonel. When the Yugoslav army disintegrated, Mihajlovic organized resistance in the name of King Peter II, who was in exile in Egypt. His army was called the Yugoslav Troops of the Fatherland, but his soldiers were commonly called the *chetniks*. Mihajlovic was loyal to the monarchy and he was pro-Western.

He had never heard of Tito (*see* Tito, Josip Broz) before the war, and thought that he was a Russian. In any case, he considered his task to be to raise a Yugoslav army and hold it in readiness for the time when the Germans were weakened and were forced to leave Yugoslavia. Above all, he considered that direct attacks on the Germans were mad; therefore, his troops conducted sabotage and minor skirmishes with the enemy. Mihajlovic, despite his hostility to communism in general, cooperated with Tito's partisans for a time. However, he deplored their recklessness which often resulted in appalling casualties among the civilian population. Finally, Mihajlovic's troops fought the partisans, and the war turned into a civil war.

In the end, Mihajlovic's lieutenants collaborated with the Germans, not because they liked them, but because they fought against the communists. Mihajlovic himself never collaborated with the enemy. Mihajlovic placed his trust in the Western Allies, but his organization was inefficient, and the Allies eventually chose to support Tito and the partisans.

The general was adopted into the Yugoslav government-in-exile in 1943, but this government was dissolved because of basic disagreements between Serbs and Croats over the postwar political settlement. Tito and Mihajlovic remained bitter enemies until the very end. Each attempted to impose his own ideology on the people. Mihajlovic's army tried to regain its prestige by sheltering Western pilots shot down over Yugoslavia; but this came too late, and it was too little. Mihajlovic was eventually captured in the Montenegrine mountains, tried for treason and executed in 1946.

Bibliography

Djilas, Milovan, *Wartime* (London, 1977); Djonlagic, Alexandar, *Yugoslavia in the Second World War* (Belgrade, 1967); Seitz, Albert B., *Mihajlovic: Hoax or Hero?* (Columbus, OH, 1953); Tomac, Peter, ed. *The Trial of Dragoljub-Draza Mihajlovic* (Belgrade, 1946); *The Trial of Dragoljub-Draza Mihajlovic: Stenographic Records of Documents* (Belgrade, 1946).

Milosevic, Slobodan (1941–). Although Milosevic's parents were Montenegrines, he was born east of Belgrade, in Serbia. His father was a theology professor, and his mother, a schoolteacher, was a committed communist. Milosevic's parents separated after World War II, and both committed suicide separately. In 1959, Milosevic enrolled at Belgrade University and joined the League of Communists of Yugoslavia. At the university, he was elected chairman of the university's committee on ideology. In 1964, Milosevic graduated with an economics degree.

He was soon employed by the Belgrade Communist party apparatus as an economic and legal adviser. In 1968, he became an executive at Technogas, the state-owned gas company, and in 1973, he became its general director. In 1978, Milosevic was appointed president of Beobanka, the United Bank of Belgrade. This enabled him to establish some Western contacts, and he even visited the United States in 1979.

In 1984, he became a full-time party worker, and he was appointed chairman of the Central Committee of the Belgrade City branch of the Yugoslav Communist party.

In May 1986, he was elected president of the Serbian branch of the party. In May 1989, he was voted president of the Serbian National Assembly, and in December he was elected president of the Socialist Republic of Serbia, relinquishing his post as party president. In December 1990, Milosevic defeated all his opponents and was reelected president of Serbia.

Milosevic is a shrewd politician. He capitalized on Serbian nationalism and on the feeling that Serbs were shortchanged in Tito's Yugoslavia. He forced through amendments to the constitution, abolishing the autonomy of Vojvodina and Kosovo, creating outrage in both provinces. He has substantial support in Serbia, since he has promised to establish Greater Serbia in place of the Yugoslav republic. Milosevic is a ruthless political manipulator who learned his tactics as a member of the communist *nomenklatura*. He is certainly responsible for the breakup of the Yugoslav federation and for the misery that has overtaken even Serbia.

Bibliography
Andrejevich, Milan, "What Future for Serbia?" *Radio Free Europe Research Report*, 1.50 (December 18, 1992), pp. 7-17; Moore, Patrick, "Conference Report: Former Yugoslavia, Prospects and Problems," *Radio Free Europe Research Report,* 1.50 (December 18, 1992), pp. 1-6; ———, "The Widening Warfare in the Former Yugoslavia," *Radio Free Europe Research Report,* 2.1 (January 1, 1993), pp. 1-11.

Mitrovic, Mitra (1912–). Mitrovic attended the University of Belgrade, but she did not graduate. In 1933, she joined the Communist party and became a white-collar worker at the secretariat of the National Assembly in Belgrade. In 1941, Mitrovic joined Tito's Partisan army, and she was a member of the Antifascist People's Liberation Council. She then married Milovan Djilas (*see* Djilas, Milovan) but they were divorced after the war. In 1945, she became minister of education in the Serbian republic. She was also a member of the Central Committee of the League of Yugoslav Communists (the Communist party) and also a member of the federal People's Assembly. She was active in the federal government as well and participated in various commissions dealing with all levels of education. In 1982, she retired to private life.

Bibliography
Byrnes, Robert F., *Yugoslavia* (New York, 1957); Hoffman, George F., and Neal, F. Warner, *Yugoslavia and the New Communism* (New York, 1962); Djilas, Milovan, *Wartime* (London, 1960).

Montenegro. *Area:* 13,812 square kilometers. *Population:* 616,000. *Capital city:* Podgorica (135,000 inhabitants). *Major ethnic groups:* Montenegrines 61.5 percent; Muslim Slavs 14.6 percent; Serbs 9.3 percent; Albanians 6.6 percent. *Major religions:* Eastern Orthodox Christianity, Islam. *President:* Momir Bulatovic. *Prime minister:* Milo Djukanovic.

In 1499, Venice and the Ottoman empire divided Montenegro between them, but neither of them could ever gain complete sovereignty over the people who moved into the mountains and prevented the establishment of effective foreign control over their land. In 1878, the Congress of Berlin, following the Russian-Ottoman war of the previous year, confirmed the independence of Montenegro. After World War I, the country joined in the new Kingdom of Serbs, Croats and Slovenes, the later Yugoslavia.

In the December 1990 elections, the Democratic Socialist party (formerly the communists) won a clear victory in a multiparty contest. On March 1, 1992, Montenegro held a referendum on the basis of which it joined Serbia under the name of the Federal Republic of Yugoslavia.

Montenegro has been the poorest republic of the former Yugoslavia. Only 4.2 percent of its land is arable, yet 75 percent of the population make their living from agriculture. The major crops include tobacco, citrus fruit, olives, and grapes. The republic also has bauxite, lead, zinc, and coal. In the 1970s, a rudimentary industry, producing pig iron and steel, took shape.

Bibliography

Avsenek, Ivan, *The Yugoslav Metallurgical Industry* (New York, 1955); Mellen, Melrad, and Winston, Victor, *The Coal Resources of Yugoslavia* (New York, 1956); Moore, Patrick "The Widening Warfare in the Former Yugoslavia," *Radio Free Europe Research Report*, 2.1 (January 1, 1993), pp. 1-11; Stojkovic, Ljubisa, and Martic, Milos, *National Minorities in Yugoslavia* (Belgrade, 1952); United States Department of the Interior, Bureau of Mines, *Mineral Resources of Yugoslavia* (Washington, DC, 1944).

Nadj, Kosta, General (1911–?). General Nadj, of Hungarian ancestry, was born in the Vojvodina. After completing elementary school, Nadj went to work in the Yugoslav aircraft factory, Ikarus, in Novi Sad. In the 1930s, he was drafted into the Yugoslav army where he rose to the rank of noncommissioned officer. A military court in Sarajevo found him guilty as being a communist agitator and sentenced him to two years in prison.

After his release, Nadj went into hiding. In 1936, Nadj fought in the International Brigade in the Spanish civil war and became commander of the Yugoslav Matija Gubec battalion. In 1939, he entered France. In 1940, the Germans caught up with Nadj and deported him to Germany. In 1941, Nadj escaped from German detention, made his way back to Yugoslavia, and joined Tito's Partisan army. In 1943, he rose in rank to become commander of the first corps of the People's Liberation Army. In 1944, he was sent to the headquarters in Vojvodina and became commander of the third corps of the Yugoslav army.

As commander, Nadj directed his forces crossing the Drava River, recaptured northern Slovenia, and crossed into Austria at Dravograd. This maneuver closed the battle, which ended in the surrender of the German southern forces that were retreating back to Germany. In 1946, he was appointed commander of the fifth corps headquarters of the Yugoslav army at Skopje, Macedonia. He was placed in charge to command the communist guerrillas in northern Greece. In 1947, he was promoted to colonel general. Three years later, he became commander of an army group, headquartered in Novi Sad, an extremely important area in case of a Soviet-led invasion of the country. He was a member of the Central Committee of the League of Yugoslav Communists. At the age of sixty-five he retired to private life.

Bibliography
Byrnes, Robert F., *Yugoslavia* (New York, 1957); Rusinow, Dennison, *The Yugoslav Experiment 1944–1974* (Berkeley, 1977).

Nationalization in Communist Yugoslavia. Tito (*see* Tito, Josip Broz) and the young communists gathered around him were motivated by the idea of Yugoslavism. This concept meant that the communists were looking forward to the establishment of a unified South Slav nation in which ethnic divisions would eventually "wither away." More important, they were dedicated to the building of a socialist society, one that would facilitate the process. Their model was the Soviet Union. The Soviet model required state ownership of all the means of production, industrial as well as agricultural. All industrial firms and land, therefore, had to be nationalized, without compensation to their owners.

In early 1946, long before a similar process began in the other East European nations, the nationalization of all industrial enterprises, banks, and trades was accomplished. The process encountered fewer obstacles than elsewhere in Eastern Europe. The Germans and Italians had confiscated most of the larger firms and banks during the occupation of Yugoslavia. Consequently, there was little opposition from the private sector when these firms were declared state property. What the communists did not expect was that nationalization of Western-owned firms would arouse opposition from the Western Allies and would eventually choke off the supply of Western goods and spare parts for Yugoslavia.

At first, Tito brushed this possibility aside, since he expected that the Soviet Union would replace the Western aid. The Soviet Union did provide some support, as well as technical assistance, but at a price. Tito soon realized that this price was the opening up of the Yugoslav economy for Soviet exploitation.

Large industrial firms were concentrated in Croatia and Slovenia; many of their foundations went back to the time when the Habsburg monarchy controlled these regions. During the late 1950s, the state bureaucracy ran these factories with relative efficiency. There were even some plans to arrange for cooperation with Hungarian and Romanian enterprises just across the borders. In the republics of Serbia, Montenegro, and Macedonia, industry consisted mostly of coal and iron ore mines. The rest of the local industry was made up by small- and medium-sized factories. The federal government combined these into large firms; however, the consolidated companies lacked experienced managers and faced a shortage of skilled workers. From the very beginning, this created all sorts of structural problems. Nevertheless, these problems did not immediately obstruct the development of industry in Yugoslavia. But there was hidden unemployment in outdated factories that was covered by state subsidies for a considerable time.

By 1965, it was obvious that fundamental changes were necessary. The economic reforms introduced that year promoted profitability (profit had been taboo before); the subsidies for firms producing at a loss were to be discontinued; and a market economy was to be introduced. In this, Yugoslavia was ahead of the Soviet Union by two decades. But the reforms did not work because they did not touch the overgrown bureaucracy. In fact, in Yugoslavia, as in the rest of the communist countries, the socialist economic system could not be reformed. It could only be abolished, which is what happened after 1989.

Bibliography

Davico, J., and Bogoslavjevic, M., *The Economy of Yugoslavia* (Belgrade, 1966); Rusinow, Dennison, *The Yugoslav Experiment 1944–1974* (New York, 1977); Vucinich, Wayne, ed. *Contemporary Yugoslavia* (Berkeley, 1969).

Panic, Milan (1929–). Panic, who was born in Belgrade, joined Tito's partisan army at the age of fourteen. He became a sportsman, a bicyclist after the war and rode to a bicycle championship. In 1956, while on his way to a bicycle race, he defected to the United States. He settled with his family in California; in 1963, Panic became a United States citizen. He attended the University of Southern California and was trained as a chemist. Between 1957 and 1959, he was a graduate teaching assistant at the university. With capital of $200, he started his own company in 1960, which burgeoned into ICN Pharmaceutical Inc., based in Costa Mesa, California. The company's annual sales amount to about $500 million. In 1986, he was one of eighty Americans awarded the Ellis Island Medal of Honor by the Congress of the United States to honor emigrants who made distinguished contributions to the United States. Although he was totally without political experience, Panic was elected prime minister of the Federal Republic of Yugoslavia (Serbia and Montenegro) on July 14, 1992, by the Federal Assembly. He promised peace and prosperity. His first effort consisted of bringing peace to the warring republics and ethnic groups, hoping that this would lead to the lifting of sanctions against Serbia by the United Nations. Panic repeatedly declared that the war in Bosnia and Herzegovina was not one of hate and ethnic conflict, but was the product of the actions of unscrupulous politicians who were benefiting from the slaughter. He also declared that not more than 1,200 hoodlums, criminals, and other assorted ugly characters were responsible for the troubles.

Opinions are divided over the relationship between Panic and Slobodan Milosevic (*see* Milosevic, Slobodan). Some believe that Milosevic has been using Panic to gain time. Panic has called on Milosevic to resign in the interest of Serbia. Although Panic survived two non-confidence votes in parliament, he subsequently lost the presidential election to Milosevic.

Bibliography

Andrejevic, Milan, "What Future for Serbia?" *Radio Free Europe Research Report*, 1.50 (December 18, 1992), pp. 7-17.

Pijade, Mosha (1889–?). Pijade was born in Belgrade and attended Belgrade University. Then he went to Munich and Paris where he studied art. In 1911, he returned to Belgrade, and changed his career from that of a fine artist to a journalist. He was one of the founders of the trade union of journalists, the Serbian Journalists' Association. In 1919, Pijade published the journal, *Slobodna Rec* (The Free Word). In 1920, when he joined the Communist party, he was the oldest member of the organization. After the suppression of the party, he was editor of the *Organizovani Radnik* (Organized Worker) and spent his energy in spreading Marxism-Leninism among trade union members. The paper was banned soon after its first issue was published. In 1925, Pijade was arrested for illegal activities and sentenced to twenty years in prison. While in Sremska Mitrovica prison, he and Radoljub Colakovic (*see* Colakovic, Radoljub) translated Karl Marx's *Das Kapital* into the Serbo-Croatian language. Pijade was released in 1939. Just before the beginning of World War II, Pijade was once again under arrest. When the Germans attacked Yugoslavia, he was freed and immediately joined Tito (*see* Tito, Josip Broz). He was sent to Montenegro where he collaborated with Milovan Djilas (*see* Djilas, Milovan) in organizing the resistance in the summer of 1941. He was exceptionally cruel toward people who were not willing to join the Partisan army.

Soon Pijade was recalled to Tito's headquarters where he was appointed chief of the administrative section. In 1943, he was appointed vice president of the People's Liberation Council. In 1945, he was named vice president of the Constitutional Assembly and later of the federal parliament. When Djilas was dismissed in 1954, Pijade took his place as president of the federal parliament. He was a member of the Politburo, and together with Alexandar-Marko Rankovic (*see* Rankovic, Alexandar-Marko) and Edvard Kardelj (*see* Kardelj, Edvard), Pijade was one of the closest collaborators of Tito. He was also named a member of the Serbian Academy of Sciences.

Bibliography

Burg, Steven L., *Conflict and Cohesion in Socialist Yugoslavia: Political Decision-Making Since 1966* (Princeton, NJ, 1983); Byrnes, Robert F., *Yugoslavia* (New York, 1957); Gellner, Ernest, "The Dramatis Personae of History," *East European Politics and Societies* 4.1 (1990), pp. 116-133.

Popovic, Koca, General (1908–?). The son of a famous Serbian family, he was related to Milentije Popovic and Vladimir Popovic, both prominent intellectuals and politicians. Popovic, a poet, studied at the University of Belgrade and attended the University of Paris as a graduate student. In 1933, Popovic joined the Communist party, and three years later, he joined the International Brigade in the Spanish civil war. When he returned to Yugoslavia, he was arrested. He was not imprisoned for long, because his family interceded for him, and he was soon released. In 1941, Popovic joined Tito's Partisan army and was appointed to various command posts. In 1942, he was the commander of the first Partisan brigade, and a year later, he commanded the first corps of the Liberation Army. By the end of the war, he commanded the second corps and had the rank of colonel general.

After the war, he was a member of the highest party- and mass-organization commands. In 1945, Popovic was elected to the Constituent Assembly. He was also chief of the general staff of the Yugoslav army, and he held this position until 1953. He was also secretary of state for foreign affairs, thus, a member of the federal government. He headed the Yugoslav delegation to the United Nations General Assembly in 1948, 1947, and 1949. He was also a constant companion of Tito (*see* Tito, Josip Broz) during the latter's visit to various countries, including England, Burma, India, Egypt, and France. He was a member of the Central Committee of the Communist party, and various other mass organizations.

Bibliography

Byrnes, Robert F., *Yugoslavia* (New York, 1957); Pavlowitch, Stevan K., *The Improbable Survivor: Yugoslavia and its Problems 1918–1988* (London, 1988).

Popovic, Vladimir (1914–?). Vladimir Popovic was born into a well-known Serbian family, related to Koca Popovic (*see* Popovic, Koca). He, too, attended the University of Belgrade and became a physician. He had communist sympathies and declared himself when, in 1932, he attended the communist-sponsored Students World Congress in Paris, as a delegate of the students of Belgrade University. When the Spanish civil war broke out, Vladimir Popovic joined the International Brigade together with Koca Popovic. He was interned after the end of the Spanish civil war and was released only when Germany defeated France in 1940.

Upon his return to Yugoslavia, Popovic immediately joined Tito (*see* Tito, Josip Broz) and was appointed to various posts in the partisan army. In 1944, with the rank of colonel, he commanded the third corps. In 1945, he was sent to Bulgaria as the first Titoist ambassador. At the end of the same year, he was appointed Yugoslav ambassador to the Soviet Union, at that time the most critical diplomatic post for Tito's government. When Yugoslavia was expelled from the Soviet Bloc, Popovic returned home and became deputy foreign minister. In June 1950, he was named Yugoslav ambassador to the United States and remained in Washington, D.C., for three years. After his return to Yugoslavia, he was named chairman of the parliament's committee on foreign affairs. In 1955, Popovic was named Yugoslavia's ambassador to communist China, a critical diplomatic post to his country.

Bibliography

Byrnes, Robert F., *Yugoslavia* (New York, 1957); Rusinow, Dennison, *The Yugoslav Experiment, 1948–1977* (London, 1977).

Post-World War II Recovery in Yugoslavia. The new Yugoslav government of Josip Broz Tito (*see* Tito, Josip Broz) faced a difficult task when the war was over. The destruction inflicted by the occupying armies was widespread. The bureaucracy and the government of the old regime simply disappeared. There were few communist cadres with technical training or experience in running administrative organs. What was in abundance was the arrogance and overconfidence of young party activists and leaders. They were all convinced that they could accomplish anything they set their minds to by applying the "scientific" theory of Marxism-Leninism.

On the other hand, Yugoslavia was receiving substantial aid from the Western Allies. Massive United Nations deliveries of food saved the country from starvation right after the war. The United States provided an immediate credit of $300 million. After the Soviet-Yugoslav break, U.S. aid eventually totalled over $2.5 billion. Hungarian and German reparations were also intended to ease the transition from the old to the new regime.

Tito and his followers were convinced in 1944 that Yugoslavia had to follow the Soviet-type development of society and economics. They established typical Stalinist institutions. They nationalized most industry, banking, and trade; ordered the collectivization of the land; and established a central planning organ to oversee all development. Emphasis was placed on the development of Yugoslavia's heavy industry. Yugoslav foreign trade was reoriented toward the Eastern Bloc. Trade with the Soviet Union alone came to more than 23 percent of the total. By 1946, more than half of Yugoslavia's trade went east. A great deal of this traffic originated with joint Soviet-Yugoslav factories whose directors were Soviet personnel. Yugoslavia was disadvantaged by this trade, because the Soviet Union paid low prices for Yugoslav products, but charged high prices for its own deliveries. The recovery was retarded by the inexperience of the new bureaucrats. Nevertheless, by 1947, the volume of industrial production exceeded that of 1938, and agricultural production was back at peacetime levels.

In 1945, a fund for recovery was set up. It was controlled by the ministry of finance conjointly with the central planning office. It received the equivalent of $428, million delivered by the West. However, the centralized planning and administration were unprepared to spend these large sums for productive investments. Coordination was faulty, and much of the machinery delivered was either mislaid or misused. A lot of the funds were spent on the upkeep of a huge military establishment. Yet, all these obstacles were somehow overcome, and the recovery continued. United Nations' aid provided tractors for agriculture, some rolling stocks for Yugoslavia's railroads, and machine tools for mining and other industries. Landing docks were built to handle deliveries, and railroad tracks were laid. Local communist cadres organized all sorts of competitions for the rebuilding of factories, and these methods proved effective in the short run to help the recovery. The central administrative and party organs encouraged these local initiatives. By 1948, Yugoslavia's recovery was almost complete.

Bibliography

Davico, J., and Bogoslavjevic, M., *The Economy of Yugoslavia* (Belgrade, 1960); Radulovic, Monty, *Tito's Republic* (London, 1948); Spulber, Nicolas, *The Economics of Communist Eastern Europe* (New York, 1957); Tomasevich, Joso, *Peasants, Politics, and Economic*

Change in Yugoslavia (Stanford, CA, 1955); Zaninovic, M. George, *The Development of Socialist Yugoslavia* (Baltimore, MD, 1968).

Pucar, Djuro-Stari (1899–?). Pucar completed his elementary schooling and became involved with the socialist labor movement early in his youth. In 1922, Pucar joined the Yugoslav Communist party and, just before World War II, he was secretary of the illegal party in Bosnia-Herzegovina. In 1941, Pucar was a member of Tito's Partisan army and assisted the leaders at their headquarters. He became a member of the presidium of the Liberation Army in 1943. In 1945, he was elected a deputy in the Constituent Assembly. When Radoljub Colakovic (*see* Colakovic, Radoljub) became a minister in the federal government, Pucar was appointed his replacement in Bosnia-Herzegovina. He remained in this position until he retired. Pucar has always been a trusted member of Tito's entourage. He was faithful to Tito (*see* Tito, Josip Broz) during the Soviet-Yugoslav break as a member of the Central Committee of the Communist party.

Bibliography
Byrnes, Robert F., *Yugoslavia* (New York, 1957); Maclean, Fitzroy, *The Heretic: The Life and Times of Josip Broz Tito* (New York, 1957); Ramet, Pedro, *Nationalism and Federalism in Yugoslavia 1963–1983* (Bloomington, IN, 1984).

Rankovic, Alexandar-Marko (1909–?). Rankovic, a Serb, was born in the small town of Drazevac. He received an elementary education and then became an apprentice tailor. It is not known whether he ever advanced in his chosen craft. While he was still a teenager, Rankovic joined the Yugoslav labor movement. In 1927, he became a member of the Serbian Communist Youth Association and joined the regular membership of the Communist party. In 1927, he was arrested and sent to prison for five years. He was jailed in the prison of Stremska Mitrovica, where Moshe Pijade (*see* Pijade, Moshe) was serving his sentence, and later he was transferred to the prison at Lepoglava, where Tito (*see* Tito, Josip Broz) served his sentence at a different time.

When Tito returned from the Soviet Union in 1937 with the task of reorganizing and rejuvenating the Yugoslav Communist party, Rankovic was included in its first Politburo. In 1941, Rankovic shaped the organization of the Partisan army of Tito; however, in one of the first engagements with German police, Rankovic was wounded and then arrested by the Gestapo. He was in a hospital when his comrades rescued him and took him to Tito's hideout.

Rankovic soon recovered and was entrusted with security arrangements around Tito. In 1945, he was appointed minister of the interior in the federal government and, thus, he was in control of both the secret police and the military police. He was vice premier and minister without portfolio in the federal government at various times. In 1953 he became vice president of the government. After 1953, he gave up the functions of the minister of the interior, and these were taken over by General Stefanovic. Rankovic, however, retained his influence in police matters.

As the 1960s progressed, Rankovic was being considered a likely successor to Tito. However, he was impatient. He suspected conspiracy against himself everywhere. He instructed the secret police to listen in on the telephone conversations not only of his suspected enemies, but also of his alleged friends. Eventually, Rankovic went too far. His men wired Tito's quarters and tape recorded the dictator's personal conversations. When these were discovered, Rankovic was expelled from all his positions in the party and the government in 1966. He was even expelled from the League of Yugoslav Communists the following year.

Bibliography

Auty, Phyllis, *Tito: A Biography* (London, 1970); Avakumovic, Ivan, *History of the Communist Party of Yugoslavia* (Aberdeen, England, 1964); Vucinich, Vayne, ed., *Contemporary Yugoslavia* (Berkeley, CA, 1969).

Religious Policies in Communist Yugoslavia. In Yugoslavia, as elsewhere in Eastern Europe, including even Czechoslovakia and Hungary, religion has been closely identified with national culture. To be a Serb means to be Orthodox Christian; to be a Roman Catholic is to be a Croatian or a Slovene. Islam is the religion of large number of Slavs in Bosnia-Herzegovina, and Albanians are also identified with the Islamic religion. The problem of religion in Macedonia is more complex because, although the population is largely Orthodox Christian, a separate Macedonian ethnicity has always been questionable.

The policies of the Yugoslav government toward the Orthodox church have always been cautious. The Communist party of Yugoslavia, especially after 1948, based its policies on safeguarding Yugoslav state interests. The party's official standpoint toward religion in general was based on atheism Nevertheless, open conflict with the Orthodox hierarchy was avoided, in spite of the obvious resentment of the party leaders of the influence of the church in Serbia. Since the communists claimed to act in the interests of Yugoslavia as a whole, the Orthodox church leaders were often rebuked for their alleged nationalism.

The hierarchy never repudiated the charge. For instance, in Montenegro, the church always insisted that there was no separate Montenegrine nationality, but the inhabitants were actually Serbs. Nor did the hierarchy budge from its assertion that Macedonians were "southern Slavs" and not a separate nation. They always spoke out in support of Serbian sovereignty over Kosovo, basing their claims on historical and national "rights." The church's nationalism was clearly exhibited in the case of the independent patriarchate of Macedonia, and its hierarchy came into open conflict with the communist federal authorities.

Macedonian national consciousness emerged late in the nineteenth century. Until 1918, the Macedonian Orthodox church was administratively subordinate to the patriarch of Bulgaria. However, his jurisdiction ended with the establishment of the Kingdom of Serbs, Croatians and Slovenes in 1918. In 1945, however, the council of Macedonian Orthodox church leaders met in Skopje and declared their church to be autonomous from the patriarch of Belgrade. Although this schism was not acknowledged by the communists then, Tito's government did not reject the idea out of hand. In 1958, the Macedonian Orthodox Christian clergy established the bishopric of Ochrid, abolished by the Ottoman Turks in 1767, and once again declared their autonomy in administrative matters. The communist government of the republic of Macedonia supported this action, and it was obvious that Tito (*see* Tito, Josip Broz) himself was not opposed to it.

The Serb church leaders were vehemently opposed to an autonomous Macedonian Orthodox Christian church and refused to acknowledge what they considered a schism. In a memorandum issued on December 3, 1966, the Macedonian church leaders warned their Serb counterparts that, unless they recognized the autonomy of the Macedonian Orthodox church, they would sever all relations with the Serb hierarchy. When the Serb patriarch continued to refuse recognition, a council was called in July 1967 in Ochrid, which declared the independence of the Macedonian Orthodox church. Two members of the Macedonian government attended the council, and Tito gave a decoration to the Metropolitan Dositej. The Serb Holy Synod condemned the move, and asserted that the Macedonians were simply "southern Serbs," who did not need a separate church organization.

While, on the one hand, Yugoslav communist leaders welcomed every move that weakened the unity of the Orthodox church (such as the independence of the Macedonian church), on the other, they readily accepted the Orthodox hierarchy's support of Yugoslav independence. They did not object to church holy days commemorating important historical events in Serbia, nor to the exhortations of the clergy trying to keep Serbs from emigrating from Kosovo province. The latter was especially important after the Kosovo riots during which Albanians destroyed Orthodox church buildings and ancient Serb monasteries. Thus, the relationship between the church and the communist government was, to say the least, ambiguous. Tito did not object to the church's standing on Kosovo; on the other hand, the communists often charged individual clergymen with nationalism, persecuting and often imprisoning them. With the collapse of communism in Eastern Europe, the Yugoslav Orthodox Christian church openly sided with Slobodan Milosevic (*see* Milosevic, Slobodan) and the Serb army in their joint effort to carve out Greater Serbia from the remnants of the Yugoslav republic. Its leaders are, therefore, equally responsible for the bloodshed and destruction practiced by the Serb irregulars and the Serb army.

The Roman Catholic church did not fare as well as the Orthodox church in communist Yugoslavia. Its hierarchy had frequently been called fascistic, and members were frequently charged with maintaining contact with Ustashi organizations abroad. Tito's government also charged the Roman Catholic hierarchy with operating a secessionist organization whose goal was the separation of Croatia from the Yugoslav state. There is no doubt about the efforts of the Catholic church to protect Croatian culture and nationality. In fact, the church was a natural target for the communists. The primate of Croatia, archbishop of Zagreb, was Aloysius Stepinac, an outspoken enemy of communism. In 1945, he issued a pastoral letter in which he declared communism the enemy of the church and the Croatian nation. In September 1946, Stepinac and other prelates were arrested and tried on charges of being the enemies of the state. The primate was also accused of having been a supporter of Ante Pavelic, prime minister of the German puppet government and the commander of the fascist Ustashi forces. He was also accused of ordering the forced conversion of Orthodox Serbs to Roman Catholicism. This was obviously a show trial in which the accused had little chance of defending themselves. There was a kernel of truth in the charges, of course. Yet the cardinal stood up against the prosecution and charged the regime of murdering hundreds of priests and of trying to end the existence of the Roman Catholic church in Yugoslavia. On October 11, 1946, Cardinal Stepinac was sentenced to sixteen years in jail. Eight other priests were sentenced with him, and one Ustashi colonel, Erik Lisak, charged in the same trial for a "better" effect, was sentenced to death. The trial created general revulsion against Tito and his government in the West. Soon all those who were involved directly or indirectly in the trial were excommunicated from the Catholic church.

Between 1967 and 1971, in spite of persecution, the Roman Catholic church was involved in what was called the "Croatian spring." This was a response to the increasingly strident Serb nationalism of the Orthodox clergy. In turn, the Catholic clergy declared its sympathies for *Matica hrvatska*, a national organization dedicated to the preservation of Croatian culture and historical traditions. The Communist party criticized the hierarchy severely and rejected their charge that the federal government was discriminating against Croatia. Criminal proceedings were instituted against some clergymen for articles published in Catholic newspapers.

In 1971, Tito removed the leadership of the Croatian branch of the League of Communists of Yugoslavia (the Communist party), including Dubcevic Kucar and Mika Tripalo, for being soft on nationalism. The publications of the Catholic church were suppressed, and *Matica hrvatska* was banned. In spite of repression, the Catholic clergy, especially the bishops, continued to insist that Croatia was an orphan in the Yugoslav federation, that Croats were underrepresented in the federal government and administration, and that federal laws were especially strictly applied in Croatia. They also dared to say that Croats received better treatment in the old, defunct Habsburg empire.

In 1971, over a quarter million Croats gathered at Nin to celebrate the eleven-hundredth anniversary of the pope's recognition of an independent Croatian state. The celebrations were presided over by archbishop Kuharic. He hailed Prince Branimir, who received the papal recognition, as a true hero of the Croatian nation. The official Yugoslav new agency then charged the archbishop with "fascist bigotry" and with being a counterrevolutionary.

The Yugoslav communists were especially incensed by the Catholic hierarchy's efforts to maintain contacts with Croatians in the West. Roman Catholic churchmen visiting Croatian exile communities abroad were smeared with the Ustashi label and were maligned in the Yugoslav press. This charge was, of course, patently untrue. The Croatian Catholic hierarchy felt compelled to defend the spiritual and national values of Croats, offering an alternative to the official atheism of the Yugoslav state. The church's position identified it with the Croatian nation once again, as had happened so many times in the past. With all the vituperation and hostility exhibited by the federal Yugoslav state toward the Catholic hierarchy, the church had fared infinitely better than Roman Catholic churches in Bulgaria and Romania.

The third religious group in Yugoslavia, the Muslims, had an entirely different relationship with the communists. The federal government treated them differently than members of other religious groups. There is no church hierarchy in Islam; therefore, the Yugoslav authorities attempted to encourage the emergence of Muslim national consciousness in order to establish a balance between Serb and Croat religious nationalism. Tito believed that Muslim identification with the Yugoslav state was a given fact; therefore, Islam could not be a competitor with the state for the believers' allegiance. In 1961, the census recognized Muslims as a separate national group for the first time. Nevertheless, until 1966, Muslims were generally treated as second class citizens. After the removal of Alexandar-Marko Rankovic (*see* Rankovic, Alexander-Marko) from the ministry of the interior, the government finally recognized the Muslims of Bosnia-Herzegovina as a nation.

Until 1972, the Muslims were supported by the Communist party. The Ulema, that is, the preachers, soon began to suggest that Bosnia-Herzegovina be declared a republic within the Yugoslav federation. They repeatedly tried to establish Muslim cultural centers, similar to the *Matica hrvatska* and the *Matica srpska*, the Croatian and Serb cultural organizations, respectively. Yet Muslim cultural and national revival was not encouraged further. Yugoslav officials clearly worried that such a revival would be encouraged by the fundamentalist Muslim regimes in the Near East. That their fears were not completely imaginary was shown by the bilateral arrangements that some Muslim-owned enterprises established with Iraq, Syria, and Libya. In 1982, Muammar Qadaffi met the mufti (spiritual leader) of Belgrade Muslims when he was on an official visit to Yugoslavia, and he promised funds for mosques to be built in the capital city. Alija Izetbegovic (*see* Izetbegovic, Alija), wrote a so-called Pan-Islamic declaration in 1983, that reinforced the fears of communist leaders of real Muslim aspirations. According to Izetbegovic, Muslims cannot coexist with other peoples in the same state. He also suggested that socialism was an alien ideology, and that it would not tolerate the existence of Islamic peoples in its territories. When Izetbegovic was elected president of Bosnia-Herzegovina in 1991, and the republic declared its independence from Yugoslavia, his declaration was remembered by Serbs living in the republic. Hence, the civil war is especially vicious in Bosnia-Herzegovina exactly because of the intolerance of religious and political minorities on both sides.

Bibliography
Fine, John V.A., *The Bosnian Church: A New Interpretation* (Boulder, CO, 1975); O'Brian,

Anthony H., *Archbishop Stepinac: The Man and His Case* (Westminster, MD, 1947); Pattee, Richard, *The Case of Cardinal Stepinac* (Milwaukee, WI, 1953); Pavlowitch, Stevan K., "The Orthodox Church in Yugoslavia: The Problem of the Macedonian Church," *Eastern Churches Review,* 4 (Winter, 1967–1968), pp. 380-381; Petrovich, Michael B., "Yugoslavia: Religion and the Tensions of a Multinational State," *East European Quarterly*, 6.1 (March 1972), pp. 122-126; Ramet, Pedro, "Religion and Nationalism in Yugoslavia," in Pedro Ramet, ed, *Religion and Nationalism in Soviet and East European Politics* (Durham, NC, 1989).

Ribar, Ivan (1881–?). Ribar, who received a doctor of law degree from the University of Belgrade, developed into one of the leading noncommunist supporters of communism. He was also a strong supporter of the Yugoslav idea, that is, that the south Slav nations should be united in a federated state in the Balkans. He was elected to the Yugoslav National Assembly in the 1920s several times and served until 1938. He was a member of the Democratic party.

In 1941, Ribar joined the partisan army of Tito (*see* Tito, Josip Broz). His two sons were with him, and one of them, Ivo Ribar-Lola, was a member of the Communist party, secretary to the Communist Youth Association. Ivo was killed fighting against the Germans in 1944. His father, Ivan, was showered with all sorts of honors. He was a token noncommunist in Tito's entourage without any influence whatsoever. When his second son was killed, he was regarded as the epitome of a father giving his all for the people's struggle. In 1943, he was appointed president of the People's Liberation Assembly, a sort of apparent parliament, and in 1945–1946, he became president of the Constituent Assembly. He then became president of parliament, a post that he held until 1953, when he retired.

Bibliography
Byrnes, Robert F., *Yugoslavia* (New York, 1957); Djilas, Milovan, *Wartime* (London, 1977).

Sandzak. In the nineteenth century and early in the twentieth, the Sandzak was known as the Sandzak of Novi Pazar. This region, earlier known as the Serbian Raska, was the center of the first Serbian state of the eleventh century. Until 1870, the whole area belonged to the Ottoman empire. Austria-Hungary occupied Bosnia-Herzegovina in 1878 and also attached the Sandzak of Novi Pazar to its territory. Serb nationalists were outraged by these actions and hoped to extend the boundaries of Greater Serbia by including Bosnia-Herzegovina and the Sandzak of Novi Pazar in their state. This was essential, according to them, in order to create a viable economy for the Serb state. When the Austro-Hungarian state finally declared the annexation of Bosnia-Herzegovina, it relinquished its rights to Novi Pazar which, then, reverted to Ottoman suzerainty.

During the Second Balkan War of 1913, Serbia and Montenegro conquered and divided the Sandzak between them, ending Ottoman control over the region. Between 1913 and 1943, the Sandzak was part of Serbia and Montenegro, thus also a part of Yugoslavia. In 1943, Tito's partisan government declared the Sandzak once again an autonomous region, but in 1945, its autonomy was withdrawn.

The Sandzak is a poor, underdeveloped region with a population of 440,789. Of these, 229,160 are Muslim Slavs; the rest are Serbs. Industrial developments since 1945 resulted in the establishment of textile factory. There is good, fertile farmland available as well as grazing meadows. Hardwood forests provide good timber. The Muslim population includes many good businessmen.

Because of the conditions prevailing in Bosnia-Herzegovina, however, a great many refugees entered the Sandzak. It has been reported that the local Serb irregulars have been conducting "ethnic cleansing" in the Sandzak, and this has altered the nature of the territorial distribution of the ethnic population. Since the Sandzak has no large cities, Novi Pazar, the largest, have 85,700 people, no dramatic reports have reached the outside world comparable to those about the siege of Sarajevo. But the conflict is continuing in the Sandzak, and the end of the trouble is not in sight.

Bibliography

Andrejevich, Milan, "The Sandzak: The Next Balkan Theater of War?" *Radio Free Europe Research Report*, 1.47 (November 27 1992), pp. 26-34.

Second Yugoslav Revolution. Yugoslavia experienced social and political ferment, similar to that experienced by other East European communist countries, during the first half of the 1960s. This was the time of China's "cultural revolution," of experiments with post-Stalinist economic reforms, and the changes in party organizations.

The ferment in Yugoslavia culminated in a struggle between liberal-minded reformers and conservative bureaucrats. It not only led to the complete overhaul of the structure of the League of Yugoslav Communists (the Communist party), but also to the reigning-in of the secret police, which was, by then, a state within the state, and the mainstay of the dictatorship of Tito (*see* Tito, Josip Broz) and the party.

By then, the Yugoslav economy was in bad shape. In spite of the break with Joseph Stalin in 1948, and the innovations introduced in the economic system after 1949, the direction of the system was too rigid and the bureaucracy was bloated and heavy for smooth economic development. The apparatus was fearful of economic reforms in Yugoslavia, just as similar organizations were in the communist camp. It prevented the necessary changes and the clear delineation of authority in economic affairs. In 1962, Tito turned seventy years old. The struggle that was taking place also involved the question of the succession to his power in which several close associates were involved. Several economic reforms were introduced in 1961. The authority of the workers' factory councils, concerning the distribution of incomes, was extended; prices were no longer controlled. The banking system was also made more independent of the federal government.

With Tito's approval, the government turned to some Western governments for loans. The United States obliged with a loan of $100 million, and the International Monetary Fund provided $75 million. The development fund of the United Nations chipped in with $27.7 million, and the World Bank came through with $30 million. The last of these loans was intended to help Yugoslavia smooth its transition to join the world markets. However, much of this amount was squandered, and the loans did not bring about the desired changes, because of the resistance of the bureaucracy. This induced Tito to retreat from the reforms.

Tito realized that at least part of the argument of the conservative bureaucrats was true; namely, economic changes would unquestionably result in the reduction of the Communist party's influence in Yugoslavia. Tito was also uneasy about joining the Western democracies in these matters since it would finally mean a clear break with the "socialist camp." In September 1961, he proceeded with a sharp criticism of the United States, after accepting the U.S. loan, at a meeting of nonaligned states in Belgrade and emphasized the leading role of the League of Yugoslav Communists in society. He also saw an opportunity to regain some of his standing in Moscow damaged during the Hungarian Revolution of 1956. Andrey Gromyko, the Soviet foreign minister, was cordially received in Belgrade and later on Leonid Brezhnev visited Tito on the island of Brioni, his retreat from the cares of the world.

In March 1962, a meeting of the Politburo was the scene of bitter arguments between reformers and conservatives, led by Alexandar-Marko Rankovic (*see* Rankovic, Alexander-Marko). Tito sided with the conservatives. In December, Tito visited Moscow, accompanied by Rankovic. In June 1963, Rankovic was elected president of Yugoslavia with Tito's approval. It was obvious that he had become Tito's chosen successor over the reformist Edvard Kardelj (*see* Kardelj, Edvard). But Rankovic was a Serb. His possible succession raised fears among Croatian and Slovene communists. A combination of reformers and nationalist communists joined hands in opposing him. Rankovic attempted to convince Tito to appoint him secretary general of the League of Yugoslav Communists (the Communist party), but strong opposition within the party prevented this from happening.

In 1964, Nikita Khrushchev was removed from the Soviet leadership, and this reflected the instability of the Soviet apparatus. No economic help was coming from the Soviet Union, and the Yugoslav economy continued its downward movement. The reformists in the communist leadership began a new effort to bring about reform. Their aim was now nothing less than the introduction of a true market economy. This effort began in 1965. Factories were now permitted to retain 71 percent of their net income, and subsidies were reduced for politically important but inefficient firms. The role of the banks in shaping the price structure was refined. The Western world once again came to the rescue of Yugoslavia, in spite of Tito's continued posturing against it. The United States shipped 1,350,000 tons of grains to the country and provided further loans for the tottering Yugoslav economy.

The reforms, quite naturally, produced a great deal of confusion. In February 1966, Rankovic sharply attacked the reforms and their advocates at a meeting of the party's Central Committee, charging that they favored Croats and Slovenes. However, this time around Tito sided with the reformists. Surprisingly, a former Rankovic ally, General Pavel Gosnjak, minister of defense of Yugoslavia, also came around to the support of the reforms.

It is possible that Rankovic was planning a coup d'etat. Tito was ready to leave the country on an extended trip to the Far East, and Rankovic would make his move while the aging dictator was out of the way. But he miscalculated. Military intelligence personnel reported Rankovic's preparations to Tito. The dictator also found out that the secret police, still dominated by his protege, had placed microphones in his offices and private dwellings and had listened in on his conversations.

On June 16, 1966, Tito berated Rankovic at a meeting of the Executive Committee (Politburo) of the League of Yugoslav Communists (the Communist party). Rankovic protested his innocence but was forced to resign from all his posts. The Central Committee of the party met and endorsed the report of the special committee charged with investigating Rankovic's activities. The report pointed out that Rankovic had turned the secret police into his personal instrument and had taken it out of the supervision of the federal government and party authorities. Rankovic had placed secret policemen in most governmental and party offices without notifying his colleagues and supervisors. Rankovic's removal was, therefore, approved, but he was not given any other punishment so as not to anger his Serb supporters.

As a consequence of the "Rankovic affair," the leaders around Tito realized that the central political and economic organs actually threatened their system. They embarked on writing a new constitution for Yugoslavia, which was promulgated in 1974. The new document provided greater autonomy for the constituent republics and the two territories (Kosovo and Vojvodina), and it recognized the economic decentralization of the federation that was introduced in the late 1960s.

Bibliography

Fejto, Francois, *A History of the People's Democracies* (New York, 1969); Petrovic, Nenad, "The Fall of Alexandar Rankovic," *Review,* 6 (London, 1967), pp. 533-551; Rusinow, Dennison, *The Yugoslav Experiment 1948–1974* (Berkeley, CA, 1977); Volgyes, Ivan, *Politics in Eastern Europe* (Chicago, IL, 1986).

Serbia. *Area:* 88,361 square kilometers (55,220 square miles). *Population:* 9,791,500. *Capital city:* Belgrade (1,700,000). *Major ethnic groups:* Serbs 65.8 percent; Albanians 17.2 percent; Hungarians 3.5 percent; Muslim Slavs 2.4 percent; Others, including Gypsies 11.2 percent. *Major religions:* Serbian Eastern Orthodox Christians, Roman Catholics, Muslims. *President:* Slobodan Milosevic. *Prime minister:* Radoman Bozovic (1953).

The medieval Serb state was a powerful organization. It lost its independence in 1389, after Sultan Murad I's Ottoman army inflicted a devastating defeat on Serb forces. Until 1815, Serbia was under Ottoman suzerainty. In 1815, it received autonomy, and in 1878, it was recognized as an independent state. Serbia became a kingdom in 1882. In 1918, Serbia, Croatia, Montenegro, Macedonia, Slovenia, and Bosnia-Herzegovina formed a south Slav state, called the Kingdom of Serbs, Croats and Slovenes. It was a mini-multinational state with many ethnic groups with diverse historical, religious, and cultural traditions. Serbia was the dominant force within the kingdom, which changed its name in 1926 to Yugoslavia, meaning the "state of the South Slavs." In 1944, Serbia was the base on which Tito built his communist power.

In September 1990, Serbia adopted a new constitution that announced the establishment of a new economic system based on the free market. It also proclaimed a consolidated Serbian state. In December 1990, the socialists (the reformed Communist party) won the elections. After the breakup of the Yugoslav federation, Serbia and Montenegro formed a new Federal Republic of Yugoslavia. Serbia's economy is mixed; it has major industrial enterprises and also fruit and vegetable production on a large scale. Livestock farming is very productive and so is the fishing industry. Kosovo's lignite fields are the largest in Europe, and this province also has lead and zinc ores. Serbia's copper ore production is also very large.

Bibliography
Moore, Patrick, "The Widening Warfare in the Former Yugoslavia," *Radio Free Europe Research Report*, 2.1 (January 1, 1993), pp. 1-11; Shoup, Paul, "Serbia at the Edge of the Abyss," *Radio Free Europe Research Report*, 1.36 (September 11, 1992), pp 7-11.

Slovenia. *Area:* 20,251 square kilometers (12,657 square miles). *Population:* 1,962,600. *Capital city:* Ljubljana (300,000). *Major ethnic groups:* Slovenes, 87.0 percent; Croats, 2.7 percent; Serbs, 2.4 percent; Muslim Slavs, 1.4 percent; "others," 6.5 percent. *President:* Janez Drnovsek. Prime minister: Milan Kucan.

In the thirteenth century, Slovenia became part of the realm of the Habsburgs. With the dissolution of the Habsburg empire, a Slovene National Assembly decided to join the Kingdom of Serbs, Croats and Slovenes (later, Yugoslavia).

In April 1990, the first multiparty elections were held since 1938, and DEMOS, a six-party coalition of center and right-wing parties, won over the former Communist party. On June 25, 1991, Slovenia declared its separation from the former Yugoslavia and was, in turn, attacked by the Serbian- dominated Yugoslav federal army. But the Slovenes defeated their adversary in ten days; they took over the former army depots in Slovenia and had ample arms and ammunition with which to defend their new state. On October 7, 1991, Slovenia declared its independence. A new constitution was adopted in late December, and the European states and the United States have recognized Slovenia as an independent state.

Bibliography
Andrejevich, Milan, "Slovenia: Politics and the Economy in the Year One," *Radio Free Europe Research Report*, 1.36 (September 11, 1992), pp. 15-23; ———, "Elections in Slovenia Maintain Status Quo," *Radio Free Europe Research Report*, 1. 50 (December 18, 1992), pp. 29-31.

Stalin-Tito Conflict. One of the factors that determined the course of communist Yugoslavia and, in retrospect, the entire history of Eastern Europe in the second half of the twentieth century was the conflict between Joseph Stalin and Tito (*see* Tito, Josip Broz). Tito started out as an "ordinary" communist ruler. He Stalinized the economy, politics and society of Yugoslavia by introducing central planning, nationalization of all industry and banking, and collectivization of the land. The secret police was developed to heroic proportions, and its agents behaved with their own people the same way as did their Soviet KGB counterparts in the Soviet Union. Alleged Nazi collaborators, most of them really enemies of Tito who had nothing to do with the Nazis, were executed. They numbered close to 300,000. Soldiers and emigres, returned by the Allies from Western prisoner-of-war camps, were also executed. Mass graves discovered in the Vojvodina in the 1990s proved that the Yugoslav army took bloody revenge on the Hungarian population for atrocities committed in Novi Sad and Subotica by occupying Hungarian troops in 1941. But Serbs suffered just as much; middle class intellectuals, liberals, and democrats were killed in large numbers. There were also some show trials such as that of the Serb Chetnik leader Dragoljub-Draza Mihajlovic (*see* Mihajlovic, Dragoljub-Draza) and the Croatian Cardinal Aloysius Stepinac.

In 1946, a new constitution was enacted. Based on the Stalinist constitution of the Soviet Union of 1936, it promised a wide array of civil and human rights for the population. Soviet military and civilian technicians helped to mold a huge Yugoslav army. The first five-year-plan which began in 1947, copied the Soviet model of industrialization, channeling the largest part of investments into heavy industry. Radical land reform was introduced and wealthier peasants were deprived of their livelihood.

In 1948, however, the system suddenly changed. By then, Yugoslav national interests were opposed to those of the Soviet Union, although the ideology of both regimes was the same. Tito's communism began to be identified more and more with Yugoslav nationalism. Tito's foreign policies were often aggressive; his conflict with Italy over Trieste brought the great powers to the brink of the third world war. His ideas about a Balkan federation of all Slavs in the peninsula ran directly counter to Stalin's policy of creating Soviet colonies in Eastern Europe. Tito eventually emerged as a statesman who had to be reckoned with, a situation not exactly to the liking of Stalin and his successors.

The Stalin-Tito conflict involved several areas, but two of these were most important. One of them was the question of who would govern Yugoslavia, Tito or Stalin. The other issue which concerned Eastern Europe as a whole, was whether the East Europeans would be able to develop their own systems of socialism, or whether they would become colonies of the new Soviet empire.

On June 28, 1948, the resolution of the Communist Information Bureau (COMINFORM) ostracized Yugoslavia, seemingly resolving the issues in Stalin's favor. Stalin's mistake was twofold: he believed that he could easily replace Tito with an obedient Soviet satrap, and he considered the Yugoslav Communist party an obedient tool of the Soviet Union. Neither of these assumptions proved correct. The fact was that the old guard of the Yugoslav Communist party, on whom Stalin would have relied, had either been killed during the war, or had been eliminated in the purges during the Stalin-Tito conflict. It has been reported, albeit never proven, that about

50,000 members of the Communist party were purged and probably killed by the Titoist secret police, the UDBA, during the controversy. Tito's new Communist party was based mostly on young peasant recruits and some urban workers. For them, Stalin was a foreigner in a remote country; Tito was one of them; he belonged to them. Thus, Tito succeeded in defying the Soviet dictator and was able to provide the first model for independent development for the East European nations.

Bibliography

Bass, Robert, and Marbury, Elizabeth, eds. *The Soviet-Yugoslav Controversy, 1948–1958: A Documentary Record* (New York, 1964); Halperin, Ernest, *The Triumphant Heretic: Tito's Struggle Against Stalin* (New York, 1958); Ulam, Adam, *Titoism and the COMINFORM* (Cambridge, MA, 1952); *White Book on the Aggressive Activities by the Governments of the USSR, Poland, Czechoslovakia, Hungary, Rumania, Bulgaria, and Albania Toward Yugoslavia* (Belgrade, 1951); Zwick, Peter, *National Communism* (Boulder, CO, 1983); Volgyes, Ivan, *Politics in Eastern Europe* (Chicago, IL, 1986).

Stambolic, Petar (1912–?). Stambolic, a Serb, became involved with the activities of the illegal Communist party while still a teenager. He became a card-carrying member of the party in 1933. In 1937, he was a close supporter of Tito (*see* Tito, Josip Broz) when he reorganized the Yugoslav Communist party. In 1941, he became a member of Tito's Supreme Headquarters, and he was entrusted with the organization of the Partisan army in Serbia. In 1943, he was appointed a member of the People's Liberation Council. Stambolic was elected a member of the Constituent Assembly in 1945. In 1946, he was elected to membership in the federal parliament and the Serbian parliament simultaneously, and he remained a deputy until his retirement. In 1952, he became prime minister of the Republic of Serbia. In 1953, Stambolic was president of the Presidium of the Serbian parliament. He was also a member of the Politburo of the League of Yugoslav Communists (the Communist party). In March 1956, Stambolic was the keynote speaker at the plenum of the Central Committee of the party. He retired into private life in the late 1970s.

Bibliography

Byrnes, Robert F., *Yugoslavia* (New York, 1957); Hoffman, George, and Neal, F. Warner, *Tito's Yugoslavia* (Berkeley, CA, 1960); Vucinich, Wayne, ed. *Contemporary Yugoslavia* (Berkeley, CA, 1969); Volgyes, Ivan, *Politics in Eastern Europe* (Chicago, IL, 1986).

Tito, Josip Broz (1892–1980). Josip Broz was born in Kumrovec, a small Croatian village, into a family of mixed Croatian and Slovenian ancestry. His father was an independent craftsman. In 1914, Broz was drafted into the Austro-Hungarian armies and fought on the Russian front. He was captured in 1915 by the Russians and joined the Bolsheviks while still in a prisoner-of-war camp. In 1918, he fought at Omsk against the Whites. The following year, he returned home, into the new Kingdom of Serbs, Croats, and Slovenes, and he participated in the establishment of the Croatian Communist party which was, at that time, a strong, effective organization.

When the Communist party was outlawed in 1922, Broz went underground and took the revolutionary name of Tito, by which he was to be known for history. Tito did not remain free for long. He was caught by the royal police, tried, and imprisoned. In 1934, however, he was freed and expelled from the country. He traveled to the Soviet Union where he became a member of the COMINTERN. In 1936, he went on a mission to France where he arranged the secret passage of Yugoslav volunteers who went to fight in the Spanish civil war. In 1937, the president of COMINTERN, Georgy Dimitrov, sent young Tito back to Yugoslavia in order to revive and reorganize a demoralized Yugoslav underground Communist party.

Tito used methods that he learned in the Soviet Union. He succeeded in creating a party with a small, but united and disciplined organization. In May 1941, after the German attack on Yugoslavia and the speedy collapse of the Yugoslav army, Tito began to put together a guerrilla organization, the so-called Partisan Army of National Liberation. The Yugoslav communists had a decisive advantage over their rivals, the chetniks of Dragoljub-Draza Mihajlovic (*see* Mihajlovic, Dragoljub-Draza), in that they had well-organized conspiratorial cells in every part of dismembered Yugoslavia. Their ruthlessness and their dedication to the cause of "proletarian internationalism" enabled them to disregard the death and destruction that followed their hit-and-run tactics against the Germans.

For a short time, the partisans cooperated with the chetniks, but their rivalry for the allegiance of the population soon turned into a bitter civil war. Unspeakable atrocities were committed by both sides, and the killings did not always follow along political disagreements. Orthodox Serbs killed Roman Catholics; Croatian Ustashi exterminated entire Serbian communities. Both sides killed Bosnian-Herzegovinian Muslims. Communists killed royalists, and the royalists killed republicans. Many hundreds of thousands of innocent people perished in this mad war from which Tito and his Partisan army eventually emerged victorious.

One of the reasons for Tito's victory lay in the fact that the British, as well as the Soviets, supplied the partisans with plenty of equipment and ammunition. The federalist principles that Tito emphasized were widely disseminated among the population and gained the partisans considerable support. His troops survived six German-Italian offensives, although the last battle almost cost him his life. By the end of 1943, the partisans had acquired the arms left behind by the Italian army which had surrendered to the Allies.

On August 8, 1944, Tito was compelled, under a joint Western and Soviet agreement to form a "government of national unity," in which both royalists and democrats would participate. Tito considered the support of the Soviet Union for this scheme a betrayal of Yugoslav interests. In any case, he did not intend to abide by the agreement. His strongest argument was the might of the Partisan army which, by then, numbered more than a half million men.

In the final count, Tito and his supporters proved to be Yugoslav nationalists first and communists only afterward. Tito was unwilling to subordinate what he considered to be Yugoslavia's national interests to those of the Soviet Union. He did not care if his Soviet friends were embarrassed by his actions. He soon forced the royalists and the democrats out of the government and sent them into exile. They could count themselves lucky to get out alive. He simply forbade King Peter II to return to Yugoslavia, and the country was declared a republic.

An open break with Stalin in 1948 cast Yugoslavia out of the Soviet Bloc, but this only enhanced Tito's authority in Yugoslavia. In order to compensate for Soviet ostracism, Yugoslavia joined the nonaligned nations, and Tito became a respected figure among the other leaders as the Egyptian Gemal Abdel Nasser and India's Jawaharlal Nehru. Tito's relations with the Western Allies were more ambiguous. On the one hand, his regime desperately needed Western economic aid and he did receive it. On the other hand, he remained, till the end of his life, a convinced Marxist-Leninist, and he often criticized the West for its policies.

During the last years of his life, Tito succumbed to the temptations of unlimited power. His ego had been fed by the sycophants around him. His luxurious life-style (he had a retreat on the island of Brioni, and he had a "royal" yacht that was furnished with all imaginable amenities), made him appear to be an oriental potentate, not the head of a relatively poor socialist country. He spent most of his last ten years on the island where he had, in addition to his luxurious castle, a nuclear bomb-proof shelter. His wife, Jovanka, much younger than the aging dictator, dabbled in Yugoslav politics, and this was greatly resented by his followers. After Tito's death in 1980, his legend was questioned more and more. His legacy certainly includes the disintegration of Yugoslavia and the brutal civil war that is currently taking place. It seems, however, that the civil war is simply a continuation of the brutal struggle that had ended in 1945, and which was only interrupted for a while by Tito's era.

Bibliography

Auty, Phyllis, *Tito: A Biography* (London, 1974); Dedijer, Vladimir, *Tito* (New York, 1953); ——, *With Tito Through the War: A Partisan Diary* (London, 1951); Maclean, Fitzroy, *The Heretic: The Life and Times of Josip Broz-Tito* (New York, 1957); Ramet, Pedro, *Yugoslavia in the 1980s* (Boulder, CO, 1985); Djilas, Milovan, *Wartime* (London, 1977); Djordjevic, Dimitrije, "The Yugoslav Experiment," in Joseph Held, ed. *The Columbia History of Eastern Europe in the Twentieth Century* (New York, 1992).

Tito after Tito. When Josip Broz Tito died in 1980 (*see* Tito, Josip Broz), his successors made great efforts to preserve his legacy. The legacy included a federal Yugoslav state with six autonomous republics and two autonomous territories, set up in order to prevent the emergence and strengthening of national passions. But the legacy also included nationalism of the constituent ethnic groups that had been suppressed during Tito's years at the helm of state.

Two laws were to serve Tito's successors to maintain the status quo. One was introduced three years before the death of the leader, in 1977, and the other, four years after he was gone. They were intended to prevent the reevaluation of Tito's role in Yugoslav history for all time to come. The aging leader introduced the idea of a collective presidency somewhat along the lines of collective leadership in the Soviet Union which followed the death of Joseph Stalin. The presidency was to be rotated among the six republican and two territorial leaders, who were also the leaders of the Communist parties in their respective regions. The octopus was intended to prevent the emergence of one single dictator and to maintain a semblance of control over the Communist party and the federal government.

But Tito had surrounded himself with sycophants during the last years of his life. They were corrupted by their closeness to power and resented the fact that they were prevented from exercising it by Tito. During much of the 1970s, Tito lived in near isolation on the island of Brioni among luxuries and fawning servants, just like an oriental despot. He tolerated the corruption that surrounded him because he, too, had become corrupt.

It must be remembered that Tito was ultimately responsible for the transformation of Yugoslavia from a backward, agricultural country into a semi-industrialized modern society. Yet the change did not alter the basic nationalistic instincts and hatreds of the people, most of which were to surface once again after the dictator was dead. It did not matter that the industrial work force increased from 1 to 7 million people. Neither did it count that the old cities had grown and that new ones had been built. Even the greatly expanded educational system was useless in creating better understanding among the ethnic groups and nations in the Yugoslav republic. Thus, Tito's successors were unable to solve Yugoslavia's most pressing problems.

Nationalist sentiments had been forced underground by Titoism, but they had never disappeared. Historical traditions, language, religion, all played their role in preventing the emergence of a truly integrated Yugoslav nation. Croats, Slovenes, Albanians, Bosnian-Herzegovinians, and, above all Serbs continued to think of themselves as ethnically different, and they all harbored resentments against all the others. The memories of killings during World War II were also revived. The ambitions of Serb communists were the direct opposite of Titoism. Serb intellectuals and simple people argued that Serbia, the largest, most populous republic in the federal state, was shortchanged under the formula of equal treatment for all republics. The failure of Yugoslavia was not very different in this sense from the failure of the Habsburg empire or of the Romanov empire of Russia. They all disregarded the aspirations of peoples with long historical memories. The consequences are too well known. These are the true legacies of Titoism in Yugoslavia.

Bibliography

Cohen, Lenard, J., Broken Bonds: *The Disintegration of Yugoslavia* (Boulder, CO, 1993); Djordjevic, Dimitrije, "The Yugoslav Experiment," in Joseph Held, ed. *The Columbia History of Eastern Europe in the Twentieth Century* (New York, 1992); Johnson, Ross A., *In the Twilight of Tito* (Beverly Hills, CA, 1974); Volgyes, Ivan, *Politics in Eastern Europe* (Chicago, IL, 1986).

Todorovic, Mijalko (1913–?). Todorovic, born a Serb, joined the Communist party in 1938, after its reorganization by Tito (*see* Tito, Josip Broz). In 1941, he organized several partisan groups in Serbia, and in 1943, he was elected a member of the People's Liberation Council. In 1945, he became a deputy in the Constituent Assembly, and he also served as a deputy in the federal parliament. In the early 1950s, Todorovic was minister of agriculture in the Serbian People's Republic and chairman of the agricultural commission of the federal parliament. A strong supporter of forced collectivization between 1949 and 1952, he headed a Yugoslav delegation to study Soviet agriculture in 1955. He was a member of the federal government and held various posts usually related to agriculture until his retirement.

Bibliography
Byrnes, Robert F., *Yugoslavia* (New York, 1957); Hoffman, George W., and Neal, F. Warner, *Yugoslavia and the New Communism* (New York, 1962).

Trieste Conflict. Trieste, an ancient city with excellent port facilities, situated on the shores of the Adriatic sea, is a natural outlet for the commerce of the Balkans and Eastern Europe. The port was developed during the nineteenth century by the Habsburg empire, which was in control of the northern Adriatic region at that time. The city has been coveted for a long time by Slovenes, Croats and Serbs. The Yugoslav communists inherited this longing.

At a meeting of the provisional government of Yugoslavia, held at Jajca in November 1943, Tito (*see* Tito, Josip Broz) announced that he planned to annex the city of Trieste and its environment to Yugoslavia because it was allegedly populated mostly by Slovenes. There was little comment on this announcement at the time by the Western Allies, who considered that the issue would be settled after the war by the coming peace conference. But the Yugoslav communists did not wait; they wanted to settle the matter themselves without negotiations.

In April 1945, the Partisan army fought its way into the city against heavy German and Italian opposition, where it met the New Zealanders who were moving north in the Poe river valley. The relations between these two forces quickly deteriorated. Tito considered the Western troops the defenders of Italian interests, and he declared that Trieste was an inalienable part of Yugoslavia. The Western Allies objected and demanded the withdrawal of Yugoslav troops from the city. Joseph Stalin was unwilling to support Tito in this matter because he did not consider Trieste worthy of a rift between the Soviet Union and the Western Allies at that point in time.

The issue became a matter of prestige for Tito whose troops were overconfident after their participation in the defeat of Germany. Without Soviet support, however, Tito was unable to face the united opposition of the Western Allies. Eventually, the Yugoslav army was withdrawn from Trieste, but Tito's government never repudiated its claim to the city.

Bibliography
Banac, Ivo, *The National Question in Yugoslavia: Origins, History, Politics* (Ithaca, NY,

1984); Hoffman, George W., and Neal, F. Warner, *Yugoslavia and the New Communism* (New York, 1962).

Tudjman, Franjo. Tudjman was a former communist official, who fought in Tito's (*see* Tito, Josip Broz) Partisan Army during World War II, and reached the rank of major general. He was a member of the communist bureaucracy after 1944 in Croatia. However, Tudjman gradually realized that Croatian nationalism was a powerful vehicle. In the 1960s, and 1970s, he became involved with Croatian nationalist organizations, and, as a consequence, he spent several years in prison. He was a founding member of the Croatian Democratic Alliance, an opposition group that operated clandestinely from 1989. This organization established offices in Croatian township, and by 1990, it had representation in 116 villages and towns. The most controversial point in the platform of Tudjman's organization was that which suggested that Serbs and Muslims, living on Croatian territory, should become members of a confederate Croatian citizenry.

In the elections of late April and early May, Tudjman's Croatian Democratic Alliance won an overwhelming victory, and Tudjman became the new president of Croatia. Croatia then declared its independence from Yugoslavia, and immediately became embroiled in a war with the Serb freebooters in the country. The war was fought with great savagery, and the Serbs had the upper hand, until the United Nations stepped in and mediated a cease-fire. Tudjman continues to direct the politics of Croatia, a country that had been recognized as an independent nation by most European states and the United States of America.

Bibliography
Cohen, Lenard, J., *Broken Bonds: The Disintegration of Yugoslavia* (Boulder, CO, 1993).

Velebit, Vladimir (1910–?). Velebit was born into a Croatian family of soldiers. His grandfather was a general of the Austro-Hungarian army, and his father was an officer in the Yugoslav army in the interwar years. He studied at the University of Belgrade and received a degree of law. Before World War II, he worked as a lawyer. While Velebit was a student at the university, he became involved with leftist causes. When Tito (*see* Tito, Josip Broz) reorganized the Yugoslav Communist party in 1937, Velebit's house was used as a secret meeting place. In 1941, Velebit joined Tito's Partisan army. Since he spoke several foreign languages, he was assigned to maintain liaison with the Allied mission. In 1944, he was sent to Egypt where he negotiated on behalf of Tito with the British Mediterranean Command for supplies for the Partisan army. In the fall of 1944, he was invited to London by Winston Churchill as a personal representative of Tito's army and his Liberation Council. This was widely interpreted as British recognition of Tito's government, although King Peter's exile government was still in existence.

After the war, Velebit was appointed deputy minister of foreign affairs. During the rupture between the Soviet Union and Yugoslavia in 1948, Joseph Stalin denounced

Velebit as an alleged Western spy. At this charge, Velebit withdrew from all his governmental positions and was appointed director of foreign tourism. In February 1953, Velebit was appointed Yugoslav ambassador to Great Britain.

Bibliography

Byrnes, Robert F., *Yugoslavia* (New York, 1957); Halperin, Ernst, *The Triumphant Heretic*: *Tito's Struggle Against Stalin* (New York, 1958); Hoffman, George W., and Neal, F. Werner, *Yugoslavia and the New Communism* (New York, 1962); Rusinow, Dennison, *The Yugoslav Experiment, 1948–1974* (Berkeley, CA, 1977).

Vukmanovic-Tempo, Svetozar (1912–?). Colonel General Vukmanovic-Tempo, a Montenegrine, graduated from the school of law at Belgrade University. In 1933, he joined the illegal youth section of the underground Communist party, and he was accepted to full membership in the party in 1935. He had become an expert in establishing secret printing shops, and was arrested several times for subversive activities. After 1937, he became a close associate of Tito (*see* Tito, Josip Broz) and joined the partisan movement at its very beginning. He was appointed Tito's personal representative in Macedonia and chief coordinating officer of the Yugoslav-Greek-Albanian-Bulgarian partisan units.

In 1943, he was appointed chief political commissar of the Partisan army. He was a deputy in the federal parliament after the war and was also appointed a member of the central planning commission. He succeeded Boris Kidric (*see* Kidric, Boris) as chief economic planner in 1952 and chaired the federal government's economic committee and the committee for energy and mines. When the constitution was changed in 1953, Vukmanovic-Tempo became the fourth vice president of the federal government. He remained an important member of Tito's inner circle throughout the 1950s and 1960s. After Joseph Stalin's death, he was entrusted by Tito with making secret contacts with Stalin's successors, and he was credited with bringing about the reconciliation between Yugoslavia and the Soviet Union in 1955. During the fall of 1955, he led a delegation of economic experts to Moscow and negotiated the details of an economic agreement between the two countries. He was a member of the Politburo and of the Central Committee of the League of Yugoslav Communists (the Communist party).

Bibliography

Byrnes, Robert F., *Yugoslavia* (New York, 1957); Clissold, Stephen, *Yugoslavia and the Soviet Union* (London, 1975).

Yugoslav Federalism. It was obvious to all concerned that Yugoslav unitarism, the system that was in practice in Yugoslavia between the two World Wars, had failed. At the end of World War II, therefore, federalism seemed a good option for the reconstruction of the state. The only question was, whether federalism should be based on the three major components of Yugoslavia—Serbia, Croatia and Slovenia—or additional units should be added to the federation.

Tito's choice was to accept the second version. Not surprisingly, most ethnic groups supported this idea. But Tito was a communist, a believer of a strong, centralized government. To reconcile these contradictory issues, the federalism Tito proclaimed in 1943 was based on the notion of the equality of nations regardless of their size or economic strength. This was essentially the Soviet model, and in Yugoslavia, the central authority was represented by the Communist party, as it was in the Soviet Union. In order to mitigate the overwhelming weight of Serbia in the federal system, Montenegro was separated from it and an autonomous Macedonia was created as a separate republic. It was expected that the new situation would establish a balance among Serbs, Croats, and Slovenes in the new Yugoslav state. However, the separation of powers was more apparent than real. The all-powerful Communist party actually governed the state, and federal and local issues were usually decided by Tito and the powerful elite around him. The underlying assumption was the old, worn-out Marxist notion that nationalism was the product of a bourgeois society and once that society was eliminated, proletarian internationalism would replace nationalist feelings. This was obviously not to be the case.

The constitution also contained several contradictions. One of these was the apparent recognition of each nation's right to self-determination and secession from Yugoslavia. But the document also asserted that the Yugoslav peoples' will was to live in a federal state. This contradiction was supposed to have been solved by the federal system. In fact, it was communist rule, not federalism, that kept the various nations and ethnic groups quiet during the Tito era. Once that era ended, nationalism once again became a dominant ideology in Yugoslavia, ending the federal system.

Bibliography

Banac, Ivo, *The National Question in Yugoslavia: Origins, History, Politics* (Ithaca, NY, 1984); Djilas, Aleksa, *The Contested Country: Yugoslav Unity and the Communist Revolution 1919–1953* (Cambridge, MA, 1991); McVicker, Charles P., *Titoism: Pattern for International Communism* (New York, 1957).

INDEX

Page numbers in **bold** indicate main entries.

About the Author

JOSEPH HELD is Associate Professor of History at Rutgers University and the editor of *The Columbia History of Eastern Europe in the Twentieth Century.*